THE CHILD
AND
THE COURTS

IAN F.G. BAXTER M.A., LL.B.

Professor, University of Toronto
Editor of Part 2

and

MARY A. EBERTS B.A., LL.B., LL.M.

Associate Professor, University of Toronto
Editor of Part 1

THE CARSWELL COMPANY LIMITED
Toronto, Canada
SWEET & MAXWELL LIMITED
London, England
1978

Canadian Cataloguing in Publication Data

Main entry under title:

The Child and the courts

ISBN 0-459-31990-6

1. Children — Law — Addresses, essays, lectures.
2. Custody of children — Addresses, essays,
lectures. 3. Parent and child (Law) — Addresses,
essays, lectures. I. Baxter, Ian F.G., 1915-
II. Eberts, Mary A., 1947-

  K700.Z9C55   346'.013   C78-001225-9

Carswell's Family Law Series

ANDREWS: *Family Law in the Family Court*

McCAUGHAN: *The Legal Status of Married Women in Canada*

BAXTER & EBERTS: *The Child and the Courts*

© The Carswell Company Limited 1978

Preface

The topics in this book of essays were chosen by the writers within an overall subject-frame, and they give the personal viewpoints of contributors from England, Scotland, the United States, Australia, Norway, Finland and Canada. The book was written under the auspices of the Connaught Programme on Family Law and Social Welfare of the University of Toronto Faculty of Law.

The role and effectiveness of the judicial process in regard to children is controversial in many countries and is a persistent law reform and social topic. The development of child welfare services in modern times has brought not only a new dimension and new expectations in dealing with children, but also a new complexity. Furthermore, it has triggered a debate on whether various problems about children are better dealt with by a judicial process or a social agency, or split between them. There is a growing involvement with interlocking sub-systems, for example: the child's family, courts, child welfare agencies, court social workers or probation officers, local authorities (for finance and other matters), institutions, foster homes, guardians, lawyers, police, schools. Within these is a great diversity of organization, power, finance, form of interest in the child, "philosophy" on child welfare and behaviour, and so on. Coordination and communications between the sub-systems and their personnel are major difficulties. Social services may fail to protect a child, and courts may return children to parents with a bad record of child abuse. The various current moves towards comprehensive family courts, with non-legal support services, also raise critically the issues of communications and working together. John Ruskin thought it indisputable "that the first duty of a State is to see that every child born therein shall be well housed, clothed, fed, and educated, till it attain years of discretion. But in order to the effecting of this the Government must have an authority over the people of which we now do not so much dream." But mere increase of state power will not bring Nirvana.

The book has two parts. The essays in the first are related mainly to the implications for children of divorce and marriage breakdown, such as custody and financial support, and the usefulness and function of courts of law in that context. The essays in the second are on situations not necessarily derived from marriage breakdowns, such as protection, wardship, adoption, and a child's rights and status.

In order to allow the contributors to meet and discuss their ideas among themselves and with others, the Connaught Programme on Family Law and Social Welfare organized a Seminar in Toronto in November 1976. We would like to thank Patricia Dawson, Ruth Hartman and Jeff Leon for their assistance in the organization and research connected with the Seminar.

CONTENTS

v

Introduction to Part I: The Child and Divorce

The Matrimonial Causes Act of 1857 made it possible for the first time in England to secure from a civil court a dissolution of marriage which would allow the former spouses to marry again. This poignant triumph of law reform was, to those interested in ending their marriages, a considerable advance over having to seek from Parliament the sort of divorce that would permit remarriage or having to be content with a divorce *a mensa et thoro,* which would not permit remarriage, from the ecclesiastical courts. With the 1857 "judicialization" of divorce did come, however, two developments which continue to trouble us. One of them is the structuring of the dissolution process along the lines of a civil trial, with the plaintiff asserting and the defendant denying, the proposition that the marriage should end. Imposing any structure at all on the complex ending of a complicated relationship is a difficult enterprise; applying as a matter of course and with little ancillary preparation the simplified adversary model is beginning to seem inhuman. This is in part due to the second legacy from our reforming past: the long necessity, now removed from the law of many jurisdictions, of establishing that the marriage should end because one of the parties to it is an offender against the marital order. Commonly, these offences have been adultery and cruelty. Proving them — and only them — as the reason for dissolution, within the charged atmosphere of adversarial litigation, is both too limited and too volatile a way to end a marriage.

The adult parties to marital disunion are often left bruised and embittered by the machinery of legal dissolution. We have become, all too recently, increasingly aware of the problems caused to the innocent bystanders of divorce, children of the marriage. Our concerns, once awakened, now cover a wide range of specific questions, at least in part because worrying about the best way of helping children through the divorce process is happening at the same time as a more general re-examination of the whole system.

We are interested, as a basic question, in finding out what actually happens to children at the time of divorce, and approach this query on at least two levels. In this collection of essays, Mr. Eekelaar of England and

Professors Lødrup and Smith of Norway present the results of empirical research designed to illumine the fate of the children of divorce: which parent becomes the full-time custodian of the child, how are the arrangements made, privately or in court, and so on. At another level, Professors Irving and Schlesinger present in their study a report of the literature describing the psychological effects on children of the break-up of their families by divorce, a survey which indicates, as one might have expected, agreement that divorce is painful and disorienting and that children, like adults, exhibit varying degrees of ability to adjust to their new reality.

Delineating the nature of the problem posed for young people by parental divorce raises, in turn, a number of questions about how best to cope with it. The need for the child to have more chance to speak up about his or her own interests is one that is quickly gaining recognition. Whether the child's interests should be advanced by way of hearing the child in person, having private counsel for the child, having an official children's advocate, or having independent research and investigation of the alternatives for the child by a trained social worker, or some combination of these, is a question addressed by Professors Lødrup and Smith, and by Professors Irving and Schlesinger, as well as by by two Judges contributing to discussions at the seminar: Judge Irwin Cantor of the Conciliation Court of Arizona and Judge David M. Steinberg of the Unified Family Court of Ontario.

These concerns about how to do what is in the child's best interests tie in with the larger inquiry about ways in which to reorganize our whole process of divorcing. The interest in a Unified Family Court, with attendant conciliation and counselling services, is a visible sign of the desire of many to move away from the adversarial approach to divorce and to solving problems like child custody which go along with it. Professor Henry H. Foster, Jr. offers in his paper a strong argument in favour of judicial resolution of these issues; Judge Cantor and Mrs. Ferguson, Mr. Justice MacQuaid and Mme Justice L'Heureux-Dubé all offer comments on the operation of the unified court with conciliation services attached.

The move toward a broadened range of services attached to the family court, and to having, as in some models, state-funded representation for children whose custody is at issue, is an increase in state involvement in family problems, state involvement aimed not just at helping the individuals resolve their difficulties but at helping them cope with the effect on them of another state process: the judicial system. In the papers of Professors Chambers and Aarnio, and Professor Foster and Mrs. Freed, we see a manifestation of this in another context. Ordering one parent to pay an amount of support to a child of the union who is in the custody of the other parent is a task that calls for a nice exercise of judgment: balancing the factors of the child's need, the abilities of the parents, the expectations for the future of each parent and the child, as well as social conditioning about roles for family members, is not an easy matter, probably exceeded in difficulty only by the custody decision itself. Getting an order of support enforced may be even more difficult: Professor Chambers reports the results of his research on how some counties in Michigan do so successfully, and Professor Foster and Mrs. Freed discuss, particularly in the appendix to their paper, the nationwide enforcement program developed in the United States under Title IV-D of the Social Security Act.

Mary A. Eberts

An Enquiry Into Custody Disposition In Divorce Cases

*John Eekelaar**

This paper makes a preliminary exposition of the principal findings of a research project undertaken at the Centre for Socio-Legal Studies, Wolfson College, Oxford. The research forms part of a wider investigation into the administration of family law in Great Britain being conducted at that Centre. In itself, the project was limited to discovering, from court records, what arrangements concerning the custody of children in divorce proceedings were being either made or approved by courts and how the legal process operated in those cases. After this paper was written, the full results of the project were published in *Custody after Divorce* by John Eekelaar and Eric Clive, with Susan Raikes and Karen Clarke,[1] to which reference should be made. The author acknowledges the support of the Social Science Research Council and his co-researchers in the project.

The researchers examined the court records of divorce cases where there were one or more children under sixteen in ten courts in different parts of England and Wales. The courts were chosen to reflect a broad cross-section of the divorcing population and at the same time to give room for the detection of regional variations should they occur. The English sample was taken from petitions filed during 1974. In Scotland, however, all divorces are granted by the Court Session in Edinburgh, and the Scottish sample of divorces involving children under sixteen was taken from divorces granted in 1975. A total of 855 cases were examined, 652 in England and Wales, 203 in Scotland. During 1974, a total of 29,232 decrees *nisi* were granted in the courts selected in England and Wales, and it was estimated that between 14,995 and 16,762 (51.3% and 57.3%) involved children. The sample population of 652 cases in England and Wales lies between 3.8% and 4.3% of the estimated number of children cases in the selected courts; that is, about one in twenty-five of such cases.

This paper is based primarily on the data relating to the English courts and the references are to that data unless otherwise stated.[2]

John Eekelaar is a fellow of Pembroke College, Oxford.

5

THE DIVORCE SETTING

Although the reformed divorce law of 1971 introduced the fact of irretrievable breakdown of marriage as the sole ground on which divorce could be granted[3] the parties may prove this only by alleging and proving one or more of the following "facts":[4]

(a) that the respondent has committed adultery and the petitioner finds it intolerable to live with the respondent (hereafter "adultery")

(b) that the respondent has behaved in such a way that the petitioner cannot reasonably be expected to live with the respondent (hereafter "behaviour")

(c) that the respondent has deserted the petitioner for a continuous period of at least two years immediately preceding the presentation of the petition (hereafter "desertion")

(d) that the parties have lived separate and apart for a continuous period of at least two years immediately preceding the presentation of the petition and the respondent consents to a decree being granted (hereafter "two years separation")

(e) that the parties have lived apart for a continuous period of at least five years immediately preceding the presentation of the petition (hereafter "five year separation").

In the sample, the proportion of wife petitioners (72.7%) to husband petitioners (27.3%) closely approximated the proportion for all petitioners during that year (68% - 32%). There were slight divergences from the national figures for all divorce petitions when the "facts" relied on are examined. A rather higher proportion relied on the "fault" conditions of adultery and behaviour, and a noticeably lower proportion relied on five year separation perhaps because, since this last fact can be used only by parties who have been separated for a long time, in many cases their children, if any, will have exceeded the age of 18 by the time of the petition (Table 1).

The retention of "fault" criteria within the rubric of a divorce law ostensibly based on breakdown is controversial. It may not be possible to obtain conclusive evidence of the effects which fault-based allegations have on divorcing parties and their children, but some of the findings of the research are highly suggestive in their consistency. They seem to show that the choice of "fact" may in itself have repercussions affecting the interests of the children.

It was discovered that respondents were far more likely to react to the petition by expressing an intention to defend when behaviour was alleged than in other cases (Table 2). Although in most cases respondents did not persist in their intention to defend (only 2.1% of the cases were defended at the hearing) nevertheless the initial hostile reaction seemed not only to render agreement between the parties more difficult but also to protract the course of litigation. It was far less likely for the petitioner to declare that the parties had made a voluntary agreement for the future support of the children in behaviour cases than in any other except desertion and five year separation (when the parties have usually long been parted). The contrast with adultery and two year separation is particularly striking (Table 3). The same relationship was found with regard to the question whether the petitioner proposes that the other party should exercise access to the children (Table 4). Behaviour cases also had a greater tendency than any other category to be prolonged. Drawn out struggles were more frequent in behaviour cases than in others and it was almost twice as likely that adultery or consent cases be settled within three months than a behaviour case. Indeed 38.8% of behaviour cases took longer than 6 months from petition to custody settlement compared to 20.2% of adultery cases and 18.2% of two year separation cases. As many as 61.2% of cases where behaviour is combined with other facts lasted over six months.

Only thirteen petitions or cross-petitions were defended at hearing. Six of these were based on behaviour alone and five on behaviour in combination with another ground. The number of contested custody and access cases was not large, but in spite of that, the proportion which were within the context of behaviour was noticeably higher than for the other recriminatory fact, adultery (Table 6). Similar findings were made in Scotland.

Although it must often be true that respondents in cruelty and behaviour cases are not the kind of people who would in any case be inclined to co-operate over a divorce, nevertheless it appeared that factors other than the activities of respondents might influence the choice of the behaviour ground. There were, for example, considerable regional variations in the choice of "facts" which did not seem to be related to an urban (industrial) rural (agricultural) dichotomy. In Scotland, where some variables were tested against the firm of solicitors used by the pursuer, differences were found between some firms concerning the grounds alleged. It also seemed clear that, in England and Wales, adultery and behaviour were preferred to two years separation because they can be alleged before the parties have separated for two years. Once two years after separation had passed, only 8.8% of petitions were based on adultery and 10.6% on behaviour (or combination thereof) whereas 46.9% were based on two year separation and 20.1% on five year separation.

The conclusion must be that, if the separation ground was available earlier, it would be used in many or most of the cases which are presently brought under adultery or behaviour. Parties are using those grounds to obtain divorces within two years sometimes very soon after separating. Behaviour was used for 61.3% (and adultery for 38.7%) of petitions brought within six months of separation. Insofar as the research indicates that, among fault-based grounds, allegations of unreasonable behaviours encourage hostility, or at the very least, fail to promote co-operation between the parties, then their availability seems to be a factor which may seriously harm the interests of many children. If this is true, the implications for divorce law reform are serious for it is a factor which must be weighed against the alleged benefits of obtaining a fault-based ground to "facilitate" quick divorces in cases of apparent urgency.

THE POSITION OF THE CHILDREN AT THE TIME OF PETITION

Nearly three-quarters of the children were living with the wife at the time of the petition. As will be seen, this *de facto* situation was crucial to the outcome of the custody issue. In 10.3% of cases they were with the husband and in 6.6% of cases the parents were still living together. It was uncommon for the children to be divided between the parents (3.7%) and there were occasional cases (4.8%) where a child might be with other persons, *e.g.* grandparents. Just over 1% of cases concerned a child who was in care. No relationship was found between family size and the person or persons with whom the children were living.

It was not easy to discover what other people were living with the children. Despite the fact that this information should be recorded in the documentation, that supplied was usually so imprecise that a "Don't Know" margin of 17.8% was returned. Nevertheless, instances of the custodian parent and the children living with other people (usually the custodian's parents) were recorded in 23% of cases and husbands and wives resorted to this equally. In only 11.2% of cases were the parties prepared to acknowledge the presence of a cohabitee. It is difficult to know whether this is a serious underestimate as the presence of a "stable cohabitee" might be thought to be favourable to the petitioner's application for custody and would therefore be disclosed. Nevertheless, in 43.1% of cases it was recorded that the custodian parent was living alone with the children.

The petitioner is also expressly asked to state whether access by the absent parent is taking place. Although a clear answer was usually given, a 7.5% "Don't Know" margin indicated a disturbing lack of precision on the part of a number of solicitors in either answering the question intelligibly themselves, or in ensuring that it was properly answered by their clients. The exercise of access on a regular basis at the time of petition was acknowledged in less than one-half of cases in the total sample (Table 7). There seems little reason why either party should not reveal that access is taking place if it is exercised. Further confirmation of the surprisingly low degree of the exercise of access after separation is suggested by the finding that, of the 502 cases in the sample where the petitioner proposed to keep at least one child, the respondent indicated that he or she did not intend to apply for access in 197 (39.2%) of those cases.

Since the children are usually resident with the wife, the absent parent will normally be the father, but it did not appear that either sex, when an absent parent, was more prone than the other not to exercise access, and nor did it appear that it mattered who else was in the home with the children. There was no apparent connection between not visiting and the ages of the children, although it was found that the custodian parent was more likely to *refuse* the other access when the child was under four (Table 8). A slight tendency not to visit girls was detected, perhaps because most absent parents are fathers, but it was not a strong factor. As would be expected, the extent to which access was exercised declined the longer the parties had lived apart, but not very steeply. When related to the facts relied on for divorce, it was found that access took place most frequently when the fact alleged was adultery, and least often, as may be expected, in desertion and five years separation cases. Even in two years separation cases, access was stated to be exercised in only just over one half of the cases.

It is hard to know what is the correct interpretation of the low degree of access revealed by the court records, which was also found in a separate study.[5] It is possible that the absent parent often withdraws during the emotionally charged period when the divorce proceedings start but later resumes contact with the children. This is not excluded by the finding that access had declined the longer parties had separated because the long separation cases in the sample would mostly include cases of total desertion of a family. It is also controversial whether it is beneficial for children to maintain contact with their absent parent.[6] More research into this problem is urgently required.

THE PROPOSALS MADE FOR THE CHILDREN

Overwhelmingly, petitioners sought the courts' approval for the continuation of the present arrangements. In 87.7% of cases there would be no substantial alteration of the existing situation, and to this must be added 5.7% of cases where the only change would be the departure of one of the parents from the home. In only 4.8% of cases (30) was any change in the residence of the child proposed.

The research shows that wives are far more likely to challenge their husband's continued possession of the children than *vice versa*. In 478 (73.3%) cases the children were living with the wife. In only 49 of them (10.3% of all cases where the wife had the children) did a husband express an intention to challenge this, although only twelve were clearly actually contested at the hearing. However, in no case did a court make an order transferring the residence of a child from a wife to the husband. Where the child was living with the husband at the time of petition (67 cases), this was challenged by the wife on no less than 23 occasions (34.3%). Eleven of these were recorded as contested at the hearing. However, in only one case did a court make an order transferring a child from a husband to a wife. Wives were clearly more prone to question their husband's suitability as a custodian and although, as will be seen, the courts shared this suspicion, their minimal success rate suggests that the courts had regard to other factors when making their final disposition. Of the 502 petitioners in the sample who proposed to keep at least one child with them, 405 (80.7%) stated that they were willing to allow the absent parent access. There is a considerable disparity between this figure and the extent to which access is actually said to be exercised and it is probable that petitioners exaggerated their reasonableness in this regard. This is accentuated by the fact that 95% of those petitioners willing to allow access would allow "reasonable" access and not specify defined limits.

Where a petitioner is proposing to retain possession of a child, he or she will usually seek a custody order with respect to the child. But where the proposal is that the child will reside with someone else (*e.g.* the other spouse) normally the petitioner will not seek an order, but the respondent will do so. In a surprisingly high number of cases, no order was sought by the petitioner (35.1% of cases) and a major reason for this is that a magistrates' court order already exists settling the custody issue.

THE LEGAL PROCESS (UNCONTESTED CASES)

Under the English procedure, the custody issue is usually settled when decree nisi is pronounced. Six weeks must then elapse before the decree *nisi* can be made absolute, and this can be done only if the judge issues a certificate stating a) that the arrangements for the children are satisfactory, b) that they are the best that can be made in the circumstances or c) that it is not practicable to make arrangements for the children.[7] The certificate of satisfaction may be issued although no custody order is made. The judge may decide, however, that before he can be satisfied with the arrangements, there should be an adjournment for further investigation; or, if some issue is contested, he may in any case adjourn the issue for decision in chambers. Sometimes a registrar will have ordered a welfare officer's report at either an earlier or later stage in the proceedings. A welfare report may also be ordered at the request of the parties.

There are thus two functions for the court to perform. One is generally to oversee that the child's interests are protected during the upheaval caused by the divorce between the parents. The other is to adjudicate on a contested issue, but the criterion for decision will be that the child's interests should come first.[8] From April 1, 1977 undefended cases will normally be processed under the "special procedure" under which a registrar certifies that the ground for divorce has been established on the basis of the allegation made in the documents alone and the judge pronounces decree *nisi* without either party having to be present.[9] But the supervisory function has been retained because, where there are children, the registrar should normally make an appointment for the parties to see the judge in chambers for him to "interview" them about the arrangements for the children.[10] In order to obtain a clear view of how the "supervisory" and "adjudicatory" functions operate, this section is concerned solely with the operation of the legal process in the 607 uncontested cases. The questions examined are: (a) time from petition to settlement of custody and access; (b) the circumstances in which courts adjourned the issue on decree *nisi;* (c) the steps (if any) taken on adjournment and (d) the time from adjournment to settlement of the custody and access issues. The next section deals with the contested cases.

(a) Time from petiton to settlement

Over two-thirds (68.2%) of the cases were settled within six months of filing the petition. Regional variations showed that most courts were quicker than the average figure given above, which was slightly depressed by the greater time taken at the Principal Registry in London. These figures should not, however, be interpreted as suggesting that the entire matrimonial litigation is finished at settlement of custody and access, for disputes over finance and property may be adjourned to a chambers hearing before a registrar after decree *nisi*.

(b) In what circumstances did the court settle the custody and access issue at decree nisi and in which circumstances did it adjourn?

Nearly one in ten of uncontested cases was settled only after an adjournment (Table 9). Possible factors [11] which might have influenced such adjournment were whether the petitioner was proposing a change in the residential *status quo* for the child; whether the child was living with the husband or the wife (they adjourned more often if the child was with the husband); whether the child's residence had altered between separation of the parties and petition and whether it was proposed that the husband or wife should have custody (adjournment was more frequent in the former case).

(c) Steps taken on adjournment

When the custody or access issue was not settled on decree *nisi* it was usually because the court adjourned in order to obtain further information. The most common step was to seek a report from a court welfare officer, but in half as many cases the court was satisfied merely with further affidavits (Table 10). However, the court may also have the benefit of a welfare report at decree *nisi* since it may have been ordered prior to the hearing. This happened in eighteen uncontested cases, and the result was that, in the 607 uncontested cases, the court had the benefit of further affidavits in nineteen (3.1%) and of a welfare report in 50 (8.2%) of them. Hence, in one in ten cases the court looked further than the initial documentation. In view of their considerable workload, it is suggested that this demonstrates that the courts place considerable importance on their supervisory role.

The following factors appeared to have a possible association with the acquisition of a welfare report:

(i) the number of children in a family; in one in three cases where there were more than five children involved, a report was called for;

(ii) whether the child had remained with the same parent or custodian in the period between separation and petition;

(iii) whether the petitioner was proposing that the child's residential situation should alter; it was three times more likely that a report would be ordered in such a case;

(iv) whether non-relatives (other than a cohabitee) were stated to be present. Nearly one-half of these cases were investigated, as were nearly one-third of those where the children were living in different households;

(v) a report was obtained in every case where a child was living with someone other than his or her parents.

(d) Length of adjournment

Three-quarters of the investigations in non-contested cases led to dispositions within six months; only a handful of cases took over a year, and then may have been due to matters outside the control of the court. Welfare reports were reasonably quickly produced, half of them (48.3%) in under three months. Affidavit evidence took longer to produce, but this was sometimes due to the inaccessibility of the sources.

OUTCOME OF THE PROCEEDINGS

The courts have a number of choices before them when disposing of the custody and access issue. Custody may be ordered to one or the other spouse, or to them jointly, or children may be divided between them. Care and control can be separated from custody. Access is amenable to many permutations. Custody may be ordered to a third party, the child may be committed to the care of the local authority, or be made subject to a supervision order. The court may, of course, make no order at all. The final outcome of the custody issue is set out in Table 11.

(a) Custody and residence

The relevance of a custody order to the supervisory function of the court may be measured by assessing the impact of the order on the child's residence. It was therefore necessary to consider the order against the child's residential background. Doing this, the following pattern emerged:

(i) in no case was custody ordered in favour of a husband if the child was resident with the wife at the time of the petition, although in twelve such cases joint custody was ordered.

(ii) where a child was resident with the husband at time of petition (67 cases) (10.3%), in half of them custody was ordered to the husband, in 24 no order was made, in six custody was ordered to the wife and in four cases joint custody was ordered.

(iii) of the 24 cases where the children were split, in one half custody was divided, in seven custody was ordered to the wife, in one to the husband and in four cases no order was made.

(iv) of the eight cases where the children were in care, in five, custody was ordered to the wife and in three no order was made.

At first sight, this pattern appears to reveal a tendency to favour the wife. If this was so, it would have been necessary to examine more closely the criteria used by the courts in deciding whether it is better for a child to be with the husband or the wife. But closer examination reveals a different process at work. This is shown by the highly significant fact that in only thirteen (2.0%) cases in the total sample was the child's residence different after the proceedings from what it was at their commencement. Moreover, of these thirteen cases, only six (0.9%) came about as a result of the court order. Eight of the thirteen cases were uncontested; in four of them the change came about as a result of the court order. But two of them did not involve fitness between parents. They were in reality child welfare cases. The other two did appear to involve a qualitative judgment between the two households, but in neither was the matter thoroughly investigated nor the advice of a welfare officer sought. In view of the drastic and, on the findings of this research, unusual nature of this outcome, this is most surprising.[12]

(b) Supervision orders and committals to care

Apart from making an order moving the child, the court may exercise its supervisory function by making a supervision order with respect to the child. This was done in only 24 cases (3.5%). Seven of them were contested cases. It was done in none of the cases which involved a residential change for the children. So when and why were supervision orders made? The answer seems mainly to depend on the readiness of the welfare officer to recommend this course. Isolated cases were found where a judge made a supervision order even if this had not been recommended in the welfare officer's report, and a few (mostly in the Principal Registry in London) where no supervision order was made despite a recommendation that it should be. But mostly judges followed the recommendation, although the proportion of cases in which such recommendations were made varied from 6.9% in one court to only once in 68 uncontested cases in another.

(c) Joint custody orders

Although, on divorce, a child must necessarily reside with one parent or the other, it has been thought that, if the parents are prepared to co-operate, their relationship with each other and towards the child could be assisted if, instead of confining the granting of custody to one parent, a joint custody order is made. This course was warmly recommended by Wrangham J. in *Jussa v. Jussa*.[13] The courts, however, make very little use of it. Of the 607 uncontested cases, joint orders were made in only eighteen (3.0%) cases. In eight of them this solution was proposed in any case by the petitioner and agreed between the parties, which means that in only ten cases in all did the proposal come from the court (and even this might be an overestimate for the suggestion might have been made orally to the court and not recorded in the documents).

(d) Access

Recent judicial dicta in England have expressed the view that access should be considered the right of the child rather than the parent.[14] The documents on the file revealed cases where access was fought out in court, but did not allow any estimate to be made as to how frequently this question had been the subject of informal bargaining or arrangement between the parties. But it was possible to record the orders the court made. The results were unexpected. In 214 of the 406 cases (52.7%) where the divorce court made an order, provision was made for access. But to obtain the overall picture of the complete sample, it is necessary to include the 145 cases where access was granted by magistrates' court. Access was provided for, therefore, in 359 cases, or 55% of the whole sample.

There were good reasons for supposing that the orders made about access bore little relation to the realities. In the usual case in a magistrates' court, the printed form on which the court's order is recorded contains an express statement that "reasonable access be granted to the defendant" which must be specifically deleted if the court wishes to deprive a parent (or child) of the access right. But the form on which the custody order of a divorce court is recorded has no formal provision about access; any such provision must be *written in* by the clerk. This difference in the stationery may go far to explain the finding that no provision was made for access in only 13.2% of instances where the outcome of the magistrates' decision was known, compared to 36.7% of the total number of cases where the outcome was known.

The absence of a provision for access does not, of course, render the absent parent liable to any enforcement action if he exercises it. That can only happen if access is expressly barred, or if the defined conditions of access are contravened. Another explanation, therefore, is that a court may prefer to make no order about access and leave it to the parties to make their own arrangements. An indication that court policy may be a relevant factor is provided by the wide disparity between the courts in England and Wales, and between those courts and the practice in Scotland, on the question whether the divorce court made provision for access. In England and Wales, the percentage of occasions when the divorce court made provision for access in a custody order varied from 79.3% to 16.2% and in Scotland such a provision was made in only 7.9% of orders.

(e) No order made

Of the total sample in England and Wales, no order of any kind was found in 58 (8.9%) cases. The reasons for this varied.[15] The most usual was that neither party had applied for access. Other situations where this happened included cases where the children were over sixteen or were abroad or resident with third parties. However, in about one-third of these cases, no clear reason for the failure to make an access order appeared from the documents.

THE CONTESTED CASES

Thirty-nine cases (6.0%) were classified as being contested on custody at the hearing and a further six as contested on access. The tenacity of wives in seeking custody compared to husbands is reflected in the fact that only 3.5% of the cases where the children were resident with the wife were contested on the custody issue compared to 17.9% where they were resident with the husband. Where access was exercised by the absent parent, this was as frequently done as in the uncontested cases, but where it was not exercised (which was slightly less than in uncontested cases) the reason often was that it had been refused by the custodian parent (Table 7). Eight of the contested cases were in the context of a defended divorce case. As only thirteen petitions were defended in the whole sample, this perhaps accounts for the much longer time that contested cases took to reach settlement. Nearly one-third took over a year (this omits seven cases in which no outcome was recorded).

Well over half the contested cases were adjourned on decree *nisi* (Table 9). In nearly half of those adjourned, a welfare report was ordered, but in just over a third no steps were recorded in the documents, probably because further negotiations took place between the parties (Table 10). Because of the smallness of the total numbers, factors especially associated with the

ordering of welfare reports in these cases were not readily apparent. There
was some indication that a report was more likely to be ordered if the child
was resident with the husband, if it was proposed that the child should
move. This might indicate that the courts will look more seriously at
proposals that a child should move from the husband than at proposals
that it should move from the wife.

Of the 39 custody contests, custody was awarded to the husband in four
cases, to the wife in seventeen, to the parties jointly in five, and the children
were divided in four cases. In one, custody was awarded to the husband's
sister and in seven others no order was made. In three of the five joint
awards, care and control was given to the wife and in the other two to the
husband. But in only five cases was the child's residence different from
what it had been when proceedings started. Since this was so in only
thirteen instances in the whole sample, it is clear that if such a change is to
take place, it is likely to be in the context of a custody dispute. However, of
those five cases,[16] in only two of these was the change the result of the court
order. Both of these were in favour of the wife and one of them also re-
united separated siblings. It is notable that in one of them the judge ignored
the recommendation in the welfare report and in the other there was no
report. Although, therefore, the study provided evidence of a certain
judicial caution about allowing husbands to look after children, apart from
these two cases, the principle in favour of the *status quo* prevailed even
when contested by the wife.

In *Jussa v. Jussa*[17] Wrangham J. said that a joint custody order with
care and control to one parent "is an order which should only be made
where there is a reasonable prospect that the parties will co-operate." It
may seem somewhat surprising, then, that the outcome of five of the 39
contested custody cases was a joint custody order. In three of the cases,
however, it seemed that this solution was eventually reached after
negotiation between the parties, but in two of them (in the same court) it
seemed likely that this solution was imposed by the court.

In seven contested cases, no resolution was recorded. In four of them
the court allowed a prior order by a magistrates' court in favour of the
husband to stand. In three it seemed possible that the proceedings were still
in progress, and this was the case in two others. Since the coding was done
some two years after most of the petitions were filed, this underlines the
length of time contested cases can take. In one case no clear reason
appeared from the documents why no order was made.

In five of the six cases where access was contested, the children were
resident with the wife. In three of them, the custodian parent had refused
access in two and permitted limited access in the third. These cases involved
lengthy litigation lasting over a year, including later variation applications.
In each of them, welfare reports were obtained, but in one the welfare

officer advised against access but the judge nevertheless ordered it in closely supervised circumstances.

CONCLUSIONS

In dividing the sample between contested and uncontested cases, it was possible to focus attention on the different functions of the courts in each of those circumstances. In exercising their supervisory role both English and Scottish courts are required by statute to be satisfied that the arrangements made for the children are satisfactory or the best in the circumstances. The English courts were reasonably assiduous in trying to obtain evidence to enable them to discharge this obligation. In contrast, the Scottish courts were prepared to express themselves "satisfied" on very meagre information indeed. But despite this discrepancy, the outstanding finding in the research lies in the fact that the outcome of the uncontested cases in both jurisdictions was almost identical. Although in England isolated instances of an apparent preference for the wife was detected, the overwhelming principle on which the courts in both jurisdictions acted was that the *status quo* should be maintained. As to access, the Scottish courts rarely concerned themselves with it and the English courts varied widely in their readiness to make orders about it.

In uncontested cases, therefore, the ability of the courts to exercise a true supervisory role must be seriously questioned. Even if fully informed of the circumstances, there are few alternatives open to the divorce judge. He may make a supervision order if one is recommended or commit the child into care. But these orders seem properly to belong within the ambit of child welfare law, not the divorce jurisdiction. In any case the family's true needs may lie in social assistance and advice. The ample evidence of the difficulties facing one-parent families, especially after divorce,[18] suggests that social resources may be better spent in providing for their needs than in providing information for a judge who cannot help them.

As for contested cases, in which the court's adjudicatory role is central, the evidence suggests that these are not dealt with as quickly or possibly as efficiently as they should be. The outcome of the cases indicates that, although wives more often perceive themselves as being the proper custodians of their children rather than their husbands, the courts on the whole do not necessarily share this view if it would mean disturbing the child's existing environment. In the relatively few cases where a child is moved, it is agreeable that this should never happen without investigation by a welfare officer. It is suggested that if the resources of the court welfare officer were re-directed from investigated uncontested cases to dealing mainly with disputed cases, the courts could perform their adjudicatory function more efficiently. Futhermore, since the courts so seldom, even in these cases move a child, the role of the welfare officer is likely to develop towards that of a counsellor and away from an officer investigating a case on behalf of the court. This, it is suggested, is the right way forward.

Table 1

Facts relied on for divorce

Petitions filed in 1974 National figures	Facts relied on	Decress nisi granted on 1974 petitions Project sample
%		%
27.4	Adultery	30.1
28.4	Behaviour	30.9
5.1	Desertion	4.8
23.0	2 year separation	21.0
12.6	5 year separation	8.7
2.5	Combination behaviour	3.1
0.5	Other combinations	1.4

Table 2

Respondents signifying intention to defend case

Facts		Did respondents signify intention to defend?		
		Yes	No	Total
Adultery	No.	3	193	196
	%	1.5	98.3	100
Behaviour	No.	36	166	202
	%	17.6	82.2	100
Desertion	No.	2	29	31
	%	6.5	93.5	100
2 year separation	No.	2	135	137
	%	1.5	98.5	100
5 year separation	No.	3	54	57
	%	5.3	94.7	100
Combination behaviour	No.	8	12	20
	%	40.0	60.0	100
Other combinations	No.	0	9	9
	%	0.0	100.0	100

Table 3

Voluntary support arrangements

Facts	Did the parties make voluntary support arrangements?	
	Yes %	No %
Adultery	42.9	57.[1]
Behaviour	20.3	79.7
Desertion	9.7	90.3
2 year separation	43.1	56.9
5 year separation	7.0	91.2
Combination behaviour	10.0	85.0
Combination other	11.1	88.9
	n = 652	

(1) Including 0.5 coded Don't Know

Table 4

Proposals about access

Facts	Is access proposed or permitted?			
	No	Yes, defined	Yes, reasonable	Don't Know
	%	%	%	%
Adultery	7.1	4.1	81.6	7.1
Behaviour	16.3	7.9	69.8	5.9
Desertion	25.8	3.2	54.8	16.1
2 year separation	10.9	2.2	83.9	2.9
5 year separation	33.5	3.5	59.6	3.5
Combination behaviour	15.0	5.0	80.0	0.0
Combination other	11.1	0.0	88.9	0.0
	n = 652			

Table 5

Time from petition to settlement of custody (usually decree nisi)

(settled cases only)

Facts	Time in months							Total cases settled
	Under 1	2-3	4-6	7-9	10-12	15-24	over 24	
	percentage settled							
Adultery	0.0	43.0	36.8	11.7	4.4	4.1	0.0	179
Behaviour	0.5	25.0	34.9	20.4	9.8	8.1	0.5	186
Desertion	0.0	46.4	25.0	10.7	10.7	7.2	0.0	28
2 year separation	0.0	42.1	39.7	8.3	3.3	6.6	0.0	121
5 year separation	2.1	28.2	32.6	15.2	6.7	15.2	0.0	46
Combination behaviour	5.5	11.1	22.2	22.2	5.5	28.0	5.5	18
Combination other	0.0	44.4	22.2	11.1	0.0	22.2	0.0	9

n = 587

Table 6

Cases where custody or access contested, by divorce facts

Facts	Custody or access contested		Total cases in sample	
	No.	%	No.	%
Adultery	11	24.4	196	30.1
Behaviour	23	51.1	202	30.9
Desertion	0	0.0	31	4.8
2 year separation	5	11.1	137	21.0
5 year separation	2	4.4	57	8.7
Combination behaviour	3	6.6	20	3.1
Combination other	1	2.2	9	1.4
Total	45	99.8	652	100.0

Table 7

Access by absent parent

Whether access exercised	Uncontested cases % n = 607	Contested cases % n = 45	All cases % n = 652
Access exercised	44.9	44.4	44.5
Access not exercised because custodian refuses	1.8	13.3	2.6
Access not exercised, other reasons	31.0	11.1	29.6
Parties residing together	5.7	17.7	6.6
Access infrequent (1)	8.9	13.3	9.2
Don't Know	8.0	0.0	7.5

(1) Once or twice in previous year

Table 8

Access refused by custodian parent, by ages of children

Ages of children	Access refused		Total sample	
	No.	%	No.	%
0 — 4	12	44.5	280	21.0
5 — 11	12	44.5	701	52.2
12 — 15	3	11.0	270	20.1
16 — 18	0	0.0	91	6.8

Table 9

Whether custody or access settled on decree nisi

Whether Settled	Uncontested Cases		Contested Cases	
	No.	%	No.	%
Settled on decree nisi	505	83.2	12	26.6
Settled after adjournment	51	8.4	28	62.2
No settlement recorded	51	8.4	5	11.1
Totals	607	100.0	45	

Table 10

Reasons for adjournment on decree nisi

Reasons for adjournment	Number	%	Number	%
Further affidavits alone	19	18.4	6	13.3
Welfare report ordered	32	31.1	21[1]	46.6 [1]
Further proposals to be submitted	3	2.9	2	4.4
Awaiting outcome of related proceedings	2	1.9	2[2]	4.4
Nothing recorded	47	45.6	15	35.5
Totals	103		46	

(1) In four of these cases, further affidavits were also required. In one, wardship proceedings were also in progress.
(2) This includes one case (wardship proceedings) shown also among the 21 welfare reports.

Table 11

Final outcome of custody issue

Outcome	No.	%
Custody to husband	47	7.2
Custody to wife	496	76.0
Joint custody	22	3.4
Custody divided	26	4.0
Custody to third party	1	0.2
Child committed to care	2	0.4
No order	58	8.8
Totals	652	100.0

---

1 Social Science Research Council (1977), obtainable from the Centre for Socio-Legal Studies, Wolfson College, Oxford (£1.50 plus postage).

2 For a full examination of the Scottish data and a comparison between the two jurisdictions, see *Custody After Divorce,* Part Two.

3 Divorce Reform Act 1969, s. 1, now Matrimonial Causes Act 1973, s. 1(1).

4 Matrimonial Causes Act 1973, s. 1(2).

5 See Susan Maidment, "A Study of Child Custody" (1976) Family Law 195 at 236.

6 See Joseph Goldstein, Anna Freud and Albert J. Solnit, *Beyond the Best Interests of the Child* (New York, 1973).

7 *Supra,* note 4, s. 41.

8 For a critical analysis of these two functions, see Robert H. Mnookin, "Child-Custody Adjudication: Judicial Functions in the Face of Indeterminacy" (Summer 1975) 39 Law & Cont. Prob. 226.

9 Matrimonial Causes Rules 1977, rule 48.

10 *Ibid.*

11 For full analysis, see *Custody after Divorce,* Ch. 4.

12 For full analysis of these cases, see *Custody after Divorce,* Ch. 5.

13 [1972] 2 All E.R. 600 at 605, [1972] 1 W.L.R. 881.

14 *M. v. M.,* [1973] 2 All E.R. 81.

15 For a full analysis, see *Custody after Divorce,* paragraphs 5-12 to 5-14.

16 Analyzed in *Custody after Divorce,* Ch. 6.

17 [1972] 2 All E.R. 600 at 603.

18 See Elsa Ferri, *Growing-up in a One-Parent Family* (Atlantic Highlands, N.J., Humanities Press, 1976).

The Child In The Divorce Situation — Factors Determining The Custody Question And The Use Of Experts In Custody Cases In Norway

*Lucy Smith and Peter Lødrup**

INTRODUCTION — BACKGROUND

In 1973, the number of divorces in Norway reached 4,664, an increase since 1969 of about thirty per cent. The number of children involved was 7,194, compared to 4,634 in 1969. The figures must be viewed in the light of a population of four million people. Children in divorce situations are being subjected to strain, the extent of which varies from child to child. The task of a legal system dealing with family breakdown must be to formulate rules with the aim of reducing this strain as much as possible. Of equal importance is the safeguarding of the child's future — and the central issue in this connection is which one of the parents shall have custody of the child.

In this paper we will discuss some of the crucial issues in custody cases. We have confined ourselves to an analysis based upon Norwegian law. This approach, though it may seem rather narrow, has been chosen because we feel that a discussion of these problems which, of course, are common to us all, should have a concrete basis.

There is today in most countries a clear tendency to let the interests of the child be decisive in custody cases. The welfare of the child is the fundamental issue; the paramount question is the child's needs. It is generally recognized that the welfare concept comprises both the physical and the psychological wellbeing of the child. In many cases it is the latter which creates the most serious problems for the judge.

The Act on children born in wedlock, of December 21, 1956, states in section 8, paragraph 2:

"The decision shall primarily take into account what is best for the

* Lucy Smith and Peter Lødrup are Professors at the Institutt for Privatrett, University of Oslo, Norway.

child. Where the child is small, the mother should as a rule have the custody, if the court does not find that it would be better for the child to stay with the father. Next, weight should also be attached to the wishes of the parents."

When the law, as in this case, directs the courts to make their decision on the basis of discretion, some standardization will develop regarding the factors relevant to the assessment and their relative weight. The application of the "what is best for the child" rule illustrates this. The different factors which the courts have designated as relevant will be discussed below. When considering the value of these factors, it should, however, be borne in mind that they have a different bearing from case to case. An element which in one case might be decisive could be set aside in another. Precedents in this field have limited effect, and new research on child behaviour may influence the relative weight of the factors.

The decision in a custody case is built upon a prediction. Empirical studies as well as psychoanalytic theory confirm the limited possibilities of predicting a solution which always will be best for a child — even if that is the goal. The factors upon which the prediction is built must therefore be considered as ingredients of a *smorgaasbord* representing generally applicable knowledge and from which the judge may choose those elements which have a bearing upon the case. Consequently, the establishment of general rules about which factors must be considered when determining what is best for the child may have unfortunate consequences. They may entail the dangers that not every aspect of the case is thoroughly deliberated, and that the concrete circumstances are not considered as far as is desirable.

A decision based on the criteria of Section 8, paragraph 2, quoted above, presupposes a dispute between the parents as to who shall have custody of the children. Where the parents agree, their agreement is decisive as to the child's future. In practice, agreement between the parents is attained in the great majority of divorces. A study carried out by Lucy Smith in 1970 shows that in the Oslo area custody agreements were reached in about 93 per cent of the cases where the parents were divorced during the previous year. There is little reason to believe that this figure has changed in recent years, or that the situation is different in other parts of the country. It is interesting to note that in about 92 per cent of these cases the mother obtained custody of the child, in about seven per cent it was decided to let the father have the child, and in about one per cent of the cases the children were distributed between the parents. The causes of this distorted distribution have not been investigated, and we have no information about the considerations on which the agreements were based. In many cases, the child's interests may not have been the major concern — it is hard to believe that parents should think fathers so much less suited to take care of a child than mothers. It is tempting to advance the hypothesis that the fathers give up, partly because it is often most practical to let the mother have the children, and partly out of sheer traditional thinking: this is the normal way of arranging it, this is how it is usually done. In the majority of cases the mother is still the one who has taken care of the duties in the home prior to divorce, and who continues to do so after the divorce. There may be changes in this pattern in the future.

Before turning to consider judicial determinations of custody, we must first clarify the terminology used in this paper. The central concept here is "custody". The most common definition of the concept, and the one we are using, is that custody is the sum total of the rights, duties and powers with respect to the person of the child. Among other things this includes physical care and control of the child, involving feeding and clothing him or her, the choice of residence, control of his or her social life, choice of a name, determination of his or her education, and so on. Colloquially speaking, the central issue in this connection is probably the "possession" of the child.

The word custody is also used in a broader sense, almost equivalent to guardianship. By the term guardianship, we mean the right and duty to take care of the property of the minor, to represent him or her in contractual relations, and other attributes of what is sometimes called "proprietary guardianship". The word custody is also sometimes used in a narrower sense than outlined above. In the so-called "split-order" cases, the "custody" and the "care and control" are separated. The parent with "custody" will have a voice in the child's upbringing even if he or she does not live with the child and the other parent has the "care and control". The term "parental rights" or "parental authority" includes all the rights, duties and powers which a parent has with respect to the child.

RELEVANT FACTORS IN CUSTODY DECISIONS

In Norway, custody decisions are made by the ordinary courts where there is no agreement between the parents. The idea of establishing courts specifically for family matters has never met with much support in Norway. The parents may, however, agree to refer the matter for an administrative decision by a county governor, a method involving a simplified procedure, although this is seldom done in practice.

When deciding what is best for the child, many varying factors will be considered by the courts: the child itself, the parents, the relationship between the child and parents, the surroundings of the family, educational possibilities, the future prospects of the parents, and so on. The legislation does not state any preference for one factor over any other. The only guidance to be found in the legislation is that normally the mother shall have custody of small children unless the court should find that "it would be better for the child to stay with the father". It follows from this, however, that when the child in question is small, the court must make an assessment of the ability of both parents to care for it.

When studying the practice in custody cases, one must bear in mind that each decision is the result of a concrete evaluation of the facts of the particular case. It is also submitted that the reasons for judgment of the courts in many cases do not provide an adequate expression of the motivation of the judge. We feel that the reasoning of the court often serves just as much to defend as to explain the judgment. In many cases the more personal impression of the parties upon the judge and even intuition may be as decisive as more tangible factors. Sometimes this is said straight-forwardly as it was in this extract from an unreported judgment of the Court of Appeals in 1975:

"Finally, there is to say that both the behaviour of the parties after the break and the impression the Court of Appeals has been able to form of the parties during the two days of proceedings, clearly tend to show that the father must be the one who is fit to take care of the children and have custody."

One must also take into account that the wish to avoid hurting the losing party will make itself felt when the opinion is formulated.

Notwithstanding these difficulties, a study of the practice of the courts may produce a sort of catalogue of factors that may be of significance in the individual case. Norwegian legal practice shows that there are certain factors that are common to most determinations of what is best for the child.

In Norway, as in most other countries, there have been two noticeable trends in the law's changing approach to custody cases. The most important one of these is the increasing promotion of the interests of the child. It is now generally accepted that the welfare of the child shall be the decisive issue in custody cases. This means that the wishes of the parents must yield to the interests of the child. A further consequence of this is that the "moral guilt" of the spouses is no longer of interest in custody cases. The statement that "the benefit and interest of the infant is the paramount consideration, and not the punishment of the guilty spouse" from *Mozley Stark v. Mozley Stark and Hitchins*[1] is now more or less universally accepted. Also, the children's opinion and even consent must be provided on important matters affecting them.

The other trend, which actually is a consequence of the first, is the tendency to institute equality between husband and wife in relation to their children.

In the following we shall go into more detail on these points and undertake an analysis of the various factors which most frequently are considered important.

THE STATUTORY PREFERENCE FOR THE MOTHER

The statutory presumption favouring custody to the mother has in many ways a specific significance among the factors to which weight must be attached. Firstly, it is the one and only factor beside the quite subsidiary regard for the wishes of the parents which is mentioned in the Act. Furthermore, in Norway as in most other countries it has strong historical roots, at least as regards physical care and control. Although the preferential position of the mother gradually has become weaker, it still plays an important part. On the other hand, the preference has now become a controversial issue to a greater extent than most of the other factors that are taken into account.

The statutory presumption favouring the mother was weakened by an amendment to the Act on children born in wedlock made in 1969. It applies only where the child is small and will not be better off with the father. The Act thus presupposes an assessment of the father's capability of taking just as good or better care of the child than the mother. According to the prevailing law it is therefore not sufficient to find out whether the mother is fit to take care of the child. Part of the motivation for the 1969 amendment was to prevent the father from engaging to a greater degree than necessary in the issue of the mother's unfitness and the mud slinging which often became part of this issue. Each party must now stress his or her own abilities rather than discrediting the other.

The amendment of 1969 confirmed a development that already had manifested itself, particularly in the practice of the Supreme Court. For some time there has been apparent a growing tendency to let the father have custody of the children. A study of the practice of Norwegian lower instance courts dating from 1959 shows that at that time the father got the children in 9 per cent of all custody disputes. The corresponding figures from 1969 are about 30 per cent and from 1974 approximately 31 per cent. The amendment has consequently had little impact in causing a new trend. The legislator may be said to have done nothing more than adjust the Act according to the actual trends. In the Supreme Court the father is granted custody in more cases than is the mother. Of a total of sixty-one cases, the father was granted custody in thirty-two, the mother in twenty-four, and in five cases the custody was divided between the parents. Futhermore, the father is granted custody of small children more frequently than is the mother and he gets custody of female children in more cases than does the mother.[2]

The figures from the Supreme Court and the lower instance courts are not directly comparable because they stem from different periods. There will of course also be a difference in the selection of cases. However, the figures seem to show that in negotiations the father is more apt to give in than is the mother, and that he will carry on the case only if he has good hopes of succeeding. The judgments in these Supreme Court decisons, moreover, give the impression that the Supreme Court to a greater extent than the lower instance courts undertakes real assessments of the father's suitability for taking care of the child. In the lower courts one can still find that a judge is satisfied with ascertaining that the child is small and that there is not sufficient reason to presume that the mother is not fit.

The figures from the Supreme Court do at any rate put an end to the general belief that it will be of no avail for the father to attempt to get the custody of the children. Moreover, the Supreme Court has presumed that a father can be just as suited as the mother to take care of small children, and in several cases the father has been granted custody of small children where the mother has been considered an unimpeachable parent.[3]

Yet a case study shows that the mother still has a preferential position where the children are small. In some decisions this preference is surprisingly dominant. As an example can be mentioned a decision by the Supreme Court in 1974[4]: the mother was awarded custody of two boys, of four and nearly six years, in spite of several circumstances which gave a less favourable impression of her conscientiousness and the conditions under which she was living. Among other things she "went steady" with a man who had recently completed a long prison sentence and who had been guilty of further punishable action while he kept company with the mother. But the children had been living with the mother for fifteen months and there was nothing to indicate that she had not taken good care of them during this period. For the court the decisive factor appeared to be the closer emotional attachment between the mother and the children.

This case also illustrates a typical conflict. One of the parents — usually the father — appears to be the most fit. He may for instance have a better education, have a stronger character, and on the whole lead a more orderly life. The other parent appears less suitable; she may for instance have little or no education, suffer from bad nerves, or be incapable of keeping a tidy house. But she may prove to be an emotionally warmer person than the other parent and have a closer emotional contact with the children. In such cases Norwegian courts have attached more importance to the emotional contact, at any rate as long as the children are small.

It may be questioned whether the mother preference is given by virtue of special qualities believed to arise because of being a woman and a mother or whether the preference is given because as a rule the mother is the one who is occupied with caring for the children because she mostly stays at home. This will be of significance in cases where the mother is working outside the home and has a job which is just as exacting as the father's. Should she still be given preference? In a decision made by Oslo City Court in 1974 it was said explicitly that the preference was given to her in her capacity as mother:

"The court does not agree that the preference of the defendant (the mother) should be revoked even though she has to go out to work. It is in her capacity as a mother that she has been given this preference. And although she may not be with her daughter in the mornings and during the first part of the day she still has this advantage over the husband in the afternoons."[5]

Although we have not seen this so clearly expressed in any other decision, our impression is that the quoted passage expresses a generally accepted view that the statutory presumption is limited to the cases where the children are small. The courts have assumed that a child is "small" up until it starts school — in Norway, at seven. However, variations in both directions can naturally be found, and this is also in conformity with the intentions of the legislators. By not fixing a definite limit, they wanted to give room for individual variations.

RISK INVOLVED IN CHANGE OF ENVIRONMENT

Risk involved in changing a child's environment is an argument which most often — either by itself or together with other ones — is being cited in the reasoning of the Supreme Court. This argument — which may be called the continuity principle — is also considered important in the lower instance courts. The risk of environment changes will, however, increase in proportion with the time that passes after the breaking up of the marriage.

The great significance attached to the continuity principle can be traced to a Supreme Court decision from 1953, in which a statement was submitted by an expert who was a prominent child psychiatrist. In this statement it was pointed out that environmental changes might have very serious consequences for smaller children, particularly if it would involve the child losing contact with the people with whom it has become involved. The Court states

"This fact has been so generally recognized that both child psychologists and child psychiatrists are of the opinion that it is better for a child to remain in an environment which in various respects may be less favourable than to be removed to a better environment if the consequence would be that the child loses contact with grownups to whom it has become emotionally attached."[6]

When such a great weight is placed on continuity, it is evidently of considerable significance to the result which one of the parents has the child living with him or her after the breakup of the marriage. This factor has also been regarded as relevant in cases where one of the parties has been keeping the child without having the right to do so, for instance when the child has been kidnapped by him or her.

A Supreme Court decision from 1958[7] concerned the custody of an eight year old girl, who had been staying with the mother after the dissolution of the marriage, and who had had a good relationship with that parent. After about three years a court settlement was established according to which the father should have the daughter staying with him during the summer holidays and then send her back to the mother. The father did not keep to the settlement, and the daughter continued to stay with him. During the proceedings the appointed expert stated that the girl had developed a neurotic fear of meeting her mother, that she was happy with the father and that she ought to be allowed to stay with him. The court decided accordingly. The Supreme Court especially stressed that a change of environment might have detrimental effects on the child. The fact that the father had been guilty of a breach of the settlement was not taken into account.[8]

Another well known case concerns the custody of two young boys whose parents were American citizens and lived during the marriage in the United States.[9] The father left the home and took the boys with him (this was the second time he did this) in 1961, and two years passed before the mother was able to trace them to Norway. The custody case was finally decided by the Supreme Court. The boys had then been living in Norway for seven and a half years. On the basis of statements by witnesses and experts the Supreme Court found that the boys were happy with their father; that they liked being in Norway, and that it might be unwise to remove them to a new environment. "And as long as the welfare of the child is going to be the decisive factor, it should not be considered significant that this was the result of illegal behaviour on the part of the father — however reproachable this might be compared to the child's mother".[10]

It is self-evident that the court will be in difficulties in cases where one of the parties illegally has taken the children away or has not sent them back to the other parent as agreed. If such illegal conduct were to be rewarded, it might of course encourage kidnapping in similar cases. On the other hand the words of the law are unambiguous: the decisive factor in each concrete case shall and must be the welfare of the child. This does, however, confront the parties and the lawyers with rather tough problems: should one risk letting the other party have the child for a visit when it might result in loss of custody? Should one consider the interests of the child in having contact with both parents when the outcome is that one loses the case and it is believed to involve problems for the child?

Problems similar to these were discussed by the Supreme Court in a decision from 1974. The question was whether the mother should lose the case because she, out of consideration for the child, had let the child stay with the father until the case was over. The dissenting judge stated:

"Out of a deep sense of responsibility the mother deemed it most correct to postpone moving B. until housing of equal standard and a nursery school had been found in the new place .... This had as result that the father has kept B. first for the one year that went by until the mother had been able to provide such housing as she wanted to give her daughter. After that the court case has entailed that the child has been staying with the father for another one and a half years. It is unfortunate if such a development, which in itself has had the one and only goal of protecting the child from the mental strain involved in the dissolution of a family, should be allowed to influence the final solution to the custody dispute."

However, the majority held that the father should be given custody of the child, first and foremost because the child had been living with him most of the time after the parents had been separated. It should be mentioned that both parents were well suited to take care of the child.

THE CHILD'S WISHES

In a custody case the child's own wishes will always be considered a relevant factor. The older the child, the more weight is attached to his or her preference. In a case concerning a thirteen year old boy, the Supreme Court held:
"It is evident that when a child is 12 years old, it must be taken into account which one of the parents the child wants to live with, and this must apply to an increasing extent proportionate with the age of the child. Although the will of the child should not be decisive as a matter of course, there must be heavy reasons for disregarding its well-founded wish.... To decide that the child should be removed from one of the parents back to the one who has custody without asking the child at all, may easily, in the case of a normally healthy teenager, result in a violation of the child's personality and may also damage the relationship with both parents...."[12]

However, several problems crop up in this connection. The child's wish may be a result of deliberate or subconscious influence on the part of one of the parents. And the smaller the child, the less well-founded its choice. It may also prove difficult to find out what the child really wants. The child may be in a muddle of conflicting loyalties and will not want to hurt either of the parents. In some cases the child may choose the parent whom it believes has the greatest need for the possession of the child, even though it might have preferred the other one. One may also hear a child say that it does not want to choose, but prefers to leave the matter entirely to the court.

Where the child's wish is quite unambiguous, but goes contrary to what otherwise must be regarded as the best solution, the question arises of how much weight should be attached to its preference. Furthermore, it is a question of at which age one should start to ask the child what it wants, and also in which manner the child should be asked.

According to Norwegian law a child of twelve years or more shall be heard in cases concerning its person. This means that the opinions of the child *must* be obtained in custody cases. If this is not done, it is regarded as an error of procedure which may result in an annulment of the decision.

The law does not say how the child's opinion is to be obtained. It is not obligatory for the court to seek the opinion. Where an expert has been appointed in accordance with Section 9 of the Act of 1956 (see *infra*, p. 42) he or she will normally be the one to speak with the child. The expert will naturally be better qualified to elicit this information. If no expert has been appointed, the judge, (or one of the judges, in lower instance courts) talks privately with the child. In cases where the children are older they may be asked to appear as witnesses, but in that event everyone except the judges shall leave the courtroom.

Opinions of children below the age of twelve will also be of interest, except where it is a case of very small children. There are instances where the judge has spoken to children as young as six years, but this is unusual. In such cases the opinion of the child will as a rule come by way of witnesses, experts or statements by the child welfare officer. Sometimes older brothers or sisters voice a view as to where the younger ones wish to stay. It is difficult to fix a definite age limit for when a child's opinion should be heard. To a non-expert it appears that one ought to avoid as much as possible asking the child directly when it is below twelve years of age. Legal practice also shows that the opinion of the child is rarely stated or taken into account until they have reached school-starting age (seven years) and are approaching the age where their opinion *shall* be heard.

In her book *Barn og skilsmisse* (Children and Divorce) (Copenhagen 1973) Gudrun Brun gives an illustrative description of a conversation she had with a seven year old boy in a divorce case. The boy understands that he has to make a choice between his mother and father, and is very unhappy. He tries to make it understood where he would prefer to live without saying so straightforwardly. However, as he is not quite sure that he has succeeded, he ends up by saying confusedly: "I don't want to say where I would rather be, but I would like most to be with my father, but that must be a secret." In our opinion it seems almost cruel to expose a seven year old child to such a strain as having to choose between his mother and father. But of course the court is obliged to consider reliable reports and statements on the child's happiness and welfare with either of the parents.

Norwegian law does not directly prescribe how much weight should be attached to the opinion of the child. This must of course depend on the strength of the child's wishes and the reasons for these wishes. It emerges quite clearly from court practice, however, that the child's own wish is considered important, and the importance increases with the age of the child. Only in very few cases has the court made a decision contrary to a clearly stated and explicit wish of a child who is past the age of twelve. One example is a decision made by the Agder Court of Appeals in 1969. This was a matter of custody of a sixteen year old boy who wanted to live with his mother. The court found, however, that this could not be considered, because it was not obvious that a 16 year old boy would be able to make a wise choice concerning his own future. What evidently tempted the boy was the free and easy life he would be able to lead at his mother's home where no one seemed to think much about going to school, doing homework or keeping clean and where there were no restrictions on alcohol and parties. The father's home was a good one, a fact which also the mother admitted. The boy's three older sisters lived happily and securely with the father, whereas the situation in the mother's house was almost indescribable. In addition, the stepfather had previously resorted to very brutal methods of punishment, and was obviously not fit to guide a sixteen year old boy. The result in this case was obvious. However, there is not much reason to believe that the decision was respected. The boy declared that he would run away to his mother anyway, as he had done several times before. And this is probably an essential point in this connection. It is hard to dictate to an independent youngster, at any rate an independent Norwegian youngster, where he or she shall live.

SEPARATION OF SIBLINGS

A study of court practice reveals that only in very few cases are brothers and sisters separated. Where the custody question is resolved by agreement of the parents, it also appears that the children are kept together. It is often stated as a main rule that there should be no separation of the children of a family. The court may decide that it shall be done where the children have been separated already so that some are living with the mother and some with the father. The leading statement in this matter was delivered by Chief Justice Terje Wold in 1960:

"This (the fact that the brothers and sisters should be kept together as far as possible) is in many cases the most valuable circumstance which is left to the children when the marriage of their parents goes to pieces, especially where the children are as old as in this case and have become used to living together as a family."

It may seem, however, that in certain cases the court has stretched the point of not separating brothers and sisters *too* far. The relationship between children of one family is not always idyllic, and where one or more of them may have a better contact with the father and the other(s) with the mother, it is imaginable that a separation will be for the best. The parents will in that case have more time to take care of each individual child. Especially where there are several brothers and sisters, it may prove hard for one single parent to give them all proper care.

Another factor in favour of separation is that it may make it easier to comply with the right of access. Both parties may be more eager to cooperate if they know that this will affect their own right of access. A separation of the brothers and sisters may also help when it comes to reducing the bitterness between the parents. And this will in turn benefit the future relationship between the children and the parents.

Here as elsewhere the question will primarily depend on the concrete circumstances, such as the difference of age between the children, the sense of belonging together, their age, sex, and the opportunity of continued contact in case they are separated.

THE WISHES OF THE PARENTS

Section 8, paragraph 2 expressly states that the wish of the parents is a relevant factor: "Next, weight should also be attached to what the parents wish". This reference to the wishes of the parents may at first sight appear surprising. In a custody case the wishes of the parents will go in opposite directions. We believe that the law must be interpreted to the effect that *due regard* must be paid to the parents, which means that where no one of the solutions appears most favourable for the child, the court may take into account which one of the parents has the greatest need for keeping the child.

This factor rarely emerges from the reasoning of the courts. Yet we do not doubt that in many cases it is included in the assessment of the court without being explicitly stated.

The fact that the question of which one of the parents is most in need of keeping the child is a very difficult one to settle, is a different matter. But there will be cases where one of the parties quite obviously is less fit to stand the loss of the children than the other, for instance because he or she is psychologically not so well equipped, or because, contrary to the other, he or she to some extent has few other interests in life that can make up for the loss of the children, such as an interesting job.

In a court decision from 1971 the expert stated that "to lose" the children would involve a terrible strain on the mother and might drive her into insanity. On the other hand it would in his opinion have a favourable effect on her mental state if she were allowed to keep the child. The judge said in this connection: "In the opinion of the court this is an important additional factor which must be taken into account when deciding the question of custody."

THE SEX OF THE CHILD

Seen from a statistical point of view the sex of the child appears to play a small part in Norwegian court practice. In the Supreme Court cases from the years 1957 to 1975, mothers have been awarded custody of more boys than girls, and fathers of more girls than boys. And yet it is evident that in many cases the sex of the child is a factor regarded by courts as important. Here are some typical statements from various court decisions: "D is now nearing the age (14 years) where the boy's need to have a father who can aid and guide through the adolescent development of personality, in questions of education and as regards other problems that might arise at this stage, is becoming more prominent". "However, where, as in this case, a girl is involved who has not yet reached the age of seven ... I believe it would be most natural to give the mother preference without having to take a stand as to whether the child is still 'small'." "But children are girls, and they will naturally feel a closer emotional attachment to their mother than to their father". "She will now, and even more so in the future, have a need of daily and close contact with her mother". On the other hand, another Court of Appeals decision emphasized the natural state of conflict which experience shows will develop in many cases between mother and a daughter in her teens. This was used as part of the argument for granting custody to the father.

On the whole it seems that the sex of the child is considered by the court to be a factor of comparatively minor importance, at any rate as long as there are small children involved. In several instances there is no mention of the sex of the child at all. However, where older children are involved, the court is more apt to emphasize this factor. It is beyond doubt that a child needs both its mother and its father, and therefore one major goal in custody cases must be to arrive at a solution whereby the child will be able to keep in contact with both parents. To say whether a boy generally is more in need of a father or a girl in need of a mother, is hardly possible.

MORAL GUILT

Norwegian law has never contained any provisions to the effect that the moral guilt for the end of the marriage shall be considered significant in custody cases. Yet one will find that the court has relatively often taken into account which of the parents broke out of the marriage. This has not been due to some thought of revenge, but because such an act will tell something about that person's sense of responsibility and ability to bring up children.

However, in Norwegian theory and practice, as in many other countries, there has been a growing recognition of the fact that it is almost impossible to point to any one of the parties as "the guilty one" in these cases. Although one of the spouses may have shown clearly deplorable conduct in connection with the breakdown of the marriage, this will as a rule be ignored. In one case, the judge held:

"The court finds that what has been substantiated about the mother's uncontrolled behavior in the home while the spouses were living together, has a direct bearing on the specific problems of this marriage and the situation in which the mother found herself, and that consequently it would not be correct to conclude from this as to the mother's usual ability to control herself, far less as to her fitness for bringing up her child."[13]

The Supreme Court agreed and stated:

"A number of the factors which previously have warranted objections to Mrs. B.'s conduct and treatment of the child seem to have disappeared as she has become more mature, has come out of that unhappy marriage to A and has settled down properly together with her new spouse in a happy marriage."

Similar views can be found in many court decisions. There will, however, naturally be cases where the behaviour of one of the parties unveils personal qualities which are apt to make him or her unfit for taking care of the children.

CHARACTERISTICS OF THE PARENT

The parent's personal qualities will, of course, be of great importance in custody disputes and are brought up in most court cases. It must also be presumed that this factor plays a more significant part than may appear from the courts' reasoning. The Norwegian Supreme Court usually shows reticence concerning its own views on this point because the Court does not have personal contact with the parties.

In the assessment of which one of the parents is most fit to take care of the child, primary consideration is given to the moral qualities of the parents and to their ability to provide a good home for the children. In addition one will take into account the parents' possibilities of mentally stimulating the children, their intelligence and their intellectual capacity.

In some cases the age of the parents is said to matter, especially where the age difference is particularly marked. It is generally supposed that in such cases it will be best for the children under otherwise equal circumstances to stay with the younger of the parents.

Furthermore, the psychological and physical health of the parties will of course count. Bad health may prevent one of the parties from giving the children satisfactory care. In a comparatively large number of cases one of the parents — most often the mother — has been suffering from nervous problems. In the instances where this has been due to marital difficulties, and the person later has recovered, the court will usually disregard this altogether. "And now, when the troubles in the relationship with the spouse after the separation no longer exist, there does not seem to be any reason to assume that the parties will have special psychological problems in the future."[14]

OTHER FACTORS

There are certain circumstances in addition to those already mentioned which are always brought forth in a custody case. These are housing conditions, the possibilities of attending nursery schools, the entire school situation, whether there will be any playmates for the children and on the whole the situation in which the child is to grow up. Very often the court tries to find out whether there will be other grownups in the neighbourhood who can be of help to the child and the parent who is given custody. If the parent in question for instance has his or her own parents, brothers and sisters or other relatives living nearby, this will be considered important.

Previously, Norwegian legal theory maintained that the fact that one of the parents were to remarry would be an element in *disfavour* of granting that person custody. Court practice reveals, however, that an accomplished or a future remarriage of one of the parties quite frequently would strengthen that persons' position. The philosophy is that he or she then is supposed to be able to offer the child a safe and more stable home.

The religion or faith of the parents is almost never considered. In a couple of cases, however, the fact that the mother has been a member of Jehovah's Witnesses has come up. In one instance this was cited as the decisive argument for not granting custody to the mother, whereas in two other cases, one of which was a Supreme Court decision, this was not taken into account. The Supreme Court stated:
"As it cannot be proved that the mother's religious views have had any detrimental effect on the children, the fact that she holds a diverging religious belief cannot bring about a result other than that which would be warranted by the other circumstances of this case."[15]

In several decisions the court has stressed as a decisive argument that the child should maintain the closest possible contact with both parents. A Court of Appeals decision from 1974 is a typical example. The court granted the mother custody in contradiction of the expert statements. The court considered it decisive that the father had demonstrated an irresponsible attitude by keeping the child away from the mother, and that it must be assumed that in the future he would not uphold her right of access. The mother, on the other hand, was obviously quite prepared to be cooperative on this point.

An unusual factor in Norwegian legal practice was brought up in a much discussed Court of Appeals case from 1974[16] concerning the custody of a four year old girl. There was a boy of three in the marriage as well, but it was agreed that he should stay with the mother. The mother was a coloured American citizen, and two years before the divorce she had moved from Norway to California. The daughter had remained with the father. Both parents were regarded as well suited to take care of the child. The Court of Appeals found that the mother ought to have custody, and it is evident that the court attached importance to the fact that the daughter was coloured:

"The Court of Appeals will emphasize that, with the future in view, it will be best for B. to stay with her mother. She will then grow up in the x/y area where they are used to people of various races, mixed races and colours, and where this does not attract unwanted attention. In Norway she would be noticed because of her skin colour, her features and her hair; and may perhaps be made to suffer in other ways on account of her appearance. Although it must be hoped that such offensive conduct will not occur, she will on account of her appearance not be able to feel quite at home in our country. This feeling must be presumed to become stronger as she grows older and will move outside the protected surroundings where she now lives."

Thus, in this instance the court found that the child should stay with the mother notwithstanding the fact that this would mean a radical change of environment for the child, and that the father had been regarded as very well suited to have the child in his care. Quite surprisingly, the father was not allowed to proceed with the case before the Supreme Court.

JOINT CUSTODY

It seems that the courts now, at least in some countries, are reluctant to deny a parent all rights over his or her children. This is in conformity with recent legislation in several countries, which has taken care to equalize the rights of husband and wife over their children. In England there have for instance been several so-called "split order" cases, that is to say, an order according to which the responsibility for children is divided between the spouses, either by a joint order for custody with care and control to one person, or an order for custody to one of the spouses solely, with care and control to the other.

In Norway this development started in 1973 with a letter from the Ministry of Justice to all county governors who decide custody disputes where the parents do not wish to have the question decided by the courts. In the letter it is stated that the passage quoted above from Section 8 does not prevent the parents from agreeing, in the event of separation or divorce, that they shall have joint custody. However, it was also said that according to Norwegian law one of the parents cannot have sole custody, while the other at the same time has only care and control. Thus, pursuant to Norwegian law, a "split order" must involve joint custody.

After this letter it has evidently become more and more usual that the parents agree on joint custody. Court settlements are also made to this effect. In May 1976 a lower instance court decided upon the wish of the father to give the parents joint custody notwithstanding the fact that the mother did not agree; she wanted sole custody. This is, for the time being, the only decision we have found where the court has dictated joint custody although the parents did not agree about it. In this connection it may be mentioned that in Sweden a bill has been presented which will make it possible to give the parents joint custody. Existing Swedish law does not permit this. However, according to the bill joint custody shall be granted only in cases where the parents agree to it. It seems to us that there can be no objection to an order for joint custody provided both parents consent. In many ways it appears unreasonable that a wholly unimpeachable father or mother should lose all rights concerning the child only because the parents have left each other. To many parents it is emotionally important to be able to maintain the same legal relationship towards their children after a separation or a divorce. Joint custody may also help to avoid conflicts of prestige. However, one condition for a joint-custody order should be a reasonable prospect of cooperation between the parents. For this reason it may be questionable to grant joint custody in cases where one of the parents opposes it.

A split order, according to which one of the parents — as a rule the mother — has the care and control, and the other the custody, appears in our view rather unfortunate. It seems fair that the parent who has the child living with him or her also should be permitted to take part in the more important decisions concerning the child. We are therefore a bit surprised at a statement in the English case of *Jussa v. Jussa*,[17] where the settlement of one parent having care and control and the other having sole custody is considered to be "the more normal form of split order". We are more in favour of the Norwegian rule which says that it should not be possible to give one parent only care and control and the other parent only custody.

USE OF EXPERTS

In Norway there is no specific court and no special rules as to the composition of the court in custody cases. It is sometimes maintained that such matters are not suited for the ordinary courts which follow the general rules of procedure. The issue is of such a character that persons with a background other than a legal one might be better equipped to reach the best decisions. It must, of course, be admitted that the study of law provides inadequate qualifications for judging which one of the parents is most fit to have custody of the children. Mr. Justice Leivestad of the Supreme Court has expressed it in the following terms:
"Cases concerning custody of children and the right to be with the children are frequently among the most difficult cases a judge has to face. Not from a legal point of view, the legal problems involved are as a rule not very complicated. But seen from a human angle they are often so important that they make the responsibility involved in making the decision a very heavy one; the law contains few guidelines, it leaves most of it to the discretion of the court."[18]

However, the general view is that a decision made by a judge with a legal education according to ordinary court procedure is the best way to handle custody cases. This point of view must be considered in the light of two factors: the kind of aid the judge can and must obtain from experts, and the alternatives which might be available.

It is of course necessary for the judge to be presented with the required factual material on which to base a decision. For the most part this material can be supplied by the parties to the case — although perhaps by each in his or her manner. To this must be added that Section 9 of the Act of 1956 says that "if and when required, the child care inspectorate or experts shall have brought forth their opinion before the question (of custody) is decided." This means that one has the instruments both for providing further facts and — what is equally or more important — for analysing these facts on the basis of the special knowledge of the experts, who submit their recommendations to the judge.

In our opinion this system takes care of two fundamental requirements: the negotiations are conducted according to the adversary process — a principle of central significance in the law of procedure and consequently a safeguard against arbitrary decisions. And yet the psychological expertise is given a central place. It should be added that psychologists and psychiatrists are not much in favour of the idea that they should sit on the bench — they are, they say, no part of the judiciary and do not wish to become involved in the decision making. If they were to act as judges, it would be rather far-fetched to imagine that they should also undertake the investigations on which the decision is to be based. The danger of the psychologist becoming an amateur lawyer is no less than the danger of the lawyer becoming an amateur psychologist.

As mentioned above, agreement between the parents is in the great majority of cases decisive regarding the question of where to place the children. In these cases there is no testing of whether the agreement of the parents brings the result which will prove to be most beneficial for the children. It must probably be admitted that in very many cases the motives of the parents are quite different from this goal, as in each concrete case they are apt to stress what is most practical for themselves. It is a striking contrast to the fact that in the cases where the parents do *not* agree, extensive legal machinery is normally set in motion, with investigations of persons and families, assessment of environment and educational facilities, and frequently highly qualified psychological and/or psychiatric help. This contrast is often emphasized by the experts — particularly when they state their reservations about being involved in a dispute. In this connection it may also be mentioned that experts maintain that their time can be put to better use than to provide material for and an assessment of where it will be best for the child to live in cases where both parents are suited to take care of the children. In our opinion we are here touching on a very central issue which may give rise to several trains of thought. The fundamental fact is: with a few exceptions both parents are suited to have custody. In some cases one of them is better suited than the other, but in most cases the child will be able to lead a happy life — according to the circumstances — with either one of them. Can it be said to be a fair use of meagre public resources to weigh one of the parents against the other when they are both qualified to take care of the child? Why set the big machine in motion in disputes, when no control is being exercised where the parents agree? The answer is probably that it will not be possible to investigate in a proper manner about five thousand divorced couples each year — this would at any rate have to be done at the expense of other social commitments. Moreover, it may be said that the fact that the parents agree is more important than which alternative they choose. Where they agree, there is likely to be less bitterness and better chances of a good relationship between the children and both parents. In any case, the fact that the child welfare officer and experts are being engaged in disputes is a natural result of the formalizing of the conflict which takes place and our tradition that the courts are to do a thorough job and to be provided with as much information as possible in each case. The paradox is still there, however. We must also take into account the strong wish of the judges to have the best possible expert aid. Justice Leivestad thus strongly advocates a strengthening of expert assistance for the courts,[19] a wish which contrasts heavily with the experts' view as to their role in custody disputes. A Danish psychiatrist has stated that, where Denmark is concerned, the situation so far has been that child psychiatrists and child psychologists have not displayed much interest in custody disputes. The reasons given have as a rule been shortage of time, or in other words, that it would be a waste of time.[20] It should also be mentioned that the use of expert statements in custody cases is often criticized by the psychologists. The experts maintain that their statements apply to the one case in question only, and that their statements should therefore be supplied with a date and should not be referred to in later custody disputes.

For the expert it will always be a question of putting first things first — wouldn't expert assistance be more valuable before the divorce is a fact, or to help others who may be in difficulties? Another problem may arise from the expert's professional ethics: the work of the psychologist and the psychiatrist is based on a relationship of trust which may be broken up if the knowledge of the experts is placed at the disposal of the courts.

STATUTORY PREFERENCE FOR THE MOTHER

As regards the existing statutory presumption favouring the mother, we agree that in the majority of cases small children will usually get the best care from the mother. This does not, however, justify the preference as it is expressed in Section 8. The reasoning behind the preference will of course be valid even if it is not expressed in the Act. As long as the mother preference is statutory, there will be a risk of the court resorting to this provision without undertaking a thorough examination and comparison of the parents' possibilities of providing a good home for the child. It is an easy way out for the court in difficult cases just to assert that this is a case of "small children in need of a mother's care". The law should not admit this possibility.

Furthermore, it is a fact that there is no longer substance in the presumption that small children always will benefit from staying with the mother. One of the reasons for the mother preference was that it would be easier for her to care for the children because she did not as a rule go out to work. However, in recent years there has been a radical change in this situation, as an increasing number of women are taking up work in addition to their domestic duties; if a woman has not done this before, the divorce will often force her to go out to work for economic reasons. If the mother's work demands just as much of her as the father's job does of him, then we are right back to the question of whether the mother ought to have a preferential position on account of her special qualities as a woman and a mother. In our opinion there can be no doubt that in most cases the mother will feel a greater responsibility towards the children than the father, whether this might be due to biological relations or upbringing and tradition, or to a combination of these factors. However, this will far from always be the case, and each case should be decided on its own merits. As a consequence of women's general engagement in professional life, young people today evidently base the rearing of their children more on cooperation, where the mother and father both share the care for the children. Consequently, the close contact from which important emotional factors are derived is no longer a mother's monopoly. In this connection it might be of interest to refer to a statement by an expert in a decision by the Court of Appeals from 1974. He said that the father would be able to offer the children a more "tenderly 'maternal' care than the wife", and for this reason he advocated the granting of custody to the father.

There is reason to believe that a repeal of the statutory presumption will result in the father getting the children more often than is the case at present, although the mother still probably will have an actual preferential position. We do not consider it a goal in itself that the father should be granted custody in a larger number of cases. But we do believe it is desirable that the courts make a free choice based on an evaluation of the personal capacities of the parties and their possibilities of providing a safe and good home for the children.

When the 1969 amendment was drafted, the question of a statutory preference was much discussed. It should be noted that the Norwegian Association of Judges was against a total repeal of the preference, and thus favoured the proposal of the Family Law Reform Committee, which later became the new text. The Association pointed out that the then proposed statutory preference was limited to cases where small children were involved and that it would be of consequence only where it would be impossible to tell which parent would be best for the child. It would not apply where the court or the county governor finds that the father can show evidence that it will be better for the child to stay with him. The proposal also seemed, in the Association's view, to imply that where older children were concerned one cannot stick to the presumption that the child will be better off with the mother. The judges concluded that the limited mother preference could hardly be of any significance in practice. One would, regardless of a statutory preference, find it most beneficial for a small child to live with its mother. Only in rare cases would it be impossible for a court to decide where it would be best for the child to stay.

Notwithstanding these objections, the Association decided to agree to the Committee proposal because they believed that, on the basis of previous legislation in the field, it seemed natural to maintain a mother preference where small children were concerned. If any prescription as to preference were to be excluded, they thought, the exclusion might easily be judged to carry more weight than intended.

THE BEST INTERESTS OF THE CHILD: SOME REFLECTIONS

When the rule says that the result shall be anchored in the "what is best for the child" standard, it is evident that the judge has a duty to weigh one of the parents against the other. But it must be proper to ask — at any rate in some cases — whether one should not also consider the situation of the parents — after all, three human fates are involved, those of the father, the mother and the child. If we assume that the child will be well off with one of the parents, but possibly a little better with the father, the result is obvious: the father will be given custody. However, if this situation will result in the mother having a breakdown, should not that fact be taken into account as well? Is it more important that an eight year old boy will be a little happier even if the consequence is that his thirty year old mother becomes a psychiatric case, than that the mother gets custody and remains a healthy human being? We think that the courts — in more marginal cases, anyhow — should consider more explicitly than is being done in practice today the consequences of a decision for the parent who loses the case. This will demonstrate the contrast between the role of the judge and the roles of the psychiatrist and the psychologist: to the former the case is closed when judgment has been passed, whereas for the latter it will be necessary to regard father, mother, and child as potential patients in the future.

We share fully the view expressed by a Norwegian professor of child psychology:
"The grownups concerned here are human beings too, aren't they — and must have a right to their share of consideration — or, in other words — one must find the least detrimental solution for them as well. Considerations must be balanced against each other, although as a rule the regard for the children should come first."[21]

Both where the parents agree as to which one of them is to have custody and also where the courts decide the question, it is being maintained that the child ought to be represented by a person who could take care of its interests. In cases of agreement this will probably not be of much help unless this person's arguments might influence the opinion of the parents. It is hard to say whether this would be the outcome in many cases. As regards the court procedure, it may appear paradoxical that the parents are the parties to the case, and fight each other to convince the judge that the child would be better off with one or the other, whereas the child has no spokesman at all. Should not the child as well be represented by counsel? The question has lately been posed in many quarters in Norway. In our opinion the answer should be no. If the efforts of a lawyer representing the child are to be limited to ensuring that all information of significance is presented to the court, his or her importance will be minimal. If, on the other hand, the lawyer pleads the child's case and propounds an opinion as to who should have custody, the judge may easily be put in a delicate position. Should he pass a judgment against the assertion of the child's counsel, when the aim is a decision where the essential factor is the welfare of the child? In many cases the person representing the child would thus be the one who actually decided the case, without his opinion being the result of an adversary procedure.

A discussion of the "what is best for the child" rule cannot dodge the continuity principle mentioned above. As maintained there, the courts are reluctant to grant custody to the parent who has not had the child with him or her since they parted company. Thus the parent who after the divorce has had care of the child will have a considerable advantage. This means that the dispute about custody is not solved exclusively by means of assessing which one of the parents would take best care of the child. Considerable weight is attached to the circumstance that it would be unfortunate for the child to have to move out of the environment where it has been living since the divorce, and especially to be parted from a person to whom the child has been very close. Moreover, if the child is in good hands already, why the change? Consequently, the fact that court proceedings take time works in favour of the parent who has care and control of the child until the case is over. This may encourage delays and appeals. We are of the opinion that reforms in this field are necessary. Still another factor may explain the courts' adherence to the continuity princple, *i.e.* that the removal of the child in itself may prove a dramatic and disturbing event, if the parent who so far has been keeping the child opposes the move. The truth of this is illustrated by the following court case from 1976. During divorce proceedings a seven year old girl had been staying with the father but the parents agreed that the mother was to have custody. When the mother asked to have the child given to her, the father refused with reference to the fact that he no longer believed that the child should stay with her. The mother got a court order saying that the sheriff's office should enforce the surrender of the child. When the sheriff came to the father to get the child, the following happened, according to the report of the sheriff:

"When we came to get the child, she cried despondently, and the mother asked permission to speak to her alone. The father of the child refused at first, but gave in when I carried the child out into the kitchen and asked the mother to follow. They were together for about half an hour, and we could hear the child crying and pleading, she wanted to be with her father.

When I fetched them back in again the child cried as if her heart would break and she clung desperately to his legs, and he let it be quite clearly known that he did not intend to let the child go. All attempts to persuade him were of no avail. I then took hold of the child and asked the mother whether she still wanted the child to be taken by force. The representative of the child care inspectorate protested, and when Dr. Svarstad was asked whether this should be allowed to happen, he answered that it should not. This was also agreed to by the plaintiff in the presence of everybody."

The father has now brought a court action for custody, and the mother has consented to having the daughter live with him until the matter has been decided.

The value of upholding a strict continuity principle is today debated by psychiatrists, psychologists and lawyers. The statement from 1953 cited above has been used too indiscriminately in later cases. We maintain that one cannot state as a matter of principle that a change of environment is detrimental. It will depend on a number of factors, such as the age of the child, its mental sturdiness and also the preparation and implementation of the change. It should for instance be obvious that where small children are concerned, a change might prove detrimental just because it is impossible to prepare a child for what is going to happen. It must be said that critics of the statement have gained support. Everyone agrees, of course, that the quite small child will have special problems if it is torn away from the surroundings it is used to. However, these problems will lessen when the child reaches the age where it is possible to prepare it for the change. It is therefore suggested that to stress the importance of maintaining continuity may be too shortsighted a view. The decision may for instance be taken when the child is four years old, but it has consequences for many years to come. A decision which at the moment may seem harsh, may in the long run prove the most favourable.

Another aspect of the continuity principle is the question of whether the custody can be changed, either by way of agreement between the parents or by a new court decision. Pursuant to Norwegian law, an agreement for a transfer of the custody will be decisive and there is also the opportunity of bringing a new court action, the outcome of which may be the granting of custody to the other parent. These provisons have not been subjected to criticism and in practice it happens quite often that custody is transferred to the other parent without this involving considerable problems for the child.

Editor's Note

Courts in Canada have considered the question of divided custody orders, referred to in the papers of Mr. Eekelaar and Professors Smith and Lødrup. In general, there appear to be two basic types of order made by courts in this country, the split order and the joint order. In *Jussa v. Jussa* (1972) 10 R.F.L. 263, at 266, Mr. Justice Wrangham of the English Family Division observed that the usual form of a split custody order provides for custody in one parent and care and control in the other. The implications of such a split order were outlined by Mr. Justice Johnson of the Saskatchewan Court of Queen's Bench, in *Huber v. Huber* (1975) 18 R.F.L. 378. At page 382, he stated:

"Therefore if the power of care and control is given to one parent and custody (in its widest sense) to the other the latter has all the powers inherent in custody except physical care and control."

The parent with custody in its "widest sense"

". . . retains the right of supervising the education, religious training and general upbringing of the children and the making of decisions having a permanent effect on their lives and development."

The parent with only physical care and control would not, in theory at least, have this legal authority to make key decisions, but would have a great deal of actual influence over the course of the child's development.

In *Huber v. Huber,* the Court awarded custody to the father and care and control to the mother. Another decision of the Saskatchewan Court of Queen's Bench, *Charko v. Charko* (1974) 17 R.F.L. 343, illustrates the use of the split order in a case involving a parent and third parties. There, custody in its widest sense of his son and step-son was awarded to a father after the children had been placed in a foster home because of their mother's neglect. Physical care and control of the children was to move from the foster home to the father after a period of two or three months to allow the father and children to become better acquainted and adjust to the change. In this case, the father's serious physical handicap would necessitate the making of some special arrangements for his care of the children.

Other types of orders that can be based on the distinction between the full "bundle" of rights and obligations toward a child (custody in its "widest sense") and physical care and control have been referred to as joint orders. One kind of joint order provides that both parents have custody in the broad sense of that term, with one parent only having care and control. Mr. Justice Wrangham in *Jussa v. Jussa* stated that this type of arrangement is of more recent origin than the split order. He would date its appearance in England from *Clissold v. Clissold* (1964)

108 S.J. 220, a case in which Karminski J. refused to make one. Two reported decisions of the Manitoba courts exemplify the use of the joint order described here. In *Miller v. Miller* (1974) 17 R.F.L. 92, the Court of Appeal upheld an order of Nitikman J., awarding custody of the children jointly to the mother and father, with physical custody to the father. The factors taken into account by the Court do not, unfortunately, appear in the brief report of the case. In *Farkasch v. Farkasch* (1972) 1 W.W.R. 429, 4 R.F.L. 339, 22 D.L.R. (3d) 345 Matas J. of the Manitoba Queen's Bench awarded joint custody of the young son to both mother and father with actual physical custody to the father and reasonable access to the mother. The father, he said, was more mature and more aware of the responsibilities of a parent and appeared to have more carefully formulated plans for caring for the boy. A variant of this type of order was affirmed by the Manitoba Court of Appeal in *Parker v. Parker* (1975) 20 R.F.L. 232. Custody in the widest sense was allowed to both the mother and the father of the child, with physical care and custody to the mother during the school year and to the father during the summer and access each Sunday of the year for the non-custodial parent. Although the report of the decision is somewhat brief, it appears as if one of the reasons for stipulating joint custody may have been to give the father a veto on any unconventional plans the mother may have considered for the children. Chief Justice Freedman stated that the father of the children was apprehensive that they might "fall under the control of" the Ecumenical Institute, an organization of which the mother was a member and on whose premises she lived with the children. The Chief Justice continued: "It was probably to allay such fears that the learned trial judge ordered that no commitment in regards to the said children be made to the Ecumenical Institute unless it be a commitment made jointly by the petitioner and the respondent." (p. 232).

This last sort of arrangement is somewhat similar to a second type of joint order. In this type, parents alternate in their possession of the full bundle of powers: for part of a year, one parent may have "custody" with "care and control" and for the other part of the year, custody with care and control will shift to the second parent. Mr. Justice Bayda of the Saskatchewan Court of Queen's Bench made this sort of order in *Buchko v. Buchko* (1973) 11 R.F.L. 252, stipulating that the mother should have "custody and control" from September through June, inclusive, each year, with the father having "custody and control" in July and August, and the non-custodial parent from time to time having reasonable access to the youngster. The court found that there was "really not all that much to choose" between the home offered by the father and that offered by the mother, although it was satisfied that the mother should have the dominant role for the time being. Perhaps one of the reasons for stipulating that the father should have both custody and control, rather than mere physical custody or an extended period of access in the summer, was the fact that the father resided in Saskatchewan and the mother in Ontario. Although the reasons do not explicitly state so it is not unreasonable to suggest that the court was mindful of the difficulties of having children that far from their legal guardian during two summer months, when they might, for example, need medical attention. In conclusion, Mr. Justice Bayda offered at p. 254 an observation which might be applied to almost any case where divided custody is ordered:

". . . I certainly hope that neither party regards this order as a personal victory or as a victory for the other party. Custody matters should not be viewed in that light. If there is a victory aspect to this order at all — and I have considerable doubt that there is — it should be deemed a victory for the children."

Mr. Justice Weatherston of the Supreme Court of Ontario, on the other hand, refused to make an order of this sort in *McCahill v. Robertson* (1974) 17 R.F.L. 23. He stated that his decision was based on the "very strong feeling" that divided custody is "inherently a bad thing." Refusing a request by the father, a Vancouver resident, for sole custody one quarter of the year of the couple's son who lived in Ontario with his mother, Mr. Justice Weatherston said, at pp. 23-24,

"A child must know where its home is and to whom it must look for guidance and admonition and the person having custody and having that responsibility must have the opportunity to exercise it without any feeling by the infant that it can look elsewhere."

Obviously, a divided order of custody will not be suitable in all, or even many, cases. It is apparent, however, that the divided order is a device of considerable flexibility: in relying upon the divisible nature of custody, the court can fashion solutions to take advantage of the strengths and minimize the weaknesses of the parental situation. It is probably not wise to attempt to choose the "best" type of divided custody order. One feels an initial resistance to the split order, which locates only physical care and control in one parent and places all the other aspects of legal custody in the other. The physical custodian may not relish the idea of being formally excluded from the critical decisions about education, religion, and upbringing, as if he or she were only a hired nursemaid. The parent with legal custody may on the other hand become frustrated if the actual influence of the physical custodian undermines his or her efforts at making key decisions, or if he or she does not succeed in remaining close enough to the child to appreciate its evolving aspirations. On the other hand, however, the real usefulness of the split order can be seen when it is contrasted, not with other types of divided orders but with the conventional order placing custody and control in one parent only. The conventional order effects a much more complete severance of the relationship between the non-custodial parent and the child than does the split order.

The problem with the split order may best be illuminated by asking when it is proper for a court to deny legal custody to the parent with physical care. This question, again, is only relevant where the court is also prepared to continue the relationship between the child and the non-custodial parent by continuing that parent as legal guardian of the child. In almost all cases, it is suggested, if a parent is suited to have physical care then that parent should probably also be legally entitled to be consulted about the important matters relating to legal custody or guardianship. Only where it seems for quite a particular reason not to be in the child's best interests to give the physical custodian full legal custody as well should that be withheld. One can perhaps envision a few instances where this might be the case. A parent may give signs of wanting to use rights as a legal custodian to obtain a passport for the child and remove him or her from Canada. A parent who is well suited for physical custody may seem ill-suited or possibly harmful for the determination of matters related to the child's property or, as in *Parker v. Parker,* religion. On the other hand, however, one would think that denying this parent legal custody, if he or she is found fit for care and control, might be too drastic in light of a readily available option: leaving legal custody in both parents, with care and control in one. This approach leaves both feeling involved in the future of the child, and allows the child to benefit from the wisdom and experience of both, while perhaps ensuring that the excesses of either one will be mitigated by the necessity to act jointly. The divided order is one that will only work where both parents want it to work. Having established the existence of this sort of cooperation, and decided to make some sort of divided order, there seems little reason for a court to deny to the physical custodian the position of legal custodian as well. At least, the reasons for doing so should be very clear and compelling. Lord Denning offers one rationale for the split, as opposed to the joint, order in *Wakeham v. Wakeham* [1954] 1 W.L.R. 366 at 369, [1954] 1 All E.R. 434:
"Cases often arise in the Divorce Court where a guilty wife deserts her husband and takes the children with her, but the father has no means of bringing them up himself. In such a situation the usual order is that the father, the innocent party, is given the custody of the child or children, but the care and control is left to the mother. That order is entirely realistic."
This, with all due respect, does not seem to be a sound basis on which to deny the mother legal custody, although in this sort of case it is eminently desirable to see that the father is not excluded from continued involvement merely because of the impracticability of his making arrangements for care.

1 [1910] P. 190 at 194.
2 On an average, the Supreme Court deals with four to five child custody cases annually. This number is, of course, too small to make a basis for an annual survey. The figures quoted cover the aggregate practice of the Supreme Court in the period from 1957, when the new Children Act was passed, up to 1976.
3 Norsk Retstidende 1970, pp. 592 and 1407, 1971 p. 1103 and 1973 p. 1396.
4 Rt. 1974.1343.
5 It must be assumed that this statement only refers to cases where the parents otherwise are in an equal position.
6 Rt. 1953.1375.
7 Rt. 1958.664.
8 The following year the case was reopened at the request of the mother. It then appeared that the father was a drug addict and had been so during the Supreme Court proceedings. The girl was then sent back to the mother, and the change did not seem to have any negative effects on the child.
9 Rt. 1968.368.
10 Also in this case there have been later developments. The father remarried in Norway, and then he sent the two sons of his first marriage back to the United States. A year later he left his second wife and illegally took their child with him to America. He has not yet been traced.
11 Rt. 1974.1112.
12 Rt. 1974.1339.
13 Rt. 1964.317.
14 Oslo City Court, 1974.
15 Rt. 1973.1113.
16 Rettens Gang 1974.310.
17 *Jussa v. Jussa* [1972] 2 All E.R. 600, [1972] 1 W.L.R. 881.
18 Leivestad, Psykologisk sakkyndige i barnefordelingssaker, Lov og Rett 1969, s. 370.
19 LoR 1969, pp. 370-372.
20 G. Brun, Faglig hjelp i barnefordelingssaker.
21 See *Ase Gruda Skare* Lov og Rett 1975 p. 31. The comment is made in a review of the Book *Beyond the Best Interests of the Child* by Joseph Goldstein, Anna Freud and Albert J. Solnit (New York, 1973) where the view that the interest of the child should be the sole and paramount consideration is strongly advocated.

Trial Of Custody Issues And Alternatives To The Adversary Process

Henry H. Foster, Jr.*

From the viewpoint of an American lawyer, just as a declaration of war is too important a matter to be left to the generals, custody decisions cannot be abdicated to the experts. The rule of law, rather than the postulates of behavioural science, must determine and control. Alternatives, of whatever specie, may at most be utilized to assist or to supplement the judicial process. This is especially true where only a dispassionate justice may calm deep emotions and vigourous contention.

On the other hand, if one looks at child custody determinations from the point of view of the social worker, or expert on child behaviour and development, one is tempted to short circuit the adversary process, if that is possible, and to substitute an "expert" for the court.[1] From this perspective the ordinary judge is ill-equipped to make a decision on an "expert" matter because he or she is too poorly informed on child behaviour and development.

A few years ago I visited Utrecht in The Netherlands and observed the procedures followed by their correction system in the disposition of convicted offenders. Utrecht had a forensic science institute on the European model and there was a screening of all convicted persons in order to determine where they would be assigned on indeterminate sentences, *i.e.,* at the Queen's pleasure. Depending upon the then attitude of the convicted person, and a decision as to whether he or she would cooperate in a rehabilitation program, a given person would be sent to a minimum or a maximum institution, or placed in a half way house, or on probation. There was no right to habeas corpus. Again, the term served was "at the Queen's pleasure." Moreover, the prestige of the director, or senior professor, of the institute, was such that when he spoke, or a decision was issued in his name, it rarely was challenged, since he was top man on the pecking order.

For those of us conditioned by the common law and our Anglo-

---

* Henry H. Foster, Jr. is Professor of Law, New York University, and Chairman, Family Law Section, American Bar Association.

American tradition, the Utrecht model is Kafkaesque. The absence of criminal due process and judicial checks in the system, and the unavailability of habeas corpus seem, to us to sell a birthright for a mess of pottage, no matter how eminent the senior professor of the Institute staff may be in behavioural science. We can visualize a momentarily embittered and sullen offender being shunted off to maximum security for life while the glib con artist gets probation regardless of the real rehabilitative prospects.

A current case I am involved with also illustrates the problem of experts gone mad. In this case there was a custody dispute between a divorced father and mother over the visitation rights of the father. There was a son aged thirteen and a daughter aged eleven. The mother brought an action to have the father's visitation rights terminated, alleging that he manipulated or "brainwashed" the children so that the mother's relationship with them had deteriorated to the point where there was continuous and open hostility. To buttress her claim, the mother had two prominent psychiatrists take the stand, one of whom sat at her counsel table and advised and consulted with her lawyers throughout the trial. The substance of their testimony was that the father showered too much attention, love, and affection, and in that way he set up an invidious comparison which made the mother look bad. One of these experts, when asked if there was any authority to support his recommendation that the father be denied further visitation rights, cited the controversial book *Beyond the Best Interests of the Child* and a passage (at p. 38) which gives a custodial parent an absolute veto right over visitation by the other parent.[2] The trial judge, impressed by this expertise, but not completely sold, suspended the father's visitation rights for six months.

Since that decision, which is now on appeal, the mother has seen the children only once for a period of an hour or so. The father has not seen them at all. They are staying in the suburbs with mutual friends of the family. The mother's one contact with them was chaotic. No explanation has been given for her failure to reclaim the children, and in the meantime, they have not attended their old school but are temporarily enrolled in a school in the neighbourhood of the family friend who is caring for them. The practical result is that the court's order made orphans out of the children. They do not see either their father or their mother.

From my biased point of view, the expert witnesses were wrong from the beginning, and the principal witness spoke as an advocate or team man. In fact, in my opinion, alienation from the mother was due to her inadequacies and her emotional and mental conditon, rather than manipulation by the father. Her treatment of the children had been outrageous, she had physically abused them, locked them in her townhouse, denied them adequate food, and to put it mildly, had been eccentric and erratic in her behavior. All of this was glossed over by her witnesses in their scapegoating of the "narcissistic" father, and the fact that this wealthy woman had spent several weeks at the Payne Whitney Hospital for a "nervous breakdown" was all but ignored.

There may be several reasons why the trial court entered an unprecedented order suspending the visitation rights of a concerned father. The major reason is that the process was not truly an adversary one. Counsel for both the mother and the father deferred to the experts and instead of a contest the proceeding resembled a seminar. Cross-examination was minimal. Significant facts and circumstances were never developed. Even though prior New York decisions suspended or terminated visitation rights only where there was parental unfitness, abandonment, or child abuse, in this unprecedented case the court decreed a six months' suspension of visitation with the father in order to give an erratic mother an unrealistic opportunity to win their love and respect. Ironically, she herself rejected the opportunity and has had nothing to do with the children whose hostility towards her continues unabated. Obviously, love and respect cannot be coerced even by a court, and the experts were in grievous error regarding their evaluation of the mother and the human relationships involved.

The same sort of contamination of the adversary process occurred in the famous case of *Painter v. Bannister*.[3] There Dr. Glenn R. Hawks, a child psychologist, was the only expert witness appearing in the case. Dr. Hawks and I later were on a panel which discussed *Painter v. Bannister,* and I also received a copy of the transcript in that case covering his testimony. There was no meaningful cross-examination, Dr. Hawks was permitted to ramble, and as he put it, he said "many things I had not intended to say," and engaged in a free wheeling discussion and a lot of conjecture. He never had an interview with the father. There was no attempt to bring out the reasons for his conclusions. In order for the adversary system to work properly, there must be competent counsel and there must be a searching cross-examination. The system relies on each party and the court for proper performance of assigned tasks.

The impartiality of most experts also is in doubt. My good friend, Dr. Milton Helpern, says there is no such thing as an "impartial" expert, except perhaps in rare instances where the expert is the court's own witness, rather than a witness called by a party. Even a court's so-called "impartial expert", who is said to be "draped with the mantle of infallibility," is bound to have a personal bias, and where the question asked calls for a political or social judgment or conclusion (such as "sane" or "insane") usually the expert answers on the basis of a private rather than an expert opinion. Political, moral, or social judgments are the raw material out of which policy is shaped by the courts in the common law system, and a consensus of the community, however determined,[4] has more relevance than the personal opinions of medical experts or psychiatrists, who, on such issues, have no more expertise than anyone else.

Even though the adversary system does not always function smoothly, and its proper working depends upon a competent discharge of a division of labour where each part gives satisfactory performance, this is no reason for abandoning the system. Experienced trial lawyers and judges are convinced that the adversary system is the best yet devised and that it is here to stay.[5] Non-lawyers who regard it as antiquated or "unscientific", and would favour the substitution of a panel of experts or some other process, often do not reckon with constitutional questions[6] or with the dangers inherent in suggested alternatives. As the history of juvenile courts amply illustrates, the judicial process gets into difficulties when it becomes a social service agency rather than a court.

Previously it was suggested that the adversary system could be adapted to serve the special needs of custodial determinations. This may be done by several devices which make available for the court's consideration relevant material that is needed for a fair and sound decision. Foremost, the court may receive investigations, evaluations, recommendations, and reports from its staff, or from welfare or other similar agencies. Second, the court may interview children in chambers and discuss with them their feelings and family relationships. Finally, the court may assign a staff person or appoint a guardian *ad litem* to represent the interests of the children. Each of these devices has advantages and disadvantages.[7]

The utilization of investigation and reports is subject to varying due process limitations in American jurisdictions.[8] In some instances there may be a conflict between the fundamental notion that court decisions must be based on evidence produced in open court at a fair trial and the need of the court to have sufficient information to make a wise decision in a custody case.[9] Some writers and judges have stressed the "need to know" and have minimized due process problems.[10] Behavioral scientists generally share this view.[11] On the other hand, some lawyers and some court decisions inveigh against "secret evidence" and insist that everything considered by the judge must be on the record.[12]

The obvious way out of this dilemma is to add another exception to the hearsay rule, on the assumption that still another exception will not matter, but at the same time to provide a procedure whereby the author of the report is subject to confrontation and cross-examination, and opportunity is given to introduce rebuttal evidence. Some statutes authorize this procedure[13] which is more common in juvenile delinquency cases than in custody disputes.[14] Those who object to such procedure argue that it imperils confidential sources and occasions delay.[15] These arguments are not convincing.

An astute observer, Dr. Andrew S. Watson, commented a few years ago:

"There was an amazing difference between these two groups of records. Those in which adoption was contemplated clearly had been studied more thoroughly, the data were well organized, and well articulated goals and procedures for handling were set forth. The foster care records, on the other hand, were chaotic and nearly impossible to analyze in any detail. The same workers had handled both sets. *It was obvious that mere awareness that the adoption cases were to be subjected to an adversary procedure with a judge evaluating the data was sufficient to increase professional proficiency. It was apparent that the impact of authoritative surveillance is of some importance, even to professionals.*"[16] (emphasis supplied)

I would go further: what Dr. Watson calls "surveillance" is not merely important — even to professionals; it is the very core of our democratic system. The system of checks and balances and the concomitant doctrine of separation of powers are the matrix of what we call a free society. There must be an opportunity to check and verify bureaucratic or administrative procedures or the rule of law will be replaced by the whim of the secretariat. But we need bureaucrats, administrators, and even law deans, so that the rest of us may function effectively; and the problem is to have our cake and eat it too. That neat trick may be done by affording the opportunity to confront the author of an evaluation or report and to cross-examine as to the basis for recommendations, along with the privilege of introducing rebuttal evidence.

The case law in the United States on "hearsay" reports is most interesting. It illustrates how the compromise has been worked out in many states. An excellent comment in the University of Chicago Law Review[17] shows the pattern. Appellate courts should and do distinguish between reports made available to all interested parties and those outside the record. The general rule is that on factual questions not subject to judicial notice a court may not consider material unknown to the parties.[18] Where a report is not secret, albeit technically hearsay, it should be received and considered in custody cases. An overwhelming majority of appellate courts have held that no error occurs when a report is admitted by stipulation or consent of the parties.[19] Moreover, many, if not most, courts have held that there is no prejudicial error if the record contains other evidence sufficient to support the findings.[20] The sound approach, in view of the purposes behind the hearsay rule and the real need for investigations and reports in custody cases, is that followed in Ohio,[21] and some other states.[22] In such states, reports from a probation department or a court-appointed psychiatrist may be received into evidence and made part of the official record without stipulation. Copies of the reports are given to the parties in advance of the trial, and, upon request, the authors are made available for examination and cross-examination. However, secret reports are not admissible. The Model Code of Evidence and the Uniform Expert Testimony Act are in accord.[23] However, there are decisions which still insist upon consent or stipulation before hearsay reports may be considered.[24]

Judicial interviews with children in chambers, outside the presence of parents and counsel, again raise the problem of "secret" evidence. Where the parties agree and stipulate to the procedure, no serious legal issues are raised. Moreover, courts differ in their answers as to what should be done after the interview. Some courts have a transcript made and then make it part of the record. Perhaps more commonly, the judge summarizes the substance of the interview on the record.[25]

The real danger of in camera interviews is that they may be traumatic for the children if a clumsy judge asks the child to choose between parents. Although some judges may acquire skills adequate to the task, not all judges are sufficiently trained or sensitive enough to be aware of the psychological pitfalls implicit in making children choose and reject a parent.[26] The interesting thing about such interviews is that the voiced preferences of the children are accorded but little weight and at most are but a factor to be considered.[27] This is surprising, because especially in the case of an older child, rejection of a strong preference may be unrealistic and he or she can frustrate the court's order in one way or another.[28]

The third device utilized by some courts to ameliorate the adversary process is the assignment of an independent counsel or a guardian *ad litem* to represent the children in custody cases. At least in theory, children should be so represented in contested custody cases, and perhaps even where there is no contest there should be a "watch dog" or some independent check on agreed upon custodial, visitation, and child support terms.[29] The theoretical reason for independent counsel is obvious. The children are real parties in interest, and there may be a conflict of interests between the child's needs and the wishes of each parent. The adversary process postulates that interested parties will have counsel. In practice, however, there are limitations on the provision of independent counsel, and for such a system to work, there must be approval by the court, the bar, and the community.[30] Also, there is the practical matter of who pays the counsel fees for the independent counsel.

The Uniform Marriage and Divorce Act wrestled with this problem and its draftsmen concluded that it was more practical to make the provision of independent counsel discretionary with the court.[31] In effect, the result has been that in most states having the Uniform Act, independent counsel are appointed rarely if ever. This may be due in large measure to the traditions and habits of bench and bar, plus the fact that many judges regard themselves as the protectors of the best interests of children, and assume that they need no assistance. On the other hand, in states such as Wisconsin, where representation of the children is routine, the bench and the bar accept the process and have found that the interjection of a third party (counsel for the children) facilitates the mediation and resolution of custodial disputes.[32] The system may not work, however, where it is mandated over the opposition of the local bench and bar.[33]

I have attempted to outline the devices commonly used to mitigate the rigours of a pure adversary system in custody cases. The devices I have described do constitute a recognition that child custody and visitation are issues which call for some special treatment in order to bolster the fact finding and decision making function of our courts. Adaptation of the adversary process so that it will be functional in custody disputes probably is the most that lawyers are likely to accept.

One possible area for expansion, however, is the arbitration of post-decree disputes as to custody or visitation. New York has advanced from a completely negative attitude towards arbitration of custodial issues to the point where there is judicial encouragement of arbitration so long as the ultimate issue — the best interests of the children — remains the court's responsibility.[34] Arbitration cannot be binding on that issue and the court cannot be ousted from its *parens patriae* jurisdiction.[35] However, New York courts accept arbitration awards as to the details of custody and visitation where consistent with the child's welfare.[36] It has become common for separation agreements or similar documents to contain arbitration clauses and this limited alternative may save time, money, and serve as a welcome option for non-litigious parents.

The use of psychiatrists, doctors, the clergy, or other third persons, as arbitrators on custodial matters has been encouraged by various authorities.[37] The American Arbitration Association recently instigated a program to provide such a service.[38] Certainly where courts have over-crowded dockets, and there is an unconscionable delay in getting a hearing, arbitration has much to commend it, and it may be anticipated that its use will increase, even though the parties to the dispute, if either desires it, may obtain a court hearing on the ultimate issue of the best interests of the child.

At least in the United States, constitutional considerations probably foreclose removal of custodial or visitation issues from the courts and the reference of them to "expert" tribunals.[39] For that reason there is no need to further discuss such an alternative as the "Utrecht Institute." My concluding remarks will be directed at some of the techniques and problems of custody litigation.

The most encouraging thing about custodial decisions in the United States is the increasing sophistication of the judiciary. We are rapidly approaching the point where the court goes through a weighing and balancing process, without rules of thumb, and awards custody and visitation on the basis of the evidence before it and in accordance with the perceived best interests of the child. Moreover, the psychological factors receive emphasis and the psychological parent-child relationship, as distinguished from the biological, is being given recognition.[40]

No longer does a fit natural parent automatically prevail over a so-called "stranger," meaning anyone who is not a biological parent. New York, which for many years has had a covenant running with the child to the biological parents,[41] in the *Bennett* case[42] recently held that the trial court must give great weight to a long association with a foster parent and must decide the matter in accordance with the child's best interests. The Court of Appeals rejected the argument that the natural mother had exclusive rights, provided she was a fit parent. Since New York in the past had stressed parental rights, this was a major concession. The New York rule now appears to be that the best interests of the child control a custodial decision if the natural parent is shown to be unfit, guilty of abuse or neglect, or abandonment, or there are extraordinary circumstances, such as placement with a surrogate parent for a substantial period of time.

New York custodial litigation within the past decade has involved a tremendous increase in the use of psychological and psychiatric testimony. A case I was involved with will illustrate the point. One day an attractive couple showed up at the law school and told me that they were living together in Greenwich Village. The man was separated from his wife, who had obtained a legal separation decree awarding her alimony and custody of three children. Under New York law, either party, if in substantial compliance with the separation decree, could obtain a divorce after living separate and apart for one year. The couple told me about the mental and emotional conditions of the mother who had custody and the effect it was having on the three children.

I suggested that the mother and children, and the father, should regularly consult a therapist, and that the father, who wanted custody, should concentrate on building up medical proof of the facts he claimed were true. The mother was amazingly cooperative. In addition to child abuse at home she managed to throw a tantrum in the office of the family psychiatrist and beat her nine year old son over the head with her spiked heel. A few days later the children called the father and asked him to rescue them from another assault by their mother.

There was considerable apprehension by myself, and the lawyer who appeared for the father on the case, when the judge assigned to hear the matter was an elderly spinster judge, past retirement age. Our concern was unnecessary. The judge awarded custody to the father, even though he then was admittedly "living in sin" with the woman he later married after the divorce decree was entered. Since then the children have thrived. The point is, medical proof won the case, and even a most unlikely judge was willing to stress the best interests of the children rather than private morality. Ten or twenty years ago, priorities would have been different.

In addition, American courts are beginning to show increasing deference to prior custodial decisions. One of the most distressing things about custody law in the United States is the absence of little if any full faith and credit obligation to prior adjudications by sister states.[43] The prevalent rule is that if there has been a change, or substantial change, in circumstances, then a custody matter may be heard anew, sometimes *de novo*.[44] Although the Uniform Child Custody Jurisdiction Act tackles this problem, the Uniform Act unfortunately has been enacted in only a few states.[45] Hence, usually the problem is one of comity or *forum non conviens*.

A case in point is one where we represented the father and also indirectly the solicitor of the High Court of Justice of England. The father was an American, the mother English, and the child had been born in England. The parties had lived there before the mother surreptitiously took the child and fled back to New York where she moved in with her former husband. Before the flight, the parties had been involved in a matrimonial action in England, including a controversy over custody, but had reconciled and the action had been dropped. The High Court of Justice asserted a questionable continuing jurisdiction over the mother and child, which later was perfected by personal service on her in New York and included an offer by the husband to pay her expenses back home.

The major difficulty in the case was the trial judge's sympathy for the natural mother and the fact that the child and mother then were in New York. We convinced the court on reargument to defer to the English court and to adopt a *forum non conviens* policy because the English court was in the best position to hear the matter and to protect the child.[46]

Such experiences have convinced me that the function of trial counsel in custody cases is to focus on the child's best interests and to marshall evidence and proof directed at that end. When convinced that his client's and the best interests of the children coincide, there is no problem. However, where custody or visitation for his client is not in accord with a child's best interests, and this is clear, partisan advocacy is questionable. The lawyer is faced with a dilemma, and perhaps withdrawal from the case may be the best option, unless there is a guardian *ad litem* or independent counsel to represent the child.[47] In the latter event, the adversary process ordinarily may be relied upon to take care of the matter.

Where the children are unrepresented, there are special problems. I am reminded of a case which had been lost at trial by a member of one of the feminist law firms in New York. The woman lawyer called and asked me if I would help on her appeal. She had represented a mother who had been awarded custody rights with alternative weekend and summer visitations to the father. He had not exercised his visitation rights, and the mother wanted some weekends free, and a summer vacation, sued to force the father to provide visitation. My response, I hope tactful, was to explain to her that she could not win on the argument that celibacy made the mother climb the walls, and if she hoped to win, the less doctrinaire argument would be that the children needed a continuing association with the father, and that if it was not too late, persuasion should be directed toward that end.

In conclusion, I would like to point out that the law of custody and visitation is responding to changing life styles and mores. Automatic rules of thumb no longer dictate decisions, rather, courts are committed to a weighing and balancing process which stresses the affectionate relationships of the child. At least to some extent, the law of custody is being desexed. The "tender years" doctrine is being lowered if not abrogated.[48] It no longer is assumed that "blood is thicker than water."[49] The child's preference carries added weight.[50] The psychological parent-child relationship, as distinguished from the biological one, gets priority in many states.[51]

Our courts, so long as they are responsive to social change, and are willing to hear and check out the insights and experiences of behavioural scientists, are the best tribunals to hear custodial disputes. It is rare to find a judge who does not approach such a task with dedication. A very wise New York judge, Justice Bernard Botein, once said that "A judge agonizes more about reaching the right result in a contested custody issue than about any other type of decision he renders."[52] Competent trial counsel can reduce some of the agony even though there is no ecstasy when courts determine difficult custodial matters.

Editor's Note

The question of the use and confidentiality of investigate reports was addressed by the Law Reform Commission of Canada in its Working Paper #1: The Family Court, published in 1974. The commission highlights the dilemma that lies at the heart of policy-making in this area. The use of investigative reports does bring before the court information which may be useful in arriving at the decision about custody, access, or maintenance. On the one hand, requiring inspection of the report and cross-examination of its authors is in keeping with our respect for natural justice and would be effective in ensuring that unfounded statements, hearsay, or remarks actuated by malice do not form the basis of a decision against a party. On the other hand, the Commission points out, the content of the reports might inflict psychological harm on the parties, or disclosure might discourage either candid response or any response at all on the part of sources who feared identification.

The Commission points out that practice with respect to disclosure of investigatory reports varies considerably across Canada, ranging from full rights to the parties to inspect the report and subject its authors to cross-examination to witholding of the reports at the discretion of the judge. In Ontario, for example, The Matrimonial Causes Act, s. 6(5) as enacted by 1972 (Ont.), c. 50, s. 1(2) requires that where a party disputes the facts contained in the report of the official Guardian in a custody matter or divorce involving custody, the Official Guardian may, or shall when directed by the Court, attend the trial on behalf of the child and cause the person who made the investigation to attend as a witness. That person is required by subsection 6(4) of The Matrimonial Causes Act, R.S.O. 1970, c. 265, to make as an exhibit to the report submitted to the Court, an affidavit "verifying the report as to such facts as are within his knowledge and setting out the source of his information and his belief as to any other facts . . . ."

The Law Reform Commission of Canada recommends, at page 48 of its Working Paper on the Family Court that

". . .investigative reports should be made available to the lawyers of the parties or, if the parties are unrepresented by counsel, then to the parties themselves. The Commission further concludes that the authors of reports should always be available for cross-examination and that, in the discretion of the judge, persons constituting the primary sources of information contained in the investigative reports should also be available for cross-examination."

Recommendations for changes in dispute settlement in the family law area also include the recommendation that conciliation services form part of the whole approach to resolving the problems of the separating family. This conciliation goes further than the reconciliation counselling now provided for in section 8 of the Divorce Act, R.S.C. 1970, c. D-8, which is aimed at giving the parties one last chance to save their marriage before the divorce is heard. Conciliation counselling may well include such opportunities in some models of the united family court, but its other aim is to encourage agreement between the separated persons on as many of the issues outstanding between them as possible. Candour is essential in approaching conciliation, whether it be for reconciliation or for ensuring a more amicable settlement. There is some recognition in Canadian legislation even now of this requirement for fostering full disclosure between the parties and to the advisor assisting them. Section 8(1)(b) of the Divorce Act, R.S.C. 1970, c. D-8, provides for the court appointment of a marriage counsellor or some other suitable person to assist the parties with a view to their possible reconciliation, where "it appears to the court from the nature of the case, the evidence or the attitude of the parties or either of them that there is a possibility of such a reconciliation." Section 21(1) of the Act stipulates that a person so nominated is not competent or compellable in any legal proceedings to disclose any admission or communication made to him in his capacity as the nominee of the court. Section 21(2) provides that evidence of anything said or any communication made in the course of an endeavour to assist the parties is not admissable in any legal proceedings. There are limitations to the range of protection afforded by the section. In *Robson v. Robson* [1969] 2 O.R. 857, 7 D.L.R. (3d) 289, and *Cronkwright v. Cronkwright* [1970] 3 O.R. 784, 2 R.F.L. 241, 14 D.L.R. (3d) 168, Mr. Justice Wright of the Ontario Supreme Court pointed out that the section will not preserve any communications made to one not appointed by the Court under section 8. There is also a suggestion in *Robson* that where the statements are not made in the course of a reconciliation effort, but during some other kind of counselling, the section is inapplicable. In the *Robson* case, the statements sought to be admitted were made to a John Howard Society counsellor during efforts to rehabilitate the husband, a drug user and former prisoner. No question of court appointment under section 8 arose. There might, in another case however, be difficulty should the court appoint as a reconciliation counsellor someone who had been counselling one of the parties for a different purpose, particularly if that separate counselling continued after the reconciliation efforts began.

Limited as the protection in section 21 appears following *Robson* and *Cronkwright,* Mr. Justice Wright in those cases suggests another way in which confidences during counselling might be protected. In *Cronkwright,* the court refused to order an Anglican clergyman who was not a court nominee under s. 8(1)(*b*) to answer a question regarding admissions made during a reconciliation attempt. The decision was based not on any legal privilege but on the judge's discretion to refuse to receive evidence which would otherwise be admissable. In *Robson,* Mr. Justice Wright refused to take this approach, declaring in the circumstances of this particularly repellant parental situation:

". . . I consider the public policy involved in this action, namely the welfare and future of the infant child, predominates over any of the public policies that have been urged before me in argument . . . ." (p. 295)

Among the other policies was the contention that refusing to receive evidence of the confidence would preserve the relationship of trust between a former prisoner and his John Howard Society advisor.

This argument seems to have been taken from the argument in *Dembie v. Dembie* (1963) 21 R.F.L. 46, where Mr. Justice Stewart of the Supreme Court of Ontario made an interesting and influential ruling on the compellability of a psychiatrist called to testify in a domestic proceeding.

The court indicated in the course of the trial that he would not cite for contempt a psychiatrist who refused to reveal a wife's confidences given during treatment. The court noted that although there was no privilege in law against the disclosure of confidential communications to a psychiatrist or physician, the common law position had evolved when "the surgeon was basically a barber and the physician little more than a herbalist" (p. 49). It shocked the conscience of the court that the legal provisions about privilege would enable one spouse, having undertaken marital counselling by a psychiatrist along with the other spouse, to require the disclosure of damaging statements in later court proceedings.

Proposals for reform of the family court seem to be tending in the direction of greater protection of confidentiality in conciliation. The Law Reform Commission of Canada states at page 49 of its Working Paper #1: The Family Court, its opinion that "... if disclosures at intake and during counselling are to be full and frank, confidentiality must extend to all statements or communications made." The Ontario Law Reform Commission, which recommended that voluntary conciliation services be attached to a unified family court, stated at page 75 of its Report on Family Law: Part V: Family Courts (Toronto, 1974):

". . . complete confidentiality must be preserved if people are to be encouraged to resort to the Court's conciliation service. We recommend that a joint privilege attach and that it belong to the spouses. Without the consent of both parties, information gained at the counselling sessions should not be brought before the Court. Conciliation officers should not be compellable as witnesses in a subsequent legal action."

---

1 See Henry H. Foster, Jr., "Social Work, the Law, and Social Action," (July 1964) 45 Social Casework 383, reprinted as "The Law and Social Work" (1964) 53 Kentucky L.J. 229, and reproduced by Children's Bureau, Welfare Administration, U.S. Dept. of Health, Education, and Welfare (1964), for an attempt to describe to laymen the reasons behind procedural due process.

2 "Once it is determined who will be the custodial parent, it is that parent, not the court, who must decide under what conditions he or she wishes to raise the child. Thus, the noncustodial parent should have no legally enforceable right to visit the child, and the custodial parent should have the right to decide whether it is desirable for the child to have such visits. What we have said is designed to protect the security of an ongoing relationship — that between the child and the custodial parent." Compare, *Pierce v. Yerkovich,* 363 N.Y.S.2d 403 (Fam. Ct., Ulster Co., 1974).

3 258 Iowa 1390, 140 N.W. 2d 152 (Supreme Court of Iowa, 1966) cert. denied, 385 U.S. 949.

4 For an interesting discussion of how the moral consensus of a community is determined, see Edmond N. Cahn, *The Moral Decision,* (Bloomington, U. of Indiana Press, 1955) 300-312.

5 In *Joint Anti-Fascist Refugee Committee v. McGrath* (1951) 341 U.S. 123, 179, Mr. Justice Douglas pointed out that "It is not without significance that most of the provisions of the Bill of Rights are procedural. It is procedure that spells much of the difference between rule by law and rule by whim or caprice. Steadfast adherence to

strict procedural safeguards is our main assurance that there will be equal justice under law." In *Malinski v. New York* (1945) 324 U.S. 401, 414, Mr. Justice Frankfurter said that "The history of American freedom is, in no small measure, the history of procedure."

6 Compare attempts to eliminate the insanity defence and to have a tribunal of experts determine criminal responsibility. All such efforts have failed to pass constitutional barriers. See *State v. Strasburg*, 110 Pac. 1020 (Supreme Court of Wash., 1910); and *Sinclair v. State*, 132 So. 581 (Supreme Court of Miss., 1931). See also, *Stanley v. Illinois* (1972) 405 U.S. 645.

7 For example, Section 310 of the Uniform Marriage and Divorce Act provides for discretionary appointment of independent counsel for children where their custody or support is at issue in divorce cases. The Family Law Section of the American Bar Association stipulated mandatory designation of independent counsel in such cases. Neither result is satisfactory. Where appointment is discretionary, such appointments are rarely made; where mandatory, the device has not worked in hostile jurisdictions.

8 See Henry H. Foster, Jr. and Doris J. Freed, "Child Custody (PartII)" (1964) 39 N.Y.U. L. Rev. 615, 615-622, and Comment, "Use of Extra-Record Information in Child Custody Cases" (1957) 24 U. Chic. L. Rev. 349.

9 Compare, *Williams v. New York* (1949) 337 U.S. 241, where the Supreme Court held in a questionable decision that due process was not violated by a judge's use of secret probation reports at the sentencing stage of a criminal trial.

10 For example, see Hon. Henry J. Sweney, "Habeas Corpus — Custody of Children" (1949) 22 Temp. L. Q. 289, 299; Pfaff, "Domestic Relations Investigations" (1961) 36 Los Angeles B.A. Bull. 192, 213; and Kolaska, "The Scope of Interaction Between Law and Psychology" (1963) 35 Pa. B.A.Q. 65, 67.

11 For example, Dr. Hirschberg of the Menninger Clinic has said: "If the court has available information about the case, the litigants, and the child, gathered by skilled personnel such as social workers, then the judicial work will be easier, and the judgments will be sounder. The cost in time and money will be minimal compared to the cost of mistaken judgment about custody, which affects the life of the child and his eventual work in society." "Symposium on the Child and the Law — Custody" (1962) 10 University of Kansas L. Rev. 555, 559.

12 For a recent expression of this view by an outstanding trial lawyer, see Mulligan, "The Lawyer's Viewpoint" (1976) 48 N.Y. State B.J. 451.

13 See Henry H. Foster Jr. and Doris J. Freed, "Child Custody (Part II)," (1964) 39 N.Y.U. L. Rev. 615, 618-621 citing statutes and cases.

14 Nanette Dembitz, "Ferment and Experiment in New York: Juvenile Cases in the New Family Court" (1963) 48 Cornell L.Q. 499, 518, explains the difference in the use of reports in delinquency and custody cases by saying that custody cases involve adjudication of competing rights of the parents, rather than an exercise in judicial discretion, and that due process therefore requires a basis in the evidence.

15 See Foster and Freed, *op. cit. supra* note 13 at 618.

16 Andrew S. Watson, "Family Law and Its Challenge for Psychiatry" (1962) 2 J. Fam. Law 71, 82.

17 Comment, "Use of Extra-Record Information in Child Custody Cases" (1957) 24 U. Chic. L. Rev. 349.

18 See *Kesseler v. Kesseler*, 10 N.Y. 2d 445, 180 N.E. 2d 402, 225 N.Y.S. 2d 1 (Court of Appeals, 1962); *Rea v. Rea*, 195 Ore. 252, 245 P.2d 884 (Supreme Court of Oregon, 1952); and Lloyd D. Mazur and Charles P. Rose, Jr., "Comment: The 'Adversary' Process in Child Custody Proceedings" (1967) 18 West. Reserve L. Rev. 1731.

19 See Foster and Freed, *op. cit. supra* note 13 at 620.

20 *Ibid.*

21 The Ohio statute is discussed in Henry H. Foster, Jr., "Note: The Family in the Courts" (1956) 17 U. Pitt. L. Rev. 206, 251.

22 See *Gumphrey v. Gumphrey*, 202 Minn. 515, 115 N.W. 2d 353 (Supreme Court of Minnesota, 1962); and *Sanchez v. Sanchez*, 55 Cal. 2d 412, 10 Cal. Rptr. 261 (Supreme Court of California, 1961).

23 Rule 403(b), and 404.

24 See sections 3, 5-7.

25 See Bernard Botein, "The Future of the Judicial Process: Challenge and Response" (1960) 15 N.Y. City B.A. *Record* 152, 159, where an able jurist says:

> "In the extra-judicial investigations conducted by our family courts, the state invades the private lives of children and adults in a fashion that would never be tolerated in a court handling litigation of a purely adversary nature . . . . Those reports [of probation officers] are based upon investigations made by nonjudicial personnel out of the presence of the court or counsel, and reflect social science disciplines and techniques which are unrelated to the procedures and rules appertaining to the judicial process. No doubt Constitutional considerations will set boundaries for judicial use of these types of investigations; but within those boundaries we must expect considerable enlargement of the technique."

26 For a recent discussion of *in camera* interviews with children, see Slifkin, "The Judge's Viewpoint" (1976) 48 N.Y. State B.J. 450. Such a device was approved of in *Lincoln v. Lincoln* (1969) 24 N.Y. 2d 270, 247 N.E. 2d 659, 299 N.Y.S. 2d 270. See also, John M. Suarez, "The Role of the Child's Choice in Custody Proceedings" (July-August, 1968) 73 Case & Comment, p.46; and S. Bernstein, "Annotation: Propriety of court conducting private interview with child in determining custody" (1965) 99 ALR 2d.

27 Compare, Utah Code Ann. § 30-3-5 (1953), which provides in part that "if any of the children have attained the age of ten years and are of sound mind, such children shall have the privilege of selection of the parent to which they wish to attach themselves." However, in *Smith v. Smith*, 15 Utah 2d 36, 386 P.2d 900 (Supreme Court of Utah, 1963), it was held that the child's choice will not be given effect if the parent selected is immoral or unfit.

28 For example, see *Rothman v. Jewish Child Care Assn*, 166 N.Y.L.J., p. 17, cols. 2-4 (Nov. 1, 1972). This case is discussed at length in Chapter six of Joseph Goldstein, Anna Freud, and Albert J. Solnit, *Beyond the Best Interests of the Child* (New York, 1973).

29 See Henry H. Foster, Jr., *A "Bill of Rights" for Children*, (Springfield, Ill., 1974), p.45.

30 Connecticut, after a brief trial, abandoned its hybrid system of mandatory and discretionary appointment of counsel for children in custody cases, convinced that the mandatory system would not work.

31 See s. 310.

32 See Wis. Stat. Ch. 245.001(2), and *Wendland v. Wendland*, 29 Wis. 2d 145, 138 N.W. 2d 185 (Supreme Court of Wisconsin, 1965). See also, Robert W. Hansen, "The Role and Rights of Children in Divorce Actions" (1966) 6 J. Fam. Law 1.

33 See note 30, *supra*.

34 See *Sheets v. Sheets*, 22 A.D. 2d 176, 254 N.Y.S. 2d 320 (1st Dept., 1964); and J.F. Ghent, "Annotation: Validity and Construction of Provision for Arbitration of Disputes as to Alimony or Support Payments, or Child Visitation or Custody Matters" (1968) 18 ALR 3d 1264. Compare, *Agur v. Agur*, 32 A.D. 2d 16, 298 N.Y.S. 2d 772 (2d Dept., 1969), which rejected the *Sheets* case, *supra*.

35 *Ibid*.

36 In addition to *Sheets* and *Agur, supra,* see *Freidberg v. Freidberg*, 23 Misc. 2d 196, 201 N.Y.S. 2d 606 (Sup. Ct. N.Y. Co., 1960) (dispute regarding education of son); *Schneider v. Schneider*, 17 N.Y. 2d 123, 216 N.E. 2d 318, 269 N.Y.S. 2d 107 (Court of Appeals, 1966) (child support); and *Kleiner v. Sanjenis*, 46 A.D.2d 617, 359 N.Y.S. 2d 791 (1st Dept., 1974). The Second Department, however, still is in conflict with the First Department and refuses to honour arbitration of custody disputes. See *Nestel v. Nestel*, 38 A.D.2d 942, 331 N.Y.S.2d 241 (2d Dept. 1972) (mem.). There also appears to be confusion in the trial courts. See *Fence v. Fence*, 64 Misc. 2d 480, 314 N.Y.S.2d 1016 (Fam. Ct. N.Y. Co., 1970). It should be noted that the earlier New York cases rejected arbitration for custody or visitation disputes. See *Hill v. Hill*, 99 Misc. 1035, 104 N.Y.S.2d 755 (Sup. Ct. N.Y. Co., Part I, 1951), and *Michelman v. Michelman*, 5 Misc. 2d 570, 135 N.Y.S. 2d 608 (Sup. Ct. N.Y. Co., Part I, 1954).

37 The leading article is the Note, "Alternatives to Parental Right in Child Custody Disputes Involving Third Parties" (1964) 73 Yale L.J. 151; see also Note: "Committee Decision of Child Custody Disputes and the Judicial Test of 'Best Interests'" (1964) 73 Yale L.J. 1201.

38 In May 1976, the American Arbitration Association announced its "Arbitration Rules for Voluntary Separation Without Fault," which includes in Rule 11(d) a provision that if the parties were unable to agree as to custody or visitation rights, the arbitrator shall determine those custody arrangements which will be in the best interests of the child, after considering all relevant factors including: (1) the wishes of the respective parents; (2) the wishes of the child; (3) the interaction and interrelationship of the child with parent or parents, the child's siblings, and other persons who may affect the child's best interests; (4) the child's adjustment to home, school, and community; and (6) the mental health of all individuals involved. It is further provided that the arbitrator shall not consider the conduct of the proposed custodian that does not affect relationships with the child. Rule 12 permits the arbitrator to interview the child privately in order to ascertain the child's wishes as to custodial arrangements and visitation. These rules were developed in cooperation with the Family Mediation Association of Atlanta. Of course, the binding effect of such arbitration depends upon state statutes and decisions as previously indicated.

39 See note 6, *supra.*

40 For example, see *In re Adoption of a Child by P and Wife,* 114 N.J. Super. 584, 277 A. 2d 566 (Superior Ct. of N.J., 1971), and *In re Revocation of Appointment of a Guardian of a Minor Surrendered for Adoption,* 271 N.E. 2d 621 (Mass. Supreme Judicial Court, 1971).

41 The most familiar example is *People ex. rel. Scarpetta v. Spence-Chapin Adoption Service,* 28 N.Y.2d 185, 269 N.E.2d 787, 321 N.Y.S.2d 65, (Court of Appeals) cert. denied, 404 U.S. 805 (1971). Compare, *Scarpetta v. DeMartino,* 254 So. 2d 813 (Fla. Dist. Ct. App., 1971), 262 So. 2d 442 (Fla. Sup. Ct., 1972), cert. denied, 93 S. Ct. 437 (1973).

42 *In re Bennett v. Jeffreys,* 176 N.Y.L.J., p. 1, col. 6 (Sept. 27, 1976).

43 See Henry H. Foster Jr. and Doris J. Freed, *Law and the Family: New York* (Rochester, 1966) § 29:34, and Leonard J. Ratner, "Child Custody in a Federal System" (1964) 62 Mich. L. Rev. 795.

44 For example, see *Scarpetta v. DeMartino, supra* note 41. See also *Bachman v. Mejias,* 1 N.Y. 2d 575, 136 N.E.2d 866, 154 N.Y.S. 2d 903 (Court of Appeals, 1956).

45 As of July 1976, the Uniform Act had been enacted only in California, Colorado, Hawaii, Maryland, Michigan, North Dakota, Oregon, and Wyoming, but the act was being considered by several legislatures. For a discussion of the problem, see Foster and Freed, "Child Snatching, Custodial Rights," 175 N.Y.L.J., p. 1, col. 1 (April 23, May 28 and June 25, 1976).

46 See *Turner v. Ratnoff,* 358 N.Y.S.2d 586 (Sup. Ct. Rensselaer Co., 1973).

47 Many lawyers would adopt an opposing view and insist that their sole duty was that owed to their client. See Mulligan, *op. cit. supra,* note 12.

48 See *State ex rel. Watts v. Watts,* 350 N.Y.S.2d 285 (Fam. Ct. N.Y. Co., 1973), but compare recent cases from Illinois and Virginia reported in 1 Family Law Reporter 2420 (Virginia) and 2 Family Law Reporter 2839 (Illinois).

49 See *In re Bennett v. Jeffreys, supra,* note 42.

50 *Ibid.*

51 See *supra,* note 40.

52 Bernard Botein, *Trial Judge* (N.Y., 1952) p.273.

Child Custody: Canada's Other Lottery

Howard H. Irving, D.S.W., *
Benjamin Schlesinger, Ph.D. **

INTRODUCTION

The Oxford dictionary defines a "lottery" as: "arrangements for distributing prizes by chance among purchasers of tickets; thing that defies calculation".

During the past two years Canadians have taken to lotteries with a vengeance on a national and provincial level. Millions of ticket holders await the results of the "wheel of chance" with eager anticipation.

The Canadian lottery dealing with the custody of our children, however, involves a different game, namely, the "wheel of life". Usually, one finds in this game of chance few winners and many losers. The problem then becomes whether we can raise up the odds so that we will have many more winners in the years to come, and eventually, disband "Canada's second lottery".

This paper will examine some of the current socio-legal aspects of child custody in Canada. A review of the relevant literature on the effects of divorce on children has been included. Some recommendations have been prepared for consideration and further study.

THE NATURE OF THE PROBLEM***

Although the statistics on family breakdown are well known, and it is fashionable to discuss "the death of the family", in reality the family remains the basic unit of our society. That the family is the primary source of psychological security and personality development is more than obvious to those agents of society who pick up the pieces of family breakdown. Lawyers, police, social workers, and psychiatrists, among

---

* Howard H. Irving, D.S.W., is an Associate Professor, Faculty of Social Work, University of Toronto.
** Benjamin Schlesinger, Ph.D., is a Professor, Faculty of Social Work, University of Toronto.
*** The material in this section appeared in substantially this form in Howard H. Irving and Barbara G. Irving, "Conciliation Counselling in Divorce Litigation", (1974) 10 Reports of Family Law 256 at 257, 264-65.

others, deal daily with such psychological and sociological consequences of family breakdown as increased child abuse, juvenile delinquency, and second generation divorce.

Divorce litigation is unique among all legal actions in that it is almost invariably accompanied by the most intense and intimate emotions. It is rarely a cut and dried piece of business with a clear-cut beginning and end which can be handled and filed away. It is a painful process for all concerned — not the least of whom is the lawyer. When the psychological factors which affect the situation are not dealt with throughout the divorce process, the resulting complications come back to plague the lawyer again and again — bitter acrimony around child custody and visitation, non-payment of alimony and support, etc.

"The Canadian Law Reform Commission has called the Canadian divorce system 'anachronistic, unrealistic and demanding'. The fault, says the Canadian Commission, is that the system is guilt-oriented, reinforced by an adversary system which demands for these family disputes, that one party is essentially innocent and the other guilty."[1]

A major cause of pain in most divorces is that the two parties are seldom at the same level of readiness to terminate the marriage at the point when one consults a lawyer. Most commonly, one has left or is about to leave, and the other party feels rejected and abandoned. It is typical for the spurned spouse, who may see himself or herself as having been made to suffer all sorts of indignities, to seek revenge in the form of money, or much worse, by using the children as a means of punishing or "getting even" with the other spouse. Children are always the casualties of their parents' marital battles. Parents frequently use their children to salve their own bruised egos, or they vie for their children's favour, thus forcing the children into conflicts of loyalties which more often than not have permanent debilitating effects upon their developing personalities.

Even when both parents are aware of these dangers and make a conscious effort to prevent them, their own high level of anxiety throughout the entire divorce process certainly damages their parenting abilities. Post-divorce depression, not unlike a mourning period, is common and can last for a considerable period of time. Naturally, the children will be affected by this. The vital importance of involving the children at certain points in the therapeutic process is obvious.

REVIEW OF THE LITERATURE****

In examining the available literature on divorce and children, one

****The material in "Review of the Literature" and "Effect of Divorce on Children" has also appeared in Benjamin Schlesinger, "Divorce and Children: A Review of the Literature (1976) 24 R.F.L. 203, at 203-209, 214-215.

comes very quickly to the conclusion that very little scientific data is available which documents the effects of divorce on children. Although the main focus of our discussion is custody, one cannot separate this topic from the effect on children. The following review attempts to pull together the major highlights of selected studies dealing with the effect of divorce on children.

"Much effort is being invested these days in saving marriages, and this is all to the good, so long as we remember that what we are trying to save is not solely the form of marriage, but its spirit. A marriage can be saved at too great a cost, especially to the children. It is the children who pay the heaviest price, for they pay not only in present unhappiness, but also in future maladjustment and perhaps the failure of their own marriages to come."[2]

When changes to divorce laws in Canada were under study in the nineteen-sixties, the Committee of the Senate and House of Commons on Divorce stated the following in relation to provisions regarding children: "Your Committee, therefore, believes that no divorce should be granted until arrangements have been made for the care and upbringing of all minor children, and that such arrangements are satisfactory or are the best that can be devised in the circumstances. This would be to follow existing British practice. All minor children should be taken to mean all children in the family whether they are the offspring of the couple before the court or only of one of them by a former union, or of the family by adoption."[3]

It is of interest that seven years later, Wheeler in his discussion of "no fault divorce", feels that in most divorce courts children are seldom seen and never heard.[4] Many marriages in Canada and the United States which end in divorce involve families with minor children. The husband and wife may know what they want and be able to hire lawyers to help them get it; but no one speaks for the children, even though they have at least as much at stake in the divorce as do their parents. The adults are most likely to be preoccupied with their own problems and to be in a position where what is best for them is not necessarily best for their children. Moreover, the emotional stress during the last days of a dying marriage can be such that the parents do not really know what is best for themselves, let alone for anyone else.

Almost by default the courts have been given the responsibility to see that children are not the innocent casualties of matrimonial warfare. If the children have been injured by conflict between their parents, the court is expected to heal the wounds. Unfortunately, it rarely does.

Wheeler also points out that:

"Ironically it is concern for the welfare of children that often sparks interest in improving our family laws, yet, after the dust of reform has settled, relatively little has been done for them. The California legislature made sweeping changes in its divorce law by eliminating the fault grounds and restructuring property rights; but, after much debate, it left the custody laws virtually unchanged."[5]

EFFECT OF DIVORCE ON CHILDREN

The literature reports both positive and negative effects of divorce on children of all ages. In a study of twenty-nine children of divorced or divorcing parents, Sugar suggests that divorce is a crisis for children. The symptoms include separation anxiety, and feelings of helplessness and mourning. He also reports symptoms of loss of appetite, disinterest in studies and playmates, and feelings of embarrassment and shame. He feels that
"If in spite of their own emotional upheaval the divorcing and divorced parents are alert to the child's confusion, depression or anxiety and to his needs, they may be able to effect prophylactic and helpful measures."[6]

Toomim[7] notes the following losses which the child experiences upon divorce: loss of faith and trust, loss of the child-mother-father relationship, loss of the predivorce mother, loss of the predivorce father, loss of environmental supports, and loss of the predivorce child. McDermott[8] examined sixteen nursery school children whose parents were being separated or divorced. He summarized his findings as follows:
"To the majority of children of this age divorce has a significant impact and represents a major crisis. There is often an initial period of shock and acute depressive reactions. Clinically observed regressive phenomena were followed by restoration of previous skills and subsequent resolution and mastery both in play and verbally.

"Sex differences were noted, with boys demonstrating more dramatic changes in behaviour, characterized by the abrupt release of aggressive and destructive feelings. Boys seemed more vulnerable to gross disruption of identifications already in process than the girls. Some of the children, principally girls, seemed to show a tendency to identify with selected pathological features of the parent of the same sex."

In addition to concluding that the school might have an obligation to intervene at this stage, involving the teacher in identifying and working with troubled children, Dr. McDermott concluded that the
". . .mental health consultant may be able to pick up signs and symptoms of the behavioural changes from the teachers, to assess the severity of these, and to advise the teacher. He may also be available to discuss with the parents how to cope with the effects on the child via explanation and to emphasize the importance of school for the child during this period. The children should not stay home because they are bored or diffusely irritable. The consultant may also coordinate the preventive work

with the child between the school and home in order to help the child resume the normal tasks of maturation."[9]

A longitudinal study of the effects of parental divorce was begun in 1970 by Wallerstein and Kelly. Their sample consisted of 131 children and adolescents, from sixty families. The researchers observed them shortly after the parents' separation and again one year later.

One of the reports of this study dealt with the experiences of the pre-school child.[10] There were in the total sample thirty-four pre-school children from twenty-seven families. The authors reported that within this group they identified three subgroups of children, distinguished on the basis of chronological age and developmental and cognitive maturity. The effects on each group were described as follows:

"1. In the youngest group, family disruption triggered regression, fretfulness, cognitive bewilderment, heightened aggression and neediness. These symptoms were found to be temporary, if continuity of physical and loving care was restored and maintained either by the parent or a competent substitute caretaker. The acuteness of the regression or other behavioural change seemed unrelated to the outcome. The most enduring symptom was that of pervasive neediness. The more vulnerable children in this youngest group showed depressive reactions and/or constriction and delays in their development.

2. In the middle group, [3¾ to 4¾ years] divorce appeared to cogwheel with early superego development, specifically burdening the child's self-esteem and self-image. His view of the dependability and predictability of relationships was threatened; his sense of order regarding the world disrupted. Some children suffered with feelings of responsibility for driving the father away. Poor outcome here included early signs of depressive illness and, again, developmental inhibitions.

3. In the oldest pre-school children [five to six years] it became possible for the first time for a child to experience family turbulence and divorce without breaking developmental stride. In the main, such children seemed able to find gratifications outside of the home, and to place some psychological and social distance between themselves and their parents. In the vulnerable children, we saw particular difficulty in bringing resolution to oedipal conflicts, and consequent delay in beginning the tasks of latency. Poor outcome in girls in this group was related to the overuse of denial through prolonged oedipal fantasy and the turning away from reality tasks. Of particular concern is the early disruption in learning which may be difficult to reverse.

Of the total sample studied, 44% . . . of the children were found to be in a significantly deteriorated psychological condition at the follow-up a year later. This finding is of particular concern, since none of the children in this study had any prior history of psychological difficulty, and we considered that all of them had achieved appropriate developmental and cognitive milestones .... In particular, a diminution in the quality of the mother-child relationship occurred in almost half of our families, and was found to be strongly associated with the deterioration in the psychological condition of the child. Father-child relationships, on the other hand, often tended to improve over the first year, but this did not prevent the deterioration."[11]

A second report by Kelly and Wallerstein dealt with the reactions of twenty-six children in early latency, defined by the authors as age seven and eight at the time of the initial interview. They observed a wide range of responses in the children, including "the most striking response": "pervasive sadness".[12] Most of the children were frightened about both the instability of the current family situation and their futures, and many had pervasive fantasies of deprivation.[13] More than half these children missed their father acutely;[14] those most profoundly hurt by the loss of the father tended to be those who were also most enraged at the mother.[15]

At the time of the follow-up of these early latency children, Kelly and Wallerstein found that fifty per cent of the children had either improved their overall level of psychological functioning, or had maintained their previous development, fifteen per cent had consolidated the difficulties initially observed, and twenty-three per cent of the children were in significantly worsened or deteriorated psychological condition in comparison with their level of functioning at the initial interview. One characteristic which distinguished these younger latency children from those in older latency and adolescence was the tenacity, after a year, of their loyalty to the absent father.[16]

A report on the reactions of thirty-one later latency children, aged nine and ten, also contains the results of an initial interview and of a follow-up study one year later. The authors found many of these nine- and ten-year olds to be poised and resourceful in functioning simultaneously on two very different levels: the one of managing and the other of "profound underlying feelings of loss and rejection, of helplessness and loneliness."[17] The authors observed that the "single feeling that most clearly distinguished this group from all the younger children was their conscious intense anger."[18] In common with the adolescents, however, the later latency children coupled their anger with a sense of moral indignation at what they considered immoral or irresponsible actions on the part of the parents,[19] and with a sense of shame at the divorce and family disruption.[20]

The report on the later latency children at follow-up contained the following observations:
". . . . In about half the children. . .the disequilibrium created by the family disruption . . . had almost entirely subsided. But even these children with the apparent better outcomes, who seemed relatively content with their new family life and circle of friends, including step-parents, were not

without backward glances of bitterness and nostalgia. In fact, the anger and hostility aroused around the divorce events lingered longer and more tenaciously than did any of the other affective responses. Of the total group, ten (or one-third) of the children maintained an unremitted anger directed at the non-custodial parent; of these, four did so in alignment with the custodial mother, the other six on their own....

"Although some of these children who were doing well continued to harbor reconciliation wishes, they mostly had come to accept the divorce with sad finality. Some seemed to be unconsciously extrapolating from these reconciliation wishes to plan future careers as repairmen, as bridge builders, as architects, as lawyers....

"By contrast, the other half gave evidence of consolidation into troubled and conflicted depressive behaviour patterns with, in half of these, *more* open distress and disturbance even than at the initial visit. A significant component in this now chronic maladjustment was a continuing depression and low self-esteem, combined with frequent school and peer difficulties. One such child was described by his teacher at follow-up as 'A little old man who worries all the time and rarely laughs'. In this group, symptoms that had emerged had generally persisted and even worsened. For instance, phobic reactions had, in one instance, worsened and spread; delinquent behaviour such as truancy and petty thievery which had surfaced remained relatively unchanged; and some who had become isolated and withdrawn were even more so. One new behaviour configuration that emerged during the first post-divorce year in these nine- and ten-year olds was a precocious thrust into adolescent preoccupation with sexuality and assertiveness, with all the detrimental potential of such phase-inappropriate unfoldings. And amongst all the children, both in the groups with better and with poorer outcomes, relatively few were able to maintain good relationships with both parents."[21]

In examining the twenty-one adolescents in the sample, Wallerstein and Kelly found that divorce is an acutely painful experience for the teenager. They concluded that "...adolescents who appeared to do best were frequently those who were able, at the outset, to establish and maintain some distance from the parental crisis and whose parents, whether willingly or reluctantly, permitted them to do so."[22] The investigators discovered over time that these were the youngsters who were able, within a year following parental separation "to develop that remarkable combination of realistic assessment of their parents along with compassion, which augurs well for their future."[23]

POSITIVE ASPECTS OF DIVORCE

In his book *Creative Divorce,* Krantzler attempts to show that we have overestimated the effect of a divorce on children. His arguments include the following points:

"1. Children are resilient . . . and can survive any family crisis without permanent damage . . . if they can sense some continuity and loving involvement on the part of their parents.

2. The impact of divorce on children is far less severe than the consequences of remaining in an unbroken but troubled home.

3. With or without divorce, the process of growing up is often stormy.

4. A two-parent home is not the only emotional structure within which a child can be happy and healthy."[24]

Steinzor points out what are, in his view, advantages of divorce:

"1. The emotional smog bothering the whole family in an early spiritual death is cleared away. . . .

2. The broken home makes it possible for the child to form his own views on each parent unobstructed by the smoke screen thrown up by each in front of the other.

3. Divorce is an honest and above-board admission that the adults cannot get along and there is no use pretending that they can provide their children with a model of a loving relationship.

4. The child's belief that he is guilty of causing his parents to fight and that only he can save them from hurting each other will be laid to rest by divorce."[25]

Gettleman and Markowitz, in their discussion of the "courage to divorce", state:

"We have considered and subsequently rejected general attitudes and opinions about the inherent dangers in divorce and have substituted a thesis that divorce is in itself a "neutral" experience for children, which can be made into a "good" experience or a "bad" experience. . . .

"It is clear that there is a destructive relationship between contemporary parental indoctrination on divorce and the handling of children in divorce. Most of the advice given to parents implies that divorce is not an honorable state, and parents in turn become the major determinants of their childrens' acceptance of it. . . .

"In the end, observations by youngsters of the beneficial effects of divorce on their parents will enable them to conclude that, for themselves, divorce was a blessing, even if at first it was a blessing in disguise. A child cannot cope successfully with divorce, though, when a parent feels that something catastrophic has happened."[26]

SUMMARY

In a recent review of the literature on one-parent families, Schlesinger[27] found only a handful of actual research studies relating to the child and divorce. Most of the references were opinions, pronouncements, advice, and assessments of children who came to the attention of social and health agencies. Thus, it is possible that the existing evidence is based on biased samples.

On the other hand, the present available findings appear to agree that divorce is a crisis for children, and that professionals should be aware of the social, emotional, and psychological impact of divorce on children. The courts in their deliberations may have to spend more efforts in safeguarding the rights of children of divorce. Sanctuary and Whitehead expressed the dilemma of children of divorce when they stated:

"In the whole drama of divorce, facts and feelings are nowhere more uncertain or more dangerously confused than as they concern the children. For them, the divorce of their parents may be better than living in a home full of hostility and discord. But often this is arguable, and in any case their well-being is still going to be very much affected by what happens *after* the divorce. Where will they live, and with whom? How much will they see of the absent parent, and where will they fit into the second marriages their parents may make or second families of which they are suddenly a part?

No parent can look dispassionately at his or her own child, and it is recognised that in this situation, where passions run high, children would be at risk if their future were left entirely in the hands of their parents."[28]

We need more research to examine the important phenomenon of the effect of a divorce on children of all ages.

CURRENT SCENE

The legal questions of custody, access and maintenance are often not the real issues but rather are the means divorced people may use to continue their involvement with each other. Wars need battlefields. Some divorced couples use the courts as battlefields for acting out their need to strike back at each other and to gratify their need for revenge. There are, undoubtedly, many other reasons motivating such couples to rush to court, reasons which are as yet not fully understood and require more research. The court process into which they rush has serious drawbacks. Judge Lindsley describes it this way:

"The adversary process, historically effective in resolving disputes between litigants where evidentiary facts have probative significance, is not properly suited to the resolution of most family relations problems. It may be that by the traditional adversary process we may come close to establishing what people have done or not done in the relationship. That is a far cry, however, from understanding the conduct and the dynamics behind it. When you add to this a generally irrelevant and frequently puritanical concept of fault as the necessary basis for legal dissolution of a marriage or for deciding questions of child custody and visitation...I think it not unfair to say that the mind of man could hardly have conceived any process, ostensibly concerned with the stability of marriage and the family, that would be more likely to rip husband, wife, father, mother and children apart so thoroughly and bitterly."[29]

How is the above description relevant to the current scene in Ontario? Both parents in Ontario have the same legal right to be awarded custody of the child in divorce proceedings.[30] We are repeatedly told that, given this fact, the courts consider only the best interests of the child.

"It is now clear that the courts, in considering the rival claims of the parents to custody, express the view that they are guided only by the best interests and welfare of the child."[31]

However, there is nothing in the 1968 Divorce Act that relates to the best interests of the child, nor that directs the judge to make these the prime basis for the decision. Nor is there anywhere any mention of any rights of the child that should be considered in the determination of custody. The courts may express the view that they consider only the best interests of the child, but, in reality, this is not the case.[32] This becomes clearer if we examine the nature of the divorce proceedings as they now exist in Ontario.

First, divorce legislation is directed toward the marital relationship, having as its aim the dissolution of the spouses' legal relationship. The question of custody is considered a corollary relief matter — one that is not of central importance to the issue. Thus, the focus is not on the children *per se*.

Second, divorce takes place within an adversary process, in a court room setting, as a trial before a judge. This process

". . . demands that one party sue the other for something, and that one party is essentially innocent while the other is guilty. This means that, before a divorce can be granted, the petitioner must prove grounds that likely have nothing to with the collapse of the marriage as such. Fail to prove the grounds, and the petitioner fails to get a divorce. The respondent may not have been quite cruel enough, or at least not cruel in a sufficiently acceptable and impressive way. The parties may have been separated for years, but a question arises whether the petitioner deserted the respondent and so should wait a few years more. None of these things have any relevance to the undoubted fact that the marriage is dead, never to be revived, and that one or both parties desperately want to be free of its legal bonds."[33]

These two features of the process lead us to the third feature of the system that is relevant in custody proceedings: the child is not represented as a party to the action, even though it concerns his or her future. Instead, each party supposedly represents the best interests of the child. However, when both parties are essentially out to win their own sides, as they usually are, they are not concerned primarily with the child as a person but often tend to view him or her as a pawn to use against the other spouse, either for revenge purposes, or to win more concessions. Since this is so often what happens, it is foolish of us to continue believing the child's interests are being served.

Although in theory, a judge in Ontario has an objective report on which to base his decisions regarding custody, in reality, this is not the case. The report is that of the Official Guardian of Ontario.[34] The Official Guardian is required to investigate the custody arrangements in all cases involving children under sixteen; however in most cases, this entails merely a questionnaire being mailed to the parties to the divorce. Only in some cases is further investigation done — usually only with one party. Bradbrook[35] found that the majority of the Supreme Court judges of Ontario that he interviewed did not find the report objective, nor helpful, although they felt that it had this potential. The point seems to be that, although the judge should have at his or her disposal something relating to the child's best interests, the Official Guardian's report is falling short of the mark. Further, if an expert witness, usually a psychiatrist, appears in court, he or she is hired by one or other of the parties. The expert witness is, therefore, used in order to build up the client's side, and thus testimony is focussed on the client, not on the child. If the witness should adopt a focus on the child, he or she may not be used, if this focus is detrimental to the client's case.

CONCILIATION AND ARBITRATION IN FAMILY DISPUTES*****

Thus, the court process, with its use of the adversary system, has for many the undesirable effect of entrenching the very attitudes and actions that initially brought the parties to court. The model presented in this paper is intended to provide an alternative, which avoids the adoption of adversarial roles. There are two key elements in this preferred approach: first, a system of conciliation, as a necessary precondition to any court-sanctioned divorce or separation proceedings, and second, the availability of arbitration as an alternative to the courts should the parties be unable to resolve their differences at the conciliation stage.

The model is represented graphically in Figure 1. The conciliation stage will first be discussed, including a case example based on the experience of one of the authors. Subsequently, the focus will turn to arbitration.

*****The authors wish to thank Professor Ernie Lightman of the Faculty of Social Work for his help in developing the material in this section. Readers are referred to Ernie S. Lightman and Howard H. Irving, "Conciliation and Arbitration in Family Disputes," (December 1976) 14 Conciliation Courts Review, pp. 12-22, where this material appears in more extended form.

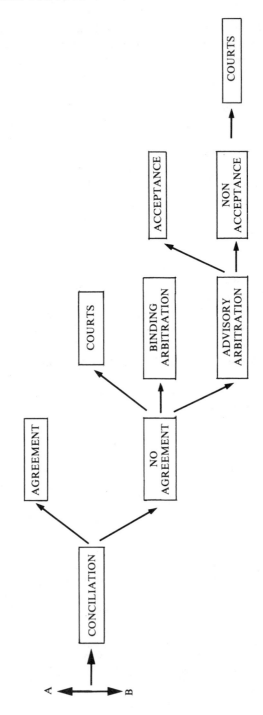

A MODEL FOR DISPUTE RESOLUTION
IN MATTERS INVOLVING A CHILD

FIGURE 1

A major, but not always successful, goal of conciliation is to help the couple become rational and responsible enough to co-operate toward compromises which are acceptable to both of them. It is a worn truism that the parents know what is best for their children more than any third party, whether that be judge, lawyer or counsellor. Voluntary settlements, which are worked out by both spouses on an emotional level as well as an intellectual one, are not only more humane than those forced by litigation, but also more practical. Mutual agreement means that neither party is the "loser" or has been taken advantage of, so there is less likelihood of revenge erupting later and leading to new and prolonged legal battles.

The subject matter for conciliation may be defined in advance by the parties but in general, will be expected to fall under three headings: questions of custody, access (visitation), and maintenance. If the parties wish to exclude one of these, they may do so in advance by joint agreement.

The primary goals of the conciliator are to help the parents arrive at an amicable settlement to ensure that "the best interests of the child" are met; to help the parties become more aware of the destructive impact their conflict has on the children; and to help the parties accept the reality that, although they are separated or divorced, their role as parents continues forever.

Even if the parties have privately resolved all the relevant issues involving the child, there is still reason to initiate conciliation. If a divorce or other resolution involving the courts is being sought, a meeting with the conciliator may be considered a crucial step; in other cases where the courts are not involved, the process would necessarily be voluntary. The reason for such an approach is that conciliation in family dispute resolution is normative: that is, the conciliator has an independent goal, apart from the narrowly-defined interests of the two parties. His or her over-riding responsibility is to ensure that the welfare of the child remains the central focus of all discussions and agreements. This approach stands in contrast to the purely accommodative goals of conciliation in labour or commercial relations; in these contexts, the acceptability of an agreement to the parties involved is the only concern of the mediator; he or she has no independent interest.

The role of the conciliator is to serve as catalyst, encouraging the parties to identify areas of disagreement and to settle their own dispute; hence, it is neither desirable nor necessary that individual lawyers be present. All meetings with the conciliator, including any information presented or offers made, should be considered confidential, and will be precluded from use in any subsequent proceedings. The conciliator will be barred from participation in any further hearings, and will not be called upon to testify or produce any documents. The conciliator will, however, be permitted to meet privately with individual lawyers, accountants, or any other relevant persons where this is considered to be appropriate. With the consent of the parents, he or she may also meet with a child who is, in the conciliator's opinion, of suitable age. Each party shall be encouraged to disclose fully all information (including financial statements, tax returns, and so on) which may be requested by by the conciliator, or, where the conciliator feels the request is relevant, by the other party.

The number, length and frequency of meetings with the conciliator should be sufficient to determine if the process can be useful, but not such as to unduly delay proceedings or increase costs.

The parties may jointly specify in advance an outer limit to conciliation in terms of either total elapsed time (*e.g.,* no more than six months from date of initial contact with the conciliator) or maximum number of meetings. These limits can, of course, subsequently be waived with the consent of the parties and the conciliator.

A minimum number of contacts may also be specified. For example, the Family Mediation Centre Incorporated, a voluntary non-profit agency in Atlanta, Georgia, requires a prior commitment of ten hours of meetings as a condition for undertaking its service. This minimum, however, can be waived by the mediator at any time, or by either party with the consent of the mediator at any time.

A minimum of ten meetings may seen reasonable in the context of a purely voluntary service such as that provided by the Family Mediation Centre. The present approach, however, contains a strong presumption that the conciliation service will be more obligatory; hence, the practices of the Los Angeles conciliation court may provide a more appropriate model. In that jurisdiction the parties are required to meet once with the conciliator in a session of approximately one and a half hours. The parties are usually seen together first, for a brief period, to enable the conciliator to establish the ground rules and to satisfy the parties of his or her impartiality. The conciliator would then be seen separately and the session would end in an extended tripartite conference. Provision might also be made for a second meeting at least, which could be required at the option of conciliator.

CASE EXAMPLE

One of the authors has made use of conciliation counselling in his private practice; a case example may illustrate the way in which this approach might operate. The names in the example have been disguised.

A couple were referred by their respective lawyers to a conciliation regarding the custody and access of their daughter. A related question concerning the child's holidays for the summer was included in the referral. The terms of the conciliation were stated as follows:

1. As the conciliator, an attempt will be made to bring about an agreement between the father and the mother as to the determination of the following question:

(a) How much time should the child spend with each of them during the forthcoming school summer vacation; and

(b) should custody of the child be changed from the mother to the father?

2. In dealing with the question of which parent should have custody of the child, they may agree to whatever arrangement is in the best interests of the child and, without limiting the generality of the foregoing, they may agree that:

(a) One or the other of them shall have temporary custody for a trial period; or,

(b) Both of them shall have custody as joint custodians and the child shall live with one or the other of them or first one then the other, during the periods that are specified and set out in the agreement.

(c) Neither of them shall have custody of the child, but the periods of time the child is to be with each parent are to be specified and set out in the agreement.

These alternatives are mentioned for the purpose of emphasizing that the parties are free to choose whatever arrangement is in the best interests of the child. Their choice may be one of these alternatives or any better that might emerge from the mediation.

3. The separation agreement previously entered into shall not be binding on the parties insofar as the questions of custody and access are concerned.

4. The question of the child's maintenance or financial support is excluded from mediation and if it arises, shall be referred back to Counsel for determination.

5. In attempting to bring about an agreement, the conciliator may meet with and speak to the father, the mother, and the child separately or jointly, and may consult such other persons and inspect such reports, records or documents as necessary.

6. Any agreement reached shall constitute a settlement of the subject matter of the agreement and be produced for the information of the court in the legal proceedings pending between the father and the mother in the Supreme Court of Ontario or in any other relevant legal proceedings.

7. In the event that no agreement is reached within the period established for mediation, both parties shall have the right to pursue their legal remedies in the action pending between them in the Supreme Court of Ontario or in such other action or proceeding as they or either of them may be advised to take.

8. The period of time allowed for the mediation shall be established by

the conciliator in consultation with both Counsel, after both parents have been interviewed, but in no event, shall be for more than six weeks from the date of this letter.

9. Evidence of anything said or of any admission or communication made in the course of the mediation is not admissible in the pending or any other legal proceeding.

10. The conciliator will not be called as a witness by or on behalf of either parent in the pending, or any other legal proceeding to give any opinion or to disclose any admission or communication made in the course of the mediation.

11. Except to inform Counsel that —
(a) No agreement has been reached; or
(b) What the terms of the agreement are; there shall be no report made of the mediation.

12. The fee for the mediation shall be borne by the parents in equal shares and payable on such terms as are determined.

A statement of agreed facts was attached as an appendix to provide the conciliator with background information. Counsel specifically raised none of the allegations made by the parties in support of their respective claims.

DISCUSSION OF CASE

The first step in this conciliation process was to discuss with the lawyers for both sides the conciliation agreement. The lawyers were encouraged to share with the conciliator their perceptions of their clients' concerns. The latter, in turn, clarified his role as it related to their clients. This dispelled the myth about working as an agent for one lawyer. This approach underscored the concept that the conciliator was acting as the child's advocate throughout the conciliation process.

Following the discussion with the lawyers, the parents were interviewed individually. Then the child was seen alone. General impressions were that the parents, as well as the child, were suffering from battle fatigue. There had been a long hard series of conflicts with nothing but a hollow victory looming in the far distance. It was interesting to note that the parents were relieved that the conciliator did not get into the game of the "expert witness" (*e.g.,* psychiatrists) and was not to determine who was the most suitable parent, but instead to create a climate for negotiation.

By the end of the interviews with the parents, it was apparent that they sincerely wanted what was best for the child and were prepared to commit themselves to conciliation. As the child was interviewed, her obvious relief was centred around the absence of the kind of questions previously asked by expert witnesses, such as "Who would you like to live with, your mother or your dad?" She was told that, after a few sessions with the family, her parents together with the conciliator, would decide what kind of living arrangements would be in her best interest at this time. She was also assured that whatever she told the conciliator would be held in confidence and would not be the subject of any report made to the court at a later time.

The most important result of the conciliation process was that for the first time the parents worked together to arrive at a recommendation for their daughter. And for the first time, they made a decision for her without giving this eleven-year old a Hobson's choice which had previously led to guilt and conflict for her.

THE ARBITRATION OPTION

In many cases the conciliation process will result in agreement and resolution of the matters in dispute. Alternatively, the parties may reach an impasse and not be able to reconcile their differences. In the latter case, the conciliator will simply report that he or she has met with the parties and that they have been unable to effect a settlement.[36] As has been indicated, the conciliator now passes from the scene, and all information acquired to this point remains privileged.

The parties now have available to them three options, indicated in Figure 1. They may choose to go to the courts as is current practice, with all proceedings commencing *de novo;* this avenue also represents the default option, the course which will be followed if the parties are unable to jointly agree on one of the other two possibilities.[37]

These two alternatives are binding arbitration and advisory arbitration. In the former case, the parties agree in advance that the decision of the arbitrators will be binding on them, with the same force as an order of the courts; in the latter case, the decision is presented to the parties and they are then free to accept or reject the substance of the award. If they choose to accept, the decision then becomes binding; if they opt for rejection, they are then free to proceed to the courts for final determination. In this latter case, however, there is a proviso that the award of the arbitrator will be made available to the courts. As the court then examines the matter, it can utilize the decision of the arbitrator along with any other new information deemed relevant to determining the best interest of the child. In the absence of compelling new evidence to the contrary, however, it may be assumed that in the majority of cases the courts would uphold the arbitrator's decision.

That is, under normal circumstances the advisory arbitration award will ultimately become binding upon the parties. The difference in practice between advisory and binding arbitration may then become largely psychological or emotional: the parties may wish to feel that they have the option or the freedom to reject the decision of the arbitrator and keep open the possibilities of going to court — even though they will undoubtedly be aware that the decision is likely to be reinforced by the courts.[38]

The attractions of arbitration as an alternative to the courts should be considered: most fundamentally, the goal of arbitration is not the determination of guilt or innocence, as results from the adversary processes used in the courts. Arbitration may be considered a form of social investigation similar in orientation to adoption proceedings, pre-sentence hearings, or delinquency cases. In none of these contexts — including that of the present model — is Truth being sought; in every case, the object is to find the best possible remedy to a social problem.

To bring about this result, recourse can be had to all relevant information without adherence to rigorous courtroom standards and formalities. For example, the arbitrator can essentially set his or her own rules concerning the admissibility of evidence. If reports are authorized, the author would presumably be available to the hearing, but the confidentiality of sources will be respected. Cross-examination and rebuttal are permitted, the lawyers will probably be present, but the total atmosphere will be less formal and more flexible than in the courtroom; and

". . .the flexibility of procedure which is possible is bound to result in more imaginative treatment of the human problems that make up a custody dispute."[39]

The use of arbitration, in this context, is also in line with a modern tendency found in the courts in the United States, in particular, to support the use of arbitration for the resolution of private disputes as a supplement to the traditional court procedures. Among the other advantages of arbitration are its greater speed in resolving disputes (as opposed to the substantial time lag which is involved in getting a case to court), the probable lesser cost, and the reduced likelihood of engendering an atmosphere of conflict, anger and tension.

CHANGED CIRCUMSTANCES

Thus far, the discussion has been primarily concerned with the initial decision of the parties to separate and establish rules governing custody, access and maintenance. However, circumstances change over time and provisions could properly be made for this as well. For example, one party may wish to re-open a prior decision concerning custody or visitation, or someone's financial status may alter in such a way that a new look at maintenance levels becomes appropriate.

Figure 2 presents a model to deal with the resolution of disputes involving a child under conditions of changed circumstances.

DISPUTE RESOLUTION INVOLVING A CHILD
UNDER CHANGED CIRCUMSTANCES

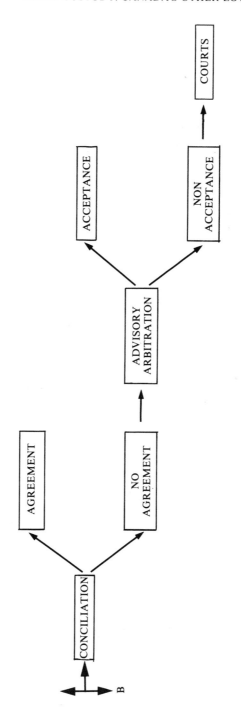

FIGURE 2

If the parties are able to settle privately the issues in question and no change in any court order is involved, the matter can rest there. If, however, the courts are to be involved, the parties must meet with the conciliator, at least briefly. As before, the process is normative and the conciliator will attempt to aid the parties in an amiable settlement of the issues in question.

If, however, the issue cannot be settled in this manner, the conciliator will then become an arbitrator, in effect, and will present a decision. The parties can then accept or reject this decision with the consequences of each alternative as described earlier for voluntary arbitration.

The two unique features of this procedure are that the conciliator and arbitrator are now the same person, and that the arbitration stage is compulsory, although the substance of the decision is not binding.

The reason for the first of these is largely economic. A one-step procedure for dispute resolution will be faster and less costly than the two-step process presented earlier. The implicit assumption underlying mandatory arbitration is that the majority of issues which arise at this stage will involve relatively minor or technical changes in an existing agreement. This stands in contrast to the more fundamental questions which must be resolved in establishing the original agreement. Of course, if either party does deem the matter of sufficient importance, he or she is free to reject the arbitrator's award and proceed to the courts, being aware that the courts are likely to uphold the decision in any case. No freedom of either party is sacrificed with the compulsory arbitration stage, as long as the decision is formally only advisory.

One interesting question which arises is whether the existence of a compulsory arbitration procedure tends to weaken the processes of accommodation by the parties. In the industrial relations context one informed observer of the Canadian scene suggests that this is in fact the case, that compulsory arbitration imposes rigidities on the parties and lessens the likelihood of agreement.[40] In the present context, it is the view of the authors that the opposite is more likely to occur; the awareness that compulsory arbitration awaits a failure to agree on their own, should act as a spur to the parties, an incentive for them to resolve the issues of dispute amiably and personally.

SOME ORGANIZATIONAL ISSUES

A fundamental question, in principle, is whether the conciliation procedure should be mandatory in all cases. Such an approach has been criticized as an attempt to legislate therapy, or, more generally, to legislate attitudes. However, there is legislative precedent in that the Canada Divorce Act requires lawyers to inform their clients who are seeking divorce of the possibilities of conciliation counselling, and a statement that this has been done must form part of the divorce petition.[41]

Unfortunately, in nearly all cases, this requirement of the Canada Divorce Act is purely *pro forma*. The implication is that if the conciliation service envisaged here is to avoid the same destiny as the Divorce Act requirement, there must be a strong presumption that it will be pursued in virtually all cases. The fundamental objections to compulsory conciliation would appear to be largely philosphical or idealogical. If some provision is to be made for opting out under specified circumstances, it is vital that the exceptions be few and very narrowly defined. If it is easy to by-pass the conciliation stage, the process will never attain credibility or viability.

In the Los Angeles conciliation court — certainly the most successful and often cited model — the conciliation service is highly recommended, rather than obligatory; yet it meets with wide public acceptance.[42]

If this conciliation service is to be virtually mandatory in cases involving a child, it is both necessary and appropriate that it operate under the auspices of the courts. Elkin describes this as the "constructive use of authority".[43]

It would follow then that the resources of the courts be available to aid in the conciliation process. For example, there should probably be lawyers and/or accountants attached to the court system who would be present or available during conciliation to advise the parties jointly without representing either individually. They will regard all information and communications obtained during conciliation as privileged and will be available, if desired, to aid in the actual drafting of a settlement should one be reached. At this stage, however, the parties may wish to involve their own lawyers or accountants, if the details of the agreement are highly technical.

The conciliators themselves must have some form of certification or sanction by the courts. In those jurisdictions such as Ontario where there is no licensing, the problems are somewhat more complex, but the list of marriage counsellors used by the Family Courts may provide a helpful model.

The conciliators can be in private practice, attached to community agencies, or employed in the public sector as a direct arm of the courts. The costs of conciliation would, in the latter case, probably be borne by the court system; in other cases the sharing of costs would be resolved as part of the final settlement. An arrangement similar to Legal Aid should also be available for the conciliation service, where appropriate.

Under normal circumstances one conciliator will be selected by the parties from the approved lists. If either party so desires, provision may be made for two conciliators, one male and one female. This same person (or persons) may later serve as conciliator/arbitrator should a dispute subsequently arise as a result of changed circumstances. Because the conciliator is familiar with the parties, he or she is probably the best equipped to aid them in matters of interpretation or in the resolution of later disagreements, ultimately making the decision, if necessary. Of course, the participation of the original conciliator at this stage is contingent upon the wishes of the two parties and they are quite free to choose a new person.

Arbitration, as well, will usually be conducted by one individual. In the United States, the American Arbitration Association maintains a national panel on which are doctors, attorneys, social workers, sociologists, psychologists, educators and other specialists in dealing with human problems. There appears to be no counterpart to this in Canada. Although there may be short-term shortages of suitably trained personnel, it is expected that over time there will develop a body of people with experience and with this experience will come expertise.

CONCLUSION

The approach suggested in this paper will, of course, require further exploration and research. A number of practitioners in both law and the behavioural sciences have begun to implement some of the ideas contained in this model, and preliminary results appear promising. It is the view of the authors that any scheme for family dispute resolution which replaces formality and adversarial roles with openness, flexibility and candour, to the maximum extent possible, can only represent a significant step forward.

In considering new approaches to an old problem, we must avoid the present lottery system involved in the custody of children in divorce actions. The human ramifications of divorce are too complex to be dealt with by a single profession. Co-operative effort would result in less fragmentation and a more comprehensive and meaningful service to clients.

1   Wayne Clarke, "Divorce by Fire," Week-end Magazine, June 5, 1976, 11.
2   Louise J. Despert, *Children of Divorce* (New York, 1962) at ix.
3   Canada, Parliament, Report of the Special Joint Committee of the Senate and House of Commons on Divorce (Ottawa, June 1967) at 151.
4   Michael Wheeler, *No-Fault Divorce* (Boston, 1974) at 72.
5   *Loc. cit.* at 96.
6   Max Sugar, "Children of Divorce," (1970) 46 Pediatrics 588 at 595.
7   Marjorie Kawin Toomim, "Understanding the Child of Divorce," Chapter 6 (pages 91-123) in Richard E. Hardy and John G. Cull, eds., *Creative Divorce Through Social and Psychological Approaches* (Springfield, Illinois, 1974) 94-107.
8   John F. McDermott, Jr., "Parental Divorce in Early Childhood," (1968) 124 American Journal of Psychiatry 1424 at 1431.
9   *Loc. cit.*
10   Judith S. Wallerstein and Joan B. Kelly, "The Effects of Parental Divorce: Experiences

of the Preschool Child," (1975) 14 Journal of the American Academy of Child Psychiatry 600.

11   *Ibid.,* at 614-616.

12   Judith S. Wallerstein and Joan B. Kelly, "The Effects of Parental Divorce: Experiences of the Child in Early Latency," (1976) 46 American Journal of Orthopsychiatry 20 at 23.

13   *Ibid.* at 25.

14   *Ibid.* at 26.

15   *Ibid.* at 28.

16   *Ibid.* at 31.

17   Judith S. Wailerstein and Joan B. Kelly, "The Effects of Parental Divorce: Experiences of the Child in Later Latency," (1976) 46 American Journal of Orthopsychiatry 256 at 258.

18   *Ibid.* at 260.

19   *Ibid.* at 261.

20   *Ibid.* at 259.

21   *Ibid.* at 268-269.

22   Judith S. Wallerstein and Joan B. Kelly, "The Effects of Parental Divorce: The Adolescent Experience," in E. James Anthony and Cyrille Koupernik, eds., *The Child in His Family: Children at Psychiatric Risk* (New York, 1974) pp. 479-505, at 504.

23   *Loc. cit.*

24   Mel Krantzler, *Creative Divorce* (New York, 1974) at 191-193.

25   Bernard Steinzor, *When Parents Divorce* (New York, 1970) at 53-56.

26   Susan Gettleman and Janet Markowitz, *The Courage to Divorce* (New York, 1974) at 110-111 (footnote 14, page 111 in original, omitted from passage cited.)

27   Benjamin Schlesinger, *The One-Parent Family: Perspective and Annotated Bibliography* 3rd. edition (Toronto, 1975).

28   Gerald Sanctuary and Constance Whitehead, *Divorce and After* (London: 1970) at 134.

29   Byron F. Lindsley, "Custody Procedures: Battlefield or Peace Conference," (1975) 13 Conciliation Courts Review 1, 1.

30   The Divorce Act, R.S.C. 1970, c. D-8, section 11(1)(c).

31   Ontario Law Reform Commission, *Report on Family Law. Part III: Children* (Toronto, 1973) at 102.

32   N. Galoon, *Custody Cases in Divorce,* Unpublished Paper, Toronto Faculty of Social Work, 1974.

33   Malcolm C. Kronby, *The Guide to Family Law* (Toronto, 1972) at 123.

34   The requirement for an Official Guardian's investigation and report where a petition or counter-petition for divorce contains particulars of any child under sixteen is found in s. 6 of The Matrimonial Causes Act, R.S.O. 1970, c. 265, as amended by 1972 (Ont.) c. 50, s. 1.

35   A. Bradbrook, "An Empirical Study of the Attitudes of Judges of the Supreme Court of Ontario Regarding the Present Child Custody Adjudication Laws" (1971) 49 Can. Bar Rev. 557, 561-2.

36   There exists, of course, a third possibility: though the primary purpose of the conciliation is not the reconciliation of the parties, they may nevertheless decide to stay together again, either as a result of the conciliation or simply during the time when it takes place. If this outcome results, the parties should have access to the conciliator to aid in the resolution of future difficulties on a voluntary basis.

37   A variation on the model involves more radical change and would remove the court option entirely. Disputes would then necessarily be dealt with by administrative panels such as are described in the text.

38   It should be explicitly noted, of course, that in all proceedings, whether before the courts or in arbitration, the parties always retain access to the court of appeal. However, it is only the lawyers who appear in the court of appeal, the proceedings are brief, and the onus is clearly on the petitioning party to indicate the grounds for re-opening the dispute. Mere dissatisfaction with the substance of the award is not sufficient. Under present conditions, a substantial majority of all petitions is denied by appeal courts, and it may be

anticipated that this trend will continue even with the additional option of arbitration.
39 Case Note, (1965) 33 Fordham Law Rev. 726, 732.
40 H.D. Woods, *Labour Policy in Canada*, 2nd ed. (Toronto, 1973) at 157.
41 The Divorce Act, R.S.C. 1970, c. D-8, s. 7.
42 Meyer Elkin, "Conciliation Courts: The Reintegration of Disintegrating Families" (1973) 22 Family Co-ordinator 63 at 67-68.
43 *Ibid.* at 66.

Editor's Note

In one of the panel discussions at the seminar which gave rise to this collection, Judge David M. Steinberg of the Ontario Provincial Court, Family Division commented on representation of children in matrimonial disputes. His remarks, based on notes prepared for the occasion and on a recording of the panel presentation, are reproduced here.

Representation of Children In Matrimonial Disputes

David M. Steinberg*

I have been asked to talk for a few moments on the issue of the representation of children in matrimonial disputes. There have been over the recent past a number of developments in this area which I believe are worthy of mention. The developments can be broadly categorized into three areas:

(1) Social
(2) Jurisprudential
(3) Legislative

SOCIAL

At common law the child was more or less regarded as an appendage to his parents with no rights or voice in legal matters except insofar as they might be accorded to him by his parents. The common law gave the child no rights against his parents, not even the right of maintenance. As Chief Justice Cockburn, some many years ago, stated in *Bazely v. Forder,* ". . .except under the operation of the poor law, there is no legal obligation on the part of the father to maintain his child, unless, indeed, the neglect to do so should bring the case within the criminal law. Civilly there is no such obligation."[1]

Now, if at common law, the child had not even the right to be maintained, one would hardly expect him to be given any right to be heard in either maintenance or custody proceedings, or any other legal matter which involved his personal welfare.

With the development of the statutory application of the law of equity to the resolution of custody disputes (*i.e.* applying the best interests of the child test) and with the recent development of the philosophic concept of the "rights" of the children, the Courts have become increasingly concerned and aware of the fact that someone must speak for or represent the child in legal matters affecting his welfare.

* David M. Steinberg is a Judge in the Unified Family Court, Province of Ontario.

JURISPRUDENTIAL

This leads me into a brief survey on how some of the judges of our Courts have reacted to the need to have someone speak for the child. It should be noted that there is little, if any, legislative authority providing for such need. The judges have responded in two ways — one which might be described as traditional and the other as innovative.

THE TRADITIONAL JUDICIAL APPROACHES

The two traditional ways of trying to listen to the voice of the child have been:

(1) by having the judge speak to the child; and

(2) by placing the onus on the counsel for the parents to represent the child's interests ahead of the interests of the parents.

The first traditional approach of speaking to the child was utilized recently by Mr. Justice Keith of the Ontario Supreme Court in *Guy v. Guy*[2]. He described his use of that approach:

"In these situations the problem facing the court is one that causes the greatest anxiety. The court's basic function is to have paramount regard for the welfare of the child involved or children involved, but at the same time recognizing the natural love and affection and, indeed, rights, up to a point, of the respective parents. I have had an opportunity of having an interview with this young lady, and I use the term advisedly, in which all the conversation was taken down by a court reporter who was present throughout. I have asked that the parties do not ask for a transcript of what was said at that time until the final resolution of this matter, if ever. Since the parties are still before the Court for determination of all issues, I wish that nothing that has transpired today will in any way inhibit the ultimate decisions of the judge presiding at the trial."[3]

The second traditional judicial approach, of relying on the parents' counsel, is outlined by Mr. Justice Selby in *Clarkson v. Clarkson*,[4] a decision of the New South Wales Supreme Court. He stated

"I have pointed out on a number of previous occasions that matters concerning the welfare of children are not regarded in this jurisdiction as similar to ordinary litigation between the parties. They are, of course, contests between the parties. The rules of procedure and the laws of evidence apply. But the interests of the parties take second place. Regard for the interests of the child is the determining factor. This is what is meant by regarding the interests of the child as the paramount consideration. A proper determination of those interests cannot be made by the application of any supposed principles as to onus of proof or of presumptions which might be thought to apply in other cases. Recognized tactics of advocacy which may be in every way right and proper are not necessarily of assistance in cases of this nature. The task of counsel is a difficult one for, whilst owing a duty to his client — a duty which may be discharged by bringing out the points which indicate that to grant custody or access to his client would be in the interests of the child whilst granting them to his opponent's client would be inimical to those interests — he must always remain aware that the child's interests come before those of his client. It is therefore necessary to adduce all available evidence which might have a bearing on the matter."[5]

Both of these approaches have suffered in my view from real defects.

With respect to the judicial interview of the child, it can be brief, and at best, very unnatural in the sense that neither the judge nor the child can function very well in the stilted setting of the judicial chambers. There is a further point that should be noted: very few adults have the emotional competence to address a judge, with respect to a point which involves their entire future — that's what counsel are hired to do. Why should we require this of children, who are supposedly less able to express themselves than adults.

With regard to relying on counsel for the parents to bring out all of the important factors relating to the best interests of the children, this had obviously many faults in an adversary setting. It is my feeling that the adversarial setting cannot be utilized to achieve goals which might be described as "non adversarial". That does not mean, however, that the adversarial process has no place in family law.

THE INNOVATIVE JUDICIAL APPROACHES

It is characteristic of common law judges, when the law fails to provide a remedy for a need, to adapt judicial forms designed for another use to meet the prescribed need. We all recall the trespass upon the case, and the development of the use upon the use.

A most innovative approach to child representation has been the development of the judicial use of the concept of the guardian *ad litem*. The guardian *ad litem* is primarily a civil law concept and is the person through whom an infant has traditionally defended a civil action. His prescribed function has been to protect the property of the child. Three recently reported cases however, involve the appointment of the Provincial Official Guardian as the statutory guardian *ad litem* of children, to intervene in custody matters, matters which are really foreign in nature to the ordinary purpose of the guardian *ad litem*.

I refer to the cases of *Re Reid and Reid*,[6] *McKercher v. McKercher*[7] and *Re Dadswell*.[8] In *Reid and Reid*, Galligan J. utilized s.107(2) of The Judicature Act,[9] which reads:

"The Official Guardian shall be the guardian *ad litem* or next friend of infants and other persons in accordance with any Act or the rules or an order of a court or judge."

It is interesting that the Reid case was applied in a Family Court matter under The Deserted Wives' and Children's Maintenance Act[10] wherein a matter of child maintenance was involved. Judge Fisher in *Re Dadswell* purported to apply s.107(2) of The Judicature Act and appointed the Official Guardian to represent the child. The clear implication of that judgment is that the term "court" used in s.107(2) of The Judicature Act includes the Provincial Court (Family Division). That may be open to some question.

In that regard, in the case of *Re Helmes,*[11] the Divisional Court of Ontario rescinded an order made in a Family Court under The Child Welfare Act appointing the Official Guardian to act as guardian *ad litem* for a child. That case, however, as I recall it, restricted itself as to whether or not there was authority under The Child Welfare Act to appoint someone to act for the child. The court found there was none. No reference, however, was had to s.107(2) of The Judicature Act. As I recall the case, the Court was of the view that the Children's Aid Society was the protector of the child and was the only party who could represent the child under the Act. So *Re Dadswell* remains unchallenged to this point.

There is another innovative approach which is used by many courts, which as yet has not been documented, and which gets around any problems raised by the use of the guardian *ad litem*. That is the approach used by Mr. Justice Manning, in the Supreme Court of Alberta, in the utilization of counsel to assist the Court and the child in the capacity of an *amicus curiae*.[12]

The *amicus curiae* has been traditionally defined as "a friend of the Court — a bystander, usually a barrister who informs a judge in court on a point of law or fact on which the judge is doubtful or mistaken." Now, just as the guardian *ad litem* role has been expanded to include cases where a child is not sued, but fought over, so to speak, so the *amicus curiae* role has been expanded by many courts to cover cases where a Court needs the assistance of the independent role of a third counsel or party in those cases where the child's case must be expressed. This approach is especially helpful in child welfare and juvenile cases where the child's position is contrary to those of the Children's Aid Society and his parents. In most Family Courts where this approach has been used, Legal Aid will finance the cost of the *amicus curiae*.

LEGISLATIVE

The need for the representation of children in matrimonial disputes, aside from the *ad hoc* measures that have been devised by the judges to date, has met with a ready response in the reports of the various Law Reform Commissions both Federal and Provincial.

The Federal Law Reform Commission in its Working Paper on the Family Court states:

"Where the right or interest of a child will be directly or indirectly affected by a court proceeding, the Commission recommends that consideration be given to the appointment of independent legal counsel to represent the child. The Commission recognizes that, in many instances, there will be no conflict of interest among the parties or, on the other hand, the agreement between the adult parties will provide as adequately as is possible for the child's welfare. However, the interests of a child may require separate legal representation, particularly in matters of contested custody, contested adoption, and child neglect, and, occasionally, in maintenance proceedings. It is not good enough to rely upon the judge, the parents or the parents' counsel, to act as an advocate for the child in such matters.

The Commission envisages the development of rules of procedure under which, well in advance of the trial, there will be a review of the facts in issue and an opportunity for an appropriate officer of the court to exercise a discretionary power to appoint counsel to represent the interests of the child until the matter is concluded."[13]

A similar view has been taken by the Ontario Law Reform Commission which has recommended the establishment of a Law Guardian in its proposed Unified Family Court.

That is a brief synopsis of what is currently going on in the area of the legal representation of children in matrimonial disputes. Much will depend in Ontario on the development of a Unified Family Court concept which carries with it the resource structure to provide consistent and adequate child representation.

---

1 (1868) L.R. 3 Q.B. 559 at 565.
2 (1975) 22 R.F.L. 294 (Ont.).
3 *Ibid.* at 295.
4 (1972) 14 R.F.L. 313 (N.S.W.).
5 *Ibid.* at 315.
6 (1975) 11 O.R. (2d) 622, 25 R.F.L. 209, 67 D.L.R. (3d) 46.
7 [1975] 2 W.W.R. 268 (Sask. Q.B.) The appointment of the Official Guardian as guardian *ad litem* was made pursuant to The Infants Act, R.S.S. 1965, c.342, section 31(1) of which provides that "The Official Guardian besides acting as a guardian *ad litem* of infants under rules of court and other orders, shall perform such other duties as the court or judge may from time to time direct, or as may be fixed by order of the Lieutenant Governor in Council." See also *H. v. H.* (1976) 13 O.R. (2d) 371, 71 D.L.R. (3d) 161 (H.C.J.) in which two motions involving custody were being argued before Mr. Justice Galligan. The Official Guardian of Ontario happened to come into the courtroom as the motions were being argued, and Mr. Justice Galligan asked him to interview the children

involved, two boys aged 14 and 16, and give them independent legal advice, adjourning for some hours to enable this to be done.

8   (1976) 27 R.F.L. 214 (Ont. Prov. Ct.).

9   R.S.O. 1970, c.228.

10 R.S.O. 1970, c.128.

11 (1976) 13 O.R. (2d) 4 (Div. Ct.). The Court stated, however, that its ruling did not mean that a Judge hearing an application may not hear persons other than the Children's Aid Society on behalf of the child. A Judge hearing a custody case would, according to the Court in *Helmes*, have the right to adjourn the matter to inquire of the Official Guardian whether he wished to make representations on behalf of the child. This right, stated the Court, was derived from section 25(3) of The Child Welfare Act, which stipulates that "The judge may hear any person on behalf of the child . . ."

12 On the other hand, however, separate representation of children by a solicitor in private practice in a custody dispute between their parents was frowned on by Mr. Justice Reid of the Ontario Supreme Court in *Rowe v. Rowe* (1976) 26 R.F.L. 91. Mr. Justice Reid stated, at p.96 of the report, "Based on my experience in this case, I doubt the desirability of having children represented by counsel or advised by "their own" (the children's term) solicitor as a practice. There may well be cases where in the circumstances a trial judge considers it desirable for the children to have separate representation at trial. If that is so, the office of the official guardian would appear to be available and can be called upon at that point. Earlier involvement of solicitors for children can, I think, cause more harm than good."

13 Law Reform Commission of Canada, *Working Paper No. 1: The Family Court* (Ottawa, 1974) p.40.

Family Counselling In The Conciliation Court: An Alternative To Custody Litigation

Judge Irwin Cantor* and Patricia L. Ferguson**

THE JUDGE'S VIEW

One of the most difficult decisions a judge has to make is to determine custody of a child. Even the terminology used, such as "award of custody," is inappropriate, referring to the child as if he or she were property. The judge has been trained in law and is able to handle any legal issues that may arise, but has little or no training to deal with the human factors involved in a custody case. Not even in criminal cases do emotions play so important a role. There are many human factors that come into play — the desires of each of the parents and their present spouses, if they have remarried; the children; and all the relatives of each of the parties. It is not unusual with a young mother and father that the custody battle is really being masterminded by the grandparents.

CUSTODY INVESTIGATIONS

Because judges have recognized the fact that those in the behavioural sciences could be of assistance, there have been requests by the Court in the past for custody investigations. Usually a social worker would talk to the various witnesses, view the premises of each of the parties, and then submit a report to the Court. The report might or might not have contained a recommendation.

* Judge Irwin Cantor is the Presiding Judge of Domestic Relations, Conciliation Court of the Superior Court of the State of Arizona, Maricopa County.
** Patricia L. Ferguson is a Social Worker, Conciliation Court of the Superior Court of the State of Arizona.

In Arizona, by virtue of Arizona Revised Statute Section 25-335, the Court may order an investigation and report concerning custodial arrangements for the child when the issue of child custody is contested by the parties. Similar arrangements for independent investigations in child custody matters exist in most states in this country either by judicial discretion or pursuant to special statutory authorization in order to give the trial Court as complete a picture of the background of the child as is possible, including the financial conditions of the parents, their interests, their morals, and their dispositions, as well as any other factors which might aid the Court in determining what is for the best interests and welfare of the child.[1]

A question of whether such investigations and reports comport with notions of due process has often surfaced in custody cases in which the judicial decision is based in part on the contents of such reports. In cases in which custody counselling is used and it is necessary for the Court to make the decision due to a failure of the parents to agree, similar due process problems will be presented.

There is the fundamental principle of Anglo-Saxon law that the decision of a Court must be based on evidence produced in open Court at a fair trial. Despite the tendency of the Courts to be less formal in custody cases, the parties cannot be deprived of any of the usual attributes of a fair trial in open court. In other words, if an independent investigation is to be admitted in evidence, the requirement of due process must be complied with.[2] Hence, it is enough to say that an investigator or counsellor stands in no better position than an ordinary witness and must be available for complete cross-examination on any matter on which he or she reports at the instance of the judge.

Other Courts have even held that the Court cannot consider Welfare Department reports regarding custody of children without filing the report in evidence.[3] An exception to the strict rule of compliance with due process seems to exist when both parties consent or acquiesce in an independent investigation. In such a situation, the general rule is that a Court, in a proceeding between the parents for the custody of the children, may consider an independent investigation in making its decision without complying with the rules of fair trial where such investigation was made pursuant to a stipulation of the parties or was acquiesced to by them.[4]

Since it is clear that most jurisdictions allow utilization of investigatory reports, the question of how much weight such reports should be given has often come up.

It appears to be well settled that the report of an independent investigator is advisory only and may be wholly disregarded by the Court. Although an independent nonjudicial investigation may be helpful, such reports cannot control the decision nor relieve the Court of the duty to conduct a judicial hearing since the Court cannot delegate to anyone the power to decide custody.[5]

CUSTODY COUNSELLING

We have found the custody investigation to be very helpful in the past, but felt that it was still not enough. Regardless of the availability of such investigations and reports to the Court, this means failed to take into consideration the wishes of the child and the possibility of encouraging the parents to decide the question of custody before going to Court. Furthermore, if the child is old enough to testify, being subjected to a formal courtroom procedure and being asked to state either in open court or in chambers which parent he or she prefers as custodian, may be quite traumatic, not to mention the overall emotional climate in the family during the pendency of the dissolution. A program of custody counselling would be an aid to the Court as well as a way of reducing the emotional tension between parents and child.

Studies conducted by the various behavioural sciences on the effects of divorce on the children indicate that the child will often exhibit the detrimental effects of the divorce in substandard educational performance, contact with the juvenile justice system, subsequent marital problems or emotional problems. A process for deciding custody that has a less hostile atmosphere and affords more security to the child would minimize the emotional shock and would benefit all concerned.

A custody counselling program would encourage and ease parental agreement on custody. The Court will generally abide by such agreements in order not to run afoul of the Constitutional prohibition against the state's entering the area of family life.[6] However, one Supreme Court case[7] strongly suggests that the state has virtually unlimited power to set aside a parental custody decision to give effect to the best interests of the child, so that it is possible that an agreement reached through the mediation process can be afforded no force and effect. The court would then be free to decide the issue based upon information supplied by the counsellor, investigator or both. As a practical matter, however, parental custody decisions will be supported by the Court as long as no family member protests.

The due process requirements discussed above have dealt with the legality and propriety of independent investigations rather than with the idea of custody counselling. Since the overall use and effect of custody counselling will be the same, merely more thorough, it is logical to assume that the use of custody counselling reports and results would, as well, be subject to due process requirements.

If the counselling program is carried out pursuant to A.R.S. Section 25-

334, which states in part, "The Court may seek the advice of professional personnel.... Advice given shall be in writing and shall be made available... to counsel .... Counsel may examine as a witness any professional personnel consulted by the Court", then such a program would meet the due process requirement as set out by precedent.

It is clear that such a program would be more effective and socially more desirable than the presently used investigatory process. The process of parental custody decision-making is clearly less harmful to children than the judicial process in deciding custody. Although the parents are divorcing, their ability to work out a suitable custody arrangement for their children will assure the children of a continuing "co-parenthood" by demonstrating to the children that both parents care about them and that they are capable of planning together for their future.

It is for these reasons that the Domestic Relations Judges in Maricopa County, Arizona, refer the difficult custody cases to the Conciliation Court for a custody study. The operations of the Conciliation Court, including its custody study function, are described below.

CONCILIATION COURT: MARICOPA COUNTY, ARIZONA, STYLE

I will discuss the actual procedure exclusively used in our Conciliation Court, together with the current statistics as of December 31, 1976. Arizona passed enabling legislation in 1962. Counselling in the Maricopa County Conciliation Court at Phoenix, Arizona, began November 1, 1964. The court was activated pursuant to the 1962 Arizona legislative statute, (Section 25-381.01 *et seq,* ARS) authorizing the Superior Court Judges in each county, in their discretion to activate a Court of Conciliation. The purposes set forth in the statute are:

". . .to promote the public welfare by preserving, promoting and protecting family life and the institution of matrimony, to protect the rights of children, and to provide means for the reconciliation of spouses and the amicable settlement of domestic and family controversies."

The law has four valuable provisions. A dissolution case need not be pending in order to obtain the services. Jurisdiction attaches when one spouse files a Petition in the court. The other spouse is required under the statute to appear for counselling. If a dissolution action is pending at the time a petition for conciliation is filed, the dissolution case proceedings are stayed for a period of 60 days. Briefly, anyone at any time can file a petition in Conciliation Court whether or not a domestic relations action is pending. Secondly, the service is free. There is no charge to the individual petitioning the court or to the respondent spouse. Thirdly, all conferences in the Conciliation Court between the parties and the counsellor are confidential and informal and no information disclosed in the proceedings is available to others, not even to the Judge, in the absence of an agreement by the parties. Under these circumstances the spouses are absolutely free to discuss with the counsellor all the details of their marriage, even incriminating matters. The fourth provision is that the clerks are authorized by statute to assist the parties in preparing and filing the petition. The individuals may retain counsel if they so desire but they do not have to do so.

After the petition is filed an appointment is scheduled for the petitioner. This appointment can usually be set the same day, time permitting. If not, the time is set within a week. Following this meeting, an appointment is made for the respondent, usually within a week to ten days. Then a conference with both parties present is scheduled a week to ten days after that. These time intervals are felt by the Court to be definitely beneficial. They allow the spouses the opportunity to reflect on any new perceptions gained in the counselling and perhaps try some alternatives to their previous behaviour before coming to a decision about reconciliation or dissolution.

The Arizona statute allows co-respondents, like interfering in-laws or paramours, to be named in the petition. They also may be required to appear for a conference if the counsellor believes such an interview would be beneficial in resolving the marital problem.

COUNSELLING GOALS

The goal is to try to help the couple decide for themselves the feasibility of reconciliation. If this is their decision then efforts are made to help them make the marriage strong and lasting. In reality, the court tries to help unhappy individuals understand themselves, their limitations as well as the cause of their conflicts. Our goal is not to make a perfect marriage but to make a meaningful as well as a lasting one.

During the individual conference with each spouse the counsellor learns how each spouse perceives the other person and the marriage relationship. Counselling techniques are used to elicit significant information which is then explored with the client to develop some understanding of himself or herself. Each partner is helped to see the other in clear perspective, to understand and determine if the point of disagreement is basic or a symptom of some deeper conflict. It is important for the couple to learn that disagreement doesn't mean one is right and the other is wrong. It means only that they are different. In the joint conference with both spouses, the counsellor attempts to expose each to the differences that exist in trust level, attitudes, feelings and values. Much effort may be expended to open up acceptance that each spouse has a right to be different in tastes, attitudes and experience with neither set of "differences" more "right" or "wrong."

If both marital partners are motivated to preserve their marriage, the counsellor can help them get started in a process of better understanding and communication of individual needs and wishes. If both partners are not motivated to do so, but only one is, then the counsellor helps them to recognize the impasse. They are given an opportunity to face reality and perhaps use the conference time to try to reduce hostility and produce a more compatible parting. The ultimate outcome in both situations is also gain for the children. In dissolutions, the right to know each parent without being pulled apart by unresolved hostilities is gained. In reconciliations a happier home life with united parents is gained.

USE OF WRITTEN AGREEMENT

If at the end of a joint conference it appears that the parties are willing to reconcile, a formal agreement is presented to them. Since every marriage has certain common problems, the attitude of the parties toward these problems determines whether the marriage will succeed or not. Basic problems and help for resolving them are incorporated into the agreement. The most important item deals with the necessity of talking things over, communicating with one another. When there are special problems these are added to the agreement when appropriate.

THE JUDGE'S ROLE

After the parties sign the agreement, a call is made to one of the Conciliation Court Judges and an immediate appointment is made for the couple to see the judge. If the judge has other matters, he will recess for a few moments and see the parties privately with the counsellor. He will offer a few words of congratulations and approve the agreement. According to the counsellors this has an impact on the parties and adds more weight to their agreement. They feel that the court is interested in their problem and in helping them to succeed in their marriage. In most cases they have had no previous contact at all with the courts.

THE FOLLOW-UP SURVEY

Often the judge is asked, "Will the reconciliation last?" We all know of cases where people after talking to someone will agree to try again, only to have the same problems magnified at a later time. We understand and realize that anybody can come to a new agreement particularly when there has been intensive counselling. Hence, the court conducts yearly follow-up surveys to determine whether reconciled couples are still together one year following the reconciliation. The Judge of the Conciliation Court sends yearly follow-up letters with a questionnaire. If they are not returned, an effort is made to get in touch with the couples by telephone. It is of great significance that among the couples who reconciled and whom we are able to contact, 90% are still together one year following the reconciliation. The survey continues to reflect encouraging results in the written comments returned to us.

Of course all individuals do not complete the minimum four hours of counselling. Of those who do, approximately 50% do not reconcile. The counsellors attempt to lessen the hostilities between the parties particularly if there are children. It is pointed out to the parents that continuing the bickering and fighting will hurt the child emotionally. Our experience shows that there are fewer court battles over custody, visitation or support payments with this post-dissolution counselling.

REQUIRED PRE-MARITAL COUNSELLING

Another phase of our work is what might be called "Pre-Marital Counselling." It is rather a truism that a great many persons whose marriages are dissolved will remarry within a year or a shorter period. Since it appears that many of them will marry a person quite similar to the spouse they are now leaving, much discussion goes on relative to this matter. Rather surprisingly, fewer than 20% of all those who come to the court have ever been exposed to any type of professional counselling.

The Conciliation Court also has a program of giving premarital counselling to young couples who are required to have court approval to secure a marriage licence in Maricopa County. Briefly, according to Arizona Law, any person under the age of sixteen years may, with the consent of his or her parents and the approval of a Superior Court Judge, be permitted to marry. Conferences are held with the couple as well as their parents. It is not the goal of the court to talk a couple out of getting married. Rather, the intent is to help the individuals assess their readiness for marriage and at the same time to consider alternatives if the conclusion is that they are not ready for marriage. In this past year, 231 couples were referred to us. The court approved 171 couples for marriage and 60 couples were denied permission to secure a marriage licence or temporary postponement was recommended.

THE STAFF

Much of our success can be attributed to the quality of our staff. At present, along with three very interested Conciliation Court Judges, our professional staff consists of a director and eleven counsellors. All have either a Master's degree or a Doctor's degree in one of the behavioural sciences and more than five years experience. The clerical staff consists of an administrative assistant and five equally qualified clerical assistants.

SOURCE OF REFERRALS

In Maricopa County, a local rule has been adopted and approved whereby a person filing a petition for dissolution must submit to the Clerk of Court the names and addresses of the litigants. This information is confidential as sometimes a spouse may not wish the other spouse to know where he or she is living. This information is given to the Conciliation Court which in turn mails a pamphlet about the court plus a card from the judge extending an invitation to the litigants to use our services. About four hundred of our referrals came in response to this interest on the part of the court. It might be well to mention here that almost nine hundred of our referrals are from attorneys. We attribute a major portion of our success to their help and assistance as well as their full belief in the Conciliation Court program.

STATISTICS

During the year 1976, there were 2253 petitions for Conciliation filed. Dissolution action had already been filed in 1064 of these cases and no dissolution in 1189 of them. The total number of children involved was 3349. Reconciliation occurred in 49.5% of completed cases, involving 1535 children.

HANDOUTS AND PAMPHLETS

In our continuing education program the Conciliation Court has prepared three pamphlets: one entitled "Marriage Problems" that is sent to every litigant in a dissolution action, a second entitled "You and Your Marriage" which is given by the Clerk of Court to every couple applying for a marriage licence and the third "Till Divorce Do Us Part" that is given to those parents after their marriages have been dissolved.

"Marriage Problems" is a question and answer type pamphlet describing the Conciliation Court.

"You and Your Marriage" is an attempt at pre-marital counselling. While there is no way to test the validity or the effectiveness of this pamphlet, we have received many favorable comments about it.

"Till Divorce Do Us Part" is an attempt to help parents prevent problems concerning support, custody and visitation.

POST-DECREE COUNSELLING

The Conciliation Court also provides post-decree counselling. This occurs when couples cannot come to an amicable decision with respect to non-payment of support, denial of visitation rights or when there is a fight for modification of custody and visitation. The emphasis of these conferences is on an effort to reduce hostility between the parties, and with the help of the counsellor, an attempt to get the parties to work out an equitable agreement between themselves. The goal is to help persons adapt to the situation as it exists, keeping in mind the welfare of the child or children. However, there are situations following the dissolution of the marriage when families cannot or will not agree on terms of custody or visitation. This being the case, there is a legally separate function of the Conciliation Court which is Child Custody Investigation, upon order of a judge or commissioner in the Domestic Relations Division hearing a custody, visitation or dissolution action. After these orders are received, appointments are arranged for parents, children, and witnesses. The investigator checks on the environment of the child by a home visit, and by calls to others in contact with the child or the environment, such as doctors, school personnel, neighbours, relatives etc.

When the investigation is completed, a report is given to the referring court. If the parties have agreed, a recommendation is also made. They may also agree that this recommendation may be accepted by the court without hearing further evidence. The usual stipulation is that the report may come into evidence but either party may present additional evidence. This way the "due process" requirements are met. We feel this procedure is the way to avoid lengthy custody litigation. In 1976, we had 322 such requests by our Domestic Relation Judges and Commissioners. We do not have the statistics of the number that actually went to trial, but in my estimation less than 50 were contested.

SUMMARY

I would like to recommend strongly the use of a Conciliation Court. We have found it satisfactory in the areas in which we use it. The public, as well as the Bar, has accepted it well. The services performed by the counsellors have been an immeasurable help to the courts. It would be my opinion that even without a Conciliation Court law the court would have the power to appoint a behavioural scientist to counsel the parties. If anyone has questions, I invite you to write us. We would be very happy to show you our Conciliation Court. By the way, the climate in Phoenix during spring, winter and fall is ideal. We invite you to come and visit us.

THE COUNSELLOR'S VIEW

The unifying principle of custody cases is that custody must be awarded to promote the child's best interests. There is growing concern, however, that the welfare of the child is being ignored in custody litigation.[8] Some feel that children should have legal representation. Others feel that custody should be decided by a panel of human relations experts.

Robert Sherwin, in *Compatible Divorce*[9] states, "There is, therefore, truth in the statement that the welfare of the children is often improperly served, both by the parents and by the courts — by parents because of haste, and by courts because of insufficient judges and a trained staff to aid them".

Once the custody dispute is in progress, the family unit has disintegrated. To determine the best interests of the child, the Court evaluates evidence offered by the parents. The reliability of this evidence is highly questionable. It is coloured by parental biases. Most often, the primary concern of a parent may be to discredit the other.[10] Attorneys for the parents must have as their main concern the parents. They are not qualified to speak for the child. The Court ultimately speaks for the child but only after hearing the parents.

The best interests of a child can best be determined on the basis of objective independent evidence as to what those interests are. One writer sums up current thinking about the best way to get this evidence:

"It has been suggested that the family court, like the juvenile court, should be freed from the hostility of the adversary process, particularly in divorce and child-custody cases. In counselling sessions with staff specialists an atmosphere of seeking the best interests of the family can be established. But if attempts at reconciliation or settlement fail, the parties are relegated to the more hostile atmosphere of the courtroom."[11]

Rose de Wolf, in *The Bonds of Acrimony*, supports this suggestion. She says:

"And there is a theory that the best answer is to have counsellors working directly with the parents to help them to find the best solution for their child — even if that solution is not to their liking at the time ....[12]

"It all comes down to the fact that any situation other than that in which a child lives with two parents who love both him and each other is a less-than-perfect situation. But less-than-perfect situations exist and must be faced....

"When divorce occurs, the court's best role is to assemble the social services needed to help the divided couple help their children. Conflict over children must be expected. One can ask only that the law make things as easy as possible, not harder on all parties concerned, especially the children."[13]

Dr. Cotter Hirschberg has said:

"Our objective in custody cases is to help the child continue his normal growth and development from the point at which the unfortunate circumstances in his own family have threatened to disrupt it. It is evident that absolute principles would be extremely difficult to formulate. In each case, child and parent should be studied individually and custody should be decided on individual merits .... Such information can not be gained briefly; it can not be gained in one interview; it cannot be gained in one hearing. If the court has available information about the case, the litigants and the child, gathered by skilled personnel such as social workers, then the judicial work will be easier and the judgments will be sounder."[14]

Maricopa County Conciliation Court has developed a unique service to those undergoing custody litigation that could conceivably provide an alternative to the adversary process. When parents cannot agree on custody or visitation arrangements in regard to their children, they frequently appeal to the Court for a decision on this matter. Upon the order of a judge or commissioner, a child custody study is undertaken by Conciliation Court counsellors. Past decisions for child custody or visitation are also reviewed upon judicial request. Such services to the judicial system are a separate legal function of Maricopa County Conciliation Court.

A child custody study is not an attempt to uncover facts that would indicate one parent or the other to be "unfit". It is a study of the dynamics and existing relationship among the members of a broken family. The main focus of the study is to determine which parent and environment can most nearly fulfill the best interests of the child.

In addition, every effort is made to assist the parents in resolving the hostilities and misunderstandings surrounding the issues of child custody or visitation. Many times the lines of communication have been broken between the parents, forcing the child to assume the role of message-carrier. On occasion, the child becomes the manipulator of both parents.

Restoration of communication, elimination of hostilities and compromise within a workable framework are the desired goals. Marital relationships end when a dissolution is granted. The parental relationship endures, but of necessity, must change from one of exclusiveness to one of sharing.

The custody counsellor spends many hours talking to the principal litigants, the children, neighbours, friends, grandparents, school personnel, physicians and others who can assist the counsellor in developing an accurate picture of existing circumstances. By such dialogue, the counsellor endeavors to bring about mutual understanding and cooperation with all parties. However, if this cannot be accomplished, the counsellor is able to present a clarified picture of the circumstances to the presiding judge to aid in the decision process.

1 See, for example, *Stanford v. Stanford,* 123 N.W. 2d 187 (Supreme Court of Minnesota, 1963), where reports of the Department of Court Services were made pursuant to Minnesota L.1961, c.527, § 2 (8), and *Dayan v. Dayan,* 86 Ill. App. 2d 358, 229 N.E. 2d 568 (1967), where reports were prepared for the court with the acquiescence of the parties.

2 *Kesseler v. Kesseler,* 10 N.Y. 2d 445, 225 N.Y.S. 2d 1, 180 N.E. 2d 402 (N.Y. Court of Appeals, 1962); *Flickinger v. Flickinger,* 494 S.W. 2d 388 (Missouri Court of Appeals, 1973); *Rider v. Rider,* 493 P. 2d 679 (Colorado Court of Appeals, 1972); *Yearsley v. Yearsley,* 94 Idaho 667, 496 P. 2d 666 (Idaho Supreme Court, 1972).

3 *McGuire v. McGuire,* 140 So. 2d 354 (District Court of Appeal of Florida, 1962), and see *Dayan v. Dayan, supra* note 1, where the fact that a report was shown to counsel, filed and entered in the record was important to the court's decision that using the report was not reversible error, although the report was incompetent evidence.

4 *Thompson v. Thompson,* 55 N.W. 2d 329 (Supreme Court of Minnesota, 1952); *Burger v. Burger,* 6 N.J. Super. 52, 69 A. 2d 741 (Superior Ct. of N.J., App. Div., 1949); and see also *Kesseler v. Kesseler, supra* note 2.

5 *Prouty v. Prouty,* 16 Ca. 2d 190, 105 P. 2d 295 (Supreme Court of California, 1940); *Washburn v. Washburn,* 49 Cal. App. 2d 581, 122 P. 2d 96 (District Court of Appeal, California, 1942); *Fewel v. Fewel,* 23 Cal. 2d 431, 144 P. 2d 592 (Supreme Court of California, 1943); and *Nelson v. Nelson,* 180 Or. 275, 176 P. 648 (Supreme Court of Oregon, 1947).

6 *Prince v. Mass.,* 321 U.S. 158 (1944); *Meyer v. Nebraska,* 262 U.S. 390 (1923); *Pierce v. Society of Sisters,* 268 U.S. 510 (1925); and *Wisconsin v. Yoder,* 406 U.S. 205 (1972).

7 *Ford v. Ford,* 371 U.S. 187 (1962).

8 Robert V. Sherwin, *Compatible Divorce* (New York, Award Books, 1970 © 1969) at 183.

9 Robert V. Sherwin, *op. cit.* p. 184.

10 Monroe L. Inker and Charlotte Anne Peretta, "A Child's Right to Counsel in Custody Cases" (1971) 5 Family Law Quarterly 108 at 111.

11 Herma H. Kay, "The Outside Substitute for the Family" in John N. Edwards, ed., *The Family & Change* (New York, 1969) 260 at 268.

12 *The Bonds of Acrimony* (New York, 1970) at 67.

13 *Op. cit.* at 72.

14 "Symposium on the Child and the Law — Custody" (1962) 10 University of Kansas Law Review 555 at 558-559.

Editor's Note

Interest in the concept of the Unified Family Court, and in the counselling and conciliation services associated with such a court, is high in Canada as well as elsewhere. Practical experiments with unified family courts of different types are going on in a number of jurisdictions. The government of British Columbia established a pilot project in the South Fraser Judicial District of the Provincial Court with the enactment of The Unified Family Court Act, 1974 (B.C.), c. 99. One feature of that Act is the provision in section 8(1) for the appointment by the Attorney-General of a member in good standing of the Law Society of British Columbia to be a Family Advocate in the Court. The Family Advocate is empowered to attend a court proceeding respecting a family matter or one concerning the delinquency of a child; the Advocate may intervene at any stage of such a proceeding to act as counsel for a child who, in the opinion of the Advocate or the court, requires representation. Upon the request of the court, the Advocate may also assist any party to a family or a delinquency proceeding who is not represented.

By The Unified Family Court Act, 1976 (Ont.), c. 85 the Ontario Legislature established for a trial period of three years a Unified Family Court in the Judicial District of Hamilton-Wentworth. Section 17(2) of the Act provides that a conciliation service may be established, maintained, and operated as part of the Court. The Act merges the jurisdiction of the various levels of court in family law matters by providing that the presiding judge in the Unified Family Court shall be a judge of the county court who is also a local judge of the Supreme Court, and by further authorizing the Lieutenant-Governor in Council to permit this county court judge to exercise the jurisdiction of a judge of a provincial court, family division.

The Unified Family Court Act of Newfoundland received Royal Assent on June 17, 1977, but operations of the Court, a division of the Supreme Court of the province, have not yet begun. The Law Reform Commission of Manitoba has taken steps to initiate an experimental court of integrated family law jurisdiction in the St. Boniface County Court district. In its Third Annual Report, 1974, at page 10, the Law Reform Commission offered the following description of the interaction between conciliation services and adjudication:

"We suggested a competent conciliation service be appended to the pilot project court so that a full sequence of (1) reconciliation, if desired; (2) conciliation, if possible; and (3) adjudication, if necessary, would be available to persons who suffer family problems with legal ramifications. As with most public or private disputes in a civilized society, the ultimate, if not always the most satisfactory, solution is a judicial resolution of the dispute according to the law of the particular society.... After all skilful attempts at reconciliation and conciliation, if people still are to have their disputed rights and responsibilities determined according to law, the ultimate disposition must be judicial — compassionate, understanding, prudent and alert, but above all, judicial."

Two of those who participated at the seminar on The Child and the Courts are judges of provincial superior courts where unification is progressing. Mr. Justice Charles MacQuaid of the Prince Edward Island Unified Family Court presented an outline of the accomplishment of a unified court in that province and discussed the limitations and advantages of the approach. Madame Justice Claire L'Heureux-Dubé of the Superior Court of Québec described the proposals of the Office of Revision of the Civil Code for amending the Civil Code to amplify the rights of children and recounted experience in her jurisdiction with the first year of operation of a Family Division within the Superior Court, which, in some centres, is equipped with psycho-social reference services. Their comments, based on notes prepared for their panel presentations, are reproduced here.

The Unified Family Court Of Prince Edward Island

The Honourable Charles R. MacQuaid*

The concept of a unified family court is something which has long been advocated by such varied bodies as The Canadian Bar Association, the Law Reform Commission, and the Council of Women. In the Province of Prince Edward Island, this has now become a reality.

Like all other projects, this was long aborning, and was midwifed by a successive series of studies and reports. The more recent of these can be dated from a study of the Island judicial system undertaken by Ross McKinnie, Q.C. of Calgary in early 1973. This was followed by a more specific study undertaken by Professor William Charles of the Dalhousie University Faculty of Law, in 1974, who produced a working document for the establishment of a Family Court. A final report entitled "Blueprint For A Unified Family Court" was prepared by Professor David Cruickshank, then of the University of British Columbia, in 1975. It was on the basis of this latter report, somewhat modified, that the Court, as it presently exists, came into being.

The actual bringing into being of the Court required several steps, as well as concurrent federal and provincial legislation.

There was in the Province at the time a separate and distinct Court of Chancery[1] which had exclusive jurisdiction over, *inter alia,* infants' interests, including adoption, and the interests of mentally incompetent persons. The presiding judges, the Vice-Chancellor and the Master of the Rolls, were Judges of the Supreme Court with added Chancery jurisdiction. The first phase in developing a Unified Family Court was the abolition of this Court. Its function, insofar as infants, adoption, and mental incompetents was concerned, was transferred to the County Courts, of which there were three, one for each County in the Province.

Phase two was the merger of the County and Supreme Courts. All jurisdiction theretofore existing in the County Courts was transferred to the Supreme Court, and the three County Court Judges were elevated to

---

* The Honourable Charles R. MacQuaid is a Justice, Supreme Court of Prince Edward Island.

the Supreme Court, thus providing a bench of seven Justices to administer all the affairs of Justice within the Province, exclusive of that inherently within the jurisdiction of the Provincial (or Magistrate's) Court.

Phase three was the re-constitution of the Supreme Court into several divisions, one of which was the Family Division. While each of the Judges maintained concurrent jurisdiction, one was assigned primary responsibility for that particular division. Although he can, and on occasion does, also conduct civil or criminal cases, or even sit as a member of the Appeal Division, just as any other member of the bench may hear family matters, he is generally accepted as being the "Family Court Judge." Although not specifically so assigned, one of the other Judges acts as back-up to the primary Judge of the Family Division as circumstances and caseload demand. This he does in addition to his usual judicial functions. It should be noted that the Family Court is not constitutionally a separate, distinct and autonomous Court, but rather a Division of the Supreme Court, under the overall supervision of the Chief Justice. Within that context, however, it does, in practice, operate pretty well as a separate entity.

The jurisdiction of the Family Division is set out in the Judicature Act, as amended:

"The Family Division shall exercise jurisdiction in respect of the following matters:

(a) formation of the marriage;

(b) dissolution of marriage;

(c) judicial separation and separation orders;

(d) actions and causes concerning matrimonial property including injunctions, partition, and settlements;

(e) restitution of conjugal rights;

(f) jactitation of marriage;

(g) declarations of status including validity of marriage, legitimacy and legitimation;

(h) alimony and maintenance (interspousal) including protection orders for deserted wives;

(i) maintenance of children including affiliation proceedings and agreements;

(j) enforcement of alimony and maintenance orders including reciprocal enforcement of these orders;

(k) custody and access;

(l) adoption;

(m) charges or proceedings under the Criminal Code or any statute of the province relating to non-support or interspousal assaults, to school attendance, to neglected children, and to juvenile delinquency;

(n) juvenile delinquency;

(o) guardianship of the person and property;
(p) interspousal and familial torts;
(q) commitment and treatment of mentally ill or mentally defective adults and minors;
(r) relief for family dependants on death."[2]

The Act further provides for the unlikely contingency that the Judge charged with these duties should find himself with idle time on his hands:

"But, notwithstanding the enumeration of clauses (a) to (r), the Chief Justice may by order vest such additional jurisdiction in the Family Division from time to time as he may deem necessary, either in a particular case or on a continuing basis, to enable the Family Division to effectively carry out its jurisdiction under clauses (a) to (r)."[3]

In the result, then, the "Family Court" as it exists in Prince Edward Island has total and exclusive jurisdiction over virtually every conceivable matter involving any aspect of domestic or matrimonial problems. Rather than having to seek a remedy in one of three, four or even five separate courts of limited jurisdiction, or indeed in all of them successively given the right set of circumstances, there is now one, and only one, forum to which a person need apply to seek relief. From the point of view of those who require the services of the Court, this is a tremendous advance. On the other hand, from the point of view of the Court itself, it should be clearly pointed out that unification does not, in itself make the resolution of family problems appreciably easier; it simply concentrates the problems, it does not necessarily resolve them.

The Division is presently staffed by one full time Judge, who is one of the seven justices of the Supreme Court; one Registrar and general administrative officer, who carries the rank of Deputy Prothonotary, one Deputy Registrar-Secretary and one general Stenographer who also functions as Stenographer to one of the other Judges. The Registrar and Deputy Prothonotary's duties include the supervision of all filings, the docketing of cases, and the general administration of the division. While ultimately responsible to the Prothonotary, he carries out his day to day duties under the immediate supervision of the Judge.

In addition, there are attached to the Court three experienced social workers, who are styled "Court Counsellors". Their function is to conduct, on the initiation of the Judge, such inquiries, and to prepare such social reports as he may deem necessary or useful as background in situations where he considers it appropriate. They also do some counselling work, both domestic and financial.

A close liaison is also maintained with the field staff of the Department of Social Services, who provide similar services for the Court on matters in which they are directly involved.

Since its inception, the basic philosophy of the Court is that most domestic problems, including that of juvenile delinquency, are essentially social problems having legal implications, rather than essentially legal problems having social implications. To this end, except when statutory provisions specifically state otherwise, the Court has, whenever possible, adopted flexible procedures, acting as the circumstances of the situation would appear to demand, rather than by rigid legal formalities, in the belief that the substance is more important than the form. This is not to say that formalities have been dispensed with, for they also have an important role in any adjudication. However, substantial use of pre-hearing conferences has materially reduced the adversary aspect of many situations. This philosophy also lends itself to the opportunity to attempt a more human and hopefully more practical, approach to families either in conflict with, or seeking the remedies of, the law, and in consequence attempting to employ new departures from some of the more structured legalistic formulas in past common use.

As to the applicable Rules of Practice and Procedure of the Unified Family Court, other than the general Rules of Court applicable to all Divisions, no specialized rules have yet been finalized. It was the opinion of the Court that rather than formulate a new set of rules at the outset the more prudent course would be to operate for the first year without specialized rules. This would enable those concerned to learn through experience, and to a degree by trial and error, what type of rules would best meet the needs of the various situations with which the Court would meet, rather than first prepare rules of practice and procedure and then try to fit all cases, many of them then unpredictable in nature, into a pre-conceived framework. The Court has now reached that point where it feels that it has sufficient experience to commence preliminary work in this area.

It can be said, after one full year's operation, that in general, the Unified Family Court of Prince Edward Island is successful in its concept and operation. It is yet far too early to assess the degree of that success, however that standard may be measured. In some measure, it is still, and will continue for some time, testing what approaches and procedures work best, and by the same token, determining those which do not work. Suffice it to say that a good beginning has been made.

It is important that those jurisdictions considering the implementation of such a court bear in mind certain cautions. On the negative side, a Unified Family Court is not a panacea, a cure-all which will of itself provide instant solutions to heretofore insoluble problems. By its very nature, it simply gathers all family matters, contentious or otherwise, which formerly were dealt with by a variety of Courts, and funnels them into a single Court. From an administrative and judicial point of view, concentration should not be equated or confused with resolution. Indeed, the Judge charged with its administration must now alone suffer all of the headaches — and heartaches — which were formerly spread among several colleagues. The establishment of such a Court tends to create, as well, in the public mind, a sense that here, at last, is a forum to which it can resort where, by some mystical process, all will be made well. Public expectation will far exceed its realization.

On the positive side, it does provide one central, coordinated, and unified judicial structure at which the public, including social service agencies and police, can attend, regardless of the nature of the proceeding, be it internal domestic situations, divorce, adoption, delinquency or whatever. The need to skip from Court to Court, and jurisdiction to jurisdiction has been eliminated, and this, in itself, by its very simplification, is a major step forward in the administration of justice.

One final point: it has been the observation of the Court that one critical domestic situation frequently spawns other inter-related social problems, or alternatively, one apparent problem, (and juvenile delinquency is one good example), is often merely a symptom of a broader and more deep-rooted domestic crisis. A Unified Family Court, properly structured, and if it dares and is prepared to be innovative, has the potential, and indeed can, deal with the matter not in isolation but in an integrated manner within the total family context.

---

1 This Court was actually two Courts of concurrent jurisdiction, namely, the Vice-Chancellor's Court and the Rolls Court, and it was the only Court of Chancery continuing to exist in the British Commonwealth outside of England.

2 Judicature Act, R.S.P.E.I. 1974, c. J-3 [am. 1975 (P.E.I.), c. 27, s. 16.1].

3 *Ibid.*

Deciding Child Custody: New Developments In Quebec

*Madame Justice Claire L'Heureux-Dubé**

Few issues today are at once as sympathetic and controversial as that of the custody of children, particularly in divorce and separation proceedings. Sympathetic, because it involves children for whom we care and who remain our most precious resource. Controversial, since practically every field of human science claims a voice in its determination, and views diverge considerably among specialists as to the best approach. They range from a philosophy of judicial non-intervention to that of strict observance of the rule of law, questioning the ability of both parents and judges to resolve that difficult problem.

However, there seems to be unanimity on at least two points, that is (1) the criteria to be applied should be "the best interest of the child" (leaving open of course the question as to *what* is the best interest), and (2) the strong public concern about the ability of the law and the court system, as it functions at present, to deal with that issue.

According to the Law Reform Commission of Canada, strong public concerns about family law "range from individual dissatisfaction with the means by which family problems are presently handled to calls for changing the basic structure of the law so that it may reflect changing conceptions and realities of family life."[1]

These concerns have been echoed in the Province of Quebec at both levels of law reform and practice before the courts. The Civil Code Revision Office has established two committees, one dealing with substantive law, and the other investigating the opportunity of establishing a family court in the Province of Quebec. Both are now at the stage of final draft, and both deal with the issue of the custody of children respectively at the substantive law level and the court process level.

Meanwhile, at the initiative of the Superior Court of Quebec and its Chief Justice, practical steps have been taken with the creation in all districts of the Province of Quebec of a Family Division within the Superior Court. This Family Division is now staffed with psycho-social

*Madame Justice Claire L'Heureux-Dubé is a Justice, Superior Court, Province of Quebec.

services to deal with custody issues both in Montreal and Quebec, with provisions for extending the concept province-wide in the near future.

I intend to discuss briefly the proposals from the Revision Office and the practical experiment presently going on in Quebec at the level of the Superior Court.

In the words of the Chairman of the Law Reform Commission of Canada, Mr. Justice Lamer, "the very existence of all law reform agencies in this country is a reflexion of the fact that existing mechanisms for legal response were falling unacceptably far behind social demand."[2] Conscious of that, the Committee on the Law on Persons and the Family of the Civil Code Revision Office proposes a complete reform of family law. Its report deals with marriage under its various aspects: annulment, separation, divorce, custody and alimony, filiation by blood and by adoption, juridical conditions of persons, and specifically with minority, parental authority, the protection of incapable persons and absence. While its main objective is to adapt the law to the realities of today's society, its whole philosophy is based on the recognition of the legal equality between consorts in marriage, the abolition of all discrimination between legitimate and illegitimate children, and the protection of children in all decisions concerning them.

As regards the protection of children, the following articles have been proposed, among others, for insertion in the Civil Code:

Article 26

In every decision concerning a child, whether that decision is made by his parents, by the persons acting in their stead, by those entrusted with his custody, or by judicial authority, the child's interest must be the determining factor.

In determining the child's interest, the court, in particular, considers his age, sex, religion, language, character and family surroundings, and the other circumstances in which he lives.[3]

Article 27

In every judicial decision affecting the interest of a child, the court must consult that child unless circumstances do not permit such consultation.[4]

Article 28

The court may appoint an attorney to represent a minor in any proceedings where that minor's interests so require.

Any interested person, including the members of the court's auxiliary services, may apply for the appointment of an attorney.[5]

Article 81

Before the court rules on the merits of the case in any matter of separation as to bed and board or of divorce, it must ascertain that attempts at conciliation have been made in accordance with the rules of the Code of Civil Procedure.[6]

Article 98

Neither divorce nor separation as to bed and board affects the rights of the children.[7]

Article 132

Adoption takes place in the interest of the child.

No adoption may take place except on the conditions prescribed by law.[8]

Article 152

If the child is ten years of age or older, no adoption may take place without his consent, unless he is unaware of his *de facto* adoption and his usual behaviour towards the person adopting may be interpreted by the court as tacit consent.

Nevertheless, when a child less than fourteen years of age refuses his consent, the court may defer adoption for a period of time which it indicates, or grant adoption notwithstanding such refusal.

Any refusual by a child fourteen years of age or older is a bar to adoption.[9]

All these proposed measures are bound to affect the disposition of custody issues by insuring not only that the interest of children be safeguarded, but also that proper steps be taken in order to minimize the consequences of divorce and separation upon the children.

In addition, the report stresses that it has been prepared within the framework of a parallel reform of the court process to be brought about by the establishment of a family court provided with specialized and auxiliary services, with the hope that such a body would encourage settlements between consorts under the best conditions, with emphasis on conciliation of issues, crash-crisis intervention at all levels, input from behavioural scientists and independent evaluation.

In the view of the Committee, the creation of a family court is necessary to make up for the inadequacies of the present legal system. The Committee's analysis of the present situation in Quebec in that respect shows that current solutions are partial, inappropriate or even contradictory, due to a division of jurisdiction, the rigidity of the adversary system, a lack of coordination, and inadequate collaboration between the psychosocial and legal family services. It proposes:

(1) An overall approach to family problems, in order to humanize and personalize the legal process in family matters, appraise the conflict in all its aspects and identify the underlying problems, in summary, to ensure comprehensive, effective, and dynamic justice.

(2) An integrated court having a comprehensive jurisdiction in all matters inherent to family law and staffed with specialized auxiliary services.

This, of course, is a very brief survey of the proposed reform in matters of family law, the reports themselves covering thousands of pages. Applied to custody in particular, the proposals of the Revision Office stress that "[f]amily members must be encouraged to exercise their responsibilities by first trying to solve the problems themselves, then seeking the help of the appropriate services..... However, when the dimensions of a family conflict make a voluntary settlement of such conflict impossible, even with the collaboration of psycho-social services, an impartial arbitrator must be called in..."[10]

This arbitrator, the Committee feels, should remain a court of law, since it believes it to be the only system which guarantees due process of law, impartiality and respect of individual rights. But a court of law which, in many respects, should not be a traditional one, but a court of law the function of which should be at the same time judicial and social.

Among the measures which the Committee has recommended, some bear more directly on the custody issue while applying also to other accessory issues. Such proposals include one mandatory pre-trial interview with court personnel, the availability of conciliation and therapeutic facilities when the parties find them desirable, objective evaluation of the situation by court-connected services, and submission of unresolved issues to a mediator, in an atmosphere of informality and at a minimum cost, the decision of the mediator being subject to review by the court should the parties so desire. In addition, proposals are put forward for proper court facilities, confidentiality of files, and *in camera* hearings, which would, however, not exclude the media. Finally, and as a last resort, a judge should render the final decision, if and when the issue has not been resolved satisfactorily in the process. Even then, children should be consulted if ten years of age, and the court may resort to expert advice if found necessary and useful, and provide legal representation for children.

While the proposed court structure is innovative, it differs only on minor points from other proposals made by the Law Reform Commission of Canada and other law reform commissions throughout the country. As to substantive law, proposals tend to reproduce in the law what has been achieved in practice and, in some instances, confirmed by jurisprudence.

However, it must be stressed that by clearly associating the parents and the child with the decision process relating to custody, making available court-connected programs and facilities to enable parents to reach more mature decisions in the best possible atmosphere of serenity and privacy, and by introducing multidisciplinary services into the court process, the proposed structure departs from a very long tradition in our Code, namely that such issues are the privilege of the judge only, to be determined according to the strict standards of adversary procedure. Also, *paternal* authority, which still remains in the Code at present, is replaced by *parental* authority, but subject always to the the best interest of the child, a notion which, although well established in practice and in jurisprudence, is nowhere to be found in the Code.

It remains to be seen whether, while these proposals were received very favourably by the public, they have a chance to survive the apparent apathy of the legislator and the resistance of pressure groups who strongly oppose the specialized interdisciplinary support services.

A practical approach is sometimes the best way to achieve what the legislator is not prepared to implement at present. On January 1, 1974, the Chief Justice of the Superior Court of the Province of Quebec, the Honourable Jules Deschênes, constituted a Family Division of the Superior Court in Quebec. With the agreement of the departments of Justice and Social Affairs, and the collaboration of the Social Services Center, the Superior Court initiated a service of psycho-social expertise in Montreal on February 3, 1975, and in Quebec City on February 11, 1976. This service is housed in the Court House and staffed with social workers and psychologists. Its function is to provide, in matters of custody of children in divorce and separation proceedings, a report to be submitted to the judge, with the consent of the parties, giving an evaluation of the conflict situation of the parties, an analysis of their surroundings and circumstances, and the result of interviews with the parties and the children involved. The report concludes with recommendations as to the proper disposition of the custody case. Although the parties are not entitled to examine and cross-examine the authors of the report, they may present arguments. The judge, however, is not bound by the conclusions of the report, which forms part of the evidence.

In the first nineteen months of operation in the Montreal District, and as of August 31, 1976, 200 cases were referred to the service by judges, with the consent of the parties and their lawyers. From the analysis of those cases, it appears that 138 of them have been filed in court to date. In twenty-three cases, parties consented to judgment according to the recommendations of the service. In fifty-five cases, the court has adopted those recommendations without reserve. In eight cases, the court adopted the recommendations but with some modifications, and in eleven cases, the court has departed from the conclusions of the report.

For the district of Quebec, from February 11, 1976, to date, forty-nine cases were referred by judges to the service. While some are still pending, fifteen judgments have been rendered according to the conclusions of the service, and two judgments have adopted the recommendations with some modifications. Statistics are not available yet on the other cases. The service is currently being expanded to Sherbrooke, Hull, St-Jérôme, Rimouski, Gaspé, Chicoutimi and Trois-Rivières.

It may be too soon yet to assess the merits of such a service in its various dimensions, namely its usefulness in terms of providing additional relevant data and in-depth analysis of issues, achieving a real mediation of issues and saving fruitless, destructive and costly legal battles, and finally to evaluate the degree of satisfaction of the public, the parties, the Bar and the judiciary. But it can certainly be said that it has achieved a reasonable degree of success in promoting concensus between the parties and preventing further litigation, and this is illustrated by cases where the parties consented to judgment according to the recommendations of the service. Furthermore, from a brief survey among the judges who have experimented with the service, I can reasonably infer that they found the reports most useful. Personally, as a judge who has used such service when warranted, I must say that the input from the behavioural sciences has permitted me to grasp the issues more adequately, thus minimizing the danger of the court taking inappropriate action.

The main function of the psycho-social expertise, as I see it, is to provide the court with an objective evaluation not otherwise available, since the court relies on such evidence as the parties elect to bring before it.

The key to its effectiveness, however, remains in its independence from the court and the respect it will generate from the public and the Bar. It must be recognized that family matters are one area where the courts and the behavioural sciences can complement one another. It may well be that the real efficiency of a psycho-social expertise service also depends on the passing of adequate legislation and the addition of other complementary services.

Much, indeed, remains to be done in the way of a comprehensive approach to the issue of custody — and, for that matter, to family law and the court process. In the views of Chief Justice Deschênes, as expressed in a lecture at the University of Sherbrooke, in May 1976, the auxiliary services to the court should also include an admission service, a family counselling service, an alimony collection service, and should provide independent legal representation of children. There is indication at present that these auxiliary services may not even await the creation of a proposed family court. These new structures, of course, are part of the proposals submitted by the Civil Code Revision Office, which also advocate various other improvements to the court process.

I would not like to leave you under the impression that we have put forward the best mechanism and achieved in practice a perfect solution. But I do feel that the Revision Office has proposed a more sensible approach to family law both in its substantive and administrative aspects, and that the courts have taken positive steps in response to a real outcry for change in that respect in our province. I readily recognize, however, that there remains to be achieved a real consensus as to the best approach to custody issues.

There is a great need for imaginative and creative experiments, exchanges and discussions. The real beneficiaries can only be the children, for whom we care, and who have a right to expect that society will not short-circuit them in a decision which is likely to affect their entire lives and probably those of generations to come. This is why I am extremely grateful to have been invited to participate in this seminar on The Child and the Courts, and to share the concerns of all of you in the light of the great expertise present here today.

Any solution, however, be it the most perfect, will only be as good as the people who apply it.

1 Law Reform Commission of Canada, Working Paper 1: The Family Court (Ottawa, 1974) at 1.
2 Lecture, Canadian Club, October 18, 1976.
3 Civil Code Revision Office, Committee on Legal Personality, Report on Legal Personality (Montreal, 1976) at 35-37.
4 *Op. cit.* note 3 at 37.
5 *Loc. cit.* note 4.
6 Civil Code Revision Office, Committee on the Law on Persons and on the Family, Report on the Family, Part I (Montreal, 1974) at 243.
7 *Op. cit.* note 6 at 279.
8 *Op. cit.* note 6 at 353.
9 *Op. cit.* note 6 at 399.
10 Civil Code Revision Office, Committee on the Family Court, Report on the Family Court (Montreal, 1975) at 31-32.

Child Support Collections In Michigan — A Study Of The Effects Of Tenacity And Terror

David L. Chambers*

Note: This chapter reports part of the findings of a study** of child support conducted over a five-year period. The full results will be available within the coming year. A grant from the National Science Foundation provided funds for several stages of the study, including the stage reported here. Additional funds were provided by the Center for Studies in Criminal Justice at the University of Chicago and the William W. Cook Research Funds of the University of Michigan Law School.

The study would have been impossible without the active co-operation of the Friends of the Court in the twenty-eight counties we examined. To them, and especially to Robert Standal of Genesee County and Richard Benedek of Washtenaw County, I am immensely grateful. I am also grateful to the score of persons who have worked on the project at various times. Three require special mention here: Ray M. Shortridge, who served as my research associate from 1974 to 1976, and who shaped and oversaw the execution of much of the twenty-eight county phase of the study; Terry K. Adams, who served as research associate in earlier phases and has advised me throughout; and Priscilla Cheever, who has performed nearly all of the computer work for the last several phases of the project.

David L. Chambers, 1976

The United States has much to teach the rest of the world about collecting child support from absent parents, just as we have much to teach the world about reducing the incidence of violent crime. If interested in collecting lots of dollars and in curbing violence, other countries should observe assiduously what we have done and do almost precisely the opposite. For with both violent crime and child support, American states have in general created conditions that encourage the undesired behaviour

* David L. Chambers, University of Michigan Law School.
** This study has also been described in David L. Chambers, "Men Who Know They Are Watched: Some Benefits and Costs of Jailing for Non-Payment of Support," (1977) 75 Michigan L. Rev. 900.

and then when sin occurs — when the handgun goes off or the father fails to pay — we shake our heads in dismay and occasionally jail the offender.

With regard to child support, widespread nonpayment flows in part from America's chronic high levels of unemployment, but aspects of the legal system more within the immediate control of local legislatures must also claim much of the responsibility. In most American states, child support outside the welfare context has been enforced only by private remedy. The divorced woman not receiving welfare benefits must scramble to retain a counsel who will search for the father and bring him to court.[1] For even the most well-heeled, the private system of remedies has proven largely ineffectual. While it is, of course, possible to frame a principled defence of the system of private remedies by characterizing the obligation to pay as deriving from an essentially private debt, most judges and officials to whom I speak make no effort to do so. When they discuss criminal sanctions, for example, they have no trouble seeing a difference between jailing for failing to support one's children and jailing for failing to make payments on a refrigerator.

Over the past four years, with a series of grants from the National Science Foundation, a group of researchers and I have been gathering information about child support collections in the one American jurisdiction with a long-established public system for collecting child support on behalf of both children who are and children who are not receiving welfare benefits. Michigan's fathers apparently pay more dollars in child support than fathers in any other state. For example, within the federally-supported welfare system, the program called Aid to Families with Dependent Children, in which states are required to maintain their own systems for collecting support from fathers of children receiving assistance, Michigan's counties during the last year apparently collected more dollars per case than any other state and over three times as much per case as the majority of other states.[2] We have reason to believe the collections are at least as lopsided in the cases of families not receiving welfare benefits.

Despite my churlish opening comments, it may well thus be that the Michigan experience does have positive lessons of value for other governments both inside and outside the United States. If I have understood correctly the points made by Professor Baxter in his recent article, Ontario officials have been far from fully satisfied with the level of support payments in their own province.[3] As the brief report that follows relates, the lesson of our study appears to be that given the opportunity, many men will not pay, but that if a state sets up a system that is well organized and persistent and that relies on a substantial level of jailing, lots of money can be collected. When there is a policeman at everyone's elbow, fewer candybars are shoplifted.

In each Michigan county, there has been since 1919 a public agency known as the Friend of the Court that oversees all aspects of the child-support process in divorce, separate maintenance and paternity cases. It advises the courts on the appropriate size of the support award, receives all payments from the parent under the order and forwards them to the custodial parent or the welfare department, and chases after the nonpayers. Virtually all cases in which a support order is entered are handled through the agency. The enforcement process varies widely from county to county, but includes mailing warnings, issuing orders to show cause, securing and often serving arrest warrants (by deputized officers working for the agency), acting as prosecutor before the courts in the hearings of men charged with contempt, and, finally, acting in effect as the parole officer charged with making deals with jailed men who wish to secure their early release from jail on payment of less than the full arrearage.

The goal of our study has been to try to understand why Michigan's counties collected as a group so much more than other American jurisdictions, why, even within Michigan, some counties collect so much more than others (despite a common framework of legally available techniques of enforcement), and why within particular counties some individuals pay so much more than others. We feel we have learned a great deal. Most of what we have learned has been possible only because of the unusually detailed files of Michigan's Friends of the Court, files that include full information about men's payments, about enforcement efforts employed at various times, and about the characteristics of the men, women, and children in their caseloads. Each week the fact of a man's payment or non-payment can be determined by a glance at the payment records. If one thinks of nonpayment as possibly criminal behaviour, consider how few other criminals call in once a week to let us know whether they picked a pocket or robbed a bank.

To carry out our study, we drew random samples of around 400 divorce cases in each of 28 Michigan counties.[4] The counties we picked were those in the southern half of Michigan that had reported caseloads of at least 1,000 cases in 1973. In two counties, Genesee and Washtenaw, we gathered much more detailed information about a random sample of divorce and paternity cases, following these cases throughout their entire lives and learning as much as we could about the families affected. (In one of the two counties, we coded well over 1,000 pieces of information for each of over 500 cases).

What we have learned fills the draft of a long book that I hope will appear during 1978. I will try here to give a glimmering of some of our findings that bear most obviously on issues of public policy.

The results we wish to report derive mainly from our study of 28 counties, as opposed to our detailed inquiry into two counties. Here is how that part of the study was conducted. We first drew in each county a random sample of persons under orders of support in divorce cases. The samples averaged 430 cases, a total of about 12,000 cases across the 28 counties. For each case in each county we recorded how much the person had paid and how much he was under an order to have paid during a fixed period (typically calendar 1974). From this information, we computed how much each man had paid of all that he was supposed to have paid during the period. Not surprisingly, we found in all counties that during the given six-month or one year period, the vast bulk of men paid either nearly everything due or nearly nothing. Where the counties differed was in the portion of their caseloads at the bottom and the top.

For our purposes, we found that the portion at the bottom and the top correlated so substantially with the mean level of payments that we have used the county's mean for reporting almost all of our findings.[5] The mean amount paid by men in each county ranged from only 45 to 46% of everything due in the two lowest collecting counties to 85 and 87% of everything due in the two highest, with the remaining counties found in an expectable pattern in between.[6] Table 1 reveals the pattern.

TABLE 1

Study of 28 Michigan Counties

Mean Portions Collected of Everything Due From
Divorced Persons Under Orders of Support During
Survey Period, 1974-75.

Counties Collecting	Number of Counties	Percentage of Counties
41-50% of everything due	2	7%
41-60% of everything due	5	18%
61-70% of everything due	13	47%
71-80% of everything due	6	21%
81-90% of everything due	2	7%
	28	100%

After determining the levels of collections county by county, we then used correlation and regression analysis to determine what factors served best to sort the high from the low collecting counties. To this end, we had gathered information for each county about as many factors as we could think of that might have affected collections. We thus accumulated for each county well over 100 items of information about such matters as unemployment levels, median incomes, order sizes, crime rates, levels of church membership, indications of political conservatism, population mobility, Friend of the Court attitudes and all aspects of the collection and enforcement process that could be quantified or categorized. Our central finding has been that three factors were overwhelmingly more important than any others in separating the high and low collecting counties.

The first factor was population — the larger the county, the lower the collections: none of the seven highest collecting counties (in terms of average collections per case) had populations greater than 70,000. Nine of the ten lowest collecting counties had populations greater than 110,000.

The second factor was an aspect of the enforcement process: counties that had a policy in non-welfare cases of initiating enforcement efforts without waiting for complaints from the mothers collected more than those that relied on complaints. These aggressive Friends of the Court, which we will refer to as "self-starting," watched for three or four weeks of missed payments or the accumulation of an arrearage of a certain number of dollars (say $200) and then sent a warning notice to the non-paying parent.

The third factor was jail. Counties that jailed more, collected more.

These three factors interrelated to some degree: a self-starting enforcement policy seems to lead to the apprehension of more nonpaying men who are then brought before the judges and jailed; large counties were for various reasons less likely to be self-starters. Nonetheless each of the three factors had independent predictive importance. With these three factors alone, we could account for over 60% of the variation in the counties' payment performances.[7] In Appendix A on page 144, for those interested in the statistical information, we set forth these findings in some detail. Table 2 makes our findings clearer (though at the cost of simplifying for display the true variations in population and rates of jailing).

As Table 2 indicates, only the counties that had both attributes of being self-starters *and* high jailers collected more than other counties of their size. Having one attribute but not the other left a county no better off than having neither attribute. But having both consistently related to substantially higher returns. Eight counties had both attributes. They were the five highest collecting small counties and three of the four highest collecting large counties. The small counties that had both attributes collected an average of 30% more than did the small counties that did not have both. The large counties that had both attributes collected an average of 20% more than the large counties that did not.

TABLE 2

Interrelation of Three Most Important Factors
Relating to Collections in Twenty-Eight Michigan Counties

How much the county jails, whether Friend of the
Court initiates enforcement without awaiting complaints,
and county population

	Counties that were both high-jailing[8] and self-starting[9]		Counties that were self-starting but low jailing		Counties that were high-jailing but not self-starting		Counties that were neither high-jailing nor self-starting	
Mean portion collected during survey period of all that was ordered	82%	69%	67%	62%	57%	59%	66%	57%
	5 small counties (under 100,000)	3 large counties (over 100,000)	5 small counties	1 large county	1 small county	3 large counties	2 small counties	8 large counties

Mean collections:
13 small counties (under 100,000) — 72%
15 large counties (over 100,000) — 60%

12 high-jailing counties[8] — 71%
16 low-jailing counties — 61%

14 self-starting counties[9] — 71%
14 non-self-starting counties — 60%

5 small, high-jailing, self-starting counties — 82%
8 large, low-jailing, non-self-starting counties — 57%

The implications of these findings are murkier than might initially appear. Here are several comments on the factors that proved important.

The lower collections in highly populated areas cannot be attributed to higher poverty there. The levels of unemployment and the portions of the population living in poverty were higher and median incomes appreciably lower in the smaller Michigan counties than in the large ones.[10] The relevance of high population seems rather to lie either in attitudes of city dwellers about obligations to pay or, more likely, in a greater isolation of city dwellers from the enforcement process. In several of the small counties, but none of the large, the Friend of the Court himself knew personally a high portion of the men in his caseload, a fact that was probably appreciated by the men under orders.

That counties that initiate enforcement without awaiting complaints collect more money than other counties is hardly surprising. One anomaly nonetheless exists about the "self-starting" factor. It is that the factor serves as nearly as important a predictor of payments in the welfare cases within our county samples as it does in the caseload as a whole, even though in welfare cases the counties are nearly all set up to begin enforcement on their own initiative. This oddity suggests that the counties that are self-starting are simply more organized to collect support in both welfare and nonwelfare cases in ways other than the self-starting attribute alone. Several other attributes of the enforcement process of counties — efficiency of bookkeeping, budget dollars per case, and so forth — correlate mildly with performance and with the self-starting factor and it appears that "self-starting" may simply capture best the sum of the attributes of an efficient organization.

That organization to collect and the rate of jailing work hand in hand is also unsurprising. Under a self-starting enforcement system more men who falter are told to "pay up". The high rate of jailing seems to add, "and we really mean it". All rather tidy. We had expected, however, that the rate of jailing would not have been the only way to say "we really mean it", but at least within our study no other aggressive aspect of the enforcement system served anywhere nearly as well to explain the differences in over-all collections.

Each county's repertoire of enforcement techniques included warning letters, wage assignments, and orders to show cause (orders, that is, to appear at a hearing to explain nonpayment). The self-starting factor probably best captures the variation in the frequency of mailed warnings and we have already reported its significance. (No county kept a log of all warnings sent.) There was not enough variation in the use of wage assignments to learn what differences they could make. Of the orders to show cause, however, we did have fairly precise counts across all our counties. We hoped that the incidence of orders might prove to be a more important determinant of payments than the jail rate itself, so that we could say that a stern indication of seriousness of purpose about enforcement, which we thought these orders might appear, had a more significant effect on payment rates than the jail rate itself. In fact, neither the rate of orders to show cause nor any combination of the jail rate and order-to-show cause rate that we could contrive (to measure the conviction rate among those cited for contempt) proved anywhere near as valuable a predictor as the jail-sentence rate standing alone.

Yes, it appears that high levels of jailing, when coupled with an ardent enforcement process, do lead to higher levels of payment. But why? Several explanations are possible and different men within the same county may be affected in different ways.[11] It is likely that the more men that are jailed, the more diffused within the community is information about the use of jail, which may in turn induce men to pay out of fear or affect in some more intangible way their sense of obligation to pay. Warning letters may quickly ring hollow if they are not backed by the realistic possibility of arrest and jail. For some other men, the relation between the jail and payments will simply be that they themselves have tasted jail and found it wanting. In Genesee county, for example, a "high-jailing" county with the ninth highest jailing rate among our 28 counties, we determined that about one in seven of all the men in the divorce caseload in 1970 were sentenced to jail at least once for nonpayment during the life of their case and that one in four were arrested at least once.

Whatever the explanation, one noteworthy aspect of the jailing process bore no positive relation to collections. The counties varied widely in the lengths of sentences their judges typically imposed. (By law, judges could not impose sentences of more than one year's length and men could buy their early release by the payment of their full arrearage or some lesser part accepted by the judge.) In some counties, the initially imposed sentences averaged over three months. In many others, they averaged around thirty days. No index that we could devise that combined average sentence length with the rate of jailing or measured jail lengths alone helped to sort high from low paying counties in a way not fully and more adequately explained by the rate of jailing alone.

From other parts of our study, we have strong evidence that long sentences also do not serve more effectively than short sentences to induce sentenced men to pay substantial lump sums to buy their early release from jail. Nor are jailed men who serve longer sentences in jail more frightened into paying better upon release. On the contrary, after controlling for other factors, length of time served remains a strong predictor of poor performance after release. In short, while the jail rate itself persistently relates to higher performances, long sentences seem to serve no useful functions whatever, except for revenge. And revenge may taste less sweet when the sentence serves no utilitarian function.

What we have reported so far seems to carry some pointed messages for persons entrusted with shaping public policy. The first is that states, counties or provinces would be wise to banish half or three-quarters of their populations. If that is not feasible, it may nonetheless be possible to recapture some of the advantages of a smaller population by finding ways to make more immediate and personal the relationship between the collecting agency and the persons under an order of support. It may, for example, help to insist that a father attend a conference with an agency staff member within the early weeks of a temporary order. It may in some areas be possible to divide the area served into smaller geographic subdivisions, in the manner of neighbourhood school boards.

The second message is that collections of child support are a direct function of the degree of organization to collect. If governments care whether the custodial parent not receiving welfare benefits receives support payments, they must do more much more than leave the parent to private remedies. That advice rests on a comparison of Michigan's collections with impressions of those in other states.[12] From within our own study, we learn that even if states establish special agencies to receive payments and enforce orders, levels of collections will still vary importantly with the degree of initiative of the agency.

The final message is — or would appear to be — that jail works and that its widespread use can be a valuable aid in increasing collections of support, if, only if, it is linked to an otherwise well-organized system of enforcement. On the face of our study of the 28 counties we have nothing to challenge this claim. From other figures available to us, it also appears that the marginal dollar return from jailing exceeds the dollar costs to the counties of the use of the courts and jails for these purposes.

Despite this, there are still a number of reasons to recoil from wide reliance on jailing as a prod for the collection of child support. Most of the rest of this essay will be concerned with helping you decide whether the apparent obvious utility of jailing outweighs the harms that flow from it.

An initial doubt about jailing for nonsupport is jurisprudential. We may well decide that even wilful nonsupport is not one of those forms of human misbehaviour that ought appropriately to be dealt with through criminal sanctions. Though not one of the "victimless" offences, it is nonetheless an intrafamily offence of a sort that flows often from the continuation after divorce of patterns of behaviour that were a part of the marriage: withholding as a technique of communication. Divorced men often "forget" to pay not out of a vicious disregard for their children but from more mundane failings of jealously or anger, just as divorced women, never jailed for it, "forget" that Tuesday was the day the father was coming to visit. Recognizing the "emotional stress" of the post-divorce period and child support's connection with "an intimate personal relationship", the Committee on One Parent Families of Britain's Department of Health and Social Security thus recently recommended that Parliament eliminate jail as a permissible sanction for nonsupport.[13]

A second and more tangible reason for avoiding criminal sanctions for nonpayment of support is that jails stink. America's county jails are among our most vicious incarcerative institutions. Often jammed with far more inmates than they were built to hold, they rely on forced inactivity, breed bodily and sexual assault, and take heavy tolls on human self-esteem. The character of our jails should be seen as particularly troublesome in this setting when it is recalled how high the level of jailing is in many of Michigan's counties. Judges sentence close to 4,000 Michigan men each year for nonsupport, their number out-stripping by far in several counties the number of men sentenced to jail for drunken driving or larceny offences. It is probable that in addition at least 1,000 more men spend a day or so in jail under arrest without later being sentenced. While many men serve no more than a day or two, it is still alarming that we treat as criminal one in ten of all divorced noncustodial parents. If Michigan's aggressiveness were replicated in the rest of the country, as it may be under the new pressures the Federal government is applying,[14] we could easily find that 100,000 American parents were sentenced for nonsupport each year.

Massive jailing for nonsupport may also damage the lives of men who have never been jailed and damage their children as well. It may do so through an impact that seems plausible but that we have been unable to measure because of the nature of our file-based research — and doubt whether current social science research techniques permit full measurement in any event. What is the impact, we have wondered, of an ever-present threat of jail on the tenor of the relationship between a noncustodial parent and his child? How, that is, does a parent begin to behave toward a child to whom he feels himself tied not by affection alone but at least in part by fear. Can jail's distant possibility make even more tense the already awkward visitation often experienced between parent and child after divorce? Can it produce further reaching injuries to the child's development? Since there is little extant research on the developmental effects of various kinds of continued relations between a child and his or her non-custodial parent after divorce, there is no baseline for the particularized question I pose here. It may be at least as plausible that in many, perhaps most, cases my worries are groundless and that a jailing policy, by playing a subtle part in inducing regular payments by fathers, frequently improves rather than corrodes the relation between father and child by removing a common source of friction between the divorced parents over irregularities of payment.

There are, however, a few other aspects of a jailing process we have been able to examine and, again, the more closely we examine them the more alarming the picture they present. In Genesee County, a county of 500,000, while we found that sentenced men did frequently unearth large lump sums and a significant portion began making regular payments afterwards, we also found that large numbers served their full terms. One-third of the men sentenced during a two-year period served five full months or more. We also found that large numbers fled the county after release and were rarely seen again. We further found that a much higher portion of men in the jailed population than in the random population of divorced men (60% v. 20%) showed some signs of alcoholism. This fact raised our fears not only that jail for nonsupport was being used as an alternative to the usual and widely discredited alcohol offences, which carry shorter sentences, but also that many of the men who were being jailed had in fact been unable to pay (as they often claimed) and hence that jailing was being used inappropriately, indeed perhaps unconstitutionally, to reach a class of persons for whom payment was currently beyond their control.

Inappropriate jailing seemed almost certain to occur — inappropriate in the sense of the jailing of men who should not have been jailed under the Michigan contempt statute that permits the jailing only of those who could have been paying but "neglected or refused to do so". As a part of the study, we read the transcripts of most of the contempt proceedings in Genesee County in a two-year period, a total of over 200 transcripts. Counsel was never appointed for indigents and witnesses never sworn, indeed never even called. The defendant was typically simply asked what his excuse was, berated for his failings and jailed. The whole hearing, including "trial" and sentencing, typically took less than five minutes. Here is the full transcript of one such proceeding. A reader may find it difficult to believe that nothing has been cut. While it sets some sort of record for brevity, it is largely true to the tone of the dozens of transcripts we read:

THE COURT: In the matter of File No. 72550 entitled Ruth Ellis against Bobby Ellis.

(Whereupon the defendant came forward, was addressed by the Court as follows:)

BY THE COURT:

Q This is pursuant to the case of Ruth Ellis. Now, on April 15, 1963, a judgment of divorce was entered by this Court wherein Bobby Ellis was ordered to pay support in the amount of $16 per week for two minor children. As of October 15, 1973, he is $9,708.86 in arrears.

Do you have anything to say before the Court pronounces sentence on you?

A Yes. I have been paying this last summer as much as I possibly could and due to the weather and the work conditions I have been on unemployment now for five years.

Q Why didn't you give them some of that money?

A Well, the price of food and everything.

Q What food? They are supposed to starve?

A No, they ain't.

THE COURT: The sentence of the Court is that you be confined to the County jail for one year. You may be released on the advancement of a satisfactory method of making the payments on the support order.

Judges and Friends of the Court have defended the utter absence of procedural safeguards on the ground that these contempt proceedings are civil not criminal — mere continuations of the original divorce action — and that the defendants carry the keys to the jailhouse in their pocket. The first excuse, even if supported by some constitutional history, is senseless. A year in jail feels the same whether labeled civil or criminal, rehabilitative or punitive. The second is simply factually untrue. Pressed, the same judges and Friends of the Court then assert that providing traditional criminal trial safeguards will cripple the effectiveness of their enforcement system, miring it in technicalities and blocking the conviction of the obviously guilty. They are quite justified in their fears that the state would often find it impossible to prove beyond a reasonable doubt that a long absent man had been working or that a given unemployed man could have been working, but their point simply underscores how widely the proof of wilful non-support differs from the proof of most other offences than can lead to incarceration. We have no single event — the robbery of a grocery store, the killing of spouse — upon which our attention can focus, but rather a series of nonevents — weeks of nonpayment — the justifiability of which may be almost impossible to assess in any rigorous way in the cases of the unemployed but healthy man. If problems of proof are severe when the burden is placed on the state, they will often be no less severe when the burden is placed on the defendant.

In Michigan, most of the resistance to procedural rights in support proceedings has revealed itself in the context of the issue of the right to appointed counsel in contempt proceedings.[15] In interviews with judges and in a survey we took of Friends of the Court, I have been startled by the intensity of the opposition to appointed counsel. One fairly liberal trial judge declared that if counsel were appointed the Friend of the Court would have "to close up shop".

The judges' fears may have some rational basis. In our own survey, among men in Genesee County brought before the judge for the first time, the only significant distinction we could find between the men who were jailed and the men who were not was that the men who were not were substantially more likely to have retained attorneys. While today retained attorneys have a very different impact on their infrequent appearances than would attorneys in the future if appointed in all cases, the way that retained attorneys have achieved success — often for blue-collar clients — might carry over into an era of appointments. Counsel have succeeded not by raising technical defences or even by denying that their client was neglectful as a matter of law, but rather by evoking a picture of a client who had fallen on hard (even if not destitute) times and by offering alternative plans that seemed more likely than jailing to produce sustained payments by the particular defendant for a particular child. They thus robbed the judge of his accustomed practice of seeing the defendant as a faceless emblem of irresponsibility.

We can usually reject as groundless any claims that procedural protections, such as the right to counsel, bear much relation to the incidence of crime. How silly the claims appear that the United States Supreme Court and its decisions about confessions or searches and seizures have been responsible for a rise in the crime rate. And yet our study does offer an indirect basis for fearing that if the appointment of attorneys did lead to a substantially lower incidence of jailing for non-support, fewer dollars might be collected from the caseload as a whole. The reduction in payments would occur not because fathers would widely come to know about the availability of attorneys and conclude that attorneys would spring them. Rather, it would occur because of the impact discussed above that heavy jailing apparently exerts on the general atmosphere of a county's payment and collection process. With fewer jailings, the unseen dragon would suddenly be breathing less fire.

That procedural safeguards would in fact reduce overall collections remains, of course, wholly unproven from our study. Not even one of the counties in our study routinely provided counsel to men charged with contempt. But concern about this possible impact on collections would be unnecessary if an alternative to jailing existed that could produce as high or higher payments and governments moved largely away from reliance on fear to motivate payment.

Such an alternative does exist. Today, for the collection of income and Social Security taxes, Americans have become long accustomed to payments automatically withheld from wages. "Wage assignments" for child support have the same effect when imposed on an employer and are authorized by law in several states, including Michigan. In most states, including Michigan, however, courts may not impose a wage assignment except on a parent already in default.[16] If a system were established under which withholding occurred from the first moment of an order and travelled with a man wherever he took work anywhere within the country, the need for much of the current enforcement system would largely disappear. Payment would be nearly perfect except by the unemployed, the self-employed and those who could find employment while fraudulently evading the floating wage assignment. Evasion could be made more difficult by a computerized system tied to the man's Social Security number. Under the current system, even in Michigan's highest collecting counties, many men working full-time, especially those living outside the county of their order, pay little or no support. Their nonpayment might be largely halted.

A compulsory deduction system would, to be sure, have many troublesome aspects. It would, in the first place, be cumbersome to administer. Unlike income-tax withholding, deductions for child support would be required only for certain employees who would not look any different at the time of hiring from other employees who had no children. Further complicating administration would be that, unlike income taxes, support payments would often need to be funneled through to a recipient other than the government.

The drawbacks of a compulsory wage assignment system would not be simply ones of administration. Such a system would also obviously curtail individual liberty. Many people feel strongly about their right to decide for themselves what to do with their earnings. They would resent involuntary wage assignments for child support as as much as they would resent involuntary deductions for their utility bills, even though they would agree that it was reprehensible not to pay their bills. Whether seen as a right or not, many noncustodial parents attach importance to their weekly voluntary writing of a support check, viewing it as a way of continually affirming their love for their children.

A wage assignment system would also involve federal intrusion of another sort on privacy. We can appropriately worry about a federal computer system carrying detailed information about the failed marriages of millions of citizens. Indeed, the employer would invariably learn through the system that his or her employee was divorced or the parent of an illegitimate child. Today, agencies often hesitate to impose a wage assignment on a person who is likely to be fired because his employer either does not want the bother of making an additional deduction or dislikes a person who is divorced or is the parent of a "bastard". This troublesome problem would continue under the system proposed here.

The question in the end, however, is not the evil of such a wage deduction system in the abstract. It is whether it is better or worse than the sin-based system that we have now — the system, as I characterized it at the beginning of this piece, in which we dangle before men the opportunity not to pay, often so inviting because of the pain of continued recollection of the old family, and then, when men respond to the opportunity, clap them in jail.

If governments remain committed to compelling long-absent parents to support their children (and there may be some basis for qualms about our commitment) and if we remain determined to enforce the obligation with ardour, I for one would rather choose the compulsory deduction system than the system now found in Michigan. It would be my preference, not so much because it would probably lead to higher collections than Michigan obtains today but rather because of the doubts I have expressed about the justness of a jail-based system in operation and the atmosphere that system creates. The choice may seem easy to me because the new system does not yet exist. I do, however, find it hard to believe that a new system, however intrusive, could be as distasteful as one that depends heavily on imprisonment and the fear of imprisonment. If you have personal doubts in this regard, I suggest that you volunteer for a weekend at your nearest local jail.

1 While in most states courts can order women to pay support, such a tiny portion of court orders run in fact against women that I will frequently allude to the father rather than the "non-custodial parent", and the mother rather than the "custodial parent".

2 See Committee on Finance, United States Senate, *Child Support Data and Materials* 151 (November 1975); Department of Health, Education and Welfare, Office of Child Support Enforcement, *First Annual Report to the Congress on the Child Support Enforcement Program* 120-21 (June 1976).

3 See I.F.G. Baxter, "Family Law Reform in Ontario" (1975) 25 U. of Toronto L.J. 236-37.

4 The counties involved in the study were: Allegan, Barry, Bay, Berrien, Branch, Calhoun, Cass, Eaton, Genesee, Gratiot, Ingham, Jackson, Kent, Lapeer, Lenawee, Livingston, Macomb, Midland, Monroe, Oakland, Saginaw, St. Clair, St. Joseph, Skiawassee, Van Buren, Washtenaw, Wayne.

5 The product-moment correlation between the overall mean and the portion of the caseload paying less than 10% of everything due was -.935. The product-moment correlation between the mean and the portion of the caseload paying more than 80% was +.899.

6 While we believe our findings are reliable for the period measured, they are probably somewhat unrepresentative of Michigan collections over a period of years, for 1974 was a year of severe economic recession. In twenty of the twenty-eight counties, unemployment exceed 8.0% during our survey months. (In eleven of these twenty counties, it exceeded 11.0%.) For purposes of the research we did, we could use unemployment levels as one of the controls in explaining differences in collections.

7 In a regression analysis with the three factors only, the square root of county population (the square root being used to flatten the extremities of the population in a few enormous counties) had a Beta of -.34; a binary variable indicating whether or not the county had a policy of some years' standing of initiating enforcement without awaiting complaints had a Beta of +.44; and the number of men jailed for nonsupport as a portion of either county population or the caseload) had a Beta of +.34. The three predicted 62.4% of the variance (unadjusted) and 57.5% of the variance (adjusted). When we created a combined variable that contrasted all counties that had both enforcement attributes of being self-starting and high jailing with all other counties not having both, we could with this variable and the population variable alone account for slightly over 70% of the variance unadjusted and a shade under 70% adjusted.

8 A high-jailing county, for our purposes, was one that jailed four or more men for nonsupport during 1974 for each 1,000 persons in the county population in 1970. The mean jailing rate for the high jailing counties was 6.0 per 10,000. The mean rate for the low jailing counties was 1.7 per 10,000. See further explanation in Appendix A.

9 A self-starting county was a county that had had for some years a policy of initiating enforcement efforts in delinquent non-welfare cases without waiting for complaints.

10 We were able to explain only a small additional percentage of the variation in collections among counties by taking the unemployment levels in the county in 1970 into account. When taken into account, levels of unemployment seemed to bear a small negative relation to levels of collections. See Appendix.

11 The most thorough available study of the ways in which enforcement practices may affect antisocial behavior is F. Zimring and G. Hawkins, *Deterrence: The Legal Threat in Crime Control* (Chicago, 1973).

12 The most startling study of collections in other states was Kenneth Eckhardt's study of payments in an urban Wisconsin county in the 1950's and early 1960's in which an agency received payments but enforcement was haphazard. Eckhardt found that even in the first year of their orders, around 40% of fathers paid nothing at all and the no-payment group rose to over 70% by the seventh year. See Eckhardt, "Deviance, Visibility and Legal Action: The Duty to Support" (1968) 15 Soc. Prob. 470.

13 Great Britain, *Report of the Committee on One-Parent Families* (London, 1974; Cmnd. 5629), Volume I, pp. 128-132.
14 See the terms of recently enacted Title IV-D of the Social Security Act, prescribing the efforts that states must make to collect child support in welfare cases.
15 The Michigan Supreme Court has recently held that counsel need not be provided to indigents in child support contempt proceedings. *Sword v. Sword*, 399 Mich. 367, 249 N.W. 2d 88 (1976).
16 *Compare* Maryland Code Ann., Art. 27, Sec. 88 *and* Michigan Compiled Laws Annotated section 552.203 (both requiring default before imposing a wage assignment) *with* Wisconsin Compiled Laws section 247.265 (permitting wage assignment to be imposed "at any time.") See also 42 United States Code section 659, by which Congress recently provided that wage assignments would be honoured for employees of the United States government as if the United States were a private employer. Thus, if state law permitted involuntary wage assignments without proof of default, a United States employee could be subjected to one.

APPENDIX A

Regression Analysis of Factors Accounting for Differences in Rates of Collections Among Twenty-Eight Counties.

The measure of county performance used in the study was the mean for each county of the individual payment rates for each person in the sample for the period sampled. That measure is referred to here as the "Mean Payment Rate." This measure was used as the dependent variable here either in its natural form, its log to base 10, or its "Logit" form, as indicated.

A list of around 40 control variables tested in the analysis can be obtained directly from the author. Below are the controls used in the analyses reported here:

1. *Self-Starting Factor.* A binary variable that records whether (coded 1) or not (coded 0) the county has used for several years an enforcement system in which the agency initiates enforcement in nonwelfare cases without awaiting complaints from the mother.

2. *Jailing Rate.* The number of sentences to jail in 1974 for contempt of court for nonpayment of support for each 10,000 persons in the county population. This rate closely parallels the rate of jailing for each 250 men in the county caseload.

3. *Population.* The log^{10} of the county's population from the 1970 decennial census.

4. *Unemployment Rate.* The unemployment rate in the civilian labor force according to the 1970 census.

5. *High-Jail/Self-Start Factor.* A combination of factors 1 and 2 above into a binary variable that coded whether or not a county was both high jailing and "self-starting". Those counties that had both a jail rate of 4 or more per 10,000 and a self-starting system were contrasted with all other counties. The selected rate of 4 per 10,000 divided our counties approximately at the median and had no other conceptual foundation.

6. *Jail x Self-Start Factor.* Factor 1 above multiplied by Factor 2. The multiplication produced a 0 for all counties without a self-starting policy (regardless of their jailing rate) and their jailing rate (from 1 to 17) for all counties that did have a self-starting policy.

A. Regression on the "Mean Payment Rate"

1. *With three variables that explain most variance:*

	B	Beta	T-Ratio	Significance Level
Self-starting Factor	8.62	+0.41	2.89	< .01
Jailing Rate	0.92	+0.35	2.64	< .02
Log^{10} Population	-7.91	-0.34	2.53	< .02
Fraction of explained variance: 62.6 per cent (unadjusted)				
57.9 per cent (adjusted)				

2. *With four variables that explain most variance:*

	B	Beta	T-Ratio	Significance Level
Self-starting Factor	7.00	+0.33	2.25	< .05
Jailing Rate	0.96	+0.37	2.82	< .01
Log^{10} Population	-8.64	-0.38	1.48	< .20
Unemployment Rate	-2.35	-0.19	2.80	< .01
Fraction of explained variance: 65.8 per cent (unadjusted)				
59.9 per cent (adjusted)				

3. *With the "High-Jail/Self-Start Factor":*

	B	Beta	T-Ratio	Significance Level
High-Jail/Self-Start Factor	14.8	+.64	6.36	< .01
Log^{10} Population	-10.8	-.47	4.72	< .01
Unemployment Rate	- 2.65	-.22	2.20	< .05
Fraction of explained variance: 76.5 per cent (unadjusted)				
73.6 per cent (adjusted)				

4. *With the "Jail x Self-Start Factor":*

	B	Beta	T-Ratio	Significance Level
Jail × Self-Start Factor	+1.33	+.55	4.30	< .01
Log^{10} Population	-9.96	-.43	3.50	< .01
Unemployment Rate	-1.94	-.16	1.25	—
Fraction of explained variance: 64.4 per cent (unadjusted)				
60.1 per cent (adjusted)				

B. Regression on Log[10] "Mean Payment Rate"

With principal variables in log form:

	B	Beta	T-Ratio	Significance Level
Self-starting Factor	0.047	+0.33	2.06	< .05
Log[10] Jail Rate	0.052	+0.31	2.20	< .05
Log[10] Population	−0.059	−0.38	2.69	< .01
Log[10] Unemployment	−0.240	−0.23	1.62	< .20

Fraction of explained variance: 62.1 per cent (unadjusted)
55.5 per cent (adjusted)

C. Regression on "Mean Payment Rate" in Modified "Logit" form

$$\text{Log}^{10} \ \frac{\text{Mean Payment Rate}}{\text{1-Mean Payment Rate}}$$

With principal measures in log form:

	B	Beta	T-Ratio	Significance Level
Self-Starting Factor	+0.13	+0.30	1.91	< .10
Log[10] Jail Rate	0.19	0.38	2.75	< .01
Log[10] Population	−0.18	−0.37	2.67	< .01
Log[10] Unemployment	−0.79	−0.24	1.88	< .10

Fraction of explained variance: 63.9 per cent (unadjusted)
57.7 per cent (adjusted)

Child Support In The American Jurisdictions

Henry H. Foster, Jr.,*
Dr. Doris Jonas Freed**

Note: The substance of this article appeared in Henry H. Foster, Jr., Doris Jonas Freed and Millard L. Midonick, "Child Support: The Quick and the Dead" (1975) 26 Syracuse Law Review 1157, and also in The New York Law Journal, where it appeared in three parts, on March 24, 25 and 26, 1975.

INTRODUCTION

Although there is a consensus that parents are obligated to support, maintain, and educate their children, and this consensus is reflected in numerous statutes and decisions, the implementation and enforcement of parental obligations has been haphazard at best. The trouble with child support is that it is difficult to collect, and the elusive father may successfully avoid his obligations. Herein we will discuss the legal and practical limitations on what generally is regarded as both a legal and moral duty of the highest order.

At common law, the parental duty to support children presented a curious lacuna between moral and legal duties. Blackstone said that the duty to provide maintenance for children was "a principle of natural law."[1] If it was such a principle it was a moral duty without adequate legal remedy, although ecclesiastical courts perhaps lent their authority as a matter of conscience to force fathers to discharge their natural duty, and in chancery a quasi-contractual duty of support eventually became equitable doctrine.[2]

Unlike the situation where the wife was permitted to pledge her husband's credit for necessaries, a child had no such privilege in his or her own right, except where there was an express or implied authorization from the father according to agency principles. Otherwise, neither the child nor any creditor who had provided him with necessaries had any cause of action against the parent. An infant could not sue a parent, with or without a guardian *ad litem,* since a minor was not a legal person. No action of

* Henry H. Foster, Jr. is a Professor of Law, New York University.
** Dr. Doris Jonas Freed is a member of the New York and Maryland Bars.

assumpsit was maintainable. However, in the nineteenth century, finally it was held that a wife justifiably living apart from her husband due to his misconduct and having legal custody of the children could pledge the husband's credit and he was liable for necessaries received by the wife, including clothes for the child.[3]

The only common law remedy provided by civil law was that derived from the Elizabethan Poor Laws[4] of the seventeenth century which permitted the parish to recoup for alms or assistance given to the family. Under certain circumstances, the father might be compelled to support his children according to his ability if they became destitute and the parish provided for their maintenance.[5] Even the duty of wife support likewise depended upon application of the Poor Laws, until a seventeenth century decision became established as precedent for the wife's right to pledge her husband's credit for necessaries.[6]

Insofar as the criminal law was concerned, a father's abandonment and non-support became a common law misdemeanor, if such neglect occasioned injury.[7] Today, in the United States, every state has enacted criminal statutes that make desertion and non-support a criminal offence, generally a misdemeanor.[8] Such statutes, however, are strictly construed, and in most states are rarely used because there are alternative and more effective remedies. Typically, there is a hodge podge of civil, criminal, and quasi-criminal statutes imposing the duty of child support in order to reinforce Blackstone's principle of "natural law."

Until the present decade a primary duty of child support was imposed upon the father but not the mother, despite Married Women's Property Acts, and at most the mother's duty of child support was secondary. This remains the usual practice in New York even though most recent legislative reform elsewhere,[9] and perhaps the requirements of due process and equal protection,[10] specify mutuality of obligation. Moreover, in some states statutory liability for child support is imposed upon stepparents who stand in *loco parentis* to a minor unemancipated stepchild.[11]

The legal duty to support children exists whether or not the parents are separated or divorced. Statutory authority is conferred to order child support as ancillary relief in matrimonial actions, and it may be awarded *pendente lite* or in the final order.[12] In New York, and elsewhere, a panoply of remedies is provided for the enforcement of child support orders and for the collection of arrearages. Although these provisions may suffer in implementation and enforcement, nonetheless their very existence is in marked contrast to the lack of protection accorded to the children of a deceased parent. Since the law of the American states is substantially like that of New York, except where changed by statute, we will use New York as an example and will discuss the duty of child support in New York, legislation enacted there and elsewhere, and then recent federal legislation.

THE DUTY OF CHILD SUPPORT IN NEW YORK

As previously stated, the New York statutes place the primary duty of child support on the father and impose only a secondary liability upon the mother. In theory, if the mother is forced to support her children, she has a right to indemnification from the father.[13] These rules apply even though the mother has far greater resources or income than the father.[14] However, under Domestic Relations Law §240, in a matrimonial action, an award for child support may be made out of "the property of either or both parents." This statutory authority has been construed to leave undisturbed the father's primary obligation of child support and to merely authorize the court to consider the mother's assets in assessing the extent of the father's liability for child support.[15]

The Family Court Act in general follows the Domestic Relations Law with reference to the duty of child support. Section 413 places the primary duty upon the father, and section 414 imposes a secondary duty upon the mother. The mother may be liable for child support "[I]f the father of a child is dead, incapable of supporting his child, or cannot be found within the state," where she is possessed of sufficient means or able to earn such means. However, it also is provided that "[T]he court may apportion the costs of the support of the child between the parents according to their respective means and responsibilities," although ordinarily such power does not affect the priority of obligation. Finally, under section 415, parents have a mutual duty of support where a child has become or is likely to become a recipient of public assistance or a patient in an institution operated by the Department of Mental Hygiene, and a parent has "sufficient ability" to provide for such minor child.

Of course, the above provisions raise serious constitutional problems under equal protection principles.[16] The child support obligation under the statutory scheme and the way it works in practice is unequal and discriminatory. In practice the mother's duty, ironically, approximates that of the father only where that is necessary in order to save on welfare expenditures. Presumably, even under section 415, a mother who is forced to pay child support has a right to indemnification from the father if he can be located and has assets. The legal responsibility remains that of the father unless the mother clearly volunteers and assumes the responsibility and in effect waives her right to reimbursement from him.[17] Moreover, in practice, a mother who can least afford it is the one most apt to be ordered to pay child support under section 415.

With reference to the duration of child support, although the 1974 legislature, following the trend of at least half of the states, reduced the age of majority to eighteen, it left undisturbed the provisions of the Family Court Act imposing child support obligations until age twenty-one.[18] Thus, the parental duty of child support is terminated only when the child reaches the age of twenty-one or is emancipated at an earlier age. Emancipation will not be readily found, as is illustrated by New York decisions that entrance into military service does not automatically effect an emancipation so as to relieve a father of his duty to support his son.[19]

In 1967, New York amended the Social Services Law so as to eliminate the responsibility of parents to support disabled adult children and the liability of adult children to support indigent parents.[20] Previously, in order to reduce welfare expenditures, such obligations had been imposed. This change in welfare policy also has been applied where a sister state seeks to impose liability upon a New York parent for the support of an incapacitated adult child within its jurisdiction where such liability exists under its own law.[21]

One of the more controversial issues in the law pertaining to child support is the matter of educational expenses. Section 416 of the Family Court Act provides that "the expense of education" is an element of the duty of child support but fails to specify the extent of the obligation. If a father by contract or agreement undertakes the cost of education, such an undertaking will be enforced.[22] In the absence of contract, however, ordinarily there is no duty to pay for the education of an adult child since the support duty terminates at age twenty-one.[23] Responsibility for the educational expenses of a minor child depends upon the circumstances of the individual case.[24] If the child has shown little or no aptitude or talent, or if the father is in financial straits, courts are reluctant to order payment for private schooling or college education.[25] However, where a child has regularly attended private school, a father may be ordered to continue such an arrangement.[26]

At common law the father controlled or dictated decisions as to schooling and some vestiges of that prerogative remain. Open ended orders to pay educational expenses are frowned upon and usually the obligation is tied down to a specific amount.[27] The mother may not unilaterally and without consultation send the child to college and bill the father for that expense.[28] Moreover, the father may impose reasonable terms and conditions which must be satisfied in return for his assumption of college expenses.[29]

If the test applied in determining whether or not there is a duty to provide private schooling or college expenses is in terms of the child's needs, courts may be loath to impose such a responsibility in the absence of an undertaking to that effect. However, if the focus is on the father's means, and he has sufficient financial ability, a duty to pay special educational expenses may be imposed upon the father on behalf of a talented child, even if there was no undertaking to do so.

The measure of the father's support duty as set forth in section 413 of the Family Court Act is "a fair and reasonable sum according to his means". Under section 416 "elements of support" include necessary shelter, food, clothing, care, medical attention, the expense of education, and "other proper and reasonable expenses." Domestic Relations Law §240 sets the standard for amount in terms of "as justice requires, having regard to the circumstances of the case and of the respective parties and to the best interest of the child". The latter standard is applied where child support is awarded in matrimonial actions. The trial court has a broad discretion in setting the amount.[30]

The parents may not by agreement foreclose court determination of the amount of child support or oust a court's jurisdiction to modify a prior award deemed to be excessive or inadequate.[31] If there is a parental agreement as to the amount of child support, where helpful, the child may be deemed to be a third party beneficiary of the agreement.[32] The obligation to pay child support is not affected by a discharge in bankruptcy.[33] In short, *parens patriae* power is exercised with regard to child support and the law imposes the obligation, and confers the right to it, independent of private agreement.

A difficult human issue is presented where the father when denied visitation rights, in retaliation, stops child support payments. The New York cases hold generally that child support, in the absence of express provision, is not conditioned on the father's right to visitation, although if his visitation privileges are interfered with, he may apply to the court for relief.[34] In addition, the court may refuse to cite him for contempt for non-payment where his visitation rights were frustrated.[35] Where a teen-age child refuses to see his or her father who is divorced from the mother, there is little that a court can do to eliminate alienation unless professional counselling is available.

Another provision of New York law which has a bearing on child support is the recent amendment to CPLR §302, the so-called "long arm statute."[36] The new law provides that "a court in any matrimonial action or family court proceeding involving a demand for support or alimony may exercise personal jurisdiction over the respondent or defendant notwithstanding the fact that he or she no longer is a resident or domiciliary of this state, or over his executor or administrator, if the party seeking support is (1) a resident of or domiciled in this state at the time such demand is made, *provided that* (2) this state was the matrimonial domicile of the parties before their separation, or (3) the defendant abandoned the plaintiff in this state, or (4) the obligation to pay support or alimony accrued under the laws of this state or under an agreement executed in this state".

Thus, personal jurisdiction may be asserted on behalf of a New York mother or child even though the father has left New York, where he deserted the family in New York or the duty to pay support arose under a

New York law or agreement. A judgment rendered under such circumstances is entitled to enforcement in other states on the same basis as any valid personal judgment. Since a number of other states have enacted similar "long arm" provisions to aid in the imposition and enforcement of support obligations,[37] and to date such statutes have been upheld as constitutional,[38] the new law is not unique and should be sustained. Certainly New York has as great a concern over family obligations as it has over the business interests or automobile accidents already subject to long arm jurisdiction.

For the most part, New York law regarding the support obligations of parents and spouses reflects traditional attitudes and the economics of the nineteenth century. However, it should be noted that legislation already exists for treating child support as a mutual obligation of both parents, depending upon their respective means and income. Both the Domestic Relations Law [39] and the Family Court Act[40] grant discretion to order child support out of the property or income of both parents. In practice, however, child support continues to be regarded as the primary obligation of the father even if the mother has equal or more ability to contribute. In other words, judicial discretion ordinarily is not exercised so as to impose a mutual obligation for child support.

Finally, with regard to child support and the law, mention should be made of the common law privilege of charging necessaries. This remedy still exists in New York even though it is of limited practicality.[41] The father may be sued by a creditor to recover payment for necessaries provided to the family. However, the father will have available numerous defences including the claim that he is not liable for the necessaries because he has already adequately provided by paying the amount directed by a child support order.[42] In such event, since New York does not have a family expense statute, which would make the wife jointly liable, the creditor may have to seek recovery against the child for "necessaries" so provided.[43] It should be noted that a father who pays child support as ordered may demand an accounting by a mother who appears to be squandering the child support.[44]

LEGISLATION IN OTHER STATES

As contrasted with the prevailing New York attitude regarding the allocation of child support, recent legislation in other states firmly makes child support a mutual obligation of both parents. The Uniform Marriage and Divorce Act in section 309 makes either parent or both parents liable for child support, without regard to marital fault. Those states which have enacted the Uniform Act[45] have accepted this provision and the same concept is embodied in the law of most states that have made breakdown of the marriage an additional ground for divorce,[46] except for Alabama and Georgia.

The Uniform Marriage and Divorce Act, also in section 309, permits the court to consider the financial resources of the child in assessing the support duty of the parents, and some statutes have followed the Uniform Act in this approach in terms of needs and resources. Among these states are Arizona, Colorado, Connecticut, Kentucky, Missouri and Montana. The desexing of alimony and child support and a regard for equal protection principles is a marked characteristic of most recent divorce reform. Contemporary values call for mutuality of obligation and elimination of discrimination in alimony and support statutes, so that economic resources rather than sex, or marital fault, is the basis for familial obligations.

ENFORCEMENT PROCEDURES

The customary laxity and ineptitude in the enforcement of support orders is one of the shames of family law. Historically, there is no other area of law where there is such wholesale defiance of court orders.[47] The need to bolster and modernize enforcement techniques is obvious. A number of states have made an effort to respond to this need by tightening up enforcement machinery. One of the more effective methods is to require support or alimony payments to be made directly to a designated court official who follows up as soon as arrearages occur.[48]

Wage attachment or garnishment of the salaries of obligors in default in making payments has been effective in some states.[49] Requiring the obligor to post security after an initial default, is sometimes efficacious.[50] But none of these techniques is sure fire, especially when the obligor leaves the state. For many years the simplest method of avoiding support or alimony obligations was simply to move to another state or locale. Formerly, it was necessary to seek extradition and to return the fugitive obligor to the home state in order to collect. To remedy this situation the Uniform Reciprocal Enforcement of Support Act (URESA) was enacted in American jurisdictions other than New York and the Virgin Islands.[51] The latter jurisdictions did not enact URESA because they already had statutes that were substantially similar. The New York Uniform Support of Dependents Act (USDA) is for the most purposes identical with URESA and works in harmony with it.[51]

URESA and the USDA contemplate a two-stage procedure, the support action being initiated in the state where the dependents are located, and the record being sent to the obligor's domicile. The latter state enters the order and provides enforcement. In some states both the initial procedure and the second stage are assigned to the court's staff or the office of the district attorney so that dependents are not saddled with legal expenses. Since the obligor is permitted to raise appropriate defences before an order is entered against him in the receiving state, to date URESA has withstood all constitutional challenges.[52] The greatest deficiency of USDA in New York is that it applies only to "dependents," who are defined so as not to include ex-wives to whom alimony is owed.[53] URESA has by amendment added ex-wives to its category of "dependents".[54] USDA likewise should be so amended.

TITLE IV-D OF THE SOCIAL SECURITY ACT: THE FEDERAL CHILD SUPPORT ENFORCEMENT PROGRAM

The most effective plan yet devised for the enforcement and collection of support orders is the recently enacted federal program. It is contained in Title IV-D of the Social Security Act.[55]

The report of the Committee on Finance which led to the enactment of the new law contains substantial data on past failures in the enforcement of child support and the enhanced cost to the welfare system.[56] The report states that of 11 million AFDC recipients, four out of every five are on the rolls because of an absent parent, usually a deserting father. In 1976, there were 6.7 million children on AFDC due to the father's desertion. Moreover, from 1971 to 1973 there was a 21.7 increase in the number of AFDC families where the father was not married to the mother. It is estimated that in the past six and one-half years, families with absent fathers have contributed about 4.8 million additional recipients to the AFDC rolls.

The committee report relies heavily upon a study by the Rand Corporation[57] regarding the circumstances of deserting fathers. It was found, contrary to popular assumption, that the fugitives did not run off to California. Instead, they were usually living in the same county as their children. Thousands of unserved child support warrants were said to pile up in many jurisdictions, and even traffic cases were given a higher priority. "Many lawyers and officials find child support cases boring, and are actually hostile to the concept of fathers' responsibility for children.... 'Some of these individuals believe that child support is punitive and that public assistance programs are designed as a more acceptable alternative to the enforcement of parental responsibility'."[58]

The Rand Corporation study emphasized that affluent fathers evaded child support obligations and that a number of well-off physicians and lawyers had families ultimately forced onto welfare because of the breakdown in enforcement. Among other problems, it was noted that there was difficulty in proving the income of the self-employed, and that the immunity of federal employees to attachment hampered collection in some cases. Under-staffed district attorney's offices were found to give a low priority to child support investigations. The study concluded that much middle-class poverty is caused by the father's nonsupport and that there has been a substantial increase in the number of middle-class families seeking AFDC.

Social and economic factors thus led to the enactment of the new law and to a concerted attempt to beef up collection and enforcement of the child support obligation in order to cut down on AFDC expenditures. In effect, Congress has tried to make more effective the policies which have dominated welfare law since the time of the Elizabethan Poor Laws.[59]

The law establishes federal-state cooperation for obtaining and enforcing child support and although it is aimed principally at welfare cases it also must be available in non-welfare cases. The provisions of this important federal law are more fully outlined in the Appendix of this paper[60], but it should be noted here that it removes the immunity from garnishment formerly enjoyed by federal employees including service-men,[61] and in certain cases permits enforcement in the federal courts and the use of the Internal Revenue Service as an aid for collection. Of great practical significance is the federal parent locator service and its companion state parent locator services[62] which will cooperate in tracking down and locating fugitive obligors who have not abided by support orders.

Since 1967, social security amendments and regulations have required state welfare agencies to establish special units to assist in locating parents and to co-operate with each other in the two-stage procedure established by URESA or in New York by the USDA.[63] Little was accomplished.[64] The new law puts teeth into the program and sanctions an active leadership as well as a watchdog role by the Department of Health, Education and Welfare (HEW).

CONCLUSION

This experiment in cooperative federalism constitutes a major intrusion into family affairs which traditionally have been regarded as the proper subject of local concern. The tremendous increase in AFDC and related welfare costs precipitated Congressional action and the utilization of the full power of the federal government to aid in the enforcement and collection of family obligations. It remains to be seen whether or not a patched up Elizabethan Poor Law can adequately serve the needs of a modern industrialized nation, or whether the present scheme must be repealed and replaced by some other welfare system.

In the past, court orders for support or alimony often have been made on an *ad hoc* basis and without regard to situational equities.[66] Moreover, the support and alimony laws of many states are discriminatory against men and perhaps deny equal protection of the laws.[67] The inequity, one-sidedness, and unfairness of state support and alimony laws was compensated for — perhaps over-compensated for — by laxity in enforcement. Now the federal-state dragnet assures the collection of both fair and unfair support and alimony orders.

The problem, of course, is that most states have a dual system of family law.[68] In the ordinary support situation there are substantial defences to the imposition of a support order. The wife who separates from her husband without good cause cannot look to him for support.[69] Under the rules applying to welfare cases, where a court refused to award support in an AFDC case because of mis-conduct, the IV-D agency is not authorized to pursue the case. In the case of ordinary support or alimony, New York holds that financial hardship justifies an upward modification of a prior alimony order based upon a surviving separation agreement.[70]

In effect, the Social Security Act, as amended, uncritically adopts the premise that existing state support laws are fair and reasonable and should be enforced. Unless federal standards, which guarantee due process and equal protection in support proceedings are forthcoming from HEW or the federal courts, discrimination will be compounded by rigid enforcement. However, IV-D does not concern itself with alimony (except with regard to garnishment of federal employees' wages), and HEW is unlikely to interfere in state law.

In the past, there may have been more than a suspicion that in the battle of the sexes what the law gave with one hand was taken away with the other. Law enforcement of alimony and support obligations, as previously suggested, compensated for, or over-compensated for, the sex discrimination built into our antiquated law. The creation of effective enforcement and collection services should trigger a reappraisal of state law as to support and alimony so as to eliminate discrimination and in order to assure fairness. Self-help, in the form of flight and desertion, no longer will be a viable alternative.

Finally, with regard to both child support and alimony, recent amendments to the New York long-arm statute,[71] make it easier for an abandoned family to recover support or alimony where the requirements for personal jurisdiction are met.[72] In such cases, once a New York decree is entered, it is entitled to full faith and credit in other states, and if another state has the Uniform Enforcement of Foreign Judgments Act,[73] or similar legislation, the New York decree may be registered and then enforced in the same manner as a local judgment.

1 William Blackstone, *Commentaries on the Laws of England,* Book I (Oxford, Clarendon Press, 1765, 1st ed.), p. 435 [Reprint, 1966, Oceana Publications, N.Y. and Wildy & Sons, London].
2 See *Greenspan v. Slate,* 97 A.2d 390 (Supreme Court of N.J., 1953).
3 See *Bazeley v. Forder* (1868) L.R. 3 Q.B. 559.
4 Act for Relief of the Poor, 43 Eliz. I, c.2 (1601).
5 See *Mortimore v. Wright* (1840) 151 E.R. 502.
6 See *Manby and Richards v. Scott* (1793) 83 E.R. 268.
7 9 Halsbury's Laws of England (2d Ed.) 443.
8 For example, see N.Y. Rev. Pen. Law § 260.05. The Model Penal Code §230.5 (Proposed Official Draft, 1962) provides: "A person commits a misdemeanor if he persistently fails to provide support which he can provide and which he knows he is legally obliged to provide to a spouse, child or other dependent." See also Cal. Penal Code §270(a), (amended 1974), which provides: "If a parent of a minor child wilfully omits, without lawful excuse, to furnish necessary clothing, food, shelter or medical care for his or her child, he or she is guilty of a misdemeanor punishable by a fine not exceeding $1,000 or by imprisonment in the county jail not exceeding one year, or by both."
9 See the Uniform Marriage and Divorce Act §309, and Henry H. Foster, Jr. and Doris J. Freed, "Divorce Reform: Brakes on Breakdown?," (1973-74) 13 J. Fam. Law 443 at 483-484 for a discussion of recent state legislation.
10 On the basis of the Equal Rights Amendment to the Pennsylvania constitution several cases in that state have held that it was unconstitutional to provide that only the wife may seek a bed and board divorce and secure alimony. See *Wiegand v. Wiegand,* 310 A.2d 426 (Pa. Super. Ct. 1973); *Corso v. Corso,* 120 Pitts. L.J. 183 (Com. Pleas 1972); *Kehl v. Kehl,* 120 Pitts. L.J. 296 (Com. Pleas 1972); *Henderson v. Henderson,* 224 Pa. Super. 182, 303 A.2d 843 (Pa. Super. 1973); and *Commonwealth of Pennsylvania ex rel.; Lukens v. Lukens,* 224 Pa. Super. 227, 303 A.2d 522 (Pa. Super. 1973).
11 New York Fam. Ct. Act §415 provides that if the child is a recipient of public assistance or likely to become such "Step-parents shall in like manner be responsible for the support of children under the age of twenty-one years." See also, Henry H. Foster, Jr. and Doris J. Freed, *Law and the Family: New York* (Rochester, 1966) Vol. II, p. 131, and 1976 Supp. Vol. II pp. 119-120; and Homer H. Clark Jr., *The Law of Domestic Relations in the United States* (St. Paul, 1968), §6.2. However, see *S. v. S.,* 276 N.Y.S. 2d 663 (Fam. Ct. Dutchess Co., 1967), which denied liability where the wife had concealed from the defendant, her new husband, that she had three children from a prior marriage who were on relief.
12 See N.Y. Dom. Rel. Law sec. 240.
13 *Maule v. Kaufman,* 33 NY.2d 58, 349 N.Y.S.2d 368, 204 N.E.2d 234 (1973), where the Court of Appeals (two judges dissenting), reversed the Appellate Division, *Maule v. Kaufman,* 41 A.D.2d 729, 341 N.Y.S.2d 749 (1st Dept., 1973), and found that even where, over a long period of years, a child had been continuously supported by the mother and her second husband, the mother was entitled to recover arrearages of support payments awarded in a Florida judgment of divorce on July 29, 1961. The Court of Appeals found upon uncontradicted evidence in the record that at or shortly after the mother's remarriage she had made a demand upon the father for child support and that this "offset any inference at the outset . . . that support would be furnished without expectation of reimbursement from the father."
14 See *Libby v. Arnold,* 161 N.Y.S.2d 798 (1957), holding that the father's primary duty of child support persists regardless of the mother's financial resources. Moreover, the wife is entitled to be supported by her husband notwithstanding that she has property or earnings of her own. See *Manufacturers Trust Co. v. Gray,* 278 N.Y. 380, 16 N.E. 2d 373 (Court of Appeals, 1938), and *Grishaver v. Grishaver,* 225 N.Y.S. 2d 924 (Sup. Ct. 1961). The mother may be primarily liable for child support, however, if she voluntarily assumes their care and maintenance. See *Jeacock v. Schorb,* 265 App. Div. 147, 39 N.Y.S. 2d 51 (App. Div., 4th Dept., 1942). It should also be noted that a father's duty of child support may be imposed without regard to the resources of the child. See *Quat v. Freed,* 31 A.D.2d 627, 295 N.Y.S.2d 728 (1st Dept. 1968), holding that the fact that children had trust income "effects no diminution of the father's primary obligation to support his children." The

opposite rule applies by express statutory dispensation to the custodian of an infant's (under twenty-one years) property under the Uniform Gifts to Minors Act; a custodian parent may spend that particular type of infant's property by applying any of it directly for the infant (*e.g.* tuition) utterly without regard to the custodian's own duty and ability to support the child (E.P.T.L. §7-4.3).

15 *S. v. C.,* 70 Misc.2d 19, 332 N.Y.S.2d 773 (1972).

16 See note 10, *supra.*

17 It has been held that the mother may be liable for child support where the father fails in his duty and the children are without means. See *Haslett v. Haslett,* 25 A.D.2d 256, 268 N.Y.S.2d 809 (3rd Dept. 1966). Moreover, where the mother voluntarily assumes care and maintenance of the children she may become a volunteer. See *Jeacock v. Schorb,* 265 App. Div. 147, 39 N.Y.S.2d 51 (4th Dept. 1942). However, the usual rule is that "[a] child is entitled to support from his father not only in accordance with its needs but also in accord with the father's means. This encompasses his ability to pay in relation to his wealth." *Goldberg v. Berger,* 295 N.Y.S. 2d 975 at 977 (2d Dept., 1968).

18 Laws 1974, Ch. 937, eff. Sept. 1, 1974, amended Fam. Ct. Act §119 to stipulate the age of eighteen, but did not lower the age for support obligations imposed by §§413-415. Hence the duty of child support continues until the child becomes twenty-one. This remains also the interstate rule, protecting children up to age twenty-one, under the Uniform Reciprocal Support Act. It should be further noted that §414 authorizes the Family Court (and by implication the Supreme Court) to "apportion the costs of the support of the child between the parents according to their respective means and responsibilities."

19 See *Craig v. Craig,* 24 A.D.2d 588, 262 N.Y.S.2d 398 (2d Dept. 1965); *Wack v. Wack,* 74 N.Y.S.2d 435 (1947); and *Harwood v. Harwood,* 49 N.Y.S.2d 727, aff'd 52 N.Y.S. 2d 573 (1944). See also *Raphael v. Raphael,* 280 N.Y.S. 2d 168 (2d Dept., 1967), holding father not liable for child support during period son was employed and self-supporting. Compare *Wolf v. Wolf,* 194 App. Div. 33, 185 N.Y.S. 37 (2d Dept., 1920), holding that marriage of child below age of legal consent (eighteen years) did not effect an emancipation.

20 See Laws 1967, Ch. 184, amending Soc. Serv. Law §101.

21 See *Matter of Dabbs v. Burrell,* 53 Misc. 2d 349, 278 N.Y.S. 2d 436 (Fam. Ct. Ulster Co., 1967), and *Jones v. Jones,* 51 Misc. 2d 610, 273 N.Y.S. 2d 661 (Fam. Ct. New York Co., 1966).

22 See *Chilson v. Chilson,* 282 N.Y.S.2d 80 (3d Dept. 1967). See also *Weingast v. Weingast,* 44 Misc.2d 952, 255 N.Y.S.2d 341 (Fam. Ct. Nassau Co., 1964).

23 See *Greenberg v. Greenberg,* 279 N.Y.S.2d 363 (2d Dept., 1967).

24 See *Matthews v. Matthews,* 14 A.D.2d 546, 217 N.Y.S.2d 736 (2d Dept. 1961); *Wagner v. Wagner,* 51 Misc. 2d 574, 273 N.Y.S.2d 572, aff'd 28 A.D.2d 828, 282 N.Y.S. 2d 639, app. dismissed, 20 N.Y.2d 803, 231 N.E.2d 135 (1967). Compare *Earle v. Earle,* 205 Misc. 738, 130 N.Y.S.2d 238 (1954), with *Borden v. Borden,* 130 N.Y.S.2d 831 (1954), which held father was not required to pay private school tuition where public schools were adequate. See also *Kotkin v. Kerner,* 29 A.D. 2d 367, 288 N.Y.S. 2d 244 (1st Dept. 1968), holding no abuse of discretion to order father to pay one-half of son's tuition (not to exceed $900 per year), where son had been attending private school for thirteen years.

25 See *Dicker v. Dicker,* 54 Misc. 2d 1089, 283 N.Y.S. 2d 941 (Sup. Ct. Kings County, 1967) (poor school record).

26 See *Kotkin v. Kerner, supra,* note 24.

27 See *Furst v. Furst,* 30 A.D. 2d 955, 294 N.Y.S. 2d 102 (1st Dept. 1968). See in general, R. Douglas Wrightsel, "Comment; College Education as a Legal Necessary" (1965), 18 Vand. L. Rev. 1400, and Monroe L. Inker and Robert F. McGrath, "College Education of Minors," (1966), 6 J. Fam. Law 230. See also *Karminski v. Karminski,* 260 App. Div. 391, 23 N.Y.S. 2d 141 (1st Dept., 1940), holding that father was not subject to paying more than amount stipulated in support order to meet emergency medical expenses of child.

28 See *Grishaver v. Grishaver,* 225 N.Y.S. 2d 924 (Sup. Ct. N.Y. County, 1961).

29 See *Roe v. Doe,* 29 N.Y. 2d 188, 324 N.Y.S. 2d 71, 272 N.E. 2d 576 (Court of Appeals, 1971); aff'ing, 36 A.D. 2d 162, 318 N.Y.S. 2d 973.

30 For example, see *Saterstein v. Saterstein,* 162 N.Y.L.J., July 14, 1969, p. 1, col. 3, where

the Family Court refused to increase a prior $100 a week child support order to $235 a week, as requested by the mother, so that the son who was 17 years old could take judo and guitar lessons, acquire a surf board, and other items he would like to have. The court concluded that the boy already had been "adversely affected by a surfeit of material things." See also *Brandt v. Brandt,* 36 Misc. 2d 901, 233 N.Y.S. 2d 993 (Sup. Ct. N.Y. County, 1962), where the Supreme Court imposed an alimony and child support order on a "Long Island playboy" who came from a wealthy family but had no visible means of support.

31 See *Farah v. Farah,* 196 Misc. 460, 92 N.Y.S. 2d 187 (Sup. Ct., 1949); *Dee v. Dee,* 9 Misc.2d 764, 169 N.Y.S.2d 789 (Dom Rel. Ct. 1957), held that the mother's release of the father's child support duty was void. With regard to power to modify notwithstanding prior agreement or decree, see *Schwartz v. Schwartz,* 48 Misc.2d 859, 265 N.Y.S.2d 820 (Fam. Ct. N.Y. Co., 1965) (modification upwards), and *Goldberg v. Goldberg,* 294 N.Y.S.2d 773 (Fam. Ct. Kings Co., 1968) (modification downwards but father still liable on contract). The leading case illustrating the plenary power to modify child custody on the basis of slight change of circumstances is *Guillermo v. Guillermo,* 43 Misc.2d 763, 252 N.Y.S.2d 171 (Fam. Ct. N.Y. Co. 1964).

32 See *Ferro v. Bologna,* 38 A.D.2d 54, 330 N.Y.S.2d 126, aff'd. 31 N.Y.2d 30, 334 N.Y.S.2d 856, 286 N.Y.2d 249 (1972); *Forman v. Forman,* 17 N.Y.2d 274, 270 N.Y.S.2d 586, 217 N.E. 2d 645 (Court of Appeals, 1966); see also Vol II, Henry H. Foster, Jr. and Doris J. Freed, *Law and the Family: New York (Rochester, 1966)* §28:37, pp. 440-41, Notes 15 and 19 and 1976 Cum. Supp., pp. 262-263.

33 See *Schellenberg v. Mullaney,* 112 App. Div. 384, 98 N.Y.S. 432 (2d Dept. 1906), and 11 U.S.C. §35, the latter providing that liability for alimony or child support is not discharged by bankruptcy proceedings.

34 See *Klarish v. Klarish,* 289 N.Y.S.2d 65 (1st Dept. 1968), and *Hambleton v. Palmer,* 283 N.Y.S.2d 404 (Fam. Ct. Monroe Co., 1967).

35 See *Abraham v. Abraham,* 28 A.D.2d 864, 281 N.Y.S.2d 601, aff'd. 22 N.Y.2d 857, 293 N.Y.S.2d 118, 239 N.E. 2d 743 (1967); *Schalk v. Schalk,* 54 Misc. 2d 439, 282 N.Y.S. 2d 847 (Sup. Ct. Erie County, 1967); and *Goldberg v. Berger,* 31 A.D. 2d 637, 295 N.Y.S. 2d 975 (2d Dept. 1968). *Murdock v. Settembrini,* 21 N.Y. 2d 759, 235 N.E.2d 220 (Court of Appeals, 1968), held it was not error for the Family Court to award child support without conditioning it on visitation rights.

36 Laws 1974, Ch. 859 (eff. immediately) created a new sub-section to CPLR §302(b).

37 See Cal. Civ. Proced. Code, §410.10 (1973); (Court may exercise jurisdiction on any basis not inconsistent with Constitution of state or United States). See also: Thomas J. Yerbich, "Note: In Personam Jurisdiction: New Horizons in California" (1970) 1 Pacific Law J. 671; Fla. Stat. Ann. Code Civ. Pro. §48.193(e) (West Supp. 1975) ("matrimonial domicile" in state at time of commencement of action or defendant's residence in state preceding commencement of action confers personal jurisdiction on court with respect to proceedings for alimony, child support or property division); Idaho Code Ann., §5-514(e) (Supp. 1971) ("maintenance of matrimonial domicile" basis for jurisdiction); Ind. Trial Rule §4.4 (Supp. 1972) (living in "marital relationship" in state confers personal jurisdiction as to all obligations for alimony, child support or property settlement if other party continues to reside in state); III. Rev. Stat. ch. 110, §17(1)(e) (1968) (either "matrimonial domicile" at time cause of action arose or commission in state of any act giving rise to cause of action); Kan. Stat. Ann. §60-308(b)(6) (1964) ("matrimonial domicile" within state gives continuing jurisdiction over matrimonial action if plaintiff remains in state); Nev. Rev. Stat. §14.065(2)(e) (1971) (living in "marital relationship" in state, confers personal jurisdiction as to all obligations arising for alimony, child support or property settlement, if plaintiff continues to reside in state); N. Mex. Stat. Ann. §21-3-16(A)(5) (1964) (living in "marital relationship" in state gives personal jurisdiction in all actions for divorce, separate maintenance and annulment, as to all obligations for alimony, child support or property settlements, if one party continues to reside in state); N.Y. C.P.L.R. §302(b) (where plaintiff resident or domiciliary at time of demand and New York was matrimonial domicile before separation or defendant abandoned plaintiff in New York or obligation to pay support or alimony accrued under laws of New York or

under agreement executed in New York, personal jurisdiction against defendant); Ohio Rev. Code, §4.3(A)(8) (1971) (living in "marital relationship"within state confers personal jurisdiction as to all obligations for alimony, custody, child support or property settlement, if other party continues to reside in state); Okla. Stat. Ann. Civ. Proced. §1701.03(a)(7) (Supp. 1970) ("maintaining relation to persons within state") (see *Sanditen v. Sanditen,* 496 P.2d 365 (Okla. 1972); Tenn. Code Civ Proced. §20-235 (Supp. 1974) (personal jurisdiction may be exercised on any basis not inconsistent with constitution of state or United States) see *Sowell v. Sowell,* 493 S.W.2d 86 (Tenn. 1973); Texas Family Code §3.26 permits a Texas court to extend in personam jurisdiction over a respondent in a suit for divorce, annulment, or to declare a marriage void, although respondent is not a domiciliary or a resident of Texas (a) If the petitioner is a resident or a domiciliary of Texas at the commencement of suit and (1) Texas is the last state in which marital cohabitation occurred and suit is commenced within two years after the date on which cohabitation ended; or (2) there is any basis consistent with the federal and state Constitutions for the exercise of jurisdiction. A court acquiring personal jurisdiction under §3.26 also acquires jurisdiction in a suit affecting the parent-child relation if §11.051 of the Family Code applies, the latter section being applicable if the child was conceived in Texas, or where the child is in Texas because the person over whom personal jurisdiction is sought "caused or permitted the child to be present in Texas." Such personal jurisdiction in matters involving custody or illegitimacy also extends to persons who have actually resided with the child in Texas and subsequently have abandoned the child in Texas and have left that state; Utah Code Ann. §78-27-24(6) (Supp. 1971) ("maintaining matrimonial domicile" in state at time claim arose or committing act in state giving rise to claim, confers personal jurisdiction with respect to actions for divorce or separate maintenance); Wis. Stat. Ann. §247.057, §247.055 (1m) (1967) ("marital relationship" within state for six months out of past six years); See also Foster and Freed, "Thumbs Up for the Long Arm Amendment," N.Y.L.J., May 26, 1972, p. 6, cols. 1-2, and *Hines v. Clendenning,* 465 P.2d 460 (Supreme Court of Okla. 1970).

38 *Ibid.*

39 Dom. Rel. Law §240 provides in part: "Such direction (for child support) may make provision for the education and maintenance of such child out of the property of either or both of its parents".

40 Fam. Ct. Act §414 (dealing with the mother's child support obligation) provides in part: "The court may apportion the costs of the support of the child between the parents according to their respective means and responsibilities".

41 For example, see *O'Brien v. Springer,* 107 N.Y.S. 2d 631 (Sup. Ct., Herkimer Co., 1951).

42 For example, see *Friou v. Gentes,* 11 A.D. 2d 124, 204 N.Y.S. 2d 836 (2d Dept., 1960); *Buckler v. Wolman,* 190 Misc. 916, 75 N.Y.S. 2d 637 (Sup. Ct. Kings Co., 1947), and K.J. Roberts, "Annotation: Support provisions of judicial decree or order as limit of father's liability for expenses of child" 7 ALR 2d 491 (1949).

43 One of the exceptions to the minor's privilege of disaffirmance is his liability for "necessaries." See Note, "Statutory Problems in the Law of Minors' Contracts" (1948) 48 Col. L. Rev. 272.

44 *Rosenblatt v. Birnbaum,* 16 N.Y. 2d 212, 264 N.Y.S. 2d 521 (Court of Appeals, 1965).

45 Arizona, Colorado, Kentucky, Nebraska, Oregon and Washington. In addition California, Delaware, Florida, Iowa, Michigan, Minnesota, Missouri, and the Virgin Islands have similar legislation.

46 Including such states as Alaska, Connecticut, Hawaii, Idaho, Indiana, Maine, Mississippi, Missouri, Montana, New Hampshire, North Dakota, and Texas.

47 For a discussion of the high incidence of violation of support or alimony orders, see Foster and Freed, *Law and the Family* — New York, Introduction to Vol. II (1967). It should also be noted that a husband or father in military service may be granted a stay of execution under the Soldiers' and Sailors' Relief Act, 54 Stat. 1181, 50 U.S.C. App. §523. Cases are collected in Annot., 54 A.L.R. 2d 390, 401 (1957).

48 See Henry H. Foster, Jr., Doris J. Freed and Millard L. Midonick, "Child Support: The Quick and the Dead" (1975) 26 Syracuse L. Rev. 1157, at 1166 *et seq.*

49 *Ibid.*

50 *Ibid.*
51 For a comprehensive discussion of URESA see W.J. Brockelbank and F. Infausto, *Interstate Enforcement of Family Support* (2d ed., Indianapolis, 1971). See Dom Rel. Law §30 *et seq.* and *Landes v. Landes,* 1 N.Y. 2d 358, 153 N.Y.S. 2d 14, 135 N.E. 2d 562 (Court of Appeals, 1956), which discusses the interrelationship between URESA and USDA, finding them compatible.
52 See *Harmon v. Harmon,* 324 P. 2d 901 (Calif. App. 1958), cert. den., 366 U.S. 270 (1960); *Ivey v. Ayers,* 301 S.W. 2d 790 (Supreme Court of Mo. 1957).
53 See Dom. Rel. Law §32. It should be noted that under both URESA and USDA there is no interstate enforcement of another state's criminal conviction for non-support.
54 The amended version of URESA classifying ex-wives awarded alimony as "dependents" has been enacted in some eighteen states.
55 Social Services Amendment of 1974, Pub. L. No. 93-647, section 2, 88 Stat. 2337, amending 42 USC sections 301 *et seq.* (1935), by adding a new provision entitled "Title XX — Grants to States for Services" to the Social Security Act, 42 USCA, section 1397 (Supp. Feb. 1975).
56 The report of the Senate Committee on Finance on the new amendment in Table 5 lists several states according to the amount of child support collected on behalf of welfare recipients in 1973. New York is reported as having collected $11,978,000 as compared with $53,000,000 by California, $12,651,000 by Illinois, $17,016,000 by Massachusetts, $28,100,000 in Michigan, and $15,000,000 in Pennsylvania. The report concludes that most states have not "implemented in a meaningful way" provisions of the existing law relative to the enforcement of child support. See U.S. Code Congressional and Administrative News, No. 15, Jan. 30, 1975 at 9209.
57 The report is contained in Winston and Forsher, "Nonsupport of Legitimate Children by Affluent Fathers as a Cause of Poverty and Welfare Dependence," Dec. 1971 (Rand Corporation Study) and excerpts appear in U.S. Code Congressional and Administrative News, No. 15, Jan. 20, 1975 at 9207-9208. The report also says that the nonsupporting fathers did not have the excuse of supporting many other children. Ninety-two percent had a total of three or fewer children. Only 13% were married to other women, with another 1% divorced or separated from another or of unknown marital status. The non-welfare fathers were more likely to be still married to the AFDC mother. Where court orders had been entered, the typical order was for $50 a month, and in a third of the non-welfare cases the order called for $50 or less.
58 *Ibid.* at 9207.
59 For an important study, see Jacobus tenBroek, "California's Dual System of Family Law: Its Origin, Development and Present Status," (Part I) (1964) 16 Stanf. L. Rev. 257, (Part II) (1964) Stanford Law Review 900 and (Part III) (1965) Stanf. L. Rev. 614. See also David R. Mandelker, "Family Responsibility Under the American Poor Laws: I" (1956) 54 Mich. L. Rev. 497.
60 An analysis of the new law may also be found in Foster, Freed and Midonick, *op. cit. supra,* note 48.
61 It has been reported that since this provision became effective in January 1975, nearly 6,500 garnishments for child support have been received by the U.S. Air Force, Army and Navy. The average amount owed was $2,000, although judgments ranged from $100 to record amounts of $62,000 in the Air Force, $47,000 in the Army, and $37,000 in the Navy. Child Enforcement Report, April/May 1976.
62 Under the new law (42 U.S.C.A. §653(f) (Supp. Feb. 1975), a state's obligations include full cooperation with state courts and law enforcement agencies and in interstate enforcement. Federal standards are established and the state must maintain an effective program. A state's poor record in collecting child support will be revealed to H.E.W. or by the H.E.W. audit. An unsatisfactory record, after January 1, 1977, may lead to a reduction of federal matching funds for social services (now normally 75%) for the following year (42 U.S.C.A. §603(h)). This section requires a 5% reduction in the amount payable to a state under the program if it is found by the H.E.W. audit not to have complied with the act. The states are given a grace period to comply with the new requirements until 1977. In this connection, the following appeared in the Federal Register: *Child support.* Office of Child

Support Enforcement published a regulation to provide a one year continuation of Federal financial participation (FFP) at the 75% rate for child support services provided by State IV-D Agencies to individuals who are not eligible for AFDC assistance, p. 43150, 9/30. Office of Child Support Enforcement proposed rules relating to the requirement for an annual audit of each State's child support program and a possible penalty of five% of a State's title IV-A reimbursement. Comments by 11/1/76, p. 43414, 10/1. Social and Rehabilitation Service proposed rules to alert States to the statutorily required penalty to be imposed for failure to have an effective child support enforcement program. Comments by 11/1/76, p. 43420, 10/1.

63 47 U.S.C.A. 602(a) (1974).
64 See *op. cit. supra* note 56.
65 42 U.S.C.A. §1397a (Supp. Feb. 1975).
66 See Henry H. Foster Jr., "Dependent Children and the Law" (1957) 18 U. Pitt. L. Rev. 579, 618.
67 Traditional support laws place a primary duty of child support on the father and only a secondary duty on the mother, regardless of her income or means. Recent divorce reform legislation, however, makes the duty of child support a mutual obligation of both parents according to their respective means. See notes 9-10 *supra* and accompanying text.
68 See tenBroek, *supra* note 59.
69 See *Steinberg v. Steinberg*, 18 N.Y. 2d 492, 223 N.E. 2d 558, 277 N.Y.S. 2d 129 (Court of Appeals, 1965).
70 *McMains v. McMains*, 15 N.Y. 2d 283, 205 N.E. 2d 185, 258 N.Y.S. 2d 93 (Court of Appeals, 1965).
71 See CPLR section 302(b).
72 Long arm jurisdiction for matrimonial or support actions exists in California, Florida, Idaho, Illinois, Indiana, Kansas, Michigan, Nevada, New Mexico, New York, Ohio, Oklahoma, Tennessee, Texas, Utah, and Wisconsin, and perhaps some other states as well. See *supra* note 37. See *Lieb v. Lieb*, N.Y.L.J., July 16, 1976, p. 1, col. 8 affirming 381 N.Y.S.2d 757 (1976).
73 New York has adopted this act. See CPLR title 54. It is also in effect in Arkansas, Illinois, Missouri, Nebraska, Oregon, Washington, Wisconsin and Wyoming. In addition, California, Connecticut, Minnesota and Mississippi have procedures for adopting foreign judgments as their own. Montana has adopted some sections and omitted others of the Uniform Act.
74 For a recent example of how the act works, see *Ehrenzweig v. Ehrenzweig*, N.Y.L.J., April 29, 1976, p. 9, cols. 3-8, p. 10, cols. 1-2 (Kings Co., Heller, J.), where a divorce judgment was obtained by the wife in Connecticut and enforcement was given pursuant to title 54 of CPLR the same as if it were a local judgment. Judgment was entered for arrearages of alimony and child support but the court declined to order wage deduction pursuant to Pers. Prop. Act s.49-b, or to order posting of security pursuant to Dom. Rel. L. s.132.

APPENDIX

Title IV-D, Social Security Act

New title IV-D, Child Support Enforcement, sets up an elaborate system for the enforcement and collection of support and alimony orders.[1] It mandates full federal-state cooperation and a concerted effort to make parents pay their support obligations.[2]

Public Law 93-647 was signed by the President on January 4, 1975, having been passed by Congress on December 20, 1974. As a result of a Conference between the United States Senate and the House of Representatives, agreement was reached on this compromise measure which was then passed by Congress. In general, the Senate version was accepted with minor changes; except that use of Internal Revenue Services for collection of child support was made contingent on non-compliance with a court order and only after notice to a parent of intent to use such services for collection, and a provision was deleted that would have established regional blood-typing laboratories.[3] Portions of the new law became effective at different dates.

As enacted, Title IV-D required that the Secretary of H.E.W. establish an Office of Child Support Enforcement, and this office was established accordingly. Among its responsibilities are the promulgation of standards for effective Child Support Enforcement programs, reviewing the state programs, giving technical assistance to the states, keeping records of program operations and child support expenditures as well as collections. In addition, the Federal Office of Child Support Enforcement was required to develop and maintain a Federal Parent Locator System.[4]

Although the main target of the new law is the enforcement of the child support obligations of errant parents (usually fathers) of recipients of Aid to Families of Dependent Children, so as to reduce welfare expenditures, services are also required in non-welfare cases.[5] For example, the Federal Parent Locator Service[6] and the complementary State Locator Services may be used in non-welfare cases upon written application, and, in some states, payment of a nominal fee. Costs may be recovered from collections at state option. Since perhaps fifty or more percent of support orders are not paid at all, or are not paid on time,[7] the availability of the locator services should become a substantial aid to enforcement and collection, assuming that once found obligors have income or resources.

Each state is required to establish or designate a separate unit to administer the state IV-D program. The IV-D agency may be located within an existing department or may be established as a new state agency.[8] All but the states of Michigan, Montana, South Dakota and Wisconsin located their IV-D agencies in the existing agency responsible for the administration of the state's AFDC program.[9]

It should be noted that Title IV-D provides for 75% federal financial participation in the administrative costs incurred by the states including the costs of law enforcement officials as they relate to approved IV-D plans. The original law also provided 75% reimbursement for cases not involving AFDC recipients until June 30, 1976. P.L. 94-365, signed July 14, 1976, extended that feature for one year.[10]

As previously indicated, one of the services that a state must provide is a locator service to find absent parents. It also must provide effective machinery for the imposition of support obligations and the determination of paternity in the case of children born out of wedlock.[11] A child support unit of the state welfare department will be responsible for such activities and is required to submit to an audit by the Federal Child Support Unit.[12]

The Federal Parent Locator Service has been given the awesome authority of file search. It will have access to all federal records and files, except confidential census data, unless national security would be impaired.[13] Such access includes that to social security records and Internal Revenue Service files. In addition, under requirements of Title IV-A, applicants for assistance will have to give their social security numbers,[14] which may provide clues for subsequent investigations. This federal dragnet should eventually catch up with all but the most skilful dodgers.

In addition, there are two other significant enforcement provisions. An obligee or potential obligee applying for assistance, must assign her claim to child support to the state which in turn will seek enforcement against the obligor for payments.[15] Secondly, in interstate cases, if another state fails to undertake to enforce a child support order on behalf of the requesting state within a reasonable time, the requesting state may ask the Federal Child Enforcement Office to certify the case for use of the Federal Courts. If the application meets certain procedural requirements and it is determined that the only effective method of enforcing the order is by use of the Federal Courts, the case will be certified and the United States District Court will have jurisdiction over the case.[16]

An unsuccessful state may request that a delinquent child support obligation assigned to it, be collected by the collection service of the Internal Revenue Service.[17] If the Child Enforcement Office certifies the amount of child support owed to the Secretary of the Treasury for collection, the Federal Tax Collection Service will try to collect such amount and will be entitled to reimbursement from the state for the cost of the collection.[18] The use of the Federal Tax Collection Service is authorized only when payments are delinquent.[19]

Assignment to the state of child support obligations should provide an added incentive for collection and the availability of I.R.S. will provide more effective machinery for enforcement. In addition, as explained above, Federal District Courts at times may be utilized, and this should prove effective.[20]

Still another highly significant feature is the elimination of the immunity of federal employees to garnishment.[21] Federal employees and members of the armed services as of January 1, 1975 became subject to garnishment for alimony and child support payments and any monies due from or payable by the United States are subject to attachment. Thus, an employee of any federal agency or corporation, as well as members of the armed services, are subject to wage attachment for past due support or alimony, and in addition to salary, income from any other federal source, such as pension income, may be reached. Removal of the federal immunity will facilitate the collection of support or alimony in the District of

Columbia, in states having large military installations, and in those having significant numbers of federal employees where there is no countervailing state law.

In order to assure maximum cooperation by welfare recipients and state welfare officials, an elaborate system of incentives, and penalties is created by the new amendment. Techniques of both the carrot and the stick are used. Between August 1, 1975 and September 30, 1976, the welfare mother received a bonus in the form of a payment of forty percent of the first $50 a month in support obligations collected from the father so that such amount is disregarded for determining the amount of assistance payable to the family.[22] If she refuses to cooperate, she may be denied assistance, although her children on AFDC are not penalized.[23] If the amount collected is more than that needed to offset the current month's AFDC payment, the additional amount up to the sum specified in a court's support order, goes to the family.[24]

Comparable techniques are applied to the states in order to assure effective child support collection and enforcement. If a collection is made, the collecting and enforcing political subdivision receives a bonus of twenty-five percent for the first twelve months of collection, and a bonus of ten percent on subsequent collections after the incentive payment is made to the recipient.[25] This incentive payment is also made in inter-state cases to the responding state. Thus, a local agency which actually carries out location and collection functions is rewarded and since there may have been an assignment of the obligee's claim to the state, it is assured of payment of the bonus.

If a state has a poor record on collecting child support, such will be revealed in its financial reporting to the Office of Child Support Enforcement or by its audit. An unsatisfactory record, after January 1, 1977, may lead to a reduction by five percent of federal matching funds for Title IV-A (mostly the AFDC) for each unsatisfactory federal fiscal year.[26]

It has been reported that during the past year a series of training sessions, joint meetings of department staff and other means have succeeded in overcoming to a large degree difficulties experienced by the states at the outset of the program, especially in the areas of staffing and financing.

In announcing the results of the first year, the Director, OCSE, said that the nation wide Federal-State Child Support Enforcement Program got off to an extremely successful start. Although originally it had been anticipated that the program would do well to break even, its first year collections far exceeded these expectations. As of October 23, 1976, more than two hundred and eighty million dollars in child support was collected by the states for the eleven months ending June 30, 1976, with total expenditures for the program amounting to about one hundred and thirty four million dollars in the fiscal year 1976.[28] States estimate that in the fiscal year 1977, child support collections will be in excess of four hundred million dollars, whereas the cost of running the program will decrease markedly in future years in proportion to collections.[29]

During the fourth quarter of 1976 (April 1 to June 30), which is the most recent period for which data are available, the states reporting the heaviest collections were the ten states of Michigan, Ohio, New Jersey, Pennsylvania, Massachusetts, Washington, California, Minnesota, Maryland and Illinois, which had an annual collection rate of close to two hundred million dollars.[30]

Considering the fact that prior to the beginning of the program, many states had made little or no effort to collect child support on behalf of AFDC (the country's major cash assistance welfare program), this progress demonstrates a remarkable achievement.

The Director further pointed out in his report that a great many parents, the majority of whom are welfare mothers, have been attempting to raise their children without any financial aid from the absent parent. This has become an increasingly grave problem existing in about 2.8 million families, recipients of AFDC. It has been estimated that half of the absent parents are financially able to support their children and that the cost in welfare payments to the families of delinquent parents has been over one billion dollars a year.[31]

"More and more the IV-D program has resulted in a social benefit to the child, the absent parent and the taxpaying public. Shifting responsibility to those who are legally liable for child support and [who are financially able to pay] . . . , reduces the actual number of families needing to be on AFDC, but more importantly, it can have a positive effect on the absent parent and the child. [The . . .] staff have been able to report examples where the assumption of child support responsibilities has led to the absent parent resuming contact with the family and taking a greater interest in other aspects of the child's life."[32]

---

1 See OCSE Annual Report to the Congress, June 30, 1976.
2 U.S. Public Law 93-647, 93rd Congress, H.R. 17045, contains the "Social Services Amendments of 1974", and inserts a new Title IV-D entitled "Child Support Programs for Services" at the end of the Social Security Act. §2001 (42 USC 11397).
3 See H.R. Rep. No. 1643, 93d Cong., 2d Sess. 29-30 (1974).
4 §453(a) (42 USC 653).
5 §454(6) (42 USC 602) requires that a state plan for child support must provide for use of its services in non-welfare cases upon payment of an "application fee" of a reasonable amount, as determined under the regulations of the Secretary.
6 §453 (42 USC 653) provides for the establishment of a "Parent Locator Service" which shall be used to obtain and transmit to "any authorized person" information as to the whereabouts of any absent parent. The definition of "authorized person" includes a state

court authorized to issue child support orders and the parent, guardian, or attorney of a child in a non-welfare case.

7 See Foster-Freed, *Law and the Family — New York,* Introduction to Vol. II (1967).

8 §454 (42 USC 654).

9 See Washington Report, American Public Welfare Assn., Vol. 11, No. 8, p. 7, Sept. 1976.

10 *Ibid,* p. 6.

11 See §454(4)(A) (42 USC 602).

12 See §452(a) (42 USC 652).

13 See §453 (42 USC 653). Sub-section (b) provides in part that "No information shall be disclosed to any person if the disclosure of such information would contravene the national policy or security interests of the United States or the confidentiality of census data."

14 See amendments to Part A of Title IV (42 USC 602), which makes it a condition to eligibility that "each applicant for or recipient of aid shall furnish to the State agency his social security account number (or numbers, if he has more than one such number), and (b) that such State agency shall utilize such account numbers, in addition to other means of identification it may determine to employ..."

15 See §402(a)(26) (42 USC 602). As a condition of eligibility for aid, each applicant or recipient will be required "(A) to assign the State any rights to support from any other person such applicant may have (i) in his own behalf or in behalf of any other family member for whom the applicant is applying for or receiving aid, and (ii) which have accrued at the time the assignment is executed."

16 §452(a) (42 USC 652).

17 Subchapter A of Chap. 64 of the Internal Revenue Code of 1954 (relating to collection of taxes) as amended by new §6305 (26 USC 6305) provides that upon certification from HEW under §452(b) of the Social Security Act, IRS will collect child support in the same manner as it collects tax obligations. The Secretary of HEW may so certify when he has received a request from a state for aid in the collection of arrears due under a court's child support order, and the state shows that despite "diligent and reasonable efforts" it has been unable to collect and agrees to reimburse the United States for any costs involved in making the collection. HEW, after consultation with the Secretary of the Treasury, is to make regulations concerning the limitations and frequency of requests for the use of IRS in child support collections.

18 *Ibid.*

19 §452(b) (42 USC 652).

20 See §460 (42 USC 660). The action to collect child support in federal court "may be brought in any judicial district in which the claim arose, the plaintiff resides, or the defendant resides."

21 §459 (42 USC 659) which became effective January 1, 1975, and provides that "Notwithstanding any other provision of law... moneys (the entitlement to which is based upon remuneration from employment) due from, or payable by, the United States (including any agency or instrumentality thereof and any wholly owned Federal corporation) to any individual, including members of the armed services, shall be subject, in like manner and to the same extent as if the United States were a private person, to legal process brought for the enforcement, against such individual of his legal obligations to provide child support or make alimony payments."

22 See §457(a) (42 USC 657).

23 See §406(f) (42 USC 606).

24 §457(a)(3) (42 USC 657). See also §457(c) which provides that a cooperative family even though assistance stops may continue to receive support payments collected under the act from the obligor for a period not to exceed three months after assistance terminated. At the end of such three month period, upon request the state may continue to collect support payments from the absent parent and after deducting costs of collection pay the amount so collected to the family.

25 See §458(a). When more than one jurisdiction is involved in the enforcement and collection of child support, incentive payments are allocated between them.

26 See §403(h) (42 USC 602) which requires a five percent reduction in the amount payable to

a state under the program if it is found by HEW audit not to have complied with the Act. However, the penalty may not be incurred until 1977 since states are given a grace period until then to comply with the new requirements.

27 *Washington Report, American Public Welfare Association,* Vol. 11, No. 8, p. 7, Sept., 1976.

28 *H.E.W. New News,* U.S. Dept. of Health, Education and Welfare, p. 1, October 23, 1976. 1976.

29 *Ibid.*

30 *Id.,* at p. 2.

31 *Id.,* at p. 2.

32 *Washington Report, American Public Welfare Association,* Vol. 11, No. 8, p. 8, Sept., 1976.

"Sufficient Maintenance" In The Finnish Law Of Support

Professor Aulis Aarnio*

FINNISH LEGISLATION ON THE FAMILY

Finnish society changed very much after the Second World War. The change began later in Finland than in some other industrialized countries of Western Europe, but the pace of change has been very rapid. Within a short time, legislation had to be adapted to such problems as industrialization, urbanization, and population growth. Family law reform was needed, because, for example, changes in the age structure, the grouping of the population, and housing problems affected the durability of marriage. An increased divorce rate not only influenced marriage law proper but constituted a problem for the whole of the legislation relating to the family.

Most of the current family law legislation in Finland dates back to the 1920's or to an earlier period, that is, to a period when the structure of Finnish society was completely different from what it is now. The Marriage Act was enacted in 1929 and it predecessor, the Spouses' Property Relations Act, which is still partly in force, in 1889. The Illegitimate Children Act, 1922, was in force until 1st October 1976. The Adopted Children Act, 1925 and the Guardianship Act, 1898, are both in force although their provisions are in many respects behind the times. These statutes no longer meet the requirements of our time. Finnish family law in the 1970's has been characterized by intensive law reform. A proposal for amending the Marriage Act has been finished (part I in 1972 and part II in 1976) as have proposals for amending the Guardianship Act and the provisions connected with it (in 1972 and 1974) and a proposal for regulating the legal status of the child (1974). So far only the last mentioned proposal has been enacted: the Establishment of Paternity Act, the Child Maintenance Act, and the statutes connected with them came into force on October 1st, 1976. Legislative reform concerning adoption is being prepared, and a rather comprehensive committee report on reforming the legislation relating to succession and the law of wills (1975) has been

---

* Professor Aulis Aarnio is a Professor at the University of Helsinki.

completed. The report contains, among other things, recommendations to consolidate the position of the surviving spouse.

This essay is limited to some of the problems connected with the 1976 Child Maintenance Act (referred to as CMA). The focus is on the criteria used by the courts to assess the amount of maintenance. This question is interesting because the Child Maintenance Act attempts to give more precise instructions than before on how the amount of maintenance should be assessed, and on how liability for maintenance might be divided between the parents. This approach raises the question of the function of legislation concerning maintenance orders: is it possible to direct the assessment of maintenance by means of precise legal rules?

Finnish legislation and court practice does not offer a precise answer to these questions. But a transitional period, such as the one that Finnish law on children's maintenance is passing through, offers some insight on the question of what stand to take on open attributes in the legislation like "necessary", "fair" or "sufficient".

PREVIOUS LEGISLATION ON CHILDREN'S MAINTENANCE

Until recently the law on children's maintenance was dispersed over several statutes, and the provisions on maintenance depended on the child's parentage. Children were divided into two categories: (a) children born in wedlock (and adopted children) and (b) children born out of wedlock. In the former case the husband was presumed to be the father unless this presumption was rebutted in specific legitimacy proceedings. Children belonging to the second category had no legal father. The law did not give the illegitimate child the means to establish his parental origin in a positive way.

Up till now, inequality between the two categories of children has been characteristic of Finnish legislation. To some extent this inequality is also found in the provisions on maintenance of a child and in those defining the maintenance duties of the parents.

Under the Marriage Act of 1929 either spouse must participate, according to his or her ability, in maintaining the family by working at home, by contributing money, or in some other way. What is needed for the education of the children, according to the family's standard of living is part of the cost of maintenance. These general provisions have practically no importance so long as the marriage continues. If during the marriage a spouse makes a claim for enforcement of the maintenance obligation this indicates that the relationship between the spouses is badly ruptured. There is no statutory provision stating a maximum age for child maintenance.

However, the courts have adopted a rule that a child can receive maintenance until he attains majority. In Finland the age of majority has recently been lowered to 18 years.

Under the former Illegitimate Children Act (ICA) the child was entitled to receive maintenance from the mother and from the putative father. This shows a principal characteristic of previous Finnish law: an illegitimate child's paternal origin could not be established; the putative father could only be ordered to maintain the child. Maintenance was assessed mainly according to the mother's standard of living, but when the putative father's standard of living was higher, the court could take this into account when making its decision. Under the ICA the obligation to pay maintenance ceased when the child became seventeen years old, unless it was extended beyond this limit for some special reason, for example, because of the child's chronic illness or disability. The liability for maintenance had to be divided between the mother and the putative father according to their respective ability to pay.

In general, then, the legitimate child has been in a better position than the illegitimate child, as far as the amount of maintenance is concerned. A legitimate child's maintenance has been assessed according to the standard of living of the family, which means in practice that the amount of maintenance has generally been related to the husband's financial position. On the other hand, the maintenance granted to the illegitimate child was mainly related to the mother's standard of living. Statistics show that illegitimate children have been granted less maintenance than legitimate children in divorce proceedings. There was also a noticeable difference in duration between the two kinds of maintenance obligation: the illegitimate child's right to receive maintenance ceased earlier than the legitimate child's.

THE CHILD MAINTENANCE ACT, 1975

The law reform concerning the child's status has aimed at putting an end to inequality. This required amendment of the provisions on the establishment of paternity, because of the different treatment applied to different categories of children. Consequently, under the Child Maintenance Act a specific action aimed at establishing the defendant's obligation to pay maintenance for an illegitimate child can no longer be taken. All legal consequences, maintenance included, are linked with the establishment of paternity. The Act provides two ways in which paternity can be established: by a man making an admission of paternity in the way the Act has laid down; or by paternity proceedings. In both cases the legal consequences are the same. This implies that the man's duty to contribute to the illegitimate child's maintenance is based on the kinship between the child and the man and not — as was the case up till now — on presumed sexual intercourse between the man and the child's mother. By adopting these principles Finnish legislation has taken the same stand as the other Scandinavian countries.

The purpose of the new statute is to give the child sufficient and continuous maintenance irrespective of his parentage. Consequently, the assessment of the amount of maintenance is based on the child's needs.

Although the assessment of maintenance is based on the child's needs, the parents' ability to pay maintenance cannot be disregarded. These two factors, however, may have opposite effects. If the court assesses maintenance, taking into account the parents' ability to pay, the maintenance may be too small to meet the child's needs. This has been provided for in the legislative drafts, which start from the principle that society has to provide sufficient maintenance for the child in all cases where the obligation of maintenance based on civil law does not suffice to cover the child's needs. This is the aim of the recent Finnish legislation, *viz.* the Child Maintenance Guarantee Bill, which was enacted in 1977. Under the Bill a child less than eighteen years old has the right to obtain support from society if his parents are living separately. Maintenance support is paid on the claim of the person taking care of the child when the person ordered to maintain the child has failed to pay or when his means are such that the maintenance he has been ordered to pay is smaller than the required amount. In the latter case, support consists of the difference between full support and the amount of maintenance adjudged by the court. The illegitimate child is also entitled to support when it has not been possible to determine the father.

In 1977 the amount of support is 150 marks per child per month. Each year this amount is adapted to the changes in the cost of living. When support has been granted because the person liable to pay maintenance has failed to pay, the maintenance support paid is generally reclaimed from him. In other cases the expenses caused by support are paid by the state.

These observations are important from the point of view of principle: they show us that the efficiency of the civil law maintenance system depends on factors outside civil law, namely on financial resources. Although the legislator's aim is to secure sufficient maintenance for the child, this cannot be achieved if the parents liable for maintenance are not able to fulfil the obligation, and if society cannot, for economic reasons, fully discharge its share of responsibility. Information is needed on prevailing social conditions before one can determine the meaning of concepts like "necessary", "sufficient" or "the parents' ability to pay". The private and public systems together indicate how efficiently a given society actually takes care of the child's interests. The civil law maintenance system has only a relative significance.

STATEMENT OF THE PROBLEM

When the court assesses the maintenance to be paid by the non-custodial parent, then according both to the previous Illegitimate Children Act and to the new Child Maintenance Act, two problems should be addressed: (a) finding the total amount of maintenance the child needs and (b) determining the parties' liability for paying maintenance. These problems will be referred to by using the terms "amount of maintenance" and "dividing the liability for paying maintenance". If the "amount of maintenance" is denoted by M, and "the way in which the liability for paying it is divided" by K, we obtain the following formula:

$$S = f(M,K).$$

This means that the assessment of the maintenance S to be paid by one of the parties — usually the man — is a "function" of two factors, the amount of maintenance and the way to divide the liability for paying it.

It is therefore essential to know which criteria the court uses when solving the problems of the amount of maintenance and of the division of liability. Both the ICA and the CMA contain a list of criteria; the lists are similar as to their structure, but the legislator has attempted to define more precisely than before some of the criteria included in the CMA. Criteria used in the Illegitimate Children Act to assess the amount of maintenance are:

1. The maintenance should suffice to cover the child's needs: indicated by the letter p.

2. The maintenance has to be assessed according to the mother's standard of living (s_m).

3. The putative father's standard of living (s_f) has to be taken into account if it is higher than the standard of living of the mother.

The criterion used in the I.C.A. to divide the liability for paying maintenance is that the maintenance has to be related to the payer's ability (q) to support.

Under the new Child Maintenance Act, the following criteria are used to assess the amount of maintenance:

1. The amount of maintenance should be sufficient, and maintenance should contain provision for the child's material and intellectual needs as well as for the care and education the child needs.

2. When assessing maintenance, the court should take into account the child's ability to maintain himself.

3. The court should also consider other factors diminishing the parents' liability for paying maintenance.

The criterion used under the CMA is that the amount of maintenance should be in proportion to the parents' ability to pay maintenance. When evaluating this ability the court should take into consideration, among other things, the parties' age, ability to work, and wealth.

Both lists of criteria give the impression that the assessment of the amount of maintenance should be based on comprehensive rules. But is this what happens in practice? Let us first examine the situation under the previous Act. The Act stated clearly that in each particular case the court had to establish separately the contents of the different criteria and put these criteria into an order of relative importance. Under the Act the court had to assess the amount of maintenance (M) by using three criteria, the child's need (p), the mother's standard of living (s_m) and the putative father's standard of living (s_f). The division of liability again depended on the parties' ability to pay (q). Consequently, the formula mentioned above takes the form:

$$S = f (p, s_m, s_f, q)$$

We may now specify as follows the questions we used as a starting point:

Do the Finnish courts act as they should according to the law, and will some fundamental change take place in the decision-making of the courts because the list of criteria in the CMA has been formulated more precisely?

The answer to the former question reveals something of how the courts have "observed the law" up till now in cases such as maintenance proceedings. The answer to the latter question again sheds light on the general meaning of the list of criteria in the Child Maintenance Act. More generally, it reveals to what extent it is possible, in the field of maintenance, to create law by statutory means and to what extent the courts as well necessarily create law in a "codified" system.

THE ICA IN PRACTICE

From 1969 onward a research team working under my supervision at the University of Helsinki — partly financed by the Finnish Academy — has been investigating the juridical and social position of families supported by only one parent. The problems related to maintenance now being examined are an important part of the investigation, during which the assessment of maintenance granted (a) to children in divorce proceedings, and (b) to illegitimate children, was investigated by empirical methods. The investigation was mainly based on the records of certain courts. The Finnish court organization consists of three levels. At the base of the hierarchy are the rural District Courts and the urban Town Courts. The decisions of these local courts may be appealed to the Courts of

Appeal, and there are four Courts of Appeal, one of which is in Helsinki. Further appeal lies to the Supreme Court. However, decisions concerning maintenance have been in a special position, and no appeal to the Supreme Court has been possible.

The first phase of the research focused on the assessment of maintenance to illegitimate children. The main part of it was finished in 1970, but everything indicates that the research shows the same trend in the subsequent practice of the courts in maintenance proceedings. The investigation was limited to the practice of the Court of Appeal of Helsinki from 1963 to 1967. The practice of the Town Court of Helsinki from 1967 to 1969 was also examined to obtain a comparison. This research radically changed our initial conception of the problem, which had been based on knowledge of the text of the Act and other juridical material. First, the Court of Appeal very rarely altered the amount of maintenance assessed by a local court, and when it did so the alteration was only a small one. We also found that only about ten per cent of the decisions were appealed. Therefore it seemed interesting to examine the amounts of maintenance assessed by the local courts. This examination also produced a suprise: in 110 cases out of 185 the Town Court of Helsinki, to which we had limited our examination, assessed the amount of maintenance according to the plaintiff's, *i.e.* the mother's, claim. In one third of the cases the amount was assessed at 100 Finnish marks and in almost as many cases at 80 Finnish marks. The amount was very rarely assessed at 70 or 110 marks. The general conclusion was that the assessment of maintenance had become standardized. This research shows that the court's deliberation of the amount of maintenance is not as comprehensive as one would assume from a mere examination of the Act. The criteria given in the Act are not used in the way they are meant to be used; rather the court applies a relatively simple "rule of thumb" to assess the amount.

It is important to take into account a Finnish rule of procedure under which the court cannot grant the plaintiff more than what is claimed. Consequently, the plaintiff's claim is a decisive factor in maintenance proceedings. Therefore we tried in our investigation to elucidate the process by which the plaintiff formulates the claim. The Children's Officer, under the ICA, apparently played a central part. According to Part 3 of the ICA each illegitimate child had an official custodian whose salary is paid by the municipality. This official was entitled to act — without any special commission — as the trustee of every illegitimate child living permanently in the municipality, which means, among other things, that the Children's Officer acted as the mother's counsel in the maintenance proceedings. When the ICA was in force, the Children's Officers adopted some rules, based on experience, indicating the amount of maintenance it was realistic to claim. The claim was specified in such a way that there was good reason to believe that the defendant would actually pay the amount the court would order him to pay. Indeed, the Children's Officers knew from experience that an excessive amount of maintenance leads to neglect of payment and, consequently, the total amount of maintenance actually paid remains smaller than what it might have been if the claim had been realistic. And because the court cannot grant the child a larger amount of maintenance than has been claimed on his or her behalf, it seemed that the Children's Officer's preliminary decision had a significant influence on the decision of the court.

But this does not exhaustively explain why the assessment of maintenance became standardized nor why the amounts of maintenance granted were statistically on a lower level than the amounts of maintenance granted to legitimate children in divorce proceedings. However, our investigation yielded some interesting additional results: when we compared the amounts of maintenance granted by the court with the mother's income, we noticed that the amounts of maintenance varied directly according to the variation of this income. The larger the income the mother had, the larger the amount of maintenance was on the average. On the other hand, we observed that the average income level and social position of the mothers of the illegitimate children was relatively low. These factors are apparently significant if we want to find a complete explanation of the problem. Indeed, the courts have rather strictly observed the rule requiring them to assess the maintenance to be paid to the illegitimate child according to the mother's standard of living, and because this standard of living is generally rather modest, the limits within which most of the amounts of maintenance vary are close.

When we compared the amounts of maintenance with the putative father's income the result was entirely different. The larger the income the man had, the smaller the percentage of his income the maintenance constituted. For example, when the man's income ranged from 1700 to 3400 marks (according to the price level prevailing at the end of the 1960's) the maintenance constituted only 6% of his income, whereas in the income class ranging from 400 to 600 marks the proportional share was 16% of the total income. This is quite plausible when we think of the standardization of the assessment of maintenance: the proportion should vary in precisely this way when we compare a relatively constant sum (maintenance) with a varying sum (income). The concept of "the putative father's standard of living" has not been relevant to the assessment of maintenance. This interpretation is corroborated by the fact that, according to our investigation, the mothers of the illegitimate children generally belonged to lower economic levels than the men. Moreover, the men's position is clearly demonstrated by the fact that the putative fathers were often quite "well-off".

Finally, we think of what a Finnish child normally consumes, and try to find a standard roughly indicting how much money is required on the average to cover his or her needs. Even when we tally the amount of maintenance granted and the mother's contribution, the sum obtained covers only a part of the child's needs.

Consequently, we use the previous symbols to formulate the new function

$$S = f(s_m)$$

This function, which can be empirically tested, shows that the criteria laid down by the Act have not been adopted in practice. In practice the deliberations on which decision-making has been based have been rather stereotyped.

EVALUATION OF THE NEW PROVISIONS CONCERNING MAINTENANCE

So far as knowledge of the present may be used to predict the future, one should adopt a reserved attitude when evaluating the significance of the new Child Maintenance Act. However, the criteria on which decisions have to be based are more precise than in the old Act and the number of criteria has been increased.

The criteria referring to the child's needs in the ICA were not observed in practice. In the new Child Maintenance Act these criteria have been replaced by others which I shall call the criteria referring to "sufficiency" because according to the CMA the child is entitled to sufficient maintenance. In principle, the way the expression has been changed is significant and important. However, when we consider the matter from the point of view of the judge who has to give a decision in maintenance proceedings, the significance of the change seems less clear. Indeed, "sufficiency" does not in itself give any directions on how the amount of maintenance should be assessed. The legislative drafts do not indicate how the term "sufficient" should be understood.

Consideration of so-called consumption investigations may offer a solution. These investigations indicate how much money is required — according to the prevailing cost level — to provide, for example, for the child's food, clothes, and lodging. In this way the term "sufficiency" becomes measurable, an amount of money which shows the objectively defined average need. But is this what the Act means by the expression "sufficient amount"? Further, is it possible to measure the sufficiency of maintenance by means of consumption investigations, when we know how intricate standard of living indicators are? Neither the Act nor its legislative drafts answer these questions. At the most "sufficiency" in the Finnish system might be an argument serving to justify a decision already made.

In the new Child Maintenance Act the list of criteria no longer contains reference to the mother's or, correspondingly, to the father's standard of living. Because we know that earlier the amount of maintenance depended rather directly on the mother's standard of living, it seems proper to replace the expression "necessary maintenance according to the parents' standard of living" by the expression "sufficient maintenance". If it is impossible in practice to give an unambiguous meaning to "sufficient maintenance" and if the correlation with the mother's standard of living is eliminated, how then should we determine the amount of maintenance? As far as the division of liability is concerned, the Act emphasizes the parent's "ability to maintain", which it specifies in different ways; when evaluating ability the court should take into account among other things, the parent's age, ability to work, opportunities for work, and wealth. Of these factors, ability to work and opportunity to work for wages are concepts which depend on interpretation and require specific consideration in individual cases. Criteria of this kind can provide only general directives. The Act does not indicate what significance the court should attach to the age factor when making its decision. Consequently, it seems that the only unambiguous factor in the evaluation of the parent's ability to pay maintenance is constituted by his wealth, that is his income and property.

Let us follow this line of thought a little further. If the assessment of maintenance is linked more closely than before with the father's resources, it seems possible that the practice of the courts concerning maintenance will be altered. Indeed, according to our investigation, the men liable for paying maintenance belonged on the average to higher economic levels than the mothers. Thus, if the concept "the mother's standard of living" is replaced by the concept "the father's resources", the average amount of maintenance granted may increase, even relatively speaking.

In previous maintenance proceedings it has sometimes been difficult to establish the man's income in a reliable way. This has been the case when men have had no regular salary, but have practised various trades. When assessing a party's ability to pay, the property of the party is important.

Generally, we may reformulate the maintenance function as follows:

$$S = f(s_f).$$

In other words, the amount of maintenance depends directly on the father's total resources. If the judges adopt this view in the future, the amounts of maintenance will probably increase. In the opposite case, the danger is that the Child Maintenance Act will be only a reform of the written law. The general policy of the reform will not materialize.

Introduction to Part 2

The essays in the first part of this book deal with situations where there is a breakdown of the marriage between the parents, for example, in issues relating to custody or financial support. The essays in Part 2 however, are related to situations where there is not necessarily a breakdown of marriage (for example, in issues such as wardship or protection, adoption, delinquency) and also the discussion of general questions such as: the value of the formula "the best interests of the child", which has achieved such a wide usage in both statute and judge-made law in the Common Law jurisdictions; whether we need a theoretical framework as a foundation for the making of effective and sensible decisions about children; whether it would be a good idea to construct a code of children's law; what kind of general principles of private international law are desirable and practicable in regard to children. A variety of interesting and important questions for study and discussion are indicated directly or indirectly throughout the essays in part 2, and the following are some of them.

A fundamental set of problems that lie behind many of the specific issues regarding children that come before the courts (or other machinery for making such decisions) are those concerning the boundaries of the intra-familial domain in the settlement of disputes involving children. The attitude of the English common law was to regard decision-making in regard to children almost entirely as within the internal jurisdiction of the family unit, and as being an area in which the courts should not intervene except in cases of serious child abuse or the like. Now that the basic common law has been considerably supplemented by statute, the problem is more that of determining the boundaries between the resolution of problems internally within the family, and the making of decisions by public authorities and services, such as child welfare officials. Perhaps it is not too fanciful to draw a very rough analogy with the concept of the "corporate veil" in company law, and to think of a "family veil" constructed by the English common law of parent and child. Of course, a great many family disputes are still settled internally, within the family and behind the "family veil", and the state and its agencies (such as the courts) intervene in the exercise of specific legal powers, for example, where there is neglect or ill-treatment of a child, or in a dispute arising out of a breakdown in the adult relationship.

These problems give rise to difficult questions as to the family/state boundaries, and the correct role of the state and its courts and agencies in regard to children. Professor MacDougall discusses these matters generally in his essay, and stresses the importance of the traditional nuclear family in the process of bringing up children. Professor Cruickshank wishes to see family courts and state agencies being more positively supportive of families, and less active (in his view) in separating them. On the other hand, of course, one of the main raisons d'être of courts and agencies in regard to children ought to be to protect them effectively from danger, and especially to protect them as far as this is possible from the private, and often secret, danger of serious abuse from a parent. Professor MacDougall raises this point. Recent cases in England and Ontario have caused concern as to whether family courts and child welfare agencies are adequately exercising this important role. It may be that both the courts and the child welfare agencies become hesitant to intervene to protect a child by reason of too much public stress on the sanctity of so-called "parents' rights", and a "non-interventionist" social climate regarding the authority and powers of parents over their children. Dr. Stone mentions the Maria Colwell case in England in this connection.

Clearly when more than one system of law may be involved in the resolution of an issue, the analysis can become more involved, and private international law in regard to children has always been a difficult and unsatisfactory area. The basic problem seems to be to obtain some measure of consistency between the common concern about the best interests of the child in different countries, and the feeling that this is a matter on which the domestic law and courts should hesitate and subordinate themselves to the rules and decisions of other countries, and on the other hand the usual attempts to make general rules of conflict of laws. Professor Swan, in his essay, makes a contribution to the development of principles of private international law regarding children.

One of the most elementary questions to be asked in relation to decision-making on issues involving children is — who should make the decision? Dr. Stone's view, which is shared by others, is that the decision should normally be left to the child's parents, at least in regard to a young child. But in the context of this book, we are concerned mainly with what may be termed the "pathology" of the law of parents and child, that is, situations where internal resolution of the problem within the family has not worked or is not desirable.

The normal public decision-maker of last resort in issues concerning children is the legally trained judge. In Canada, the Ontario Law Reform Commission in the 1974 Report on Family Courts recommended (at page 61) "that no person be appointed a Family Court judge who is not legally qualified. We would define a legally qualified person as one who is a member of the Bar of one of the Provinces of Canada." There was also an emphasis on legal qualifications for a judge of a family or juvenile court in the Ontario Royal Commission Inquiry into Civil Rights (McRuer Commission) in Chapter 40, Volume 2, of Report No. 1. This emphasis is different from the approach in the United Kingdom, where substantial use is made of the lay judge or magistrate. Recommendations such as those in Ontario, which were framed by lawyers, seem to regard the need for legal qualifications in family law matters as self-evident. But there are those, particularly among the lay public, who raise questions about the essential value of legal training for making decisions on issues involving children. It is argued that the special value of legal training is to give expertise in assessing the veracity of witnesses, in interpreting rules of law, and so on. But, in practice, most of the issues concerning children that come before a family or juvenile court involve social issues rather than legal questions proper, and the rules to be administered are mainly judicial discretion (and the application of a discretionary formula about the "best interests" of a child). Further, much of the work of a family or juvenile court judge in regard to children is concerned with the (social) question of making orders about the child's future, for example, in regard to such matters as protection, wardship, custody, access, delinquency. Does a legal training give a person any special wisdom to help in ordering the disposition of a child and the direction of its future? Does being a lawyer make a person any less likely to make wrong decisions about what is best for the future life of a young child? The essay by Professors Mnookin and Coons emphasizes the vagueness of the "best interests" formula and Dr. Stone appears to see it as really just a general denial of the concepts of parental "possession" of the common law. Is it possible that, in the last decade or so in particular, society has become too optimistic about the ability of courts, lawyers, and law to solve the problems of tangled marriages and children in difficulty?

There are important questions about the manner of presentation, to a court, of an issue involving a child. Should a child be represented in such proceedings, and if so by whom? Does the court need the services of someone (legally trained or otherwise) in an *amicus curiae* role in some or all cases involving children? Professor Dickens discusses the present situation in this regard, as well as law reform recommendations which have been made. Professor Spencer examines the use of a "reporter" in the Scottish practice in regard to children, and Professor Bromley discusses the concept of an independent reporting officer in regard to the adoption of children. Dr. Stone and Mr. Lowe mention the proposal by "Justice" for a children's ombudsman.

There are a number of basic problems about a scheme for the representation of a child or of a child's "best interests". One obvious problem is connected with the financial cost and the administrative format for any such scheme, whether the value of a Law Guardian or similar office would justify the expense, and so on. Another problem would be connected with the attraction of suitable personnel into such an office. Some critics have suggested that the office would fail to attract persons of the right calibre for the work involved. Is there any merit in the concept of a law firm, with the partners on a salary basis paid by the state, designed particularly to provide services in this and similar areas of family law? State law firms having a general practice (mainly in family law and criminal law) are beginning to function in Sweden. Another question is whether the *amicus curiae* or representative of the child has to be a lawyer, or might have another kind of training. Along this line, there is the United Kingdom idea of having social workers appointed to family and juvenile courts.

In what kind of cases would a Law Guardian be needed? If one says that a Law Guardian is needed whenever there is a conflict of interest between the parent and the child, then how and by what procedures are such conflict of interest cases to be separated from the others? This would seem to indicate some selection or sorting process, but it might be possible to identify certain areas of children's law in which conflict of interest situations are most likely to arise.

Some of the contributors discuss evidentary and procedural matters in cases involving children. For example, Dr. Stone examines the difficult problem of, if, when, and how to interview a child as to its own wishes. Professor Bromley discusses a similar point in regard to adoption. Dr. Stone considers the critical problem of whether the parents should have access to what the child had said, for example, to the judge in chambers in connection with the custody application. There is also the matter of what weight should be given to a child's preferences in regard to such matters as custody, access, adoption, protection or wardship. How competent are children (of different ages) to assess all the implications of a decision about their future in such matters?

Some of the contributors discuss the general area of *parens patriae,* wardship, and "kidnapping" of children. There is, from long tradition, a general duty in the state to protect children within its boundaries. The difficulties of operating this general duty in the context of specific cases tends to lead back to a lack of settled, accepted principles in the law regarding children. Professors Mnookin and Coons raise a question whether there is a need for a better theoretical framework as a foundation for the law on children, and Professor Stoljar gives consideration to the possibility of providing a codification of children's law. Mr. Lowe and Mrs. Weiler contribute information on the present state of the law on the "kidnapping" of children in the United Kingdom and Canada. The domestic *parens patriae* duty to protect children, and to advance their "best interests" as seen in the discretion of the forum court, have generated a reluctance to enforce, automatically, foreign orders regarding children, and so a "kidnapping" case tends to produce an awkward confluence of foreign judgment and *parens patriae* duty.

An adoption is perhaps the most final decision that can be made in relation to a child's upbringing and future. Professor Bissett-Johnson discusses "foster adoptions" and the variety of sensitive problems that arise when a parent has remarried and there is an application to make the child a legally adopted child of the new union, thereby cutting-off the child legally from the other natural parent. Professor Bromley discusses the new English legislation on adoption and there are a number of possible interesting comparisons between this legislation and the roles on adoptions in other jurisdictions. English law, for example, has a principle of parental consent (unless dispensed with by court order for one of the statutory reasons). Ontario, Canada, also has statutory provisions for dispensing with parental consent under Part 4 of The Child Welfare Act, but under Part 2 of the same statute a child who is made a Crown Ward, as being a child in need of protection, only requires the authorization of the Director of Child Welfare in order to be placed for adoption, and in the case of a Crown Ward parental consent to the adoption is not required. As Professor Cruickshank points out in his essay, this Part 2 procedure for the adoption of a Crown Ward accounts for about two-thirds of all Ontario adoptions.

There are many basic questions on the law regarding children that are still controversial, and that are currently topics of law reform discussion and legislative review. Ontario has passed The Children's Law Reform Act, 1977, and the Ontario Ministry of Community and Social Services is preparing new long-range legislation in children's law.

Ian F. G. Baxter

Children And The Law: The Limited Effectiveness Of Legal Process

Donald J. MacDougall*

FAMILY, SOCIETY AND THE LAW

"When men demand much of law, when they seek to devolve upon it the whole burden of social control, when they seek to make it do the work of the home and of the church, enforcement of law comes to involve many difficulties. Then few can comprehend the whole field of the law, nor can they do so at one glance. The purposes of the legal system are not all upon the surface, and it may be that many whose nature is by no means anti-social are out of accord with some or even with many of these purposes. Hence today, in the wake of ambitious social programs calling for more and more interference with every relation of life, dissatisfaction with law, criticism of legal and judicial institutions and suspicion as to the purposes of the lawyer become universal."[1]

Dean Roscoe Pound made these comments in an address in 1916, and he referred to the law relating to children to illustrate his comments.

"In modern law not only duties of care for the health, morals and education of children, but even truancy and incorrigibility are coming under the supervision of juvenile courts or courts of domestic relations. But note that the moment these things are committed to courts administrative agencies have to be invoked to make the legal treatment effective. Probation officers, boards of children's guardians and like institutions at once develop. Moreover one may venture to doubt whether such institutions or any that may grow out of them will ever take the place of the old-time interview between father and son in the family woodshed by means of which the intangible duties involved in that relation were formerly enforced."[2]

Society has changed since those words were written. Woodsheds have disappeared and a widespread scepticism has developed about the effectiveness of the behaviour—modification techniques that were

* Donald J. MacDougall is a Professor, Faculty of Law, University of British Columbia.

employed in that legendary location. Nevertheless most western countries still rely on the family as the primary agent for the socialization of the child.[3] It must be admitted that the family is not secure and unchallenged in that role. The family today is significantly different from the family that existed when Pound wrote. An increasing number of children are living in single-parent households, often in conditions of social and economic deprivation. In two-parent families it is rare to find any adult other than the parents and frequently both parents work. Urie Bronfenbrenner, the Cornell psychologist, has suggested that in North American society many parents abdicate their parental responsibilities and that the socialization process is controlled, to a disturbing extent, by the age-differentiated peer group.[4]

Bronfenbrenner wrote later that: "(1) Over the past three decades literally thousands of investigations have been conducted to identify the developmental antecedents of behaviour disorganization and social pathology. The results point to an almost omnipresent overriding factor: family disorganization. (2) Much of the same research also shows that the forces of disorganization arise primarily not from within the family but from the circumstances in which the family finds itself and from the way of life that is imposed on it by those circumstances."[5]

Let us assume, for the moment, that those generalizations are accurate. What should be society's response? Clearly we may have to deal with both the symptoms (behaviour disorganization and social "pathology") and the cause (family disorganization). We need a remedial as well as a preventive programme. The point is that we need both.

How effective have our remedial programmes been? Pound had a healthy scepticism about society's abilities to provide substitutes for the functioning family. Since he wrote, however, modern science and technology have pushed back the empirical limits (with which Pound was concerned) on the law's effectiveness. Modern behaviour — modification techniques (and I include here psychotropic (mind-altering) drugs, electrical stimulation of the brain (ESB), psychosurgery, and organic conditioning techniques as well as the more common psychotherapeutic techniques) have placed awesome new powers in the hands of state officials, doctors and psychiatrists. Fortunately there is a growing appreciation of the political, ethical and social problems that accompany the use of these techniques.[6] When state or professional intervention is suggested, a critical question must be the propriety, as well as the probable effectiveness, of the proposed intervention. I believe that modern behaviour modification techniques should not be used, except in a limited number of situations and subject to strict controls, and that the effectiveness of the more common psychotherapeutic techniques is a critical issue. Unfortunately it is very difficult to measure their effectiveness.[7] There is evidence that some of them work to some extent — but the statistics on child abuse and juvenile delinquency should caution as against making extravagant claims concerning their effectiveness.

We must be modest in our expectations of what the law, and the health and social science professionals, can achieve under the best of circumstances. Moreover, these experts are expensive, and work most effectively when their caseload is kept within strict limits. Our first objective must be an effective preventive programmme to ensure that the number of cases requiring remedial action are kept to the minimum practicable level. We must do what we can to buttress and support the family. Here the British have demonstrated a better appreciation of the grubby realities confronting families in our industrialized cities of the twentieth century. Money, of course, is the basic problem.

Second only to financial difficulties, and to a considerable extent exacerbated by them, housing is the largest single problem of one-parent families.[8] I do not want to catalogue the other social services that are needed or desirable, but I do want to express a concern about excessive reliance on government services, because we also need the voluntary organizations, such as the Boys' and Girls' Clubs. We need to create a "caring" society. If people generally do not feel any responsibility to preserve and improve the quality of life in their community, there is no professional group that can hope to cope with the social problems. Finally we need educational programmes to prepare young people for their role as parents. We have worried too much about the biological facts of life and too little about educating young people on the responsibilities and rewards of being a parent.

But no preventive programme will be completely successful, and remedial measures are required. Here the law fulfils an essential function. To a considerable extent it will determine when, and what, remedial action will be taken. Before we can determine the law's proper role, however, we need a better understanding of the interests that require legal protection.

WHOSE INTERESTS? LIVING IN AN ADULT WORLD

In "Social Dimensions of Law and Justice" Julius Stone attempted to compile an inventory of the interests actually asserted in our society. He was careful to warn us against assuming that any interest was fundamental, or paramount, in the sense that it would automatically prevail over any other interests. But he began his discussion of the inventory of interests with the following comment:

"It is clear immediately that the claim of personality, so far as it concerns personal physical integrity, is persistently made and in large part legally supported in British countries and in America. In a sense, physical integrity is pre-supposed by all other claims."[9]

There should be no doubt that one of the principal functions of any legal system is the control of violence against the person. An elementary study of legal history supports this view. Anglo-Saxon law seems to consist of little more than a tariff of compensation for different types of physical injury. "If an ear is struck off, the bot (compensation) is twelve shillings; if an ear is pierced, three shillings; if an eye is knocked out, fifty shillings."[10] It is only in more sophisticated systems that the law attempts to prevent more subtle injuries to our feelings and sensibilities.

Thus, if we were drafting a new children's code, our first concern would be to protect the physical integrity of the child. If there is anything which clearly justifies dramatic state intervention in family affairs, it is child abuse. In fact the law has given the child inadequate protection against physical abuse. Criminal sanctions contained in the Canadian Criminal Code are rarely invoked. The family is dealt with, if at all, under provincial child welfare legislation. Child abuse is regarded as an illness which will respond to appropriate treatment by doctors, psychiatrists, social workers and/or trained community volunteers employing a variety of psychotherapeutic techniques. Most of the literature on the subject is devoted to discussions about which of these treatments is most effective.[11] The tragic fact is that in Canada, every year, a large number of children die or suffer permanent injury because this type of response was made and it was ineffective and inadequate. Do not misunderstand me. There are many situations where such psychotherapeutic techniques will be sufficient. But there are many cases where the proper response is prompt removal of the child from the situation and/or the use of more drastic behaviour modification techniques. No doubt errors of judgment cannot be avoided. The available statistics are limited, but they suggest that we rely too much on psychotherapeutic techniques of uncertain effectiveness. There are too many cases of repeated abuse. Why are we so timid? Is it because children lack an effective spokesman?

Compare this with the elaborate machinery that has been constructed to deal with juvenile delinquency. Is theft or vandalism more important than a child's broken arm or leg? Yet we allocate more of our community resources to dealing with juvenile delinquency than to dealing with child abuse. We do not hesitate to remove a delinquent from his home and place him in a training school or otherwise under the supervision of a government official. Yet we hesitate to remove a battered child from his home. Why? Which child is at greater risk?

Let me suggest a possible answer. The law is a reflection of adult, rather than children's, interests. We are all potential victims of juvenile delinquency. Many of us have been actual victims. We are effective in asserting our interest in protection from such anti-social behaviour. Child abuse is another matter. We are no longer potential victims. Any legal regulation in this area is likely to restrict our freedom, as parents, to deal with our children as we see fit or require us to take action (*e.g.* reporting our client or our neighbour) which we consider distasteful. And children, especially young children, do not have an effective voice in any of the authoritative conclaves of our society.

Can I give you another example. Divorce, today, is a common event. Inevitably divorce entails financial adjustments between the parties. There has been considerable discussion of the need to reform matrimonial property law to ensure greater equity between husband and wife. None of the discussions contain any expression of concern for the economic interests of the children in the family property. Is it so utterly inconceivable that they should be given a legal share of any property owned by the husband and wife? For some time courts in Australia have had power to make orders settling property "for the benefit of all or any of the parties to, and the children of, the marriage".[12] A court, for example, could settle the matrimonial home on the wife for life and thereafter to the children absolutely. In Canada the discussion over matrimonial property law reform has been so strident that it has drowned out any tentative suggestions that it might be appropriate, in some cases, to give children a share in the family assets.

I have reached two tentative conclusions that I would like to put before you.

(a) Many law reformers have set their goals unrealistically high. They have sought to use the law to protect interests of personality (autonomy, privacy, feelings and sensibilities) which are still struggling uncertainly for legal recognition. If adults have been unable to devise legal rules to protect these interests adequately surely it is unreasonable to hope that the breakthrough will come with children where the problems are more subtle and complex. In general, all that the law can do is select one secure adult-child relationship (by custody, adoption or some similar process) and hope that the selected adults will fulfil their roles as the parental guides, protectors, and advocates for the child. No doubt we can improve the processes for selecting the best available adults, but once the selection is made and the relationship established, the legal system is ill-equipped to exercise a continuing supervisory function. Unfortunately excessive concentration on unrealistically high objectives has diverted attention from more limited, but more practical, goals (*e.g.* protecting the child's interest in his physical integrity; in fair treatment from persons in a position of authority; and his economic interests).

(b) Where the interests of children coincide with the interests of at least some adults (as in custody, adoption, etc.) it is likely that the law will recognize the child's interests. On the other hand where this coincidence does not occur (for example, in cases of child abuse, cases involving economic claims by children and, to some extent, juvenile delinquency) the law has been slower to recognize the interests of children and sporadic in its enforcement of their rights. Who sees the law from the child's perspective and who speaks on his behalf? If we are seriously interested in using the legal process to protect children we must put more emphasis on these neglected areas of the law.

A CHILDREN'S CODE?

These days it is fashionable to call for more precise definition of the legal rights and responsibilities of children. It is difficult to object to such requests. The legal system is a coercive system, and those subject to it (whether children or adults) are entitled to demand that any laws affecting them be as clear and precise as possible. However the advocates of a comprehensive children's code would not be satisfied with a mere clarification and codification of existing law. They want to use the legal system as an instrument of social change. What is proposed is a redefinition of the rights and responsibilities of the child *vis-à-vis* his parents, other adults, and the state.

There is nothing improper about these objectives. However it must be seriously questioned whether legal regulation is an appropriate way of pursuing them. We may hope that parents will love and educate their children (in the broadest sense) and that children will love and respect their parents and other adults. Converting those broad objectives into enforceable legal rules is fraught with difficulty. Over the years there have been several attempts to formulate a list of children's rights. Some of the early attempts were laudable but legally unenforceable, being statements of social policy.[13] More recently there have been attempts to define children's rights in more precise, and legally enforceable, terms.[14] Moreover the balance between rights and responsibilities has disappeared. The perceived need is to circumscribe adult power in order to protect the interests of the child.

For example, in British Columbia, the draft Children's Act, 1976 prepared by the Family and Children's Law Commission, contains a list of children's rights (Part III, Section 2). Section 3 requires parents, persons responsible for the child (defined to include *inter alia* teachers, social workers and probation officers) and the Provincial Government "to take all reasonable measures" to ensure that the rights of the child are fulfilled. By Section 4 either the child, or someone acting on his behalf, is entitled to seek a declaratory order specifying the measures best suited to fulfilling the rights of the child.

It would be easy to make some minor criticisms of the list of rights. For example, one of the rights is a right to play and recreation. When is a parent, or a teacher, entitled to curtail that right? Similarly parents and teachers who attempt to discipline a child may find that they have contravened Section 2(b) which provides that a child has a right to an environment free from "physical abuse, exploitation and degrading treatment". Is a scolding degrading treatment?

But these are debating points. In truth we would not anticipate many actions against parents. Actions against teachers, social workers, and probation officers are a little more likely. Most actions would be brought by the parents on behalf of a child, against the government. Consider, for example, the following situation. A family is on welfare. In its opinion the welfare payments are insufficient for the parents to fulfil their children's right "to food, clothing and housing in order to ensure good health and personal development". Proceedings are initiated. What is a court to do? It is entitled to make a declaratory order specifying what further additional measures should be taken? What if the government disregards, as it may, such a declaratory order? Obviously the procedure set out in the draft bill raises serious questions about the relationship between the legislature, the executive and the judiciary. One Supreme Court judge has suggested that the enactment of the draft Children's Act, in its present form, would be like requiring the courts to drink a cup of hemlock.

One flawed model is not evidence that the concept is unworkable. The practicality of a children's code must be debated in principle. I am reminded of the continuing legal debate over the advantages and disadvantages of incorporating a Bill of Rights in a written constitution. Are individual liberties better protected in the United States, which has such a Bill of Rights, or in England, which does not?[15] There are other countries where the adoption of the Universal Declaration of Human Rights and the incorporation of a Bill of Rights in the constitution did not prevent serious violations of the civil rights of citizens of those countries. A Bill of Rights may have some value, but the most effective guarantees of individual liberties are the social and political values held within that community. There is still a great deal of force to the argument that "stateways cannot change folkways".[16]

The same comment can be made concerning efforts to create a children's code, or a bill of rights for children. The needs and capacities of children vary greatly depending on the age and maturity of the individual child. They need love and affection, guidance and training. The socialization process is a complex one and not one that is easily converted to a system of legal rules and regulations. Indeed a great deal is lost in the attempt. Once an abstract principle is expressed in legal terms the legal rule tends to become the accepted measure of the parties' rights and responsibilities. In a society that values and respects its children, a Bill of Rights for children is unnecessary. In a society that does not value or respect its children, a Bill of Rights for children is unlikely to be effective. The same comments apply with equal validity to proposals for a comprehensive children's code.

Moreover attempts to codify the law relating to children involve complex social and political questions about the state's involvement in family affairs. The British Columbia Family and Children's Law Commission gave three reasons for emphasizing children's rights and by-passing children's obligations.[17] The reasons given were:

(1) The common law already gives guardianship powers to the parents which vest in them complete control of the child's custody, care and property.

(2) The child's obligations to the society outside his family have already been defined (in the Criminal Code and the Juvenile Delinquents Act).

(3) A definition of children's obligations could lead to an abdication of parental rights and responsibilities. If parents are constrantly able to turn to the government to demand enforcement of their children's obligations within the family there could be an overwhelming demand on the services of the police, social services and the courts.

We could have a debate about the validity, and the relevance, of the first two reasons given but I want to focus attention on the third reason. Similar consequences would flow from an attempt to give children comprehensive legal rights against their parents. We should be aware that any attempt to implement a bill of rights for children, or a comprehensive children's code, would effect changes in the basic structure of our society — especially the role and function of the family.

OR SPECIFIC LEGISLATION?

On the other hand there is an urgent need for legislation more limited in scope but more specific in content. Many adults deal with children. Their relationships are not subject to the checks and balances of familial ties. All too frequently we hear of arbitrary action by teachers, social workers or probation officers. In Vancouver, for example, I have heard of juveniles held in a detention centre when adults charged with a similar offence would have been out on bail. The immaturity and inexperience of young people in asserting and defending their interests against an adult in a position of authority justify the imposition of specific procedural checks on any adult empowered to exercise coercive authority over a child. Unfortunately many of these adults see themselves in a quasi-parental role and will regard these procedural checks as "legal technicalities" and unnecessary "red tape". As lawyers we must insist that these "legal technicalities" are central to our concept of justice under the law. We should remember the comments made by Foster and Freed on the *Gault* case, but the distasteful thing about *Gault* is not that the minor was deprived of numerous constitutional rights but that he was treated so unfairly while being subjected to a process which supposedly was geared to his own welfare.[18]

Some of the greatest injustices have been commited under the cloak of paternalism. Thus, I greet with enthusiasm some of the provisions of the draft Young Persons in Conflict With The Law Act — for example, Section 5 (containing rules governing detention not pursuant to disposition); Section 6 (notices to parents, relatives and friends); and Sections 30-34 (providing for review of dispositions). I would quibble over the wording of some of those provisions but I am in complete agreement with the basic objective — to ensure that informality is not a cloak for injustice. Similarly I welcome the restrictions contained in the draft British Columbia Children's Act, 1976 on the power to apprehend neglected children and the very specific time limitations imposed on persons acting under the authority of that Act (see Part V, Sections 29 and 31).

INTRA-FAMILY DISPUTES

Different considerations apply to attempts to regulate relationships within the family. The arguments in favour of a secure family enclave are strong. Children can sue parents to protect interests in property, or for damage inflicted either intentionally or negligently.[19] In that sense there is no parental immunity principle. But I am concerned to limit, rather than expand, the law's role in intra-family disputes. The mind boggles at the possibilities. How many possible actions for intentional infliction of nervous shock, negligence and breach of contract arise in the ordinary functioning of the normal family? Fortunately the law does not require continual parental supervision of every child under threat of a verdict in negligence.[20] The courts will hold quite happily that most family arrangements were not intended to be legally binding. The law should be reluctant to intervene except to protect established property interests or in cases of physical injury where the conduct of the parent clearly falls below that expected of an ordinary, prudent parent.

In *Poel v. Poel*[21] the mother, who had been given custody of her three-year-old son in divorce proceedings, had remarried and wished to emigrate with her son from England to New Zealand. This would effectively destroy any possibility of a relationship between the child and his father. Nevertheless, the Court of Appeal granted permission, Winn L.J., observing:

"I am very firmly of opinion that the child's happiness is directly dependent not only on the health and happiness of the mother but on her freedom from the very likely repercussions, of an adverse character, which would result affecting her relations with the stepfather and her ability to look after her family peacefully and in a psychological frame of ease, from the refusal of the permission to take the child to New Zealand which I think quite clearly his welfare dictates."[22]

A similar "hands-off" policy was evidenced in a British Columbia decision, *Re Malat*.[23] A testator left his entire estate to his wife. The Public Trustee sought to have himself appointed guardian of two children (girls aged 12 and 17) in order that a claim could be made on their behalf under the Testator's Family Maintenance Act. Meredith J. refused the application, stating:

"In any event I do not think it has been shown, nor should it be assumed, that, even if proceedings under the Testator's Family Maintenance Act were to result in some special provision for the two children out of the estate, such provision would in net advance the welfare of the children. Proceedings under the Act would effectively pit the children against their mother, thrust upon the estate unwanted costs, occasion anxiety, pre-occupation and other strains on all sides, to say nothing of the risk of family discord. The possible disruption might well be much more harmful to the children than any benefit they might possibly receive from the estate.

I have not the slightest reason to suppose that Mrs. Malat will do other than the best for all her children during her life-time. Nor should I speculate that she will do other than make adequate provision for her children out of what may remain of her assets, including those inherited from her husband, on her death."

It is respectfully submitted that these decisions reflect a wise reluctance to interfere in the parent-child relationship and a proper appreciation of the legal system's ability to regulate family arrangements. Several studies have indicated the value of secure parent-child relationships. Indeed this is one of the conventional arguments in favour of adoption as compared with placing children with foster parents or in institutions.[24] A similar, albeit narrower, argument was put by Goldstein, Freud and Solnit when they argued that the non-custodial parent's opportunities for access should be controlled by the custodial parent rather than the court,[25] but it is questionable whether they considered the social consequences of such a rule.[26] My own view is that there is a good argument for court control of access or visitation rights. But I agree with the general sentiment underlying their argument. The law should refrain from officious meddling in family matters.

There are, of course, real parent-child conflicts. Parents may forbid their children keeping company with individuals they dislike; drinking beer or taking drugs; smoking cigarettes; reading "adult" magazines and books; having sexual intercourse; staying out after hours; going on unauthorized trips, etc. How are these rules to be tested by a child who considers a particular rule unreasonable? How is the rule to be enforced by a parent? In our society we expect parents to do their best to curb and control delinquent or anti-social behaviour by their children. Where the act involved is a criminal offence (*e.g.* taking drugs) the parent can obtain assistance from the police. However many parents will be reluctant to take such drastic measures and their children, aware of such reluctance, are unlikely to take mere threats seriously. What other procedures are available to deal with the rebellious or emancipated child? The problem is to devise a procedure which maintains a proper balance between the need to buttress the natural authority of the parent and the child's legitimate aspirations for personal autonomy. Marks has documented the dramatic shifts that have taken place in our attitudes to emancipation.[27] Prior to the nineteenth century, children were often emancipated in fact long before they had reached the lawful age of majority. Between 1870 and 1920 the parental role was expanded and prolonged — reflecting the additional educational, and other requirements to prepare a child for life in an industrialized society. More recently adolescents have begun to challenge the limits imposed on their personal autonomy by parents and other adults while recognizing their continued need for financial support. How is this conflict to be resolved? Frequently the only realistic sanction available to a parent is an economic, or financial one. Should he be able to use this to tyrannize a child? There comes a time when the conflict is so irreconcilable that someone has to intervene. At present the only legal procedures available relate to "unmanageable" or "incorrigible" children or "persons in need of supervision". In some respects these provisions have achieved too little. In other respects they have gone too far. If the goal was to provide professional, state-sponsored supervision instead of parental supervision, it is debateable whether that is what is required or what has occurred. It may be that we need a formal doctrine of emancipation permitting children over a certain age (school leaving age, perhaps) to be free from control by either their parents or the state. There may, however, be a need for some special state services for children in an "in-between" group (16 to 19). Unfortunately legal and social policies in this area are often developed on an *ad hoc* basis and without a proper consideration of their consequences.

In British Columbia, the Protection of Children Act applies to children under the age of seventeen. Suppose a 16-year-old is having difficulty with her parents. Is it appropriate for her to approach the local representative of the Superintendent of Child Welfare and ask to be placed in a group home? I have heard reports of cases where proceedings were taken under Section 65 of the Protection of Children Act (B.C.) not because of any defect or fault in the parents, but because the children wished to escape parental supervision and constraint. Is this an appropriate use of community resources?

Who should be responsible for the maintenance of the "emancipated" child? Under Section 15 of the Family Relations Act (B.C.) maintenance may be ordered until a child reaches the age of 19. Under Section 2 of the Divorce Act (Canada) maintenance may be ordered for a child "sixteen years of age or over...but unable...to provide himself with the necessaries of life". To what extent should a parent be compelled to support his independent, or even rebellious, child? In *Downing v. Downing*,[28] the parents were divorced in 1966. Over the years their eldest daughter became estranged from both of them. From 1971 she attended a boarding school and her relationship with her parents became so bad that she chose to remain at school during the school holidays. In due course she qualified for admission to a university. She was eligible for a county council grant, but neither of her parents would make any contribution to her living expenses or, in fact, cooperate in her application to the county council. In those circumstances the daughter sought, and received leave, to intervene in the divorce proceedings. The judge did not have to determine what financial provision should be made, because the parties (at that stage) entered into a compromise.

Although it is common to find statements to the effect that only a party to divorce proceedings under the Divorce Act can claim maintenance,[29] in some provinces the Divorce Rules would permit the procedure used in *Downing v. Downing* (in British Columbia, see the Divorce Rules, 1975, Rule 18(2)). The decision on the merits is much more difficult in cases such as these. The court has the power to award maintenance, but whether it is "fit and just to do so" in the particular circumstances of the case is sometimes a very difficult question. It is a question that often confuses agencies responsible for administering various types of social assistance programmes. In British Columbia children between the ages of 16 and 19 may experience difficulty in collecting social assistance, even though it is quite clear that they are living independently of their parents. The assumption is made that such children have a right to financial support from their parents. This is not an accurate statement of what the law is, or should be. In determining whether to award maintenance to an independent or rebellious child a court may consider that the relationship between the parent and the child constitutes a "reasonable excuse" for refusing maintenance (within Section 17 of the Family Relations Act (B.C.)) or circumstances which would prevent an award being "fit and just" within Section 11 of the Divorce Act (Can.). We should be wary of stripping parents of their authority and influence in these borderline cases. It would be far better to develop special programmes to meet the needs of those between 16 and 19 who are unable to support themselves or remain in their parental homes. One of the main functions of any legal system is the resolution of conflicts. But it need not attempt to resolve every conflict. There are times when a policy of judicious non-intervention is more appropriate.

JUVENILE DELINQUENCY

Many children will have their first contact with the law in a criminal setting. Yet conferences on children and the law often neglect this very important area of children's law. In fact the Juvenile Delinquents Act (Can.) is a perfect illustration of my basic theme — that we should not expect the legal system to remedy all our social ills. The history of the Juvenile Delinquency Act is a history of hopes unrealized and promises unfulfilled.

Roscoe Pound called the Illinois Juvenile Court Act of 1899 "one of the most significant advances in the administration of justice since the Magna Carta".[30] A similar optimism pervades Canada's Juvenile Delinquents Act, which has remained substantially unchanged since it was first enacted in 1908. Under Section 3(2) of the Act a child is to be treated "not as an offender but as one in a condition of delinquency and therefore requiring help and guidance and proper supervision" and by Section 38 "the care and custody and discipline of a juvenile delinquent shall approximate as nearly as may be that which should be given by his parents". Delinquency is thought of as an illness which will respond to proper treatment.

Nearly everyone concerned with the administration of the Juvenile Delinquents Act would admit that it has failed to achieve the high hopes originally held by its sponsors. Why has it failed?

Many of the professionals — particularly the social workers and others involved in the treatment side of the court's functions — have tended to place the blame for the juvenile court's failure (to the extent that they will admit that it has failed) chiefly at the feet of the community arguing that it has been the community's unwillingness to provide the court with the necessary services — the staff, the facilities, and the concern — that has prevented the court from realizing its potential and resulted in it taking on many of the undesirable features of the adult criminal courts. Undoubtedly, there is some validity to this argument.... However, the lack of these resources is clearly not the only explanation. Rather, it is submitted that the primary reason for the juvenile court's failure to live up to its rehabilitative and preventive goals was the extremely unrealistic nature of those goals based as they were upon the over optimistic view of the court's earliest proponents as to what was and what could be known about the phenomenon of juvenile criminality and as to what even a fully equipped juvenile court could do about it. There is no doubt that the problem of delinquency has proved itself to be infinitely more complicated than the 19th Century reformers thought. Not only has the attempt to develop effective rehabilitation programmes met with only very limited success, but even the causes of delinquency itself have remained substantially a mystery.[31]

If these comments are valid, and I believe they are, how should we set about the business of redrafting the Juvenile Delinquents Act? There is now an extensive literature on juvenile delinquency and I could not hope to review all of it. Let me select some items which I believe are especially pertinent.

There is evidence, for example, that delinquency is not an uncommon phenomenon. American studies, based on a self-reporting system rather than official statistics, suggest that 88% of the adolescent children in that country have committed a delinquent act,[32] and that these percentages have not changed dramatically over the years.[33] Most of these offences were undetected. I know of no comparable Canadian studies, but I suspect that the results of such a study would be similar. This research suggests that we should be reluctant to make hasty decisions on the basis of official statistics. Increases in recorded rates of juvenile crime may reflect nothing more than changes in the demographic structure of our society, improved police detection methods, improved record keeping or an increasing tendency to invoke institutional supports to deal with anti-social behaviour by juveniles. Clearly we should not attempt to design a system which would deal with every technical delinquency. We must assume that much delinquent behaviour will be handled within the family or within the community generally. Only serious, or repeated, offences should be handled within the juvenile justice system.

A contrary argument is sometimes put. In summary form it would read like this: "The delinquent act is not important in itself. But its occurrence identifies a family at risk. We may then conduct an investigation and offer the family the services it needs."[34] In my view there are two basic fallacies in this paternalistic argument. First, it fails to distinguish between the provision of governmental services on an elective basis and coercive state intervention. As a general proposition we should expand the community services available on a voluntary or elective basis and restrict coercive state intervention to cases where there is a demonstrable need for such intervention. I shudder to think how much time, money and effort has been spent on the investigation of petty thefts and other minor delinquencies which could have been used to expand other social programmes of a preventive nature. The second fallacy in the paternalistic argument is its facile assumption that the intervention will be successful. Intervention under legislation like the Juvenile Delinquents Act carries the risk of negative, as well as positive, consequences. A debate rages about the effect of "labelling".[35] Given the limited evidence of the positive advantages of intervention, we should hesitate to intervene unless we are satisfied that such intervention is necessary and proper.

The problem, of course, is to identify the cases in which intervention is required. I have suggested that intervention should be limited to cases involving serious offences or repeated offences. Obviously we must have some method of distinguishing isolated offences from repeated offences. While I have an aversion to record-keeping (because of the danger that the information will not be kept confidential) I accept the necessity for police records, under appropriate safeguards, in order that an informed judgment can be made about which cases require intervention and which do not. It is the lesser of two evils. The alternative is an undiscriminating and inefficient system of enforcement.

Today, the "in" concept is "diversion", but it is not always clear what this concept involves. Many so-called "diversions" merely divert within the system. For example, the "screening agency" proposed in Section 9 of the draft Young Persons in Conflict With The Law Act is an example of diversion within the system. Juveniles may be dealt with, informally, by the screening agency or, more formally, by the court. I have serious objections to the screening agency proposal. My most serious objection is that it involves an inappropriate allocation of our community resources. Many of the cases that would come before such a screening agency should be diverted right out of the system. They should have been handled by parents, teachers, school counsellors, police and other adults involved in the particular incident. What I am concerned about is a possible misallocation of public funds and community resources — with an increase in the resources allocated to the juvenile justice system accompanied by reductions (or inadequate increases) in other key areas (e.g. public education and child welfare). In my view that would be a tragic mistake. There is a natural tendency to refer young people who need the support of community services to the institution or organization with the greater resources. This has undesirable consequences for the young person who is stigmatized by his involvement in the juvenile justice system. Moreover, it perpetuates the present confusion about the role and function of the juvenile justice system.

Minor and isolated acts of anti-social behaviour by juveniles should be dealt with within the family. It is important to emphasize that the family is still our primary resource, and usually our most effective resource, in the socialization of the child. Where the family fails or is ineffective, the police, teachers, school counsellors and other adults involved in the situation should accept a responsibility to offer the child guidance and direction in a humane and understanding context. The juvenile justice system should be our last resort. Precious resources should not be wasted on cases that can be adequately dealt with within the community. There are enough "serious" cases to exhaust the modest resources available to the juvenile justice system. We have little accurate information about the effectiveness of the various treatment programmes currently in use, but one conclusion is clear. No programme will work effectively if it is overloaded. The trend towards increasing institutionalization of juvenile delinquency problems threatens to sabotage whatever success the existing programmes have achieved. Have we been bemused by numbers? An argument can be made that we have not devoted enough attention to the problem of dealing with young persons who have committed serious, or repeated, offences. A juvenile justice system must attempt to rehabilitate the offender. Indeed one of the principal arguments for the separation of the juvenile justice system from the adult criminal justice system is that extraordinary efforts at rehabilitation are justified in the case of young offenders. But even a parent, if he is wise, will make it clear to an offending child that he is responsible for his conduct. Moreover the juvenile justice has an important subsidiary function. It must protect the community itself. Of late there has been increasing public criticism of its lack of success in fulfilling this function. One disappointment that I have about the report on "Young Persons in Conflict With The Law" is that it offers no encouragement to searches for new methods of dealing with seriously delinquent behaviour.

CONCLUSION

The theme of this paper is a simple one. The happiness and welfare of a child depend, first, on his family and, secondly, on the community in which he lives. The law can play only a limited role. There is evidence that the "childsavers", whose efforts led to the present juvenile justice system, expected too much of our legal system. It cannot regulate the intimate relationships upon which the healthy growth and development of the child's personality depend. I have suggested to you that many of today's law reformers are making the same mistake and that their goals are unrealistically high. Does this matter? It may be that proposals for a children's code or a bill of rights for children serve an essential educational function. My only concern is that such campaigns may divert attention from more limited, but quite practical, proposals. In the past the law has not served children well. It has protected adult interests, rather than the interests of children. It can and should do more — for example, in the fields of child abuse and juvenile delinquency. But our primary concern must be to strengthen and support the family. There are not enough lawyers, psychiatrists or social workers available to cope with the problems that will arise if our basic family structure is unable to survive.

1 Pound, "The Limits of Effective Legal Action" (1917) 3 A.B.A. Journal 55 at 56.
2 *Id.* at 66. See also Pound, *Jurisprudence* (1959) Vol. 3, at 357-358.
3 See generally Bell and Vogel, *A Modern Introduction To The Family* (rev. ed., 1968) at 7-9.
4 Bronfenbrenner, *Two Worlds of Childhood: U.S. and U.S.S.R.* (1970).
5 Bronfenbrenner, "The Origins of Alienation" (1974) 231 Scientific American 53.
6 For a definition of these terms see Shapiro, "Legislating The Control of Behaviour Control: Autonomy and the Coercive Use of Organic Therapies" (1974) 47 S. Cal. L. Rev. 237 at 240-245.
7 Crane, "The Power of Social Intervention Experiments To Discriminate Differences between Experimental and Control Groups" (1976) 50 Social Science Review 224.
8 Report of the Committee on One-Parent Families (the Finer Committee Report) (1974) Cmnd. 5629, vol. 1, 528.
9 Stone, *Social Social Dimensions of Law and Justice* (1966) at 200.
10 Windeyer, *Lectures on Legal History* (2nd ed., 1949) at 19.
11 See, generally Bakan, Eisner and Needham, *Child Abuse: A Bibliography* (1976). Note, especially, pp. xxi and xxii.
12 Matrimonial Causes Act, 1959-1965 (Cth.), s. 86.
13 See for example, the Children's Charter, drafted at the White House Conference on Child Health and Protection (1930) and the United Nations Declaration of the Rights of the Child (1959). Both of these documents are reprinted in Bremner, *Children and Youth in America,* Vol. II, at 106-108 and Vol. III, at 225-227.
14 See the Royal Commission on Family and Children's Law (B.C.), Fifth Report, Part III, "Children's Rights", and Foster and Freed, "A Bill of Rights For Children" (1972) 6 Family L.Q. 343.
15 Tarnopolsky, *The Canadian Bill of Rights* (1966) at 12-13.
16 A *dictum* credited to the American sociologist, William Graham Sumner, by Rose, "Sociological Factors in the Effectiveness of Projected Legal Remedies" (1959) 11 J. Legal Ed. 470.
17 *Supra* note 14 at 23-24.
18 *Supra* note 14 at 353.
19 For a recent illustration of this principle see *Teno v. Arnold* (1976) 11 O.R. (2d) 585, 67 D.L.R. (3d) 9; leave to appeal to Supreme Court of Canada granted at 11 O.R. (2d) 585n, 67 D.L.R. (3d) 9n (S.C.C.).
20 Thuillez, "Parental Nonsupervision: The Tort That Never Was" (1976) 40 Albany L.Rev. 336. Note, however, that there may be differences between Canadian and American law.
21 [1970] 1 W.L.R. 1469, [1970] 3 All E.R. 659 (C.A.).
22 *Id.* at 1473.
23 Unreported, B.C. Supreme Court, August 21, 1975.
24 See generally Yarrow, "Separation From Parents During Early Childhood" in Hoffman and Hoffman, *Review of Child Development Research* (1964).
25 *Beyond The Best Interests of The Child* (1973) at 38.
26 Katkin, Bullington, Levine, "Above and Beyond The Best Interests of The Child" (1974) 9 Law and Society Review 669 at 680.
27 Marks, "Detours on the Road To Maturity: A View of The Legal Conception of Growing Up and Letting Go" (1975) 39 Law and Contemporary Problems 78.
28 [1976] 3 W.L.R. 335, [1976] Fam. 288, [1976] 3 All E.R. 474.
29 See *Power on Divorce* (3rd ed., 1976) vol. 1 at 169.
30 Quoted in "National Probation and Parole Association", *Guides For Juvenile Court Judges* (1957) at 127.
31 Wolfson, Juvenile Delinquents, Young Offenders and Young Persons in Conflict With The Law: A Study of Juvenile Delinquency in Canada" (1976) (unpublished LL.M. thesis) at 43-44.
32 Gold and Williams, "From Delinquent Behaviour To Official Delinquency" (1972) 20 Social Problems 209.
33 Gold and Reimer, "Changing Patterns of delinquent behaviour among Americans 13 through 16 years old: 1967-1972" National Survey of Youth Report No. 1 (1974)

University of Michigan Institute For Social Research.
34 See also Baxter, "Recent Developments in Scandinavian Family Law" (1977) 26 Int'l & Comp. L.Q. 150 at 165-166.
35 Mahoney, "The Effect of Labeling Upon Youths in The Juvenile Justice System: A Review of The Evidence" (1974) 8 Law and Society Review 583.

Court Avoidance In Child Neglect Cases

*David A. Cruickshank**

In Canada, most lawyers think of "Family Courts" (in their presently existing form) as "inferior courts", presided over by provincially-appointed judges. Previously known as Magistrate's Courts, they cannot grant divorces and generally cannot act beyond the jurisdiction given to them by statute (but there are recommendations and experiments in Canada about the concept of a comprehensive family court with a full "family law" jurisdiction *e.g.* in Ontario). Maybe the label "Family Courts" is a statistical description for the Canadian provincial family courts; they were the first legal institutions to deal with the majority of Canadian family law cases.

I wonder why we call these Canadian provincial courts "Family Courts". They separate children from their parents and parents from each other. They are certainly not there on behalf of families. They are courts of law but few lawyers enter them. The lawyers who do attend these courts may know some law, but they rarely have the knowledge of those who work with families. Perhaps these courts protect families from the state, but the state rarely loses a case.

As a legal institution, it may be convenient shorthand for us to call them Family Courts. As a social institution the more appropriate title is: "A Legally Authorized Body Regulating the Futures of Family Members." Fortunately for their place in history, no master plan was drawn to give us the family courts that now adjudicate child neglect and abuse cases. Indeed, no plan could have designed an institution to be so completely inept at directing the future of a family involved in a child neglect proceeding.

Professionals working in the Family Court forum must bear some of the responsibility for this development. When child care workers bring the clearest case of physical abuse to the Court, they claim that the lawyers' use of evidence and technicalities prevent a finding of neglect. Lawyers hearing their clients' stories of long-term removals of children without review are

---

* David A. Cruickshank, B.A., LL.B. (Western Ontario), LL.M. (Harvard), Professor, Faculty of Law, University of Calgary; Counsel to Ontario Ministry of Community and Social Services, Children's Services Division.

rushing to the dusty precedents to revive parental rights doctrines. The judge is reviewing the evidence of parent-state conflict, but he or she may have a more subtle conflict to mediate — the tension between the professional goals of the lawyer and the child-care worker. This interstitial professional conflict produces many results which damage the public reputation of the Family Court as a competent arbiter of child neglect cases. In my view, this perceived incompetence is a product of some serious misunderstandings about the utility of the court and some equally serious misallocations of legislative power in child care matters. It is my thesis that in Canada we are on the threshold of developing legislative mechanisms to avoid court proceedings in the great majority of neglect and abuse cases and that this development is to be welcomed.

Court avoidance is a praiseworthy objective for lawyers, child care workers, children and parents. In fact, two expressions of that objective have practically become cliches for the professionals involved. First of all, we go to court "as a last resort". Secondly, the goal of intervention, before or after court proceedings, is "family re-unification". Considered against the outcome of hundreds of cases, these aims have been myths.[1] Court is not the light at the end of a long tunnel; it is more often the destructive explosion at the end of a short fuse.

This is not to say that Family Courts have no place in child neglect cases. They are charged with the application of compulsory state intervention in family matters and they take an important position in child welfare services. But that place should no longer be a central location, draining the main energies of child care professionals. The court should retreat to one end of a wide spectrum of child care services. A range of services exists now, but many are not recognized as formal methods of family intervention. No province has yet collected and legislated the spectrum of alternatives available in child care practice in Canada. Until this happens, I suggest that the courts will, by force of history, predominate in the handling of many child neglect cases which should never come before the bench.

In the province of British Columbia, a Royal Commission on Family and Children's Law has reported on the range of alternatives that could be implemented in child neglect cases. Their 1975 report on "Children and the Law" recommended legislated rights of children as part of a comprehensive code of children's law.[2] In the Part concerning protection of children, the possibilities for avoiding judicial intervention were outlined: the offer of services by the government, custody by agreement, voluntary surrender of guardianship, the child care conference, and short-term custody.[3] These legislative devices are now contained in a draft Children's Act, 1976[4] which awaits action by the government of British Columbia.

EXISTING LEGISLATION AND NEW DIRECTIONS

The child welfare legislation in Canadian provinces reveals the operative child care systems only to those who can read between the lines. In most provinces, an antique statute has been patched and expanded to cover immediate crises. In Saskatchewan[5] and Manitoba,[6] there is evidence of a comprehensive revision and a change of philosophy in the statutes, but the diehard premises of state intervention remain the same. The familiar trademarks of quasi-criminal procedures, language derived from the Poor Laws,[7] broad administrative discretion, and an obsession with financial matters still characterize child welfare statutes. And yet, behind the legislation, there are some dynamic efforts being made in Canada to strengthen troubled families without judicial intervention.

Some case examples will illustrate the operation of existing statutes at their worst. In British Columbia, when the capable parents of a physically handicapped child cannot afford the therapy and mechanical devices necessary for rehabilitation, they go to the Department of Human Resources. The child care worker will inform them that only children in care may receive such financial assistance,[8] and, to obtain this, if the parents are not on social assistance themselves, they must submit to the indignity of a court proceeding in which they admit to being "unfit, unable, or unwilling to care properly" for the child.[9] The child is then declared "in need of protection" and returned to the parents under a supervision order.[10]

This is a bureaucratic conspiracy between the federal Canada Assistance Plan and the provincial child welfare authorities. In order to keep tidy, manageable categories for financial assistance, legislation forces the family through a costly, inappropriate court hearing. At a minimum, British Columbia might adopt the voluntary relinquishment sections of some provincial legislation.[11] In those procedures, no court hearing is required, but the child comes into care by agreement and can receive financial aid. But the root assumption — that state custody and supervision must always accompany financial assistance — should be challenged. Otherwise, this misdirected use of legislative authority and court proceedings will continue to alienate parents and swell the child care caseloads.

In the *Mugford* case, the Child Welfare Act of Ontario was found wanting when the natural mother sought return of her child after an adoption placement.[12] But the *ad hoc* response of the legislative amendments in 1969[13] have re-routed cases through legal hoops that are not designed to serve children as much as they are calculated to facilitate a smooth-running adoption system. Briefly, the mother in this case wanted her child back after consenting to Crown wardship. The Children's Aid

Society resisted because the child had been placed for adoption. The mother's circumstances had changed to the degree that she was clearly ready and able to care for her child. Nevertheless, the parties embarked upon two years of litigation before it was decided (in the Supreme Court of Canada) that: 1) a natural mother could apply under the Child Welfare Act to terminate a Crown wardship;[14] and 2) the mother, on the merits of the application, was entitled to custody of her child.[15]

The Legislature of Ontario responded to the decision by granting time-limited rights of appeal to parents who seek termination of Crown wardship. The limits work in two ways. First, the parents may appeal from the original decision within 30 days.[16] Failing that step, they may apply for termination of wardship at any time before an adoption placement. However, once the adoptive parents have executed a notice of intention to adopt, the Crown wardship cannot be terminated and the parental rights to guardianship are extinguished.[17]

For the immediate crisis, the solution seems to be sound. Parental rights are recognized, and the integrity of an uninterrupted adoption system is preserved. But the costs of this patching job may be greater than its short-term benefits. A startling number of Ontario adoptions, instead of being authorized by the adoption consents that have always been available to achieve the same end under a different Part of the Child Welfare Act, are now being processed as neglect (*i.e.* "wardship") cases.[18] The natural parents are subjected to a legal process which reinforces the guilt associated with abandonment of their child. The child too can suffer; if an adoption placement breaks down, only the Crown, through the Director of Child Welfare or a Children's Aid Society, has a legal relationship to the child. A series of damaging placements may lie ahead and the natural parents are at this point legal strangers in the eyes of the agency. Finally, there is little evidence to suggest that adoptive parents will become an extinct species if the authorities use conventional adoption consents which avoid court hearings for the natural parents.[19]

In the *Mugford* case, the Legislature failed to project the consequences of their one-shot answer. In so doing, they have allowed the courts to become an instrument of the child care agencies for the wrong purposes and at the wrong time. I suggest that in many cases of uncontested adoption placements, the intervention of the courts at this stage is serving neither the parents or the children involved. Neglect proceedings should be confined to actual facts related to neglect or abuse. In the alternative, the neglect and adoption provisions of the Child Welfare Act should be completely re-cast to allow for termination hearings in which parental rights can be tested against any placement proposed by the agency. Surely the courts cannot be blamed for this legislative misallocation and agency exploitation of judicial power.

A third illustration from the Alberta Child Welfare Act[20] highlights a frequent problem in Canada concerning the delays in child neglect proceedings. When a child is apprehended or taken into care under the Alberta Act, a hearing does not have to be held until twenty days from the date of apprehension.[21] Even at that first presentation of the case, the child does not have to be present or be represented by counsel.[22] The judge can, and often does, adjourn the hearing on neglect for "such further period" as he "may direct".[23] Accused persons under the Criminal Code get far better attention to their fundamental freedoms.[24]

Child welfare organizations will complain that it takes time to notify parents of the hearing and to prepare the agency's case. In many cases, one parent is out of the jurisdiction or the legal requirements of serving notice cannot be met within the necessary ten days preceding the hearing.[25] But child welfare authorities must also acknowledge the extent of their unfettered power during the twenty day period. They have sole discretion to determine whether the child should be detained in custody, placed in a temporary home, or returned to the parents.[26] Also, the maximum period has become the standard rule for processing apprehensions, not the outside limit; as a result, an unsupported apprehension canot be challenged for at least three weeks. Finally, the practice of "withdrawing" an apprehension just before the court appearance has the effect of shielding the authorities from any judicial scrutiny of their original intervention and subsequent twenty days of work with the family.

In adult criminal matters, an abuse of the arrest power by a common practice of "withdrawing" would lead to civil actions against the police for false arrest. The parents in a child welfare apprehension would have difficulty proving a similar charge on behalf of their child. The apprehension may not even be like an arrest because it is undertaken to protect the child. The broad grounds for apprehension exclude any notion of a "reasonable cause" criterion. Finally, the release of the parents from court proceedings is no doubt sufficient to dampen their wishes for vindication in the courts.

This example of delay mandated by legislation raises many serious questions of civil rights for parents and their children. But more importantly, it points to a legislative failure to give individual attention to different types of cases. A documented case of repeated child abuse may well require a twenty-day period of preparation. However, leaving a child unattended in a parked car for an hour may call for only a one-day period preceding minimal judicial intervention. The sweep of present legislation fails to separate legitimate, short-term extra-judicial intervention from cases which require the full protections of a court hearing.

The courts have a dual role to play in child neglect cases directed to them by legislation. Their existing role calls primarily for the legitimation of the child welfare authority's activities prior to a hearing. This is done explicitly by confirming agency actions with a disposition that matches agency expectations. It is done implicitly by a failure to examine closely the work of the authority during the pre-hearing delay. The second role, as watchdogs over the child welfare authorities, is not encouraged by Canadian legislation. In my view, it is proper for the courts to hold the administrative agencies accountable for compulsory intervention in family lives. Our legislation needs to make this mandate precise without returning to the shackles of "parental rights over best interests".

The malfunctions of existing legislation must be faced with a comprehensive response. The *Mugford* case leaves behind the dangers of streaming cases through the courts that don't belong there until the day of a final adoption order. The handicapped child in British Columbia becomes a court statistic in order to receive financial aid. The delays built into Alberta child neglect apprehensions apply to all children, regardless of their individual needs. Advocates of law reform must, therefore, meet demands for individualized, non-adversarial child care; but they must also find the fulcrum between court avoidance as an aid to therapy and court intervention as an accountability feature of child care systems. The British Columbia Royal Commission proposals must be tested with these goals in mind.

THE OFFER OF SERVICES

The most basic duty of child welfare authorities — to provide supportive services to families — is rarely reflected in Canadian legislation. The British Columbia Commission saw this duty as the starting point for a new group of legislative options. The Commission recommended that the government and its child care agencies should be obligated by legislation to offer child care services to families who cannot meet the needs and rights of their children and that this offer of services should be accompanied by legislative protections for the persons who are carrying out the services.[27]

This recommendation has been carried out to some degree in Saskatchewan, where the Minister of Social Services "may, in order to enable a parent to maintain a child in his home and in order to prevent the child from becoming a child in need of protection, assist the parent by providing such welfare services as the minister considers necessary and advisable."[28] The goal of preventive services is laudable, but the Saskatchewan legislation has not left the direction in the hands of the people who actually deliver child care services. Ministerial discretion is subject to political restraints and tends to be reserved for special cases. The motive behind ministerial control is undoubtedly the need for budgetary restrictions. However, an annual budget for preventive services could be established without imposing ministerial discretion on its day-to-day application. The drafting of a statutory service always carries financial implications,[29] but these should be balanced with the opportunity to re-formulate the whole doctrine of *parens patriae* through an "offer of services" clause.

The practising doctrine of "the state as parent" centres around the need to substitute legally the state as a parent. The rationale for intervention is to protect the child because of the state's interest in future generations. Wherever compulsory intervention seems necessary, the courts are relied upon to give a fair hearing and attendant legal rights for those objecting to the state's interference. Yet, at an earlier stage, before courts even become entitled to hear a case for intervention, there should be statutory protections which reflect a new doctrine of *parens patriae*.

The developing doctrine could be termed the "family support" theory of state intervention. It holds that no compulsory intervention by the courts should be permitted unless the family has first been offered supportive services in the home. Furthermore, in the event that services are refused or would clearly be late and inadequate, the neglect finding of the court should always be tested against the available dispositions and resources. If the child cannot get a proper placement through the child care agency, the finding of neglect should be vacated and the child returned to the parents. It has also been suggested that the judicial finding should be one of "family intervention," not "neglect," in order to remind child care workers of the family re-unification goal.[30]

This "family support" theory cannot be found in Canadian legal literature. Social workers and other child care professionals have been negligent in their failure to educate lawyers, judges and legislators about the trends in their practice which keeps families together and away from courtrooms. Lawyers are unlikely to learn from their colleagues about child abuse programmes involving lay therapists, parents' anonymous groups, crisis nurseries and homemakers.[31] Law schools which take a multidisciplinary approach to their family law courses are beginning to remedy this situation for future lawyers. In the meantime, it is submitted that an evolutionary doctrine of *parens patriae* could be founded by new legislation that requires attempts at supportive services to precede judicial intervention.

In the United States, the "family support" doctrine has received attention as a "right to remedial services," which in turn can be traced to the "right to treatment" cases.[32] The emerging right is derived in part from the intention clauses of the state child care statutes; in terms of federal policy, there is increased financial backing for those agencies which can demonstrate better community prevention services and well-organized service delivery.[33] The contribution of the "right to treatment" cases to the "right to remedial services" has been described by one writer as follows: "The basic premise of the theory is that, since noncriminal confinement can be justified only by the provision of treatment, where adequate treatment is not provided the authority for state intervention is vitiated and the state may not restrain the individual."[34]

Although the theory stated here has only been applied to American cases involving institutional settings, it has attractions as a legislative device for court avoidance. If the British Columbia recommendation is to be adequately implemented, the "offer of services" legislation will have to contain a number of guarantees which are consistent with the "family support" theory. First, the statutory conditions leading to a finding of neglect need to be revised. The broad net of the existing standards has been criticized in many quarters.[35] The Family and Children's Law Commission recommended more narrow grounds for neglect which could be called "emergency neglect."[36] Perhaps the best general statement of the proper reform goals was made by Sullivan in 1968:

"In summary, the court should find neglect only when parental action or condition has or is likely to have an effect on the child which conflicts with the self-perpetuating interest of the state and which effect the child is not likely to overcome without the protection of the state."[37]

By restricting the gateway to court intervention, an increasing number of cases will have to be handled in a rehabilitative service environment which cannot deny parental participation. At the same time, it would be unwise to make supportive services a necessary prerequisite for all apprehensions or findings of neglect. There will always be some serious cases of abandonment or continuing abuse, which have come to the attention of the agency for the first time, and which require agency-supervised placement following a court order.

However, the "family support" theory need not be abandoned on the courthouse steps. A second guarantee of prevention can be drafted in the disposition sections of new legislation. When a judge is prepared to order supervision or guardianship, he should order that care and control "which the child is unlikely to receive unless the court makes an order."[38] This legislative phrase would require the court to review the efforts previously made by child care workers, and to examine the less coercive measures that could be made available before the court orders some form of guardianship. This proposed change in the disposition powers and the re-writing of grounds for apprehension again point to the need for a comprehensive approach to legislation. Preventive measures cannot be isolated from court powers.

A third safeguard attached to the "offer of services" should be a "right of refusal" by parents or guardians.[39] If child care services proceed on the basis of consulting the community which is served, workers should have little difficulty in accepting the right of parents to turn down an offer of service. The approach to the family is a voluntary one and should carry no threat of compulsory intervention. Therefore, a legislative guarantee of a parental right to refuse should not only be found in the books, but also in the information passed by child care workers to their clientele. In the event of a refusal of services, the crucial thrust of child care practice should be toward revised methods of prevention, not an immediate leap to legal proceedings.

From the child-care worker's viewpoint, another guarantee should attach to the "offer of services". The worker needs legal protections from certain actions in tort when working in the home. In recent amendments to Canadian legislation this concern has been reflected in the protections for homemaker services.[40] The homemaker may enter the home in the absence of the parents and immunity from liability has, therefore, been granted in matters such as trespass and the exercise of "reasonable control and discipline" over children.[41] The specific mention of homemaker services allows these protections to be advanced, but it also dampens flexibility in preventive services. The homemaker provisions only apply where the parents are absent from the home; the continuation of services depends upon a judicial order, not a voluntary compact between the parents and the child care worker.[42] The Saskatchewan legislation seems to be more flexible in the provision of homemaker services where it stipulates that ". . . the officer or person may in lieu of removing the child take such steps as he considers necessary to provide for the safety or welfare of the child."[43] If this pattern is followed, the legal protections for child care workers will have to be drafted in a similarly flexible vein.

In summary, we must go back to the starting point of child welfare services — the duty to provide supportive and preventive child care services. This must be a legal duty, prescribed by statute and resting on the shoulders of government generally, not in the discretion of one minister. The existing statements of intention in child welfare legislation have produced no significant legal results because they have no force in the daily processing of cases. If an "offer of services" becomes a prerequisite to judicial intervention, except in serious emergencies, new legislation will contain the roots of a new "family support" doctrine of *parens patriae*.

CUSTODY BY AGREEMENT

Custody by agreement, or non-ward care, is becoming an established legislative device for court avoidance in many Canadian provinces.[44] Even those jurisdictions which do not authorize non-ward care agreements by statute have been using them for years.[45] This absence of legislative

authority in British Columbia prompted the Family and Children's Law Commission to make the following recommendation:
"New legislation should provide for custody by agreement between parents and the Superintendent of Child Welfare. The maximum period for custody by agreement should be fifteen months."[46]

The fundamental aims of custody by agreement are sometimes expressed in legislation; but more often Canadian legislation has lost sight of those goals and is presently in danger of undermining the trust that resides at the centre of this device for court avoidance. Custody by agreement aims at agency child care for a temporary period, during which time the parents are expected to work with the agency toward re-unification of the family. Normally, there should be no evidence of continuing, wilful neglect or abandonment of the child. The parents should have a positive attitude toward their future responsibilities and should be willing and equal participants in child care decisions during the period. For these goals to be fulfilled, the parent must remain in close contract with the child and the agency must encourage that contact through geographic proximity in their placement of the child. In British Columbia, the self-imposed question of child care workers sums up many of these objectives: "What can we offer a child committed to care by the Court that we cannot by non-ward care?"[47]

The serious omissions of existing legislation offer little comfort to those who advance custody by agreement as a short-term means of family re-unification. Some statutes have no limit on the term of the agreement.[48] A more common technique is to allow one-year agreements which are renewable for an indefinite number of terms.[49] Although the parents and the child welfare authorities are supposedly equal partners in the agreement, some statutes only allow the director of child welfare to terminate an agreement.[50] Furthermore, the termination by the director in Alberta or New Brunswick is deemed to be an apprehension of the child.[51] In other words, the parents are asked to relinquish custody on a basis of a mutual trust which can be unilaterally violated at any time by child care authorities.

The Manitoba statute contains some progressive elements of custody by agreement,[52] but no Canadian legislation has met all the key issues of this form of child care. First of all, there should be an initial term of three months for the agreement. This term, renewable for six months, would meet the convincing argument raised in *Beyond the Best Interests of the Child* — that a child's sense of time should govern placement decisions.[53] For a pre-school child, three months' absence from parents can feel like the adult equivalent of two years. The law should take account of the child's perceptions and demand that child care practice accommodate the child, not the convenience of workers.

Moreover, if the parent-agency agreement is truly being used to facilitate a family reunion, there should also be a maximum term which prevents automatic renewals for an indefinite period. The Manitoba legislation stipulates eighteen months,[54] in Ontario, a twenty-four month aggregate term is the upper limit.[55] In British Columbia, a fifteen month term has been recommended.[56]

The fifteen month limit, composed of a three month initial term and two potential renewals of six months each, would be sensible as part of a broader spectrum of child care options. In the existing legislative milieu, where nothing but judicial intervention can supplant an agreement, it is easy to see how non-ward care has expanded to a medium and long-term child care method. The "circumstances of a temporary nature"[57] which initiate an agreement, are not being applied to the actual length of many non-ward care agreements.[58] The fifteen month maximum would return custody by agreement to its original short-term goals. Furthermore, the frequent renewals within that term would serve as a regular measure of accountability for both the parents and the agency.

Accountability is the second main issue to be faced in non-ward care agreements. Because the courts are not involved in monitoring these agreements, the balance between the parents and the agency must be fair and equal. A minimum requirement should be an equal right to terminate the agreement. This is possible in Ontario and Manitoba, where the parents are allowed to give notice in writing, to terminate the agreement, and to regain custody of the child.[59] Even in provinces where the parental right to terminate is not clear, it is difficult to see how an agency could resist a writ of *habeas corpus* for the return of the child.[60] The agency must, therefore, satisfy the parents that the services for the child are in fact directed toward returning the child. Policies such as strictly limited parental visits cannot survive where parents have a right to regain custody that is easily exercisable.

The equal partnership concept can be empty unless the parents are confident that their past incapacities will not be used against them. The legislation in Ontario, Alberta and New Brunswick allows a child to be brought before a judge as a child in need of protection immediately upon termination of custody by agreement.[61] In most of these situations, the evidence justifying apprehension and protection relates to a time preceding the original agreement. As a result, the agency holds a Damocles' sword over the parents. Even a legitimate case for termination of the agreement by the parents could be upset by the agency going immediately to court. In order to maintain parental confidence in custody by agreement, the threat of apprehension should be removed from the non-ward care sections of legislation. If the child is truly in present danger by returning to the parents, the clauses reserved for all cases of neglect will be sufficient to bring about protective measures.

The third major issue surrounding non-ward care is the provision of services to children with special needs. Custody by agreement should be a device for the accommodation of the needs of someone like the handicapped child in British Columbia. The parents are not forced into the courtroom and yet they can receive shared federal-provincial funds for their child.

Some provinces have properly distinguished the "provision of services" agreement from the ordinary case of non-ward care.[62] This distinction should be made within the general framework of custody by agreement because the degree of agency supervision and control should be significantly reduced in cases of services for the child with special needs. Ideally, the mentally or physically handicapped child should reside at home and be a recipient of the "offer of services" proposed earlier in this paper. However, recognizing the existing fiscal structures and the need for agency custody in some programmes, legislation should contain the alternative of a "special needs agreement", as one option within custody by agreement.

VOLUNTARY SURRENDER OF GUARDIANSHIP

The technique of court avoidance that is probably most open to administrative abuse is the voluntary surrender of guardianship. The complete absence of a means to surrender permanent guardianship without a fault-oriented court proceeding was noted by the British Columbia Family and Children's Law Commission when they made the following recommendation:

"New legislation should provide for the voluntary surrender of guardianship, without the necessity of a court appearance. This administrative process should be reviewable by a Provincial Court judge within thirty days of the surrender."[63]

This recommendation was made in contemplation that adoption consent procedures would remain in child care legislation. As the *Mugford* case illustrated, the purposes of wardship and adoption proceedings are often confused. Where permanent guardianship orders become a routine step in an adoption process, that confusion reaches an apex. Voluntary surrender of guardianship is susceptible to this same kind of abuse, and it must receive careful attention from the legislative draftsman.

At the outset, adoption consents need to be kept distinct from voluntary surrender of guardianship, although both can have the same purpose of giving legal rights of guardianship to the Crown.[64] Because of case law developments, the adoption consent is thought to be a "weaker" means of terminating parental rights. In some provinces, the parent can apply to revoke a consent until the day of the adoption order.[65] There must be a serious effort made to obtain the consent of a known father of an illegitimate child or an Ontario Crown wardship order may be ineffective as a basis for an adoption order.[66] Child welfare authorities have complained that adoption placements can be disrupted by the uncertain legal position of the natural parents. Consequently, the use of judicial permanent guardianship proceedings seems to be the "safe" way to shut the door on the claims of natural parents, even when they agree to an adoption placement.

The next step toward court avoidance would be to substitute court proceedings for permanent guardianship with a voluntary, administrative means of surrendering guardianship. This step would respond to critics who say that it is unfair to subject the parents to a fault-finding judicial hearing. Canadian Legislatures to date have answered in two ways: (1) they retain a court hearing, but remove the fault orientation by allowing the parents to submit to the court's orders without an admission of fault,[67] or (2) they allow permanent guardianship to be surrendered by agreement or by an instrument of surrender which does not have to be reviewed by the court.[68] Some legislation covers both bases of voluntary relinquishment.[69] The British Columbia Commission recommended that the second avenue be included in new legislation.[70]

However, existing legislation has not reserved the voluntary surrender of guardianship for legitimate cases of continuing Crown wardship. A "legitimate case", in my view, is one which does *not* have an adoption placement secured at the time the voluntary surrender is executed. This could involve a handicapped child, an adolescent, or any child who is not in high demand for adoption. Child welfare authorities need to make an early placement in an environment where the child can learn to feel secure. Such a placement could mean a permanent foster home or a residential treatment program. The concept of shared guardianship between psychological parents and the Crown can also serve these children.[71] In all of these cases, no future involvement or rehabilitation of the natural parents would be contemplated. Otherwise, custody by agreement would serve the purposes of the agency. The agency must, therefore, be satisfied that the parents are fully informed of their abdication of parental rights and that they have no opposition or hesitancy in using non-judicial procedures to terminate parental rights. Indeed, a child care worker should be looking for positive benefits to be gained by court avoidance before recommending voluntary surrender.

Insistence on separate streams for adoption consents and the voluntary surrender of guardianship should not cut the child off from adoption if he is made a Crown ward. In a permanent foster home, for example, the parents may be prepared to adopt the child if assisted by a subsidized adoption programme. But it is important to remember that this plan for the child may not emerge until years after the initial placement. When it does emerge, the agency is unfettered by the rights of natural parents. In the British Columbia proposal, only inheritance rights would remain between the child and the natural parents until the day of the adoption order.[72]

Nevertheless, the parents would have a time-limited opportunity to reconsider a hasty decision about voluntary surrender. Within thirty days, they could go to the Provincial Court for a review of the administrative process in the voluntary surrender. Grounds for review will have to be developed, but it should be noted that unlike adoption, this would not be a parental request to revoke the surrender on the basis of the child's best interests.[73] Instead, it is an opportunity for a judge to determine that the parents fully understood the process, and gave their informed consent to the termination of parental rights. Beyond the Provincial Court, an appeal would lie to the Supreme Court within sixty days of the first judicial decision.[74]

At the present time, no Canadian statute contains all these proposed requirements of a voluntary surrender of guardianship. Only Manitoba, Saskatchewan and Alberta allow voluntary surrender to take place outside the courtroom.[75] The Alberta and Saskatchewan provisions seem tied to an adoption placement and do not have the flexibility advocated here for Crown wardship through a surrender.[76] The Manitoba Act has not linked voluntary surrender to adoptions, but that statute, along with the Alberta Act, omits any reference to judicial review. It is submitted that this latter omission could be fatal to the success of any voluntary surrender provision because the normal legal rights to judicial review of administrative action will be available to any parent wishing to get a voluntary surrender re-examined by a court.[77] New legislation in those provinces which do not have voluntary surrender provisions should establish this new form of wardship as one that has legal protections within a reviewable administrative framework.

Two parallel reform efforts should be made. First, adoption consents should be given a legal status that terminates parental rights at a fixed time well before the adoption order is finalized.[78] The present use of neglect proceedings to smooth the adoption process would be unnecessary if parental rights were terminated by adoption consents well before the final order. After a reasonable period for the revocation of consents and an appeal period following an unsuccessful revocation attempt by the natural parents, full guardianship of the child should vest in the Crown. Secondly, child care authorities should develop understandable administrative procedures to accept a voluntary surrender of guardianship. The "indenture" used in Alberta for this purpose is a fine example of what should be avoided.[79] The technical eighteenth-century language of the indenture is more unwieldy than a land deed. Child care workers who deal with these cases should be experienced and educated in the legal significance of the procedures. Above all, they should appreciate when a case needs to be referred to a lawyer or converted into a voluntary appearance before a judge.

In summary, voluntary surrender of permanent guardianship should be enacted as an administrative child neglect proceeding. There are appropriate cases for this type of court avoidance; they cannot be handled by adoption consents because the child is difficult to place in an adoptive home. Voluntary surrender also presents a challenge to child care workers, who must develop fair administrative procedures, and accept the need for judicial review in some cases.

SHORT-TERM CUSTODY

In many child abuse and neglect cases, there may not be the time or co-operation necessary to engage the parent in a voluntary programme designed to protect the child. For example, absent parents cannot be consulted when a young child is lost and apparently forgotten at the local fairground. In the "bad old days" of child protection, such a child might be apprehended as one "found wandering about at late hours"[80] and made a ward of the Crown. That apprehension, as we noted in Alberta, can lead to a twenty day separation from the parents. In more enlightened child care practices, the worker who finds the parents shortly after an apprehension often withdraws the apprehension and the child is quickly returned. No Canadian legislation addresses itself adequately to the withdrawal of apprehensions or the accountability of child care workers in this practice.

This situation, along with a legislative idea from the Yukon, motivated the British Columbia Commission to recommend that:
"Under new legislation, designated child care workers should be empowered to take custody of a child in emergency circumstances for a single period of forty-eight hours. The workers should be guided by specific grounds for use of this short-term custody and they should be accountable to the Family Court."[81]

In the Yukon, where weather conditions and travelling distances often overrule the finer legalities of a child neglect case, the forty-eight hour period was introduced as a pragmatic means of reducing the judicial caseload that would result from a literal application of the Child Welfare Ordinance.[82] The section outlining this technique of court avoidance reads:
"16(4) Where a child is apprehended pursuant to sub-section (1), the person who apprehends the child is not required to bring the child before a justice if the child is returned within forty-eight hours of the apprehension to his parents or the person having the actual care and custody of the child at the time of the apprehension."[83]

The Ontario Child Welfare Act bears some resemblance to this provision where it instructs workers to either go before a judge or return the child to the parents "as soon as is practicable and within five days of detaining a child in a place of safety."[84] This "hurry-up" direction for all apprehensions stands in sharp contrast to the much-abused twenty day delay in the Alberta statute.

In a spectrum of child welfare legislative reforms, short-term custody has an important role. However, if it is to be freed from a court hearing, some strict limitations must be placed on its application so that it does not become a powerful form of child arrest. Specific cases which justify short-term custody have therefore been proposed in the British Columbia Draft Children's Act, 1976 as follows:

"(a) a dependent child has left his home and no adult person appears to be exercising necessary care and control over him,

(b) the child appears to be in physical danger or represents a potential physical danger to himself or others,

(c) a child under 12 years of age is apparently unattended, and

(d) a child incapable of giving his own consent for medical treatment must, for his own protection, in the opinion of the person apprehending the child, be taken immediately to a medical facility for assessment and diagnosis of his condition, and no parent or other person is willing or able to take alternative remedial action."[85]

It is also clear from the draft legislation that a worker must have a short custody period in mind, not a regular apprehension followed by court proceedings.[86] Short-term custody should not become a regular "pre-apprehension" step which gives the agency a new period of contemplation. This suggestion is not to discourage the normal reflection and change of circumstances that often lead an agency to withdraw an ordinary apprehension. But the proposed forty-eight hour custody term may well divert cases from the court-oriented conveyor belt and reduce the incidence of withdrawn apprehensions.

Two themes emerge once again from this recommendation:

(1) if adversarial proceedings can be held off in certain cases, preventive and remedial work can be immediately substituted before the child care agency is perceived as "the enemy";[87] and

(2) without accountability features, legislative power which has a compulsory element can be misallocated and abused.

This latter theme was of such concern to the British Columbia Commission that they introduced several checks on short-term custody.[88] First, the workers entitled to exercise this power would have to be specially designated by the Director of Child Care. Presumably they would be properly trained for these cases and would be familiar with temporary custody facilities that are completely divorced from juvenile delinquency resources. Secondly, the repeated use of short-term custody would be discouraged. Each time a child was detained on this basis, a written report would have to be filed with the Family Court in the locality. Those reports could then be reviewed by a judge as part of a child's case history; repeated inaction by child care workers, following previous uses of short-term custody, would be scrutinized by the court. Finally, if the period extends beyond forty-eight hours, the designated workers must either return the child to a parent or make an apprehension and go before a judge within seven days. If the apprehension is to be withdrawn, the worker will have to explain that step in person to the judge on the day the case is called.

In conclusion, the short-term custody device could be a valuable, though dangerous, piece of legislation. It carries the benefit of fast intervention without being committed to the one-way street that so often begins with the first court appearance of the family. On the other hand, particularly in the area of controlling potential criminal activity by young persons, the power could be irresponsibly used. Careful evaluation of the uses and effects of short-term custody should accompany the already cautious legislative drafting of this power.

THE CHILD CARE CONFERENCE

A stroke of the legislative pen can sometimes convert the "obvious" or "commonplace" solution into the "bold, unprecedented" measure. The conversion can occur without political chicanery and noisy announcements because the "new" idea has always been right before our eyes. With regard to the child care conference idea, the British Columbia Family and Children's Law Commission was well aware that it was re-discovering the case conference used commonly by social workers. The Commission recommended:

"New legislation should introduce the child care conference as a voluntary means of resolving child care cases. The conference should be chaired by a mediator who can assist the parties in reaching a child care agreement. The discussions in the conference should be confidential and informally structured."[89]

The proposal of an informal method of dispute resolution is not revolutionary among child care professionals. Lawyers, too, negotiate the outcome of a child neglect case before they enter the courtroom. But the child care conference invites a middle alternative to both the child welfare and legal processes. The cases most amenable to such a solution will be those where family re-unification is possible and the parents have a strong concern for the protection of their interest in the child. When preventive measures have been exhausted and the removal of a child by non-ward care is not desirable, the existing notion of a case conference often requires a consideration of only the judicial orders available. If the exclusive professionalism of these conferences was broken down and the court alternatives were momentarily set aside, there would be new hope for a resolution, evidenced by a formal agreement in writing, that could satisfy both the parents and the child care authorities.

The legislator will immediately face the question of how formalized the conference should become under legislation as opposed to unwritten guidelines. Who should initiate and control the conference? Who should attend? Will the conference have a professional orientation, a community base, or a family-centred composition? What will be the legal significance of discussions and agreements arising from the conference? There is very little precedent for legislation on these issues, and it may take considerable amendment in future years to accommodate new developments in this concept of negotiation.

The province of Quebec has taken a parallel initiative in the establishment of their "Comité pour la protection de la jeunesse."[90] Although this committee is not limited to negotiation and it has some powers of compulsion, the goal of court avoidance by assiduous use of child welfare professionals is the same. The ten person committee of professionals has broad powers to under-take preventive programs, investigations, and the disposition of some cases of reported child abuse.[91] Insofar as the Quebec committee diverts cases from court, the function is similar to the child care conference. However, the institutional character of the committee and its power to refer cases directly to court set it apart from the British Columbia proposal.[92]

The only regular and continuous participant in a child care conference would be the mediator.[93] He or she must be a person with adept communication skills and experience in negotiations. The mediator should be independent of the child care system, but must respond to the system's request for a child care conference. Independence is preserved by the fact that the parents would also have the right to ask that a conference be convened. Furthermore, the parents could control the invitations of professionals who should attend the conference. Once assembled, the mediator would aim to facilitate discussion of the common ground between the parents and the various professionals interested in the child's future — the teacher, the public health nurse, the homemaker, the social worker and others called to assist.

A significant departure from the present case conference would be the active participation of the parents in the child care conference. This method of court avoidance would not compel their attendance. They would speak for themselves; the involvement of lawyers would be discouraged. Supportive friends and relatives would be invited to assist the parents in working toward the child care agreement. If the child in question is sufficiently mature, his or her views should also be heard. In this consultative process, the mediator's most difficult job will be to keep the family's views afloat and credible in order to balance the tendency of the professionals to overwhelm the parents with mounds of articulated and written evidence.

The parties should, at the conclusion of the conference, seek to record their areas of mutual agreement. Although the discussions in the conference would be held in total confidence, it is recommended that the written agreement should be admissible in any subsequent court proceedings. A breach of the agreement by either the parents or the agency would be helpful to the court upon disposition of a case.

There would only be one means of compelling parents to participate in a child care conference. The British Columbia Commission recommended that among the court disposition powers, the judge should be able to refer the parents to a child care conference for a mediated solution.[94] It must be remembered that the case would come to court in the ordinary way — where a child is "in need of care". Obviously this disposition would be fruitless if a child care conference had failed previously. However, where the parental attitude has changed and there is a willingness to negotiate, rather than oppose, some form of agency intervention, the judge should be able to direct the convening of a child care conference.

Finally, the child care conference must be immunized from the criticism most often levelled at the courts — the delay in processing cases. The proposal calls for the conference to take place within four weeks of the date it is initiated. The mediator would also limit the time for the session; it would be the rare case that consumed more than half a day.

Lawyers may find the concept of the child care conference unpalatable. The parents are fully exposed and without a champion for their rights. The agreement may prove to be lop-sided in favour of the agency. While the agreement is admissible in a later court hearing, it is not enforceable by judicial proceedings. The final card is held by the agency, which can apprehend a child if a child care agreement breaks down and the child is in jeopardy. Despite these potential objections, it is submitted that lawyers would be wiser to join the movement toward negotiated child neglect matters. In my view, the child care conference is the future setting for a majority of child neglect cases. Lawyers have negotiation skills and should be welcome to apply them in this forum, as long as their adversarial robes are left in the corridor.

CONCLUSION

My original militant stance against Family Courts has mellowed. I have made no attempt to advocate an alternative which fully removes the functions of the Family Court. Nor has the term "court avoidance" been used to suggest that the court is to be approached like a tank full of piranhas. In considering alternatives to the judicial process, the argument is simply this: we must have a broader range of legislative alternatives to handle the unique features of each child neglect case; the Family Court is but one alternative reserved for contested matters or cases of abandonment, where parental rights must be removed or diminished. The techniques should be legislative, in order to promote uniformly high standards within a provincial child care system and to guarantee that child care administration will be accountable to families and to the public interest. Furthermore, alternatives like those recommended by the Family and Children's Law Commission have some precedent in Canadian legislation or child care practice. The collection and refinement of these techniques is a logical development that child welfare systems and provincial governments should be prepared to accept in the near future.

Law reform efforts directed at the unification or demolition of the Family Courts we know today are not in conflict with the proposals made here. In British Columbia, an experimental panel system, consisting of a judge and two lay persons for child neglect cases was attempted at the same time that the Commission worked out its recommendations for court avoidance.[95] But the courts now represent too much of the core of existing child welfare systems, and wholesale reform of judicial institutions is notoriously long in coming. Therefore, we should be looking at the "front end" of child neglect problems, where a spectrum of alternatives could be developed more quickly and where successes could produce a demonstrable reduction in judicial caseloads.

Finally, the issue of tension between lawyers and child care professionals deserves comment. The repeated argument for accountability is directed to this problem. Lawyers must be ready to accept a greater movement into the administrative realm in child neglect matters. However, they will insist on the protection of parental and children's rights even within that administrative process. Child care workers, in response to this demand, need not become "legal beagles". However, they should be willing to articulate procedures and policies which make their actions open to parental scrutiny and, in some cases, open to judicial review. Furthermore, these policies, guided by new founding legislation, will only be successful if they are anticipatory. Too often, child care professionals meet situations like the *Mugford* case which make them revile lawyers for another decade. But when the parents of a child have had no recourse within the administrative system they can hardly be blamed for going to the courts. An understanding of the need for court avoidance and the parallel need for accountability may help both professional fields to unfold a broader concept of teamwork in cases of abuse and neglect.

1 A 1974 study in the District of Columbia revealed that out of a random sample of 100 child abuse or neglect complaints, 89 complaints were followed by petitions for court action. In 82 of the 89 cases, the children were removed from their homes for the period of time prior to the court hearing. Burt, *The System for Neglected and Abused Children in the District of Columbia* 10, quoted in Areen, "Intervention Between Parent and Child: A Reappraisal of the State's Role in Child Neglect and Abuse Cases" (1975) 63 Geo. L.J. 887.

2 The Fifth Report of the Royal Commission on Family and Children's Law, "Children and the Law", Queen's Printer, Victoria, B.C. (1975) contains seven parts: I. The Legislative Framework II. The Status of Children Born Outside of Marriage III. Children's Rights IV. The Special Needs of Special Children V. The Protection of Children (Child Care) VI. Custody, Access, and Guardianship VII. Adoption.

3 The Fifth Report of the Royal Commission on Family and Children's Law, "Part V, Protection of Children (Child Care)", (1975) at 10-25.

4 This draft was completed by Cruickshank and Adamson in December 1975, and is a supplement to the Commission's Fifth Report.

5 The Family Services Act, 1973 (Sask.), c. 38: *e.g.* s. 5(1) — "Subject to the approval of the Lieutenant Governor in Council, the minister may do such things as he considers advisable to promote the growth and development of community services and resources designed to support families in the proper care of their children and to prevent circumstances that lead to family breakdown."

6 Child Welfare Act, 1974 (Man.), c. C-30.

7 Fraser, "Children in Need of Protection" in *Studies in Canadian Family Law,* (1972 ed. Mendes da Costa) Vol. 1, Butterworths, Toronto, 1972, at 72-73. The frequent use of the term "ward" to describe children before the courts first appeared in the time of Henry VIII, when he established a Court of Wards to sell the guardianship of children and (more importantly) their estates to the highest bidder. The clinging attitude toward children as chattels and objects of financial concern remains a reality in our present use of the term. See: Areen, "Intervention Between Parent and Child: A Reappraisal of the State's Role" (1975) 63 Geo. L.J. 887-937.

8 "Services Policy and Procedures Manual", Department of Human Resources, (1976) at 8:01.

9 Protection of Children Act, R.S.B.C. 1960, c.303, s. 7(k) [re-en 1968, c. 41, s. 3].

10 *Ibid.* ss. 7, 8(9)(*a*)(i) [re-en. 1968, c. 41, s. 4].

11 *E.g.* Child Welfare Act, R.S.O. 1970, c. 64, s. 23*a* [am. 1975, c. 1, s. 15]:
"(2) Subject to the approval of the children's aid society having jurisdiction in the area where the parent resides, or the Minister, a parent,
(*a*) who through circumstances of a temporary nature is unable to make adequate provision for his child; or
(*b*) who is unable to provide the services required by his child because of the special needs of the child, may voluntarily place the child into the care, custody or under the supervision of the society or of the Crown, as the case may be."

12 *Mugford v. Children's Aid Society of Ottawa* [1969] S.C.R. 641, 4 D.L.R. (3d) 274; reversing [1968] 2 O.R. 866. *Re Mugford* [1970] 1 O.R. 601, 9 D.L.R. (3d) 113. Affirmed [1970] S.C.R. 261 (*Sub nom. Children's Aid Society of Ottawa v. Mugford*), [1970] 1 O.R. at 610n, 9 D.L.R. (3d) at 123n. See Green, "Re: Mugford — A Case Study of the Interaction of Child-Care Agency, Court and Legislature" (1971) 1 R.F.L. 1; Baxter, Law and Domestic Relations, (1973) 51 Can. Bar Rev. 137 at 145.

13 Child Welfare Amendment Act, 1968-69 (Ont.). c.9[now Child Welfare Act, R.S.O. 1970, c. 64, ss. 32, 36].

14 *Mugford v. C.A.S. of Ottawa, supra* note 12.

15 *Re Mugford, supra* note 12.

16 Child Welfare Act, R.S.O. 1970, c. 64, s. 36.

17 *Ibid.* s. 32.

18 Because of a change in reporting methods, only the years 1969-72 give a statistical picture of the number of Crown wards who were discharged from care via adoption. The following statistics are relevant:

Year	Crown Wards Adopted	All C.A.S. Handled Adoptions
April/69 - Mar/70	4,192	5,947
April/70 - Mar/71	3,986	5,877
April/71 - Mar/72	3,273	5,265

Source: Annual Reports of the Ontario Department of Social and Family Services, Queen's Printer, Toronto, 1969-72.

19 *E.g.* in British Columbia, where parental rights are never foreclosed until the day of the adoption order, the normal adoption route is attractive enough to have a waiting list of hundreds. See Fifth Report of the Royal Commission on Family and Children's Law, Part V, at 42-44 and Part VII, at 2-6.

20 R.S.A. 1970, c. 45.

21 *Ibid.,* s. 18(1).

22 *Ibid.,* s. 18 requires no attendance of the child and counsel is only appointed at the request of the Director of Child Welfare.

23 *Ibid.,* s. 18(1).

24 Criminal Code (Can.), 1976, s. 454(1) requires an accused to be brought before a justice within twenty-four hours of the arrest in most cases; s.465(1)(b) requires that no remand can be longer than eight clear days without the consent of the accused and the prosecutor.

25 Child Welfare Act, R.S.A. 1970, c. 45, s. 19(1).

26 *Ibid.,* s. 16(1) [am. 1972, c. 18, s. 4].

27 See notes 2, 13.

28 Family Services Act, ss. 1973, c. 38, s. 6.

29 The usual objection to preventive services is their expense. There is no demonstrable return and they are often cut from government budgets. However, some recent cases in the U.S. have brought to light the greater expense of foster care and institutional care as opposed to state-supported home care for children. See Thomas, "Child Neglect Proceedings — A New Focus" (1974) 50 Ind. L.J. 60 at 60-63.

30 Areen, "Intervention Between Parent and Child: A Re-Appraisal of the State's Role" (1975) 63 Geo. L.J. 887 at 934.

31 One of the few articles directed to lawyers concerning non-legal alternatives in child abuse cases was written by a lawyer: Fraser, "A Pragmatic Alternative to Current Legislative Approaches to Child Abuse" (1974) 12 Am. Crim. L. Rev. 103 at 122-124.

32 Thomas, see note 29, at 71-78. See also "The Relationship Between Promise and Performance in State Intervention in Family Life" (1972-73) 9 Columbia Journal of Law and Social Problems 28; Levine, "Caveat Parens: A Demystification of the Child Protection System" (1973), 35 U. Pitt. L. Rev. 1 at 36-37.

33 Thomas, see note 29 at 72-76 (table of state statutes).

34 Thomas, see note 29, at 77. The author cites the "mutual compact" theory enunciated by Judge Ketcham, in which the absence of promised governmental care breaks the agreement between parents and state, resulting in the loss of legal or moral justification for asserting state control over the child. See Ketcham, "The Unfulfilled Promise of the American Juvenile Court" (1962) Justice for the Child 22 at 25-27.

35 *E.g.* Foster and Freed, "Unequal Protection: Poverty and Family Law" (1967) 42 Ind. L.J. 192; Katz, "Foster Parents Versus Agencies: A Case Study in the Judicial Application of the Best Interests of the Child Doctrine" (1966) 65 Mich. L. Rev. 145; Sullivan, "Child Neglect: The Environmental Aspects" (1968) 29 Ohio St. L. J. 85; Note "The Custody Question and Child Neglect Rehearings" (1968) 35 U. Chi. L. Rev. 478 at 480-84.

36 Fifth Report of the Family and Children's Law Commission, *Part V: Protection of Children (Child Care),* (1975) at 29-32. See also Draft Children's Act, 1976, Queen's Printer, Victoria, B.C., Part V, s. 1.

37 Sullivan, "Child Neglect: The Environmental Aspects" (1968) 29 Ohio St. L. J. 85 at 93.
38 This phrase is close to that used by Sullivan, see note 37, at 9. It has also been used in the Family and Children's Law Commission Report, see note 36, in the definition of "emotional neglect" (p. 27 of Report).
39 Fifth Report, see note 36 at 13-14:
    "4. Recommendation: Parents or guardians who are offered child care services on a voluntary basis should have the absolute right to refuse the services offered."
40 E.g. The Child Welfare Act, S.M. 1974, c.C-30, s.12; The Child Welfare Amendment Act, S.O. 1975, c.1, s.15.
41 The Child Welfare Amendment Act, 1975 (Ont.), c.1, s.15 [enacting s.22a(3)].
42 Ibid., s.22a(7).
43 The Family Services Act, 1973 (Sask.), c. 38, s. 17.
44 E.g. Child Welfare Act, R.S.O. 1970, c. 64, s. 23a [am. 1975, c. 1, s. 15]; Child Welfare Act, R.S.A. 1970, c. 45, s. 35, [am. 1973, c. 15, s. 7]; Child Welfare Act, R.S.N.B. 1973, c. C-4, s. 16; Child Welfare Act, 1974 (Man.), c. C-30, s. 13; Family Services Act, 1973 (Sask.), c. 38, ss. 8, 10.
45 British Columbia has used non-ward care agreements for over eight years; most children discharged from care in the first six months are in non-ward care: Fifth Report, see note 36, at 6-7 (App. III).
46 Fifth Report, see note 36, at 15.
47 "Non-Ward Care: Policies and Procedures," Vancouver Resource Board, November 1974.
48 E.g. Alberta, Saskatchewan, New Brunswick, see note 44.
49 E.g. New Brunswick, Saskatchewan, see note 44.
50 E.g. Alberta, New Brunswick, see note 44.
51 Alberta, New Brunswick, see note 44.
52 Manitoba, see note 44: the legislation has an eighteen month maximum term, termination rights for parents, and no automatic tie to apprehension if the agreement breaks down.
53 Goldstein, Freud and Solnit, Beyond the Best Interests of the Child (1973) at 40.
54 See note 44.
55 See note 44.
56 See note 46.
57 Child Welfare Amendment Act, 1975 (Ont.), c. 1, s. 15 [enacting s.23a(2)(a)].
58 The wording of all Canadian legislation and policy directives seems to indicate the temporary nature of non-ward care. However, as a British Columbia study pointed out, 14% of children in non-ward care remained in care after two years: Fifth Report, see note 36, App. III, 7.
59 Ontario, Manitoba, see note 44.
60 None of the legislative provisions for custody by agreement allow the parents to relinquish fully their rights to custody. Unless the agency has obtained a voluntary surrender of guardianship or a court order, they would have to return the child to the persons having the primary legal right to custody.
61 Ontario, Alberta, New Brunswick, see note 44.
62 E.g. Child Welfare Amendment Act, 1975 (Ont.), c. 1, s. 15 adding s.23a(2), see note 11. Saskatchewan has a similar bilateral agreement in s.8 of the Family Services Act ss. 1973, c. 38, but in s. 7 they also allow for the unsupervised unilateral provision of services by the minister:
    "7. The minister may make such payments as he considers necessary to or for the benefit of a parent, child or other person where special services or moneys are considered by the minister essential to enable the parent to care for the child."
63 Fifth Report, see note 36, at 18. The Commission recommendation for the voluntary surrender of guardianship on a temporary basis is not discussed, because of the similarity to non-ward care.
64 E.g. Family Services Act, 1973 (Sask.), c. 38, s. 11(8) (voluntary surrender) provides for complete termination of parent rights:

"Except as provided in this section and section 12, a committal of a child made under this section is irrevocable and the parent is not thereafter entitled to the guardianship or custody of the child or to any control or authority over, or any right with respect to, the child."

However, adoption consents, before the adoption order, give less explicit rights of guardianship. This can be seen from s. 56(4) of the Act, which provides that adoptive parents who have not made a timely application to adopt must return the child to the director of the social services department.

65   *E.g.* Adoption Act, R.S.B.C. 1960, c. 4, s. 8(5). See also Child Welfare Act, R.S.O. 1970, c. 64, s. 73(1).

66   Children's Aid Society of Metro. Toronto v. Lyttle, [1973] S.C.R. 568, 10 R.F.L. 131, 34 D.L.R. (3d) 127. See also Cruickshank, "Forgotten Fathers: The Rights of the Putative Father in Canada" (1972) 7 R.F.L. 1, 41.

67   *E.g.* Child Welfare Act, R.S.O. 1970, c. 64, s. 20(1)(*b*)(i).

68   Child Welfare Act, R.S.A. 1970, c. 45, s. 30; Family Services Act, 1973 (Sask.), c. 38, s. 11; Child Welfare Act, 1974 (Man.), c. 30, s. 15.

69   Child Welfare Act, R.S.A. 1970, c. 45, ss. 14(*e*)(xv), 30; Family Services Act, 1973 (Sask.), c. 38, ss. 11, 13; Child Welfare Act, 1974 (Man.), c. 30, ss. 15, 16(a)(ii).

70   See note 63.

71   Fifth Report, see note 36, at 55-57.

72   Fifth Report, see note 36, at 17.

73   *E.g.* Adoption Act, R.S.B.C. 1960, c. 4, s.8(5). The case law on revocations indicates that a best interests test will prevail over "parental rights": *Re Wells* (1962) 33 D.L.R. (2d) 243, 37 W.W.R. 564 (B.C.C.A.). In practice, very few revocation attempts by a natural mother are successful; in British Columbia, one application out of ten was successful in the period 1970-74: Fifth Report of the Family and Children's Law Commission, Part VII, Adoption, Appendix A, Table III.

74   Fifth Report, see note 36, at 17.

75   See note 68.

76   Child Welfare Act, R.S.A. 1970, c. 45, s. 30(1):

"Where a parent, by instrument of surrender . . . surrenders custody of a child to the Director *for the purpose of adoption* . . . ." (emphasis added).

See also: Family Services Act, 1973 (Sask.), c. 38, s. 11(3) (return of child after one year limited to child placed for adoption).

77   Although no reported case has tested the voluntary surrender sections on administrative law grounds there is some support for bringing the prerogative writs in analagous areas: *M.T. v. Family and Children's Services of Lunenburg County* (1975) N.S.R. (2d) 348 (C.A.) (mandamus to compel Director to reveal time and place of adoption hearing to natural parents); *Kociuba v. Children's Aid Society of Halton* (1971) 18 R.F.L. 286 (Ont.) (habeas corpus to compel delivery of child to father, who had no notice of Child Welfare Act proceedings); *Re Child Welfare Act; Worlds v. Director of Child Welfare* (1967) 61 W.W.R. 513, [1968] 2 C.C.C. 88, 65 D.L.R. (2d) 252 (Alta.) (habeas corpus with certiorari in aid to examine permanent committal order and court record). In a voluntary surrender, the availability of judicial review depends on whether the function of the administrative procedures is classified as "administrative" or "quasi-judicial". If the latter classification prevails, remedies such as certiorari will be available to review the procedures. Under a voluntary surrender clause, a key problem may be the doctrine of waiver, which holds that a person's conduct in consenting to certain procedures may result in the forfeit of rights to a later hearing. See Reid, *Administrative Law and Practice,* (1971) at 111 *et seq.,* 159-161, 214.

78   This was recommended by the British Columbia Family and Children's Law Commission: Fifth Report, Part VI, Adoption, at 13-15. The Commission cited the survey of the English Houghton Report which stated that 84% of mothers giving up their children wanted their consents to be irrevocable.

79   Alberta Department of Social Services and Community Health, Child Welfare Branch, Edmonton, Form H.S.D.33A:

"*e.g.* Now Therefore this Indenture Witnesseth that the Party of the First Part doth voluntarily commit and make over the said child to the care and guardianship of the Party of the Second Part, and doth resign all claim to the custody or any control or authority over or any right to interfere with the said child."

80   Protection of Children Act, R.S.B.C. 1960, c. 303, s. 7(1)(*h*).
81   Fifth Report, see note 36, at 25.
82   Child Welfare Ordinance, c.C-3, Rev. Ord. of N.W.T. 1974, s. 16(1), (2).
83   *Ibid.*, s. 16(4).
84   Child Welfare Amendment Act, S.O. 1975, c. 1, s. 16.
85   Draft Children's Act, 1976, Part V, s. 21 (Supplement to Fifth Report, B.C. Family and Children's Law Commission).
86   *Ibid.*, s. 21(3): (3) Notwithstanding subsection (2), no person must apprehend a child under this section where, prior to apprehension, that person has concluded that it will be necessary to proceed for an order under section 37 (children found in need of care).
87   *Ibid.*, s. 21(5): (5) Subject to subsection (4), a person acting under this section *must assist the parent or other person to remedy the situation which gave rise to the apprehension* and must return the child to that parent or other person within 48 hours of apprehension (emphasis added).
88   All the checks discussed herein are mentioned at pp. 22-25, Fifth Report, see note 36.
89   Fifth Report, see note 36, at 22.
90   Youth Protection Act, R.S.Q. 1964, c. 220, as amended by Bill 78, 2nd sess., 30th Legislature, National Assembly of Quebec, 1974.
91   Bill 78, see note 90, ss. 14b, 14c, 14g, 14n.
92   *Ibid.*, s. 14n.
93   The main features of the child care conference discussed herein are outlined in the Fifth Report, see note 36, at 18-22, and Appendix V.
94   Fifth Report, see note 36, at 54-55.
95   The Use of Lay Panels in the Unified Family Court, Third Report of the British Columbia Family and Children's Law Commission, (1974). See Also: The Family, The Courts, and the Community, Fourth Report of the British Columbia Family and Children's Law Commission, (1975) 92-98.

The Welfare Of The Child

*Olive M. Stone**

This essay deals with the assessment, representation, and promotion of child welfare in judicial proceedings. In 1972, John Eekelaar found a general acceptance throughout the Commonwealth that in custody cases the welfare of the child is to be considered the first and paramount consideration.[1] I will refer to this as the "welfare principle". Even as far afield as Kenya it predominates over the local custom of unfettered discretion in the husband.[2] Bradbrook[3] cited s. 1 of the English Guardianship of Infants Act 1925[4] and added: "This English principle is equally applicable over the whole of Canada, as legislation and case law has produced the same result".[5] Frank Bates also agrees in his article in the Australian Law Journal in March 1975,[6] in which he applauds both the approach adopted and the decision reached by the New South Wales Court of Appeal in *Barnett v. Barnett*.[7] Here custody of a boy aged eight and a girl aged five was entrusted to their father in preference to their mother after a divorce, reversing the decision of the trial judge that the children should be separated, the boy to be in his father's and the girl in her mother's custody. In these Commonwealth jurisdictions the 'welfare principle' is also generally approved by academic writers.

South of the 49th parallel, however, the situation appears otherwise. In their seminal contribution of 1973: *Beyond the Best Interests of the Child,* Goldstein, Anna Freud and Solnit have suggested that the United States equivalent of the 'welfare principle', *viz.,* 'in the best interests of the child'[8] may be positively harmful in that it engenders too euphoric an attitude by the court to what must be a situation highly detrimental to the child. Before any forum is required to decide with whom and under what imposed conditions, if any, a child shall live during his minority, the child's stability and long-term welfare have been endangered. For this reason these writers have suggested the criterion of "the least detrimental available alternative for safeguarding the child's growth and development",[9] to bring home to all concerned that damage may have already been done and more threatens.

* Dr. Olive M. Stone, LL.B., B.Sc. (Econ.), Ph.D., of Gray's Inn, Barrister-at-law, former Reader in Law at the London School of Economics where she taught law since 1950.

This formula has already found its way into the decisions of tribunals within the Union.[10] To Caleb Foote, Robert Levy and Frank Sander, "the best interests of the child" is the guiding shibboleth[11] used by the courts in custody disputes.[12]

No sufficient evidence is available to enable us to say whether the courts in the different Commonwealth jurisdictions considered are more or less aware than their counterparts in the United States of the dangers to the child inherent in any judicial determination as to the child's care and upbringing. Nor can it be assumed that there is a constant level of awareness in any one of the jurisdictions considered. It can only be hoped that this very salutary warning from the United States will be heeded in all jurisdictions, whatever the formula enunciated by the legislation or the courts.

This essay examines: (1) What, if anything, is or should be the meaning of "the welfare of the child" or "the best interests of the child" as applied today in Commonwealth and United States courts in the various kinds of cases concerned with arrangements for the custody or upbringing of a child; (2) the implications of the principle for the nature of the proceedings and the gathering and presentation of evidence, including the relevance of the great social divisions such as religion, race, nationality and sex; (3) the range of judgments or remedies available at the tribunal; and (4) the constitution and nature of the tribunal required for such hearings.

The differences between the approach in much of the United States and in the more progressive, at least, of the Commonwealth tribunals, are unlikely to be considerable. One reason is that the "welfare principle" cannot be a precise formulation. The principle is intended only as a guideline. It has and should continue to have a variable content. This is by no means to deny the increased breadth and clarity brought to our understanding of the problems in the law relating to children by the skilful and concentrated research in the United States in recent years. It is to say that to lay down fixed general rules is to make the same kind of mistake as Dr. Spock has admitted making in his early works. In *J. v. C.* Lord Upjohn said that the law and practice in relation to infants "have developed, are developing and must, and no doubt will, continue to develop by reflecting and adopting the changing views, as the years go by, of reasonable men and women, the parents of children, on the proper treatment and methods of bringing up children; for after all that is the model which the judge must emulate, he must act as the judicial reasonable parent".

In decisions relating to children more curbs should be placed on the accusatorial nature of the proceedings, and efforts should be made to take greater account of the individual child and his unique situation, so that the child's interests are not subordinated to those of either or both of his parents when there is a real conflict between them. On the other hand, the pitfalls awaiting the inquisitor, and the frailty of human knowledge, cannot be disregarded. In this, as in many other areas, particularly of family law, the range of effective choice is more circumscribed than we like to admit, and the sanctions available are few and weak.

The making of decisions, after hearing details of the alternatives available, is a "judicial" role. In other words, I suggest that however much we may wish to encourage solutions by agreement, however many or radical the changes we may wish to see in the kind of evidence heard, the persons from whom it is heard, the time when, place where, and atmosphere in which it is received, and the kind of person or persons who eventually reach a decision, the proceedings will in the end be "judicial" proceedings. There is no alternative to some form of judicial process, however much or little it may differ from the type of judicial process with which we are most familiar.

I shall confine my consideration of these problems to England and Wales, Canada, Australia and the United States of America. There are two main reasons for starting with England and Wales. First, as the jurisdiction in which I ordinarily reside and with which I am most familiar, it is my normal base-point. It is also the only unitary jurisdiction included for present purposes, and is therefore the simplest to present. The United States is not only the largest group of jurisdictions, but it has the largest and most complex body of available research material, so that consideration of its provisions in short compass can be proportionately little more than fragmentary. Both Canada and Australia now have a federal Divorce statute, but in the United States family law (with quite minor exceptions) is a matter for state legislation, and although the National Conference of Commissioners on Uniform Laws has produced a number of important model uniform family law acts,[13] which have achieved varying degrees of state recognition, this recognition has not yet advanced sufficiently to achieve much simplification of the richly-varied scene relating to children.

THE MEANING OF 'THE WELFARE OF THE CHILD' OR 'THE CHILD'S BEST INTERESTS' IN THE VARIOUS PROBLEMS CONCERNED WITH CHILDREN

In England and Wales it was the Court of Chancery, exercising the prerogative jurisdiction of the Crown as *parens patriae* over minors constituted Wards of the Court, that first introduced consideration of the child's welfare.[14] It did so as a means of introducing in very unusual circumstances exceptions to the near-absolute right of the father to control and direct the custody, upbringing and education of legitimate children. Sir

George Jessel M . R . [15] considered that, after the passing of the Custody of Infants Acts 1839 and 1873, what was formerly the absolute right of the father became subject to the discretionary power of the judge. He expressed in a few words the function of the 'welfare principle' in equity, namely, to introduce another principle which, in a very restricted number of cases, might be applied as an exception to the sacred right of the father to have his every whim in relation to his children enforced without question by the courts. The equitable "welfare principle" (at first only in the rarest circumstances) was intended to subject the absolute right of the father to the discretionary power of the judge. *Re Agar-Ellis*[16] is a reminder of how narrow were the exceptions to the sanctity of paternal rights, even a year after Parliament had restored to a married woman the power to deal with her own property of which the wedding ceremony had previously been held to divest her. In that case, the Court of Appeal held[17] that the court would not interfere with the father's exercise of his parental authority except (1) where by his gross moral turpitude[18] he had forfeited his rights, or (2) he had by his conduct abdicated his parental authority,[19] or (3) he sought to remove the ward from the jurisdiction without the consent of the court. Sir William Brett M . R . added:[20] "I am not prepared to say that the patience of the Court, *in the case of its Ward*, might not be exhausted by other conduct of the father — by cruelty *to a great extent, or pitiless* spitefulness *to a great extent* ... but the court could not interfere on such grounds as that except *in the utmost need and in the most extreme case.*" Eighty-seven years later, a member of the Judicial Committee of the House of Lords would describe this case as "dreadful", and one in which "the Court of Appeal permitted a monstrously unreasonable father to impose upon his daughter of 17 much unnecessary hardship in the name of his religious faith".[21]

The English Guardianship of Infants Act 1886, which first gave actual parental rights to the mother, provided by Section 5 that the court might, on the application of the mother of any infant, "make such order as it may think fit regarding the custody of such infant and the right of access thereto of either parent, having regard to the welfare of the infant, and to the conduct of the parents and to the wishes as well of the mother as of the father..." The Guardianship of Infants Act 1925 further extended the principle by providing in Section 1: "Where in any proceedings before any court ... the custody or upbringing of an infant, or the administration of any property belonging to or held on trust for an infant, or the application of the income thereof, is in question, the court, in deciding that question, shall regard the welfare of the infant as the first and paramount consideration..." Historically, it seems quite clear that all the statutes sought to do was (1) to extend the range of exceptional cases in which the courts might intervene between the will of the father and his children, at first in favour of the mother (to whom actual rights were first given in

1886), and (2) the statutes sought to allow the discretionary power of the judge (as so extended) to prevail over the absolute right of the father in all custody cases in all courts, and not only in the Chancery Division of the High Court. Unfortunately the 1925 Act was the first of several ill-drafted statutes on the point.[22] It is now established[23] that the welfare principle applies not only between one parent and the other, but also between one or both parents and a stranger to the child, and that the Acts extend to illegitimate children, except as regards their maintenance.[24] Under the Guardianship of Minors Acts, however, only a parent or guardian may apply to the court,[25] which may be the High Court, county court or magistrates court.[26] There is also now power for either parent to apply to the court for adjudication on any specific question affecting the child's welfare on which the parents cannot agree, and the court may make such order as it thinks proper, but this does not extend to orders for the child's custody or access to him.[27]

Since the Guardianship of Minors Act 1971 clearly applies the welfare principle to all proceedings in all courts in England and Wales regarding the custody or upbringing of a minor or the administration of his property, there is no specific provision in the Matrimonial Causes Act 1973 or the Matrimonial Proceedings (Magistrates' Courts) Act 1960 regarding the welfare principle. However, the divorce courts[28] in matrimonial causes,[29] and the magistrates' courts in separation and maintenance applications now have jurisdiction extended to "children of the family" of the spouses.[30] In both the English jurisdictions also, the courts may make orders for the custody and upbringing of the children of the family even if they do not grant the matrimonial relief for which application is made.[31] By the Matrimonial Causes Act 1965 the earlier description of orders relating to custody and upbringing of children as 'ancillary relief'[32] was for the most part discarded, and orders relating to children were categorised as such.[33] The vocabulary used in respect of orders relating to children is, however, outmoded.[34] On divorce the most important safeguard for children is contained not in the Matrimonial Causes Act, but in the Rules,[35] which provide that the petition for divorce must state the number of children of the family in existence, giving the full name and date of birth if under full age. The Act provides[36] that the court shall not make absolute a decree of divorce or nullity, or grant a decree of judicial separation unless it has first by order declared that it is satisfied either (a) that there are no children of the family or (b) that the only such children are named in the order and that the arrangements for their welfare are either satisfactory or the best that can be devised in the circumstances, or that it is impracticable for such arrangements to be made by the parties before the court, or that the court is unable to make any of these declarations, but has obtained a satisfactory undertaking from the parties to bring the arrangements for the children before it within a specified time. Once the court has made one of these declarations, its validity cannot afterwards be challenged on the ground that the prescribed conditions were not met, but if the court makes absolute a decree of divorce or nullity or makes a grant of judicial separation without making a declaration about the children, the decree or order made is absolutely void.

Unfortunately, in the magistrates' courts, the legislation still makes it clear that the court must first decide the questions arising between the spouses, and only thereafter may it cause enquiries to be made before deciding on custody of the children.[37]

Under the Canadian Divorce Act 1967, the jurisdiction relating to children of the marriage is exercised in the manner the court thinks 'fit and just', having regard to the conduct of the parties, and the condition, means and other circumstances of each of them.[38] In *Re Moores and Feldstein*[39] the Ontario Court of Appeal reversed a decision at first instance and held that a married woman who had placed her extra-marital child with foster-parents about ten days after its birth could not recover the child four years later.[40] The decision has been hailed[41] as "the first occasion in Ontario where the welfare of the child was regarded as separate from the biological mother's wishes and was objectively given paramount consideration".

In Australia, the federal Family Law Act 1975[42] provides that in proceedings with respect to the custody or guardianship of, or access to, a child of a marriage, the court shall regard the welfare of the child as the paramount consideration. By Section 62, where there is a child of a marriage below eighteen years in respect of which 'proceedings for principal relief' have been instituted, or there are contested custody or guardianship proceedings in respect of a child under eighteen, the court may at any stage of the proceedings direct the parties to attend a conference with a welfare officer to discuss the welfare of the child, and to endeavour to resolve any differences between the parties as to matters affecting the welfare of the child. 'Proceedings for principal relief' are defined[43] as proceedings for a decree of dissolution or nullity of marriage. Proceedings for custody, guardianship or maintenance of, or access to a child of a marriage are included in the definition of matrimonial causes, and further subdivided as 'financial or custodial proceedings'. By Section 61(4) of the Act, a considerable lacuna is filled in Australia that still remains in England. It is provided that on the death of a party to a marriage in whose favour a custody order was made in respect of a child of the marriage, the other parent is entitled to the child's custody only if the court so orders on that other parent's application. This seems admirable. In England the only safeguard possible is for the custodial parent to appoint a testamentary guardian to act after her or his own death. The testamentary guardian then stands on an equal footing with the non-custodial parent, and in case of disagreement may apply to the court. In the absence of such an appointment it has been held[44] that a step-parent has no parental rights, and the court may appoint a guardian only for a minor who has no parent or guardian and no other person who has parental rights with respect to him or her.[45]

In the United States, the sheer volume of custody litigation has itself created a crisis.[46] In 1973 there were 913,000 divorces, and the million mark may well have been passed by now.[47] The draft Uniform Marriage and Divorce Act[48] lists as the fourth of the underlying purposes of the Act, "to mitigate the potential harm to the spouses and their children caused by the process of legal dissolution of marriage". Section 402 provides that the court shall determine custody in accordance with the best interest of the child, and shall consider all relevant factors including: (1) the wishes of the child's parent or parents as to his custody; (2) the wishes of the child as to his custodian; (3) the interaction and interrelationship of the child with his parent or parents, his siblings, and any other person who may significantly affect the child's best interest; (4) the child's adjustment to his home, school and community; and (5) the mental and physical health of all individuals involved.[49] The section specifically provides that the court shall not consider conduct of a proposed custodian that does not affect his relationship to the child.

In Title 2 of the revised Family Code of Texas on Parent and Child enacted in 1973,[50] efforts were made to amend the vocabulary of the law, and section 14.01 provides that in any suit affecting the parent-child relationship, the court may (and if it finds that the parents are or will be separated it shall) appoint a 'managing conservator', who shall be a parent unless the court finds that such an appointment would not be in the best interest of the child. The law also provides that in determining which parent to appoint, the court shall consider the qualifications of the respective parents without regard to the sex of the parent. It may be interesting to see how this provision operates when the court is considering custody of a child say within the first year of life. I venture to suggest that it is not possible to consider the qualifications of any individual for any purpose 'without regard to' that individual's sex, or age, or disposition, or in many cases their social (including racial and religious) background. Evils arise not when these factors and all others are considered impartially, but when the courts act on presumptions for which there is no evidence, and which are frequently at variance with facts.

There is a tradition in the United States that when the parents cannot agree on the religious or social upbringing of a child, although they live otherwise in amity, the courts will not intervene.[51] Such a neutral stance may be desirable, and the English courts may yet find themselves faced with non-justiciable issues in applications by one parent under the Guardian-ship Act 1973, Section 1(3) for a direction on individual questions affecting the child's welfare. On the other hand, failure by the court to intervene may well favour the more affluent and determined parent.

Both the English and the American jurisdictions have also been faced with parental refusal, on religious and social grounds, to comply with the general educational requirements of their countries, but in somewhat different circumstances. Convictions against members of the Old Order Amish communities for violating their State's compulsory school attendance law were quashed as unconstitutional when they withdrew their children from school after completing the eighth grade of elementary education.[52] It is surely relevant that the Amish are reasonably numerous and prosperous communities, able to offer their members a fairly full life within the community, despite lack of formal education. The English Mrs. Baker, on the other hand,[53] could offer the children she deprived of education nothing but a chance of solitary labour for strangers without hope of advancement. Her stand seems to have been based largely on personal arrogance and failure to consider the welfare of her children.

There are two areas of legislation in which the interests or welfare of the child are not generally regarded as paramount. They are adoption and the removal without parental consent of a child from the care of his physical parents when they are living together (or one of them when they are living apart) and the parents cannot adequately care for him, or when the child has come into conflict with the law. In England it is clear that the child's welfare is not paramount in adoption, the principal reason being that Parliament fears a possible interpretation of the 'welfare principle' that might enable the rich to adopt the children of the poor against the wishes of the physical parent by demonstrating that it was for the child's welfare to be rich, or at least richer than his physical parent. The rule is that the parent is entitled to refuse consent to the adoption of her or (more rarely) his child unless withholding of consent is unreasonable.[54] The welfare of the child is a factor of which account must be taken in deciding whether the parent is acting unreasonably.[55] Now by the Adoption Act 1976 Section 6[56] "In reaching any decision relating to the adoption of a child a court or adoption agency shall have regard to all the circumstances, first consideration being given to the need to safeguard and promote the welfare of the child throughout his childhood; and shall so far as practicable ascertain the wishes and feelings of the child regarding the decision and give due consideration to them, having regard to his age and understanding." It has been held[57] that this provision means that "the welfare of the child is to be regarded as of first importance in an objective assessment of the reasonableness or unreasonableness of a parent, but is not to be paramount in the sense that it will rule upon or determine the course to be followed".

The wording of the new provision was held not to change the law as it was under the Adoption Act 1958 in respect of dispensing with parental agreement (thought to be a different word for the identical concept of consent). The court must still not substitute its own judgment for that of the parent. The new wording has been attacked as obscure,[58] but in my view it is a mistake to consider welfare as susceptible of any clear or precise definition.

In Canada also, none of the Adoption Acts nor the Child Welfare Acts dealing with adoption[59] provides for the child's welfare to be the first and paramount consideration. It is frequently provided[60] that the Director of Child Welfare shall enquire into the suitability of the proposed adoption, and that the order shall be made if the judge is satisfied that it should be made or is satisfied with the propriety of the adoption and the fitness of the petitioner.[61] The fact that two of the Provinces (Alberta and British Columbia) specifically mention the welfare of the child probably makes no difference to the way in which adoption is administered in those as compared with other Provinces. The general position about the need for parental consent (or agreement), the possibility of dispensing with it if unreasonably withheld, and the need for the court to be satisfied that the adoption will be for the child's welfare (or beneficial) appears to be much as in England and Wales.

In Australia the position is different in that all the State adoption laws except that in Western Australia provide that the welfare and interests of the child concerned shall be regarded as the paramount consideration. This has not resulted in the mass adoption by the better-off of the children of the poor, although there are some allegations that aboriginal children are removed from their parents, with or without adoption, more freely than other children. Social conditions in Australia are, of course, different from those in England. Australia did not live through several centuries of feudalism, and its class system is less monolithic and established than that in England. In New South Wales and the Australian Capital Territory a child over twelve years must consent to his adoption unless special reasons are shown.

In the United States of America, the revised Uniform Adoption Act provides in Section 6 for dispensing with the parental consent normally required for adoption only if the parent has voluntarily relinquished his right to consent, or if his rights have been judicially terminated under some other legislation. This appears more restrictive than the provisions in any U.K. jurisdiction.

As regards children in public care, the powers of the local authorities in England have been extended and the position of foster-parents somewhat improved by legislation[62] following the killing of Maria Colwell by her stepfather just before her eighth birthday in 1973. Her physical mother had succeeded in recovering the child from the care of foster-parents with whom she had lived happily for almost six years, following which she subjected the child to continuous abuse and ill-treatment for the fifteen months until her life was brutally ended. The inquiry which an enraged public forced on a reluctant government found that "it was generally believed that natural parents had the 'right' to have their child back from (public) care once they had established that they were fit to receive it",[63] with the result that the physical mother's application to the magistrates' court for the child's return to her "went through on the nod". The new legislation brought into operation on 26th November 1976 improved the statutory position, but it cannot be assumed that the position of children in this kind of situation will be greatly altered. The current cliché concerning the Colwell case is that it showed a "failure of the system". This is undoubtedly true, but however faulty "the system", the most important factor was that a considerable number of professional people, including social workers, teachers, magistrates and doctors, failed in their duty to protect a small child from violent and drunken adults. Only if the knowledge of this and similar cases brings home to them and others their individual responsibility, will the situation improve. The position seems comparable in other jurisdictions, and probably in none of them would a Colwell case be impossible, or even extremely unlikely.

An admirable review of Child Neglect Law in America was published in Volume IX of the Family Law Quarterly for Spring 1975, proper consideration of which would require several essays.

When children have come into conflict with the law, an attempt must be made to balance the child's welfare against the injury to the public caused by the anti-social behaviour of the child. Indeed it may be said that the child's welfare requires prevention of his damaging the community. Here we have the clear contrast between the English approach outlined in the Children and Young Persons Act 1969 and that of the United States courts as laid down in the decision of the United States Supreme Court in *Re Gault*.[64] The English system is based[65] on an attempt to keep the erring child outside the courts as far as possible, which is more fully realised in the Scottish system of Children's Hearings (see Professor Spencer's essay in this volume). The approach in the United States is based on ensuring due process of law for the juvenile during his trial.[66] If it is true (as some have suggested) that the United States system has led to less children being placed on trial and more being dealt with informally by social workers, this would imply that in both jurisdictions large numbers of children are dealt with informally, but that in England such dealings are much more closely controlled by the legislation.

It is now beyond doubt that the legislation and its implementation in England have run into serious difficulties.[67] The local authorities were given the responsibility without the means of discharging it. They had inadequate accommodation of any kind for delinquent children; there was a grave shortage of secure accommodation, there was overall shortage of welfare workers, and an acute shortage of trained personnel, particularly to staff residential accommodation. Expertise amongst the social workers has been diluted,[68] and the continuing financial stringency will ensure that the present shortage will not be quickly relieved. In particular, the problem of the persistently delinquent youngster has been seriously underestimated,[69] and at least until the age of 17 some of these children have been given in effect a licence to prey on their local community.[70] The public have responded by trying to make the local authority responsible for some of the damage done, even though the resources available to prevent the damage were inadequate.[71] The role of our longest-established social workers, the police force, has been seriously underestimated, and the need for close co-operation between the police and other social workers needs enforcement at all levels.

The Children Act 1975 has now amended the 1969 Act[72] to permit the Secretary of State to make grants to local authorities in respect of expenditure incurred in providing secure accommodation in community homes other than the assisted community homes provided for in Sections 39-40 of the 1969 Act. The Minister has also been given extensive powers to inquire into the functions of local authorities and social services committees, voluntary organisations running voluntary homes or specialist homes for the accommodation of children in the care of local authorities.[73]

It is where the child's home background is deficient and anti-social that it is most difficult either to formulate clearly the 'welfare principle' or to make it effective.

THE IMPLICATIONS OF THE 'WELFARE PRINCIPLE' FOR THE ASSEMBLY AND PRESENTATION OF EVIDENCE AND THE NATURE OF PROCEEDINGS FOR THE CARE OF CHILDREN

There are certain guidelines usually observed by the courts which profoundly influence the kind of evidence presented to them in child custody cases. Many if not most of these have already been referred to, and they are here summarized:

(a) Parental rights

The 'welfare principle' was originally introduced to derogate from the almost-absolute right of the father to decide on the custody and upbringing of his children so that the right of the father became subject to the discretionary power of the judge. The case of Maria Colwell has demonstrated that parental custody is still too strongly favoured in many cases. In *J. v. C.* the situation was summed up thus:[74] "While there is now no rule of law that the rights and wishes of unimpeachable parents must prevail over other considerations, such rights and wishes, recognized as they are by nature and society, can be capable of ministering to the total welfare of the child in a special way, and must therefore preponderate in many cases. The parental rights, however, remain qualified and not absolute for the purposes of the investigation . . . ." While there may be no substitute for the normal loving parent, however deficient she or he may be in many ways, there are few fates worse than that of the child in the hands of the spiteful, self-indulgent or brutal parent. The child's welfare, and that of society, depends on distinguishing the one from the other.

In Canada, Australia and the United States of America also, the question seems to be to what extent parental 'rights' are still weighed too heavily in the balance. There is still a tendency to regard parental control as normal, and then see if there is strong countervailing evidence to displace it. But the correct approach is to take into consideration the wishes of the parents, together with all the other evidence available. It is a poor parent who needs a presumption in his favour.

(b) The bias in favour of the mother for very young children and for girls

This is noticeable in the jurisdictions under consideration, and until recently there were jurisdictions in the United States that favoured maternal custody for all children.[75] In England and Australia[76] the father has in general far greater hope of obtaining custody of a boy of more than about six years of age.[77] It seems to be generally accepted that formerly most American parents, on separation, agreed that the mother should have custody of the children, but that recently this situation has changed in that more fathers are anxious to have, and more mothers are prepared to relinquish custody of their children, so that more fathers are being awarded custody.

(c) Parental (especially maternal) behaviour

In England,[78] Canada[79] and Australia[80] there are examples of courts depriving the mother of custody of her children in order to punish her for her marital behaviour, without much consideration of the probable effect on the children. With reference to the United States, Foote, Levy and Sander state: "Some commentators believe that most judges no longer decide custody issues solely on the basis of the mother's adultery; but data either to support or refute that claim are simply unavailable. It does seem likely that judges' attitudes vary more in accordance with their personal philosophies than with the latest pronouncements of the appellate courts. . ."[81] An even more difficult question is how heavily parental kidnapping of the child and transporting him to another jurisdiction should weigh in the balance.

These considerations are linked with the usual gender roles in our societies under which it is normal for the husband and father to earn his living away from the home, whilst the wife and mother normally spends most of her time within the home, and therefore in more frequent contact with the children. In the past,[82] and even today[83] in England, awards of custody are frequently made to the father provided he can show that there is a woman in his household who will be able to provide for the day-to-day and hour-to-hour needs of the child for food, supervision and attention. In the majority of reported cases where the father is given custody, which, of course, form a small minority of the cases decided in private (as are all cases of child custody in England) the woman who will be actually in charge of the child for most of the daylight hours has never met the child, and no evidence is offered or required as to the relationship, if any, between the child and that woman, who can be replaced at the whim of the person granted custody. Similar situations arise in respect of mothers awarded custody of young children when the mother works outside the home. The children are then frequently looked after by some other person about whom the court has no information. It is thought that the situation is not markedly different in the other jurisdictions.

(d) Ascertaining the views of the child

The courts in the British jurisdictions are here moving very slowly, largely because of the complication of how far the physical parents are entitled to demand as of right to be told everything said by the child. On the one hand, a young child cannot always be handed over to the far-from-tender mercies of a parent who has just been told of the child's criticisms.[84] On the other hand, children are given to romancing, especially where their own egos are involved. With the older child, there is always the possibility of undue influence by another adult for his or her own purposes. I welcome the decision of the House of Lords in *Re K*.[85] that a parent is not absolutely entitled to see all the evidence before the court in relation to a custody application, but that knowledge of such evidence should only rarely be withheld, and only when the judge personally has considered the matter and decided that disclosure of the evidence to the parent would not be for the child's welfare. Where a local authority is involved, it has been held that a parent is not entitled to demand disclosure of local authority records.[86] On the whole, however, judging from reported cases, the judges in England rarely interview the child. One of the few cases in which this was done with noticeable effect was *Re S.*,[87] in which Cross J. talked to a boy aged 13½ years, as surely any reasonable parent would have done. In *H. v. H.*[88] a county court judge had talked to two boys aged thirteen and eight under a pledge not to divulge anything they told him except to an appeal court, and the Court of Appeal sent the case back for re-hearing, saying that no pledge of secrecy should be given to children in such circumstances. In the magistrates' courts, Sir G. Baker P. said in *Re T.*[89] that since there is no statutory authority for magistrates to see children in custody cases in their private rooms, they must not do so. It seems extreme to assume that those entrusted with responsibility for deciding whose evidence to accept in disputes between adults are incapable of assessing a child's evidence as to the home in which his life should be spent. To the writer's knowledge, leading members of the medical profession have expressed the opinion that children aged six or seven years, even if below normal intelligence, may have decided ideas about their custodian, and should be heard. The fact that Maria Colwell was right, that all the professional people who forced her back to the "care" of her physical mother were wrong, and that it was the child's life that was forfeit as a result, might induce us all to re-examine present practices in a mood of some humility.

In British Columbia, the two boys concerned in *Saxon v. Saxon*[90] were interviewed, as they were in Australia in *Priest v. Priest,*[91] and in Ontario Professor Bradbrook found the judges aware of the percipience of even young children on the matter of their custody.[92] In the United States, the Uniform Marriage and Divorce Act provides in Section 404 that the court may interview the child in chambers to ascertain the child's wishes as to his custodian and as to visitation (access), it may permit the presence of counsel, and it shall cause a record of the interview to be made and to be part of the record in the case. It is hoped that judges will ensure that the child knows that his or her views may be relayed to his parent. In *Lincoln v. Lincoln*[93] the Court of Appeals of New York dissented in 1969 from the view of the Appellate Division that it was an error for the trial court to interview three children in the absence of counsel despite parental objection.

Some American State Codes provide specifically for the court to consider the child's views, but usually the provision is linked to the child's age. In California "if the child is of a sufficient age to form an intelligent preference the court may consider that preference in determining the question".[94] In Ohio if any child is fourteen years of age or more, it may be allowed to choose which parent it prefers to live with, unless the court finds that the parent so selected is unfitted to take charge.[95] In Utah, if any of the children have attained the age of ten years and are of sound mind, such children shall have the privilege of selecting the parent to which they will attach themselves.[96] In Australia, the Family Law Act, 1975 Section 64(1)(b) now provides that, where the child has attained the age of 14 years, the court shall not make a custody order contrary to his wishes unless satisfied that this is necessary by reason of special circumstances. It will be very interesting to watch the interpretation put on this provision.

(e) Psychiatric evidence

This is becoming gradually less suspect than formerly in all the jurisdictions under consideration. After the unfortunate suggestion by Harman L.J. in *Re C.* (M.A.) (An Infant)[97] that a distinguished member of the medical profession would give evidence favourable to the party who called him, the medical profession was able to demonstrate that it was the practices of the lawyers that prevented their seeing both sides, as they would prefer.[98] Since then the Court of Appeal has said that disputing parents should, where possible, co-operate in obtaining expert medical opinion,[99] and much of the former controversy has subsided. In the United States, the psychiatrist's evidence was crucial in the very controversial case of *Painter v. Bannister.*[100] The psychiatric evidence in that case was against a change of custody, and it may well be that it was the increasing realization of the importance of stability at home for a young child that weighed heavily with the court.[101] In Australia, Hutley J.A., in *Barnett v. Barnett* adopted a more sympathetic approach to psychiatric evidence than that evidenced in some previous Australian decisions.[102]

(f) Welfare reports

The judicial conversion to the desirability of welfare reports has been more thoroughgoing in England than that to psychiatric evidence. Perhaps the social workers constitute less of a potential threat to the judges. The Court of Appeal has insisted that there be one welfare report by one officer on both possible homes, and not two separate reports by different people.[103] The courts have required a welfare report before the custody of young children is given to the father,[104] and have given guidance on how these reports should be presented.[105] In Australia, the very existence of the federal Family Court is likely to give a considerable boost to the importance of welfare reports, and the Family Law Act, 1975 also contains specific provisions enabling the court to direct all parties to attend a conference with a welfare officer to discuss the welfare of the child. There seems to be accumulating evidence from the different jurisdictions that the training of many social workers produces an approach that is too obscure than to clarify thought, and a lack of intellectual and temperamental cutting edge can result in children's early sorrow. In the United States, the Uniform Marriage and Divorce Act provides in Section 404(b) that the court may seek the advice of professional personnel, whether or not employed by the court on a regular basis, and that counsel may examine as a witness any professional person so consulted. There are also provisions in Section 405 for investigation and report by various social welfare agencies.

(g) Other rules sometimes applied

The New South Wales Court of Appeal affirmed in *Barnett v. Barnett*[106] the general rule applied in all the jurisdictions that brothers and sisters should not be separated from each other, although in rare cases this may be done.[107] In recent years the English courts have emphasised the need for speed in dealing with children's cases,[108] and castigated those legal advisers who exploit the overlapping jurisdiction of different courts to delay decisions relating to children.[109] The Divisional Court has asked to be told the reasons for abandoning appeals from magistrates, particularly where the order made is unusual on its face.[110] The rule in Texas, that either party to a custody dispute may apply for jury trial,[111] seems unlikely to arouse much support in other jurisdictions.

(h) Custody and access

The stresses inherent in disputes between parents are frequently played out as between the custodial parent and the other granted access or visitation rights. Here again, the quest for general rules does not yet seem to have proved satisfactory. The suggestion in *Beyond the Best Interests of the Child*[112] that the parent not granted custody should have no right of access has not been widely supported. In England access for a parent is very rarely refused, and it is becoming more usual to give custody to both parents, with care to one.[113] In a report by Justice on Parental Rights and Custody Suits,[114] a Proposed Visiting Code drawn up by a distinguished psychiatrist was appended, and it was recommended that this be both handed and explained to all parents at the conclusion of custody suits, to supplement the work of the Children's Ombudsman, whose appointment was recommended. The Visiting Code would certainly be helpful in emphasising to parents the need their children have to love and be loved by both their parents in security, but there is likely to be a residue of cases in which one parent feels real hatred and bitterness towards a former spouse, or fears the influence of the other parent on a child. When everything possible has been done to reduce such enmity, there is likely to be a residue of cases in which nothing but the power of the state exercised through the courts will ensure reasonable parental behaviour.

(i) The implications for custody suits of recent developments

Recent developments point towards far greater emphasis on thorough, but speedy, enquiry into the facts relating to children, and decisions by those trained to evaluate evidence, and to suppress bias as far as possible, whilst recognizing that it is rarely entirely eliminated. The accusatorial nature of proceedings regarding custody of children should probably be modified,[115] and not only the court, but the parties and their counsel[116] should have the paramountcy of the child's interests brought constantly home to them.

With a view to ensuring this paramountcy, the Justice Committee referred to, suggested that there should be one official, who might be called the Children's Ombudsman (although no stress was laid on his exact title), whose duty it would be to receive and collate all the evidence relating to children, so as to eliminate the kind of gaps in the system demonstrated in the Maria Colwell case. The committee envisaged that the establishment of such an office might be linked with that of a Family Court, as recommended by the Finer Committee on One-Parent Families.[117] A Family Court in England could operate only at the level of an inferior court, combining the jurisdiction now exercised by the divorce county courts (which may grant divorce) and the magistrates' courts (which may grant only separation and maintenance). Both courts may now deal with custody of a child. The possible objection is the same to both the Children's Ombudsman proposal and the Finer proposal for a Family Court. If there is only one channel of information, or only one tribunal dealing with such matters, there is always the possibility that the channel or tribunal might be captured by proponents of a particular viewpoint or ideology. It is thought that this danger is particularly acute in dealing with the family. Our history is replete with schools of thought convinced that they knew precisely how families should be constituted, and what the relations should be between men and women and between parents and children in all cases. Since I am persuaded that most of these theories were seriously wrong and caused much distress, in the final analysis I cling to diversity rather than uniformity in jurisdiction relating to the care and upbringing of children. Rationalisation is desirable, uniformity is to be shunned.

THE RANGE OF CHOICE AVAILABLE IN THE CARE OF CHILDREN

When all the possibilities for decision in child care have been canvassed and the latest developments evaluated, it is salutary to remind ourselves that the range of choice available is in the last analysis, as in most areas of family law, very restricted, and the sanctions available are weak. As Foote, Levy and Sander point out: "The alternative to leaving the child in the charge of the parent would be to try to find a suitable relative or friend who is willing to undertake the (care of the) child, or failing that, that the local authority [the welfare department] should receive the child into care; and it is obvious that conditions would have to be really bad before one of these courses could be justified."[118] This is true. There is as yet no rival to the even moderately successful parent. In most cases the courts have only to choose between mother and father, or at most between physical and foster-parent. As these authors point out, in the great majority of cases parents are the best judges of their children's welfare. However, the law is not concerned with the great majority of cases, and for this reason I would regard as dangerous the further conclusion drawn by these authors that where the parents are agreed upon the arrangements for the children "very strong evidence indeed would be required to justify setting aside their proposals". All the evidence is that this insistence upon "very strong evidence indeed" to displace what parents propose has caused great distress and hardship in the past, and was indeed the reason for the introduction of the "welfare principle", and the authority given to the judges to impose it against the parents' wishes when necessary. It was this approach that "very strong evidence" was necessary to displace a parent's wishes that three years ago in England caused at least one little girl much unnecessary humiliation and suffering culminating in a violent death.

For this reason, and following the Maria Colwell case, there was considerable support in England for separate legal representation for children in all cases where their interests might be at variance with those of their parents. The Justice Committee in paragraph 31 of its Report called for separate legal representation of children in all contested adoption, guardianship and custody proceedings affecting them. Because of financial stringency, the provisions in the Children Act, 1975, Section 64 are limited to allowing the court to order separate representation of the child in certain cases under the Children and Young Persons Act, 1969 in which it appears to the court that there is or may be a conflict between the interests of the child and those of his parent or guardian. My own view is that a blanket provision for separate representation of the child is neither necessary nor sufficient. The essential factor is that the court itself should realize that the interests of parents may differ from those of their children, and ensure that, where this is likely to be so, the children have a real possibility of putting their views before (I do not say have them followed by) the court. In particular, I would like the present hesitancy about the court interviewing the child separately to be discarded. It may also be that arrangements could sometimes be made for an unbiased person who knows the child (such as a schoolteacher) to ascertain the child's views and report on them to the court. A child is more likely to talk freely to someone he already knows. It would in all cases be essential either to make it clear to the child that whatever he said would be made known to his parent(s) or if, as I would prefer, it was decided that his views could be made known in private, to ensure that this privacy was unequivocally maintained.

THE CONSTITUTION AND NATURE OF THE TRIBUNAL DECIDING ON CHILD CARE

There is also much criticism today of the court consisting of a single judge, particularly on questions where partiality may be so pervasive and so damaging as in relation to the care of children. Two of the few favourable features of the magistrates' courts in England (apart from their cheapness, which is their overriding advantage) are the facts that for matrimonial proceedings the bench is required to consist of not more than three magistrates, and that so far as practicable they shall include both a man and a woman.[119] This is very real advantage in dealing with young children, having regard to the virtual exclusion of women from judicial office in England. Although the position is now improving in all the jurisdictions considered, women are in a tiny minority in most tribunals dealing with children.

From time to time the possibility of having a lawyer sitting in company with lay assessors for these and similar cases is canvassed. The hollowness of these proposals is usually made clear when it is suggested that the lawyer should not invariably preside. The insistence on the invariable presidency of the lawyer makes it manifest that the final decision is intended always to be his. The presence of the lay magistrates is, for the most part, window-dressing. I cannot think that it is ever desirable in the law that things should be other than they seem. If one person is to decide, I think he (or she) should be seen to decide. What is important is to bring home to all involved that entrusting a young child to the care of an adult is to give that adult greater power over the child than one person can exercise over the person and the mind of another in any other area of our society. The entire future of the child is at stake. Such decisions must never be rushed. It should be impossible ever again for a Government committee to find that a proposal about care of a child was agreed by tribunal "on the nod". It is only human beings, conscious of their responsibilities, who can make "the welfare principle" really operative.

1 *Annual Survey of Commonwealth Law* 1972, 311-2.

2 *J. Mule Nzoka v. B. Mwikali* [1971] K.H.C.D. 90 (H.C. Kenya).

3 "An Empirical Study of the Attitudes of the Judges of the Supreme Court of Ontario Regarding the Workings of the Present Child Custody Adjudication Laws" (1971) 49 Can. Bar Rev. 557.

4 Now s. 1 of the Guardianship of Minors Act 1971, *viz:* 'Where in any proceedings before any court . . . (a) the custody or upbringing of a minor; or (b) the administration of any property belonging to or held on trust for a minor, or the application of the income thereof, is in question, the court, in deciding that question, shall regard the welfare of the minor as the first and paramount consideration . . .'

5 Mr. Bradbrook cites the Domestic Relations Act, R.S.A. 1955, c. 89, s. 49; Equal Guardianship of Infants Acts, R.S.B.C. 1960, c. 130, ss. 5, 22; Child Welfare Act R.S.M. 1970, c. 80, s. 100(1); Infants' Custody Act, R.S.N.S. 1967, c. 145, s. 2; Infants Act R.S.O. 1970, c. 222, s. 1.

6 "Custody of Children: Towards a New Approach" (1975) 49 A.L.J. 129.

7 [1973] 2 N.S.W.L.R. 403, [1973-4] 2 A.L.R. 19.

8   *E.g.*, California Civil Code (1954), s. 138: "In awarding the custody [of a child in divorce and separate maintenance actions] the court is to be guided by the following considerations: (1) By what appears to be for the best interests of the child; and if the child is of a sufficient age to form an intelligent preference the court may consider that preference in determining the question". (Reproduced in Ploscowe, Foster & Freed: *Family Law, Cases and Materials* (2nd ed. 1972) p.905). In *Ragan v. Ragan* (Mo.1958) 315 S.W.2d 142, 147, the court said: "the paramount and controlling consideration in every child custody case, to which all other principles and presumptions must yield, is the welfare of the child", and in the immediately following passage the term "the best interests of a child" is used as synonymous with "the welfare of the child". In many decisions, such as *People v. Glendening* (1940) 19 N.Y.S.2d 693, the court combines the terms, *viz:* "the boy's true welfare and best interests". The two expressions will therefore be considered synonymous, especially as it will be argued that they are not precise (and are not intended to be so).

9 *Beyond the Best Interests of the Child,* Ch.4, "As an overall guideline for child placement we propose, instead of the 'in-the-best-interests-of-the-child' standard, 'the least detrimental available alternative for safeguarding the child's growth and development'".

10 *E.g., DeForest v. DeForest* (1975, S.C., N. Dakota) 228 N.W.2d 919: "there is testimony which could support a finding that Peggy needs both parents and that a split or alternating custody award is the least detrimental to her welfare."

11 "Shibboleth" was the Hebrew test-word used by the men of Gilead after their victory over the Ephraimites, to distinguish their own men from the Ephraimites, who could not pronounce the "sh". Judges, 12, v. 4-6. Like this ancient distinction between "ours" and "theirs", "the best interests" test is not only weighted in favour of the parents, but may even import a racial bias.

12 Foote, Levy and Sander: *Cases and Materials on Family Law* 2nd ed. (1976) p.408 of some opinions in *Lucas v. Kreisher* (Pa.1972) 289 A.2d 202, 221 Pa.Super 196. The Pennsylvania Supreme Court in 1973 at 299 A.2d 243, 450 Pa.352, adopted much of the dissenting opinion of Hoffman J. (Spaulding and Cercone JJ. concurring) in the lower court, and held that the remarriage of the (so-called "caucasian") mother to a (so-called "black") man after divorce was not an adequate reason for depriving her of custody of her three children (aged nine, eight and six years) of a former marriage. It had been argued that the children would be the victims of the "almost universal prejudice and intolerance of interracial marriage".

13 *Viz.,* Revised Uniform Adoption Act (1969); Child Custody Jurisdiction Act (1968); Juvenile Court Act (1968); Marriage and Divorce Act (1970, amended 1971 and 1973); Parentage Act (1973); Reciprocal Enforcement of Support Act (1950, amended 1958 and 1968), and Uniform Probate Code (1969). All but the last-mentioned have been collected by Foote, Levy and Sander in the Statutory Appendix to the 2nd edition of their *Cases and Materials on Family Law.*

14 See *J. v. C.* [1970] A.C. 668 *per* Lord Guest at 697: ". . . in my view the law administered by the Chancery Court as representing the Queen as parens patriae never required that the father's wishes should prevail over the welfare of the infant. The dominant consideration has always been the welfare of the infant". Similarly Lord Upjohn at 721A: ". . . in respect of infancy matters, while recognising the dominant consideration of the welfare of the child, in practice in the presence of the early Victorian pater familias, equity too dutifully followed the law". John Hall dissents in "The Waning of Parental Rights" 31 Camb. L.J. (1972B) 248, 249 n.8, but I suggest the difference of opinion depends on different views of the welfare of the child.

15 *Re Taylor* (1876) 4 Ch.D. 157, 159, applied in *Re Elderton* (1883) 25 Ch.D. 220.

16 (1883) 24 Ch.D. 317.

17 The summary here given follows, for the sake of brevity, the headnote to the report.

18 "Mere" adultery by the father was never sufficient to deprive him of his rights, although any act of adultery by the mother (which was never 'mere') deprived her even of the right of access to her child until after the decision in *Re A and B (Infants)* [1897] Ch.786 (C.A.). The solution adopted in that case, of giving the child into the custody of each parent for

half of each year, was soon discarded as inimical to the child's welfare.

19 This could not be effected by contract. Until the Custody of Infants Act 1873, s.2 was passed, any clause in a contract by which a father agreed to surrender to anyone else the custody or control of his children was not only itself void and unenforceable, but so contrary to public policy that it invalidated the whole of any agreement of which it formed part. Nor did failure to maintain the child constitute abdication of parental authority. Only allowing others to bring up the child for a considerable time and usually to settle property on the child constituted such abdication: see e.g. Lyons v. Blenkin (1820) J. & C. 245, and especially Lord Eldon at 255, 258, and In re Fynn (1848) 2 de G. & Sm. 457, where the lack of a settlement was decisive. Even today the courts enthusiastically enforce the "rights" of fathers who have failed to support their children. In In re D. (Minors) (Adoption by parent)[1973] Fam. 209 a father who had deserted his wife and children and left them dependent on social security until the mother remarried after a divorce was allowed to refuse consent to adoption of the children by the mother and step-father. Without an adoption order the physical father could almost certainly obtain access to these children.

20 (1883) 24 Ch.D. 317, 328 (italics supplied).

21 Per Lord Upjohn in J. v. C. [1970] A.C. 668, 721E.

22 The provision that the welfare of the child was the first and paramount consideration "in any proceedings in any court" meant that until the question was before the court the statute was inoperative, and the common law, by which paternal rights were paramount, remained in full operation, except that if the mother did not agree she could apply to the court. When the matter was before the court, the child's welfare became paramount for the first time. Hence after s.1 of the Guardianship of Infants Act, 1925 had been incorporated in s.1 of the partial consolidation of the Guardianship of Minors Act 1971, the Guardianship Act 1973 s.1 was passed, providing that "In relation to the custody or upbringing of a minor... a mother shall have the same rights and authority as the law allows to a father, and the rights and authority of mother and father shall be equal and be exercisable by either without the other." This gave rise to the anomaly of two adults each with equal rights to the sole custody of a minor child. The Children Act 1975 s.85(3) (in operation from the beginning of 1976) now provides that "Where two or more persons have a parental right or duty jointly, any one of them may exercise or perform it in any manner without the other or others if the other or, as the case may be, one or more of the others have not signified disapproval of its exercise or performance in that manner". There may still be some tricky questions about what constitutes timely and adequate signification of disapproval. For example, if baby Caroline is living with either parent and there is no custody order in existence, is the other parent (with whom the custodial parent has had no communication) entitled to seize the child in exercise of his or her separate and equal rights?

23 J. v. C. [1970] A.C. 668, was the first case in which foster-parents were allowed to prevail over physical parents against whom no offence against the child could be proved. Lord Guest at p.697H considered that s.1 of the Guardianship of Infants Act 1925 was "of universal application and is not limited in its application to questions as between parents". Lord MacDermott agreed at 710C, Lord Upjohn at 724D-E, and Lord Donovan at 727E. It has always been clear that the inherent wardship jurisdiction of the High Court could override any common law right of the father.

24 Guardianship of Minors Act 1971, s.14, expressly excluding maintenance under s.9(2) of the Act.

25 Except that by s. 12(2) of the 1971 Act, a person over 18 but under 21 years of age may apply if he has, whilst a minor, been the subject of a guardianship order.

26 Ibid. s.15 but by s.15(2) the magistrates have no jurisdiction to make orders in relation to minors over the age of 16 unless the minor is physically or mentally incapable of self-support; nor may they consider applications involving the administration or application of any property belonging to or held in trust for a minor or the income of such property.

27 Guardianship Act 1973, s. 1(3)(4).

28 Principally the divorce county courts (including the Registry of the Family Division of the High Court in London, which is a divorce county court for this purpose) in which all

petitions in matrimonial causes must now be launched. Only the few defended petitions and certain others showing complications are then transferred to the Family Division of the High Court. There are some exceptional provisions for hearings at the Royal Courts of Justice in London.

29 Those, other than divorce, are of minor importance. In 1974 there were filed: 131,662 divorce petitions, 949 nullity petitions and 696 petitions for judicial separation; an additional 134 divorce petitions and one for judicial separation were granted during the year, having been filed before 1974: Civil Judicial Statistics, Annual Report 1974, Cmnd. 6361, Tables B(12) and B(12)(ii).

30 Unfortunately "children of the family" are differently defined in the two statutes concerned. The Matrimonial Causes Act 1973, s. 52 defines a "child of the family" in relation to the parties to a marriage as: "(a) a child of both of those parties; and (b) any other child, not being a child who has been boarded out with those parties by a local authority or voluntary organization, or who has been treated by both of those parties as a child of their family". For matrimonial proceedings before magistrates the unamended definition in the Matrimonial Proceedings (Magistrates' Courts) Act 1960 s. 16(1) is: (a) any child of both parties; and (b) any other child of either party who has been accepted as one of the family by the other party. In its Published Working Paper No. 53 (1973) on Matrimonial Proceedings in magistrates' courts the English Law Commission drew attention to numerous anomalies between the provisions of various statutes governing the custody and maintenance of children, and made recommendations, including a uniform child custody and maintenance statute. The Law Commission's Report on the subject (following reactions to the Working Paper) is awaited.

31 Under the Matrimonial Causes Act 1973, s. 42, the divorce court may make orders for the custody and education of a child of the family under the age of eighteen before or on granting a decree or at any time thereafter, or where any such proceedings are dismissed after the beginning of the trial. The court may also direct that the child be made a Ward of Court. Under the 1960 Act s. 2(1) the magistrates may make orders for a child "on hearing a complaint" and by s. 4(1) when the court has begun to hear a complaint or an application for the variation of a matrimonial order it may make orders in respect of a child "whether or not the court makes the order for which the complaint is made".

32 Meaning subservient or subordinate, derived from *ancilla,* a female slave or maidservant.

33 Matrimonial Causes Act 1973, Part III, Protection, Custody, etc. of Children. But the "ancillary" approach still lurks in Rule 49 of the Matrimonial Causes Rules 1973 (S.I. 1973 No.2016), covering the "Right to be heard on ancillary questions," (a) to (c) of which deal with custody, care or supervision of and access to children. It has been re-introduced in the Recognition of Divorces and Legal Separations Act, 1971, s. 8(3) of which refers to "maintenance, custody or *other ancillary* order made in any (divorce or separation) proceedings".

34 For example, in the Guardianship of Minors Act, 1971 s. 1, orders are for "custody and upbringing" of the minor, and ss. 9, 10 and 11 refer also to "right of access" to the minor. By the Guardianship Act 1973 the court may "commit the care of" the minor to a specified local authority. In the Matrimonial Causes Act 1973 s. 44(1) there is reference to a period during which the child is "committed to the custody of any person". The Child Act 1975 has defined such terms as "legal custody" and "actual custody" of a minor.

35 By Rule 9 every petition shall contain the information required by Form 2, which requires *inter alia* in para. 4 full names of all children of the family now living, with date of birth if under full age, and if over 16 whether receiving instruction at an educational establishment or undergoing training for a trade, profession or vocation.

36 Matrimonial Causes Act, 1973 s. 41.

37 Matrimonial Proceedings (Magistrates' Courts) Act 1960, s. 4(2): Where on hearing a complaint (including an application for variation of an existing order) "the court, *after* it has made any decision which falls to be made on the complaint" with respect to separation or maintenance if it considers that it has not sufficient information to make decisions about the children, may call for a report by a social welfare worker on such matters as it may specify.

38 Ss. 10-11.

39 [1973] 3 O.R. 921, 12 R.F.L. 273, 38 D.L.R. (3d) 641 (C.A.).
40 This was a stronger decision than that of the English House of Lords, *J. v. C.* [1970] A.C. 668, on which much reliance was placed, because the foster-mother was a married woman unable to marry the foster-father until her husband died. The foster-parents married each other in December 1972, shortly before the hearing. This was the reason why no legal adoption was possible, but a 'consent to adoption', recognized by both parties as unenforceable, was signed before the child was handed over. The mother had wanted an abortion, but for this, at the time, she required the consent of her husband, and he refused it although all agreed he was not the child's father.
41 By K.M. Weiler and G. Berman (1974) R.F.L. 294. See also Weiler (1974) 12 Osgoode Hall L.J. 207-221.
42 S. 64 in operation since 6th January 1976.
43 Family Law Act, s.4(1).
44 *In re N (Minors)*, The Times Newspaper, 13.6.73.
45 Guardianship of Minors Act 1971 s. 5(1). By the Children Act 1975 s. 33(3) a step-parent is among those entitled to apply for a custody order, but only if he applies with the consent of a person having legal custody of the child and the child has had his home with him for three months preceding the making of the application. The only way in which an English court could award custody to a stepfather would be under the prerogative wardship jurisdiction of the High Court. Contrast *Root v. Allen* (1962) 377 P.2d 117 (Colorado).
46 See B.M. Bodenheimer, The Rights of Children and the Crisis in Custody Litigation: Modification of Custody in and out of State (1975) 46 U. Colo. L. Rev. 495.
47 In 1963 there were 428,000 divorces in the United States, so that the increase over the ten years has just exceeded 113%. In England and Wales the increase was from 32,304 decrees nisi granted in 1963 to 106,522 in 1973, an increase of almost 230%. In England and Wales the Finer Committee on One-parent families found that nearly two-thirds of a million parents were looking after one million children single-handed. Since then the number of divorces has risen from 70,500 in 1970 to 130,000 in 1974, but the extent of the increase, if any, in one-parent families is not known. Many parents separate well before divorce.
48 1970, as amended 1971 and 1973.
49 These factors will be considered in greater detail under heading II.
50 See *The Anatomy of a Family Code:* (1974) VIII F.L.Q. 105, especially Smith, *Parent and Child — the Texas Family Code* at 135.
51 *Kilgrow v. Kilgrow* (1959) 268 Ala.475, 107 So.2d 885; *People ex rel. Sisson v. Sisson* (1936) 271 N.Y. 285, 2 N.E.2d 660.
52 *Wisconsin v. Yoder* (1972) 406 U.S. 205.
53 *In re Baker* (Infants) [1962] Ch.201, C.A. The legislation was also defective in that the Education Act 1944, ss. 36-37, 40 and 76 provided for conviction of a parent who persistently refused to allow his child to attend school (with the usual provisions for appeal, enabling the determined parent to delay final conviction until the child had passed the school-leaving age), but no effective means of compelling the child's attendance. Some amendments were effected by the Children and Young Persons Act 1963, Sched. 3.
54 The English courts have always stoutly defended the parental right to refuse consent to the child's adoption, and held that the parent must be shown to be acting unreasonably *as a parent* in refusing consent. The House of Lords' decision in *Re W* [1971] A.C. 682, [1971] 2 All E.R. 49 was a breakthrough in holding it unnecessary to show culpability or callous or self-indulgent indifference or failure or probable failure of parental duty or potential lasting damage to the child before parental refusal could be held unreasonable. In *Re D (An Infant) (Adoption: Parent's Consent)* [1976] 3 W.L.R. 12, the Court of Appeal held that a homosexual father was entitled to refuse his consent to the adoption of his son aged 8 by the mother and her then husband, but it was not agreed on whether the test of unreasonableness should be that of a homosexual or of a heterosexual father. The decision was reversed by the House of Lords, which found the refusal of consent to adoption unreasonable, at [1977] 2 W.L.R. 79, [1977] 1 All E.R. 145.
55 *Re W* [1971] A.C. 682. In *Re C(L)* [1965] 2 Q.B. 449, [1964] 3 All E.R. 483 the Court of Appeal affirmed the decision of a county court judge that the mother of an extra-marital child was unreasonable not to take account of the psychological effects of withdrawing her

child aged 2 from the home of the adopters, with whom he had lived for 18 months, when she herself had little hope of providing him with a stable home.

56 Formerly Children Act 1975 s.3, in operation from the beginning of 1976.

57 In *Re B* (An Infant) (Adoption: Parental Consent) [1976] Fam.161, 166G, [1976] 3 All E.R. 124 *per* Cumming-Bruce J.

58 Cretney, *Welfare in the New Adoption Law* (1976) New L.J. 671.

59 There are separate Adoption Acts in British Columbia; New Brunswick; Nova Scotia and Quebec. In the other provinces the adoption of children forms a separate part of the Child Welfare Act.

60 *E.g.* R.S.N.B. 1952, c. 3, s. 11; R.S.N.S. 1967, c. 2, s. 8; R.S.O. 1970, c. 64, s. 75; R.S.S. 1965, c. 268, s. 73.

61 R.S.A. 1970, c. 45, s. 57 reads: "if the judge is satisfied with the propriety of the adoption having regard to the welfare and interests of the child" the order shall be made. British Columbia in 1960 provides "if the court is satisfied of . . . the propriety of the adoption, having regard to the welfare of the child"; New Brunswick, s. 14, "if the judge is satisfied as to the fitness and propriety of the adoption"; Nova Scotia, s.9, "if the court is satisfied . . . that it is proper that the adoption should be made." In Ontario by s.73(5) the court can dispense with parental consent if satisfied that it is in the best interests of the child. In Quebec by s.12, the judge is to make a thorough enquiry, and if of the opinion that the adopters have the qualifications necessary to fulfill the obligations and duties of a parent towards his child, and that the adoption would be of advantage to the latter, may make the order. In Saskatchewan by s.78(4) the judge may dispense with parental consent if this is in the interests of the child, and by s.81, if satisfied that the order should be made may make the adoption order. Saskatchewan appears to be the only Province providing (s.74) that the religion of parents and adopted must be the same.

62 Children Act 1975, Part II (introducing the 'custodianship order', which will enable a temporary custodian to exclude removal by a parent or guardian) and Part III, which requires a parent or guardian to give 28 days' notice before removing a child from a local authority in whose care the child has been for a year; it extends the circumstances in which local authorities may vest parental powers in themselves and in which juvenile courts may uphold such resolutions, and provides for separate representation of the child in certain cases of possible conflict between parent and child.

63 Report of the Committee of Inquiry into the Care and Supervision Provided in Relation to Maria Colwell, Department of Health and Social Services (1974), paras. 62 and 226. On any showing, there was a relaxed interpretation of Pauline Colwell's 'fitness to receive' the child. In para. 39 the majority of the Committee points to the very apposite contrast between the stringent requirements which a prospective foster parent must satisfy and the lack of interest in the man with whom this mother was living.

64 (1967) 387 U.S.1.

65 See in particular Cmnd. 2742 (August 1965) "The Child, the Family and the Young Offender," replaced by Cmnd. 3601: "Children in Trouble", on which the 1969 Act is based. The 1969 Act is itself only one in a long line of amendments of the Children and Young Persons Act 1933, and a consolidation of the legislation has been needed for at least the last 25 years.

66 In particular, a young person alleged to have acted in a way that in an adult would constitute a criminal offence must have four rights secured to him on adjudication, *viz.* (1) the right to notice of the charges; (2) the right to counsel, at public cost if necessary; (3) the right to silence and (4) the right to confront and cross-examine witnesses. It is right (3) that is considered particularly questionable in British jurisdictions. The subsequent decision in *Re Winship* (1970) 397 U.S. 358 requires proof beyond reasonable doubt and not on a balance of probabilities: to be retroactively applied in cases under appeal: *Ivan V. v. N. Y. City* (1972) 407 U.S. 203. *McKeiver v. Pennsylvania* (1971) 403 U.S. 528 establishes that a juvenile is not entitled to trial by jury.

67 See Berlins and Wansel, *Caught in the Act* (1974), the "Eleventh Report from the Expenditure Committee", and "Observations thereon by the Home Office and Welsh Office", D.H.S.S. and D.E.S., Cmnd. 6494 (May 1976), para. 35.

68 Following the Seebohm Report on "Local Authority and Allied Personal Services" Cmnd. 3703, the Local Authority (Social Services) Act 1970 disbanded the Children's Officers from 1971 and they were absorbed into Social Services Committees. After 1973 the local authorities were themselves reorganized under the Local Government Act 1972.

69 Berlins and Wansel estimate that secure accommodation is required for some 2,500 instead of 730 'hard-core' persistent offenders below the age of 17, who commit a disproportion-ately large number of offences.

70 Below the age of 14, the only kind of proceedings possible are "care" proceedings, and these were originally intended to be normal until the age of 17. Care proceedings may result in the child being placed in the care of the local authority, under a "care" order, which replaced the old "fit person" order. About half the cases coming before the juvenile court are still, however, disposed of by the infliction of fines. The local authority has no suitable accommodation for most of the children, and when children are placed in its care, sends them back to their unsatisfactory homes and their teenage neighbourhood gangs. When they are discovered in later infractions of the law, the procedure is repeated again, and again. Magistrates tell of 12-year old children with 400-500 offences admitted or proved.

71 In *R. v. Croydon Juvenile Justices* [1973] Q.B. 426, [1973], All E.R. 476, the local authority was held liable for fines for the damage done, but the courts have resiled from so drastic a solution in later decisions, *e.g. Somerset County Council v. Brice* [1973] 1 W.L.R. 1169, [1973] 3 All E.R. 438, *Lincoln Corporation v. Parker* [1974] 1 W.L.R. 713, [1974] 2 All E.R. 949, *Leicestershire County Council v. Cross* [1976] 2 All E.R. 491 and *Somerset County Council v. Kingscott* [1975] 1 W.L.R. 283, [1975] 1 All E.R. 326. According to the annual Report by the Secretaries of State for Social Services and for Wales, at 31st March 1975 a total of 99,100 were in care, of whom 44,200 were under a "care" order made under the Children and Young Persons Act 1969, and a further 1,800 under an interim care order.

72 Children Act 1975, s.71, inserting s.64A into the Children and Young Persons Act 1969.

73 Children Act 1975, s.98.

74 [1970] A.C. 668, 715. For Australia see *McKinley v. McKinley* [1947] V.L.R. 149, 168 *per* Lowe J. and *Barnett v. Barnett* [1973] 2 N.S.W.L.R. 403, 411. The situation seems very close to that in England.

75 Roth, "The Tender Years Presumption in Child Custody Disputes" (1976-77) 15 J. Fam. L. 423. *State ex rel. Watts v. Watts* (1973) 77 Misc. 2d. 178, 350 N.Y.S. 2d 285, *per* Sybil Hart Kooper, Family Court judge: "Although in theory, a father has an equal right with the mother to the custody of his children, in well over ninety % of the cases adjudicated, the mother is awarded custody." In California in particular, I have seen the mother awarded custody in cases in which I doubt very much if she would have received it in England. Professor Wadlington (in his paper presented at Nottingham, England to the U.K. N.C.C.L. Colloquium on Social Security and Family Law on 21.9.76.) considered that the old 'tender years' presumption is giving way to a process of individualized judicial determination of what would be in the best interests of the child under the particular circumstances.

76 The High Court of Australia reaffirmed the preference for the mother of very young children in *Kades v. Kades* (1961) 35 A.L.J.R. 251. See now Hutley J.A. in *Barnett v. Barnett* [1973] 2 N.S.W.L.R. 403, 412-3. The Supreme Court of Canada in *Talsky v. Talsky* (1976) 21 R.F.L. 27 decided that it is not incorrect to regard the view that children of tender years should be given to the mother as not a rule of law but as a principle of common sense, subject to the paramount consideration, which is the welfare of the child.

77 In *Re B* (An Infant) [1962] 1 W.L.R. 550, [1962] 1 All E.R. 872 (C.A.), with Donovan L.J. dissenting, a boy of four was removed from the care of the mother, with whom he had always lived, and handed over to the care of his father, recently retired from the Royal Navy, who had a married couple keeping house for him. The father could, of course, dismiss the married couple at any time, and replace them or not at his choice. The decision might not be followed today for so young a child. In *W. v. W.* [1968] 1 W.L.R. 1310, [1968] 3 All E.R. 409 (C.A.), the court said a boy of eight was better with his father, but the fact that the mother had committed adultery may also have been considered relevant. In the Canadian cases of *Saxon v. Saxon* [1974] 6 W.W.R. 731, 17 R.F.L. 257 (B.C.) and *Lowe v. Lowe* (1974) 15 R.F.L. 244 (N.S.C.A.), the father was given custody of boys of six and

seven, and of a boy of four. For Australia see *Priest v. Priest* (1963) 9 F.L.R. 384, *Byrnes v. Byrnes* [1958] S.R. (N.S.W.) 323.

78 In *Re L.* [1962] 1 W.L.R. 886, [1962] 3 All E.R. 1 (C.A.) the father was given custody of two girls aged five and three years after the mother had committed adultery and deceived the father by representing she had ended her illicit relationship. Similarly in *B. v. B.,* The Times Newspaper, May 15, 1975, the Court of Appeal awarded custody of the children to the father because of the mother's marital behaviour. The Court of Appeal has on several subsequent occasions declared that *In re L* is no longer binding authority; see *S.(B.D.) v. S.(D.J.)* [1977] 2 W.L.R. 44; *In re K (Minors) (Children: Care and Control)* [1977] 2 W.L.R. 33; *W. v. W.* The Times Newspaper, November 26, 1976.

79 In *Re Moilliet* (1966) 56 W.W.R. 458, 58 D.L.R. (2d) 152, the Court of Appeal of British Columbia upheld the award by Branca J. of custody of four girls to their father. The girls were born in July 1951, April 1953, July 1956 and July 1958. I do not find this an easy case to understand. The husband had assaulted the wife three times in two weeks, but the judge spoke of her "arbitrary action" in leaving home in 1961 with the children, and one for which he "could find no logical explanation". There was no suggestion of adultery by the wife, and her "fault" apparently consisted in insisting on earning her own living and not being utterly dependent on her husband, as he wished, and of sometimes refusing "demands" for sexual intercourse.

80 See *Chisholm v. Chisholm* [1966] 1 N.S.W.R. 125; [1966] A.L.R. 1101; 7 F.L.R.347, and the criticism of this approach by Hutley J.A. in *Thompson v. Thompson* [1966] 2 N.S.W. 534, 540 and *Barnett v. Barnett* [1973] 2 N.S.W.L.R. 403, 411; and Sornarajah, "Parental Custody: The Recent Trends" (1973) 90 A.L.J. 131, 143-4.

81 Foote, Levy, Sander, 411; see note 11 *supra*.

82 In *Re Thain* [1926] Ch. 676 (C.A.) a girl aged six was taken from the only home she had ever known, with her maternal aunt, and handed over in theory to her father. In practice the crucial person in the life of a girl of this age would be the stepmother, who was neither seen nor heard by the court, and had never met the child. The finding of Eve J. at 684 that the child would be as happy and well cared-for in the one home as in the other could not be substantiated. What kind of relationship the stepmother would establish with the child was unknown and disregarded. Another matter ignored in the judgment was the fact that the deceased mother had, by her will, left some £12,000 to her husband for life or until remarriage and thereafter to the child. It is more than doubtful if any of the parties involved ignored this.

83 *Re C.* (M.A.) [1966] 1 W.L.R. 646, [1966] 1 All E.R. 838 (C.A.) represents an advance on *Re Thain* in that custody of an ex-nuptial boy aged 17 months was there awarded to the putative father largely because of the personality of his wife, with whom he had become reconciled. Here again, however, she had never seen the child, and since her care was considered crucial, one may well ask why custody was awarded to the putative father alone.

84 One element in the physical mother's continuous abuse and ill-treatment of Maria Colwell may have been that this clean, well-mannered and well-spoken child was known to despise the dirty, violent and drunken family she had been forced by the public authorities to rejoin.

85 [1965] A.C. 201, [1963] 3 All E.R. 191. It is thought the decision overrules that in *Fowler v. Fowler* [1963] P.311 [1963] 1 All E.R. 119 (C.A.) that in custody on divorce a judge should not interview the welfare worker in the absence of the parties and their advisers.

86 *Re D.* (Infants) [1970] 1 W.L.R. 599 [1970] 1 All E.R. 1088 (C.A.). A recent disturbing decision of the Court of Appeal in *D. v. N.S.P.C.C.* [1976] 3 W.L.R. 124 [1976] 2 All E.R. 993 (C.A.) that the National Society for the Prevention of Cruelty to Children was not entitled to withhold the name of an informant to the effect (erroneously, as it appeared) that a child was being ill-treated, is now under appeal to the House of Lords. Lord Denning's dissenting judgment in this case seems much to be preferred.

87 [1967] 1 W.L.R. 396, [1967] 1 All E.R. 202.

88 [1974] 1 W.L.R. 595, [1974] 1 All E.R. 1145 (C.A.).

89 The Times Newspaper, January 16, 1974. In its Published Working Paper, 53, the English

Law Commission made no recommendation for the magistrates' court to be given power to interview children.

90 (1975) 17 R.F.L. 257.

91 [1965] V.R. 540; (1963) 9 F.L.R. 384. The court there said that such interviews should preferably be conducted with the consent of both parties.

92 *Op. cit.* note 3, 49 Can. Bar Rev. 557, 560.

93 (1969) 24 N.Y.2d 270, N.Y.S. 2d 842, 247, N.E. 2d 659, cited by Paulsen, Wadlington and Goebel, *Domestic Relations, Cases and Materials* 599.

94 California Civil Code, (1954) s.138.

95 Ohio Revised Code, s.3109.04.

96 Utah Code (1953) s.3-3-5, all cited by Ploscowe, Foster and Freed, "Family Law, Cases and Materials."

97 [1966] 1 W.L.R. 646, 675 at B.

98 Normally the solicitor of the opposing party would refuse any request to interview his client. The judges refused to have court experts appointed, preferring conflicting evidence from experts retained by each party, which allowed them greater flexibility in reaching their decisions.

99 *B(M) v. B(R)* [1968] 1 W.L.R. 1182 at 1184, [1968] 3 All E.R. 170 (C.A.), confirming the observations to this effect of Cross J. in *Re S.* (Infants) [1967] 1 W.L.R. 396, 407D.

100 (1966) 258 Iowa 1390, 140 N.W.2d 152, cert. denied, 385 U.S.494. That court reversed the award of custody of a 7 year old boy to his father, whose style of life was bohemian and somewhat unsuccessful, and declared that he should remain with his maternal grandparents, with whom he had been living for more than two years since his mother's death. The grandparents were prosperous, certainly elderly and probably dull. The father had dissipated the mother's estate of about $4,300 which she had intended for her children's education. Two years later, when the child was visiting his father, he expressed a preference for that home, and remained in it by agreement.

101 See Brigitte M. Bodenheimer, "The Rights of Children and the Crisis in Custody Litigation: Modification of Custody in and out of State" (1975) 46 U. Colo. L.Rev. 495. Several states have moved to prohibit rapid changes in arrangements for children's custody. The Uniform Marriage and Divorce Act, s.409 prohibits changes within two years of the order except in unusual circumstances.

102 See note 76. See also *Lynch v. Lynch* (1965) 8 F.L.R. 433 and *Neill v. Neill* (1966) 8 F.L.R. 461.

103 *C. v. C.* The Times Newspaper, Nov. 9, 1972 (C.A.), *B. v. B.* The Times Newspaper, Jan. 24, 1973. (C.A.).

104 *Re O* (Infants) [1971] Ch.748 [1971] 2 All E.R. 744 (C.A.).

105 In *Thompson v. Thompson,* The Times Newspaper, March 12, 1975, (C.A.), Buckley L.J. is reported as saying that if hearsay is included in welfare reports, particularly on controversial matters, that fact should be made explicit. Judges have been heard to emphasize to magistrates that welfare reports should be made by the signatory to them, and not "improved" or "amended" by some person higher in the hierarchy who did not see the homes about which the report is made.

106 [1973] 2 N.S.W.L.R. 403.

107 As in *Re O (Infants)* [1962] 1 W.L.R. 724, [1962] 2 All E.R. 10 (C.A.). The husband was Sudanese and the mother English. The mother had at first instance been awarded custody in England of both children, but the Court of Appeal found this unjust to an unexceptionable father, and held he was entitled to custody of the boy. See also Sir G. Baker P. in *Bell v. Bell,* The Times Newspaper, Dec. 10, 1975.

108 *Practice Direction (Wardship Applications)* [1966] 1 W.L.R. 1384, [1966] 3 All E.R. 144; *Re W* The Times Newspaper Jan. 28, 1972 and *M. v. M.* The Times Newspaper, Nov. 30, 1972.

109 *Jones (E.G.) v. Jones (E.F.)* [1974] 1 W.L.R. 1471, [1974] 3 All E.R. 702 (C.A.).

110 *Bell v. Bell,* The Times Newspaper, Dec. 10, 1975. The magistrates had entrusted the father with custody of one child and the mother with the other.

111 Now in Title 2 of Tex. Laws 1973, c.. 543, s.11.13, which provides that "In a suit affecting

the parent-child relationship, except a suit in which adoption is sought, any party may demand a jury trial", but the provision is not new.
112 At pp. 35, 38, 101.
113 This was done in *Jussa v. Jussa* [1972] 1 W.L.R. 881, where despite their differences both parents were clearly anxious to maintain the children's contact with both. Since the Guardianship Act, 1973 s.1 provided that the rights and authority of mother and father are equal, custody is usually given to both.
114 Published May 1975, Chairman of Committee Gerald Godfrey Q.C. The writer was one of twelve members of the committee.
115 The Finer Report, Cmnd.5629, para.4.405 pointed out that the two forms of "accusatorial" and "inquisitorial" procedure are not mutually exclusive, and that in matters affecting children the court has to have regard to the child's paramount interests, which are not determined by the contending parents. But the parents may noticeably limit the evidence presented to the court. Members of the medical profession in particular frequently express intense dislike of the accusatorial process, which in many cases resolves itself into inappropriate behaviour by counsel.
116 This is a matter on which professional practice might well be more effective than any rule of law. For example, what is the position and duty of the solicitor or counsel who quite accidentally becomes aware that his client, who is demanding sole care of a young child, is an alcoholic, or has an addiction to drugs that might soon become more serious?
117 Cmnd. 5629, part 4, sections 13 and 14, pp. 170-223.
118 *Cases and Materials on Family Law* (2nd ed. 1976) 399.
119 Magistrates' Courts Act, 1952 s.56(2).

Children's Hearings In Scotland

John C. Spencer*

I propose to examine the principles and practice of the Scottish system of children's hearings[1] which are responsible for taking decisions on children who are in need of "compulsory measures of care".[2] This system is now only in its sixth year and the fruits of research are severely limited.

It is correct to see the Scottish system of hearings as an alternative to the model of the juvenile court, but it is wrong to assume that the judicial process, in the form of the Scottish criminal courts, both sheriff courts and the High Court, has no part to play in dealing with the young offender. Three sets of decisions for juvenile offenders are reserved for the criminal court, the finding as to guilt,[3] sentencing in the case of certain serious offences,[4] and the hearing of appeals.[5]

The discussion of my subject takes the following form: first, the antecedents to the system and its legislative development, second, the characteristic features of the hearing system and in particular the relationship between the hearings and the courts, third, the experience of their working during the first five years, and finally the relevance of the Scottish system for contemporary issues in juvenile justice.

One of the most interesting features of the development of the contemporary Scottish system is its divergence from the English system after many years of sharing a common history. The Children's Act of 1908 applied to England and Scotland alike, and this legislation led to the introduction of juvenile courts attached to the Justice of the Peace courts and was designed to keep children out of the adult courts. But the growth of juvenile courts in Scotland was extremely slow and by the nineteen-sixties only four had been established.[6] In England, by contrast, although the quality of juvenile courts varied considerably, they had developed steadily, particularly in London and in the main metropolitan areas.

The two main committees established during the nineteen-sixties, the Ingleby[7] committee in England and the Kilbrandon[8] committee in Scotland, therefore, faced a rather different situation, although based

* John C. Spencer, M.A., Ph.D. (Lond.), Professor of Social Administration and Head of Department, University of Edinburgh; Vice-President, Scottish Council of Social Service; Member, Scottish Advisory Council on Social Work to the Secretary of State for Scotland.

initially on common legislation. The impetus to reform stemmed largely from a concern over the fragmented nature of the services available to young offenders and children in need of care. It was no accident, therefore, that the reforms which followed these two reports were as much focussed on the structure of the child and family welfare services as they were on the structure of the decision-making body. This point will certainly not be lost on Canadians whose constitution provides for the responsibility for justice and for welfare at separate levels of government. But it is certainly a firm reminder that systems of justice, above all in the case of children, cannot be divorced from the structure of the social services responsible for the assessment and care of the offender and in particular of his family.

Given the rather different situation which prevailed in Scotland, the Kilbrandon committee found itself faced with a more open range of options. In its recommendations it favoured neither the extension of the juvenile court system nor reliance on the sheriff courts. It pointed out that the existing system was unevenly balanced between the traditional crime-punishment and a welfare or educative principle. Their conclusion was unequivocal: "we do not believe that the present system, resting as it does on an attempt to retain the two existing concepts in harness, is susceptible of modification in any way which would seem likely to make any real impact on the problem."[9]

The main feature of the Kilbrandon proposals, therefore, was to divorce the task of adjudication on the facts of the case from the decision-making function as to disposal. The former would remain with the courts while the latter would go to a new "duly constituted public agency" which would not be a criminal court.[10] The committee, in proposing this model, had noted that only 5% of young delinquents before the Scottish courts pleaded not guilty.[11] The Ingleby committee, on the other hand, was less radical in its proposals and recommended the retention of the juvenile court as the main decision-making body in England with responsibility for dealing with delinquents but with modifications to meet the needs of the deprived.[12] The subsequent history of the English juvenile court has shown the uneasy, and sometimes strongly critical, response of magistrates to a compromise of this kind. Nevertheless the Report of the Expenditure Committee of the House of Commons (1975) on the Children and Young Persons Act 1969, recommended no change in the existing English system, though recognizing the delicate balance between society's demand for protection from the serious offender and the disappointing consequences of custodial treatment.[13]

In October 1966 the government published a white paper, giving its views on the Kilbrandon recommendations.[14] While it accepted the committee's plan for a new system of children's hearings it rejected the idea of a new social education department as the matching field organization, and placed this responsibility on the new unified departments of social work which would be established in the local authority. The care of deprived and delinquent children was to be closely linked with related work with parents, families and communities to which children belong. Co-ordination of social work services and a preventive approach to welfare and to community development were to constitute major functions of the new departments. The underlying principle of the new model was that of welfare[15] and the proposals subsequently were enacted in the Social Work (Scotland) Act 1968.

There are two main elements in the Scottish system: the panel members who constitute the children's hearing[16] and decide on the treatment of the children appearing before them and considered to be in need of compulsory measures of care, and the reporter[17] who acts both as a gateway to the children's hearings and also as their executive arm. The essential characteristics of the hearing itself, attended by child and parents with the reporter and three panel members of whom at least one must be a man and one a woman, sitting as a working group around a table, are informality and privacy. They will certainly be joined by a social worker involved in assessment and supervision, and occasionally by a school teacher and by a friend of the child or parent: while lawyers may appear in this capacity, their function is not to give legal advice.

The role of the reporter is perhaps the most interesting and certainly the most innovative part of the Scottish system. This function (distributed about equally among men and women) arises from the Kilbrandon report which expresses the concept as follows: "Since it seems to us that the referral of cases to the juvenile panels should be in the hands of an independent official competent to assess both the legal issues and also the wider question of the public interest, he should preferably be an officer combining a legal qualification with a period of administrative experience relating to the child welfare and educational services."[18] Not only would he decide on individual referrals to the panels — acting as a kind of sieve — but also would act as their legal adviser.

His appointment is made by the local authority, subject to the approval of central government, without whose consent he cannot be removed from office. The role has substantial independence. His statutory duties are prescribed under the 1968 Act but above all these he has a substantial measure of discretion, acting as he does as the gateway to the system. His discretion operates at several stages:[19] first, in the initial investigation when a referral (by "any person" with reasonable cause to believe that a child may be in need of compulsory measures of care) is made. He may consult, for example, police, school or social worker. Second, he must decide whether a family should be brought to the hearing, or informal guidance is required. Third, he has the duty to communicate to the family and to the person bringing the case that "no further action is required". Among the options used in this third task one should note particularly the possibility of inviting restitution in some form.

But over and above all this he is responsible not only for arranging the hearing and attending at its proceedings to ensure that the correct procedure is observed, but also, in cases of appeal, of taking the case before the sheriff (who is a judge in Scotland with a wide jurisdiction) and providing the family with access to free legal aid. (This right of appearance was challenged by defence lawyers in 1975 and the challenge upheld by the High Court.[20] The government subsequently placed regulations before Parliament under the Children Act 1975 (Section 82) giving the right of appearance in the sheriff court to any reporter with at least one year's service.)

He is also responsible for arranging a review hearing for every case in which a supervision requirement is made. Reviews must take place within a year, but may be requested earlier by social worker or family. It is pertinent at this point to emphasize the importance of this built-in system of reviews, but with the essential proviso that their value is greatly dependent on continuity in the panel membership so that the members who originally heard the case can review their original decision and also get the benefit of feed-back.

The diversity of skills required by the reporter has taken time to develop: legal competence as well as skill in assessment and in social work understanding are clearly required.[21] Reporters have been drawn primarily from law and social work and their association has been active not only in clarifying their role but also for arranging for appropriate training.

As regards the lay members of the panel considerable emphasis has been placed on their selection as a cross-section of the community and their ability to represent community opinion.[22] Responsibility for selection rests with independent Advisory Committees who are also concerned with the fitness and general working of the panels, with public relations and with research.[23] The process of selection involves a general system of public advertisement and a multi-stage selection process for which professional advice may also be used. Following this the selected members are required to undertake a period of organized training before taking up their work.

Criticism has been directed mainly towards the composition of the panels which have not fulfilled the hoped-for objective of a balance in age, education, occupation and sex: in short, few of the members have been drawn from the neighbourhoods in which delinquents live, but are concentrated largely in the higher social classes.[24] Their task in decision-making is clearly difficult and it is not therefore surprising that applicants are largely drawn from the middle-class for work that is unremunerated even though travelling and loss of time at work may be compensated.

But perhaps the most significant characteristic of the Scottish system is the relationship between the hearings and the courts. The Kilbrandon committee recommended that all juvenile offenders under sixteen, subject only to very exceptional cases should be referred to panels. These exceptional cases were those in which "the Lord Advocate may under common law direct, exceptionally, for grave reasons of public policy that they be taken in the Sheriff Court or for that matter in the High Court of Justiciary." It is clear that the committee had in mind only the gravest crimes for which trial under criminal procedure was essential.[25]

When the Lord Advocate issued instructions to chief constables and procurators-fiscal in August 1970, he defined seven categories of offences for which prosecution might be required.[26] But in doing so he opened the door to a system which has extended the range of children prosecuted by the Procurator-Fiscal (who prosecutes in the sheriff courts in Scotland), and which has carried with it a number of unsatisfactory consequences. One is the retention of the courts' right to fine children (a policy rejected by Kilbrandon) and another the difference in the courts' policy for sending children away to a residential school without provision for a review.

The Kilbrandon committee had dismissed the age of criminal responsibility as "a largely meaningless term",[27] leaving it at eight years and preferring instead to put forward recommendations for a fundamental reconstruction of the system dealing with children through a form of non-criminal procedure. But the much-publicized case of Mary Cairns (a nine-year-old Glaswegian girl) raised in an acute form the need for close collaboration between reporters and procurators-fiscal.[28] The government subsequently directed procurators-fiscal not to prosecute children under thirteen without reference to the Crown Office nor against children alleged to have committed an offence in company with an adult except where joint prosecution was essential.[29]

It is in this context that recourse to the courts is most controversial, as I argue later. But one must also mention the role of the sheriff in chambers in making a finding as to whether such grounds for referral to the reporter as are not accepted or understood have been established. The sheriff too may issue a warrant for the child's apprehension if he fails to attend the hearing of the application. This adjudication on the grounds of referral is clearly fundamental to the whole system.

So also is the right of appeal to the sheriff against decisions of the hearings together with a right of appeal to the Court of Session on points of law arising out of decisions by the sheriff. At this stage we should note, however, that the number of appeals against the decision of the hearings is extremely small, amounting in the three years 1971-72-73 to no more than 0.2% of the total number of decisions.[30]

How successful has the Scottish system been? In a study of four areas of

Scotland recently published, we used six broad criteria.[31] But we have not been able to take the further essential step of measuring the precise effect of the new system on the subsequent behaviour of those who have experienced it.

Briefly the six criteria were:

a. Communication between the professionals who operate the system.

b. The discriminatory power of the hearings in the process of decision-making.

c. Their intelligibility to the clients of the system.

d. Respect for the rights of the child.

e. The availability of a wide variety of positive treatment measures.

f. The nature and extent of community involvement.

Hard indeed as these criteria are to assess in a fair and accurate manner it seemed to us essential to apply to the system criteria which reflect the breadth of purpose in a system of this kind of which the essential focus is children in trouble or in need, against the background of family and community. To reduce the purpose of systems of juvenile justice, however, to the rigid terms of a punishment/treatment dichotomy is to gloss over the subtleties of the distinction and to incur the risk of observing inevitable differences in perception. One man's treatment is another man's punishment. But over and above the difficulties of the punishment/treatment dichotomy there is the obvious though frequently overlooked fact that systems of justice are just one factor in the wider climate of social and economic change as well as of public opinion and moral judgment.

The subject of collaboration immediately draws attention to the large number of different kinds of professionals and laymen involved, as well as to their differences in purpose, in language, in training and in assumptions. The categories involved include the panel members, social workers, schools, police, reporters and procurators-fiscal and the courts.

Given the differences between the four areas (two urban and two rural) it is hard to generalize but certain conclusions seem justified. The most tenuous links, in our view, were between teachers and social workers and between procurators-fiscal and reporters though it is, of course, in these areas that the opportunities for collaboration are most important. Attitudes of procurators-fiscal, as indeed of sheriffs also, differed widely as regards the desirability of prosecution and relationships between courts and hearings were most difficult where both prosecutor and sheriff favoured a policy of prosecution.

For the police, the establishment of the system of children's hearings was a "quiet revolution"[32] but general attempts at re-education were hardly undertaken in Scotland. Although virtually all police forces had established community involvement branches since 1971, for which liaison with social workers and reporters was a recognized task, the police have found the new system hard to understand. But in particular the retention of a dual system (of hearings and courts) seemed to the police to imply that hearings were responsible for only minor offences and that the courts were expected to deal with serious delinquents.

Research by Alison Morris and Mary McIsaac suggests that hearings are paying more attention to the needs of the family than to the seriousness of the offence.[33] It is interesting to note that their system of scoring "needs" criteria and "deeds" criteria showed a very high correlation between the two in the emphasis placed on them by the hearings when making decisions. They also observe that hearings reach different decisions for two or more children involved in similar offences, not merely on the grounds of differences in their involvement, but also because the children's parents have different capacities for coping with them.

In broad terms the conclusion is that the hearings are capable of greater discriminatory and diagnostic competence (in spite of considerable variations between areas) than the juvenile court. At their best panel members have used the informal context of the hearing, with an average time-span of about 40 minutes for each family, to achieve a relationship with children and their parents and to gain that ease of communication which enables both child and parent to speak. It is clear, however, that continuity in the membership of hearings, particularly for the purpose of reviews, is essential so that this relationship may facilitate freedom of discussion, in which expression of hostility may play an important part.

To say this, however, is in no way to under-estimate the difficulties of a panel of ordinary citizens, faced with the task of taking decisions on information provided by social workers and occasionally by psychiatrists. They have the responsibility of balancing the diagnostic criteria related to treatment in terms of children's needs with lay concepts of justice prevalent in the community from which they are drawn.[34] It is at this point that the consequences of training deserve such careful analysis.

The criterion of intelligibility received little guidance from Part III of the 1968 Act, which prescribes no more than that decisions should be in the best interests of the child. Nor does the continuance of the dual system make the problem any easier. The formality of the juvenile court has frequently been criticized for lack of intelligibility to children. In particular, there are the barriers that arise from differences in accent and language. Then too there is the crucial question of time and the consequences of delay in procedures. In 1974, the proportion of cases dealt with by a hearing in which the total interval was greater than eight weeks was 51% compared with 47% in the previous year.[35] Both the time span and the number of appearances are increased when the grounds of referral are not accepted or when there is an appeal to the sheriff.

There is a general concern at the present time that juvenile courts should make better provision for ensuring that children's rights are preserved. There are some also — from whom I dissent — who make the same criticism of the hearing system. Nevertheless it remains true that a belief in informality and free communication does not necessarily carry with it a neglect of individual rights. The problem is not an easy one, and it arises not only in the procedure of the hearings but also in the use of the reporter's discretion. The communication of social history reports from social worker and school is a case in point. Hearings have an obligation to inform the child and his parents of their substance provided that the contents are "not detrimental" to his interests. On the other hand, in the case of an appeal, both of these reports would be seen by the sheriff and by the lawyer who represents the family. As yet there has been little, if any, discussion of separate representation of the child, as in the case of proceedings under the Children Act 1975. Nor has more than very slight use been made of the provision for the child or family bringing a friend as a representative.

Nevertheless, in our own study, we were in general impressed by the care which hearings took over certain basic rights. Informing the family of their right to appeal is one example: the right to confidentiality is another: there is also the care taken in informing the family that they are known to a member of the hearing in daily life and a request made as to whether they should stand down. This latter point is most likely to arise in smaller communities.

The development of the Scottish system of decision-making has not been accompanied by a corresponding extension of resources and by the necessary range of treatment options. The same observation has justifiably been made in reply to those critics of the English system who have attacked the adverse effects of the Children and Young Persons Act 1969.[36] This point deserves the strongest possible emphasis, and the shortage of treatment facilities, both in number and in the range of alternatives, has certainly done "great damage to the credibility of the system."[37]

In a climate of shortages and cut-backs, moreover, the pressure of demand for stringent measures of punishment, for better custodial and facilities, and in general for greater "teeth" for the decision-making body, be it juvenile court or welfare tribunal, becomes all the stronger. It is welcome, therefore, to see the recent revival of demand for an increase in forms of "intermediate treatment" in which innovative measures of community care are an essential element.[38]

The idea of community involvement was clearly predominant in the Kilbrandon proposals for a lay panel. The idea was further developed in the White Paper when the concept of children's panels as representing the community was suggested. The concept is both challenging and difficult to achieve. Although the expected balance in social class, age and sex has only been achieved to a very limited extent, panel members have nevertheless been conscious of their responsibility to the community. Clearly there are varieties of interpretation among different members and different areas, but one of the most significant consequences of the system has been a sharpened awareness of the real problems faced by children living in families and neighbourhoods of deprivation. Our hope is that panel members who are appointed in the first instance for three years will not continue to hold on to their position but that membership will rotate. In this way the number of former members will be able to play other roles in the life of the community and in initiating new ways of helping children in trouble.

A word should be added about their potential function as a pressure group in the face of severely restricted resources and facilities for prevention and treatment. Here also experience varies but already there are to hand some useful examples of the ways in which panels have been putting pressure on the local authority to do more by way of experiment and innovation, especially in the field of intermediate treatment and community care.

CONCLUSIONS

What conclusions can be drawn which have a wider and more general relevance than for Scotland alone? I pass over the changes which experience suggests might usefully be made in the Scottish system, though it will be clear that we favour a diminution in the present form of the dual system. Our own proposal is that children under 14 should no longer be prosecuted in a criminal court and that in the case of the age-group 14-16 the hearings should be given power to remit the child to the court if the protection of society appears to make this necessary.[39] This is a very controversial suggestion.

But the main point of general interest in the system at the present time, particularly in Canada, is surely its implication for policies of diversion. There appears to be a substantial measure of agreement with those sociologists who have emphasized the damaging consequences of the stigma attached to a court appearance and to the growth of a sense of delinquent identity through a process of labelling.[40]

A policy of diversion clearly aims at restricting the gateway to the criminal court and systems of police cautioning have clearly proved themselves as one important form of diversion. Yet much remains to be done. There is, for example, that important group of children on the threshold of a delinquent career of whom the police are aware as in need of help, but with no formal proof of delinquency. This group, moreover, which includes children who are at risk from abusive parents, has been noticeably absent from the Scottish hearings since few of them have been referred to the reporter. It is certainly abundantly clear that any policy of diversion must take account of existing police practices.

But over and above diversion by the police, there remains the important question of ways in which the screening process could best be extended and developed. For diversion is a futile policy if it *merely* means a speedy and trivial system of disposal and of lightening the load on the courts. Screening clearly implies diagnosis and the diagnostic function can only properly be fulfilled by those trained to carry it out.

The device of a hearing for children through a lay panel, carefully selected and trained and, above all, served by the office of the reporter, is one approach to juvenile justice which should commend itself for comparative study. I have placed particular emphasis on the role of the Scottish system in facilitating a policy of diversion through a process generally known in Canada as screening. But I have perhaps dealt too casually with the important function of the children's hearing as an opportunity for mediation in the affairs of a family, and in which the family members play (or certainly ought to play) a significant part in the discussion. We have come to recognize, both in social work and more gradually in law, how essential it is that the parties to a dispute (sharing in a common problem) should be themselves actively involved in the taking of the decision. Decisions in family affairs, such as where children are in trouble, are more likely to be accepted and to be acted upon when the family itself, both parent and child, feel themselves committed to the decision taken.

At the same time, we must recognize that no system in this field is free from stigma, and that there is still a risk that it will be present in any alternative system to the juvenile court. Treatment, moreover, is an elusive concept and the "rehabilitative ideal" of which Francis Allen[41] wrote so clearly is a goal which is all too rarely achieved. There is always the danger of treatment goals being displaced by control, and even by coercion. It is with this reality in mind, therefore, that new policies must be examined.

Appendix

Flow Chart of Procedure relating to Deprived Children (S 15-26)
and Children in need of Compulsory Measures of Care (Part III)

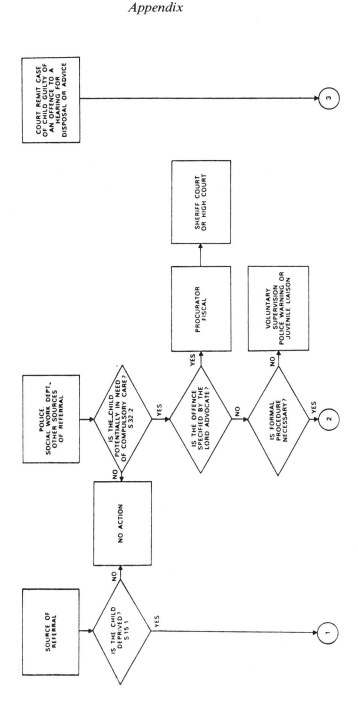

Appendix

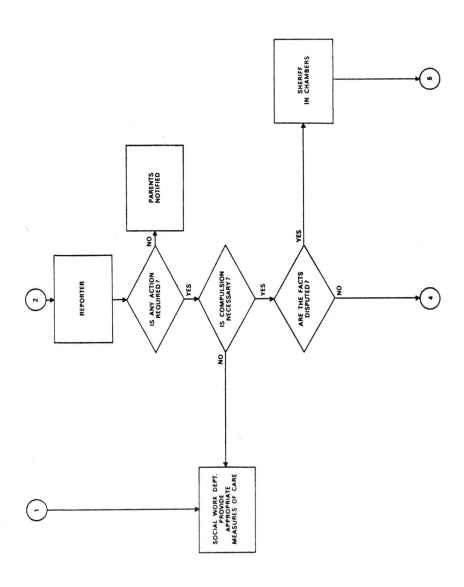

Appendix

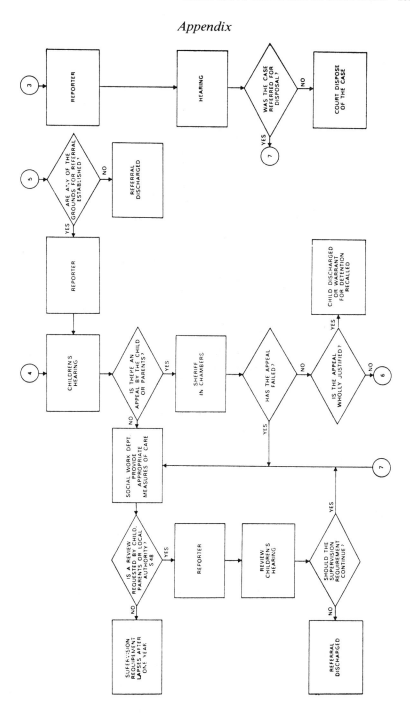

Appendix

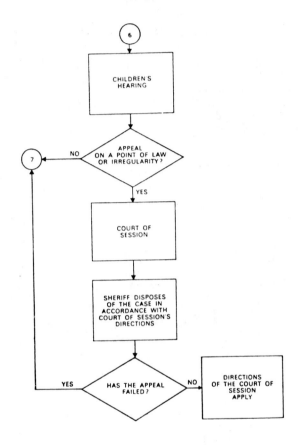

1   The study from which material for this paper has been drawn was discussed in Bruce and Spencer, *Face to Face with Families* (1976). Macdonald: Loanhead, Scotland.

2   There are eight categories under which a child may be deemed to be in need of compulsory measures of care (which include protection, control, guidance and treatment) and referred to the reporter for the local authority area. S. 32(2) Part III of the Social Work (Scotland) Act 1968 (subsequently referred to as "the 1968 Act"). The statistics of the grounds of referral show that in 1973 and 1974 the proportion of children referred by the police for an offence amounts to 87% of the total. Truancy represents 7% and has shown a slow but steady increase during the last four years. Social Work Services Group, Scottish Social Work Statistics 1974, Table 2.62, H.M.S.O. 1976.

3   1968 Act, s. 42(6).

4   *Ibid.* s. 31.

5   *Ibid.* s. 49(1).

6   Scottish Home and Health Department and Scottish Education Department. Children and Young Persons, Scotland, Report of the Kilbrandon Committee (1964), para 44. Cmnd. 2306.

7   Home Office. The Child, the Family and the Young Offender, Report of the Ingleby Committee (1965) Cmnd. 2742.

8   Children and Young Persons, Scotland, Report of the Kilbrandon Committee (1964) Cmnd. 2306.

9   *Ibid.* para. 80.

10   *Ibid.* para. 72.

11   *Ibid.* para. 73.

12   Report of the Ingleby Committee, paras. 104-112.

13   House of Commons Expenditure committee, Report on the Children and Young Persons Act 1969, (1975) para. 167.

14   Scottish Education Department and Scottish Home and Health Department. Social Work and the Community (1966) Cmnd. 3065.

15   *Ibid.* para. 61, Chapter III.

16   1968 Act. s. 34(1).

17   *Ibid.* s. 36.

18   Report of the Kilbrandon committee, para. 98.

19   1968 Act. s. 39.

20   Bruce and Spencer, *op. cit.*, 34.

21   It is important to note that children's hearings are subject to the scrutiny of the Council of Tribunals. The Council, in its Annual Report for 1971-72 (paras. 69-71) indicated that it had been consulted over the procedural rules and took a special interest in their working. It was concerned over two matters:
        1) the role of the reporter in regard to the selection of chairman and members of the hearings. The committee was satisfied that in practice reporters took little part in this.
        2) tribunals should not have to rely on legal advice from qualified reporters. Chairmen differed widely in their views. Some favoured using the reporter.
     The committee agreed to keep this under review.

22   Social Work and the Community, paras. 76-80.

23   Constituted under Schedule 3 of the 1968 Act. See Haldane, "Children's Panel Advisory Committees: development of function and responsibilities" (1971) Vol. 11 Brit. J. Criminol., 359-370.

24   See, for example, Smith and May, "The appointment of the Aberdeen City Children's Panel" (1971) 1 Brit. J. of Social Work, 5-25; Mapstone, "The selection of the Children's Panel for the County of Fife" (1972) Vol. 2 Brit. J. of Social Work, 445-470.

25   Report of the Kilbrandon committee, paras. 125, 126.

26   Bruce and Spencer, *op. cit.*, 72.

27   Report of the Kilbrandon committee, para. 65.

28   Bruce and Spencer, "Children's Hearings and the Scottish Courts: some lessons from the case of Mary Cairns", in Jones (ed), *The Yearbook of social policy in Britain 1973* (1974). Routledge.

29   Bruce and Spencer, *op. cit.*, 72-73.

30 Social Work Services Group. *Scottish Social Work Statistics 1974.* (1976). Table 2.72 analyses the small number of appeals made to sheriffs against disposals by hearings.

31 Bruce and Spencer, *op. cit.,* Chapters 5 and 6.

32 *Ibid.,* 89.

33 Morris and McIsaac, *Scottish Juvenile Justice* (forthcoming publication).

34 Stewart Asquith (Department of Criminology, University of Edinburgh) discusses some of the implications of this point for policy in an unpublished paper given at the University in September 1976.

35 The delay in procedure is particularly open to criticism in the light of the considerable emphasis placed on "crisis intervention".

36 House of Commons Expenditure Committee, Report on the Children and Young Persons Act 1969 (1975) paras. 167, 168.

37 See, for example, Drucker and Mackintosh, *A roof over their heads?* (1976) Department of Social Administration, University of Edinburgh, Edinburgh panel members were asked to note cases, between August 1973 and August 1975, where they would have taken a different decision if other resources had been available. In the first year, a List D placement (*i.e.* in Canadian terms, committal to a Training School) was required for another 90 young people, a small children's home for another 25 and a hostel for older children for another 23. They were unable to make satisfactory arrangements — either residential or non-residential — for one-fifth of children. During the early part of 1975 the proportion of unsatisfactory arrangements increased to nearly one-third.

38 The literature on "intermediate treatment" has rapidly outgrown the extent of the work actually carried out under this broad category of treatment. For a useful discussion of its aims and methods see the special number of Social Work Service, No. 11. October 1976. Dept. of Health & Social Security, London.

39 Bruce and Spencer, *op. cit.,* 157.

40 See, for example, Rock, *Deviant Behaviour* (1973) Hutchinson. University Library, London.

41 Allen, *The Borderland of Criminal Justice* (1964) University of Chicago Press.

Representing The Child In The Courts

Bernard M. Dickens*

Decisions of utterly fundamental, lifelong and at times life-shortening effect[1] upon children have traditionally been made by courts before which they have not been represented. Judges fashion children's destinies upon child abuse or neglect, termination of their parents' marriages and applications for adoption, and so on, usually acting in the uncritical belief that determinations of disputes between contending adult parties discharge judicial duties to children, whom the judges often do not hear in court, or in chambers.[2] Sometimes judges merely put the seal of their approval upon the terms of an out-of-court agreement already reached between adults. Concepts that children might have opinions and interests separate and different from those of adults urging claims over them, and that those opinions and interests might be both worthy and capable of independent legal representation, have been advanced only in relatively recent times, and even now do not prevail in all quarters. Where these concepts are acknowledged in procedural jurisprudence, moreover, no uniform pattern of accommodation exists.

My purpose is to consider ways in which the opinions and interests of children may be identified, advanced and defended in judicial proceedings, including in particular those to which the children themselves are not parties.[3] I am primarily concerned with protection, wardship, custody and adoption proceedings,[4] and I refer to juvenile delinquency proceedings, where rights to representation are in principle established[5] only by way of analogy. A brief survey of some existing and proposed systems of representation in Canadian provinces will be followed by consideration of the more advanced model of the Law Guardian introduced in New York and proposed for Ontario.

Reference will be made to conditions in the United States and, for instance, in Britain, but the intention is to have a Canadian and in particular an Ontario orientation. Developments in the jurisdictions covered have followed a relatively uniform evolutionary pattern, however,

* Bernard M. Dickens, LL.M., Ph.D. (Lond.), of the Inner Temple Barrister-at-law, Research Professor, Faculty of Law, University of Toronto, Canada.

and are separated more by time than space. Legal systems have progressed from initially treating children as adults' property[6] to allowing them the status of persons but lacking, for instance, the protection against cruelty afforded to animals,[7] and later to acknowledging their interests as defined by adults or protectively motivated agencies litigating or agreeing about their control. The most developed systems see children as persons in their own right, whose welfare is to be determined not only in terms of the claims of others but also by reference to their situation unaffected by any other's advantage.

United States' jurisdictions, and especially that of New York, led the way to recognizing children's independent needs in litigation, but as recently as 1962 a commentator observed that participation of lawyers, on behalf of any interest in abuse proceedings, was still considered by some to be incompatible with the objectives of the family court.[8] By 1974, when the Law Reform Commission of Canada recommended "the appointment of independent legal counsel to represent the child" where his rights or interests will be directly or indirectly affected by a family court proceeding[9], an experienced Ontario family lawyer described this as a concept "which has for several years attained widespread support and can hardly be the subject of debate".[10] The comparable development of provisions for child representation in Britain and Australia[11] shows the relative speed in adjustment of legal systems to common expectations, and suggests a high level of cultural, or at least jurisprudential, osmosis in the English-speaking world. Provision for representation in Canada may become a matter of increased urgency, however, since upon implementation of proposals for "no fault" divorce,[12] the interests of children may be at increased risk of becoming submerged or neglected in a welter of property allocations.[13]

Modern legal literature on divorce and custody hearings is replete with narratives of acrimonious attitudes of marital partners, locked in adversarial conflict, rendering control of children the prize of combat.[14] One parent venomously attacks the other, at times in the presence of their child, hoping to deprive the other of custody and visitation rights; and, at times, a father with little interest in custody or visitation will claim such rights as a bargaining counter, to trade off against relief from maintenance obligations in a divorce settlement. It is evident, and needs no emphasis, that highly personal litigation of this nature does not provide a favourable or even a suitable environment in which to identify children's best interests.[15] It does not follow, however, when the role of individuals is reduced and protection or wardship proceedings are initiated by agencies or institutions such as children's aid societies, that their interests are more impersonal and relevantly focused.

Agencies serving to protect and promote children's interests, such as

Canadian children's aid societies, may too easily persuade weak or disadvantaged parents, or a single parent, to consent to, or not to resist, a request for a judicial order which society personnel consider fitting. Moreover, in consensual instances and particularly on occasions of parental resistance or non-cooperation, indications for an order may be found more in the behaviour of the parents than in the needs of their child.[16] No adverse criticism is intended of the Ontario Association of Children's Aid Societies in referring to their Guidelines for Practice and Procedure in Handling Cases of Child Abuse, published in July 1976.[17] In explaining the use of the courts, the Guidelines observe that:

"Court authority is generally requested for removal of the child from the home under the following circumstances:
— When there is risk of further injury
— When the parents reject help
— When the parents refuse access to the child or refuse to release the child
— When the parents are too irrational or psychotic to participate in working out a plan".[18]

Parental refusal of "help" or of access to or release of their child does not in itself show the parents' position to be indefensible, and the assessment that they are "too irrational or psychotic" may be questionable when made by a psychiatrist, and is far more so when made by a social worker; a society's capacity to prevail over parents in out-of-court arrangements when it is satisfied of such conditions may not necessarily serve the child's long-term and overall interests. Similarly, whatever representations parents may advance before a court when they are respondents to a society's application (if indeed they appear at all as respondents), the child's opinions and interests may justify separate consideration. This is more so since courts are being encouraged to turn from the euphoric "good-better-best" gradation of "seeking the best interests of the child", to acknowledge the grim reality of having to decide on a "bad-worse-worst" scale, and find "the least detrimental alternative."[19]

A children's aid society alleging a child's home to be unsatisfactory, may be unable to show the likelihood of offering a better total environment. The society may be expected to improve upon material standards, of course, and to remove certain dangers of physical abuse, neglect or, for instance, undernourishment, but it may be unable to replace the child's emotional environment.[20] A child's material and, for instance, nutritional advantage, may have to be balanced against the risk of maternal and other emotional deprivations institutionalized children have been shown to suffer,[21] as have those experiencing lack of continuity in adult relationships. Societies' good intentions to "rescue" children[22] may desensitize them to the delicacy of this balance. Equally, at the other end of the spectrum, a society's financial constraints may persuade it to seek a child's most economic (usually non-institutional) disposition rather than his safest and most satisfying management compatible with the society's means. In all such circumstances, an advocate for the child may have a contribution to make to the child's advantage that neither the society nor his parents may be able or willing to present.

Not only may a representative independent of a children's aid society be able to consider more objectively the society's position and its potential for furnishing a better total environment for the child, but, as a trained advocate, he may also be able to cause the court itself to face its own preconceptions and prejudices. It has been observed in California, for instance, that "juvenile [court] judges and referees ... find it difficult to release a child to the parents when there is any risk at all to the child. This protects the judges from criticism ... but in many cases it may not be the best disposition and may in fact be more harmful to the child than a return to the family."[23] A children's aid society may fail to make a court aware of this consideration, and a representative of a parent may sound self-serving and unconvincing in proposing this as an objective ground for restoration of the child. The child's own representative may, however, display a concern both for the child's security and for his interest in growing up in his own family that will encourage a judge to be appropriately sensitive to potential risks and advantages, and to be somewhat self-analytical as to his motives in determining disposition.

LEGAL REPRESENTATION IN CANADA

For purposes of litigation, individuals appear as parties, witnesses and third persons. Parties have an obvious right to legal representation, but the practical advantage they can take of this may depend upon their financial means. If these are inadequate, legal aid may be available at public expense, to supply a private lawyer or representation through a system of duty counsel. The principle expressed in the United States in *Argersinger v. Hamlin,*[24] that there can be no lawful trial of an imprisonable criminal charge in the absence of counsel for the defendant, does not apply in Canada, but where a defendant on a charge of any gravity lacks counsel the court would be expected to make suitable provision for him, by appointing counsel for the party or as *amicus curiae.*

In principle, the same expectation should arise regarding a juvenile appearing in a Juvenile Court charged with a criminal offence,[25] but in practice such defendants are often unrepresented. The Ontario Legal Aid Plan, established by the Legal Aid Act,[26] provides for counsel to be available to a juvenile upon parental initiative,[27] but if the parents are not disposed to respond to their child's need, he may go without this advantage.[28] In civil proceedings regarding, for instance, custody and protection against abuse and neglect,[29] there is in the United States no constitutional right to counsel,[30] and the rights of parties to such proceedings in Canada are no better.

Witnesses have a limited protection in that section 2 of the Canadian Bill of Rights enacts that "no law of Canada shall be construed or applied so as to... (d) authorize a court, tribunal, commission, board or other authority to compel a person to give evidence if he is denied counsel". This may protect an unrepresented party, of course, since he frequently gives evidence as a witness, but the effect of the language of the section is to protect a person *qua* witness.[31] The safeguard of the Bill of Rights is confined, however, to federal legislation, as opposed to provincial legislation which governs most family matters, and even in federal affairs is limited to protection against self-incrimination.[32] The capacity of counsel giving such protection to participate in the general currency of the trial is restricted, moreover,[33] so that the general right to legal representation enjoyed by a witness may be considered to exist in Canada only to a very limited effect.

The rights of third persons to representation at judicial proceedings have become recognized in Canadian law only quite recently, and only at the very highest judicial level regarding public matters going beyond the immediate interests of the litigants. When the Supreme Court of Canada heard the civil case of *Attorney General of Canada v. Lavell*,[34] which raised an allegation of discrimination by reference to sex, contrary to section 1 of the Bill of Rights, the Supreme Court permitted the intervention through counsel of third person groups such as the Native Council of Canada, the National Indian Brotherhood, and University Women Graduates. The role of these groups was not to call evidence to dispute facts, but to advance constitutional contentions as to the scope and application of the Bill of Rights. In *Robertson and Rosetanni v. R.*,[35] the Lord's Day Alliance of Canada intervened in a criminal appeal with permission of the Supreme Court. But more significantly, in the much publicized criminal appeal to the Supreme Court in the abortion trial of *Morgentaler v. R.*,[36] intervention was allowed by a variety of bodies including the Canadian Civil Liberties Association, the Foundation of Women in Crisis, and the Alliance for Life.[37] Participation was confined, however, to argument on issues of public law concerning legislative power and the effect of the Bill of Rights, the intervenors being granted no *locus standi* regarding the quality of the appellant's conduct or the fact of his unique conviction on appeal following acquittal by a jury.[38]

Counsel for the groups permitted to address the Supreme Court in these cases appeared in a partisan capacity, to urge their clients' specific convictions upon matters of general public importance, but in so far as they assisted the Court's deliberations, they appeared in a role analogous to that of *amicus curiae.* The institution of *amicus curiae* is of long standing in Common Law procedural case law, having its origin in the inherent jurisdiction of the court to request its officers, and particularly the available lawyers to whom the court affords exclusive rights of audience, to be of aid to the court by presenting contentions of law upon identified issues. The *amicus* soon ceased to be a lawyer available to the court by chance, moreover, and came to be appointed because he was a legal practitioner enjoying great eminence and the confidence of his colleagues; traditionally in England the Attorney General, who ranks as head of the Bar, was appointed *amicus curiae.*[39]

In cases before the Supreme Court of Canada involving constitutional issues, there is an established practice of the appropriate provincial Attorney General appearing as *amicus curiae,* even when there is no point upon which he wishes, or is invited, to address the Court. In the *Morgentaler* case, indeed, the Attorney General of Canada was represented separately from the Attorney General of Quebec, who had appeared through counsel in order to undertake the trial and the appeals. There had been no practice until these recent cases, however, of lawyers representing private groups and interests seeking leave to appear to argue public points of law as *amici curiae* before federal or provincial courts. This shows how unlikely a spontaneous development allowing such counsel to appear on behalf of a third person in a family court is, to contest or supplement the factual evidence and to urge the court to adopt a particular disposition.

There are many historical precedents for an Attorney General presenting the *parens patriae* concept,[40] and there is impressive twentieth-century authority that might, if extended, permit Attorneys General to intervene as *amici curiae* on behalf of children. They have adopted the practice in the United States of appearing in courts to speak for the interests of the otherwise defenseless, particularly members of minority groups. Modern use of the *amicus* concept in the United States[41] has been found, however, to have been made more by quasi-public bodies, originating in the case of *Ah How v. United States* in 1904,[42] where counsel appeared for the Chinese Charitable and Benevolent Association of New York. The American Civil Liberties Union, the American Jewish Congress and the Catholic Council on Civil Liberties have been active for the disadvantaged, as has been the National Association for the Advancement of Colored People. The Association's first involvement in litigation has been traced back to 1913 in *Guinn v. United States,*[43] but Charles J. Bonaparte, as United States Attorney General from 1906 to 1909, developed the practice of using the Department of Justice to assist negro interests.[44] For the Attorney General of a Canadian province to appear as *amicus curiae* in a family court to promote the cause of children seems, therefore to be within the traditions of his office.

What "might have been" establishes a contrast with the inadequacy of what has actually existed to the present time. Nevertheless, recourse to public officials has been shown to be available, and if no better provision is made along the lines of current proposals, such as for an office of the Law Guardian,[45] existing officials, in particular provincial Official Guardians, may be propelled into the breach. The potential for this was recently confirmed in Ontario when the Attorney General noted that judges have begun to request such legal representation for children in custody issues.[46] In *Re Reid*[47] the Ontario Divisional Court, in ordering a new trial of a custody application, observed that section 107(2) of the provincial Judicature Act[48] contains statutory authority for the independent representation of children. It enacts that:

"The Official Guardian shall be the guardian *ad litem* or next friend of infants and other persons in accordance with any Act or the rules or an order of a court or judge".

In addition, the Divisional Court noted that in its own right as a court of equity, it enjoys inherent power, representing the Sovereign as *parens patriae,* to protect the rights of any person under a legal disability. In the event, however, the Court appointed the Official Guardian as guardian *ad litem* of the three children involved, "with full power to act for the infants as though they were parties to these proceedings",[49] his costs to be at the discretion of the subsequent trial judge. This welcome development in Ontario may be compared with the functions of the Official Solicitor in England.[50]

Certain provinces may have recourse to the *parens patriae* concept mentioned in *Re Reid* where inherent judicial power reinforced the statutory power arising under the Judicature Act. The United States Supreme Court in the *Gault* case,[51] however, rejected the traditional doctrine that the child's interest would be protected merely by the judge as the embodiment of the *parens patriae* doctrine[52] in juvenile delinquency proceedings. The theory that a benevolent judge acting alone would furnish the best protection for juveniles was considered inadequate to secure the child's constitutional rights. A Canadian child's "constitutional rights" are arguably less than those of a child in the United States, but equally in Canada reliance cannot be placed upon a judge undertaking the investigations and enquiries required by proper representation of a child's interests. Protection must come from an advocate acting as such by preparing and presenting a case before a court, with full powers of obtaining, for instance, pre-trial discovery, and of managing all relevant aspects of the pre-trial, trial and post-trial processes.

CHILD REPRESENTATION IN CANADIAN PROVINCES[53]

The appointment of lawyers to serve as "family advocates" was enacted in British Columbia in 1974 by the Unified Family Court Act,[54] section 8 of which gave such advocates power, notwithstanding any other Act, to:

"(a) attend a proceeding in a court respecting a family matter or a matter respecting the delinquency of a child;

(b) intervene at any stage in a proceeding under clause (a) for the purpose of acting as counsel for a child who, in the opinion of the family advocate or the court, requires representation by counsel; and

(c) upon the request of a court, assist any party to a proceeding under clause (a) who is not represented by counsel."

Three models of legal representation have been identified in juvenile matters,[55] namely the adversary, *amicus curiae,* and social work models. The adversary role is traditionally combative in urging the client's case under strict rules of law and procedure, striving to establish the virtue of his cause by the fact of prevailing. The *amicus curiae* model is comparably legalistic but neutral as to outcome, seeking to assist the administration of justice by advising on law and fact in the hope of countervailing more distorting partisan contentions and leading to the best resolution of issues. The social work model is concerned to help the child affected by litigation, as party or otherwise, by proposals, concessions and collaboration to put the child expeditiously into the most satisfactory condition that can be achieved.

The British Columbia family advocate does not really conform to the adversary model, but may come within the social work model, or is perhaps between the *amicus curiae* and social work models. It may be noted that he acts not to initiate proceedings but only in response to proceedings initiated by others. In such cases, he intervenes at his own initiative or upon the court's instruction, from which it follows that the child's right to his representation is not absolute, and is, in a sense, at the mercy of judicial discretion of the court or of administrative discretion of the family advocate. Representation may be lacking, therefore, not only in particular custody or protection proceedings, but also in delinquency proceedings.

In 1975 the Fifth Report of the British Columbia Royal Commission on Family and Children's Law, Part III, Children's Rights, recommended that children be afforded the right to legal assistance in all decisions affecting their guardianship or custody, or in determination of their status.[56] Clearly, the design of such assistance would have to be at the representative's unaided discretion, since children affected by such decisions or determinations would often be too young to have or to express significant opinions. Compatible with this recommendation is the proposal in Part IV of the

Fifth Report, Custody Access and Guardianship, that the family advocate be preserved to act for children, and to protect their interests by advancing proposals designed in their best interests.[57]

Alberta has no legislation comparable to British Columbia's, but in 1966 courts in the province recognized the need of independent representation for children in some custody cases. In *Woods v. Woods*,[58] Manning J. made an innovative order appointing counsel to represent the minors who were the subject of custody proceedings before him. He ordered that not only should counsel have power to make a comprehensive and independent investigation of the circumstances on behalf of minors, but should also appear at the trial representing only the minors. They would conform to the traditional adversary model of representation in that they would participate fully in the proceedings by calling evidence and by examining and cross-examining witnesses. Since *Woods v. Woods,* this practice has been followed in Alberta on many occasions.[59]

A 1976 study by S. McKeown of the Alberta Institute of Law Research and Reform, entitled "Representation of the Infant in Legal Proceedings — Who Speaks for the Child?" identified a pilot project under the provincial legal aid system for duty counsel to attend juvenile courts. For custody and other civil proceedings it was felt, however, that such a provision would not be feasible in the circumstances of Alberta. The British Columbia family advocate approach was favourably considered, but it was recommended that an office of Amicus Curiae be established, permitting the court to appoint, at its own discretion or at the request of a party, a person to represent the infant. Such officer would be able to make recommendations to the court on the basis of investigations, which he could commission, for instance from social workers or psychiatrists. He would be able to tender in court not only such reports but also additional evidence to assist the establishment of an impartial opinion as to the child's best interests. The recommendation was that such officer's intervention be made mandatory in all cases of alleged abuse or neglect as well as in disputes as to custody, access and guardianship. These are cases in which parental claims may not embody or coincide with a child's best interests, but for delinquency proceedings, where the child is a party and the parents may be expected to have no adverse interest, intervention of the *amicus curiae* was not recommended to be mandatory. The matter will have to be seen, of course, in light of the results of the duty counsel project.

A Saskatchewan court has followed the practice in *Woods v. Woods* in a way that may suggest its potential for achieving by judicial innovation what legislatures may be slow to implement. Legislatures may become alerted, however, and even alarmed, at the implications for provincial budgets of such a development in the exercise of judicial discretion. In *McKercher v. McKercher,*[60] Bayda J. appointed the Official Guardian under section 31(1) of the Infants Act[61] to represent four children in a custody application, granting the officer as wide powers of participation in the proceedings as the parties enjoyed. Neither the contending mother nor the father objected to the Official Guardian's intervention, but the officer herself protested that section 31 applied only to matters affecting the property and estate of an infant, but not to his custody, and that if the judge did have jurisdiction to appoint the Official Guardian to act in custody cases, it should be declined on the grounds that there was no precedent for its exercise in such cases, and the officer had no budgetary or other facilities to provide that service.

In Manitoba the legal aid scheme includes aid for defendants before provincial juvenile courts, but representation, while not strictly confined to the actual court appearance, is not as of right. Under the Legal Aid Services Society of Manitoba Act,[62] Regulations provide as follows:[63]

"JUVENILE COURT DUTY COUNSEL

57. Duty counsel, who shall be solicitors, may be appointed by the board, on a part-time or full-time basis, to attend at one or more Juvenile Courts in the province.

58. The board may appoint graduates-at-law to assist duty counsel as permitted by law.

59. Duty counsel assigned to a Juvenile Court shall

(a) provide information to the general public, and in particular to minors, about the law as it relates to minors;

(b) advise children who have been charged, or who may be charged, with delinquencies under the Juvenile Delinquents Act;[64]

(c) subject to this regulation, and in his discretion, represent children in Juvenile Court proceedings, or arrange, through the office of the area director, for the appointment of solicitors, in accordance with this regulation, to represent children charged with delinquencies; and

(d) advise and assist adult persons charged, or liable to be charged, under the Juvenile Delinquents Act, including taking applications for legal aid."

The provision has several features of interest in regard to possible extension into civil litigation affecting families and particularly children. The Manitoba Child Welfare Act[65] provides in section 25(7) that, in protection proceedings, the judge may order that legal counsel be provided to represent the interests of the child. There is no comparable provision regarding such matters as custody and adoption proceedings, however, and even in the area of protection, proceedings must reach the judge before legal counsel is provided. The juvenile court proposal provides a precedent for dealing with the child at a period some time before court proceedings (which the child may not actually attend), to obtain reports and opinions relevant to the child's best interests. Whether this power might go to the extent of including the power to obtain pre-trial discovery is unclear, but the existing scheme appears principally court-based, in that duty counsel may be appointed "to attend at" court, to "advise children who have been charged, or who may be charged", and to "represent children". The scheme also provides for duty counsel to "advise and assist adult persons" charged or liable to be charged before the court, which may suggest that, if extended to family court settings, counsel would be routinely available to parents. Duty counsel must "advise and assist adult persons", but only has to "advise children", having a discretion as to undertaking or otherwise arranging their representation.

The Committee on the Family Court of the Quebec Civil Code Revision Office has recognized "that the presence of a lawyer at the Family Court constitutes a necessary means for protecting the rights of the parties concerned, ensuring respect of the rules governing the evidence given before the court, assisting the judge in his choice and appreciation of pertinent facts, and helping the parties to better understand, and even accept, the decision taken."[66] This recognition may seem to distinguish legal services to parties from services to non-parties, but the reference to "parties concerned" may go beyond the strict *inter partes* dispute and include children affected by the nature and outcome of proceedings. This is not clear from the implementing recommendation that "every person before the Court be entitled to retain the services of a lawyer of his choice, or to make use of the services provided under the Legal Aid Act if he is entitled thereto",[67] but seems to follow from the recommendation "that every child involved in proceedings before the Family Court be entitled to legal aid services if he so desires, if his parents so request and cannot meet the legal costs involved or if the judge, the mediator or the Admission Service, assigns *proprio motu,* a legal advisor, or a lawyer to that child".[68] This proposal does not give the child legal assistance as of right, nor does it outline the means by which the child is to be made aware of the rights or facilities available to him, and it may fail to provide for his interests to be observed at a sufficiently early stage.

It has been seen that in Ontario, as demonstrated in *Re Reid,*[69] courts have become prepared to provide for protection of children's interests by separate representation through the office of the Official Guardian, acting as guardian *ad litem* rather than as *amicus curiae.*[70] In fact, some statutory instances exist which recognize the principle that in contests involving a child, a court should not always be satisfied only with evidence relating to the child presented by persons whose interests may not be exclusively those of the child. For instance, the Matrimonial Causes Act[71] provides in section 6(2) that:

"Where a petition or counter-petition for divorce or the statement of claim in an action for the annulment of a marriage contains particulars of any child of the marriage who, at the time of the commencement of the action, (a) is under sixteen years of age . . . the Official Guardian shall cause an investigation to be made and shall report to the court upon all matters relating to the custody, maintenance and education of the child".

Further provisions of section 6 permit the Official Guardian to engage another to conduct such investigation, to bring the findings before the court and, when the facts so produced are disputed, call the investigator as a witness.

Regarding adoptions, section 70(4) of The Child Welfare Act[72] enacts that:

"For the purpose of an application for an order for the adoption of a child under eighteen years of age, other than a child who has been placed for adoption by a children's aid society, the court shall appoint a guardian *ad litem* of the child".

The Official Guardian acts in this capacity, and he may commission reports comparable to those made under section 6 of the Matrimonial Causes Act. It is significant that a survey published in 1971[73] showed that the majority of judges of the Supreme Court of Ontario feel that the social workers who compile the Official Guardian's reports lack objectivity, and it appears that in some cases only one of the parties is interviewed. Some judges feel that the reports do not always present information which is helpful to the court in its resolution of the particular issue at hand.

The confinement of the mandatory appointment of a guardian *ad litem* under section 70(4) to private adoptions may be justifiable, especially since under section 75 of The Child Welfare Act, the provincial Director of Child Welfare must certify the suitability of the adoptive parents, whether by private adoption or adoption through a children's aid society. Indeed, referring to some confusion as to whether the guardian *ad litem* should also satisfy himself as to suitability of the proposed adoptive parents, the Ontario Law Reform Commission observed that "we are of the opinion that the guardian *ad litem* should not duplicate this function".[74] Nevertheless, there may be an argument that an independent guardian *ad litem* should consider the suitability of prospective adoptive parents, either as well as, or even instead of, the Director of Child Welfare, since a disturbingly high proportion of children found "in need of protection" under the Child Welfare Act[75] are under the guardianship of adoptive parents. This seems to raise some questions about the standards applied by the Director and the depth of scrutiny undertaken by those whose proposals he affirms. Clearly, the provision of section 76 of the Act, that: "Upon the hearing of an application for adoption, where the child is seven or more years of age, the court shall inquire into the capacity of the child to appreciate the nature of the application and shall, where practicable, hear the child", is inadequate to ensure that the child's interests are fully considered in isolation from other interests, such as that of a children's aid society in placing a difficult child for adoption.

The Ontario Law Reform Commission took a materialistic approach, in noting that:

"A useful function which the guardian *ad litem* could perform is to evaluate whether adoption is in the best interests of the child. We have in mind here the possibility, admittedly probably remote, that the child would be better off financially by remaining the child of its natural parents, although not necessarily remaining in their care. The child may have an expectation of inheriting a substantial legacy from the relatives of the natural parents. It is appreciated that this gift could be preserved if it were to be given *nominatim* but adoption could remove the incentive for making the gift.

That this evaluation should be conducted by a lawyer is a proposition which we regard as elementary. Only a lawyer, we believe, can safely be said to have the capacity to appreciate the rules of succession and their effect for the child in question".[76]

When considering children liable to be found "in need of protection", the Commission noted that section 25(3) of the Child Welfare Act provides that "The judge may hear any person on behalf of the child", but stated that "after consultation with numbers of knowledgeable people, we have come to the conclusion that the interests of the child may not be adequately represented at the present time".[77] This conclusion was fully vindicated in the August 1976 decision of the Divisional Court in *Re Helmes*.[78] A Family Court judge invoked the authority of section 25(3) to appoint the Official Guardian to act as guardian *ad litem* of the four year old child, but the Divisional Court quashed that appointment, on the grounds that "the Children's Aid Society is a society appointed by the community to act in matters to protect the interest of children",[79] and that a Family Court judge has no power to impose upon the Official Guardian a parallel or competing duty.

The Court proposed, however, by way of compromise, that "if the Judge is concerned as to whether the interests of the child are being properly protected, the Judge hearing the case would have the right to adjourn the matter, contact the Official Guardian and ask him if he wished to make representations. It would then be up to the Official Guardian if he wished to make representation". Thus, the courts cannot order representation on the guardian *ad litem* model, but may invite and permit the Official Guardian to address the court as *amicus curiae,* with more circumscribed rights of participation at trial.

The Divisional Court's reading of section 25(3) may appear realistic, at least in eliminating duplication of functions, but its confidence in children's aid societies was not fully shared by the provincial Law Reform Commission in its 1973 Report. The Commission observed that:

"in contested cases the Children's Aid Society, on the one hand, asserts an institutional viewpoint of the child, while on the other hand the child's parents assert their own view of what is best for the child. In non-contested cases only the institutional viewpoint of the Children's Aid Society is available to the court. In neither case does the court have a means by which it can attempt its own independent inquiry or be confident that it has access to all possible views of what would be in the best interests of the child".[80]

The Commission was aware "of some ambiguity in the differing roles which a Society is called upon to play in the course of [protection] proceedings",[81] and of institutional dynamics that may lock an institution into pre-conceptions or attitudes fixed by purely internal institutional considerations, perhaps affected by personal relationships. The Commission concluded that:

"both the court and the child could be assisted by the presence in the proceedings of a person who would represent the child by an independent viewpoint of the best interests of the child, testing the evidence of the Children's Aid Society and on occasion calling his own independent evidence. Under the present system it is the Judge who must assume the burden of all these tasks if they are to be performed at all, and we are acutely aware of the dangers of the Judge descending into the arena of any proceedings".[82]

Since these dangers are present in every case, the solution recommended was to put representation beyond discretion and introduce an officer who, "through continuous involvement with [protection] proceedings . . . would be better equipped to represent a child than counsel retained on an *ad hoc* basis".[83] It was sympathy with this view that persuaded the Divisional Court in the custody case of *Re Reid*[84] to appoint the Official Guardian to represent the child. The Family Law Study and the Ontario Law Reform Commission, in formulating their respective recommendations in regard to the development of an office of Law Guardian in Ontario, took into consideration the institution created in 1962 in New York State.[85]

THE NEW YORK LAW GUARDIAN[86]

The 1962 Family Court Act[87] established the system of Law Guardians in New York State following recommendations in a study conducted by the Committee on the Domestic Relations Court of the Bar of the City of New York, with the cooperation of the Legal Aid Society. Responding to the findings of this committee, section 241 of the New York legislation states that:

"This act declares that minors who are the subject of family court proceedings should be represented by counsel of their own choosing or by law guardians. This declaration is based on a finding that counsel is often indispensable to a practical realization of due process of law and may be helpful in making reasoned determinations of fact and proper orders of disposition. This part establishes a system of law guardians for minors who often require the assistance of counsel to help protect their interests and to help them express their wishes to the court. Nothing in this act is intended to preclude any other interested person from appearing by counsel."

Although the Act is not definitive of law guardians' functions, it has introduced a concept of legal representation, divisible into three separate activities:

(i) as an advocate, the guardian defends his client's legal and constitutional rights;

(ii) as a guardian, he takes into consideration the general welfare of the child as well as his legal rights;

(iii) as an officer of the court, he has the duty of interpreting the court and its objectives to both child and parent, of preventing misrepresentation of facts, of making full disclosure to the court of all relevant facts in his possession, of working closely with the court's probation and other ancillary services to reach a proper disposition and, where necessary, to help in getting a child or family to understand and accept the purposes of such disposition.

(a) In delinquency proceedings

The law guardian rarely enters the picture prior to the filing of the petition, all work at the intake level being handled by the probation staff. The petition may be filed by a peace officer, by an individual who has allegedly suffered injury as a result of the acts complained of, by a parent or by authorized agencies. The petition must contain a full description of the nature and circumstances of the particular complaint.

In those localities which have a permanent law guardian staff (see c below), counsel is usually assigned after the petition is filed and before the first hearing. In other localities, counsel will not usually be assigned until requested at the initial hearing. The loyalty of the law guardian is to the child he represents, in traditional adversary fashion.

In New York family courts, hearings in juvenile cases are held in two parts. The legal aspects are first determined in an "adjudicatory hearing" and the social aspects are considered later in a "dispositional hearing". No final adjudication can be made until both hearings have been held.

In the adjudicatory hearing, the issue is generally well-defined and limited, namely, whether the respondent committed the particular act or acts alleged. In cases where the facts are admitted, as a general rule, counsel should interview at least the complaining witnesses so that he can verify the true extent and nature of the child's complicity. Where there is insufficient evidence to sustain the petition, the law guardian may on occasion find himself subjected to pressure from the judge not to seek dismissal on the ground that the child requires the court's "help". There is no justification for counsel to submit to this pressure: the legislation does not make amenability to "help" from the court a ground for jurisdiction. At the conclusion of the adjudicatory hearing, either the petition must be dismissed or else the court must find on a preponderance of evidence that the acts on which the petition is based have in fact been committed by the respondent.

The Act permits the commencement of a dispositional hearing immediately after the adjudicatory hearing has been completed; the dispositional hearing may also be adjourned until a social, medical and/or psychiatric assessment has been made. Unless it is clear that this type of assessment is not required, counsel will usually request an adjournment of the dispositional hearing until the results of these investigations are available. The law guardian should be aware of the broad range of dispositional powers available to the court and should seek to obtain the best possible treatment for his client, on the basis of his own findings and those contained in the social investigation.

(b) In neglect proceedings

Family courts in most of the counties throughout New York have automatically appointed law guardians to represent children in all neglect proceedings. Unlike delinquency proceedings, the parent or parents are the respondents, not the child, and since there is considerable possibility of conflict between the interests of the parents and the child's welfare, counsel cannot adequately represent both. In a neglect proceeding, counsel's role as guardian rather than as advocate becomes apparent. He is not called upon to defend, but rather to ascertain where the best interests of his ward lie and to strive to secure the disposition which in his view would best serve those interests.

The law guardian enters the picture once the petition is filed (as in delinquency proceedings). Neglect hearings are held in two stages — adjudicatory and dispositional. The adjudicatory hearing is designed to determine whether the allegations of the petition are supported by a fair preponderance of the evidence while the dispositional hearing determines what order of disposition should be made.

It would appear to be counsel's duty to make as complete an independent investigation as possible of the background of the neglect charges. At the adjudicatory hearing his position will be almost completely non-adversarial — to present the evidence to the court. At the dispositional hearing, the role of the law guardian is similar to that performed by him in the dispositional stage of juvenile proceedings.

(c) Generally

The law guardian system has now been operating in New York State for fifteen years. In large urban centres, there is a permanent staff of law guardians, but in rural areas, a panel of practising lawyers recommended by the local Bar association is available. All are paid by New York State, under the terms of an agreement with the Legal Aid Society. The participation of the law guardian in family court proceedings has proved valuable and the family court judges of the state of New York advocated the expansion of the role of the law guardian to all cases involving children. Nevertheless, the system is not without its critics, and some within the legal profession have complained that it affords areas of patronage.

ONTARIO APPLICATIONS OF THE LAW GUARDIAN MODEL

The Ontario Law Reform Commission envisages a Law Guardian fulfilling a number of roles. The Commission considered that the child who is the subject of an adoption application should have the benefit of counsel to evaluate whether adoption is, in fact, in the child's best interests. Section 70(4) of The Child Welfare Act permits appointment of a guardian *ad litem* for a relinquishing parent aged under eighteen. It is proposed by the Commission that this should fall outside the Law Guardian's competence, however, since assumption of this function would lead to a pronounced conflict of interest with the responsibility to the young parent's child, even if an Office or Department of the Law Guardian contained a number of independent law guardians.

In custody and guardianship matters where the existing Official Guardian is introduced under The Infants Act or The Matrimonial Causes Act, his practice is to employ a staff of social workers, to send questionnaires to the parties involved, and to analyse the responses to determine whether further investigation is required. If so, it is undertaken in Toronto by the Official Guardian's own social workers, and in other areas by local children's aid societies. The Official Guardian acts as a reporter to the court, and does not generally express a view (outside of the report) on where he considers the child's best interests to lie; he similarly does not call witnesses apart from the person who prepared the report, and does not cross-examine other witnesses.

The Ontario Law Reform Commission thinks this approach might be suitable regarding children's property interests, but unsatisfactory regarding the new functions of representation on the merits and disposition of custody and guardianship matters. It is, therefore, proposed that the Law Guardian should be vested with new powers to discharge the new functions, in the expectation that he will be able to develop new techniques. His role before a court in a custody dispute should be analogous to that of an *amicus curiae* rather than that of the child's advocate in the strict sense, but he should nonetheless be responsible for forming an independent opinion on the best interests of the child and assisting the court to reach its own conclusion on these interests, in the context of a proceeding in which both parents are represented.

In protection proceedings, the Commission favoured a Law Guardian to represent the child by forming a viewpoint of his best interests independent of the guardian of the child and/or of the children's aid society, testing the society's evidence and on occasion calling independent evidence. The Office or Department of the Law Guardian may be expected in time to accumulate a body of expertise in handling such cases, and a stock of experience of past cases that may be of service to all concerned, including the court. The Law Guardian should have the power, now existing under section 4(3) of the Matrimonial Causes Act in favour of the Official Guardian, to engage any person's assistance, giving him access to the advice of psychiatrists, psychologists, social workers and others who may be able to guide him in forming his judgment.

As an advocate, the Law Guardian would as of right obtain notice of any proceedings, either actual or pending, involving a minor and would receive all relevant information regarding it, such as documents and reports. Accordingly, the Commission favoured children's aid societies making their evidence available to the Law Guardian before the proceedings to aid his evaluation of the position of the child. This is not to further the Law Guardian's assumption of a strict adversary position in the proceedings, but to assist him in adopting the stance of an *amicus curiae* acting creatively to aid the court, through having access to relevant knowledge and time to consider its application to the actual and potential circumstances.

THE ADVOCATE FOR THE CHILD

Representation for children is being provided today under a number of legal systems, and is being urged in more. No uniform pattern exists, however, for the construction, powers or role of the office of a representative charged with promotion in court of a child's best interests. In some instances and proposals he is an officer of the court itself, reinforcing the court's *parens patriae* supervision or acting as standing *amicus curiae,* while in others he is specially designated but established independently of the court service, appearing in court as *amicus curiae* or in a traditional role as an advocate of his client. In some systems, the representative has no special designation, but is drawn *ad hoc* from the ranks of the practising legal profession, or from the ranks of non-lawyers such as social workers. The New York law guardian is a lawyer acting as an officer of the court, enjoying access to its ancillary services such as are provided by social welfare and probation personnel.

The Law Reform Commission of Canada, however, in its Working Paper on the Family Court[88] considered that "Counsel for the child should be independent of the court".[89] The federal Commission added that the counsel should have direct access to the court's investigative services so that he would obtain as much relevant evidence as possible for a proper disposition of the proceedings. Recognizing that under federal-provincial legal aid agreements in force in most provinces, counsel may be provided for juveniles in certain criminal or delinquency proceedings, the Commission favoured comparable protection for children at need in civil or quasi-criminal matters. It does not follow that counsel should appear for a child in all proceedings, but the recommendation "underlines the importance of an investigation at an appropriate point to determine whether there is or may be a conflict of interest between the child and the adults in the proceedings and whether separate counsel should be appointed to protect the interests of the child".[90] To implement this concept, the federal Commission recommended that full-time or part-time lawyers be made available in and to Family Courts through a suitable agency, to provide legal advice to individuals presenting themselves to, or otherwise coming within the notice of the Court, who require it, and, where necessary, to refer prospective litigants to appropriate community legal services. Agency lawyers would fulfil the further function of being available to advise court personnel upon legal aspects of intake, counselling, investigative and enforcement services.[91]

The federal Commission proposed separation of counselling and advocacy roles, and envisaged that the rules of procedure of the type of family court it proposed would develop in such a way that, well in advance of any trial, the facts in issue would be reviewed and an appropriate court officer would exercise a discretion to appoint counsel from the independent agency to represent the interests of the child until the matter before the court is concluded. Counsel would be a full participant in all matters affecting the child, with full rights and privileges, for instance to call and cross-examine witnesses, and to enjoy direct access to the court's investigative services to provide the relevant evidence he needs. Such counsel would not be expected to appear for a child in all proceedings, but would be present where a conflict of interest might arise between the child and adults involved in proceedings; it has been seen that in practice such a conflict might be presupposed to exist in all child abuse or neglect proceedings.

The concept of a judge or other court officer determining whether to refer a case to an independent representative of the child underlines the scheme of protection of the interests of children and young persons introduced in Britain by the Children Act, 1975.[92] Section 64 of the Act[93] aims to safeguard the interests of children and young persons in care and related proceedings in Juvenile Courts and in appeals therefrom to Crown Courts. The court may by order disqualify parents from claiming to represent their children when it finds an actual or potential conflict of interest. Such disqualifications may be made by courts before or in the course of proceedings, or by single justices before hearings of certain applications for care orders. Upon disqualifying the parents, the court or a single justice, unless satisfied that to do so is not necessary for safeguarding the interests of the child or young person, shall appoint a guardian *ad litem* of the minor for the purposes of the proceedings. Section 64 provides that in unopposed applications for the discharge of care or supervision orders,[94] there is a greater onus on the court to make an order that the parents shall not represent the child, and to appoint a guardian *ad litem*. Section 58 of the 1975 Act[95] extends the concept of separate representation of the child to proceedings involving a child welfare authority (that is, a local government authority) makes resolutions as to parental rights, where the child may be made a party to the proceedings.[96]

The Act, which covers by no means all litigation affecting children's interests, and does not include custody proceedings, does not make representation mandatory, but leaves the guardian's appointment to the court's discretion. This may seem appropriate, and conforms to the observation of the Law Reform Commission of Canada that representation may not be required in all cases.[97] The distinction is, however, that the federal Commissioners required the representative to be a lawyer, whereas the British Act is silent as to the guardian's qualifications. An initial expectation was that representatives, if not lawyers, would engage solicitors in private practice, but the Department of Health and Social Security envisages[98] that representation will be by specially selected, experienced social workers who are independent of any parties to the proceedings. Local government authorities will be required to appoint, and will have power to dismiss, members of panels of potential guardians.

The questions raised by this arrangement are legion, and can be answered only by experience drawn from evolving practice. It may be asked whether appointed guardians will engage legal counsel, and whether non-lawyers would have the necessary procedural and other perceptions to give adequate protection and representation, whether local government authorities are suitable to make panel appointments, and whether those so appointed will feel independent when resisting local government authority applications.[99] As against this, a new body of legal paraprofessionals may emerge, the child advocates, who will blend the lawyer's procedural "know-how" with sensitivities to children's needs and the capacity to maintain an instructive rapport with the child that a traditional lawyer may lack.[100]

In Australia, the initiative of a voluntary organization, named Action For Children, has led to recognition of a right of children in custody disputes to be separately represented by legal counsel, and has resulted in a social worker being judicially appointed to mediate between a child and the court. In *Dewis v. Dewis*[101] the Supreme Court of Tasmania granted leave for counsel to intervene on behalf of children, and for the president of the organization to be appointed as their guardian *ad litem,* in attachment proceedings arising out of a custody application. This decision was followed in 1975 in *Rosen v. Rosen,*[102] where the Family Law Division of the Supreme Court of New South Wales ordered that a member of Action For Children serve as guardian *ad litem* of a thirteen-year-old boy in a custody dispute, and ordered a qualified social worker to interview the child, submit relevant affidavit evidence to the court, and attend the proceedings for cross-examination. This decision anticipated the federal Family Law Act, 1975,[103] section 65 of which provides that:

"Where, in proceedings with respect to the custody, guardianship or maintenance of, or access to, a child of a marriage, it appears to the court that the child ought to be separately represented, the court may, of its own motion, or on the application of the child or of an organization concerned with the welfare of children or of any other person, order that the child be separately represented, and the court may make such other orders as it thinks necessary for the purpose of securing such separate representation".

In conclusion, consideration may be given to the qualities required of an advocate for a child when they differ from those of an advocate in general litigation. It has been noted that "a child may have less need for a litigation specialist than for a lawyer who has competence and familiarity with non-legal resources",[104] and that some knowledge of child psychology and mental development would seem to be required beyond the usual skills of a litigation lawyer. The child advocate should know how to interview his young client, how to listen and how to perceive when the child is repressing, misdescribing or deflecting his concerns. If his client is too young to speak, the advocate must be able to comprehend specialists' reports predicting the child's future in different potential environments. He should gain a sense of what the child who can communicate considers important in making assessments, while also having the vision to accommodate immature judgment in determinations having longer-term effects than a child has the experience to recognize.

Dangers are present, however, not only in a lawyer whose professional training and experience have not inculcated such qualities having suddenly to exercise them, but also in a lawyer or other representative whose career comes to depend upon demonstrating such skills falling under the spell of fashionable theories and dogmas that cause him to apply preconceptions and stereotypes to the individual child in whose life he has gained considerable influence. Inept and doctrinaire advocacy may too easily become the norm when the court is satisfied that simply by appointing a representative for the child the court has safeguarded his interests. The appointment of an independent representative may be essential to serve the child's best interests, but, like the right to a fair trial, is not in itself the substance of those interests. The judge must carefully observe his duty of listening to all sides, and should no more presume that the advocate for the child has comprehensively identified the child's best interests than that a parent has done so. The judge should acquire more profound and relevant evidence through a child advocate, but the decision as to disposition of the child remains his.

The advocate's function is clearly to protect and advance the interests of the younger child, but when the child is of an age to express opinions and preferences, the advocate's role becomes less clear, and may present him with conflicting duties. It must be asked whether he is to express to the court simply the views the child holds, or the views he holds as to the child's best interests. If he acts as a traditional advocate conforming to his client's instructions, he may have to advance views he disfavours and thinks immature and potentially disastrous, because his duty is to speak for his client and not to superimpose his own preference as to what the client should want. If he expresses his own views, based on his independent research and experience, he may be opposed by the child whose advocate he is appointed to be. Further clarification is needed on the principles by which he is to function. If he departs from the traditional model of an advocate in favour of serving a welfare role, the purpose of his creation may be frustrated. The only person whose judgment appears in hindsight to have been correct in the Maria Colwell tragedy was the girl herself, aged just under eight at her death.[105] It would be a sad irony if, when represented by an advocate, a child's views were still to be unheard and unheeded.

---

1 See, for instance, the circumstances of the death of Maria Colwell, described in Dr. Olive Stone's essay in this volume, and the death of a one-year-old congenital drug addict within one month of his court-ordered return to his parents in Devine, "A Child's Right to Independent Counsel in Custody Proceedings" (1975) 6 Seton Hall L. Rev. 303.

2 Practice on the interviewing of children by judges is discussed in Dr. Olive Stone's essay. See also Stone, Family Law, (1977), 209.

3 This essay will not consider children themselves giving evidence or information, for instance as to their preferences, in open judicial hearings or privately to judges. See generally note 2, *supra*. On the topic of lawyers in defence of children in the U.S. see generally Katz (ed.), The Youngest Minority, Vol. 1 (1974) and Vol. 2 (1977).

4 The issue of legal representation of a child facing mental health commitment is part of the wider issue of inadequate legal representation for adults in such proceedings, even though proponents of a child's commitment may be his parents or other guardians. See, however, Panneton "Children, Commitment and Consent: A Constitutional Crisis" (1977) 10 Fam. L.Q. 295.

5 See generally *Re Gault* (1967) 387 U.S. 1.

6 For a recent decision treating parental rights as a property interest, see *Turner v. Turner* (1959) 334 P. 2d 1011 (Cal. C.A.). See generally Bates, "Redefining the Parent/Child Relationship: A Blueprint" (1976) 12 Western Aust. L.R. 518.

7 In 1874 in New York, eight-year-old Mary Ellen Wilson was found to have been systematically starved and beaten by her step-parents, but no obvious law appeared to have been violated. The New York Society for the Prevention of Cruelty to Animals took up the case, arguing (successfully) that children are members of the animal kingdom. Within months, a Society for the Prevention of Cruelty to Children was formed in New York. The Metropolitan Toronto Children's Aid Society dates its origin to 1875.

8 Isaacs, "The Role of the Lawyer in Representing Minors in the New Family Court" (1962) 12 Buffalo L.R. 501.

9 Law Reform Commission of Canada, Working Paper 1, The Family Court (1974) 40.

10 Ferrier, comment in (1975) 7 Ottawa Law Rev. 247 at 249. See generally, Westman (ed.) *Proceedings of the University of Wisconsin Conference on Child Advocacy* (1976).

11 See *infra*, "The Advocate for the Child".

12 Law Reform Commission of Canada, Report on Family Law (1976).

13 See Freed and Foster, "The Shuffled Child and Divorce Court" (May/June 1974) 10 Trial 26, who note that, under no-fault divorce concepts, there is "an enhanced tendency to treat custodial ... problems in a *pro forma* fashion" (at 41).

14 Few articles consider the professional duty of a parent's lawyer engaged to represent parent and child when he realizes the possibility of a conflict of interest between both clients; but see Genden, "Separate Legal Representation for Children: Protecting the Rights and Interests of Minors in Judicial Proceedings" (1976) 11 Harv. Civ. Rights — Civ. Lib. L. Rev.565 at 586 *et seq.*

15 For a brief but acute analysis of the problem, see, Judge Levin, "Guardian *Ad Litem* in a Family Court, (1974) 34 Md. L. Rev. 341. He cites the inadequacy of the traditional adversary system to respond in the letter he reproduces, written in a childish hand, reading: "Judge Levin, My parents case, ... v. ..., is currently being heard in your court. As these are my parents and my family I am directly involved with all rulings handed down by you, therefore I would like to have an appointment to see you and discuss the situation. Sincerely, Tommy . . ." (at 343).

16 For a critique of the statutory expression of such indications in Ontario, see Dickens, "Legal Issues in Child Abuse" (1976) Working Paper of the Centre of Criminology, University of Toronto 5 - 17.

17 Indeed, the Association is to be praised for analysing the practice of the fifty children's aid societies in Ontario, and for seeking greater standardization.

18 At Guidelines, 42.

19 See the seminal book by Goldstein, Freud and Solnit, *Beyond the Best Interest of the Child* (1973) especially Ch. 4.

20 See generally Stoetzer, "The Juvenile Court and Emotional Neglect of Children" (1975) 8 U. Mich. J. Law 351, and materials listed at note 39 of the article.

21 See note 30, *supra*. Under-stimulation of institutionalized children was recognized by Goldfarb, "Effects of Psychological Deprivation in Infancy and Subsequent Stimulation" (1945) 102 Am.J. of Psychiatry 13, and "Psychological Privation in Infancy and Subsequent Adjustment" (1945) 15 Am. J. of Orthopsychiatry 247. On maternal deprivation, see also J. Bowlby, *Maternal Care and Mental Health* (1951).

22 A "rescue" syndrome affecting social workers is described in Platt, *The Child Savers* (1969) Tamilia, "Neglect Proceedings and the Conflict Between Law and Society" (1973) 9 DuQuesne L.R. 579 585, and Wald, "State Intervention n Behalf of 'Neglected' Children: A Search for Realistic Standards" (1975) 27 Stan. L. Rev. 985, note 117 at 1005.

23   Goodpaster and Angel, "Child Abuse and the Law: The California System" (1975) 26 Hastings L.J. 1081 at 1119.
24   (1972) 407 U.S. 25. For a Canadian contrast, see *Re Ewing and Kearney and R.* 18 C.C.C. (2d) 356, [1974] 5 W.W.R. 232 (*sub nom. R. v. Ewing*) (B.C. C.A.).
25   The U.S. Supreme Court held in *Re Gault,* note 5 *supra,* that a juvenile in a delinquency proceeding has a right to counsel (see 31-57).
26   R.S.O. 1970, c. 239, as amended by 1973 (Ont.), c. 50.
27   See Little, "A Guarantee of Legal Rights of Children through Legal Aid" (1970) 4 Law Soc. Gaz. 217.
28   See Steinberg, "The Young Offender and the Courts" (1972) 6 Review of Family Law 87.
29   It was confirmed in *Re B and Children's Aid Society of Winnipeg* (1975) 64 D.L.R. (3d) 517 (Man. C.A.) that protection and wardship proceedings are civil in character.
30   See *Re Robinson* (1970) 87 Cal. Rptr. 678, cert. denied (1971) 402 U.S. 964. Some states have, however, developed a system creating a right to counsel for both a child and an indigent parent in neglect proceedings, notably Arizona; see Singleman, "A Case of Neglect: Parens Patriae Versus Due Process in Child Neglect Proceedings" (1975) 17 Ariz. L. Rev. 1055.
31   See generally *R. v. Bencardino and de Carlo* (1973) 2 O.R. (2d), 351.
32   *Curr v. R.* [1972] S.C.R. 889, 18 C.R.N.S. 281, 7 C.C.C. (2d) 181, 26 D.L.R. (3d) 603.
33   See *R. v. Hawke* (1975) 7 O.R. (2d) 145 at 182-3, 29 C.R.N.S. 1, 22 C.C.C. (2d) 19 (C.A.).
34   (1973) 11 R.F.L. 333, 23 C.R.N.S. 197, 38 D.L.R. (3d) 481 (S.C.C.).
35   [1963] S.C.R. 651, 41 C.R. 392, [1964] 1 C.C.C. 1, 41 D.L.R. (2d) 485.
36   (1975) 30 C.R.N.S. 209, 4 N.R. 277, 20 C.C.C. (2d) 499, 53 D.L.R. (3d) 161 (S.C.C.).
37   See Dickens, "The *Morgentaler* case: Criminal Process and Abortion Law" (1976) 14 O.H.L.J. 229 at 244.
38   *R. v. Morgentaler (No. 5)* [1974] Que. C.A. 129, 17 C.C.C. (2d) 289, 47 D.L.R. (3d) 211.
39   For a modern analysis of the office, see Angell, "The Amicus Curiae: American Development of English Institutions" (1967) 16 Int'l. & Comp. L.Q. 1017.
40   See Edwards, *The Law Officers of the Crown* (1964) at 7, 155.
41   See Angell, note 39 *supra* at 1018.
42   193 U.S. 65. (Angell dates this in error as 1916).
43   238 U.S. 347.
44   See Angell, note 39 *supra* at 1018.
45   The recommendation of the Ontario Law Reform Commission for the creation of the office of Law Guardian in connection with a comprehensive Family Court of Ontario is discussed later in this essay.
46   See *Toronto Star,* October 14, 1976; contrast protection proceedings, as explained in *Re Helmes,* note 78 *infra.*
47   (1975) 11 O.R. (2d) 622, 67 D.L.R. (3d) 46 (Div.Ct.).
48   R.S.O. 1970, c. 228.
49   At p. 630.
50   There may be restraints, in the absence of clear statutory authority, upon the Official Guardian acting not upon judicial direction but entirely at his own initiative to institute protective litigation. His office is closely comparable to that of the English Official Solicitor, and in *Re D (a minor)* [1976] 1 All E.R. 326, Heilbron J. reviewed his traditional functions as "the officer of the Court to take all measures for the benefit of the infant in the litigation in which he appears as next friend". She concluded, however, that "it is not the duty or function of the Official Solicitor to institute wardship proceedings" (at 336).
51   See note 5 *supra.*
52   For the history of this doctrine, see Judge Levin, note 15 *supra,* at 353-4, note 69.
53   In preparing this part I have been indebted to Jeffrey S. Leon for affording me access to the paper prepared by Katherine A. Catton and himself under the auspices of the University of Toronto's Child In The City Project, entitled "Legal Representation and the Proposed Young Persons in Conflict with the Law Act" (1977) 15 O.H.L.J. 107.
54   1974 (B.C.) c. 99.

55 See generally Dootjes, Erickson and Fox, "Defence Counsel in Juvenile Court: A variety of Roles" (1972) 14 Can. J. Crim. Corr. 132, and Stapleton and Teitlebaum, *In Defence of Youth: A Study of the Role of Counsel in American Juvenile Courts* (1972) ch. 1.
56 At 7.
57 At 33.
58 Unreported, Supreme Court of Alberta, File No. 41784.
59 See *Re Reid,* note 47 *supra* 629.
60 [1973] 2 W.W.R. 268, 15 R.F.L. 39, 41 D.L.R. (3d) 760. (Sask.).
61 R.S.S. 1965, c. 342.
62 1971 (Man.), c. 76.
63 Man. Gazette, Regulations (1972), 101 (32) at 285.
64 R.S.C. 1970, c. J-3. To be replaced in 1977-78 by the Young Offenders Act.
65 1974 (Man.), c. 30.
66 Quebec Civil Code Revision Office Committee on the Family Court, *Report on the Family Court* (1975) at 128.
67 *Ibid.* at 129.
68 *Ibid.* at 132.
69 See note 47, *supra.*
70 In *Re Reid,* Galligan J. noted that "Although there are no reported decisions in Ontario where orders have been made ordering representation for infants in custody cases, I am advised that the Official Guardian has been appointed to represent them in a number of cases by Judges of this Court"; note 47 *supra* at 629-630. In a later case involving a custody issue, children were, apparently for the first time, represented by private counsel. The judge expressly noted, however, that, "Based on my experience in this case, I doubt the desirability of having children represented by counsel or advised by 'their own' (the children's term) solicitor as a practice. There may well be cases where in the circumstances a trial judge considers it desirable for the children to have separate representation at trial. If that is so, the office of the official guardian would appear to be available and can be called upon at that point. Earlier involvement of solicitors for children can, I think, cause more harm than good." Reid J. in *Rowe v. Rowe* (1976) 26 R.F.L. 91 at 96. The children were aged twelve, ten and six.
71 R.S.O. 1970, c. 265, as amended by 1972 (Ont.), c. 50, s. 1.
72 R.S.O. 1970, c. 64, as amended by the Age of Majority and Accountability Act, 1971 (Ont.), c. 98, s. 4(1).
73 Bradbrook, "An Empirical Study of the Attitudes of the Judges of the Supreme Court of Ontario Regarding the Workings of the Present Child Custody Adjudication Laws" (1971) 49 Can. Bar Rev. 557.
74 Report on Family Law (1973), Part 3, Children, at 126.
75 R.S.O. 1970, c. 64, s. 20(1) (b).
76 Report, note 74 *supra,* at 126.
77 Report, note 74 *supra,* at 82.
78 (1976) 13 O.R. (2d) 4 (Div.Ct.).
79 *Per* Morand J. at 5. For the potential role of such a guardian, see Fraser, "Independent Representation for the Abused and Neglected Child: The Guardian Ad Litem" (1975) 13 Cal. Western L.R. 16.
80 Report, note 74 *supra,* at 128.
81 *Loc. cit.*
82 *Ibid.* at 129.
83 *Loc. cit.*
84 See note 47 *supra.*
85 See Ontario Law Reform Commission, Report on Family Law, Part 3, Children (1973) C. 5.
86 This part is based on the Appendix to C. 4 of Vol. X of the Family Law Study (1969), prepared for the Ontario Law Reform Commission.
87 L. 1962, c. 686, as amended by L. 1970, c. 962.
88 See note 9 *supra.*
89 *Ibid.* at 40.

90   *Loc. cit.*
91   *Loc. cit.*
92   See Bissett-Johnson, "Protecting the Interests of the Child in Custody and Related Proceedings" (1976) Justice of the Peace, 190.
93   Which operates by adding ss. 32A and 32B to the Children and Young Persons Act, 1969 (U.K.), c. 54.
94   As in the Maria Colwell case, note 1 *supra.*
95   Adding ss. 4A and 4B to the Children Act, 1948 (11 & 12 Geo. 6, c. 43).
96   Children are parties to proceedings under the 1969 Act (note 93 *supra*) and are therefore entitled to legal representation, if appropriate representation is available.
97   See text at note 90 *supra.*
98   See Fourth Consultative Paper, noted in Freeman, "Children in Care: The Impact of the Children Act, 1975" (1976) 6 Family Law 136 at 140.
99   The Report of the (British) Departmental Committee on the Adoption of Children (Chairman: Sir William Houghton), for instance, recommended the appointment of guardians, but proposed that "the court should appoint the guardian from a panel of officers, approved by the court, comprising senior social workers drawn from the staffs of local authorities, the probation service, or other social work organizations in the area. The court should be precluded from appointing a guardian concerned with an agency or local authority involved in the case"; Report Cmnd. 5107 para. 254, at 71.
100 See Manchester, "Custody, the Child and the Legal Process", (1976) 6 Family Law 67 at 70, and Freeman, note 98 *supra* at 140.
101 (1973) 47 Austl. L.J. 548.
102 (1976) 50 Austl. L.J. 145.
103 Aus. Stats. 1975, No. 53.
104 Genden, note 14 *supra* at 589. For an indication of data to be gathered, see Goodman, "Child Custody Adjudication; The Possibility of an Interdisciplinary Approach" (1976), 50 Austl. L.J. 644.
105 See note 1 *supra.*

Wardship In The Law Of England

*Nigel V. Lowe**

In the midst of a statutory jungle in the law of England relating to children, the wardship jurisdiction is as yet relatively untrammelled by legislation.

Wardship is exclusively a High Court jurisdiction being in origin part of the inherent jurisdiction delegated by the Crown *parens patriae* to protect children. The general basis of this inherent jurisdiction lies in the concept that it is the Sovereign's duty to protect his subjects, particularly those, such as children, who are unable to protect themselves.[1] The jurisdiction was entrusted to the Lord Chancellor as representative of the Crown and through him to the Court of Chancery. When the courts were reorganized in 1875 the Court of Chancery's jurisdiction was exercised by the judges in the Chancery Division of the High Court and in turn this jurisdiction in respect of minors was taken over by the Family Division.[2]

Although ancient in origin, wardship has adapted well to modern problems so that today it is a significant and extensively used jurisdiction.[3] A number of factors help to make wardship a unique and effective jurisdiction useful to disparate applicants. In brief these factors are: (1) wardship vests considerable control in the court over the child both during and after the proceedings (2) the court has wide ranging and largely non-statutory powers to protect its ward (3) wardship orders can be effectively enforced (4) the court will be well informed about the child's interests principally through the services of the Official Solicitor (5) wardship can be invoked relatively easily and, where necessary, quickly by any one having a legitimate interest in the child (6) the court has a wide jurisdiction to entertain wardship applications both domestically and internationally so that, for example, it can be invoked even though the child is in the care of a local authority or where he is the subject of a valid subsisting foreign court order.

I propose to discuss the extent and significance of these factors, to illustrate the scope of the jurisdiction and finally to discuss the limits and limitations of wardship.

* Nigel V. Lowe, LL.B. (Sheff.), of the Inner Temple Barrister-at-law, Lecturer, Faculty of Law, University of Bristol, England.

THE CONCEPT OF WARDSHIP — CONTROL VESTED IN THE COURT

Wardship is conceptually different from all the other jurisdictions concerned with children since the court is not merely called upon to resolve a dispute concerning the child's care or welfare but it becomes the ward's legal protector and guardian and is thereby vested with special control over both the ward's person and property. As Lord Haldane L.C. said[4] the court:

"is really sitting primarily to guard the interests of the ward . . . Its jurisdiction is in this respect parental and administrative, and the disposal of controverted questions is an incident only in the jurisdiction".

More recently Cross J. described the jurisdiction in these terms:[5]

"Wardship proceedings are not like ordinary civil actions. There is no 'lis' between the parties. The plaintiffs are not asserting any rights; they are committing their child to the protection of the court and asking the court to make such order as it thinks is for [the ward's] benefit".

One should be wary of making too much of this conceptual difference for in practical terms there is a great similarity with the other child jurisdictions at least with regard to the court's function in disposing of the "controverted question". In all disputes concerning the custody or upbringing of a minor the court is statutorily enjoined to regard the welfare of the minor "as the first and paramount consideration".[6] This means, as the House of Lords emphasized in *J. v. C.*,[7] that once a child's upbringing is in issue before the court the overriding consideration is the child's welfare. Hence it is true to say of any jurisdiction concerned with children that the parties are not asserting any "rights" but are asking the court to make such orders as it thinks best for the child. On the other hand it is as true of wardship as of any other jurisdiction that counsel will be concerned to argue in favour of their clients in forwarding suggestions for the care or upbringing of the child in question. In all cases the judge will have to resolve the question of what he thinks is best for the child in the light of the evidence produced. In this respect, the role of the judge, counsel, parties and the position of the child is really no different in any of the jurisdictions concerned with custody or upbringing of children.

What makes wardship outstandingly different is the fact that the court's role is not confined to resolving disputes for, in becoming the ward's guardian, the court is empowered to supervise the child's welfare both during and after the proceedings. Of course being under the court's protection does not mean that the ward is physically in the court's care but simply that the ward and those having *de facto* care and control are subject to the court's direction. The effect of a wardship order is perhaps best summed up by saying that it throws a "ring of care around the ward". The immediate and automatic consequence of this "ring of care" is that no one may take the ward out of the jurisdiction or marry the ward without the court's consent.[8] But the control is not confined to those examples. Indeed Cross J. has said[9] that once a child has been made a ward "no important step in the child's life can be taken without the court's consent". On this basis it has been held that a ward cannot be psychiatrically examined,[10] sterilized[11] nor adoption proceedings be brought[12] without the court's consent.

THE POWERS OF THE COURT

The degree of control that the court enjoys over its ward is in itself significantly wider than any other jurisdiction concerned with children. In addition the court has the widest possible powers to make such orders as are necessary to secure the ward's best interests. Moreover since these powers are largely non-statutory the court is thereby freed from legislative constraints and technical argument based on statutory interpretation.[13]

Illustrative of the wide powers is *Re D*[14] where the court prohibited the sterilization of an 11 year old girl despite parental consent. On a less dramatic level the court can make detailed orders for care and control and access which can be supervised by the Official Solicitor.[15] It can make provisions as to where the ward should reside and where he should be educated.[16] It has the power to make a wide range of orders, for example, to restrain the ward's removal from the jurisdiction,[17] to restrain a person from continuing an association with a ward or from harbouring or molesting the ward[18] and to order one party to transfer the custody of the child to another.[19]

As well as these common law powers the court is vested with certain statutory powers. Under section 6 of the Family Law Reform Act, 1969 the court can order maintenance to be paid by one parent to another or by either or both parents to any other person awarded care and control. It is specifically provided[20] that such payments cannot be ordered where the child is illegitimate and this seems a major gap in the court's powers. Under section 7 the court can commit the ward to the care of a local authority or place the ward under the supervision of an "independent person". In either case the court must be satisfied that there are "exceptional circumstances making it impracticable or undesirable for a ward of court to be, or continue to be, under the care of either of his parents or of any other individual".[21]

WARDSHIP AND THE LAW OF CONTEMPT

Considerable protection is afforded to a ward by the law of contempt. As Cross J. said:[22] "Any action which tends to hamper the court in carrying out its duty [in protecting a ward] is an interference with the administration of justice and a criminal contempt". The classic instances of contempt are marrying a ward and removing a ward from the jurisdiction without the court's consent. In each case the offence is one of strict liability and will be committed whether or not the defendant knows that the child is a ward of court.[23] It is a contempt to disobey any of the specific orders or directions which the court may make in respect of a ward though in these cases a *mens rea* will be required.[24] Because punishment for contempt may be imprisonment and or a fine, (in each case there is no statutory maximum) these powers offer a considerable inducement to obey the court orders. In addition the High Court can draw upon the services of the Tipstaff to secure compliance with any direction relating to a ward.[25]

The fact that such orders are enforceable makes a wardship order a useful supplement, for example, to local authorities' powers in respect of children already in their care or even to a magistrate's court.

ASCERTAINING THE WARD'S INTERESTS

Another advantage of wardship is that the court will be well informed about the child's interests. It derives all the advantages of being a High Court jurisdiction which generally means that the cases are better prepared than in the lower courts. It also enjoys wide powers to ascertain the child's interests. To this end the Rules for making a child a ward are so designed as to ensure that the court is properly informed as to all matters relating to the ward. Hence the parties are required to state, if known, the whereabouts of the minor.[26] Indeed the court may summarily order any person who is in a position to give information as to the child's whereabouts to attend before a court.[27] Even a solicitor is obliged to divulge to the court any information which may lead to the discovery of the ward's whereabouts.[28] In the case of a missing ward the court may also derive assistance from the Department of Health and Social Security which will be prepared to disclose directly to the court the ward's address or that of the person with whom the ward is believed to be.[29]

In addition to these powers the court may also call upon the court welfare service and the services of the Official Solicitor to augment further its knowledge of the facts.

THE COURT WELFARE SERVICES

A welfare officer, who is a qualified probation officer, can only act upon the court's or registar's direction, but a report can be called for at any stage of the proceedings. Welfare officers do not represent the ward's interests, their function is to make a report on the facts as they see them. To this end they will visit and interview the various parties, including the child.

The report should contain a statement of the facts and while obviously reflecting the officer's views it need not contain any specific recommendations, indeed, it is usual for it not to do so.[30] The report is intended as an aid to the court's decision but it has been held,[31] though not in wardship, that where the court differs from the officer's views it is essential to give the reasons. It is perhaps doubtful whether this applies to wardship but it does serve to show the regard which is paid to the welfare officer's views.

THE OFFICIAL SOLICITOR

Unlike the welfare officer, the Official Solicitor *is* called upon to represent the ward's interests. The value of the Official Solicitor's services is that it gives the court the assistance of an experienced and impartial person whose only interest is the child's welfare.[32] Whenever it is thought desirable that a ward should be separately represented, he is joined as a party and the Official Solicitor is appointed, subject to his consent to represent the interests of and act as guardian *ad litem* to the child.[33] It is to be noted that the consent of the Official Solicitor is a prerequisite to his acting for the ward.[34] In practice such consent is rarely withheld, though it may be justified if his appointment might involve him in a conflict of duties as, for example, where he already represents an adult party who is under a mental disability, or where due to pressure of work he is unable to accept further appointments. This latter situation has yet to arise though the number of referrals are increasing each year. In 1975 of the 521 orders confirming wardship 161 were referred to the Official Solicitor compared with 106 referrals out of 410 confirming orders in 1974. That the Official Solicitor must consent before acting for a ward is just one example of the unique nature of the office. By the Supreme Court of Judicature (Consolidation) Act, 1925, the office has quasi corporate status, its holder must be of ten years standing and its tenure is similar to that of a High Court Master or Registrar. When appointed to act as guardian *ad litem,* the Official Solicitor is in the words of Goff J.[35] "not only an officer of the court and the ward's guardian but he is a solicitor and the ward is his client". But it has since been held that while he is a practising solicitor he does not seek clients and only acts on behalf of minors who are the subjects of existing procedures.[36]

Subject to his consent, the Official Solicitor may be appointed at any stage of the proceedings either upon the request of one of the parties or pursuant to a registrar or judge acting on his own motion. He is almost invariably appointed where the dispute is between a teenage ward and parents (*e.g.* where the parents wish to restrain a particular person from continuing a relationship with their child). His appointment is common where the child has been brought from a foreign jurisdiction, but in other cases, involving very young children or where the dispute concerns a local authority, his appointment is less common but not unknown. One example is where parents cannot agree on whether their child should be examined by a psychiatrist.[37] Another, involving local authorities, might be where there is such animosity between the parents and the authority that it would be an advantage to have a fresh unbiased view. But these are not the only instances, for as Heilbron J. said,[38] his appointment is desirable whenever "it is possible that the interests of the infant may take second place to the evidence and arguments of the adult adversaries". One advantage of the appointment is that the Official Solicitor's intervention can take the heat out of a situation and at the same time insulate the children from the effect of the conflict between the warring parties. No formal order of appointment is necessary, but it has been said that his instructions should be embodied in some document or at least reduced to writing.[39] In practice his instructions will vary depending on the particular judge and the circumstances. Upon his appointment he will receive the court files which should highlight the areas or problems that need to be investigated. His principal task is to place before the court, usually in the form of a report, evidence which he considers to be material on the child's behalf. To this end he undertakes a very full investigation and will interview all the parties concerned including, where appropriate, the child and any other persons such as specialists who may be relevant to the case. His role is not merely to rubber stamp the parents' views but to make an objective and independant assessment of the child's interests. This is particularly important in teenage wardships.[40]

THE REPORT

The Official Solicitor's report will contain a statement of the facts as he sees them and will normally, though not necessarily, contain specific recommendations. It has recently been argued[41] that the report should be confined to giving an unbiased view of the facts and should not contain any specific recommendations. Baker P. emphatically rejected such an argument saying:
"It would be a great disservice to the interests of children and in respect of information available to the court, if it were thought that the Official Solicitor was in any way inhibited in making a recommendation to this court ... either in a report or when he has heard the evidence and the cross examination of the parties".
When completed the report is sent to the court and a copy is usually sent to the parties. However, it was held by the House of Lords in *Official Solicitor v. K*[42] that parties do not have an absolute right to see the report and the judge is entitled to act upon it without disclosing its contents.

When, in the Official Solicitor's opinion, disclosure of the report would be harmful to the ward, the report can be submitted confidentially to the court leaving it to the judge's discretion whether to withold its contents. Confidential submission is not, however, adopted as a matter of routine but only in exceptional circumstances and according to Lord Evershed,[43] on such occasions, the Official Solicitor should explain to the judge the reasons which have persuaded him to adopt such a course. It is to be emphasised that confidential submission still leaves the judge with a discretion whether to disclose the contents and a common practice, and one which was recommended in *Official Solicitor v. K.*, is for the judge to disclose the report to the parties' counsel only. It should be added that the practice of confidential submissions does not apparently extend to reports of other persons acting as guardian *ad litem*.

The Official Solicitor's function is not confined to investigating the facts and making reports. He must instruct counsel to present the case in court. He may also be called upon to act after the court hearing has been completed, for example, the court may order that access should be controlled by his office.[44] In this way his office will maintain contact with the ward after the hearing. It is also established that he may institute contempt proceedings in the course of his duties. This was done in *Re F. (A Minor)*[45] where proceedings were brought against certain newspapers for their alleged contempt in publishing details of a wardship hearing and referring to reports made by the Official Solicitor and a social worker. It is important, however, to distinguish this situation from instituting wardship proceedings themselves which is outside his powers.

It would be hard to overestimate the value of the Official Solicitor's services. The office has acquired considerable and unique experience of interviewing parties, and as the Latey Committee commented[46] the Official Solicitor and his staff execute their often difficult and delicate tasks with humanity and expertise. The court is not bound by the Official Solicitor's views or recommendation but his report is treated with respect and ensures that the ward's interests are specifically brought to the court's notice. The fact that the holder is a senior ranking solicitor[47] adds to the efficiency of the office since his views and authority are more respected. The point should be made, however, that it is doubtful whether, as presently constituted, the office could handle a vast increase in cases and an expansion of his office might detract from its efficiency and humanity. In this respect as a matter of policy it was probably correct to hold that the office was not empowered to initiate wardship proceedings since that power might have involved a considerably increased work load with questionable benefits.

PROCEDURE FOR MAKING A CHILD A WARD OF COURT

The procedure for making a child a ward was both simplified and unified by the Law Reform (Miscellaneous Provisions) Act 1949, s. 9.[48]

The scheme under the Act is that primarily no child can become a ward unless the court makes an order to that effect, but under s. 9(2) a child becomes a ward immediately an application is made, though for a limited period only. Wardship will lapse unless an application for an appointment for the hearing of the summons is made within 21 days of the issuing of the summons.[49] If no application is made within the 21 days then a notice must be left in the registry stating whether the applicant intends to proceed with the summons.[50]

An application to make a child a ward must be made by an originating summons which may be issued out of the Principal Registry in London or a District Registry.[51] The summons can be issued in a matter of hours and in cases of extreme urgency an application may be made (even on Sunday) for an injunction *prior* to the issue of the summons. This was established in *Re N*[52] where a mother applied on a Sunday to a High Court judge at his private residence for an order preventing the father from removing the children from Switzerland (where by agreement they went to school) to Australia. The order was granted on terms that the originating summons should be issued the following day, which it was. Stamp J. endorsed this order holding that the court retained its inherent jurisdiction to protect children even though no summons had been issued and in any event it had authority to grant the injunction under the rules of the Supreme Court.

DURATION OF WARDSHIP

Once a child has become a ward the order will only cease upon a court order to that effect, unless the order lapses under s. 9(2) or the child reaches the age of majority which is now 18.

S. 9(3) specifically provides both for applications to be made to the court for a child to be dewarded and for the court to deward on its own motion. Although the court will not hesitate to order a child to cease to be a ward where the continuation of the order would serve no useful purpose it has also been said that so long as there is a need for control by the court it is a mistake to discontinue the wardship.[53]

WHO CAN APPLY?

Following *Re Dunhill*[54] where a night club owner applied to make one of his models a ward purely for publicity purposes, it is now[55] provided that an applicant must state the relationship of the plaintiff to the ward when producing the summons to the recording officer. If the officer is in any doubt as to the propriety of the application he will immediately refer the matter to a registrar who will dismiss the summons if he considers the application to be an abuse of process or he can refer the matter to a judge.[56] It is also established[57] that the Official Solicitor cannot institute wardship proceedings but, subject to these provisos, *anyone* having an interest in the child may apply to have him or her made a ward of court. Applicants are not therefore restricted to parents or even parties with whom the child is living, but may include, for example, local authorities and, as *Re D*[58] shows, persons attached to the local authority. In addition the court itself has the power to direct that a child be made a ward.[59] The fact that wardship can be invoked by a wide range of people distinguishes it from other child jurisdictions which in the main provide an avenue only for natural parents. For most non-parents wardship is the only means or the only practical means by which they can apply to the court even for the care and control of a child they have been looking after for some time.[60] It is true that those parties looking after the child could apply for adoption but that is a much more drastic order which the parties themselves may not desire or which the courts may not grant. Persuading the parents to agree to adoption may well cause disputes. Indeed another use of wardship is by would-be adopters whose adoption application having failed, because of the withdrawal of the natural parents' agreement which the court has refused to dispense with, nevertheless wish to retain care and control of the child.[61]

CUSTODIANSHIP ORDERS

Undoubtedly inroads into the wardship jurisdiction will be made by the Children Act, 1975 Part II, which, when in force will provide a procedure whereby *non*-parents can apply for what, somewhat confusingly, will be known as custodianship orders. Since a custodianship order will vest in the applicant rights almost equivalent[62] to a custody order it will obviously be a powerful alternative to wardship and in view of the fact that such applications may be made to a magistrates' court or to a county court and not simply the High Court it is likely, where applicable, to be preferred. However, it is doubtful whether custodianship orders will provide a panacea for all non-parental applications and it is unlikely that wardship will become redundant in this area.

It is clear that wardship will be available as an alternative to custodianship so that any person may avail himself of that jurisdiction if he so wishes, but there will be circumstances where the applicant will have no choice but to use wardship. For example, anyone wishing to avoid the time provisions[63] must still use wardship. An applicant may initially have the consent of the person having legal custody, but if that consent is withdrawn before the hearing the result will be that instead of the three or twelve month period the child must have had its home with the applicant for three years. In any event the three year period is a long time, and there seems no reason why an applicant should wait so long since he can instead use wardship to gain care and control. Another requirement for custodianship is that the applicant must be able to show that the child has had his "home" with him for the three months preceding the making of the application. There may be cases where the child cannot be said to have had his "home" with the applicant for that period yet that person may still wish to apply for an order. The only remedy will be via wardship, where the applicant will not be troubled by the statutory definition of "home",[64] nor with any other problem of interpretation that may arise under the 1975 Act. The wisest course may still be therefore to use wardship. A further example of where an applicant would wish to use wardship is where a remedy such as an injunction is sought which is outside the powers of a court acting under its custodianship jurisdiction.

SHOULD SOME OFFICIAL BE EMPOWERED TO INITIATE WARDSHIP PROCEEDINGS?

It has already been mentioned that the Official Solicitor is not empowered to initiate wardship proceedings. Further, it has been suggested that this is correct since to hold such powers otherwise might overburden the Official Solicitor with applications. However, the question might still be asked as to whether there should be someone upon whom there is a general duty to supervise children and who, in appropriate cases, could institute wardship proceedings. The facts of Re D (A Minor)[65] may be thought to illustrate the need for such a person. An application was made to prevent an 11 year old girl from being sterilized. What made the application more unusual was that it was not made by the girl's parent since both her mother and the consultant surgeon agreed that the girl should be sterilized. The applicant was an educational psychologist attached to the education department of the child's local authority. The ward suffered from a mental condition and the proposed operation was to prevent the possibility of the ward giving birth to another mentally abnormal child. There was disagreement as to whether the ward's condition would improve or deteriorate and the concern of the applicant was that it was premature to carry out an operation which would have a permanent and irreversible effect. In the event the court agreed and prohibited the operation. One disturbing feature of the case was the rather fortuitous way in which the issue was brought before the court. Had the applicant not been conscientious enough to bring the action, there seems little doubt that the operation would have gone ahead, the disturbing implication being, that other operations in similar circumstances had already been performed. Having rejected the contention that it was within the Official Solicitor's power to initiate proceedings, Heilbron J. refused to speculate as to who should fill the gap, if indeed, there was a gap. The question remains whether there is a gap and how it should be filled.

In one sense it can be argued that there is no gap since anyone with sufficient interest in the minor can invoke wardship as *Re D* itself shows. There are two stumbling blocks to this argument. First there is the question of cost which is a powerful deterrent to bringing an action and second there is the question of whether there can be satisfaction with a system which depends for its efficacy upon the conscientiousness of others to use it. The second point argues in favour of having someone charged with the duty of looking after children's interests. Justice has recommended[66] the creation of a "Children's Ombudsman" who *inter alia,* it was suggested, should be able to act as a clearing house for complaints and as a protective service for children at risk of violence. This suggestion has been met with little enthusiasm. One of the problems is how such an office would be briefed in the first place. It seems likely that it would still depend on the conscientiousness of the individual to bring the matter to the Ombudsman's attention and in this respect cannot be said to improve the present system. It might, however, be argued that having such an official who is empowered to initiate wardship proceedings, in much the same way as the Attorney General can institute contempt proceedings, would be useful since it would relieve the individual both of the expense and the burden of bringing legal proceedings. On the other hand it may be pointed out that such a burden could be borne by existing organizations such as the National Society for the Prevention of Cruelty to Children or by a local authority. It was certainly open to either the N.S.P.C.C. or the local authority to have instituted wardship proceedings in circumstances like *Re D.* An individual can make a complaint to the N.S.P.C.C.[67] or a local authority which either can follow up or if necessary take steps to protect the child including that of making the child a ward of court. That the local authority involved did take steps to initiate wardship proceedings in *Re D* is perhaps a cause for concern though in view of the approval for this operation by the mother and the consultant surgeon it may be that the local authority should not be faulted. On the other hand it may be that it is not always appreciated by local authorities, nor, where appropriate, by bodies like the N.S.P.C.C. that in such circumstances it is open to them to institute wardship proceedings in which case it should be made clear, perhaps by means of a circular, that they do have such powers. Another improvement might be to allow the court itself to have the power to direct that the wardship proceedings, including the costs, be taken over by the relevant local authority. In this way the court's attention would be drawn to the plight of a particular child while the individual applicant would be relieved of both the expense and burden of maintaining the proceedings. The applicant in this case did in fact receive aid from the National Council for Civil Liberties.

WHO CAN BE MADE A WARD? — JURISDICTION

The court has an extremely wide jurisdiction to entertain wardship applications in respect of persons under the age of 18. Jurisdiction is based on the concept of allegiance so that any minor who can be said to owe allegiance to the Sovereign enjoys the corresponding right to protection from the Crown and may be made a ward of court. Hence any child who is a British subject whether born in or out of allegiance and irrespective of his physical location at the date of the application may be made a ward since he owes a duty of allegiance and is therefore entitled to protection.[68] The court also has jurisdiction to entertain applications in respect of alien children who are physically present in the jurisdiction irrespective of their nationality or domicile. In *Re P. (G.E.)*[69] the Court of Appeal went further holding that the court had jurisdiction in respect of an alien minor not physically present in the jurisdiction provided the child could be said to be "ordinarily resident" in England. This test of "ordinary residence" was justified on the basis of justice and convenience and some authority for it was found in the law of treason,[70] although Lord Denning M.R. characteristically commented:

"We are not to be deterred by the absence of authority in the books. Our forefathers always held that the law was locked in the breasts of the judges, ready to be unlocked whenever the need arose."

To be ordinarily resident the child must have had his home or base in the jurisdiction at the date of the application. This test is not without its difficulties, particularly where one parent unilaterally withdraws the child from the other parent, as in *Re P (G.E.)* itself. The child lived with his mother but at weekends visited his father. It was during one of these weekend visits that the father, without the mother's knowledge or consent, took the child to Israel. The mother applied to make the child a ward of court within two months of the removal. The Court of Appeal unanimously held that the English court had jurisdiction because the child's ordinary residence was still in England. The majority held that, on the facts, the father had not yet abandoned his ordinary residence in England and therefore could not be said to have deprived his son of a similar residence. Lord Denning M.R. thought that the son's ordinary residence remained that of his mother. As he said:

"Quite generally, I do not think a child's ordinary residence can be changed by one parent without the consent of the other. It will not be changed until the parent who is left at home, childless, acquiesces in the change, or delays so long in bringing proceedings that he or she must be taken to acquiesce. Six months' delay would, I should have thought, go far to show acquiescence. Even three months might in some circumstances. But not less."

EXCEPTIONS

(a) Diplomatic immunity

It is sometimes stated that the court has no jurisdiction in respect of a minor whose parent claims diplomatic immunity.[71] However, the authority relied upon, *Re C. (An Infant)*[72] might be better regarded as establishing the more limited proposition that the court has no jurisdiction over a minor who is a member of the family household of a parent claiming diplomatic immunity.

(b) Refusal to allow an alien minor to enter the country

There is some debate whether it is possible to make a ward of an alien minor, who has been refused entry to the country by immigration officials. In *Re Mohamed Arif (An Infant)*[73] Cross. J. thought it was at least arguable that such a child could not be said to owe allegiance to the Crown and hence there was no jurisdiction to make the child a ward of court. In the event he left the point open but nevertheless ordered the summons to be struck out. On appeal the decision to strike out the summons was upheld, but Lord Denning M.R. did say that "there may be exceptional cases where such a jurisdiction may be desirable" and presumably thought that there was jurisdiction to make such a child a ward. Russel L.J. thought that if the two parents were already in England and were in dispute as to the child's future then, should the removal order subsequently be cancelled, a summons issued before that cancellation might be held to have effect at least between the parties.

THE DISCRETION TO EXERCISE THE JURISDICTION

Although the wardship jurisdiction is founded upon an extremely wide basis it is important to bear in mind that the court still retains a discretion whether to exercise that jurisdiction. This discretion provides an important practical limitation on the width of the jurisdiction. For example, the court will be reluctant to exercise its jurisdiction in respect of a minor who is not present in the country even if he is of British nationality since there will be difficulties of enforcement and a risk of conflict between the English court and the foreign court in which the minor is present and resident.[74]

Even where jurisdiction is taken, the practice has been developed of making a summary order instead of investigating the full merits of the case. This practice has been developed principally to combat the problem of "kidnapping" where a child is taken from a foreign jurisdiction, where he has had his home, to England simply to further a parent's claim to the right to look after the child. In such cases it is established[75] that the court has a discretion to make a summary order for the child's return to the country from where he was taken, rather than investigate the full merits of the case.

THE LAW COMMISSION'S PROPOSALS

Despite these limitations the Law Commission feels[76] that the jurisdiction is too wide and is an encouragement to "kidnappers" to "forum shop" in the English courts. While agreeing that the discretion to make a summary order for a child's return does mitigate the unfair advantages which kidnapping can produce, it was pointed out that the discretion creates too much uncertainty and would be unnecessary if the jurisdictional rules themselves were narrowed. Accordingly, one of the proposals is that the wardship jurisdiction should be narrowed at least in the UK context[77] to cases where the child is "habitually resident" in England. Allied to this proposal is a proposed presumption that unless it is established that a child is habitually resident in some other country, his habitual residence will be in the jurisdiction where he has resided cumulatively for the longest period within the year immediately preceding the commencement of proceedings.

The Law Commission is perhaps a little sanguine about the clarity of "habitual residence" as a test.[78] Nevertheless, coupled with the above presumption, the proposal should provide a reasonably certain and workable concept. However, the certainty and arguably the value of the presumption is offset by the proposal designed to deal with kidnapping whereby no account would be taken of a child's residence where it has been changed without lawful authority during the year before the commencement of the proceedings.[79] The basic philosophy of this proposal seems to be that the best solution for dealing with kidnapping is that the court of the jurisdiction to which the child has been unlawfully taken, should have no powers to hear the case. This is surely a questionable policy since even the narrowest of jurisdictional rules will not eliminate kidnapping and in any event it seems preferable to allow the parties some redress in such courts, for even a summary order for the child's return is likely to bring more stability to the situation than is likely to be brought by a court simply refusing to hear the case.

Even if it is thought preferable to have some specific rule to deal with kidnapping, it is not at all certain that the Law Commission's proposal is ideal. Indeed it is not clear exactly how the proposal will operate.

Presumably in the case of a kidnapping of a child from the matrimonial home, say in England, provided the "innocent" party brings proceedings within twelve months, the presumption will be that the child is habitually resident in England, since in that year, ignoring the changed residence, the child will have spent the longest period in England. This in itself could produce an odd result in cases where the hearing is delayed. For example, a child may be kidnapped when it was six months old, proceedings being brought nine months later and the hearing six months after that. The presumption will be that a child who at the date of the hearing is 21 months old will be habitually resident in a jurisdiction in which he has spent only six months of his life.

Another problem relates to rebutting the presumption, as it is unclear whether a "kidnapper" will be precluded from establishing that a child is habitually resident in a jurisdiction to which he has been taken if he has spent less than a year there. To make sense of the provision it would seem that the parent would be so precluded unless he could establish that the child was habitually resident in that jurisdiction for a period *more* than twelve months prior to the commencement of the proceedings. If this is a correct interpretation, then it is submitted that the provision is too rigid, and in any event it is too long[80] a period to be ignored in a life of a young child. If this interpretation is incorrect and the "kidnapper" can nevertheless adduce evidence to establish the child's habitual residence it would seem to undermine the proposal altogether.

Another criticism is that the changed residence is only to be ignored where the child's residence has been changed "without lawful authority". There is bound to be a problem with the meaning of "without lawful authority". It was envisaged that it would apply where the residence was changed in breach of a U.K. court order or against the will of a person, such as a parent or guardian having the legal right to fix the child's residence. Authority already exists[81] that where the parent removes the children to another jurisdiction with the consent of the other, merely for a temporary visit, and subsequently changes his mind and refuses to return the children, that does not constitute "kidnapping". The question is whether it would constitute "without lawful authority". If it did then the period of changed residence would be ignored, if it did not then there would be a presumption of favour of the latter jurisdiction. It seems questionable whether jurisdiction should depend on such fine points. For these reasons it is submitted that it would be better to drop the proposal for dealing with kidnapping.

Another proposal of the Law Commission calling for comment is that for dealing with "emergencies".[82] The Commission decided that it was better not to define "emergency" since it was impossible to predict all the circumstances in which judicial intervention might be necessary. The proposal states that the child's physical presence would give the court jurisdiction "if, and only if, the immediate intervention of the court is necessary for the protection of the child". Though the difficulties of defining "emergencies" are readily apparent, it may be that in leaving the definition so open many of the difficulties and uncertainties attributed to wide jurisdictional rules, and which the Commission seeks to avoid, would simply be transferred to the category of "emergencies".[83] It seems likely that, in any event, what constitutes an "emergency" will become a justiciable issue in itself, which is one of the consequences the Commission is trying to avoid.

JURISDICTION IN THE DOMESTIC CONTEXT

In the domestic law context, wardship is an all-pervading jurisdiction in the sense that it is not ousted by the operation of other jurisdictions. In particular, the wardship jurisdiction is not abrogated by the legislation vesting extensive powers and duties in local authorities.[84] Equally the existence of an order made by justices does not destroy the High Court's prerogative powers under wardship.[85] Most recently it has been said that the fact that a child has been adopted does not preclude the possibility of the natural parents making a wardship application in order to regain care and control of their child.

In each of these cases, while the wardship jurisdiction continues to exist, it is firmly established that the court will not automatically exercise its jurisdiction. Indeed the general policy adopted by the court is not to interfere with a discretion clearly vested in some other body or court. So, for example, wardship cannot be resorted to simply to have the court review a decision made by a local authority acting under its duty or discretion vested in it by statute.[86] Similarly wardship cannot be used simply as a means of over-turning a magistrate's decision which is unpopular with one of the parties.[87] However, the existence of the wardship jurisdiction has proved to be of some importance in relation to local authorities, and to a certain extent magistrates' decisions, since it is established that the court will intervene in cases of impropriety or with regard to matters falling outside the authorities' or justices' powers. In this respect wardship operates as an important supervisory and supplementary jurisdiction.

AS A SUPERVISORY JURISDICTION

No matter what power[88] a local authority is purporting to exercise the court will be prepared under its wardship jurisdiction to review the decision if some impropriety can be proved as, for example, by showing that the authority has acted in breach or disregard of its statutory duties. A good example is *Re L (A.C.)*.[89] A Section 2 resolution was passed on the grounds that the mother had a permanent disability rendering her incapable of looking after the child. The authority duly served the mother with written notice of the resolution and she gave written notice of objection. The authority then made a complaint to the Juvenile Court.[90] Subsequently a doubt was raised about the competence of the sub-committee to pass the resolution, and accordingly a second resolution was passed though by a different committee. Although the mother was again duly served with a notice, the authority led her solicitor to believe that, as the second resolution was a technicality, the mother's first objection would be treated as applying to the second resolution. Hence a second objection was not at first lodged, but when it was, the authority said it was out of time. The mother was forced to rely on sub-section 4(3) of the 1948 Act whereby she had to prove that the authority had no ground for passing the resolution, whereas had she objected in time, under sub-section 2(3) the authority would have had the burden of proof. It was after the failure of her action under sub-section 4(3) that she applied to have the child made a ward of court. It was held that the court should exercise its wardship jurisdiction and investigate the merits of the case since (a) the authority had not followed the correct statutory procedure and had thereby deprived the mother of real protection under the Act, and (b) there was a doubt about the validity of the resolution since the committee was either unaware or confused about a material fact, namely, that in spite of her infirmity the mother was capable of looking after the child.

A local authority decision may also be impeached on the grounds of improper motives. As Lord Evershed M.R. said:[91]

"There may be cases in which a local authority, acting by its committee, may be moved by improper motives, for example, of personal hostility to some person concerned, so that the resolutions or decisions they arrived at can be impeached as not being bona fide exercises of their power."

Allegations of impropriety will normally be difficult to substantiate and the courts have discouraged such allegations being made simply to support a wardship application.[92]

Another example of wardship being successfully invoked to challenge a local authority decision is *Re Cullimore (A Minor)*[93] which concerned a Place of Safety Order.[94] The issue before the court was whether the several fractures suffered by the ward were the result of non-accidental injury caused by the parents or by reason of the fact that the child suffered from brittle bones. As an issue of fact, the case highlights a matter of some importance since many feel that there is a danger of parents wrongfully being deprived of their children on the grounds that injuries suffered by a child are thought to be deliberately inflicted by the parents. *Re Cullimore* seems to prove that those fears can be justified since the medical evidence as to the cause of injury in the case in question was conflicting. As Baker P. said:

"Many doctors had seen the child and gave different diagnoses. At least one paediatrician changed sides, bowing, it seemed, to the greater knowledge and experience of a senior. Social workers and others were apt to see the matter in black and white, and some could make no allowance in their own minds for the possibility that the parents were not at fault.

The dilemma was that if the injuries were wrongly held to be non-accidental, the parents . . . could suffer unjustly and be held in hatred, odium and contempt and pilloried in public while the child would be deprived of the loving care of parents and spend its formative years in an institution. If a diagnosis of "brittle bones" was made and that was wrong the child was gravely at risk if allowed to continue living with brutal parents."

It was held, after a five day hearing, that on the balance of probabilities the child was suffering from brittle bones and accordingly the place of safety order was discharged. However, whilst granting care and control to the parents the wardship order was continued to enable the Official Solicitor to act as the child's guardian *ad litem*.

In many ways this was an ideal case to be decided via wardship since the High Court was clearly able to deal with the complexity and had the requisite powers to meet the situation. In particular the court was able to keep the case under review by the appointment of the Official Solicitor. The disturbing feature of the case is that had not the father been properly advised to bring wardship proceedings then in all probability the case would have been decided by the Juvenile Court under the 1969 Act. It is doubtful whether such a court would have been well equipped to deal with such a complex case. The constitution of the magistrates' courts:[95]

"makes them a somewhat unsuitable tribunal to deal with cases in which a prolonged investigation into disputed facts are called for or in which the court may have to give and enforce detailed directions as to the upbringing of children."

There must therefore be at least a suspicion that had not the child been made a ward the parents might have lost the case.

AS A SUPPLEMENTARY JURISDICTION

(a) Magistrates' Decisions

Provided the relief sought falls outside the powers of either justices or local authorities to grant, then recourse can be had to wardship. In other words the jurisdiction can be used to supplement the powers of magistrates or local authorities. Illustrative of these supplementary powers in relation to the magistrates' jurisdiction is *Re H (G.J.)*.[96] Following a decision to award custody to the mother and access to the father, the father tried to take the child out of the jurisdiction. The mother instituted wardship proceedings with a view to restraining the father from taking the child out of the jurisdiction. As the magistrates have no such powers[97] the relief prayed for was granted and in addition it was specifically directed that the child should reside with her mother at her address and should continue with her present education. Stamp J. commented that the magistrates' order:

"in no way precludes this court from making orders, in the exercise of prerogative powers of the Queen in relation to infants, not inconsistent with orders made by the magistrates' court. What I am asked to do today is merely to make an order which will supplement the order which has already been made in relation to the infant by the magistrates' court and this I will do."

Wardship may fill another gap in magistrates' powers, namely, the power to enforce effectively their orders. The only power available to magistrates to enforce a custody order is to fine the person disobeying the order £1 for every day the default continues up to a maximum of £20 or commit him to prison until he remedies his default up to a maximum of two months.[98] There is no direct power to ensure that the child is physically returned. The High Court on the other hand has more effective means of enforcing its orders, in particular the court can draw upon the services of the Tipstaff to secure compliance with any direction relating to a ward.[99] Illustrative of the use of these powers is *Re P (A.J.)*.[100] A mother took *habeas corpus* proceedings to enforce a magistrates' order granting her custody against her husband who had neither appealed against nor complied with her order. The father responded by making the child a ward of court and as a result, the *habeas corpus* proceedings were adjourned. Although Cook J. refused to interfere with the magistrates' decision he ordered that the child should not be dewarded unless and until the father complied with the High Court order to return the child and in the meantime the mother was given liberty to apply to the court, if the father remained obdurate. It was held that such an order could be made as it supplemented the order of the justices, and it saved the mother the expense of having to revive the *habeas corpus* proceedings.

(b) Local Authorities

In the local authority context, wardship is perhaps more usually thought of as a means by which other parties may challenge an authority's decision, but there is a growing realization that wardship may usefully be invoked by the authorities themselves. As Ormrod L.J. said:[101]

"I feel bound to say that I think that local authorities might find, if they look into it, other situations in which it would be positively to their advantage to invoke the wardship jurisdiction themselves. It would sometimes avoid their having to take unpleasant, awkward decisions themselves which sometimes cause great pain and anguish."

There are a number of situations where wardship might be useful. First, the jurisdiction can be used as a means of supplementing their powers over children already in care. A good example is *Re B*[102] where there was a danger that the child's stepfather, who had already been convicted of causing the child bodily harm, might discover her whereabouts and attempt to molest her again. Hence although the court refused to interfere with the authority's decision to place the child with foster-parents, it nevertheless ordered that the wardship order should continue, thereby enabling the authority to have immediate recourse to the courts in the discharge of their duties. As Lane J. said, an application could be made: "for an injunction restraining the stepfather from endeavouring to ascertain the whereabouts of the child, or from approaching within a specified distance of the place where she lives, or from making any contact with her. Further if there were any breach of such an order, the court could commit the stepfather to prison for contempt of court."

Lane J. concluded:

"as a matter of general application, it seems to me that there may be various circumstances in which a local authority would be grateful for the assistance of a court exercising wardship jurisdiction. Local authorities are sometimes faced with difficult and onerous decisions concerning children in their charge; responsible officers of their welfare departments may be subject to various pressures from within or from outside the authority itself. I consider that there would be no abandonment of, or derogation from, their statutory powers and duties were they to seek the guidance and assistance of the High Court in matters of difficulty, as distinct from the day-to-day arrangements with which, as the authorities show, the court will not interfere."

Although it is perfectly proper for authorities to use wardship to supplement their powers they should only do so for good reason. As Lane J. said in *Re B* the jurisdiction should be used sparingly and in a vast number of cases the application would serve no useful purpose. Moreover there are practical reasons for authorities to be wary about invoking wardship. One disadvantage from the authority's point of view is that a ward is subject to the directions of the court and that increased interference might be considered to be a hindrance.

A second use of wardship is to enable local authorities to have children *placed* in their care. Although authorities are given wide powers to assume the care of children there are situations where an authority feels that a child should be in care, yet there are no statutory grounds, or none that can be proved, to enable them to assume that care. In such situations it would be quite appropriate for the authority to make the child a ward and to ask the court to commit the child to the authority's care.[103]

A third use of wardship is to enable local authorities to *retain* children already in their care. This is particularly useful in the case of children received into care under the Children Act, 1948, chapter 43, section 1 since their powers come to an end upon parental request for their child's return.[104] In such cases rather than simply allow the parent to recover the child[105] it is permissible for the authority to make the child a ward and seek the court's sanction to keep the child in care.[106] Indeed, of the various devices[107] used by authorities to frustrate parental requests, wardship is the most satisfactory. Another option open to the local authority to oppose a parental request for the child's return is to support (either actively or passively) a wardship application by foster parents seeking to retain care and control.[108]

The usefulness of wardship is not confined to retaining the care of section 1 children since it may be used to review a magistrates' decision to discharge a care order[109] and, if it is submitted, a refusal to uphold a section 2 resolution.

CONCLUSION

The present and future scope of wardship

From the foregoing discussion it is evident that the scope of wardship extends beyond its Gilbert and Sullivan image of protecting wealthy orphans. In summary, wardship is currently used in three separate ways: as an original jurisdiction; as a supervisory jurisdiction and as a supplementary jurisdiction. The last two uses have just been discussed and it is sufficient to conclude that the development of wardship in these respects have been beneficial to the system. As a supplementary jurisdiction, wardship complements the other jurisdictions, and as a supervisory jurisdiction the limited power of intervention seems sufficient both to deal with any proved improprieties and to deter improprieties in the first place. It is likely that this aspect of wardship will continue to expand as it is doubtful whether its full potential has been realised.

On the other hand various changes have either been made or proposed which will have the effect of reducing the use of wardship as an original jurisdiction. One inroad was the lowering of the age of majority to 18, which has reduced the number of "teenage wardship" cases whereby parents try to prevent their child from continuing an undesirable relationship. The usual reason for such actions is to prevent the continuation of a personal relationship and ultimately the marriage, and this use has declined. But it could also be used to prevent the child from associating with "undesirable" groups such as hippies, drug addicts, or religious sects and this use might well expand.

A further inroad will be made when custodianship orders come into force giving non-parents the right to apply for an order in relation to children that the applicants have been looking after. However, as has been suggested, though third party applications (at present a major use of wardship) will be reduced, it is unlikely that such a use will disappear since advantage might still be taken of the court's wider powers.

Various reform proposals by the Law Commission would, if implemented, also reduce the need to have recourse to wardship. One proposal will affect applications made to prevent a parent removing the child from the jurisdiction. At the moment this is a frequent use of wardship and, indeed, where no other proceedings are pending[110] wardship is the only means open to the parties. Many believe that the current procedure is too restrictive since many cases particularly those involving threatened removal are unnecessarily raised to the High Court level. The Law Commission[111] has recommended that magistrates should be given such powers, and undoubtedly this proposal would reduce wardship applications. It is to be hoped that this proposal will be implemented.

Another proposal by the Law Commission[112] as we have seen, is to narrow the jurisdiction so that the court would not be competent to hear many of the so-called kidnapping cases. It is to be hoped that this proposal will not be implemented, since the power even to make a summary order for the child's return seems a valuable one and preferable to declining jurisdiction altogether. Nevertheless it has to be conceded that there is great uncertainty as to the type of order the court may make. It is clear that time is of the essence in such cases and it is disturbing that parties can procrastinate during the proceedings and although it is within the court's powers to state time limits within which evidence must be produced, there must still be a suspicion that the "innocent" party can suffer a disadvantage. Perhaps reforms should be made in this respect.

Despite these inroads or possible inroads, it is likely that wardship even as an original jurisdiction will remain important. It will remain, as at present, an alternative to other jurisdictions, and parents may wish to take advantage of the court's wider powers. Moreover, because wardship is much wider than any other jurisdiction, it will remain useful as a reserve jurisdiction to be used as a last resort, for example, in cases of complexity and it will remain competent to handle novel applications. In this respect, however, the decision of *Re X*[113] has reduced the possible scope for expansion. A stepfather of a girl aged 14 applied for an order that she should be made a ward, and that an injunction be granted restraining the publication of a book containing details about the ward's dead father's alleged sexual predilections and behaviour. It was contended that, as the girl in question was psychologically fragile, were she to read the book or hear about it from others, it would be grossly damaging to her. The Court of Appeal refused to grant the injunction, holding in effect that the interests of the child could not be allowed to prevail over the wider interests of freedom of publication. That the case established that there are limits to the protection which the court can afford its ward comes as no surprise, for as was said, it is impossible to protect a ward against everything that might do her harm. The interest of the case lies in exactly where the line should be drawn, and in particular whether as a matter of principle the lawful activities of others completely unconnected with the ward can be restrained in the interests of a ward. Although it has been argued[114] that there has never been a power to restrain the activities of those unconnected with the ward it is submitted that it is premature to seek to limit the jurisdiction in these terms.[115] Certainly the judgments in *Re X* leave open the possibility of further developments. Perhaps the key to the limits lies in the wording of section 1 of the Guardianship of Minors Act, 1971 which provides that the child's interest is the first and paramount consideration where the custody or upbringing or the administration of property belonging to the minor is in issue. In *Re X* itself Sir John Pennycuick[116] thought that section 1 was inapplicable to the issue of whether a publication could be restrained in the ward's interests. It is, therefore, possible that once it can be shown that the ward's interests are within the terms of section 1, the court will be prepared to extend its protection even to the extent of restraining the activities of those unconnected with the ward. Developments in this regard will be awaited with interest.

Wardship has proved to be a particularly useful and versatile jurisdiction especially since 1949, and it is likely that it will continue to play an important role in the future. It is doubtful, however, whether the jurisdiction could handle a vast increase in cases without detracting from its efficiency and for this reason it is likely to be confined to handling a relatively small number of cases.

---

1   See *e.g. Hope v. Hope* (1854) 4 De G.M. & G. 328, 43 E.R. 328 and *Re D.* [1976] Fam.185,
    [1976] 1 All E.R. 326 at 332. But any minor actually in England may be warded even
    though he is neither domiciled here nor a British subject. Bromley, *Family Law* (5th ed.,
    1976) at 397.
2   Administration of Justice Act 1970, c. 31, s. 1(2) and Sched I.
3   The number of applications has steadily increased. In 1975 there were 1203 originating
    summonses involving 1929 children. (Civil Judicial Statistics 1975, Cmnd. 6634. Table
    C.13) This compares with 959 summonses in 1974, 622 in 1971, 258 in 1961 and 74 in
    1951.
4   In *Scott v. Scott* [1913] A.C. 417 at 437.
5   *Re B. (J.A.) (An Infant)* [1965] Ch. 1112 at 1117, [1965] 2 All E.R. 168 at 171. See also the
    extra judicial comment by Cross J. in the same vein: "Wards of Court" (1967), 83 L.Q.R.
    200 at 207.
6   Guardianship of Minors Act, 1971, c. 3, s. 1.
7   [1970] A.C. 668, [1969] 1 All E.R. 788 (H.L.).

8   See Lord Eldon L.C. in *Wellesley v. Duke of Beaufort* (1827) 2 Russ. 1 at 20, 38 E.R. 236 at 243. "[Wardship] is founded on the obvious necessity that the law should place somewhere the care of individuals who cannot take care of themselves, particularly in cases where it is clear that some care should be thrown around them." See also Marriage Act 1949 (12, 13 & 14, Geo. 6, c. 76), s. 3(6).

9   *Re S.* [1967] 1 All E.R. 202 at 207, [1967] 1 W.L.R. 396.

10   *Ibid.*

11   *Re D.* [1976] Fam. 185, [1976] 1 All E.R. 326.

12   *F. v. S. (Adoption: Ward)* [1973] Fam. 203, [1973] 1 All E.R. 722 (C.A.).

13   See, for example, *Re D.* [1977] 2 W.L.R. 1006.

14   [1976] Fam. 185, [1976] 1 All E.R. 326. On the other hand it seems clear that the court can overrule parental *refusal* to allow their child to undergo medical treatment, for example, Jehovah's Witnesses refusing to allow their child to have a blood transfusion. Compare The Child Welfare Act, R.S.O. 1970, c. 64, s. 20(1)(x).

15   See *e.g. Re R. (P.M.)* [1968] 1 All E.R. 691, [1968] 1 W.L.R. 385.

16   See *e.g. Re H. (G.J.)* [1966] 1 All E.R. 952, [1966] 1 W.L.R. 706.

17   Including, for example, the power to restrain specific airlines from carrying the ward. See *Re Harris* (1960) The Times, May 21.

18   See *e.g. Re B. (J.A.)* [1965] Ch. 1112, [1965] 2 All E.R. 168.

19   Importantly such an order can be enforced via the Tipstaff see R.S.C. Ord. 90 r. 3A. A Tipstaff is an officer attached to the Supreme Court, appointed by the Lord Chancellor and the Lord Chief Justice. His functions are largely confined to arresting persons guilty of contempt of court.

20   C. 46, s. 6(6).

21   "Exceptional circumstances" are not defined but see *F. v. F.* [1959] 3 All E.R. 180, [1959] 1 W.L.R. 863 and *G. v. G.* (1962) 106 S.J. 858. If the court does commit the child into care it retains the power to make detailed provisions as to the ward's access. *Re Y.* [1976] Fam. 125, [1975] 3 All E.R. 348 (C.A.).

22   *Re B. (J.A.) (An Infant)* [1965] Ch. 1112 at 1117, [1965] 2 All E.R. 168.

23   For marrying a ward see e.g. *Herbert's case* (1731) 3 P. Wms. 116, 24 E.R. 992 and *Re H.'s Settlement* [1909] 2 Ch. 260. For removing a ward out of the jurisdiction see *Re J.* (1913) 108 L.T. 554. In *Re F.* [1977] 1 All E.R. 114 (C.A.), Lord Denning M.R. commented (at p. 122) that neither case should be a strict offence. For comments on the case see Lowe (1977) 93 L.Q.R. 180.

24   *Re F.* [1977] 1 All E.R. 114 (C.A.).

25   R.S.C. Ord. 90 r. 3A.

26   R.S.C. Ord. 90 r. 3(4). Concealing the ward's whereabouts is a grave contempt: See *Mustafa v. Mustafa* (1967) The Times Sept. 11 and 13.

27   *Hockly v. Lukin* (1762) 1 Dick 353, 21 E.R. 305 and *Rosenberg v. Lindo* (1883) 48 L.T. 478.

28   *Ramsbotham v. Senior* (1869) L.R. 8 Eq. 575.

29   *Practice Direction* [1973] 1 All E.R. 61: see Supreme Court Practice 1976, Vol. 1 at 138 para. 90/3/6.

30   See *Re W. & W.* (1975) Fam. Law 157 (C.A.).

31   *Clark v. Clark* (1970) 114 S. J. 318.

32   Heilbron J. in *Re D.* [1976] 1 All E.R. 326 at 335, [1976] Fam. 185.

33   R.S.C. Ord. 90 r. 3(2).

34   Established by *Re D.,* note 32, *supra.*

35   *Re R. (P.M.) (An Infant)* [1968] 1 All E.R. 691 at 692, [1968] 1 W.L.R. 385.

36   Per Heilbron J. in *Re D.,* note 32, *supra* at 336.

37   Per Cross J. in *Re S.* [1967] 1 All E.R. 202 at 208, [1967] 1 W.L.R. 396.

38   In *Re D.,* note 32, *supra* at 335.

39   *Re Caton, Vincent v. Vatcher* (1911) 55 Sol. Jo. 313.

40   See the account given in the Latey Report (1967) Cmnd. 3342, paras. 208-211.

41   *Re W. & W.* (1975) Fam. Law 157 (C.A.).

42   [1965] A.C. 201, [1963] 3 All E.R. 191 (H.L.).

43   [1965] A.C. 201 at 222.

44 As in *Re R. (P.M.)* [1968] 1 All E.R. 691n, [1968] 1 W.L.R. 385.
45 [1977] 1 All E.R. 114 (C.A.).
46 Para. 218. See note 40, *supra.*
47 He must be a solicitor of at least ten years standing: Supreme Court of Judicature (Consolidation) Act 1925, Fourth Schedule.
48 For the position prior to 1949 see *e.g.* Simpson *The Law of Infants* (4th Ed. 1925) at 165 and Pettit in *A Century of Family Law* (1957, ed. Graveson and Crane) at 82, 38. See also the comments of Stamp J. in *Re N.* [1967] Ch. 512, [1967] 1 All E.R. 161 at 168.
49 R.S.C. Ord. 90 r. 4(1)(9). The hearing takes place before a registrar.
50 R.S.C. Ord. 90 r. 4(3).
51 R.S.C. Ord. 90 r. 3(1).
52 [1967] Ch. 512, [1967] 1 All E.R. 161 endorsed by Simon P. in *L v. L* [1969] P 25 at 27, [1969] 1 All E.R. 852 *cf. Re E.* [1956] Ch. 23, [1955] 3 All E.R. 174, where Roxburgh J. had held that following the 1949 Act the Court had no inherent jurisdiction prior to the issue of a summons.
53 *Baldrian v. Baldrian* (1973) 4 Fam. Law 12 (C.A.) per Buckley L.J. See *e.g. Re Dunhill* (1 9 6 7) 111 S. J. 113 (frivolous application); *Re M.* [1961] Ch. 328, [1961] 1 All E.R. 788 (C.A.) (parental rights vested in local authority by an order made under statute) *Re H.* [1966] 1 All E.R. 886 [1966] 1 W.L.R. 381 (C.A.) (foreign court already seized of jurisdiction), and *Re O.* (1977) The Times, April 6 (natural parent wishing to get round the effect of an adoption order).
54 (1967) 111 S. J. 113. The application was struck out as an abuse of process.
55 *Practice Direction* [1967] 1 All E.R. 828.
56 An abuse of process can be considered a contempt of court, see Borrie and Lowe: *The Law of Contempt* (1973) at 248 *et seq.*
57 *Re D.* [1976] Fam. 185, [1976] 1 All E.R. 326.
58 *Ibid.* The applicant was an educational psychologist attached to the local authority.
59 Matrimonial Causes Act, 1973, c. 18, s. 42(1).
60 It may be possible (i.e. where one or both parents are dead) for a non-parent to apply to become a guardian. Even then, however, wardship may still be more effective see *Re N.* [1 9 7 4] Fam. 40, [1974] 1 All E.R. 126.
61 See *e.g. Re E.* [1963] 3 All E.R. 874, [1964] 1 W.L.R. 51. Occasionally wardship proceedings may be commenced by the parents to frustrate the adoption application see *Re F.* [1970] 1 All E.R. 344, cf. *Re O.* (1977) The Times, April 6, 1977.
62 For a discussion of the nature of a custodianship order see *e.g.* Freeman, (1976) 6 Fam. Law 57. See also "Custodianship and Wardship" (1977) 7 Fam. Law at 116 by the same author. At the time of writing it is not known when Part II of the Children Act, 1975, c. 72, will be in force, though various other sections are already in force.
63 If the applicant is a relative or step-parent and has consent of a person having legal custody, the child must have had his home with them for three months. Any other person (excluding the mother and father) must have looked after the child for twelve months. Without the requisite consent the period is three years: Children Act 1975, c. 72, s. 33.
64 "Home" is defined by s. 87(3) of the 1975 Act: "unless the context otherwise requires, references to the persons with whom a child has his home refers to a person who, disregarding absence of the child at a hospital or boarding school and any other temporary absence, has actual custody of the child."
    Suppose the applicant allowed the parent to look after the child for what was intended to be a short holiday, but the parent then refused to return the child. With whom does the child have his "home"?
65 [1976] Fam. 185, [1976] 1 All E.R. 326.
66 "Parental Rights and Duties and Custody Suits", 1975. Another suggestion is to have a Ministry of Children: see Jackson, New Society, Jan. 15, 1976, p. 94.
67 Moreover it is now established that the N.S.P.C.C. is entitled to treat its sources of information as confidential, see *D. v. N.S.P.C.C.* [1977] 1 All E.R. 589 (H.L.).
68 See Sachs J. in *Harben v. Harben* [1957] 1 All E.R. 379 at 381, [1957] 1 W.L.R. 261.
69 [1965] Ch. 568 at 583, 586, [1964] 3 All E.R. 977 (C.A.). The parties were in fact stateless but it is submitted that this was not material to the decision that jurisdiction can rest on

ordinary residence. However, the fact that both father and son retained travel documents entitling them to return to England provided an alternative ground for holding that there was jurisdiction.

70 Foster's Crown Cases 1792 (3rd Ed.) at 185 and *Joyce v. D.P.P.* [1946] A.C. 347 at 352.

71 See *e.g. Rayden on Divorce* (12th ed.) at 1028.

72 [1959] Ch. 363, [1958] 2 All E.R. 656. Query whether the child in question was a member of his father's household.

73 [1968] Ch. 643; affirmed [1968] 2 All E.R. 145 (C.A.).

74 See Pearson L.J. in *Re P (G.E.)* [1965] Ch. 568 at 587, [1964] 3 All E.R. 977 (C.A.) citing *inter alia Nugent v. Vetzera* (1866) L.R. 2 Eq. 704, *Re Willoughby* (1885) 30 Ch. D. 324 and *Harben v. Harben* [1957] 1 All E.R. 379, [1957] 1 W.L.R. 261.

75 See *e.g. Re H.* [1965] 3 All E.R. 906 per Cross J. approved on appeal [1966] 1 All E.R. 886, [1966] 1 W.L.R. 381 (C.A.). For the current approach, see *Re L.* [1974] 1 All E.R. 913, [1974] 1 W.L.R. 250 (C.A.) and *Re K.* (1976) The Times March 9.

76 See English Law Commission, Working Paper No. 68 "Custody of Children — Jurisdiction and Enforcement within the United Kingdom" (1976). See also Scottish Law Commission Memorandum No. 23.

77 The proposals are confined to cases where the child is habitually resident in some part of the U.K. A second working paper will be published to cover "international" problems.

78 The concept has yet to be fully tested in the courts. *Cruse v. Chittum* [1974] 2 All E.R. 940, (1974) 4 Fam. Law 152 merely stated that "habitual" residence indicated quality rather than the period of residence. An earlier Law Commission (No. 48 Report on Jurisdiction in Matrimonial Cases Para. 42) conceded that "habitual" residence is not a "sharp definition". See also Dicey-Morris, *The Conflict of Laws* (9th ed., 1973) at 97.

79 Paras. 3, 76-77. See note 76, *supra*.

80 Lord Denning M.R. in *Re P. (G.E.)* [1965] Ch. 568 at 586, [1964] 3 All E.R. 977 (C.A.) envisaged much shorter periods (e.g. six months) to show acquiescence in the change.

81 See *Re A.* [1970] 1 Ch. 665, [1970] 3 All E.R. 184 (C.A.).

82 Discussed at paras. 3, 92-95, see note 76, *supra*.

83 Would it, for instance, be an "emergency" if one parent threatens to remove the child from the *de facto* control of the other? What powers should the court have in an emergency? Should it have the power only to maintain the *status quo* pending the outcome of proceedings in the court of habitual residence or should it also be able to make summary orders for the return of the child?

84 *Re M.* [1961] Ch. 328, [1961] 1 All E.R. 788 (C.A.).

85 *Re H. (G.J.)* [1966] 1 All E.R. 952, [1966] 1 W.L.R. 706.

86 *Re O.* (1977) The Times, April 6; reversed 121 S.J. 710 (C.A.).

87 See *Re K. (K.J.S.)* [1966] 3 All E.R. 154, [1966] 1 W.L.R. 1241.

88 Local authorities are vested with considerable powers under the Children Act, 1948 (11 & 12 Geo. 6, c. 43) (as amended by the Children Act, 1975, c. 72) both to receive children into care under s. 1 and to pass a resolution to keep children in their care under s. 2. Authorities may also apply to the Juvenile Court for a care order under the Children and Young Persons Act, 1969, c. 54.

89 [1971] 3 All E.R. 743. For an example involving magistrates see *Re D.* [1973] Fam. 179, [1973] 2 All E.R. 993.

90 For the statutory procedure for serving notices etc. see the Children Act, 1948, ss. 2 (2) and 2 (3).

91 *Re M.* [1961] Ch. 328 at 341-342, [1961] 1 All E.R. 788 (C.A.).

92 See the comments of Russell L.J. in *Re T (A.J.J.)* [1970] Ch. 688 at 695, [1970] 2 All E.R. 865 (C.A.).

93 (1976) The Times, March 4.

94 Issued pursuant to the Children and Young Persons Act, 1969, s. 28 which in cases of emergency empowers a local authority to remove a child from parental control for a maximum period of 28 days.

95 Cross (1967) 83 L.Q.R. 200 at 204.

96 [1966] 1 All E.R. 952, [1966] 1 W.L.R. 706.

97 *T v. T* [1968] 3 All E.R. 321, [1968] 1 W.L.R. 1887. It has now been recommended that

they should have such powers, see Law Com. No. 77 Paras. 10.1-10.10 and see cl. 27 of the Draft Bill.
98 Magistrates Courts Act 1952 (15 & 16 Geo. 6 & 1 Eliz. 2, c. 55) s. 54. The Law Commission recommends that the pecuniary penalties should be increased to £10 per day with a £400 maximum — Law Com. No. 77 Paras. 5.48 — 5.53 and see C1.42 of the Draft Bill. The High Court has, under its contempt jurisdiction, unlimited powers to fine or imprison an offender.
99 R.S.C. Ord. 90 r. 3A.
100 [1968] 1 W.L.R. 1976.
101 *Re Y.* [1975] 3 All E.R. 348 at 352, [1967] Fam. 125 (C.A.).
102 [1974] 3 All E.R. 915 at 921, [1975] Fam. 36.
103 Under the Family Law Reform Act, 1969, c. 46, s. 7(2).
104 Under s. 1(3) and *B. v. B.* (1975) 6 Fam. Law 79 (C.A.).
105 Once the child has been in care for six months, 28 days notice must be given to the Authority before the child can be removed. Children Act 1975, c. 72, s. 56.
106 See *Re G.* [1963] 3 All E.R. 370, [1963] 1 W.L.R. 1169.
107 *E.g.* to pass a s. 2 resolution or to apply for a care order under the Children and Young Persons Act, 1969 and as an interim measure keep the child under a Place of Safety Order. For a criticism of these devices see Freeman (1976) 6 Fam. Law 136 and White (1976) 6 Farm. Law 141.
108 See *e.g. Re R. (K.)* [1964] Ch. 455, [1963] 3 All E.R. 337 (joint application), *Re S.* [1965] 1 All E.R. 865, [1965] 1 W.L.R. 483 (C.A.).
109 *Re D.* [1977] 2 W.L.R. 1006.
110 Either party may apply at any time after filing a petition in matrimonial proceedings for an order prohibiting the removal of any child of the family (see Matrimonial Causes Act, 1973, c. 18, s. 52) out of England and Wales M.C.R., 1973 r. 94(i).
111 Law Com. No. 77, paras. 10.1-10.10, and see cl. 27 of the Draft Bill.
112 Law Com. Working Paper No. 68 and Scottish Law Commission Memorandum No. 23.
113 [1975] 1 All E.R. 697, [1975] Fam. 47 (C.A.).
114 Everton, "High Tide in Wardship", (1975) 125 N.L.J. 930.
115 In any event orders have been made against strangers — see *Re Harris* (1960) The Times, May 21.
116 See note 113, *supra,* at 707.

Kidnapping Of Children: A Note On Canadian Cases

*Karen M. Weiler**

The issue of custody, difficult to determine at best, is rendered more complex when inter-jurisdictional problems arise.[1] Basically, one parent will be seeking to regain custody of the child which has been "snatched," while the other will attempt to obtain judicial sanction for his or her actions. The extent to which a court will intervene in settling the dispute is often unpredictable by virtue of the fact that a court may assume jurisdiction on several different bases.

The welfare of the child is paramount in most jurisdictions in custody or wardship questions, but there is a lack of statutory guidelines to assist a judge in the exercise of his broad discretion.

A foreign judgment may not be relied upon for enforcement in a subsequent jurisdiction elsewhere, unless it is final, binding, and not subject to variation in the forum pronouncing it.[2] A custody order is always subject to variation and cannot in its nature be final.[3]

THE TRADITIONAL APPROACH

Jurisdiction Based on Domicile Yielding to Jurisdiction Based on Physical Presence of the Child

Beginning with *Masterson v. Masterson,*[4] the Saskatchewan Court of Appeal rejected the exclusive test of domicile as the sole basis for assuming jurisdiction in custody disputes and took jurisdiction on the basis of the presence of the infant. The court held that a mother who had established a residence in Saskatchewan for herself and her children was entitled to make application for their custody in that province and that the proceedings ought not to be stayed to allow the father to take similar proceedings in the courts of his domicile.[5] Since then, Canadian courts have come to rely less and less on domicile as the basis for assuming jurisdiction.

* Mrs. Karen M. Weiler, of Osgoode Hall, Barrister-at-law, Counsel, Policy Development Division, Ministry of the Attorney General of Ontario.

But in *Heslop v. Heslop*[6] the Ontario Court of Appeal relied substantially on the fact that the father was domiciled in Ontario. Notwithstanding that the father had forcibly removed the child from the *de facto* custody of its mother in Michigan, where she had instituted divorce proceedings claiming custody, Roach J.A., held that the Ontario courts should assume jurisdiction in the case. Although the decision is based on the fact that the father was domiciled in Ontario, the infant was also physically present in Ontario.

Jurisdiction was assumed on the physical presence of the child in the Privy Council decision in *McKee v. McKee*. The essential point was whether Ontario courts should enforce a California order granting custody to the mother of a child when the father, who had invoked the jurisdiction of the Californian courts and, in defiance of the outcome, had taken the child to Ontario and applied for custody.[7] The Californian decision was reopened and the question of custody re-examined in a full evidentiary hearing on the merits before an Ontario trial judge. While the Californian judgment was given consideration, the best interests of the infant required that the court should look beyond circumstances in which the jurisdiction of the foreign court was invoked, and examine all the circumstances, from the evidence available in the new forum, and form an independent judgment.[8] The Privy Council said that, if the matter came before the court within a very short time of the foreign judgment and there was no new circumstance to be considered, the weight to be accorded the foreign judgment might be so great as to justify its enforcement.[9]

Following *McKee* the Nova Scotia Supreme Court in *Re Wright*,[10] reopened the question of custody which had been granted to a mother in Manitoba. The father had kidnapped the child to Nova Scotia one month after the decision, but, at the time of the return of the writ of habeas corpus, the child had been living with the father and his common law wife for two years, and the trial judge was concerned that removal of the child from its present surroundings would be detrimental.

In *Stalder v. Wood*[11] the parties were married in England and the Magistrates' Court gave custody to the mother in 1970. In March, 1974 the father petitioned the Scottish courts for custody, and an *ex parte* order of interim custody was granted in his favour. In May of that year, the mother applied to set aside the *ex parte* order, but her application was refused. The mother, through her solicitors, gave an undertaking to the courts not to remove the child from the jurisdiction. Later, the parties agreed that the child could spend the school vacation in Canada with the mother, and that she was to return the child after 45 days. When she did not do so, the husband applied to the Manitoba courts for an order for custody or an order that the child be returned to Scotland. The trial judge declined jurisdiction and stated that the relevant evidence was mostly available in

England, and partially in Scotland, and that a Canadian court would not as readily have information before it for a proper decision. But, Freedman C.J.M., of the Manitoba Court of Appeal took the view that the custody issue could effectively be dealt with in Manitoba and on the ground that the welfare of the child was the paramount consideration, he remitted the matter to the Manitoba trial judge for a full examination and hearing of the custody issue on the merits.

Jurisdiction on the basis of the ordinary residence of the child

In *Re Lyon and Lyon*,[12] a wife who had unsuccessfully claimed custody in divorce proceedings in Alberta, later removed the children to British Columbia forcibly and sought a custody order there. Kennedy Co. Ct. J., declined jurisdiction notwithstanding the *McKee* case, and considered that a principle that courts should assume jurisdiction based on the physical presence of the child, would create confusion. Any parent possessing ample financial means and sufficiently lacking in respect for orders of the courts and for his own undertaking, could, by moving from province to province, prolong litigation as to an infant's custody until such infant attained his majority.[13]

In *Nielsen v. Nielsen*,[14] Mrs. Nielsen filed a petition for divorce in Ontario claiming custody as corollary relief. Her husband counter-claimed for custody. At the opening of the trial, the husband's solicitor advised the court that his client had removed the three youngest children from Ontario to British Columbia where they were now residing and where the husband had employment opportunities. He argued that the Ontario court no longer had jurisdiction to deal with the issue of custody. Mr. Justice Galligan found that, apart from section 11 of the Divorce Act, the Ontario courts had jurisdiction because the children were ordinarily resident in Ontario at the time of institution of the proceedings. He felt it would be wrong if a husband, properly served in Ontario and after appearing, defending, and invoking the jurisdiction of the Ontario courts by counter-claiming for custody, could frustrate the jurisdiction of the court by removing the children from the province.[15] Mr. Justice Galligan concluded that the child's ordinary residence is the last place in which the child resided with his parents and that, unless there were exceptional circumstances, the court in which the child has his ordinary place of residence has jurisdiction to deal with the custody of infants, even though the infant is not within the territorial bounds of the jurisdiction of the court.[16] Galligan J. did not deny the jurisdiction of the courts where the child was physically present.[17] He considered that the courts of the jurisdiction where the child is physically present should recognize and give effect to the orders of the courts of the place in which the child is ordinarily resident, unless in exceptional circumstances the court was satisfied beyond a reasonable doubt that serious harm could result to the child.[18]

Hunt J., of the Manitoba Court of the Queen's Bench, in *Prosser-Jones v. Prosser-Jones*[19] ordered that children who were the subject of custody proceedings in England, and who had been kidnapped to Manitoba by the father, should be returned to England because the preponderance of evidence necessary to determine the future of the children was available in England and not in Manitoba. It was further ordered that the costs of the mother in pursuing the children to Canada and her return to England, as well as the costs of transportation of the children, be paid for by the father.

In *Re Ridderstroem*[20] and *Re Loughran,*[21] the Ontario Court of Appeal declined to take jurisdiction on the basis that the child was not ordinarily resident within its boundaries. The question, therefore, arises as to whether the notion of domicile is being reintroduced under cover of residence.[22]

In *Kemp v. Dawson*[23] the court felt that so long as the father and mother were living together in the matrimonial home, the child's ordinary residence was the home, and that this would still be the case even when the child attended a boarding school. A slightly different approach was taken by the Ontario Court of Appeal in *Ritchie v. Ritchie.*[24] The husband and wife entered into a separation agreement giving the husband custody of the child. The husband continued to reside in Waterloo County, but made arrangements for the infant to be looked after by its paternal grandparents at their home in the County of Oxford. The wife took up residence in Sudbury and subsequently removed the infant there without the husband's consent, at the same time commencing proceedings for custody in the Surrogate Court. Under the Infants Act[25] the Surrogate Court of the county or district in which the infant resides has jurisdiction to decide custody disputes. The court found that the infant was below the age at which he could form any intention with regard to his own residence, but physical presence in Sudbury and the fact of dwelling in the custody of a parent did not change the ordinary residence of the child.[26] The rule that a child's ordinary residence cannot be changed by the unilateral act of one parent unless the other parent acquiesces in the change (or delays proceedings to such an extent that he can be assumed to acquiesce) was adopted. But the court did not find the child to be ordinarily resident in the County of Waterloo with its father. Instead, Mr. Justice Kelly was of the opinion that immediately prior to the date of the kidnapping, the residence of the infant was in the County of Oxford where he was dwelling on a reasonably permanent basis.[27]

Jurisdiction based on ordinary residence is not an exclusive test. The courts where the child is physically present also have jurisdiction over the child, but will decline this jurisdiction unless there is a danger of serious harm to the child in returning it to its parents.[28] While Galligan J., in *Nielsen* indicated that such danger must be beyond a reasonable doubt,[29] it remains to be seen whether the court will require so high a degree of proof. In *Re Walker*,[30] a father, formerly resident in Vancouver and later in California, kidnapped the children back to Vancouver when an investigation by the probation department did not confirm his allegations of unfitness on the part of the mother. The British Columbia Supreme Court nevertheless assumed jurisdiction to decide the issue of custody. In *Re D.J.C. and W.C.*[31] a Manitoba court awarded custody of the children to the father, with access to the mother for a period of one month in the summer. The mother came to Ontario and, after exercising her access rights, refused to return the children to the father, making allegations regarding the father's conduct with respect to the children. The Ontario Court of Appeal ordered that interim custody of the children be given to the mother provided that proceedings would be taken within a month before the Manitoba Court of Queen's Bench to vary custody.

Jurisdiction based on ordinary residence can promote a decision by the jurisdiction with which the child has the closest connection, and where most of the evidence pertinent to the dispute lies. It can also result in a wider recognition in other jurisdictions. Because of this, the court of the child's ordinary residence may not be as loathe to assume jurisdiction where the child is not physically present and/or the person in whose charge he is, is not within its boundaries, on the basis that such an order is not enforceable in the foreign jurisdiction because it is an order in personam.[32] The child's ordinary residence accords generally with the increasing emphasis placed by legal writers and the courts on the importance of continuity and stability of the child's environment.[33]

THE EXTRA-PROVINCIAL CUSTODY ORDERS ENFORCEMENT ACT

The need for some predictability in inter-jurisdictional custody disputes induced the Canadian Commissioners on Uniform Laws to draft The Extra-Provincial Custody Orders Enforcement[34] Act, and to adopt it at their 1974 proceedings. To date, it has been enacted by the legislatures of Manitoba, British Columbia, Nova Scotia and Prince Edward Island. The Act requires enacting provinces to recognize and enforce extra-provincial custody orders, unless it is satisfied that at the time the custody order was originally made, the child did not have a real and substantial connection with the jurisdiction in which the order was made. If there was no real and substantial connection with the jurisdiction making the order, or if the child and all parties affected by the custody order are resident in the enforcing jurisdiction, the court may vary the custody order and in so doing shall give first consideration to the welfare of the child. A person is deemed not to be a resident of the jurisdiction if the sole reason for his physical presence there is to make or oppose an application to vary. The court may also vary a custody order where it is satisfied that a child would suffer serious harm by being restored to the custody of the person named in the order.[35]

The mere physical presence of the child with one parent claiming custody does not, therefore, result in a new inquiry and a full-scale investigation as to the merits of the previous custody order. Instead, subject to the three conditions already mentioned, the court will give effect to the foreign order.

For its application, the Act does not rely on reciprocal enforcement with another jurisdiction. Thus, the Act is a significant deterrent to parental kidnappers bringing the child to that province.

---

1   *Re P. (G.E.)* [1965] Ch. 568 [1964] 3 All E.R. 977 (C.A.).
2   *McKee v. McKee* [1951] 2 D.L.R. 657, [1951] A.C. 352, 2 W.W.R. 181; *Lear v. Lear* [1973] 3 O.R. 935, 38 D.L.R. (3d) 655. 13 R.F.L. 27, Dicey and Morris, *The Conflict of Laws* (9th ed.), 1973 1037.
3   *Skjonsby v. Skjonsby* (1974) 15 R.F.L. 251 (Sask.).
4   [1948] 2 D.L.R. 696, [1948] 1 W.W.R. 642 (Sask. C.A.).
5   *Ibid.* at 699.
6   [1958] O.R. 183, 12 D.L.R. (2d) 591 (C.A.).
7   This case is noted at (1948) 26 Can. Bar Rev. 1368; (1949) 27 Can. Bar Rev. 99; (1951) 29 Can. Bar Rev. 536; (1973) 11 Alta. L. Rev. 15.
8   Note 2 at 363, 364.
9   Note 2 at 665.
10   (1964) 49 D.L.R. (2d) 460 (N.S.); See also *Menasce v. Menasce* (1963) 40 D.L.R. (2d) 114, 48 M.P.R. 281 (P.E.I.).
11   [1975] W.W.D. 76, 54 D.L.R. (3d) 157, 20 R.F.L. 214, Even if the court of the jurisdiction to which the child has been brought considers that it has jurisdiction it may decide that the other jurisdiction is more convenient and appropriate. *Cochrane v. Cochrane* (1975) 8 O.R. (2d) 310, 57 D.L.R. (3d) 694, 20 R.F.L. 264 (C.A.). See also *Desilets v. Desilets* (1975) 60 D.L.R. (3d) 546, 22 R.F.L. 87 (Man. C.A.); *Desilets v. Desilets (No. 2)* (1975) 22 R.F.L. 304 (Sask.); *Martin v. Martin* (1975) 24 R.F.L. 304 (N.S.); *Paschke v. Paschke* (1975) 26 R.F.L. 324 (Alta T.D.).
12   (1969) 72 W.W.R. 156, 3 R.F.L. 71, 10 D.L.R. (3d) 287 (B.C.).
13   *Ibid.* at 289-290.
14   [1971] 1 O.R. 541, 5 R.F.L. 313, 16 D.L.R. (3d) 33.
15   *Ibid.* at 36.
16   Note 14 at 38-39.
17   Note 14 at 39.
18   Note 14.
19   (1972) 7 R.F.L. 150 (Man.).
20   [1972] 2 O.R. 113, 6 R.F.L. 18, 25 D.L.R. (3d) 29 (C.A.).
21   [1973] 1 O.R. 109, 9 R.F.L. 255, 30 D.L.R. (3d) 385 (C.A.).
22   (1973) 11 Alta L. Rev. 15 at 23.
23   (1974) 3 O.R. (2d) 605, 15 R.F.L. 359, 46 D.L.R. (3d) 321.

24 (1974) 5 O.R. (2d) 520 (C.A.). See also *Leatherdal v. Ferguson* (1964) 50 W.W.R. 700, 50 D.L.R. (2d) 182 (Man. C.A.).

25 R.S.O. 1970, c.222, s.2.

26 Note 24 at 522.

27 *Ibid.* at 523.

28 Note 14 *supra.*

29 *Ibid.* at 37.

30 [1974] 3 W.W.R. 48 16 R.F.L. 98 (B.C.).

31 (1975) 8 O.R. (2d) 310, 20 R.F.L. 264, 57 D.L.R. (3d) 694 (C.A.).

32 *Elash v. Elash* (1963) 45 W.W.R. 94, 43 D.L.R. (2d) 599 (Sask.); *Re Vadera* [1972] 1 O.R. 441, 23 D.L.R. (3d) 289, 6 R.F.L. 33; The contrary view which is perhaps now outdated is expressed in *Hannon v. Eisler* (No.2) (1954) 13 W.W.R. 565 (Man. C.A.) and *Re Overholt* [1960] O.R. 314, 24 D.L.R. (2d) 157 (C.A.).

33 Freud, Goldstein and Solnet, *Beyond the Best Interests of the Child,* (1973) 456-459; Yarrow, "The Crucial Nature of Early Experience" Glass ed. (1968) *Environmental Influences.*

34 Proceedings of the Fifty-Sixth Annual Meeting of The Uniform Law Conference of Canada, August 1974, p. 114.

35 *Ibid.* sections 2, 3, 4.

Step-Parent Adoptions In English And Canadian Law

*Alastair Bissett-Johnson**

A few years ago adoption centred around the needs of families who wanted to enlarge by adopting a young child. Certainly in England[1] (and probably Canada) the position has changed. Fewer young children are available for adoption, due to changes in social attitudes, making it easier for parents to raise their illegitimate children. The real need is for adoptive homes for older and handicapped children, "the children who wait" in foster homes or community homes and whose plight in England has been graphically referred to by Jane Rowe and Lydia Lambert.[2] Although in England the numbers of adoptions have only shown a modest decline from a peak of 26,989 in 1968 to 22,502 in 1974, these figures conceal the fact that around a third[3] of adoptions now involve the joint adoption of a child by one of his natural parents (usually his mother) and a step-parent (usually his step-father, though step-mother adoptions do occur and create virtually the same problems as step-father adoptions). This normally occurred after the child's natural parents' marriage ended in divorce and one or both of the parents remarried. Clearly all this was not envisaged by the legislature when adoption was introduced in England in 1926. The position in Canada shows a similar pattern. The Quebec Civil Code Revision Office[4] has reported that one-third of adoptions in Quebec involve a new consort of the child's mother or father.

Unlike the 'adoption simple' of French law,[5] an adoption in British and Canadian law generally operates to extinguish all ties between the child and his natural parents and replaces them with new ties between the child and his adoptive parents.[6] In the case of the natural mother/step-father adoption this has the effect of cutting off the legitimate child from his father, whom he may know and love, as well as from the child's wider family who can be all too easily overlooked such as his paternal grandparents, aunts and uncles, etc., with whom the child may already have had valuable contact. It is true that in England there is a power to

* Alastair Bissett-Johnson, L.L.M. (Michigan), of the Inner Temple, Barrister-at-law, Professor, Faculty of Law, Dalhousie University, formerly of the Faculty of Law, McGill University.

impose conditions permitting access of parents and grandparents to the child even after the making of an adoption order,[7] but the power is difficult to enforce, and indeed is contrary to the whole ethos of adoption, which is to create a new relationship between parent and natural child. The very existence of such conditions, and the inquiries of social workers may inhibit the development of the new ties.

The essence of adoption in the Common Law world has generally been the creation of legal ties where none previously existed, soon after a custodial transfer of the child occurred. In practice (as opposed to law) step-parent adoptions usually change very little. The child is already legitimate, and so there is no stigma of illegitimacy to remove. The main effect of adoption in such a case is exclusionary: the exclusion and extinguishment of the natural father's rights. In 1968 in England, Judge Grant, delivered a judgment[8] setting his face against the principle of allowing step-parent adoptions in 'run of the mill' cases. This was taken up by the English High Court, by the Houghton/Stockdale Committee on Adoption[9], and by Parliament in the Children Act, 1975.

MOTIVES BEHIND STEP-PARENT ADOPTIONS

In many cases the reasons behind the application involve insecurity and a lack of confidence (particularly after a failed marriage) in the relationship between the child and the step-parent, and a desire to make the step-child a part of the step-parent's family.[10] Coupled with the step-father's desire to have extra standing as a result of adoption, there is often the feeling that if adoption is granted, the natural father will cease to maintain the child (that burden being transferred to the step-father), that visits will cease and that as the children grow more remote from their natural father they will grow closer to the step-father. This is often associated with an element of competition between the natural parent and the step-parent. Even if the natural father wishes to rid himself of the obligation to support his children, it is questionable if that *per se* is a good reason for adoption.

Fundamentally, all this is a matter of psychology and perhaps involves a failure in society and the law to come to terms with step-parenthood. This point is well made by Brenda Maddox in her instructive and sensitive book *The Half-Parent*.[11] She points out that the step-parent has not been described in a flattering way in literature from Hansel and Gretel through Cinderella to Snow White and the Seven Dwarfs.[12] Such myths do not make it easy for step-parents to find a satisfactory role and the law has been slow to define the rights and duties of the step-parent. Mrs. Maddox also discusses the problems of double-parenting and grand-parenting and the problem whether to have a new baby and the effect of this on the step-children. A related reason is to give the child the same name as her mother and her step-father, and indeed the question of the name often has a symbolic importance which those practising outside this area of family law totally fail to comprehend. It symbolises the sort of relationship that it is hoped to create within the new family.

The adoption of the child also gives the child rights of succession and maintenance against his or her step-father and at the same time gives the step-father rights of custody to the child. The desire of the step-parent for continued custody of the child should a natural parent die is another potent factor. Some of these rights can be achieved in ways which do not involve adoption e.g. testamentary guardianship,[13] but sometimes this involves some difficulty, and these ways may not have the right psychological feel for those involved. Indeed, particularly in Canada, the desire to make a step-parent a legal parent of the child, who can act as such after the death of the natural parent (their spouse) may be an important factor in many adoption applications.[14] The problem is compounded by the fact that, whilst the law on testamentary guardianship in England[15] is clear, the position in some Canadian Provinces is less clear. In Ontario for instance there is a split of authority[16] on whether a testamentary appointment of a guardianship is effective and the Ontario Law Reform Commission recommended clarification of the position.[17] However, one of their recommendations was that only the appointment by a surviving parent should be effective. This could raise considerable problems where a child was living with its mother and step-father, and where the mother died having appointed the child's step-father testamentary guardian but where the natural father was still living. The position in Alberta[18] by which a parent may by deed or will appoint a testamentary guardian to be a guardian of the child after his or her death seems more desirable. The step-parent in such a case acts jointly with the surviving parent.

THE DEVELOPING LAW

Both in England and in Canada, over a period, there was at first a move to regulate the duties of step-parents towards their step-children. This has been done in England by imposing duties to support children whom they have *treated* or *accepted* as children of their family.[19] This clearly included step-parents. In Canada much the same result was achieved by the condition that the parent and child stand in *loco parentis*.[20] Another possible approach (although not commonly used in Canada or in England until the Children Act) would be for courts to award care or custody of a child not only to the natural parent but also the step-parent with whom the child is living.[21] Legislation may give the step-child in Ontario,[22] and has already given him in England,[23] succession rights against his step-parent's estate. A final approach is to expressly include step-children within the

Provincial support provision.[24] However these changes in the law largely concern themselves with the imposition of duties on the step-parent. However convenient a beast of burden the step-father might be, it is probably necessary to grant him some *rights* to accompany the duties imposed upon him, without cutting one of the child's parents out of his life. It has been this feeling that underlies much of the recent British Children's Act and the codification of English adoption law in the Adoption Act 1976.

In 1972, the Houghton/Stockdale Report[25] suggested that it would be more appropriate, in the majority of cases, if rights short of adoption were conferred on a step-parent who married a person with children by a prior marriage. These rights would not involve extinction of the ties with the natural parent and would be open to periodic review. The concept was to be termed "guardianship". In the end when the Children Act, 1975 was passed, the term "guardianship" was dropped in favour of the less felicitous name of "custodianship". (The reason being that a guardian would have acquired certain rights [*e.g.* to deal with his ward's property and to give consent to adoption] which the legislature did not wish to confer on the custodian). Moreover under section 10(3) of the Children Act, 1975 a court dealing with an adoption application involving a parent and a step-parent is directed to dismiss the application if it considers that the matter could be better dealt with by referring it back to the divorce court, so that that court could vary the post divorce custody order to include the step-parent in the custody arrangements.[26] The legal rights created would be identical to those of the custodian (which are discussed later) though the name custodian is not used in such cases. Custodianship orders in their purest form are restricted to cases (a) involving illegitimate children where the mother subsequently married or (b) cases where the parent of a legitimate child remarried after the death of his or her spouse. In other words where there is no Divorce Court to refer the case back to and so the case must be dealt with *de novo*.

Even before the Children Act was published, whether influenced by the Houghton/Stockdale Report or working independently, the English High Court, in a number of decisions, made clear their misgivings about step-parent adoptions.

In *Re D.*[27] the Divisional Court disagreed with both the *guardian ad litem* and the justices that the adoption of the children by the mother and her new husband would be for the welfare of the girls. Sir George Baker P. was at a loss to see how:

"the adoption orders would be for the welfare of the girls when the expressed object was to give them the mother's new surname. All too often that course was taken by the mother to disguise from her new neighbours that she had been involved in a failed marriage."

Perhaps more important was the decision in the unreported case of *Re M.*[28]

in which even though the first husband's consent to the adoption had been dispensed with on the ground that it was being unreasonably withheld, the Divisional court set aside the adoption order made by the justices apparently on the ground that there was no evidence that the adoption order, if made, would be for the benefit of the children as required by section 7 of the 1958 Act. Ormrod J. said:

"In this present case it is essential to bear in mind that it is an application by a natural mother to adopt her children and it is therefore an entirely different case from one where a stranger is applying to adopt. Start by asking this question: In what way will adoption affect these children's lives? In none. They will continue to live with their natural mother and step-father as they have been doing. The step-father has accepted them as children of the family and therefore their position *vis-à-vis* him is the same morally and legally as if he were their adopted father."

There is not, however, the same objection to the adoption of a child by his mother and step-father after the divorce of the child's natural mother and father, if it is unlikely that the natural father (and his family) will have any future beneficial contact with the child. This situation arose in *Re S.*[29] and Megaw L.J. and the Court of Appeal stressed that if the facts showed, as here, that the father had intentionally broken off all contact with the child and if there was no suggestion of there being any member of the father's family with whom the child could have advantageous contact now or later, adoption might be appropriate. In *Re S.* the father consented to the adoption order being made after deserting and neglecting to maintain his wife and child, which made it quite different from *Re D.*[30] and *Re H.*[31] where the fathers and the wider family wanted to retain contact with their children with whom they had had beneficial contact over several years. Moreover there was real affection between step-father and child and the natural father had abandoned the child at an early age and wished to be relieved of the burden of having to support him.

The feelings of the English judiciary are perhaps summed up in three recent cases; one (discussed in Child Adoption[32]) appeared under the heading "Two Fathers Better Than Adoption"; another, one of the few successful step-parent adoption applicants, involved a successful attempt to dispense with the need for a homosexual father to consent to the adoption of his child;[33] and the third involved an attempt to dispense with the consent to adoption of a father in prison for armed robbery.[34] Against this background it seems unlikely that in many cases the courts will consider that adoption by a parent jointly with a step-parent is more appropriate than rearranging the custody arrangements. Even the desire of a natural parent to rid himself of a financial burden and his consent to the adoption of his child is not conclusive evidence that adoption is in the best interest of the child.

The movement in Canada has parallelled that in England. Some of the earlier cases seem to distinguish "stranger adoptions" where the need to protect parental ties are strongly recognized, from cases where the adoption is sought by a parent acting jointly with natural parent. Amongst the most important of these cases have been those which involved the Manitoba legislation which provides [35] that a judge shall not make an interim order for approval of adoption unless written consent in prescribed form is obtained: "where both parents are living but their marriage has been dissolved or annulled . . . and the custody of the child has been given to one parent by order of [the] court, by the parent to whom the custody was given."

In Re Pshebnicki Adoption[36] this was used to allow an adoption even though it was opposed by a parent utilizing rights of access granted by Court order. In a later case *R. v. Co. Ct. Judge, Ex Parte Sobering*[37], although feeling constrained by precedent, Tritchler C.J. Q.B. expressed reservations about the *Pshebnicki case:*

"Again with respect, had it not been for the decision in *Pshebnicki,* I should have questioned the propriety of a Judge acting under s. 99C of the *Child Welfare Act* when there was outstanding an order of this Court respecting the custody of and access to the child. A Judge of this court, after careful inquiry and assisted by reports of social workers attached to the family Courts may award custody to one parent with a carefully spelled-out right of the other parent to weekly visitation and to have the child during weekends and holidays. It would seem inappropriate for a dissatisfied parent, instead of applying to vary or appealing the order, to set it at naught by an application for absolute adoption under s.99C of the Act. A more orderly course would be an application to the Judge of this Court to vary his order, if circumstances have changed, to suspend the right of access or to provide that it be subject to termination in the event of a decree absolute of adoption."[38]

A further factor in the Manitoba cases is that the local legislation[39] makes the best interest of the child the test in deciding whether or not to dispense with the need for parental consent, and thus different from the approach in other jurisdictions where this rule is not present. This factor was referred to by the court as a reason for its decision in *Goldstein v. Brownstone*[40] to allow the adoption of a child contrary to the wishes of her father. The father, a doctor, had seen little of either his wife or his child during the marriage, and his attempts to exercise access had emotionally disturbed the daughter. Nevertheless termination of access for a time might have served the Court's aims just as well, and step-parent adoptions are not necessarily in the best interest of a child.

Decisions favouring step-parent adoptions can be found in other jurisdictions. In *Re Sharp*[41], an adoption order was made against the mother's wishes. The mother had paid little or no attention to the children aged 7 and 9 at the time of the proceedings in the six years in which she had been separated from her husband. She was not of good character, and such visits as she had made to the children were found to be harmful and disturbing. The majority paid attention to the fact that the mother had no suitable home for the children and was merely being obstructive in seeking custody. Clearly these issues are relevant in relation to the custody proceedings but not necessarily in relation to adoption proceedings. The dissenting judgment of Davey J.A. has much to commend it. He said[42]:

"I do not for a moment doubt that the children are happy and secure in their father's and step-mother's care. But I do doubt that their welfare will be advanced by the adoption order in view of the present order for custody and, in effect the lack of access by the appellant. In fact, the main purpose of the adoption order seems to be, not so much to benefit the children, as to buttress the father's present right of custody without access by the mother, by severing the appellant's legal relation to her children and substituting his present wife as the mother. In so far as the adoption order will prevent the Court from reviewing the present orders for custody and access in the event of any change in circumstances through death or remarriage of either of the respondents, or change in their material fortunes, it would work against the interests of the children. The male respondent is the natural parent and does not need the adoption order. He has the legal custody of the children with no present access by the appellant. He may appoint his present wife, if he should pre-decease her, to be guardian of his children along with the appellant. If his wife should predecease him and he should remarry he would after the adoption order be the sole guardian of the children unless his present wife should appoint someone else to act with him. If the survivor of them should remarry, the atmosphere in the new home might be quite undesirable for the children, yet after the adoption, the appellant would have no status even to inquire, let alone intervene. These possibilities are probably remote, but nonetheless real.

In my opinion it is not the intention of the *Adoption Act* that it should be used without grave reasons over the objections of a parent to create a new family unit of parents and child following divorce of the natural parents and remarriage of one of them; still less that it should be used to terminate the power of the Court to review and vary the provisions for custody and access contained in the decree."

This same confusion between custody and adoption proceedings also emerges in the decision of O'Hearn Co. Ct. J. in *Re Application for Adoption*.[43] The natural mother and step-father of an eight year old child were allowed to adopt him notwithstanding that the natural father had in no way misconducted himself. It was true that difficulties had emerged over maintenance for the child but these were linked to problems over the

exercise of rights of visitation. Hearn Co. Ct. J. started by stressing that
"It should be stressed that this is not a case of a contest between natural
parents and strangers, but a contest between natural parents themselves in
the very unnnatural situation created by divorce."[44]
He admitted that the child would lose certain rights by adoption.
". . . the surname he was given at birth, the protection and care of his
natural father, and the prospect of inheriting from him, as well as legal
connections with his parental kindred . . . [and] the religious denomination
with which he was baptized . . . he will have a stable and loving home which
is of primary importance in bringing up a normal and well-adjusted child to
become a normal and well-adjusted adult, and parents who love and care
for him well . . . and whom he loves and looks up to."[45]

Although Margaret Hughes describes the judgment as enlightened[46], it
is not clear that the judge could articulate any clear positive advantages
that were being achieved by adoption. Even in the absence of adoption the
child would have remained in the stable home environment of his mother
and step-father. Perhaps the most undesirable feature of this case was the
relatively short period between the mother's remarriage and the adoption
application, a period of only 17 months. With divorce figures growing
amongst first as well as subsequent marriages one would hope that courts
will assure themselves so far as possible of the stability of the subsequent
marriages, and will not expose children to the risk of multiple adoptions
following multiple divorces.[47] The superficial neatness of step-parent
adoptions must not preclude an enquiry by the courts into the factors
operating below the surface in such cases. A skimpy treatment of these
issues is not in the best interest of the child. The finality and severance of the
ties involved in adoption makes custody cases a most questionable
analogy. It seems probable that some judges have a certain subconscious
predisposition to favour (or disfavour) step-parent adoptions; it is,
therefore, no surprise to find that in Re A.E.C.[48], O'Hearn Ct. Co. J. again
favoured a step-parent adoption despite the opposition of the natural
mother, whom the judge described as a charming and intelligent woman,
and though he attached no blame to her conduct and attitude. The benefits
attaching to the adoption were described as:
". . . supplying an element of stability and authority that is now lacking
in their lives, and it will not deprive them of the love and affection of their
natural mother although, of course, her legal right of visitation is
terminated by an adoption order. Nevertheless, there appears to be no
danger of a refusal of access to her, although it cannot be legally
guaranteed."[49]

Unfortunately the judge does not make clear what was the element of
stability which would be protected by the making of the order. No change
in custody was sought or threatened, and again the new marriage was only

of relatively short (15 months) duration. Although the decision was justified by reference to the Superior Court decision in *Block v. Benight*[50], which emphasized that under s.5(g) of the Nova Scotia Adoption Act[51] parental consent can be dispensed with "in the interest of the person to be adopted", it is also interesting that that case affirmed the decision of Anderson Co. Ct. J. that adoption would not make a positive contribution to the welfare of the child but would rather deprive the child of the love and affection of her natural father. Finally it is perhaps too optimistic to refer to rights of access that may continue, despite there being no obligation on the part of the applicants to do so, against a background in which the severance of the ties of the non-custodial parent is often a feature not far from the surface in the adoption application. This decision was affirmed on appeal under the name *Re Children of Alexandra Edith Carter*[52]. Although the trial judge's decision was affirmed, the majority seemed in the main to base their decision on the ground that a trial judge's decision should not be set aside unless he had applied wrong principles. Nevertheless the basis of the applicant's case seemed to be that adoption was necessary for the step-mother's feelings so that she need no longer fear that she was a mere surrogate mother[53]. However, in a powerful dissenting judgment, Coffin J.A. stressed the difference between custody and adoption cases, and said that the applicants had not satisfied him that the evidence justified depriving the children of the love and affection of their natural mother. Coffin J.A. was clearly not as willing as the majority of the court to accept *ex gratia* rights of access being extended to the natural mother by the applicants.

More recent cases have stressed that step-parent adoptions require special attention. In *Re Adoption Nos. 22025 to 22028*[54] Kerans D.J. indicated that the power to dispense with the need for parental consent should be used with caution:

". . . the court should not supplant its judgment that adoption is in the best interests of the child for the judgment of the objecting parent unless first it is satisfied that the parental view is utterly unworthy of consideration because the parent is guilty of bad faith, is not fit to be a parent or has discharged his parental duty in such a grossly inadequate way that it may be said that he has, in effect, abandoned the child.

. . . [G]reat care must be taken in applying this test when there has been a divorce and remarriage by the parent with custody. The law has not come to the point where adoption by the new spouse of the parent with custody is an automatic thing. Merely to have been required to yield up custody should not deprive the parent of his ultimate rights, which include the right to have custody regularly reviewed.

And, in weighing the circumstances, the court should be aware that a parent who has shed a spouse as unsatisfactory naturally is inclined to the view that the spouse is also an unsatisfactory parent and that the new spouse would be a better parent.

Also, while I am aware that it is no bar to jurisdiction, the existence of an access order must give the court some pause in adoption procedures. It is inconceivable, having regard to the test to be applied, that access would be granted in circumstances where the court ought to dispense with consent to adoption. It follows that the adoption court must be shown that the circumstances have so changed since the access order that it would not be sustained..."[55]

Thus step-parent adoptions have been refused in a number of cases[56], either directly or by a refusal to dispense with parental consent. The mere fact that a mother is prevented by illness from being able to care for her children (now or in the future) is not a sufficient reason to allow their father and his new wife to adopt the children.[57] Perhaps the case which involves the fullest discussion of the problem is *Re Munro*[58] in which a mother discouraged her former husband from visiting his children, and then applied to adopt the children with her new husband despite her former husband's objections. The judge declined to make the order sought. In doing so he relied heavily on the case of *Re Liffiton and Campbell*[59] which stated that in a case of this kind (adoption application by parent and step-parent after divorce and remarriage) "an order should not be made except for the most serious reasons". The court concluded that "no serious reasons for the adoption of (the boys) have been established. If this application is refused, custody will remain as it is. Nothing will change. If (the step-father) is sincere for the future material welfare of the boys, he need only make a will to ensure their sharing in his estate.... Until proved otherwise, I believe that child has a right to the knowledge of the existence of its natural parents, to a normal association with those parents...."

Moreover as will be seen later[60] a change of the child's name may be achieved in other ways and the Adoption Acts should not be used for this purpose.[61]

The fact that it is probably not open to a Canadian court in the Common Law provinces to impose conditions after adoption allowing a natural parent access to his children, even after their adoption by the other natural parent and their new spouse, has also been used to support a decision that adoption in these circumstances would be inappropriate.

However, although the Canadian courts have frequently declined to make adoption orders in favour of step-parents they have not yet, under the prevailing state of the law, been able to offer the step-parent the benefit of any suitable alternative order to regulate the step-parent's position towards his step-child. This is possible since the "legal custody" provisions of the English Children Act, 1975. Perhaps the nearest that the Canadian law has come to considering this problem was the suggestion by the Ontario Law

Reform Commission[62] that the effect of an adoption order should be modified so that the relationship between the natural parent and the child was not severed but permitted the step-parent/new spouse to stand in an adoptive relationship to the child.[63] However the Ontario Law Reform Commission's Report seems more concerned with the embarrassment of the custodian parent at having to join in the adoption rather than the extinction of the rights of the non-custodial parent. Admittedly, the natural parent's consent to adoption will not lightly be dispensed with by the court[64], but the desirability of step-parent adoption needs to be carefully considered even in the cases where the natural parent appears to consent to the adoption, *e.g.* but where grandparents and other relations disapprove it; it may be that it is the apparently "open and shut" cases that need most scrutiny.[65] Indeed, the latest work on adoption which reveals the deep concern of adopted children to know their origins, calls in question much of the law surrounding adoption which up till now has been based on extinguishment of parent rights in circumstances of secrecy.[66]

THE LEGAL EFFECT OF AN ENGLISH CUSTODY OR CUSTODIANSHIP ORDER

The effect of the order is only negatively stated in the British Children Act, 1975, though it seems to have strong similarities to the effect of an ordinary custody order. Section 86 of the Children Act, 1975 provides:

"In this Act, unless the context otherwise requires, 'legal custody' means, as respects a child, so much of the parental rights and duties as relate to the person of the child (including the place and manner in which his time is spent); but a person shall not by virtue of having legal custody of a child be entitled to effect or arrange for his emigration from the United Kingdom unless he is a parent or guardian of the child."

Thus, the Children Act seems to distinguish between custody and guardianship. The following rights appear to pass to the custodian: the choice of education, religious up-bringing, consent to medical operations on the child, consent to marriage,[67] but he acquires no rights over the child's property[68] and no right to consent to the child's adoption[69] nor the right to change the child's name.

It is not clear, in view of the wording of section 86, what the effect of a custodianship order would be on a care order made under the Children and Young Persons Act, 1969 or on a resolution assuming parental rights under section 2 of the Children Act, 1948 (the provisions governing neglected children or children at risk). Presumably these would be suspended, although it is difficult to think of a case in which a court would consider making a custodianship order whilst these other orders were operative and of benefit to the child.[70] Where there was already in existence a supervision order in respect of the child (made under other legislation) the court could continue the supervision under its power to make supervision orders in custodianship cases.[71]

Although an adoption order might have the effect of changing a child's domicile or nationality, a custodianship order will not. Most of the rights not falling on a custodian would fall to the legal guardian of a child which may explain the use of the word "custodianship" in the Children Act, 1975 rather than "guardianship" as proposed by the Stockdale Committee. Strangely, although a British guardian or an alien child may at the discretion of the Secretary of State, apply for the registration of the child as a British citizen[72], it is uncertain whether the legal guardian or a child (unless one of the natural parents of the child) has power to alter his ward's domicile.[73]

Under the Children Act, 1975 a child acquires no rights of succession against his custodian comparable with the rights of an adopted child; though he might acquire rights under the Inheritance (Provision for Family and Dependants) Act, 1975 to apply to a court to have reasonable financial provision made for him from his custodian's estate if he had been treated as a child of the custodian's marriage or if he was being wholly or partly maintained by the custodian at the time of the custodian's death.

Under the Guardianship Act, 1973 the parents of a legitimate child exercise their rights *equally* and *separately*. Where other people, *e.g.* custodians, share parental rights these are shared *jointly* under section 85(3) of the Children Act, 1975, though to make life easier, any one person vested with parental rights under a custodianship order can exercise them without approval of the other person having parental rights, if they have not signified their disapproval. Thus in an extreme case, consent to medical treatment could be given by one custodian without the need to consult the other. But so far as dealings with a child's property are concerned, which a guardian (but not a custodian) has power to deal with, it is doubtful if section 85(3) applies. Where one person having parental rights or duties dies, then these rights vest in the survivor or survivors jointly[74]. When the last person having parental rights and duties dies the rights lapse, though without prejudice to their acquisition by other persons under other provisions.[75]

At the time of making the custodianship order the court may also make orders relating to access and maintenance of the children.[76]

STEP-PARENTS' ASPIRATIONS

Unfortunately if any change is made in the law on step-parent adoptions which, in the past, have gone through as run-of-the-mill matters, lawyers, and social workers may have to face the problem of insecurity and dashed expectations among both adults and children. More than ever there is a case for early counselling of people about alternatives to step-parent adoption. There is perhaps a case for discussing the future of the children at the time of divorce before the new step-father has come on the scene or before hopes of adoption have arisen. It remains a fact that we have still not, as a society, fully come to terms with divorce and all that it entails.

SOCIAL WORKERS' ATTITUDES

At present in England, reports to the court are compulsory in all adoption cases and the *guardian ad litem* (the social worker who usually prepares the report) should be there to protect the interest of the child. Regrettably, as was said in *Re H.*:

"reports in too many intra family adoption cases seem to take the success of the application for granted and merely skim the surface of facts and outward appearances without any probing of underlying factors which abound in some of these adoptions and may call for remedial measures other than adoption . . ."[77]

It may even be that some social workers have read *Beyond the Best Interests of the Child*[78] and accepted the view of the authors that a complete break with the non-custodial parent is in the best interest of the child (as it sometimes is). It is arguable that the authors of that book were more concerned with the creation of a stable home for the child (particularly the younger child), than in cutting one of his parents out of the child's life. Moreover, the authors may have been concerned to overstate their case about access in an attempt to make the courts consider the problem more fully, rather than making an order for agreed access in circumstances in which it seems unlikely that agreed access will work satisfactorily.

Alternatively, inexperienced social workers may fail to appreciate that by adoption the natural father will be cut out of the child's life, and they may mislead the father into giving consent on the basis that continued access to the child will be possible.[79]

Social investigation reports are required in several Canadian jurisdictions, but the quality of the report depends on the capability of the agency involved and the presentation of a written report to the court is mandatory in only a few jurisdictions.[80]

THE SIGNIFICANCE OF THE CHANGE OF FAMILY NAME

The desire for step-parent adoptions may emanate from the step-parent himself; if he has to maintain the child and has possibly to make reasonable provision for the child after his death under the legislation already discussed, he may want to feel that this step-child is his child; or both the natural parent and the step-parent may feel the need to make the child *our* child in a way that they feel custody or guardianship does not. Such feelings may crystallize over the issue of the child's surname which may assume an importance that strangers to the adoption process fail to appreciate. The name may symbolize the applicants' perception of their new roles and the relationships between themselves and the child.

Although the Houghton/Stockdale Committee[81] believed that the question of change of name in English law was quite simple, they had not appreciated the full problem. Since *Re T.*[82] it has been clear that the mother who has been granted custody of a legitimate child normally has no power to change his surname by deed poll to that of her new husband without getting the consent of the child's father. *Y. v. Y.*[83] qualified that rule by suggesting that if a child had become known by his *new* name for a considerable number of years, then (despite the legitimate child's father's protestation) a court might hold that it was not in the best interest of the child to make him revert to his former name. These cases received confirmation by S.I. 2168 of 1974 which amended Matrimonial Causes Rule 92 and forbids a spouse who obtains custody of a child in a matrimonial cause from changing the name of the child without the consent of the other parent or leave from the court. Since early in 1975, slips reminding parents of this have generally been appended to or included in custody orders.

The situation is far from easy if the father objects and will not consent to a change of name by deed poll, or asks within a short time of an informal change of name (that on the school register is the most insidious) that reversion to the former name take place. The use of two names (a formal and an informal one) used, for example, at school is hardly to be encouraged. It may cause confusion in the child despite the fact that the use of such a device is often justified to spare a child having to explain at school why he and the parent with whom he lives have different names. Moreover, the change of name may be associated with a failure on the part of the parent to face up to the failure of marriage and a failure to explain to the child that he still has another caring parent even though he may be living away from home. When an application is made to a court requesting a change of a legitimate child's name it may not be easy to satisfy the court that such a change of name is in the child's interest. If the reason for making adoption by step-parents more difficult is the desire not to cut a child off from an important part of its life (its relationship with its father), equally the court may feel reluctant to deprive a child of the surname that symbolizes that relationship.[84] In the case of *Re D.*,[85] a case decided prior to the Children Act, 1975 but obviously influenced by the Stockdale/

Houghton Committee's Report, Sir George Baker, in refusing to dispense with the need for a father to consent to the adoption of his children, said that he was at a loss to see how "the adoption orders would be for the welfare of the girls when the expressed object was to give them the mother's new surname. All too often that course was taken by the mother to disguise from her new neighbours that she had been involved in a failed marriage".

In the Canadian provinces the rules as to change of name are usually to be found in Change of Name Acts. That for Ontario[86] will serve as a typical example. It thus appears that commonly four consents are necessary, that of both the natural parents, the child if he is over 14[87] and that of the new husband. There is power for the court to dispense with parental consent.[88] One wonders how commonly the need for the father's consent is dispensed with on the basis that the other parent does not contribute to the support of the children. In many cases the breakdown of marriage produces friction which is only dissipated over a period of time.[89] Premature applications for change of name (particularly the successful ones) may inhibit the restoration of normal relations between the children and their non-custodial father.

The requirements of the Act need to be complied with strictly. In *Jennings v. Cosgrove*[90] an order which was made by reference to section 10(3) of the Ontario Act dispensing with notice to the natural father (even though he could have been found) was set aside. Nor could this have been justified by reference to another head, of section 19(3), that the father does not contribute to the support of... the children on whose behalf the application was made, because though the father was in arrears with maintenance, he was making payments and thus supporting the children albeit inadequately.

The present position in Quebec, and as it will be when the Civil Code Revision Office's recommendations are implemented,[91] is broadly similar. As the commentary to the proposed "article 15" points out, if a mother of children, all bearing their father's surname, should petition for a change in her own family surname this change would have no effect on her children. (A married woman in Quebec retains her maiden name in exercising her legal rights [*e.g.* when making a contract or doing a judicial act][92] though for social purposes she may use her husband's name.) In fact the cases in which a change of a child's family name has been sought in Quebec have, in the main, involved immigrants whose original name gave rise to problems of pronunciation.

CONCLUSION

The problem of step-parent adoptions needs much more careful thinking out than has previously been the case, including thinking about the alternatives to adoption. Nevertheless, perhaps some further consideration needs to be given to the needs of step-parents. If the courts or the legislature prevent them being able to adopt their step-children, they may feel unhappy at being fobbed off with some legal appellation which is clearly less than adoption. The English approach of trying to divert step-parents from adopting and to accept the lesser rights of custody or custodianship may well be thwarted; it is not clear whether step-parents will wish to proceed with custody proceedings if the court refuses to allow adoption proceedings; rights of custody are clearly less than rights of adoption. Step-children may try to manipulate a situation, to portray their present natural parent as "100% right" and their step-parent as "100% wrong". Alternatively the child may retain an idealized picture of the absent natural parent and hope that the natural parents may become reconciled.

What is desirable is that the child should be able to enjoy the benefits of both the absent natural parent's affection and that of the step-parent with whom he lives. Neither should be artificially cut out of the child's life by the law until all reasonable efforts have been made to enable the adult parties and the child to come to terms with the reality of the situation. Only where it is impossible should the absent parent be completely cut out of the child's life. Counselling of more couples at the time of divorce about the problems which they face, or may face in the future, remains a desirable goal. Unfortunately, not all those who could be helped by such counselling are ready to seek it (those who need it most may be amongst the most reluctant) and even if more people sought help, it is uncertain whether the existing resources are now available.

---

1   For a fuller account of the current English adoption law see Seago and Bissett-Johnson, *Cases and Materials on Family Law*, (1976) Ch. 10.

2   Rowe and Lambert, *Children Who Wait*, (1975).

3   In England, of 9,254 legitimate children who were jointly adopted in 1973, 8,101 were adopted by couples of one of whom was their parent. Most of these were step-parent adoptions.

4   C.C.R.O. Report on the Family, Part I (1974) p.422. In Ontario in 1975 there were 2,400 adoptions by step-parents which shows indirectly the impact of the divorce and remarriage in the adoption field.

5   The effects of incomplete or 'adoption simple' under French law are dealt with in articles 363 and 364 of the French Civil Code. Basically the ties with the natural parents are retained and the child's original family name will not be replaced unless the court orders that this is to be done. See further Groffier, "Principaux problèmes de l'adoption au Canada, en France et en Belgique" (1974) Revue International de Droit Comparé, 263.

6   See further Hughes, chapter on Adoption in *Canadian Studies on Family Law* (1972) 167 *et seq.* There is, however, a difference between those provinces which use a 'divesting and imposing' approach and those which treat the adopted child as if he had been born to the adoptive parents in lawful wedlock.

7   See s. 8(7) of the English Children Act, 1975, re-enacting s. 7(3) of the Adoption Act, 1958. In Canada the position seems to be that there is now probably no express power to impose such conditions. See further Hughes in *Canadian Studies on Family Law* 160. In fact in two recent cases *Re Adoption No. H 5877* (1975) 21 R.F.L. 306 (Man. C.A.) and *Re Baker* (1975) 20 R.F.L. 392 (Sask.) the courts have concluded that in view of the finality of adoption orders and the fact that ties with natural parents are extinguished, no power exists to impose conditions on an adoption order allowing the natural parent continued access to the child. In Quebec the proposed new article 163 of the Civil Code (C.C.R.O. Report Part I 1974) would permit a court, where a child is adopted by the consort of his father or mother, to decide that a child may retain rights of succession in his original family and that they be permitted to retain rights of visitation.

8   See *Re Proposed Adoption of "J"* (printed as Appendix C to Adoption — The Way Ahead: The (British) Association of Child Care Officers monograph No. 3. The judgment is also set out in Hambly and Turner *Cases and Materials on Australian Family Law* (1971) 633.

9   Departmental Committee on the Adoption of Children, Cmnd. 5107 (1972).

10 As one step-father put it "as a step-father I have little or no authority . . . I want to be in all situations a parent rather than a guardian". This extract is taken from a judgment of Judge Grant set out in "Child Adoption", (the Journal of the Association of British Adoption and Fostering Agencies) (1975) 15. Much the same point was made in the magazine "Step-parents Forum", Issue 1 (April — May 1975) 1.

"Step-parents, too, want to feel loved and important. If their feelings are repeatedly ignored or discounted, they may easily feel quite unloved, and react with resentment and anger.

As our impromptu step-mother summed it up. 'I often feel that my husband makes the major decisions of our life with his ex-wife, and I get to just trail along, liking it or lumping it.'

Step-fathers, too, can be made to feel unimportant when their feelings are not accorded their due respect. 'I am frustrated', reports one step-father, 'when my wife demands her rights as final authority regarding my step-daughter.' "

At the same time one should not expect that the child whom the step-parent seeks to adopt will necessarily have the same perception of adoption as the step-parent. For the child the act of adoption might be seen as an attempt to displace the absent parent. The absent parent, unless he can accept the step-parent in a parenting role, may see it in a similar way.

11 Published by André Deutsch, London 1975.

12 Is there a difference between society's attitude to step-fathers and step-mothers? Consider this extract from the preview issue of Stepparents Forum (May 1975) 3: —

"STEP-MOTHERS are historically cast as 'wicked', *that woman* who broke up the marriage, and so on.

The step-father? That wonderful man who *took on another man's children*, the saviour of some poor female.

Step-fathers are social 'heroes'. Step-mothers . . .?

Think about it!

13 The appointment by a parent in a deed or will of a guardian who can act after the parent's death in the parent's place.

14 See Step-parents Forum (Jan/Feb 1977) p. 3 where a step-father explains that his decision to adopt his wife's children by a prior marriage was prompted by a fear that there was a risk that their children (2 of his wife's by a prior marriage and 2 of their own) who had grown up together for many years might be split up and that a ferocious and expensive custody suit involving the non-custodial parent might ensue.

15 S. 4 of the Guardianship of Minors Act would enable a parent to appoint the step-parent testamentary guardian so that he or she would have joint rights with the surviving parent. In the event of dispute over the exercise of the rights the matter may be taken before the courts. See further Cretney, *Principles of Family Law*, (2nd ed., 1976) 622.

16   Compare *Re Doyle* [1943] O.W.N. 119, [1943] 2 D.L.R. 315 with *Re MacPherson* [1945] O.W.N. 533.

17   Report on Family Law (1973) Part III, Children, 117.

18   Domestic Relations Act, R.S.A. 1970, s. 43.

19   See Matrimonial Causes Act, 1973, ss. 25(3) and 52(1); Matrimonial Proceedings (Magistrates' Court) Act, 1960, ss. 2(5) and 16.

20   *E.g.,* Divorce Act, R.S.C. 1970, D. 8-2(a). But note that in *L.H. v. L.H.H.* [1971] 4 W.W.R. 262, 3 R.F.L. 353, 20 D.L.R. (3d) 190 the British Columbia Court of Appeal held that there had to be more than acts of a decent step-father involved, at least where the natural father continued to exercise parental rights. The step-father had stepped in to provide financial support for his step-child after the natural father became temporarily unable, through financial difficulty, to meet his obligations under a court order to maintain his child. Compare this case with *Proctor v. Proctor* (1975) 22 R.F.L. 217, 57 D.L.R. (3d) 766 (Man.) in which Deniset J. ordered a man whose marriage began to disintegrate shortly after the honeymoon, to support his step-child. When the marriage occurred he had intended to stand *in loco parentis* to the child. And in contrast to *L.H. v. L.H.H.* the natural father was not (so to speak) in the picture.

21   The legislation in most Provinces and under the Federal Divorce Act usually empowers the court to make such orders as it thinks fit relating to the custody, care and upbringing of a child. Although Wright J. in *Robson v. Robson* [1969] 2 O.R. 857, 7 D.L.R. (3d) 289 questioned whether the wording of s.1 of the Ontario Infants Act (now R.S.O. 1970, c. 222) allowed the making of orders in favour of third parties, he achieved his desired end (that of granting custody to the child's paternal grandmother) by recourse to the rules of equity. In fact though s. 1 of the Ontario Infants Act envisages proceedings only being instituted by the parents of the child (or its next friend) once the case is before the court. It can make such order as it thinks fit including orders in favour of a third party such as a step-parent acting jointly with a natural parent. See also *Re R.* [1974] 1 All E.R. 1033 and Robinson in *Canadian Studies on Family Law* Ch. 8, 607. The fact remains that there is some doubt about the standing of third parties such as step-parents to launch custody proceedings. The power (if it exists) must be a common law power. One of the few cases recognising the power is *Re McMaster v. Smith* [1972] 1 O.R. 416, 6 R.F.L. 143, 23 D.L.R. (3d) 264. See also Ontario Law Reform Commission Report on Children at 108 *et seq.* Once a child is in the care or custody of a third person the full protection of the neglect provisions operate to safeguard the child *e.g.* s.40 of the Ontario Child Welfare Act, R.S.O. 1970, c.64.

22   See Ontario Bill 60 (Succession Law Reform Act, 1977), s.64.

A similar definition of child in s. 1(1) (a) is to be applied in proceedings under The Ontario Compensation for Victims of Crime Act, 1971. See clause 82. As originally drafted in Bill 85 express reference was made to step-children within the statutory definition of child. However the new definition will include most step-children who have lived for any appreciable period with their step-parent. Step-children are expressly included within the definition of children under s.1 of the Ontario Fatal Accidents Act, R.S.O. 1970, c. 164.

23   Inheritance (Provisions for Family & Dependants) Act, 1975. Under s. 1 of the Act amongst those who can apply to a court for reasonable provision to be made from the deceased's estate are:

"(d) any person (not being a child of the deceased) who, in case of any marriage to which the deceased was at any time a party, was treated by the deceased as a child of the family in relation to that marriage."

The mere fact that such a child is over 18 and of full age does not automatically disqualify an application to the court by the child, though it is a relevant factor for the court's consideration. The English Act also gives a right of application to mistresses (or others) who immediately before the deceased's death were being wholly or partially maintained by him.

24 In Ontario The Family Law Reform Act, 1978 (Bill 59), s. 1(a) provides that:
". . . a child born within or outside marriage, subject to sections 83 and 85 of *The Child Welfare Act* which relates to the effect of adoption), and includes a person whom the parent has a settled intention to treat as a child of his or her family, but does not include a child placed in a foster home for consideration by a person having lawful custody;"
An earlier draft specifically mentioned step-children but there is no doubt that most step-children are covered by the definition in cl. 1(a) (at least where they live with the step-parent for any appreciable period).

25 See note 9.

26 This rule is reinforced by s. 11(3) and (4) governing applications to adopt by single persons. S. 11(3) provides:
"An adoption order shall not be made on the application of the mother or father of the child alone unless the court is satisfied that —
(a) the other natural parent is dead or cannot be found, or
(b) there is some other reason justifying the exclusion of the other natural parent, and where such an order is made the reason justifying the exclusion of the other natural parent shall be recorded by the court."
This will almost certainly reduce the number of applications by mothers to adopt their illegitimate children. S. 11(4) is in terms similar to s. 10(3) above and requires a court to dismiss an application by a step-parent where the matter could be better dealt with by a custody order under s. 42 of the Matrimonial Causes Act, 1973.

27 [1973] Fam. 209, [1973] 3 All E.R. 1001. The facts of this case were that the father left the mother and children in 1969. The mother had to live on social security because the father refused to pay maintenance, though he did send Christmas presents for the children. In 1970 he saw the children 8 or 10 times at irregular intervals, meeting them outside school or at the flat where they lived. On two occasions he failed to collect the children as arranged. In April 1970 the mother filed a divorce petition alleging that the father had committed adultery; she also asked for maintenance and custody of the children. The husband did not contest the divorce and custody was granted to the mother (though nothing was said about access). The application for maintenance was delayed by the father's failure to provide an affidavit of means. The last time the father saw the children was on the day of the divorce hearing in September 1970 when he took them out.
The mother remarried in September 1971, changed the children's names to that of their step-father's and moved from London to Dover. The father traced the children and tried to see them late one night after he had been drinking, but the mother refused him access. The mother and step-father then tried jointly to adopt the children but the natural father opposed this. It was alleged that the natural father's failure to provide for the children from September 1969 amounted to a "persistent failure to discharge the obligations of a parent" and his consent could therefore be dispensed with. The justices made the adoption order, but the father successfully appealed to the Divisional Court.

28 See 124 N.L.J. 566. In England if the adoption order is not made the children cannot usually take their step-father's name. Nor did such children have any rights of intestate succession against their step-father nor any claim under the Inheritance (Family Provision) Act, 1938 though the Inheritance (Provision for Family and Dependants) Act, 1975 has recently changed the position.

29 (1974) 5 Fam. Law 88 (C.A.).

30 *Supra*, note 27.

31 The Times Newspaper, Nov. 25, 1974. In this case the parents of the two girls married in 1960 when the wife became pregnant with the eldest daughter. The couple had cohabited for some time previously. The husband was an art student dependent on his grant holiday work and gifts from his parents. The wife, as she must have been aware from before the marriage, was to be the mainstay of the home; the father spent seven years studying art. In 1965, while on a scholarship in France he met a French girl with whom he committed adultery. After a divorce in 1967 he married the French girl. It was left to his parents to pay off the family's accumulated debts. The wife remarried, but the husband kept in touch with his children by visiting the children from time to time at

weekends. In 1968 the husband was ordered to pay 5 pounds per week for the children. Shortly after this he went to Canada where he earned 4,000 pounds per annum as a teacher. He paid the maintenance regularly and in 1969 the girls visited him for six weeks in Canada. In 1970 his second wife left him and he lost his teaching post. He ceased to send maintenance, wrote only infrequently and his Christmas and birthday presents to the girls were delayed. Eventually he came to be supported by a young Canadian lady. The children retained strong links with their paternal grandparents and often stayed with them during the holidays. In one of these visits they met their father who had come to England with the Canadian lady. However, the mother and her new husband then applied to adopt the children and at that stage the mother stopped the children from seeing their father. After his return from Canada the children's father had paid maintenance, at first sporadically but from September 1973 he had regularly paid 21 pounds per month. At the time of the adoption proceedings he was unemployed and in receipt of social security. Although the magistrates dispensed with his consent on the ground that he had failed without reasonable cause to discharge the obligations of a parent, the Divisional Court reversed the finding. Although the natural father had behaved irresponsibly as a husband and a father he was nonetheless a loving father who had visited the children, and communicated with them, albeit fitfully. When in employment he had paid the maintenance due under the court order. In these circumstances it could not be proved that the instability of the father's life was such that no advantage accrued to the children from their contact with their paternal grandparents, a contact that was wholly beneficial. The main effect of the refusal to allow the adoption would be to preserve the access of the father and grandparents. The children, the court pointed out would still live with their mother and step-father and family unity would not be upset. The children had known their father for most of their lives and got on well with him. The allegation that the father was unreasonably withholding consent also failed.

32 [1975] No. 3, p. 13. The report involves a case heard before Mr. Justice Latey in the Family Division of the High Court on 25 February 1975. The judge said that a 'two-father' situation could be beneficial to children where a mother remarried after divorce. It was only in a minority of cases where it was to the children's advantage for one parent to adopt them. Merseyside justices had been wrong to make an adoption order in favour of a mother who, with her new husband, planned to take her two daughters, aged six and three, to New Zealand. The father, the mother's previous husband, won his appeal and the adoption order was cancelled.

Mr. Justice Latey said that with the soaring divorce rates it was a case of general importance. It was understandable that the new family felt more secure if the real father were excluded, in terms of the mother's wounded feelings, but did it best serve the children to give effect to those feelings? It has been wisely said 'Marriage can be dissolved but not parenthood'. The magistrates had found that the father had been unreasonable in withholding his consent to adoption. He too had remarried after the divorce. The judge said that if the magistrates were right there were many cases in which a parent would be for ever excluded from his or her children's lives for no other reason than that a new marriage had provided a step-parent and it was wished to exclude him. This was not the law, and it was difficult to believe it ever would be. The absence of an adoption order did not stop the mother and her new husband from emigrating to New Zealand. The father might not object, and it would be for the court to decide if it was in the best interest of the children.

This case seems to emphasize the value to a child as he matures of continuing close relationships with adults other than their parents — provided that there is no element of competition for roles between the adults concerned.

33 In this case named Re D. [1976] 2 All E.R. 342 a mother and her new husband applied jointly to adopt the mother's 8 year old son by her first marriage. When the boy's father would not consent to the adoption it was sought to dispense with the need for his consent. The father admitted living in a homosexual relationship with an 18 year old youth and that he had lived with other men. The County Court judge held that the father was unreasonably withholding his consent because a reasonable father would have said 'I must protect my boy, even if it means parting with him forever, so that he can be free from this danger'. The Court of Appeal, however, suggested that the judge had substituted his

personal views for those of the reasonable parent. The father loved his son, wanted to go on seeing him, was willing to support him and had agreed to ensure that the child was not subjected to homosexual advances — access would take place at the paternal grandparents home. Any access problems could be brought back to court. The position might have been different if the only alternative to adoption had been for the child to live with his father. Finally the House of Lords [1977] 1 All E.R. 145 restored the County Court Judge's decision holding that although homosexuality between consenting adults over 21 years was no longer an offence, the courts should not relax in any degree the vigilance and severity with which they should regard the risk to children at critical ages being exposed to or introduced to ways of life which might lead to severance from normal society, to psychological stresses and unhappiness and possibly, even to physical experiences which might scar them for life. A reasonable parent would want to protect his boy from those dangers even if it means parting from him forever. The trial judge had been right to dispense with the father's consent and make the adoption order. For a powerful criticism of this case see 127 N.L.J. 226 and 253.

34 *In Re W (a minor)* The Times Newspaper, Nov. 26, 1976, the Divisional Court of the Family Division refused to dispense with the father's consent in the following circumstances. In 1973 the father had been sentenced to eight years imprisonment for armed robbery. Next year the mother obtained a divorce and was granted custody of their son who was at the time of the present proceedings aged 9½. After the father was first imprisoned, the mother encouraged the son to correspond with the father but by April 1974 correspondence ceased. In October 1975, the mother remarried and she and her new husband jointly applied to adopt the child. Although the father initially consented, he withdrew his consent on learning that adoption would sever his ties with his son. The Divisional Court indicated that including the step-father in the post divorce custody arrangements was preferable to the draconian guillotine of an adoption order.

35 The Child Welfare Act, R.S.M. 1970, c. C-80, s. 86(1)(c).

36 (1967) 66 D.L.R. (2d) 82, 62 W.W.R. 251 (Man. C.A.).

37 (1969) 71 W.W.R. 283, 8 D.L.R. (3d) 575 (Man.).

38 *Ibid.* p. 580.

39 Child Welfare Act, R.S.M. 1970, c. C-80, s. 86(4)(b) Some other provincial legislation is in similar terms. See for instance the Ontario Child Welfare Act, R.S.O. 1970, c. 64, s.73(5).

40 (1970) 75 W.W.R. 193, 3 R.F.L. 4, 15 D.L.R (3d) 102 (Man. C.A.).

41 (1962) 40 W.W.R. 521, 36 D.L.R. (2d) 328 (B.C.C.A.). See also *Ex parte Lawson* [1960] O.W.N. 267 where it was not surprising that the consent of a father who had not seen his children for 12 years was dispensed with. In the Alberta case of *Re Snider* (1966) 56 W.W.R. 116, the unmarried mother of a child who had previously agreed to him being adopted, capriciously withdrew her consent to adoption after the father of the child, who was proposing to adopt him jointly, failed to send her a picture of the child. Paterson D.C.J. felt that this capricious withdrawal of consent involved an attempt by the mother to use the child, whom she had hardly seen and did not want, as a weapon. The Judge, therefore, dispensed with the consent without requiring proof of any parental misconduct. This drew some barbed criticism, see further Rabin, "Court Order Dispensing with Consent of Natural Parent in Adoption Proceedings" (1968) 6 Alta. L. Rev. 296.

"If . . . the principle of law for which this case stands is that the mere finding of a capricious withholding of consent once freely given, without regard to the conduct and character of the parent, is sufficient grounds for dispensing with such consent, then it would appear that, though the case is consistent with the intent of the *Child Welfare Act*, it is inconsistent with previous law in Alberta."

42 (1962) 36 D.L.R. (2d) 328 at 334.

43 (1967) 64 D.L.R. (2d) 538 (N.S.).

44 *Ibid.* at 553.

45 *Ibid.* 552.

46 *Canadian Studies in Family Law*, at 150.

47 The importance of the length and stability of the second marriage was emphasized in *Smith v. Harvey* (1974) 19 R.F.L. 367 (Ont. C.A.). The Court also emphasized that

adoption by a step-parent was desirable where the link with a non-custodial natural parent had been broken and was unlikely to be re-established in the future. Where, however, a past or potential future link with the non-custodial parent was involved the court should be reluctant to dispense with the need for parental consent to adoption.

48   (1975) 23 R.F.L. 398 (N.S. Co.Ct.)
49   *Ibid.* at 400.
50   (1974) 8 N.S.R. (2d) 210.
51   R.S.N.S. 1967, c. 2.
52   (1976) 15 N.S.R. (2d) 181 (C.A.).
53   *Ibid.* 215.
54   (1972) 8 R.F.L. 240 (Alta. D.C.).
55   *Ibid.* 244.
56   *E.g. Morrison v. Perry* (1973) 11 R.F.L. 214, 38 D.L.R. (3d) 304 (Alta. C.A.) *Cour de Bien-Etre Social v. X.* [1974] C.A. 372 (Q.C.A.).
57   *Re Adoption Nos.* 60-09-032424, 62-09-032106, 54-09-017846 (No. 2) (1973) 12 R.F.L. 100 (B.C.).
58   [1973] 3 O.R. 156 at 166, 167, 11 R.F.L. 21, 36 D.L.R. (3d) 180.
59   [1972] 2 O.R. 592, 7 R.F.L. 353, 26 D.L.R. (3d) 260 (C.A.).
60   *Post.*
61   *Re Wilson* (1970) 4 R.F.L. 184 (N.S.).
62   *Re Baker* (1975) 20 R.F.L. 392 (Sask.); *Re Adoption* No. H. (1975) 21 R.F.L. 306 (Man. C.A.). A contrary and unorthodox view was expressed by Miller L.J.S.C. in *Smith v. Koch* [1976] 3 W.W.R. 346, 67 D.L.R. (3d) 303 (Alta.) where the Judge made an adoption order which he admitted had the effect of severing the natural father's rights of access. The Judge then, however, restored the father's access, not under the adoption legislation but under the Alberta Domestic Relations Act, R.S.A. 1970, c. 113, s. 46 (1). In doing so he determined that the natural father remained a father within the meaning of the Domestic Relations Act notwithstanding the adoption order: *sed quaere*. See note 7 for the proposed Quebec law. For another contrary but not clearly reasoned view see *Lyttle v. Children's Aid Society of Metro. Toronto* (1976) 24 R.F.L. 134 (Ont.) esp. 136, though the authorities relied on there concerned the Infants Act rather than the adoption statute.
63   The full commentary of the Commission is as follows:
      "as the law now stands, a parent whose spouse is dead, or who has been divorced, and who has married again and wishes the new spouse to stand in the legal relationship of parent to the child is compelled to adopt his or her own child. The reason for this lies in Section 83(2) of the Act, which provides that where a child is adopted his relationship to his natural parents is severed. If, in the situation which we have outlined, the new spouse were to adopt the child without the natural parent joining in the application under section 72(3), the natural parent would no longer stand in any but the most tenuous legal relationship towards the child. This is clearly undesirable. On the other hand, it has been suggested to us on a number of occasions that natural parents find it inexplicable that they should be compelled to go through the formalities of adopting their own children. While we do not wish to detract in any way from the strength of the principle enunciated in section 83 that adoption should constitute a complete break between the child's natural and adoptive parents we think that where there is a question of a person who has been married adopting his or her own child, logic should give way to a recognition of human sensitivity.
      Accordingly we recommend that section 83 be modified to accommodate the situation where a natural parent who has been married wishes to have his or her new spouse stand in the full legal relationship between the natural parent and the child, but should rather permit the new spouse to stand in the adoptive relationship to the child while permitting the natural relationship of the natural parent to the child to be maintained."
      In similar vein see the Fifth Report of the British Columbia Royal Commission on Family and Children's Law, Part VII — Adoption, p. 25.

64 *E.g.,* See *Re Desmarais* [1969] 1 O.R. 700 at 704-5, 3 D.L.R. (3d) 617 (C.A.). This was,
    however, not a step-parent case and there are still suggestions in quite recent cases that
    joint step-parent and natural parent adoptions raise different issues, *e.g.* the statements
    by Dickson J.A. in *Sobering v. Sergeant* (1970) 75 W.W.R. 430, 15 D.L.R. (3d) 112, 6
    R.F.L. 51 at 56 (Man. C.A.) where he distinguished cases such as *Hepton v. Maat* [1957]
    S.C.R. 606, 10 D.L.R. (2d) 1, and *Re Desmarais* as involving contests between natural
    parents and strangers and continued: "[i]n such circumstances it would seem only proper
    that the right of a natural parent should not be terminated except for the most
    compelling reasons." As the instant case involved an adoption order in favour of a
    natural parent who had sole custody and the only effect of the order was "to terminate
    visitation rights, infrequently exercised, of the other natural parent", parental consent to
    the adoption was dispensed with. However, *Sobering v. Sergeant* may depend very
    much on its own facts, not the least important of which was that while the mother's
    objections to the adoption were regarded as not entirely prompted by nuisance-making
    motives, neither were they characterized as being purely maternal.

65 In *Re Adoption Nos. 63-09-024371, 68-09-012377, 65-09-011906* (1975) 22 R.F.L. 307
    (B.C.) it was suggested that step-parent adoptions required more scrutinizing by the
    courts than stranger adoptions.

66 See for example Triseliotis, *In Search of Origins* (1973). This no doubt influenced s. 26 of
    the English Children Act, 1975 which will give adopted children the right to access to the
    information on their original birth certificate. See further Seago and Bissett-Johnson *op.
    cit*, note 1, 475 and Bissett-Johnson, 140 Justice of the Peace, 290. Some more limited
    proposals have been made in British Columbia, see Part VII of the Draft Children
    Act 1976 produced by the British Columbia Law Reform Commission as a supplement
    to the Fifth Report of the Family and Children's Law Commission. Although the
    Commission recommended that a written summary of non-identifying background
    information about the natural parents be given to adoptive parents at the time of
    adoption, adopted persons would only have access to identifying information pursuant
    to a Supreme Court Order.

67 See the Marriage Act, 1949. Children Act, 1975, Sched. 2, para. 7, Sched. 3.

68 *Cf.* Guardianship of Minors Act, 1971, s. 8. These rights do not relate "to the person of
    the child", within s. 86 of the 1975 Act.

69 See Children Act, 1975, s. 12 (1)(b).

70 Should not the prior orders be discharged first?

71 Children Act, 1975, s. 34(4).

72 British Nationality Act, 1948, s. 7(1).

73 The Domicile and Matrimonial Proceedings Act, 1973, s. 4, makes a child under 16
    dependent on his mother's domicile during the lifetime of his father, if the child is living
    with the mother and has no home with the father. The Act and the common law do not
    appear to give a guardian power to change a child's domicile (see Dicey and Morris,
    Conflict of Laws (9th ed.), 120).

74 S. 85(4).

75 S. 85(3).

76 Children Act, s. 34. When the Children Act, 1975 is fully operative the appointment of a
    guardian *ad litem* will be discretionary. Normally reports to the court will be prepared by
    the placing agency or, in non-agency cases by a local authority social worker. The
    English Houghton/Stockdale Committee suggested (*op.cit.* p. 245) that the skills
    required in such cases to protect children were usually social work and not legal skills.

77 (1974) 5 Fam. Law 54 (D.C.).

78 Goldstein, Freud and Solnit, (1973).

79 See the following example taken from Child Adoption Issue no. 2 & 3, 1974, p. 3. In a
    case that has recently come to our notice a father in such circumstances gave his consent
    to the adoption of his two children, aged 7 and 8 years, having been given to understand
    by the guardian *ad litem,* who apparently was inexperienced, that he would continue to
    have access. He was fond of his children and before the adoption had maintained a close
    and affectionate relationship with them, as had the paternal grandparents and the rest of
    that side of the family. After the adoption, however, the mother and her husband refused

to allow any further contact, and presents and letters to the children were returned. Both the father and the paternal grandparents were and are very much disturbed about this state of affairs, and worried about the effect on the children of their apparent desertion. On general principles it seems urgent at least to remind judges and magistrates that a court should always ascertain that a consenting parent relinquishing the child in such adoption cases has been told and fully understands the normally sundering nature of legal adoption; and no adoption should, in any court, be made unless the court is satisfied that such severance is in the interests of the child concerned. The court should give the parent the opportunity of asking the court to make the adoption order subject to conditions which would assure continued right of access and thus a continuing informal relationship with the child.

80   Hughes, *op. cit.*, 156 *et seq.* See note 46.
81   Cmnd. 5107 (1972).
82   [1963] Ch. 238, [1962] 3 All E.R. 970.
83   [1973] 2 All E.R. 574. See In *Re B.*, (Law Society Gazette, April 7, 1976). The mother obtained a divorce decree nisi in November 1972 and she was given sole custody of their daughter then almost three years old. In February 1973 the mother remarried and then in May of the same year the father left for Singapore with his new wife. The father saw the child in February 1972 and there had been one recent visit in 1976. In February 1976 the mother applied for an order that she might change by deed poll her daughter's name to that of her second husband. The judge granted the order on the basis that the change would be in the best interests of the child. The father appealed and the Court of Appeal held that the interests of the child were paramount but it was important to maintain links with the father unless it would be undesirable for him to have access. The grounds on which the judge had ordered the change (which included the affidavits of two headmistresses) were not strong enough to amount to special reasons and the appeal was granted. For Canadian cases to similar effect see *Hoodekoff v. Hoodekoff* (1976) 25 R.F.L. 8 (B.C.).
84   As many children perceive themselves as being "part of their parents" and the changing or discarding of a child's name might be regarded by the child as the discarding of something that was not acceptable. Other children particularly those who have been "gently persuaded' may even resort to using the new name of the custodian parent in correspondence with the absent parent almost as a weapon of revenge.
85   See note 27.
86   R.S.O. 1970, c. 60.
87   Why was such a high age fixed? Compare this age fixed by law or practice in relation to consent to adoption which can be as low as 7 years though more commonly it is 12. See further Hughes, *op. cit.* 118. See note 46.
88   See s. 10(3) of the Ontario Act and s. 11 of the Alberta Act.
89   As in *Re D.* see note 27.
90   (1975) 25 R.F.L. 98, 32 C.P.R. (2d) 102 (Ont.).
91   See *C.C.R.O. Report on the Name and Physical Identity of Human Persons*, (1975).
92   *Op. cit.* 9.

The New English Law Of Adoption

*Peter M. Bromley**

In July 1969, a Departmental Committee was set up jointly by the Home Secretary and the Secretary of State for Scotland with very wide terms of reference to consider the law, policy and procedure relating to the adoption of children in England and Scotland and what changes were desirable. Its original chairman was Sir William Houghton; after his death in November 1971 the chair was taken by His Honour Judge Stockdale. This committee (usually known as the Houghton Committee or the Stockdale Committee) produced a working paper containing some provisional proposals as a basis for discussion in 1970 and presented its final report in October 1972.[1] Almost all its recommendations (with modifications in certain cases) were implemented by the Children Act, 1975. As will be seen later, the basic recommendation to establish a nationwide adoption service will involve considerable public expenditure and consequently is not likely to be introduced for some time; as many other recommendations depend directly or indirectly upon the implementation of this one, most of the provisions of the Act relating to adoption have not yet been brought into operation. The object of this paper is to make a critical examination of these provisions in the light of the Committee's recommendations, the existing law and practice, and the social need which they seek to fill.

Legal adoption (as distinct from *de facto* adoption) was not possible in England till 1927, when the Adoption of Children Act, 1926 came into force. (Corresponding legislation for Scotland was not passed until 1930.) From the first, certain fundamental principles have been clear:

(a) legal adoption can be effected only by a court order;

(b) only an unmarried minor[2] may be adopted;

(c) no order may be made without the consent of the child's parents or guardian unless the court dispenses with it on one of a number of specified grounds;

(d) a joint application for adoption may be made only by a married couple;

* Peter M. Bromley, M.A. (Oxon.), of the Middle Temple, Barrister-at-law, Professor of Law, University of Manchester.

(e) each applicant must satisfy certain requirements relating to age or relationship to the child;

(f) the effect of an adoption is to vest custody and all other personal rights, powers and duties relating to the child in the adoptive parents and to destroy any such rights and powers formerly vested in the natural parents or guardians;

(g) an adoption order, once made, is irrevocable. The law was considerably modified by a series of Acts passed during the 30 years or so following the 1926 Act and further principles have been laid down:

(h) adoption societies are now required to be registered;

(i) local authorities have been given extensive powers and duties, particularly to supervise arrangements for adoption, to secure the well-being of children placed for adoption, and to act as adoption agencies;

(j) it is necessary to appoint a guardian *ad litem* in every case to make an independent confidential report to the court;

(k) adopted children now generally rank as the children of their adoptive parents and of no other person for the purpose of inheritance and other claims to property.

The figures set out in Appendix I to this paper will give some indication of the number of adoptions made in England and Wales every year.

Before discussing the other changes introduced by the Children Act of 1975 it will be necessary to consider the establishment of the adoption service. Although the courts are not directly concerned with it, many changes which will affect their powers are intimately bound up with it. First, however, attention must be drawn to the general duty to promote the welfare of the child laid down in section 3 of the new Act.

DUTY TO PROMOTE THE CHILD'S WELFARE

Section 3 of the 1975 Act provides:
"In reaching any decision relating to the adoption of a child, a court or adoption agency shall have regard to all the circumstances, first consideration being given to the need to safeguard and promote the welfare of the child throughout his childhood; and shall so far as practicable ascertain the wishes and feelings of the child regarding the decision and give due consideration to them, having regard to his age and understanding."

This section (which is already in force) has been described as the keynote of the Act. It will be observed that it applies not only to any decision made by a court but also to any decision made by an adoption agency.[3] Just as the former must refuse to make an adoption order if it is of the opinion that the order will not be for the child's welfare, an agency must refuse to place a child or even to accept it for adoption in such circumstances.

Unfortunately the meaning of the phrase "first consideration being given to safeguard and promote the welfare of the child" is not entirely clear. Obviously, the most important aspect of this is the security, love and care which the child should find as a result of adoption and which must be the prime consideration in placing a child and making an order. "Welfare" also includes material benefits[4] and the removal of whatever social stigma and legal disadvantages still attach to illegitimacy.[5] The latter consideration doubtless accounts for the fact that between 1964 and 1973 on the average 78 illegitimate children were adopted each year by their mothers alone.[6] Conversely, as we shall see later, the necessity of taking account of the child's welfare may preclude the making of an order in favour of a divorced parent and her (or his) second spouse because it will sever the links between the child and the other parent. But the real problem is to determine the meaning to be attached to the expression "first consideration". It is to be contrasted with the wording of section 1 of the Guardianship of Minors Act, 1971 (re-enacting section 1 of the Guardianship of Infants Act, 1925) which provides:

"Where in any proceedings before any court. . .the custody or upbringing of a minor . . . is in question, the court, in deciding that question, shall regard the welfare of the minor as the *first and paramount consideration.* . ."

Construing the words underlined, Lord MacDermott has said:

"It seems to me that they must mean more than that the child's welfare is to be treated as the top item in a list of items relevant to the matter in question. I think they connote a process whereby, when all the relevant facts, relationships, claims and wishes of parents, risks, choices and other circumstances are taken into account and weighed, the course to be followed will be that which is most in the interests of the child's welfare as that term has now to be understood. That is the first consideration because it is of first importance and the paramount consideration because it rules upon or determines the course to be followed."[7]

By deliberately omitting the words "and paramount" Parliament must have intended that the child's welfare should be treated as the most important of all the considerations that the court has to take into account but that it should not rule upon or determine the course to be followed. This was the conclusion reached by Cumming-Bruce J. in *Re B.*[8] It seems, however, that this consideration will nevertheless be the determining one in all questions relating to adoption bar one — dispensing with parental consent, where the court's powers are specifically limited to the circumstances set out in the Act.[9] In all other matters (for example, determining whether the child should be adopted at all, or placing it with prospective applicants) the child's welfare must be the ruling consideration.

THE ADOPTION SERVICE

The history of adoption in England has followed the same pattern as the history of much social reform, such as education and fostering: the impetus and organization originally sprang from voluntary charitable bodies and has gradually become more and more the concern of central or local government. For about 30 years after the passing of the 1926 Act the placing of children for adoption (except where this was done directly by the mother or by a third party such as a doctor or minister of religion) was primarily carried out by a number of adoption societies, some national and some local, many of which were founded by persons or bodies connected with a particular religious faith or sect. It was not until 1958 that local authorities were empowered to provide an adoption service for children who were not already in their care, and not every authority has exercised this power. In 1972, there were 63 voluntary societies operating in England and Wales and 96 of the 172 local authorities acted as adoption agencies.[10]

The result is a service which is undesirably fragmented. The voluntary agencies are primarily concerned with the child and concentrate on selecting potential adopters, receiving and placing the child, ensuring that all necessary consents have been given, and providing a counselling service for adoptive parents. Other voluntary bodies are concerned with the provision of support, accommodation, counselling and after-care for unmarried mothers and other natural parents who may need these services. Many adoption societies are too small and too poor to be able to extend their work and do not even have the facilities to provide accommodation for children whom their parents wish to surrender but who cannot be placed immediately. Furthermore, if the society is small, it may be difficult or impossible for them to find suitable placements. Consequently, different agencies may be (and often are) involved, depending on whether the mother intends to have her child adopted, whether she changes her mind, whether the child has to be put into care temporarily, and so forth.

The Houghton Committee accordingly recommended that a comprehensive service should be established.

"[This] should comprise a social work service to natural parents, whether married or unmarried, seeking placement for a child (which would include channels of communication with related community resources); skills and facilities for the assessment of the parents' emotional resources, and their personal and social situation; short-term accommodation for unsupported mothers; general child care resources, including short-term placement facilities for children pending adoption placement; assessment facilities; adoption placement services; after-care for natural parents who need it; counselling for adoptive families. In addition, it should have access to a range of specialised services, such as medical services (including genetic, psychiatric and psychological assessment services, arrangements for the examination of children and adoptive applicants, and a medical adviser) and legal advisory services."[11]

The Act implements this recommendation by placing on local authorities the duty to establish and maintain a service designed to meet the needs of children who have been or may be adopted, the parents and guardians of such children, and persons who have adopted or may adopt a child. "Local authorities" for this purpose are the authorities which have a duty to provide other social services under existing legislation, that is, non-metropolitan counties, metropolitan districts and London boroughs. As a part of this service each authority is required to ensure the provision of, *inter alia,* (i) board and lodging for pregnant women, mothers or children, (ii) arrangements for assessing children and prospective adopters and for placing children for adoption, and (iii) counselling for persons with problems relating to adoption (which could include the natural parents, unsuccessful applicants and adoptive parents experiencing difficulty with adopted children). The facilities of this service have to be provided in conjunction with the authority's other relevant social services "so that help may be given in a co-ordinated manner without duplication, omission or avoidable delay".

These facilities may be provided by the authority itself or by approved adoption societies, and local authorities and approved adoption societies are to be collectively known as adoption agencies. An adoption society is defined as "a body of persons whose functions consist of or include the making of arrangements for the adoption of children".[12] At present it must register with the local authority in whose area its administrative centre is situated and registration may be refused only on certain specified grounds, for example that the body is not a charitable association or that its staff is insufficient having regard to its activities.[13] But if the service is to maintain the high standard envisaged, it is clear that adoption societies themselves will have to satisfy very rigorous conditions if they are to continue to operate. Leaving registration with local authorities in these circumstances was likely to create serious difficulties: standards might differ from one authority to another; the area in which a nation-wide society had its administrative headquarters might be a matter of chance and it would be unreasonable to expect one authority to control the activities of such a body; and it might be difficult for an authority to work smoothly with a society over whom it also had supervisory control. Consequently, the Act has adopted the recommendation of the Committee and in future societies will have to be approved by the Home Office. In considering an application for approval, regard will be had to the applicant's adoption programme (including its ability to make provision for children who are free for adoption), the number and quality of its staff, its financial resources, the organization and control of its operations and, if it has already acted as an adoption society, its record and reputation; and approval will not be given unless the Home Office is satisfied that the society is making or is likely to make an effective contribution to the Adoption Service.[14] Approval will last for only three years, when a fresh application will have to be made; in addition, approval may be withdrawn at any time if it appears that the society is not making an effective contribution to the Adoption Service.[15]

Some extremely important consequences flow from these changes. In future adoption societies will have to work with local authorities or perhaps, to be more precise, under their direction. There is little doubt that a number of small societies now in existence will have to stop operating because they will not be able to satisfy the stringent conditions which the Home Office is likely to lay down. This will release a pool of experienced case workers whose services local authorities will well be able to use. It may be difficult at first to overcome the administrative problems posed by this new arrangement and many societies may take time to adjust to their loss of autonomy and what they will doubtless regard as their new position of inferiority. Great tact may be required of Directors of Social Services to ensure that the new scheme works smoothly.

It will be some time before these provisions come into operation. Regulations have to be made; administrative machinery has to be set up; existing societies will have to apply for approval; and — the major stumbling block at the moment — cuts in public expenditure will probably leave too little money to finance the changes. As a result, many of the other changes contained in the Act will have to be postponed as well.

CONSENT TO ADOPTION

The Children Act, 1975 retains the principle that generally no adoption order may be made except with the consent of each living parent or guardian of the child. The term "parent" includes both parents of a legitimate child, the mother of an illegitimate child, and the adoptive parents of a child who has been previously adopted. The term "guardian" includes anyone so appointed by a deceased parent or by a court.

It will be seen that this definition does not include various people who may have some connection with the child which adoption will destroy. In the first place, it does not include the putative father of an illegitimate child. The reason is that, as all rights and powers with respect to such a child are by English law vested *prima facie* in the mother, he has no claims which adoption will extinguish.[16] He will obtain these rights, however, if he successfully applies for custody (which he may do under section 9 of the Guardianship of Minors Act, 1971), and accordingly his consent will be required so long as he has custody by virtue of an order made under that section.[17] In other cases existing rules of court give him a right to be heard in any adoption proceedings (but not to veto the application) if he is contributing to the child's maintenance under any order or agreement; if he is not doing so, the court *may* permit him to be heard and clearly should do so if he is showing genuine parental concern for the child. Although it has been judicially stated that a guardian *ad litem* is under no duty to seek out the putative father of an illegitimate child and discover his views,[18] some case workers apparently still consider that they should do so if he is known and accessible. In many cases, of course, the father will have no wish to have anything further to do with the child, but when he has, his position contrasts unsatisfactorily with that of the father of a legitimate child whose links with the child the courts have been at pains to strengthen rather than weaken during recent years.[19] If the parents separate, there is no *de facto* difference between those who have been married and those who have been living in a formerly stable but illicit union. Consequently, the father may try to prevent the adoption by applying for custody. When this occurs, the question is whether the court should make the adoption order or award custody to him; in order to ensure that all parties are heard and all relevant evidence is put before the court, both the application for custody and the application for adoption should be heard by the same tribunal which should not give judgment in either until it has heard both. Clearly the father's claims must rank high, but as the issue relates to custody, section 1 of the Guardianship of Minors Act, 1971 applies and the welfare of the child is to be the *first and paramount* consideration.[20]

Difficulty of a different sort occurs if the mother is married and it is claimed that the child is not her husband's. If it is clearly illegitimate, the husband's consent is obviously not required for he cannot be a parent; but there is a presumption in English law that a child born to a married woman is the legitimate child of her husband (unless they were living apart under a court order when the child was conceived), so that it may be necessary to establish the fact that he is not the father before the court can make an order. The husband will then become involved as a party or witness and a blood test of mother, husband and child may be desirable. In these circumstances it may be easier for the husband to consent to the adoption if he is convinced that he is not the father, and apparently some courts require the written consent of the mother's husband in all cases.[21]

The converse problem arises if a step-parent wishes to prevent the adoption of a child which is admittedly not his or hers — for example, if spouses separate and the wife wishes to have adopted a child of a previous marriage. This could occur if the step-parent had become sufficiently fond of the child to wish to have access or even care and possession. If other matrimonial proceedings are pending between the spouses (for example, divorce or an application for maintenance in a magistrates' court), the court can award either spouse custody and/or care and control of any minor who has been treated as a child of the family.[22] If the step-parent obtains care and control, this will prevent the child from being physically placed for adoption and so will effectively frustrate the other's plan; if on the other hand he obtains custody without care and control (so that all he has are the residual parental rights and powers such as the right to determine the child's education and to consent to a surgical operation), he does not thereby become a guardian of the child and his consent to its adoption is still not required. If he can establish that the parent is contemplating adoption for the child, the court will no doubt bear this in mind in deciding which of them is to have care and control, but this will help him little if he is unable to offer the child suitable accommodation and care. Unless he is liable to contribute to the child's maintenance by virtue of an order or agreement, he does not even have a right to be heard in the adoption proceedings although it is submitted that any court ought to permit him to be heard as an interested party. A much more powerful weapon that he has at his disposal is to apply to have the child made a ward of court. The effect of this would be to vest custody in the High Court (although obviously physical care and control would have to be left with an individual) and the court's leave would have to be obtained before an application for adoption were made.[23] The court would have to take the same matters into account in reaching its conclusion as in any other adoption proceedings, but at least this device would ensure that the step-parent was heard. The practical difficulty is that, as wardship proceedings can be taken only in the High Court, they are comparatively slow and expensive. It is, therefore, urged that the law should be changed so as to give anyone who has treated the child as a child of his family a *right* to be heard in adoption proceedings and to require the consent of anyone with custody to the making of an adoption order (unless it is dispensed with).

It should also be noted that consent is required whatever the age of the parent and that, if the mother (or father) is a minor, her (or his) own parents have no power to instigate or prevent adoption proceedings with respect to their grandchild.[24] Like the step-parent, a grandparent or any other relative wishing to stop an adoption must have the child made a ward of court.

Documentary evidence of consent may be given, but in the case of the mother the child must be at least six weeks old when the document is executed and it must be attested by a justice of the peace or a court officer. The Houghton Committee criticized the existing procedure on the ground that research showed that "the form is often signed in surroundings and in a manner inappropriate to so serious a step, for example, over the counter of a busy court office".[25] Consequently, they proposed the establishment of a new type of officer to be called a reporting officer who should be a senior social worker appointed by the court to interview the mother, witness her signature and report to the court whether he was satisfied that she had freely reached the decision to have the child adopted after considering the alternatives and implications. The Children Act provides for the appointment of reporting officers (who must be independent of any agency involved) who may also act as guardians *ad litem,* but as yet no rules have been made laying down their duties more particularly.

Conditional consent

It was formerly possible for a parent or guardian to give consent to adoption "subject to conditions with respect to the religious persuasion in which the infant is proposed to be brought up".[26] This reflects in part the respect which the law and the judges had for the parent's religious beliefs and in part the fact that many of the original adoption societies were religious charities concerned with protecting the faith practised by their members and, in most cases, by the parents of the children they placed. Unless the adopters gave an undertaking to the court (which was very rarely done), the condition was unenforceable, and many felt it was anomalous that the natural parent could exact such an undertaking when the effect of the order was to sever all legal links between him and the child. A more cogent argument against its retention was that it might act to the child's detriment (if one can disregard his religious upbringing in this context) because there might be no suitable applicants for adoption of the particular persuasion. Consequently the Houghton Committee recommended the abolition of the power to attach this conditon.[27] Many bodies (particularly Roman Catholics) were opposed to this and the provision ultimately introduced (which is now embodied in section 13 of the Children Act, 1975 and is already in force) is a compromise. It enacts:
"An adoption agency shall in placing a child for adoption have regard (so far as is practicable) to any wishes of the child's parents and guardians as to the religious upbringing of the child.'"
It will be seen that this duty is placed solely on the adoption agency in placing the child: the court is no longer concerned with the child's religious education in any way when making the order. It is also clear that the wording is sufficiently wide to include a wish that the child shall have no religious upbringing at all. A parent who is anxious that the child shall be brought up in a particular faith will in future have to rely on the services of an adoption society that places children with adopters sharing the same beliefs; whilst this will present little difficulty to, say, Anglicans and Roman Catholics, there will be no effective control at all in many other cases. Either the parent will refuse consent altogether so that the child will remain indefinitely in care or its religious education will have to be subordinated to its physical well-being.

Dispensing with consent

Consent may be dispensed with only by the court hearing the application. One or more of the following conditions must be satisfied.

(1) The parent or guardian cannot be found or is incapable of giving consent.

(2) He has persistently failed without reasonable cause to discharge the parental duties in relation to the child. This includes not only legal obligations (for example, to maintain the child) but also the natural and moral duty to show affection, care and interest.[28] The courts have laid down the principle that the failure must be culpable and "of such gravity, so complete, so convincingly proved that there can be no advantage to the child in keeping continuous contact with the natural parent who has so abrogated his duties that he for his part should be deprived of his own child against his wishes".[29]

(3) He has abandoned or neglected the child. This, it has been held, connotes conduct which would render the parent or guardian liable to be prosecuted under the Children and Young Persons Act, 1933.[30]

(4) He has persistently ill-treated the child.

(5) He has seriously ill-treated the child and the rehabilitation of the child within his household is unlikely. Thus it will be seen that the ill-treatment, if serious, does not have to be persistent. Rehabilitation may be unlikely, for example, because the parent has been deprived of custody as a result of the ill-treatment or because he is in prison or is precluded from living with his family for any other reason. This provision is new and, pending an authoritative decision of the High Court or Court of Appeal, lower courts may well take different views of the severity of the conduct necessary to constitute serious ill-treatment.

(6) He is withholding his consent unreasonably. In practice this is the commonest ground for applying for consent to be dispensed with and certainly gives the most trouble. In the leading case of Re W.[31] the House of Lords held that, unlike the previous four conditions, unreasonable withholding of consent does not imply culpability on the part of the parent or guardian concerned. The test, it was said, must be objective: would a reasonable parent, placed in the position of the particular parent in question, withhold consent? In some cases there will be no doubt that a parent would be acting unreasonably if he withheld consent, and in some others that he would not; between these extremes comes a whole range of situations where one reasonable parent might withhold consent and another might give it. In such a case the court must respect the decision of the individual and is not entitled to substitute its own views for his. All the facts must be taken into account but the reasonable parent will obviously give greatest weight to the child's welfare, and it seems that the court is entitled to dispense with consent on this ground if the parent has

disregarded some appreciable risk likely to be avoided or some substantial benefit likely to accrue if an order for adoption is made. Consequently, if refusal to make an order means that the child will have to be removed from applicants whom it has known and come to regard as substitute parents over a long period of time, this fact may of itself be sufficient to compel the reasonable parent to give his consent. The Court of Appeal has held that this is still the correct approach notwithstanding the provisions of section 3 of the Children Act which requires *a court or adoption agency* to give its first consideration to the child's welfare in reaching any decision relating to his adoption.[32] The decision to dispense with consent is clearly a decision that the court has to make in relation to adoption, but the only question with which it has to concern itself at this stage is the attitude of the parent and the section does not require the *parent* to give first consideration to the child's welfare. Although in practice the courts are undoubtedly paying increased attention to this fact in deciding whether or not a parent is acting unreasonably,[33] they still cannot dispense with consent and make an adoption order solely on the ground that this would be in the child's interest. Many critics of the existing law would have preferred to see the introduction of such a principle, and the Houghton Committee itself felt that the correct approach would be to regard the child's welfare as of first importance in making an objective assessment of the reasonableness of the parent's attitude.[34]

Freeing a child for adoption

Even though a parent (or guardian) has given written consent, under the existing law she (or he) may withdraw it at any time before an adoption order is made. This has been seriously criticized. Although only about 2% of children are reclaimed by the mother before the application is heard, the possibility of this is a very real source of fear to many applicants who already have care and possession of the child, and the latter's welfare is at risk so long as it may be moved. Moreover, evidence indicates that many mothers find that the delay imposes strain on them and prevents them from planning their future, and it may lead them to vacillate.[35] Consequently, sections 14-16 of the Children Act have introduced a procedure based on proposals made by the Houghton Committee which is designed to enable a parent (or guardian) to give a general consent to adoption which will in most cases be irrevocable.

In future the court will have a power to make an order freeing a child for adoption. Only an adoption agency can apply for such an order[36] and, in addition, either each parent or guardian of the child must consent to its being made or the court must dispense with his consent on one of the grounds applicable on making an adoption order. Furthermore, no application may be made without the consent of one of the child's parents or guardians unless the child is in the agency's care. The purpose of the last provision is to enable the agency to apply for an order when a child in care has been with foster parents for a long time and there is no real hope of the parent resuming any contact with the child. It also means, however, that if, say, the mother of an illegitimate child puts it in the care of a local authority because she is temporarily unable to look after it properly for some reason, she runs the risk of the authority's applying for an order freeing the child for adoption. Although this is purely theoretical, it has been suggested that it might inhibit a mother who knows the law from putting the child in care. The chances of this seem so remote that the Act has very properly put the interests of the child in long term care first.

As in the case of consent to an adoption order, the mother's agreement will be ineffective unless the child is at least six weeks old. It may also be given in writing attested by a reporting officer. In order to prevent blanket dispensations, the court may not dispense with the consent of a parent or guardian unless the child has already been placed for adoption or it is likely that it will be so placed. In order to prevent the arbitrary extinction of potential rights of the father of an illegitimate child, the court must satisfy itself that, if his identity is known, he has no intention of making an application for custody or, if he were to do so, the application would be likely to be refused.

So long as an order freeing the child for adoption is in force, parents' and guardians' consent to adoption is not necessary and they have no power to veto an application for a specific adoption. In the meantime parental rights vest in the agency. If no adoption is made, the Houghton Committee considered that on balance it would be right to enable the parent to resume care of the child in a suitable case. The Act lays down a fairly complicated procedure that has to be followed. The parent or guardian may, if he wishes, make a declaration that he prefers not to be involved in future questions concerning the child's adoption; if he does so, he is given no further information about the child at all. If he does not do so, however, the agency is required to tell him after twelve months whether the child has been adopted (if it has not already done so) or is in the actual possession of a person with whom it has been placed for adoption, and it must thereafter inform him every time the child is placed for adoption or ceases to have its home with a person with whom it has been placed. If at any time after this initial period of twelve months the child has not been adopted and does not have its home with a person with whom he has been placed for this purpose, the parent or guardian may apply to have the order freeing the child for adoption revoked on the ground that she (or he) wishes to resume parental rights and duties. As the court will be reaching a decision relating to adoption, it must obviously have regard to the principle laid down in Section 3 of the Act and give first (but not paramount) consideration to the child's welfare. If the order is revoked, parental rights and duties will revest in the person or persons in whom they were vested before the order freeing the child for adoption was made; if they were then vested in a local authority or a voluntary organization, they will revest in the person or persons in whom they were vested before that body had them. The reason for the latter provision is that the court would revoke the order only if it was satisfied that they were fit to take the child back. If the child's welfare demands that the order should not be revoked, the agency ceases to be under any further obligation to inform parents and guardians of the child's movements and the parents cannot make any further application to have the order revoked without the leave of the court. This is designed to prevent frivolous applications for revocation and to protect the agency against repeated attempts to recover the child. Consequently, the court may not give leave to make any further application unless there has been a change of circumstances or some other proper reason is adduced.

It is difficult to forecast how useful this new procedure is likely to be. It will clearly be valuable if an agency cannot place a child immediately. On the other hand, the number of persons wishing to adopt so far exceeds the number of children available that this situation will probably occur only if the child is difficult to place, for example because it is coloured or handicapped; consequently the court may be precluded from making an order on the ground that it is not satisfied that the child is likely to be adopted. If the child is placed virtually immediately after birth, little purpose will be served in obtaining an order freeing it for adoption in most cases because two court hearings will be involved instead of one and the first may come on only a short time before the second. The order may be most used if foster parents wish to adopt with the approval of the local authority or voluntary organization concerned because, if the application is unsuccessful, hopes may not have been raised so high before they are dashed. But if the child is already living with the proposed adopters, the procedure will do little to achieve two of its objectives: the anxiety now felt by applicants before an adoption rder is made will be replaced by a similar anxiety pending the hearing of the application to free the child, and the mother herself will still experience the same uncertainty and temptation to vacillate as she does at the moment.

ELIGIBILITY TO APPLY FOR AN ADOPTION ORDER

Two aspects of this question have been considerably modified by the provisions of the Children Act.[37]

Joint application

As the effect of adoption is to give the child the same legal status as the adopters' legitimate child, it has always been a principle of English law that joint applications can be made only by a married couple. An application can of course be made by one person only,[38] but if a married person is the sole applicant, no order may be made unless his or her spouse cannot be found or is incapable of giving consent or if the spouses have separated and are living apart and the separation is likely to be permanent.

The purpose of this limitation is obvious: it would be absurd in the normal case to permit one only of two spouses living together to create this new legal relationship. It was also formerly possible for a married person to apply for an adoption order with his or her spouse's consent. This, however, produced a highly artificial and therefore undesirable situation, and consequently the relevant provision was repealed when section 11 of the Children Act came into force on 26 November 1976.

Age of applicants

A further limitation is imposed to prevent adoptions by immature applicants. The old law was complex. A single applicant had to satisfy one of the following conditions:

(a) be the mother or father of the child (including the father of an illegitimate child);

(b) be over the age of 21 and a relative of the child;[39]

(c) be over the age of 25.

In the case of joint applications one of the applicants had to satisfy one of the above conditions and unless one of them was a parent of the child the other had to be over the age of 21.

Condition (a) was designed to enable a parent (particularly the parent of an illegitimate child) to legitimize the situation and, as no change of care was involved, the applicant's age was felt to be immaterial. It is difficult to see, however, why the applicant's relationship to the child should affect the age at which he could apply for an order. The Houghton Committee were told that the age limit of 25 had prevented some suitable couples from being considered.[40] They, therefore, recommended that the minimum age for all adopters (including the child's own parent) should be 21 and this was implemented when section 10 of the Act came into operation on 26 November 1976. They chose this age as a compromise so as to ensure that "teenage marriages which appear to be more vulnerable would be tested by time". Two comments on this may be made. In view of the point made above that adoption by a parent involves no change of care, there seems to be little justification in imposing any limit on a parent's age. Secondly, whilst marriages of persons under the age of 20 are at greatest risk, the divorce rate reaches a peak during the fourth year of marriage and remains high for the next two or three. It would be wrong to prevent adoption by suitable couples merely because their contemporaries' marriages are breaking down, but there seems little justification for selecting the age of 21. Two independent pieces of research indicate that adoption is more likely to be successful if the adoptive mother is aged between 30 and 39 at the time of the placement.[41] One wonders whether the evidence of a few isolated cases has brought about an unwarranted change.

Adoption by parents, step-parents and relatives

It has already been pointed out that adoption by the parents of illegitimate children has always been fairly common in order to give the children the advantage of the status of legitimacy.[42] In recent years, there has been a marked increase in the number of legitimate children adopted by a parent and step-parent.[43] Although the figures do not disclose how many of the adopters were widowed and how many were divorced, it may be reasonably safely asserted that the majority were divorced. The number of widows and widowers with young children is relatively small and divorcees have stronger motives to adopt: by doing so they may effectively conceal their earlier unsuccessful marriage and at the same time completely cut the other parent out of the child's life. In some cases this might be appropriate, for example if the other parent had completely disappeared from the scene or there was some good reason for keeping the child away from him, but in the vast majority of cases it may not be in the child's own interest to extinguish his links with half his family or to distort the true relationships. In very exceptional circumstances the link may be preserved by imposing a condition that the other parent shall continue to have access after the adoption order has been made but this will rarely be satisfactory because of the confusion and distress that it may cause the child.[44] Both the Houghton Committee and judges have criticized the practice of adoption by a legitimate child's parent[45] and the same criticisms obviously apply albeit to a less extent to adoption by other relatives.[46] Consequently, certain restrictions on such adoptions are to be found in the Children Act.

In the first place, from 26 November 1976 a court cannot make an adoption order on the *sole* application of either parent (including either parent of an illegitimate child) unless the other parent is dead or cannot be found or there is some other reason justifying his (or her) exclusion.[47] The court will be left with a complete discretion in deciding whether sufficient reason exists, but only extreme conduct can warrant completely shutting out a parent who wishes to retain contact with his child. This might occur, for example, if he had culpably abandoned, neglected or ill-treated him, or perhaps if he suffered from certain types of mental disorder or had been convicted of certain types of offence. If the father of an illegitimate child has no desire to keep in touch with it, there is no reason why it should not be adopted by the mother. Consequently, this in itself ought to be sufficient reason to justify making an order.[48]

Secondly, if a joint application is made by a parent and step-parent of a legitimate child or if the step-parent of a legitimate child is the sole applicant, the court must dismiss the application if it considers that the question will be better dealt with under the provisions in the Matrimonial Causes Act, 1973 relating to custody etc. after divorce.[49] This provision (which came into force on 26 November 1976) has two objects: the retention of the link between the child and the other parent and the desire to leave the divorce court (which will have made any previous orders relating to custody) in control of the situation. Presumably these provisions are limited to legitimate children on the assumption that their parents will have been the parties to the divorce, but as a result one of the problems mentioned earlier still remains. Support that M, the mother of an illegitimate child, C, marries H who treats C as a child of the family. M and H are later divorced and M marries X. H will have no *locus standi* in the adoption proceedings unless he is liable to contribute to C's maintenance and, as C is illegitimate, the court will not be required to consider whether the matter would be better dealt with by the divorce court.

Thirdly, the court *may* direct the application to be treated as an application for a custodianship order if it is satisfied that this would be a more appropriate means of safeguarding the child's welfare. If a relative or the spouse of either parent of the child (including an illegitimate child) applies for an adoption order, whether alone or jointly, the court must make such a direction in these circumstances.[50] A custodianship order is a novelty to be introduced by the Children Act following the recommendations of the Houghton Committee.[51] It will enable the court to vest custody in an applicant who satisfies certain conditions, even though no other proceedings are pending. But a custodian's rights and duties will relate solely to the child's person and not to the administration of his property and a local authority will be able to apply to have a custodianship order revoked;[52] consequently it would be inappropriate to give custodianship (as distinct from custody) to a parent and no order may be made in his favour. Custodianship will differ radically from adoption because the legal ties with the child's natural parents will not be severed and a parent may be given access and ordered to contribute towards the child's maintenance. It may, therefore, have two advantages over adoption if the child is to remain in the care of a relative or step-parent: the natural relationship of the child to the applicant will be preserved and a parent anxious to keep in touch with the child will be able to do so unless this is not in the latter's interest.

There is a further (and rather technical) limitation on the court's power to make a custodianship order, whether in adoption or other proceedings. On divorce or nullity the court is under a duty to afford special protection to certain children of the family who may be particularly vulnerable.[53] In order to ensure that its jurisdiction is not ousted by a step-parent's obtaining custodianship (which would effectively give custody to the parent to whom he or she is married), no order for the custodianship of a legitimate child within this category can be made in favour of a step-parent of a legitimate child unless the other parent is dead or cannot be found.[54]

The combined effect of these provisions is very complicated and is set out as Appendix II to this paper. It seems probable that adoptions by parents, step-parents and close relatives will become much rarer in the future except where the applicant (or one of the applicants) is the mother of an illegitimate child with whom the father has no desire to retain any sort of contact.

DIRECT AND "THIRD PARTY" PLACEMENTS

English practice has always discouraged placement for adoption otherwise than through an adoption agency. Although up to date statistics are lacking, a survey conducted in 1966 indicated that, ignoring adoptions by parents, about 17% of children were placed either directly by the parents or by third parties (for example, doctors, nurses and clergymen).[55] The nature of the concern felt about these placements was thus voiced by the Houghton Committee:

"The decision to place a child with a particular couple is the most important stage in the adoption process. Adoption law must give assurance of adequate safeguards for the welfare of the child at this stage, otherwise it is ineffective. This assurance rests mainly upon the skilled work of the adoption services, which includes preparation for adoptive parenthood. An independent adoption is one in which this assurance is lacking."[56]

Although no doubt a number of highly unsatisfactory placements have been made independently, there has been little research done to discover whether generally these adoptions turn out any worse than others. Despite this the provisions of the Children Act have followed the Committee's recommendations designed to discourage such placements. Commercial trafficking in children for adoption (which could be the worst aspect of direct or third party placements) is already prohibited by provisions in the Adoption Act of 1958 forbidding the giving or receiving of any payment or reward in consideration of an adoption[57] and prohibiting any advertisement indicating that a person wishes to have a child adopted or to adopt one or (except for an adoption agency) that he is willing to make arrangements for adoption. It is also illegal for any body of persons to make arrangements for an adoption unless it is an adoption agency. The Children Act contains two further relevant provisions (not yet in force at the time of writing). First, it will be illegal for anyone other than an agency to place a child for adoption or to make any other arrangements for an adoption unless the proposed adopter is a relative of the child or the person making the placement is acting in pursuance of a High Court order.[58] Secondly, in order to prevent parties getting round this provision by the parent's ostensibly placing the child with the proposed adopters as foster parents, the period for which the child must have his home with at least one of the applicants before an adoption order is made will be extended from 13 weeks to 12 months unless one of them is a parent, step-parent or relative of the child or the child was placed by an adoption agency.[59]

On the assumption that there is a need to discourage direct and third party placements, this compromise is probably the best that could be devised. One criticism of the Houghton Committee's original proposal to proscribe them altogether was that this would be an unwarranted interference with individual liberty: this can be met with the obvious reply that it is more important to protect the child than to let the mother place it where she will. More cogent was the fear that the suggestion would merely drive unauthorized placements underground. The additional waiting period involved may act as a more effective deterrent.

ACTUAL CUSTODY BEFORE ADOPTION

One further protection to be given when prospective adopters have already received the child should be noted. The child must have had his home with them for a minimum period of time immediately preceding the making of an adoption order to enable their suitability to be tested. A parent or guardian could thus defeat the application at the last minute by reclaiming the child.[60] Once the adopters have taken the formal step of applying for an order, a parent or guardian who has consented to the adoption cannot remove the child from their custody without their consent or the leave of the court. But it will be seen that the protection that this offers is inadequate so long as there has been no order depriving the parent of his parental rights and duties. A parent who had not given his consent to the adoption can always reclaim the child and *any* parent may do so before the adopters can have filed the application for the order. The prospective adopters and any adoption agency involved can always resist the claim, of course, but this may end by involving them in litigation which they may lack the means or will to entertain.

Two provisions in the Children Act will ameliorate the position when Section 29 comes fully into force. When an application to free a child for adoption has been made, it will be impossible for any parent or guardian who has not consented to the order to seek to recover actual custody without the leave of the court. This may provide an additional reason for applying for such an order before applying for an adoption order. Secondly, if the child has had his home for five years with the applicants, *no one* may now remove the child against their will without the leave of the court when they have started proceedings to obtain an adoption order or for a period of three months after their giving the local authority notice of their intention to do so.[61] The latter provision (which came into force on 26 November 1976) is intended to help children in the care of a local authority who have lived with the same foster parents for years and for whom adoption will be highly beneficial. At present, the authority may be reluctant to raise the question of adoption with the foster parents in case this leads the parent to demand the return of the child.[62] The Houghton Committee originally proposed that all foster parents who had had a child for five years should be able to apply for adoption even though the parents did not consent, but this suggestion produced considerable criticism. It was argued in particular that many parents might be inhibited from placing children in care for fear of their being adopted and that some foster parents might try to weaken the links between children and parents in order to strengthen their own claims to adoption. There is, however, ample evidence that the chance of children returning home is considerably smaller if they have been in care for at least five years and consequently in their final Report the Committee advocated the compromise proposal now embodied in the Act.[63] This is not expected to affect the decision of parents who face the need to put their children in care because their consent to adoption will still be required and it is likely to be dispensed with if they continue to show a genuine interest in the child.

WELFARE SUPERVISION

At present no adoption order may be made in respect of a child below the upper limit of the compulsory school age[64] unless three months' notice of the intention to apply for an order has been given to the local authority in whose area the applicants are residing. This provision does not apply if the applicant, or one of joint applicants, is the mother of the child or the father of a legitimate child. When notice has been given, the child becomes a "protected child" and it is the authority's duty to secure that it "is visited from time to time by officers of the authority who shall satisfy themselves as to its well-being and give such advice as to its care and maintenance as may appear to be needed".[65]

The role of the authority's case worker is vital if the child has been placed by the parent or a third party because no other agency case worker will be involved. The authority's officers have a power to inspect premises and, as the authority must be a respondent to the application, may oppose the making of the adoption order. If the child was not placed by an adoption agency, the authority may prohibit any person from receiving the child and in all cases may apply to a juvenile court for the removal of a child living with anyone unfit to have his care, or in a detrimental environment.[66] If, on the other hand, the child has been placed by an adoption society, it will be immediately apparent that the authority's case worker will merely be duplicating the job of the society's case worker; when it is appreciated that a guardian *ad litem* will also be appointed and a health visitor may also be involved, one can see that the applicants will be visited by three or four different case workers. It is not surprising that the adopters are confused and tend to see the authority's representative as an inspector rather than as a support. Moreover, the latter is not always clear what her role is and overloaded social workers are given unnecessary tasks.

The main aim of welfare supervision has been described as being "to offer a supporting service to adopters, help them to focus on the essential task of integrating the child into their family life, and look forward confidently to the future. The welfare supervisor . . . should concentrate on the particular needs of this period: the adoptive parents' preoccupation with the physical care of the child, their adaptation to new family roles and changed relationships".[67] This is best done by the agency responsible for placing the child, and bringing in two case workers will become even more anomalous once approved societies and local authorities work together in an integrated adoption service. Consequently, following the recommendation of the Houghton Committee,[68] no notice will have to be given to the local authority if the child was placed by an adoption agency when section 18 of the Children Act comes into force. In other cases the authority will be under a duty to make a full investigation and report to the court hearing the application.

The opportunity to supervise is provided by the fact that the child must have had his home with the applicants or one of them for at least thirteen weeks before the order is made. He is to be regarded as having his home with the person who, disregarding absence of the child at a hospital or boarding school or any other temporary absence, has actual possession of his person. The possibility that the child could spend the whole of this period away from home is guarded against by the further provision that the agency or local authority must have sufficient opportunities to see the child with the applicants together in the home environment.[69] Presumably this means that the agency must have sufficient opportunity to satisfy itself that the order, if made, will be for the child's welfare.

THE GUARDIAN AD LITEM

In order to assist the court and to safeguard the interests of the child, under the present law a guardian *ad litem* must be appointed by the court as soon as practicable after the application is filed. The guardian must be a member of the Social Services Department of the local authority, a probation officer or some other suitably qualified person, but in order to ensure that he is impartial, he must have taken no part in arranging the particular adoption.[70] His recommendations are contained in a confidential report to the court which may not be seen by any party to the proceedings except by leave of the court. Obviously the value of the report would be reduced if the guardian *ad litem* were inhibited by the knowledge that it might be read by those about whom he was writing, but the procedure is unsatisfactory in that an unsuccessful applicant cannot controvert any statement of fact. This can be overcome in part by disclosing portions of the report or permitting the parties' legal advisers to read it, but there is some doubt about the validity of rules which permit evidence to be given behind the parties' backs without express statutory authority. Whereas the High Court undoubtedly has an inherent jurisdiction to receive such evidence in proceedings dealing with children,[71] it is not so clear that other courts may do so,[72] and it is a pity that the Children Act did not seize the opportunity to put the matter beyond question.

Usually the guardian *ad litem* will do no more than make the same enquiries as have been made before, and provided that the initial case work has been done carefully by the adoption agency or local authority, it will rarely be necessary to have the child's interests further protected by the appointment of another social worker. Consequently, the Houghton Committee concluded that there is no need to have a guardian *ad litem* in most cases.[73] Following this, rules are to be made under section 20 of the Children Act defining the circumstances in which a guardian is to be appointed. It is difficult to forecast what these circumstances are likely to be: the Houghton Committee considered that a guardian should be appointed if the proceedings were contested (for example, by a parent who was withholding consent) and thought it more likely that one would be needed if no order had been made freeing the child for adoption. In other cases the responsibility for making the necessary enquiries and submitting the confidential report to the court will fall on the agency placing the child or the local authority. Very few adoptions appear to have been refused as a consequence of the guardian's adverse report, so that it would seem that little will be lost by the change in the law.[74] There are two points, however, to which the Houghton Committee made no reference in its report. First, the fact that an adoption agency has made a poor placement may be more apparent to an outsider than to the case worker concerned who will probably, if only subconsciously, be anxious to justify her initial decision. Secondly, the guardian *ad litem*'s function in most cases is to ensure that the mandatory requirements of the Adoption Act have been complied with. He can also give a second opinion in a really difficult case. One does not know in how many cases slips have been spotted and cured before the case gets into court or the agency has been persuaded that a particular placement is unsatisfactory and the application withdrawn. Bearing in mind that an order may be void if the Act is not complied with and that, once it is made, it is irrevocable, it is not clear that the present shortage of social workers in England justifies the removal of this check.

THE ROLE OF THE COURT

The function of the court remains the same under the Children Act as it was before: to satisfy itself (a) if the child is not free for adoption, that each parent and guardian, whose consent is not dispensed with, freely and with full understanding of what is involved, agrees unconditionally to the making of the adoption order, (b) that the order if made will be for the child's welfare, and (c) that no unauthorized payments or rewards for the adoption have been made or agreed upon.

Interim orders

The court will retain the power that it possesses at present of making an interim adoption order to last for not more than two years.[75] The effect of this is to vest the legal custody of the child in the applicants (so that the natural parent can no longer reclaim it) upon such terms for its maintenance and otherwise as the court thinks fit. The purpose of an interim order is to enable the applicants to act for a probationary period and may, therefore, be made if the court wishes to test their suitability.[76] It is an unsatisfactory compromise, however, because the future of the child's status and its relationship with the applicants remain in doubt; moreover, if a child has lived with the applicants for over two years it will rarely be in its interests to send it elsewhere. Few interim orders are made[77] and in the future it will probably be more appropriate to make a custodianship order if the court is not prepared to make an irrevocable adoption order. Nevertheless the Houghton Committee were of the opinion that on balance they served some purpose and should be retained: in particular they enabled the adoption agency to remain in contact with the child and the applicants.[78]

Refusal of adoption order

If the court refuses to make the order sought or if the application is withdrawn and in either case the child was placed in the applicants' care and possession by an adoption society or local authority, the child must be returned to the agency in question within seven days. A much needed change in the law has been introduced by Section 31 of the Children Act (which came into force on 26 November 1976) under which the court now has a power to extend the period to six weeks. This, of course, is particularly important if an appeal is pending.

In other cases there was formerly no obligation to return the child at all.[79] The reason for this distinction was that an adoption agency remains under an obligation to the parent from whom the child was received to try to secure its adoption and must, therefore, endeavour to place it with other suitable applicants. On the other hand if, say, the child was placed by its mother and she wished to reclaim it, she had to do so by bringing other proceedings (for example, under the Guardianship of Minors Act) in which the court must regard the welfare of the child as the first and paramount consideration. The result, however, was that the child might be singularly at risk, particularly if the court had refused the order because of the applicants' unsuitability. Consequently, following the recommendation of the Houghton Committee,[80] since 26 November 1976, Section 17 of the Children Act has enabled the court to place the child under the supervision of a local authority or a probation officer if there are exceptional circumstances making this desirable, or, if there are exceptional circumstances making it impracticable or undesirable for the child to be entrusted to any individual, to place it in the care of a local authority. This is an extension of the powers that the court already has in matrimonial proceedings and proceedings for custody and fills a very obvious gap.

IDENTIFICATION OF THE PARTIES

The identity of the adoptive parents can be — and usually is — concealed from the natural parents by the device of referring to the proceedings throughout by a serial number. This protects the adoptive parents and the child from any threat of interference by the natural parents and also removes any temptation that the latter might have to try to make contact with the child at a later date. A parent may, of course, refuse to consent to adoption unless the applicant's identity is revealed to him. If he makes his position clear from the beginning, no adoption agency will accept the child from him; if he discloses it at a later stage (which rarely seems to happen in practice), there is a strong case for saying that he is withholding his consent unreasonably.[81]

Current adoption rules require the application to state the names and addresses of the natural parents (if known) and to be accompanied, if possible, by the child's birth certificate. Consequently, the natural parents' identity will be known to the adopters. The Houghton Committee considered whether this practice should be changed and came to the following conclusion:

"Natural parents in general may not need the same protection of anonymity as adoptive parents, but there can be cases where the parents strongly wish to retain anonymity because they are well known or belong to closely knit communities in which the child might be placed for adoption. On balance we think that, in cases where children are relinquished for adoption, the parents should have the right, if they wish, to be completely anonymous as far as the adopters are concerned until the adoption process is completed. However, we take the view that the child's original name should not be concealed from the adopters once the adoption process has been completed, and that it should appear in full on the form of adoption order which is given to the adopters. We recognize that in the case of an unusual surname this may lessen the degree of anonymity afforded to the natural parents, but we consider that in the interests of the child this must be accepted."[82]

Whether this recommendation will be implemented depends on the rules to be made when the relevant provisions of the Children Act are brought into operation.

It will be apparent that this question is linked with another which is much more difficult, namely whether the child himself should have access to this information at a later stage. The Registrar General's records enable the entry relating to the birth of an adopted person to be traced but in England this information may not be divulged to anyone without an order of the High Court, the Westminster County Court or the court which made the adoption order. In practice such an order is made only in exceptional circumstances, for example to give effect to property rights which vested before the adoption order was made. In Scotland, on the other hand, any adopted child over the age of 17 has the right to obtain a copy of his birth certificate. Much has been written about the "crisis of identity" experienced by many adopted children, particularly at adolescence, and their desire to find out more about their background and their natural parents. Research done on those applying for birth certificates in Scotland has thrown up some interesting facts.[83] About 45 people a year on average sought the information although 17 to 25 years earlier there had been some 1,500 to 2,000 adoptions annually. Most of those who did so had learned that they were adopted only when they were eleven or more years old and many had experienced difficulty in coming to terms with the fact. Significantly, too, many had lost at least one of their adoptive parents by death, divorce or separation. About a third of the sample were upset by the information that they discovered, whether it was that they were illegitimate or alternatively that their parents, although married, had "given them away". Sixty per cent of the sample tried to trace their natural parents although less than 6% were successful in finding them.

It, thus, appears that a tiny fraction of all adopted children are likely to avail themselves of the opportunity of finding out the facts of their background and that many of these will experience emotional problems probably brought on in many cases by the adoptive parents' failure to explain to them in a sensitive way the fact that they had been adopted. Against the good that the discovery of the information may do to the child concerned must be weighed the unhappiness that could be caused to the natural parents by the appearance of the child many years after the adoption. It requires little imagination to see the possible effect on a happily married middle aged woman who had kept from her children the fact that she had had an illegitimate child before her marriage. The Houghton Committee seem to have paid scant attention to this aspect of the problem but came down in favour of freer access to background information in conformity with their wish to "encourage greater openness about adoption". Accordingly Section 26 of the Children Act (which came into force on 26 November 1976) entitles any adopted person over the age of 18 to acquire a copy of his birth certificate. It is recognized that those seeking this information may have need for more help than the knowledge of the facts will give them and consequently before supplying any information the Registrar General must inform the applicant that counselling services are available for him at the General Register Office, a local authority or, if he was placed for adoption by an adoption society, that society. There is no need for him to take advantage of these services, however, unless he was adopted before the Children Act was passed (12 November 1975) and in any case he may still insist on obtaining the information even though he is advised to the contrary.

One further and wholly uncontroversial change has been made. To prevent the possibility of an inadvertent incestuous marriage by an adopted child intending to marry in England or Wales under the age of 18, he may now apply to the Registrar General to inform him whether it appears from the latter's records that he and his intended spouse may be within the prohibited degree of relationship.

THE FUTURE

The history of the law relating to adoption in England during the past 50 years has consisted of a series of reforms implementing the recommendations of *ad hoc* committees. The Report of the Houghton Committee and the provision of the Children Act must be regarded as the latest chapter in this history. Some of their possible weaknesses have been indicated in this essay and doubtless many more will become apparent when the Act is fully brought into effect. There is certainly nothing final about them and the law will need to be modified in the future as social conditions continue to change.

It may not be inappropriate, therefore, to end this essay by mentioning one interesting and novel feature of the Children Act. In its original working paper the Houghton Committee suggested that adopters should be subsidized in appropriate cases. Reaction was mixed: whilst this might encourage adoption by foster parents who could not afford to lose the boarding out allowance they were being paid, others criticized the proposal on the ground that it would draw an unwarranted distinction between natural and adopted children and would also be regarded as unfair by some natural parents. The Committee eventually compromised by proposing that the Home Secretary should be able to approve pilot schemes to be reviewed after a limited period of time.[84] Section 32 of the Act accordingly empowers him to approve any scheme put forward by an adoption agency enabling them to pay allowances with respect to any children whose adoption they have arranged. A report on the operation of schemes approved must be published every five years and, without prejudice to any payments already promised, the power will lapse after seven years unless extended by statutory instrument.

APPENDIX I
ADOPTIONS IN ENGLAND AND WALES

Year	High Court	County Courts	Magistrates' Courts	Total
1927	133	184	2,626	2,943
1939	65	635	6,126	6,826
1953	75	4,297	8,623	12,995
1963	74	10,443	7,265	17,782
1968	39	16,499	8,293	24,831
1973	34	13,825	8,392	22,251

APPENDIX II
RESTRICTIONS ON MAKING OF ADOPTION ORDERS IN FAVOUR OF PARENTS, STEP-PARENTS AND OTHER RELATIVES
I. If the child is illegitimate

Applicant	Other parent dead or cannot be found	Other parent alive and can be found
Parent alone	No restriction	Only if special reason justifying other's exclusion
Step-parent alone or parent and step-parent jointly	Court *must* direct application to be treated as for custodianship by step-parent if appropriate. (Parent will have custody.)	
Relative alone or jointly	Court *must* direct application to be treated as for custodianship by applicant(s) if appropriate.	
All other cases	Court *may* direct application to be treated as for custodianship by applicant(s).	

II. If the child is legitimate

Applicant	Other parent dead or cannot be found	Other parent alive and can be found
Parent alone	No restriction	Only if special reason justifying other's exclusion
Step-parent alone or parent and step-parent jointly	No order if question would be better dealt with under court's powers under Matrimonial Causes Act. In other cases court *must* direct application to be treated as for custodianship by step-parent if appropriate. (Parent will have custody.)	No order if question would be better dealt with under court's powers under Matrimonial Causes Act. In other cases court *must* direct application to be treated as for custodianship by step-parent if appropriate, unless child subject of order under s.41 of Matrimonial Causes Act. (Parent will have custody.)
Relative alone or jointly	Court *must* direct application to be treated as for custodianship by applicant(s) if appropriate.	
All other cases	Court *may* direct application to be treated as for custodianship by applicant(s).	

---

1 Cmnd. 5107 (hereinafter referred to as "the Report").
2 Originally this meant a person under the age of 21; since 1970 the age of majority has been 18.
3 For the genesis of this section, see Bennion, 126 New L.J. 1237.
4 *Re A.,* [1963] 1 W.L.R. 231 at 234, [1963] 1 All E.R. 531.
5 *Re D. (No. 2)* [1959] 1 Q.B. 229 [1958] 3 All E.R. 716 (C.A.).
6 But the number is insignificant compared with the annual average number of illegitimate children adopted during this period (16,437). It is also significant that the number of illegitimate children adopted by their mothers alone dropped every year from 115 in 1967 to 25 in 1973.
7 *J. v. C.* [1970] A.C. 668 at 710, [1969] 1 All E.R. 788 (H.L.). If it is paramount in the sense that it rules upon or determines the course to be followed, the word "first" seems unnecessary.
8 [1976] Fam. 161 at 166, [1976] 3 All E.R. 124.
9 See *infra* under "Dispensing with Consent".
10 Report, paras. 32 and 33. See generally *ibid.,* Chap. 3.
11 Report, para. 38.

12   Adoption Act, 1958, s. 57. The body may be incorporated or unincorporated, but under the 1975 Act the Home Secretary will be able to make regulations prohibiting the approval of unincorporated bodies (Sched. 3, para. 27).

13   See Adoption Act, 1958, s.30. There is an appeal to the Crown Court against a refusal to register: s.31.

14   Children Act, 1975, s.4. If the society is likely to operate exclusively within the area of a particular local authority, the latter's views must be sought and they must be asked whether they support the application. There will be no appeal against a refusal to approve a society: the only remedy that an aggrieved applicant will have is to get a Member of Parliament to raise the matter with the Home Secretary who will, of course, be answerable to Parliament. The applicant must be given the reasons for the refusal of the application and may make further representations: see s.6 and Report, para. 60.

15   The Home Office will be able to give directions about arrangements for children in the care of a society whose approval expires or is withdrawn or which becomes inactive or defunct: ss.4(7), 5 and 7.

16   *Re M.* [1955] 2 Q.B. 479, [1955] 2 All E.R. 911 (C.A.).

17   See Children Act, 1975, s. 107(1) and Sched. 3, para. 39(d) (already in force).

18   *Per* Wilberforce J. in *Re Adoption Application 41/61 (No. 2)* [1964] Ch. 48 at 58, [1963] 2 All E.R. 1082.

19   See further *infra*, "Dispensing with consent," p. 368.

20   See *Re Adoption Application 41/61* [1963] Ch. 315, [1962] 3 All E.R. 553 (C.A.) and *Re O.* [1965] Ch. 23, [1964] 1 All E.R. 786 (C.A.).

21   See *Guide To Adoption Practice* (H.M.S.O., 1970) at 17.

22   A magistrates' court has jurisdiction only if the child has been *accepted* as a member of the family. This demands an agreement by both spouses that the child should be so treated: *Snow v. Snow* [1972] Fam. 74 (C.A.). In proceedings for divorce, nullity and judicial separation, the court may award custody to one of them and care and control to the other, but a magistrates' court has no power to order custody to one spouse and care and control to the other: the reason for this is technical and is to be found in *W. (C.) v. W.(R.)* [1969] P. 33, [1968] 3 All E.R. 608.

23   *F. v. S.* [1973] Fam. 203, [1973] 1 All E.R. 722 (C.A.).

24   If the mother is under the age of 17 and unmarried, the mere fact that she is pregnant may indicate that she is exposed to moral danger or beyond the control of her parents and should be brought before a juvenile court in care proceedings with a view to having her placed under the supervision or care of the local authority.

25   Report, para. 175. For reporting officers' duties, see *ibid.* paras. 176-180.

26   Adoption Act, 1958, s.4(2).

27   Report, paras. 228-231.

28   *Re B. (No. 2)* [1968] Ch. 204, [1967] 3 All E.R. 629.

29   *Per* Sir George Baker P. in *Re D.* [1973] Fam. 209 at 214, [1973] 3 All E.R. 1001. Hence in that case the court refused to dispense with the consent of a father who had drifted apart from the child for a year after his divorce. Temporary withdrawal must be common in such circumstances.

30   *Watson v. Nikolaisen* [1955] 2 Q.B. 286, [1955] 2 All E.R. 427.

31   [1971] A.C. 682, [1971] 2 All E.R. 49 (H.L.).

32   *Re P.* [1977] Fam. 25.

33   See *Re H.* [1977] 1 W.L.R. 471 at 472 (C.A.).

34   Report, paras. 205-218.

35   See Report, paras. 168-9. For the Houghton Committee's proposals, see *ibid.* paras. 167-191. They were based on similar procedures to be found in other jurisdictions, notably in the U.S.A.

36   This ties up with the policy of the Act to reduce the number of "third party" placements.

37   Two other limitations have been amended by the Children Act. One relates to the highly technical question of the applicant's domicile. The other prevented the adoption of a female child on the sole application of a man unless there were special circumstances justifying this as an exceptional measure. The latter restriction has been abolished

because it can be adequately dealt with under the court's general duty to have regard to the child's welfare.

38 About 1% of all orders are made in favour of sole applicants. About one half of these are the children's parents.

39 *I.e.,* grandparent, brother, sister, uncle or aunt, of the full blood or half blood or by affinity, and including persons so related to illegitimate children. The desirability of adoption by such relatives is discussed below.

40 Report, para. 77. See generally *ibid.* Chap. 4.

41 McWhinnie, *Adopted Children: How they grow up* p. 199; Kornitzer, *Adoption and Family Life* pp. 171-2.

42 During the years 1964-1973 a total of 164,336 illegitimate children were adopted of whom 45,930 (27.9%) were adopted by a parent. The percentage rose from 18.3 in 1964 to 43.1 in 1973.

43 Between 1964 and 1973 the number increased annually from 2,296 to 8,101. The total number of legitimate children adopted rose from 3,916 to 9,254.

44 E.g. in *Re J.* [1973] Fam. 106, [1973] 2 All E.R. 410, where the child was illegitimate, Rees J. made such an order as the only way of preventing lengthy litigation which would have embittered relations between the parties. A similar order was made in *Re S.* [1976] Fam. 1, [1975] 1 All E.R. 109 (C.A.). Because of the difficulty of enforcing a condition attached to an adoption order unless the adopters give an undertaking to the court, a condition relating to access can be attached only if the adopters consent.

45 Report, para. 105; Sir George Baker P. in *Re D.* [1973] Fam. 209 at 216, [1973] 3 All E.R. 1001.

46 Approximately 5% of all orders are in favour of other relatives.

47 S. 11(3).

48 The Houghton Committee were of the opinion that it followed that, if exceptional circumstances justified the other parent's exclusion, he should cease to be under any obligation to contribute to the child's maintenance. The Children Act implements this recommendation. But if, say, it is in the interests of an illegitimate child that he should be adopted by his mother, and his father has no interest in him at all although he is compelled to pay maintenance under an affiliation order, why should the mother lose this support?

49 Ss. 10(3) and 11(4).

50 S. 37(1) and (2). For the definition of "relative", see note 39, above. In addition the necessary consents must have been given or dispensed with.

51 See Report, Chapter 6. The detailed provisions of the Act differ in some respects from the Committee's recommendations.

52 The reason that the local authority can intervene is that many children with respect to whom custodianship orders are likely to be made will previously have been in the authority's care and it may be necessary for the latter to take action if the child becomes difficult: see Report, para. 133.

53 These are children of the family who are (i) under the age of 16, or (ii) over that age and still receiving instruction at an educational establishment or undergoing training for a trade, profession or vocation (whether or not they are also gainfully employed), or (iii) of any age if there is a particular need for protection (for example, if the child is physically or mentally handicapped). No decree of divorce or nullity may be made absolute (and no decree of judicial separation may be made) unless the court has declared itself satisfied that the arrangements for the welfare of all such children are satisfactory or the best that can be devised in the circumstances, or that it is impracticable for such arrangements to be made, or that it is desirable for the decree to be made absolute or made, as the case may be, without delay. See the Matrimonial Causes Act, 1973, s.41.

54 Ss. 33(5) and (8) and 37(5). This restriction does not apply if the child is illegitimate, nor will it apply if it has since been determined that the child was not a child of the family at all.

55 Approximately 12% were placed directly and 6% by third parties. If one disregards placements with relatives, the figures are 4% and 6% respectively.

56 Report, para. 84. See further *ibid.,* paras. 81-92.

57 But an adoption agency may be paid reasonable expenses and the court may authorize payments and rewards. In practice the court rarely does so although many voluntary societies largely depend on the payment of expenses and gifts from adoptive parents who have already had a child placed by the society.

58 S. 28(a). For the meaning of "relative", see note 39, above.

59 S. 9.

60 But he could not do so if the child were free for adoption or were in the care of the local authority. This could arise if a care order had been made by a juvenile court on one of a number of grounds laid down in the Children and Young Persons Act, 1969 (*e.g.* that the child's proper development was being avoidably prevented or neglected, that he was beyond parental control, or that he had committed a criminal offence). It could also arise if the local authority had assumed parental rights over the child. They can do this if he has been put in care voluntarily and certain other conditions are satisfied (*e.g.,* his parent has abandoned him or suffers from some permanent disability rendering him incapable of caring for the child, or the child has been in care continuously for three years).

61 *I.e.,* if the applicants do not start court proceedings within three months of giving notice to the local authority, the protection given to them by this section will lapse.

62 The position of long term foster parents is also appreciably improved by section 56 of the Children Act which came into force on 26 November 1976. This requires parents of children who have been in care for six months or more to give 28 days' notice of their intention to reclaim the child; this not only discourages frivolous demands but also enables the authority to pass a resolution assuming parental rights if a ground for this exists and it is in the child's interest. The periods of six months and 28 days may be changed by order.

63 See Chap. 7, particularly paras. 139-147 and 161-4.

64 This falls on a date fixed by statute which is not more than seven months after or three months before the child's sixteenth birthday.

65 Adoption Act, 1958, s. 38.

66 *Ibid.,* ss. 41-49. A person aggrieved by the imposition of a prohibition may appeal to a juvenile court.

67 See the *Guide to Adoption Practice,* 101.

68 Report, paras. 237-240.

69 Ss. 9 and 87.

70 Nor must he be a member, officer or servant of any local authority that has taken part in the arrangements. In the High Court the Official Solicitor is usually appointed.

71 *Official Solicitor v. K.* [1965] A.C. 201, [1963] 3 All E.R. 191 (H.L.).

72 In *Re P.A.* [1971] 1 W.L.R. 1530, the Court of Appeal held that the county court rule was *intra vires.* But Lord Denning M.R. followed the decision in *Official Solicitor v. K.* which was concerned with the inherent jurisdiction of the High Court.

73 Report, paras. 245-256.

74 The *total* number of applications refused is believed to be less than 0.5%.

75 Or two or more interim orders to last for not more than two years in total.

76 The power has also been used when the court was uncertain whether the child should be adopted or live with a parent: *S. v. Huddersfield Borough Council* [1975] Fam. 113, [1974] 3 All E.R. 296 (C.A.).

77 No reliable figures are available. In 1969, 32 interim orders were made by magistrates' courts. As they dealt with approximately one-third of all applications, the total number of interim orders was probably about 100.

78 Report, paras. 309-310.

79 But if the child is in the care of a local authority, the authority *may* require the child's return. This is of little importance because there will be very few cases where a child is in the care of a local authority but the latter have not delivered him into the applicants' possession.

80 Report, para. 308.

81 S. 5(3) of the Adoption Act 1958 expressly provided that, if a parent who had given consent to the adoption then withdrew it solely on the ground that he did not know the

identity of the applicant, he was deemed to be withholding it unreasonably. This section has been repealed from 26 November 1976.
82   Report, para. 298.
83   Triseliotis, *In Search of Origins.*
84   Report, paras. 93-4.

Toward A Theory Of Children's Rights

*John E. Coons and Robert H. Mnookin**

Children generally have less liberty than adults and are often held less accountable. Within the family, parents have legal power to make a wide range of important decisions that affect the life of the child, but are held responsible by the state for the child's care and support. Children have special power to avoid contractual obligations, but are not normally entitled to their own earnings and cannot manage their own property. Moreover, persons younger than certain statutory limits are not allowed to vote, hold public office, work in various occupations, drive a car, buy liquor, or be sold certain kinds of reading material, quite apart from what either they or their parents may wish.

Because of such legally imposed limitations on the child's power to decide, some reformers suggest that a children's liberation movement should follow the trail blazed by the civil rights and women's movements. The emancipators' rhetoric often compares the legal status of children to that of "slaves" or "property". To modify this, one child liberator endorses the adoption of "A Child's Bill of Rights"[1] that begins by proclaiming a child's "Right to Self-Determination".

"Children should have the right to decide the matters which affect them most directly. This is the basic right upon which all others depend. Children are now treated as the private property of their parents on the assumption that it is the parents' right and responsibility to control the life of the child. The achievement of the children's rights, however, would reduce the need for this control and bring about an end to the double standard of morals and behaviour for adults and children".[2]

Other reformers see salvation not through liberation, but through expansion of a child's legal rights, and through government intervention. An extreme example is found in yet another Bill of Rights for children that proposes that a child "should have a legal right to be regarded as *a person* within the family" and "to receive parental love and affection, discipline

* Robert H. Mnookin, LL.B., A.B. (Harvard), Professor of Law, University of California (Berkeley); John E. Coons, B.A. (Duluth), J.D. (Northwestern), Professor of Law, University of California (Berkeley).

and guidance, and to grow to maturity in a home environment which enables him to develop into a mature and responsible adult".[3]

It is hard to transact intellectual business in the coin of either the liberators or the child savers. A core idea of the civil rights movement and the women's movement is that a person's legal autonomy should not be made dependent upon race or sex, at least without some compelling justification, and this is straightforward and intelligible. By contrast, the broad assertion that age is also irrelevant to legal autonomy inescapably collides with biological and economic reality. Because the young are necessarily dependent for some period after birth, the relevant question is often which adult should have the power to decide on behalf of the child. The argot of the child saver has a similar ring of unreality; here the difficulty is understanding how legal claims "to love and affection" would be monitored by government or enforced by courts.

But one must avoid dismissing too quickly either the liberators or the child savers. Buried in their rhetoric are important questions. That an element of domination of children by adults is inevitable gives no licence to ignore the moral dimension implicit in the liberators' challenge: *i.e.* what are the legitimate justifications for giving one human being power over the nurture, training, and experience of another? Similarly, the problems to which the child savers point — for example the abuse and neglect of some children — are serious ones and implicitly raise an important question about the roles of government and the family in child rearing. What is the government's responsibility in protecting children? In our view, one reason the advocates for children's rights have failed to generate very clear ideas is in part because of inattention to theory. Therefore, after describing different types of theories that may be relevant, we will suggest a framework for analyzing children's rights.

One need not be a student of epistemology or the history of science to understand just how ambiguous the word "theory" is. Must a theory be capable of empirical rejection? Or, must a theory necessarily be at a level of abstraction that precludes direct testing?[4] There appears to be no consensus about general criteria for qualification as a theory. Not surprisingly, the dictionary suggests a variety of definitions of the word "theory". Some have little relevance for the law, much less for children and the law, either because they demand too much or offer too little. For example, no theory of law will ever provide "a body of . . . theorems presenting a clear, rounded and systematic view" of the subject. At the other extreme, while there may now exist a "body of generalizations and principles developed in association with practice" in this area, this unadorned body contributes little to focused inquiry. Other definitions strike closer to the mark. A theory of children's rights might provide a "coherent set of hypothetical, conceptual, and pragmatic principles forming the general frame of reference for a field of inquiry..." or "a hypothetical entity or structure explaining or relating an observed set of facts . . . ."[5]

Without attempting to define general criteria for deciding with precision what qualifies as a theory, we think there are, broadly speaking, three types of theories about children and the law, each of which could be based on a respectable jurisprudential tradition. The first is *analytic theory*. It would define terms, specify axioms, and prescribe methods of analysis in order to view the legal order largely on its own terms, as a self-consistent system. It would study the law as it relates to children as part of an autonomous, and self-contained legal system. The purpose of such an inquiry would be to infuse clarity and order into this branch of law. In the tradition of analytic jurisprudence, one might ask: How is a child defined for purposes of the law in various realms? Are age-based rules used for these definitions, or instead does the process involve a more discretionary, case-by-case inquiry? What values or norms infuse these definitions? A theoretical inquiry of this sort would examine the law as it relates to children for clarity, consistency, coherence and non-redundancy.

A second kind of theory about children and the law would focus on the *relationship* between law, on the one hand, and social, economic and pyschological conditions in the world, on the other hand. Such a theory would fall within the broad tradition of what is often called *sociological jurisprudence* and might attempt to describe or predict the effects of the law about children on the attitudes of parents, children, various organizations, on social institutions, or on the social or political environment. Alternatively, a theory in this tradition might attempt to show how various social phenomena reciprocally influence the development of substantive and procedural law.

A third sort of theory, unlike the first two, is explicitly ethical and could be called a *theory of justice*. It would evaluate and criticize the law as it relates to children in terms of the ideals and goals postulated for it. Such a theory would articulate the values that the legal order should seek to realize, and then criticize the existing legal order where it fails to live up to these values. In its nature, such a theory would focus, not on the enforceable rights of children that exist today, but instead on the question of what those rights *should* be.

The American legal tradition is premised in some substantial measure on notions of individual autonomy, and the idea that no person, especially a state official, should be able to require some other person to take some action "for his own good" where the interests of others are not implicated. If one generally accepts that principle for "adults", then a theory of justice for children would necessarily explore the ethical justifications for departing from that principle for young people.

There is necessarily a broad overlap between a theory of justice, on the one hand, and ethics and political philosophy on the other. Different values can obviously affect one's judgments and the approach influences one's conclusions about what justice requires. A utilitarian might analyze the question of whether a pregnant teenager should have the legal right to an abortion without parental consent differently than a Jehovah's Witness.

The general discussion of theories about children's rights is meant to suggest that there are very different sorts of questions one might wish to ask about children and the law. A single theory might provide analytic understanding of the legal system itself, expose the relationship of the legal system to society, and spell out a theory of justice. But that is a tall order, and it seems more likely that a variety of less comprehensive theories might explain or heighten our understanding of different kinds of issues.

What follows is a preliminary sketch for what we hope will later be a full-colored and detailed theory of children's rights. Our primary concern is with two questions: how does law allocate power and responsibility for children in our society, and how should it?

THE INDETERMINACY OF WHAT IS BEST FOR A CHILD

Everywhere one looks in debates over children's rights, there are frequent references to the notion that the guiding principle in decision-making is the best interests of the child. In divorce custody cases, for example, the best interests standard is the legal rule that is supposed to guide judicial decision. The same is true in the dispositional phase of various sorts of juvenile court determinations. In deciding what should be done with a minor who has committed a crime, or who has been neglected by his parents or has run away from home, the court is supposed to appraise the alternatives by the best interests principle. Educators often invoke the best interests principle when deciding what reading group or academic track or kind of education a particular child should have. In the current public policy debates over child care, and the extent to which it should be licenced and subsidized by government, many of the arguments both pro and con are premised on what is best for children.

One postulate of our theory of children's rights is that what is "best" for a particular child or even children in general is usually indeterminate and speculative. Deciding what is best for a child or for children as a group involves choice among alternatives. Decision theorists have laid out the logic of rational choice with clarity and mathematical rigor for prototype decision problems. Framing the question of what is best for a child by this model illustrates what we mean by indeterminancy.[6]

Suppose the decision to be made is whether a child will live with his mother or with his father. Alternatively, one could imagine that the issue was whether a child should go to one school as opposed to another school. Presumably a rational decision-maker would specify alternative outcomes with regard to different courses of action and then choose that alternative that "maximizes" the utility for the child. A judge would, for example, wish to compare the expected utility for the child of living with his mother to that of living with his father. To do this requires considerable information and predictive ability. The judge would also need some source of values to measure utility for the child. All of the three are quite problematic.

Even with substantial information about a child's past home life and present alternatives, present-day knowledge about human behavior provides no basis for the individualized prediction required by the best interests standard. There are numerous competing theories of human behavior, based on radically different conceptions of the nature of man, and no consensus exists that any one is correct. No theory is widely considered capable of generating reliable predictions about the psychological and behavioral consequences of alternative decisions for a particular child.

Even if various outcomes could be specified and their probability estimated, however, a fundamental decision would remain. What set of values should a judge use to determine what is in a child's best interests? If the decision-maker must assign some measure of utility to each possible outcome, how is utility to be determined?

For many decisions in an individualistic society, one asks the person affected what he wants. Applying this notion to custody cases, the child could be asked to specify those values or even to choose. In some cases, especially those involving divorce, the child's preference is sought and given weight. But to make the child responsible for the choice may jeopardize his future relationships with the other parent. And we often lack confidence that the child has the capacity and the maturity appropriately to determine his own utility.

Moreover, whether or not the judge looks to the child for some guidance, there remains the question whether the best interests should be viewed from a long-term or a short-term perspective. The conditions that make a person happy at age seven to ten may have adverse consequences at age thirty. Should the judge ask himself what decision will make the child happiest in the next year? Or at thirty? Or at seventy? Should the judge decide by thinking about what decision the child as an adult looking back would have wished to be made? In this case, the preference problem is formidable, for how is the judge to compare "happiness" at one age with "happiness" at another age?

Deciding what is best for a child poses a question no less ultimate than the purposes and values of life itself. Should the judge be primarily concerned with the child's happiness; or with the child's spiritual and religious training? Should the judge be concerned with the economic "productivity" of the child when he grows up? Are the primary values of life in warm, interpersonal relationships, or in discipline and self-sacrifice? Are stability and security for a child more desirable than intellectual stimulation? These questions could be elaborated endlessly. And yet, where is the judge to look for the set of values that should inform the choice of what is best for the child? Normally, the custody statutes do not themselves give content or relative weights to the pertinent values. If one looks to society at large, one finds neither a clear consensus as to the best child rearing strategies nor an appropriate hierarchy of ultimate values. There are only private views.

This lack of consensus about values — like many assertions that seem obvious — cannot be empirically proven on the basis of existing research. The idea of consensus carries with it the notion of degree of agreement or disagreement about certain values. One might fairly ask whether a given degree of agreement represents consensus or dissensus. To avoid this characteristic problem one would want either a comparison between various groups (for example, American parents and French parents) or an evaluation of the same group at two different times based on identical questions. The great bulk of research done by sociologists on parental attitudes and practices focuses on how well certain variables such as social class or ethnicity *explain* differences, not on measuring the degree of consensus. Given the inherent difficulties of conducting reliable survey research, and the questions that interest sociologists, it is not surprising that there is no body of existing research aimed at demonstrating this lack of value of consensus. Nevertheless, we believe that in an exceptionally diverse society that is deeply marked by racial and religious divisions, highly varied in economy, geography, and even in the degree of urbanization, there is no consensus about the good life for children.

THE CRITICAL QUESTION — WHO DECIDES?

Given our premise that the means and ends of child rearing are largely indeterminate, a critical question that quite naturally comes to the fore is: *Who decides?* Or, more precisely, how does law allocate power and responsibility in our society, and how should it? This question, it seems to us, must be the focus of any intelligible theory. Whoever enjoys the power of decision will influence not only the means but also the very objectives of child rearing.

Very broadly speaking, there are three locations for the power of decision: the child, the family, or the state. Moreover, decision-making power can be shared. A primary function of law in relation to children is to outline a framework for the distribution of decisional power among the child, the family and various agencies of the state. Indeed, in the tradition of analytic theory, it would be possible to evaluate the law as it relates to children from the vantage point of asking how power is distributed by law presently, and whether this distribution is coherent and consistent. Any theory of justice in relation to children must address the issue of how power and responsibility for children should be distributed.

Emphasizing *who* should decide, rather than *what* should be decided, brings into focus the problem unexplored by child emancipators. Very young children are incapable of decisions about many important questions affecting their lives. It is not simply unwise to emancipate them; it is impossible. A two-and-a-half year old will be subject to the will of either an older person or the elements. If the child emancipators are libertarians and simply want children to have the same liberty as adults, then, as suggested above, they must explain what is to become of younger children. There is no libertarian alternative until the child is competent to survive in the manner of an adult. Obviously, for many matters, therefore, the question is not whether the child should decide, but which adult should decide on behalf of the child. The emancipators fail to provide a coherent theory for determining when and how the law should give the child primary power of decision over various aspects of his or her life.

The theoretical shortcomings of the child-saver's claims are also exposed by focusing on "who should decide?" The child-savers implicitly suggest that government should have a very broad role relating to the protection of children, but they do not define the limits, if any, of governmental power. Delineating the scope of child protection by government poses profound questions of political and moral philosophy concerning the proper relationship of children to their family and the family to the state.

Like the choice (in the judicial system) of which party is to bear the burden of proof (or the risk of non-persuasion), one's starting point as to the *proper* distribution of power can profoundly affect policy conclusions, particularly in the face of factual uncertainties and value clashes. Broadly speaking, there are three basic "starting points" for analyzing policies concerning children: (1) state paternalism, which assumes the state has primary responsibility for children and ought to exercise full control over their lives, except where delegation to the family is justified; (2) family autonomy, which assumes that power and responsibility for children generally ought to be vested in private hands — essentially the family — except for cases where government rule can be justified; and (3) agnosticism, which rests on no preference and instead approaches individual policy issues somehow on their own merits. The child-savers for the most part never describe their starting point, much less develop a theory of justice to justify their preference.

CONCLUSION

Children's rights pose profound and fascinating intellectual questions. As a general proposition, one would expect that law, particularly in an area so intimately related to the family, would largely reflect the dominant cultural norms and would have a rather limited capacity to change those norms or shape individual behavior. Nevertheless, it is part of a well-established American tradition to view law as a means of producing cultural change and political response. As a general proposition, it appears that the legal process is used increasingly as a forum for debate over competing perceptions of the world, where the protagonists hope to affect on a broad scale both social values and behavior. Plainly much of the debate over children's "rights" has ramifications that are not strictly legal, and indeed these nonlegal consequences may be the primary goal for some child advocates. In all events, how power and responsibility for children are distributed, the causes and effects of today's distribution and how power *should* be distributed — these questions provide a basis for fashioning a variety of theories.

1   Coigney, *Children Are People Too: How We Fail Our Children and How We Can Love Them* (1975).
2   Farson, *Birthrights* (1974).
3   Foster, *A Bill of Rights For Children* (1975).
4   Compare Popper, *Conjectures and Refutations: The Growth of Scientific Knowledge* (1964) with Kuhn, *The Structure of Scientific Revolutions* (2nd ed. 1970).
5   See *Webster's Third New International Dictionary of the English Language,* Unabridged (1969) p. 2371.
6   The idea of indeterminacy and its relevance to child custody issues is explored in Mnookin, "Child Custody Adjudication: Judicial Functions in the Face of Indeterminancy," (1975) 39, Law and Contemporary Problems 226. Its relevance to schools and education is discussed in an unpublished manuscript entitled *Choice* by Coons and Sugarman.

A Preface To A Children's Code

*Samuel Stoljar**

Surely one matter to which we may well devote some attention begins as a purely lawyerly question yet ends up as a much wider socio-legal one, namely, whether our children's law could, or should, be usefully codified, and if so what form such a code should take: what, more broadly, such a code might emphasize, or take particular notice of at the present time.

Many may object to the mere mention of a code. Some will say that children's law should not be codified except as part of a more general family code or, still more ideally, of a comprehensive code covering the totality of civil law. Fortunately I do not here have to argue for, or against, this sort of view. For my present position claims no more than this: that our law concerning children offers an ample enough body of distinctive principles and problems which, both conceptually and socially, do warrant consideration on their own. In some respects, it is certainly true, a full law of children would necessarily have to tie in with other civil or criminal rules, those relating to incapacity or diminished responsibility in particular, which rules are of course also meant to protect the child. Still this latter protection is quite different from that envisaged in children's law. For whereas our incapacity rules are designed to shield the child from possible liability to other persons, in fact assume that the child himself has somehow been at fault, our children's law tries to protect children as children by creating special obligations and liabilities' towards them, obligations primarily attaching to parents, sometimes to guardians, wherever either display a demonstrable lack of care either with regard to the child's person or to his property. Our children's law then seeks to impose various additional responsibilities upon those who have their charge so as to protect children against hurt and harm to which, in their natural vulnerability, they are particularly prone; otherwise they would not only be injurable with impunity but also join the obscure.

There remain other and more challenging objections to the project of a code. One frequent objection is that a children's code is anyhow of little

* Samuel J. Stoljar, LL.B., LL.M., Ph.D., LL.D. (Lond.), Professor of Law, Research School of Social Sciences, Australian National University.

value since, especially in the area of family law, legal rules or principles codified or not can only play a limited or modest role, for so variable and random are the factors that influence any one member of a family that his responses often turn out to be as unpredictable as they are unique.[1] Similarly it is sometimes said that legal rules do not really catch the precise nature of family relationships since what such rules reflect is their morphology, not their anatomy, so that it becomes largely illusory to regard the principles embodied in any family code as a faithful expression of family life as it actually or normally proceeds.[2]

These objections, admittedly, contain a good deal of truth. Yet they also overlook perhaps something even more important, which is that to a lawyer, if perhaps not to all social scientists, it is the variability and morphology of social or personal relations that offer the interesting as indeed also the crucial facts of life, as it is precisely the morphological deviation from the supposedly natural or normal ("anatomical") paradigm that provides both the occasion and the justification for legal intervention and redress. Nor can the lawyer be too embarrassed by the alleged uniqueness of human responses or events. If these responses were literally unique, unique in every case, we would have to abandon all rational inquiry since there can be no such inquiry in a world of absolutely unique phenomena. So what the above objections may rather mean to convey, or in any case more legitimately convey, is that our responses are not so much absolutely as they are relatively unique, with the result that they are still broadly identifiable or knowable, at least in rough outline even if not exactly so. It follows that the lawyer must always make some attempt to bring even allegedly unique responses under some normative control, that is, he must try to evaluate the drift or significance of such responses; try to understand the reasons why certain human actions or reactions, unique or not, cause conflict or dispute. Without this sort of understanding his intervention in these situations would neither professionally nor intellectually be worth his job.

Yet, as already hinted, the objections we have mentioned do point to a feature strongly characteristic of this province of the law, the feature that our children's code can never be a full or accurate embodiment of legal certainty but can, in large part, only strive to be a statement or restatement of very broad principles in which the element of discretion will loom very large. A code is admittedly no panacea for all the possible ills in the relations between parent and child; still it can offer a good deal of practical, even if not theoretical, knowledge of the problems these relations typically involve. A code, if its work is well done, can offer such practical knowledge by virtue of its systematic clarity and its comprehensive scope, particularly in an area such as this where, as has been the case in most common law jurisdictions, our children's law has been bad simply as law merely by being so disarranged and diffuse. A code can also be of help if it were to indicate the general direction our children's law should go, if it somehow could illuminate the "policy", the *Rechtspolitik,* or (if you prefer) the "ideology" which should inform the way in which, as well as the discretion with which, we apply our principles, especially our broadest principles.

2.

Our ideal children's code would naturally divide into two principal parts, one dealing with the child's personal relations with his parents, another with his property. The property part would obviously come after the personal one; still we may deal with it first, as it is by far the simpler of the two. Speaking generally, this property area is in no urgent need of reform. The law is here based on two broad principles which have never been in doubt: that the child is entitled to own property, and secondly that it is for the parents, sometimes the guardians, to safeguard and administer it. In this administration parents are in no more favourable position than are guardians (parents are indeed called natural guardians), for both parents and guardians are essentially trustees; moreover, trustees whose managerial responsibility is virtually strict, having to exercise a very high degree of fiduciary care and circumspection, the details of which technically belong, in our system, not to children's law but to the law of trusts.

By contrast, continental codes (I am here mainly referring to West European codes), lacking as they do the special category of trust, have had to provide more specifically as to what exactly parents (or guardians) are to do in their property management. Thus, these codes require the making of inventories to separate their child's property from their own; they specify how or when the parents are to render accounts, or what sorts of gifts they can make or take out of the administered property, how they are to meet possible conflicts of interests, just as the codes also provide whether, or to what extent, parents may make transactions in respect of their child's property, including which transactions they can make independently, or which not without a court's authority. Though this is not the place to pursue these technicalities, let it be said with emphasis that we can here learn a good deal from comparative law, if only because in European law these special rules laid upon parents or guardians constitute one of the great sources of fiduciary obligations, the obligations imposed upon persons who manage property not their own.[3]

There are other things that comparative law can teach, quite apart from furnishing something of a model of how our children's property law could be more systematically arranged or organized. It can suggest one or two improvements in our law. One improvement, a purely technical one, relates to the child's representation by his parents, the latter's power to represent the child as *ex officio* agents or trustees. At common law the well-known position is that parents have no such right of representation unless this is expressly given them by a court. It is true, one should hasten to add, that even at common law parents do have certain *ex lege* rights, rights arising from their so-called "natural guardianship", to deal independently with the property of their child, though this only in respect of his personal property: they may, for example, dispose of that property, and reinvest the proceeds, if circumstances warrant this.[4] However this is a very limited and very exceptional right, nor one the exact extent of which is very clear. Hence the effective common law position is that a parent cannot incur any liability on behalf of his child and that, moreover, if he does purport so to do the liability will attach not to the child, but to the parent himself.[5] The absence of such representative rights creates obvious practical disadvantages, since a parent can never safely act, even as regards the most ordinary or simple matters, without being so authorized by a court, an official authorization that must always involve some expense and at the very least delay.

A second possible improvement suggested by comparative law is of a very different kind. Suppose a child comes into a large sum of money either through some inheritance or as the winner of a lottery-ticket, and so quite suddenly and unexpectedly becomes a very much richer person than his parents and all his brothers and sisters combined. In continental law, where the parents have a usufructuary right in or over the child's property until the latter's emancipation or majority, they are thereby also in a position to use the child's new riches for the benefit of the whole family: clearly a very useful power since it helps to eliminate what might otherwise become an almost shocking disparity in the financial or economic welfare amongst members of the same small group. The common law, it need hardly be said, has never recognized any such parental usufruct, nor is there any reason to introduce this now. But there might be a good deal more justification for doing what German law has recently done, namely, to introduce a variant of this usufruct which, while denying the parents a beneficial interest in the child's property, yet gives them a special power to use that property for the benefit of all members of the family should there be an equitable need for this.[6]

Nor would such a power be completely at odds with our law though it would still be innovatory enough. There are indeed two areas, both in the law of succession, where our courts have long been concerned with a more equitable (intra-family) distribution of property benefits. One is the situation where children somehow receive unequal portions or legacies, a situation which equity has long since tried to rectify by way of such doctrines as satisfaction, ademption and so on. The other, more recent and of statutory origin, has to do with the testator's family maintenance as regards which courts now are allotted the sometimes very complex task of assessing whether a deceased's child is left a "proper" maintenanance. The word "proper", it was remarked in a leading case, connotes something different from the word "adequate"; a small sum may be sufficient for the "adequate" maintenance of a child, having regard to the child's station in life, but may be wholly insufficient for his "proper" maintenance, while, conversely, a sum may be quite insufficient for the child's "adequate" maintenance but may nevertheless be "proper" taking all other circumstances into account.[7]

Somewhat similar considerations, though transposed into a different key, would apply to the situation of the (suddenly) unequally rich child, except that here, this being an *inter vivos* situation instead of the more usual *post mortem* one, there would be the further question as to whether the equitable redistribution of property should only be of income or could touch capital as well. If the latter, the question would then be what proportion of capital the rich child ought to contribute; for it is clear that while he may be expected to make some contribution to the common good one cannot expect of him a total or disproportionate sacrifice, as this is after all still his property which is to be kept for him until the age of majority, whether this be eighteen or twenty-one. These matters clearly deserve much further thought, just as it is also clear that our code could probably do here no more than issue a very broad principle the application of which would have to be left to the equitable discretion of a judge.

3.

Let me turn to what I called the first part of a children's code, that dealing with the personal relations between parents and child, on which it is well worth spending more time. Here, again, the broad catalogue of parental duties or powers would not be difficult to compile since there is broad agreement not only in our own common law jurisdictions but, for that matter, also in continental or even Socialist law as to what parents can or cannot do: that, more particularly, they must care for and maintain their children, clothe and feed them, give them a home, further their education, or at the very least do nothing to hinder that education while the children remain at school. We may presume, furthermore, that our code would not leave any doubt that while parents have many duties, they enjoy as parents certain prior rights: prior in that it is for them, not for the state or society, nor for relatives or neighbours, to decide how their children are to be brought up.

This prior parental right, it is easily seen, is very much a nucleus of civil liberty, since the family thus becomes something of a pocket of resistance to the overweening claims of the state. In most cultures, in fact, this prior right is usually taken for granted, control over one's children being generally accepted as a sort of paternal monopoly, the one question only being whether the mother, too, could share in this control as a matter of right. Nor, for a very long time and not until the advent of the modern totalitarian state, was it in fact within the power of European governments (confronted as they were by a mostly rural population dispersed over a considerable territory) to displace this parental control. It was the church, rather more than the political state, that had both the local opportunity and the doctrinal urge to interfere with the parents' rights, in particular with their right of education; and in effect it was only as a result of the French Revolution that parents' rights over their children came to be seen as a part of basic human rights. Parental control is prior or basic also in another sense in that it constitutes a duty, a sort of socio-legal office, from which parents cannot withdraw. There is no legal way of renouncing parental responsibility, aside of course from the special procedure of adoption and aside also from such curious institutions as the French *bureau d'abandon,* which was created during the unsettled period of World War II, and which may have been just an attempt to make legal virtue out of social necessity.[8]

As everyone knows, the parents may not overdo their powers: they have to act reasonably and with restraint, particularly with regard to their disciplinary rights, those of correcting the child, this right, too, being regarded as one of their prior rights. The right of correction goes very much together with the right to educate and bring up a child; so that the question whether or not this disciplinary or corrective right has been violated or carried to excess is best answered by asking what sort of educative purpose the correction was meant to achieve. To punish a child for reasons divorced from or unrelated to its upbringing would be clear evidence of parental cruelty, by no means a declining phenomenon even in our advanced societies as well as something which no code can really eliminate. Even so, the code could perhaps make a clear distinction between the parents' persistent cruelty and a merely occasional lack of restraint. For the latter is not always irremediable, while the problem of the wantonly abused or battered child leaves us all at our wits' ends.

As everyone also knows, parents may breach their protective or custodial duties in many other ways, intentionally and even unintentionally. In most cases, parental neglect is virtually a matter of visible proof; but in some cases, parental neglect is more apparent than real, as in the case of a vagrant or truant child, for a child may be simply incorrigible without being actually delinquent, despite the fact that the parents may have consistently been doing their best. In this situation, too, parental custody may be withdrawn, though now for quite different reasons from those where children are at risk because in neglect. The child at risk needs a better home (foster-parentage rather than institutionalization is now the usually preferred alternative), whereas the incorrigible or delinquent child may require a severer (reformatory) regime than the parents are able or willing to provide. Yet we need not pursue these matters as they are familiar enough.

What, in this connection, may be a little less familiar is the peculiar doubt that has arisen as to whether children can sue their parents in tort for harm or injury done to them by the latter through their abuse or carelessness. At common law this doubt did not exist. In the famous *Ash Case*,[9] for example, a mother, pretending that her daughter was mad, "bound her and compelled her to take physick" for three hours or so. In an action for personal trespass and false imprisonment, the jury awarded the daughter £2,000 in damages, in those days a fabulous sum which Lord Holt later reduced without, however, questioning the child's right to sue. This right has nevertheless been disputed in some American courts, largely on the ground that such suits would be as unfitting as they might be destructive of the family.[10] But this ground is misconceived as it seems to derive from the false assumption that the "family" constitutes a separate entity from the parent-child relationship: there are no "parents" without children: a childless couple are neither parents nor do they constitute a family. The family, in short, consists precisely of the relation between parents and children which, by their injurious action, the parents themselves undermine.

4.

I am however more concerned with certain other, also more subtle and complex, aspects of the relations between parents and child which an informed codifier will need to attend to, even if at the end of the day he may remain as baffled as ever as to how some of the emerging difficulties are to be met. Now we can take it for granted that a children's code would provide for some such general principle as this: that (to use the phraseology of much modern legislation) the child's "best" interests are to be served, that his interests are to be a "paramount" consideration, that parents whether acting jointly or severally must strive to promote or advance not only the child's physical but also his psychological well-being, his "moral" well-being in the broadest sense. "Best" and "paramount" interests are obviously somewhat vague expressions, but in one respect we know well enough what they are supposed to mean, namely, that in a situation of marital break-down, including a conflict or dispute over a child's custody (or guardianship), the interests or preferences of the child are to be preferred to the claims of the (divorcing or separating) parents, irrespective of which side is at fault.[11]

In most other respects, however, to speak of a child's "best" or "paramount" interests makes considerably less sense. For if you take a normal family, a family describable as a going concern, how can the child's interest be paramount there? Assuming that the parents are of limited financial or, for that matter, intellectual means, the "best" that children can expect will be only a very second best. Again assuming that the parents do everything that in the circumstances can be reasonably asked from them, how can a child claim a "paramountcy" of interest unless he were to claim, or could rightfully expect, some real manifestation of parental self-sacrifice? Children are certainly entitled to a very great deal, but their parents' total self-abnegation is not one of their rights.

It then appears that, apart from break-down situations, a child's "best" or "paramount" interest is not always a realistic or realizable one. What in fact the words "best" or "paramount" rather seem to suggest, yet so convey only in a very roundabout way, is the now well-known historical fact that the whole position of children has undergone a profound change, not just in the care and protection they are now entitled to, but more significantly in our total attitude towards them, the attitudes of parents as of society as a whole. The extent of that change is quickly seen by comparing the social situation of (say) the seventeenth century with the situation prevailing today. Then parents would often not know how many children they had, or where they were or what they did. Not, perhaps, because they were then intrinsically more unfeeling than parents are now; but rather because they were overwhelmed by some extraordinarily hard facts of life. The death of children was so frequent it became an almost normal happening (about a third died before the age of one and more than half before their teens). Not only did children die young, their parents did too. With normal life expectancies thus tragically short, there was little or no encouragement to invest psychological capital in one's children or even in one's parents: the family was too ephemeral a unit precisely because it was too short-lived. Under such conditions, it was a natural (rationally perhaps the only credible) belief that human beings deserved their harsh fate because of their essential sinfulness. Moreover, if everyone was wicked, sin also resided in the small child, so that he, too, whatever his infantile foibles, seemed to deserve the severe punishment that would strike at the very root of the evil if his ultimate chance of salvation was not to be lost.

Obviously, this is not the place to trace the socio-historical factors that brought all the relevant changes about. Suffice it to say that with material conditions constantly improving and infant and adult mortality very significantly reduced, the (nuclear) family acquired an entirely new role, not only for the upper and middle classes but for the increasingly comfortable working class as well. Thus, Professor Ariès and (more recently) Professor Plumb have been right in insisting that as a "sentimental" as distinct from a purely legal unit the family is in fact a relatively modern phenomenon not (as so often believed) an old or traditional one.[12] Of course these "sentimental" changes took a long time to evolve. Even in the nineteenth century the father's authority was still regarded as supreme or sovereign, with the courts, virtually everywhere in Europe, still most reluctant to intervene even if (according to more recent standards) that authority was deployed too rigidly.[13] Not until our own time has our whole familial setting been more radically transformed: today children have become extraordinarily cherished possessions, intensely desired for their own sake, things to be particularly loved and indulged; with the death of a child now a major disaster, not the accepted occurrence it once was; in short, the whole psychological relationship between parents and children is almost totally reversed. Children are, of course, still dependent on their parents, dependent on obvious physical and economic grounds; but parents have become dependent too, in that parents need children, no less than children need parents for their own mental health.

There is here another sociological point. Our modern family, it is important to see, could not have become the emotively interdependent unit it now is had it not also evolved as a relatively small group that both invites and develops very special, often almost exclusive, kinship bonds. In early or primitive societies a strong sense of kinship is suffused through the entire social structure, a child being, so to speak, the child of the whole group or clan, thus belongs not just to a nuclear but to a much larger network of multilateral human affections and solidarities. Only when this extended kinship weakens can the nuclear family really come to the fore. Roman law offers a good example of this. When, under the Empire, the old agnatic connections growingly decline, there appear perhaps as yet cautious yet still quite unmistakable attempts to develop the nuclear family's internal relationships. The Roman family had, of course, always been an important legal unit, in fact ever since recorded Roman law began; what is striking about the new legal measures is that they try to give the family a particular human dignity by turning it into an institution of filial piety and mutual support.[14]

This Roman image of the family largely disappeared through the long centuries of European barbarism, but gradually reemerged at the end of the middle ages, broadly the time of the renaissance. Modern society, as it developed from then on, increasingly relied on the nuclear family: this is, socially, perhaps its most distinctive mark. It is true that modern society also allows room for larger groups (indeed our political pluralism greatly encourages all kinds of groups), but their significant feature is that they are mostly divorced from kinship ties, with the crucially important result that the family has become, if not the only, then in any case the principal centre of those close natural ties of affection and affinity which are part of our most basic human needs, certainly of any normal child's needs. Not only is our modern nuclear family thus our main centre of secure human ties, it is also the place where these ties of affection are translated into concrete measures of assistance or support: measures, moreover, that can be claimed as a matter of right, of strong moral even if not always or not everywhere of fully legal right.

The greater the role of the nuclear family, the greater also the reliance of all its members *inter se.* For the children, as already indicated, the family, just by dint of its continuity and stability, responds to their essential needs, as it surrounds them with persons they can identify with, can imitate or learn from, with whom they can develop a sense of inter-personal dependability and human warmth. That all this can affect them vitally has been known for quite some time. It has been said that where orphaned or deserted children are brought up in state institutions these latter have 'for the most part produced uninspired individuals poorly adjusted for the outside world'.[15] In the remarkably concrete thinking that psychologists tell us children do, parents and home are the very embodiment of their biological nest. For the parents, too, children are now usually the very focus of their married lives. Indeed, children, as some sociologists have pointed out, seem also important to adults in another way, in that they seem to bring out the "childish" elements in their parents' personalities.[16] What is perhaps merely another way of saying that while we all grow older, children, especially our own children, somehow help us not to lose all contact with our own youth.

5.

I have so far been speaking of our relations with children in general. But of course these relations vary according to whether we deal with children of very young or tender years, or with older children, that is, adolescents or juveniles. What I now wish to suggest is that, though our relations with all our children are closely related, our ideal code would have to distinguish, for a number of purposes, between younger and older children, between (let us say) infants and juveniles, between the *impuberes* and *puberes,* as they were called in Roman law. It is with the older children, those between (say) ten and eighteen, that we are now particularly concerned.

Here, again, it is one thing to prescribe that their "best" or "paramount" interests must prevail, and quite another to provide for every conflict that may arise. Certainly, we can now say that the "best" interests of an older child require parents to do distinctly more for him than they were once expected to do. Let us further admit, what has now become quite fashionable to maintain, that there has been a definite shift from the parents' rights to children's rights, particularly in relation to teenage children who, unlike their younger siblings, may these days lead a distinctive life of their own. Let us, in sum, wholeheartedly agree that adolescents, too, are persons, that they have, or should have, rights to a personality we should do our best to recognize and respect.

Even so, we may tend to put too much emphasis upon the children's rights, for there remains a residual area of parental authority which we would do ill to overlook. There are several separable problems here. Consider, to begin with, two old cases which, however antiquarian they may appear at first sight, still contain some relevant points. A girl, eighteen years of age, was taken in labour in the house of her step-father during his absence. The mother omitted to procure for her the assistance of a midwife, as a result of which the girl died, yet it was held that the mother was not legally bound to procure any obstetric aid, hence could not be committed for manslaughter for not doing so.[17] At first sight the decision seems surprising, but is not really so. For one thing, the mother lacked the knowledge or foresight that a difficulty might occur. For another, and more importantly, she lacked the "necessary means", that is, lacked the funds to obtain a midwife at the right time. All she could have done was to go out to borrow the money, but the court was not prepared to ask her to go so far as to have to swallow her legitimate pride: borrowing money from friends or strangers, to facilitate the confinement of the mother of an apparently illegitimate child, would (in the then moral climate) have exposed her to too much shame. In the other case, which, I think, is illustrative of my thesis that even a modern children's code should not overlook the rights of the parents however much it may stress and elevate the children's rights, a rich Jew's only daughter embraced Christianity whereupon he turned her out as well as refused her further maintenance. The court rejected her application for relief since she could not bring herself within the Elizabethan Poor Law as she did not show that she was actually poor or likely to become a public charge.[18] This somewhat technical ground should not obscure its potentially wider rationale. A child, old or determined enough to choose its own religion, may well be expected to look after itself; a child choosing to injure so seriously its parents' feelings, as the daughter had done, cannot also claim to be comfortably maintained by them.

Consider next certain other disagreements, perhaps less serious or fundamental in character, which often arise in the ordinary day-to-day contacts between parents and child. To resolve such disagreements, is the child's interest always to be preferred, or are the parents to be allowed a more decisive influence, something like a casting vote? If parental authority is to count for something, they obviously need some overriding discretion, not merely a right just to express their views. But what sort of discretion would that be? Take, for example, the problem of how much freedom a juvenile may have, or how he (or she) is to be restricted in that freedom, or what the appropriate restrictive measures might be, or how much advice he may be expected to take, including advice with regard to his education, or career, or his social activities, not to mention the persons he (or she) should or should not befriend.

In considering these difficulties, we still seem to be a little over-impressed by Ogden Nash's well-known lines (in his *Family Reunion*): "Oh, what a tangled web do parents weave when they think that their children are naive". But surely the plain fact is that children often are naive, or foolish, or inexperienced or simply immature. What can make matters worse is that such disagreements may no longer be purely private, arising from purely personal differences of taste, but reflect a wider clash between two cultures, that is, between the parents' culture and the sub-culture of the children who, at least in our own affluent societies, have become an almost separate class. For adolescents (meaning children from the ages of thirteen or fourteen to those of seventeen or eighteen, assuming eighteen to be now generally the age of legal majority) share and participate in a way of life, characterized not only by their relative freedom and their special and independent pursuits, but also by their role as specialized consumers of the things regarded as desirable or appropriate amongst themselves. Clearly this is a phenomenon to which our children's code would do well to pay some heed; and this perhaps, as already suggested, simply by separating the legal treatment of younger children from that of the older ones and, more particularly, by providing for the latter a more relaxed parental regime. This, indeed, is something that some civilian codes (including the Soviet) seem to have attempted, by ending the parents' legal guardianship for adolescents and replacing it by a mere curatorship, a move certainly intended to give adolescents a greater legal capacity in their daily affairs which may also imply an intention to bestow a measure of greater personal freedom on them. Unfortunately, how this special adolescent regime has worked out in practice, how successful it has been, it is very difficult to say, so reticent are the relevant comparative sources in this respect.[19]

To urge some relaxation in the parents' day-to-day relations with their children is by no means to say that they are to surrender their residual or basic authority. That parents may sometimes need such authority is not difficult to see. For the disagreements with their children may not simply arise from sub-cultural differences of the sort adverted to above, they can derive from differences far more fundamental and intractable in character. For example, is the child entitled to smoke, cigarettes or marijuana, even at home? Is he entitled to abandon his schooling or training: thus to "drop out", to use this significantly new word in our social lexicon? Even Bazarov, the self-confessed 'nihilist" in Turgenev's *Fathers and Sons* had at least some constructive ideas on life and work compared with the totally nihilistic views some of our modern children entertain at least some of the time. Just this leads me to my last big problem concerning juveniles. For suppose we agree that parents do have a residual authority over their adolescent children, especially in matters of their moral education or social waywardness, how is this authority to be rationally justified? Are parents to retain ultimate moral or educational control? Or, to put the question differently, is such a final right of education to include a right to "indoctrinate" their children at least with regard to certain cultural or social values or attitudes?

This distinction between education and indoctrination has recently been much discussed in educational theory.[20] Even teachers at school, it is maintained, must stop short of indoctrinating children, however hard they must try to instruct or guide them to become good or at least reasonable citizens. Yet, how do we apply this distinction in the fields where fundamental disagreements or conflicts between parents and children occur? For if education does not just mean the communication or explaining of objective knowledge, but includes the teaching or transmission of the subjective or conventional values that inform the culture by which we live, how is this cultural transmission to be achieved? The only answer one can give, though even this may seem a little too vague to be completely satisfying, is this: that the communication of our cultural values must be by rational means rather than by dogmatic repetition, or propaganda, or a kind of "cultural" brainwashing, which would be indoctrination, not true education at all.

Now, admittedly, as regards very young children, those beneath or under the age of discernment (as lawyers say), some indoctrination seems always inevitable, since the very young cannot effectively be taught except by precise imperatives ("don't touch the fire", "don't hurt your little sister", etc), the reasons for which they may not understand until quite a few years hence. As regards older children, however, our adolescents or juveniles, the values, attitudes or rules we communicate cannot just be commands but must be rational prescriptions, in the sense of conveying explicit or implicit reasons or justifications as well. Only (what we may call) "reasonable rules" are apt to be morally educational, since only reason-giving rules invite and encourage questioning or discussion, thus cultivate both reflection and open minds, all quite unlike the methods of indoctrination which rather seek to close our minds by inculcating into us dogmatic and unquestioning beliefs.

All this, moreover, affects our parent-child relationships in two closely related ways. In the first place, it is an important reminder to parents that the kinds of persuasion they can use as well as the rules or injunctions they may issue should always be rational or justificatory in a moral or cultural sense. Accordingly, it would be a form of parental neglect, of intellectual neglect if you like, were parents merely to announce dogmatic or doctrinaire imperatives without any explanation or discussion of what it is, in their children's actions, they are objecting to. This would still be no magic formula automatically resolving all our difficulties. Still it is a way of reaffirming the very important "politic" and cultural role that parents play in a free society: I mean a society in which the transmission of our social culture or of our "cultural heritage" (if one may still use such a phrase) is entrusted to the (nuclear) family, not to specialized institutions, such as the church, or to other more secular but no less ideological agencies of the state. My point is that parents, though certainly possessing a prior right to bring up their children in (so to speak) their own image, are at the same time performing a more public role. This, in fact, may explain why Aristotle spoke of parents as having a sort of "royal" power over the young who need to be educated "with an eye to the state"; this, too, is why John Stuart Mill justified the denial of liberty to children long enough to make them competent citizens.[21]

In the second place, if children are to be morally educated, if they are to learn the meaning of "right" behaviour and "wrong", they must learn what moral philosophers sometimes call "the golden rule", that is, as Professor Hare has pointed out, they need somehow to realize that what is wrong for another to do to them is no less wrong for them to do to another: "Children must learn to think about what it is like to the other person. They must cultivate their sympathetic imagination".[22] For it is just this sort of imagination that will give them an understanding of what it means to do hurt and harm. Without such moral imagination, children are rather like the natural garden in Andrew Marvell's poem — the garden which unless ideally cultivated has a tendency of running wild. A concomitant aim of this moral exercise is to help children to place themselves in their parents' shoes, to understand that the latter, too, have feelings which adolescents may deplore, but still feelings that can be seriously, sometimes damagingly, hurt. A morally instructed or sensitive child may then be as ready to take note of and respect his parents' concerns as, on another level, he will respect the feelings or values of the members of his own sub-cultural group. Perhaps Bazarov, to whom we already referred, would have shown more dutiful sentiments towards his so poignantly devoted parents, had his "modernist" views not also included a quite distasteful moral insensitivity.

Not that a child's moral education has to follow a set course. It is rather by dint of living in a family, of being exposed to intimate moral criticism, of being subjected to regular praise and blame, that the child learns that his particular interests cannot always take precedence, that he must come to terms with the views and wants of others, must accept the existence of other interests or desires, not just his own. The family thus becomes a moral institution just as it has always been our most effective socializing milieu, precisely because it is a primary group which by involving its members in daily face-to-face contacts, thus teaches them, if anything can so teach, the arts of living together, including the arts of reasonable or amicable compromise.

6.

I have then been arguing for a conception of a children's code in which the legal relations between parents and children will certainly stress the great duties that parents owe, yet at the same time calls attention to the children's reciprocal duty to respect parents as parents as well as persons who, having lived a little longer, may have views on life worthy of some tolerance. In this conception, let this be clear, to ask for respect for parents is not to ask for a return to older or more traditional values, let alone a return to the old ideas, encapsulated in the notion of *patria potestas* (which notion, incidentally, so long maintained in European law under its Roman name was no less strongly influenced by the Germanic institution of the *Munt*). Rather, and more essentially, to ask for a respect for parents (*honneur et respect,* to use the words of the French civil code) is quite simply to ask for respect for different points of view, surely in its own way a most valuable preparation for the difficult business of growing up.

In thus concentrating on the family, I may have said rather too little about many other things our children's code might contain. Certainly, I have furnished no detailed blueprint of an ideal code, though I have tried elsewhere to offer something of a systematic checklist of, at any rate, the most important things such a code would have to deal with, whether with some particularity or only in the broadest terms.[23] Again, I have said far too little about procedural matters and, in particular, about the division of labour as between judges and courts on the one hand and administrative organs or agencies on the other. We hear a lot, these days, about the need for extra-judicial mediation or about the increasing role of specialized officials in this whole field; a French writer has in fact spoken of a shift from a parental to an institutional or official guardianship of children, from (what he calls) the *tutelle individuelle* to the *tutelle fonctionarisée*.[24] Nor can there be any doubt that we do need effective state agencies if the welfare of the orphaned or neglected child, and of every child at risk, is to be seen to as quickly and satisfactorily as we know how.

Still, rather different considerations surely apply in the particular area of intra-family disputes, those arising from the conflict between parental authority and children's interests. For here our business may not be so much, or at least not directly, with the actual welfare of the child, but with the delicate delimitation of human rights: parents and children may find themselves with opposing claims sometimes due to the complexities, sometimes to the varying fortunes of life. Yet, these are the very conflicts and claims so preeminently reserved for judicial discretion and even creativity; our administrative agencies would not really know how to deal with them. Suppose, to give just one example, that a child has been administratively entrusted to foster-parents because of the parents' extreme poverty and the child's attendant neglect; suppose next that the parents, never really at fault, see their situation improve dramatically whereupon they ask for the return of their child, only to be resisted by the foster-parents who have grown deeply affectionate of the child just as he of them. What is to be done? To speak of the child's "best" or "paramount" interests now reveals itself for the cliché it is, since what is his "best" interest is precisely what is so difficult to decide. Is he to be deprived of his natural parents eager, and now perfectly able to look after him? Is he to be removed from his foster-home to which he has become happily accustomed, with the *status quo* to be perhaps upsettingly disturbed?

I would not wish to propose now a considered solution of this problem except to suggest that we shall encounter it, with many factual variations yet always on the same general theme, probably more and more frequently in the years to come; already we can discern, even at common law, a distinctive line of cases that seem to grant foster-parents quasi-adoptive rights, that is, rights of practically permanent custody without a proper adoption having taken place. And this reinforces the proposition earlier advanced, namely, that our law of parents and children is morally and socially far too serious and sensitive a matter to be dealt with extra-judicially: we have a need here for judge-made decisions if only because they are our only public and published decisions which society can debate. Indeed all I have said, here and before, in this perhaps too prefatory preface is but an invitation to further legal and moral reflection and argument.

1   Cf. A.J.W. Taylor, "A Psychologist's View of Family Law" in *Family Centenary Essays* (Wellington, New Zealand, 1967) 91, 94.

2   Cf. A. Malmström, *Children's Welfare in Family Law,* Scandinavian Studies of Law, Vol.2 (1957) 123, 125.

3   For a detailed description of the comparative arrangements, see my "Children, Parents and Guardians" at 99ff. in Vol.4 of the *International Encyclopedia of Comparative Law.*

4   See 39 Am. Jur. 2d., § 122.

5   See 2 Williston on *Contracts* (3rd ed. 1959) § 314. If the guardian proves insolvent, there may be a right of subrogation in that equity may allow creditors to enforce obligations against the ward's estate provided the obligations were incurred for the child's benefit.

6   See German Civil Code (BGB), § 1649.

7   *Bosch v. Perpetual Trustee Co* [1938] A.C. 463, 476.

8   On this French bureau see Ripert et Boulanger, *Traité de droit civil* (Paris 1956), Vol.i, Nr.2524.

9   (1696) Comb. 357.

10   See on this more fully and critically, Prosser on *Torts* (3rd ed. 1964) 885ff.

11   For the manifold problems that here arise, including those where relatives dispute over the custody of orphaned children, see the comprehensive study by Brigitte W. Bodenheimer, "Uniform Custody Jurisdiction Act" (1969) 22 Vanderbilt L. Rev. 1207, 1208ff.

12   Philippe Ariès, *Centuries of Childhood* (London 1962) 10, 33 and *passim;* J.H. Plumb, "The New World of Children" The Listener, February 26, 1976.

13   See generally on this A. Trabucchi, "Patria Potesta e Interventi del Giudice" (1961) 7 Rivista di Diritto Civile 223-31.

14 See on this P. Ourliac and J. de Malafosse, *Histoire du Droit Privé* (Paris 1968) 50.

15 *White House Conference on Child Care and Protection* (Washington 1930) Section IV, 134.

16 Parsons and Bales, *Family: Socialisation and Interaction Process* (New York, 1955) 21.

17 *R v. Shepherd* (1862) Le. & Ca. 147.

18 *The Inhabitants of the Parish of St Andrew's Undershaft in London v. J. Mendez de Breta* (1701) 1 Ld. Raym. 699. The matter did not end there, for the decision immediately gave occasion to another statute (not repealed until 1846) under which the Lord Chancellor was empowered to make a proper order if Jewish parents refused their Protestant children a fitting maintenance. For this story, see Blackstone's *Commentaries* (23rd ed. 1854), i, 563.

19 For some attempt to survey these sources, see my "Children, Parents and Guardians" at 38-9. See note 3.

20 See, in particular, R.M. Hare, "Adolescents into Adults" in T.H.B. Hollins (ed.), *Aims in Education* (Manchester 1964) 47, 51ff.

21 Aristotle, *Politics* i, 2, 13; J.S. Mill on *Liberty* Chap.3.

22 R.M. Hare, *op.cit.* 63.

23 This in my study of "Children, Parents and Guardians" see note 3.

24 See R. Rodière, *La tutelle des mineurs* (Paris 1950) 34.

Determination Of The Status Of A Child In The Conflict Of Laws

*John Swan**

The problems that I want to investigate are those connected with issues of minority, and legitimacy, and with the effectiveness of adoption orders, when any of these come before a court in regard to a child. Questions about these issues have been traditionally put in an abstract form, requiring a consideration of the child's status. For example, is this person a minor or not? Is this child the legitimate child of that person? Is this person the adopted child of that person? To simplify the discussion, I shall generally assume that we are asking each question before an Ontario court, and that that court has jurisdiction to hear the case. I shall suggest that asking the abstract question is seldom a helpful way to begin the inquiry that most cases require for disposition, and that better ways must be found if we are not to do great harm to people who seek relief from the court.

A question on minority would have to be answered in the following case. Peter, aged 17, borrows money from the Friendly Finance Company. He fails to repay and is sued in Ontario. It turns out that he lives in the province of Arcadia where the age of majority is 17. Traditional conflict analysis suggests that the determination of the question whether Friendly can successfully sue or not will depend on the proper law of the contract.[1] We will assume that the proper law is that of Ontario: the contract was made here, by parties physically present here, and was to be performed here. The result would be that the contract is invalid. If we change some facts so that David, aged 18, comes to Ontario from Ruritania, where the age of majority is 19, the result is again that Ontario law governs and, this time, the contract would be valid.

Brainerd Currie[2] demonstrated that the first result is absurd and that the second may be defensible, but only if we make some assumptions that the traditional analysis does not. Briefly, the first result is absurd because it protects Peter from the unpleasant consequences of his conduct when there

---

* John B. Swan, LL.B. (U.B.C.), B.C.L. (Oxon.), Professor, Faculty of Law, University of Toronto.

is no good reason to do so. We frustrate a commercial enterprise in Ontario without forwarding any policy of any jurisdiction. Why should Ontario care to protect Peter when Arcadia says that he is perfectly able to look after himself?[3] The second question is more difficult. We may assume that Ruritania is concerned to protect people in David's position from the consequences of their weakness, and that Ontario is concerned to protect enterprises like Friendly who are doing business in Ontario and who rely on the kind of contract made here. It is now common to refer to such a case as a "true conflict"; both rules are competing for application and the purposes of both would be served by being applied in this case.[4] An answer to the problem might lie along the following lines. Ruritania and Ontario both share the policy of protecting reliance on contracts. Both acknowledge that certain people are, by reason of age, illness or other weakness, unable to look after themselves and need protection by the law. When these two policies clash, one party must bear the risk of loss. The risk should in this case lie on David, since he came to Ontario and dealt with Friendly who may (let us assume) have had no idea that the law in Ruritania either applied to David or was different from that in Ontario.[5] Of course, one can argue for a contrary result, but to do so would admit the premise that the real issue is the rational choice between competing rules.[6]

The capacity to make a will or other disposition of property presents similar problems. The traditional rule is not completely clear. Dicey and Morris state that the capacity to make a will is governed by the law of the testator's domicile at the time of making.[7] If, therefore, a person aged 18 has the capacity to make a will by Ontario law, and he or she is domiciled here, any will made by that person is valid even though that person may subsequently move to another jurisdiction, where the age of majority is, say, 21, and acquire a domicile there and die. Ontario and all common law jurisdictions share a common policy in favour of testamentary freedom: in general, wills should be upheld if possible. While wills are not bilateral in the way contracts are, it is not true that holding a will to be invalid will not hurt someone.[8] Even though the estate of a person held to have died intestate may be distributed in accordance with some statutory scheme that is presumed to be fair, as we shall see, that scheme does not protect some people who may be expected to be the concern of a testator. For example, if a person left an illegitimate child, that child can only take if he or she is a beneficiary under a will: not under the Devolution of Estates Act.

There are, therefore, two difficulties with the traditional view. The first is that there may be strong pressure to recognize as many wills as possible. The second is that the concept of domicile is not a useful or convenient one to use here. The first problem could be solved by providing that any will would be valid unless it can be shown that the purpose of the law of some relevant jurisdiction would be forwarded by holding it to be invalid and that this purpose is one, which, in all the circumstances of the case, should be forwarded. This would permit a jurisdiction where, for example, the age of capacity is 21, to apply its rule in the case of immovable property in that jurisdiction. There would seem, however, to be no need for universal validity or invalidity — a will could be valid or invalid in respect of so much of any estate as is subject to the jurisdiction of any court.

The second difficulty arises from the fact that it would be false to suggest that there is any uniformity under the traditional rules for determining domicile (particularly the domicile of minors). Domicile is not likely to be treated in an identical fashion in every court where the issue may come up. There is, for example, no uniformity in the tests used in various Canadian provinces to determine domicile[9], and it would be unrealistic to expect any more agreement throughout the Common Law world, to say nothing about the rest of the world. In general, domicile would work were it not for the more grotesque possibilities inherent in the minor's domicile of dependence, especially when coupled with the risk of revival of some domicile of origin. We need some alternative concept to replace domicile, that would indicate when a person was so closely connected to any particular jurisdiction that its invalidating rule should be applied. Perhaps the best we can do is to suggest that "settled residence" should be the test. Therefore, only that jurisdiction where a testator had a settled residence at the time of making a will should be concerned to invalidate it on the ground that the testator lacked capacity.[10] There is no reason why that determination should govern any other jurisdiction where probate is sought or the testator has property.[11] The same approach would solve any other issue of testamentary capacity.

In the case of contractual capacity this analysis has shown two things, first, that the choice of what law shall govern must be made by comparing actual rules that are in conflict; there are no choice of law rules of the kind, "capacity to contract is governed by the proper law of the contract". Second, that to make the choice we must compare the purposes behind the rules that are in conflict. Such a comparison will normally disclose either that there is no real choice: one rule obviously applies and the other equally obviously does not, or that there is a true conflict and that a difficult choice must be made. In the case of both contractual and testamentary capacity, it has been shown that there are basic policies which are available for use in the conflict analysis. If these basic policies are used, then it will often be the case that a court is shown a preferred solution which should normally be adopted unless some overriding concern exists to displace it. The only rules that will have to be developed will be rules for determining when the special concern overrides the general policy.

Can this analysis be usefully applied to the second and third questions that were asked earlier in this paper? The second question was, "Is this child the legitimate child of that person?" A typical case raising such an issue would be one where a testator leaves money in trust for his children for life, remainder to their issue. A child of the testator has had a child who was not born in lawful wedlock[12], and the question that would come before an Ontario court would be if the testator's grandchild is "issue". It is quite clear that, so far as we are concerned here, a testator can leave his money to anyone he likes. It is equally clear that whether or not any particular person can take under a will is a matter of construction of the will. There are no choice of law issues in construction: the only question is, what did the testator mean? The common law position is that the word "issue" means legitimate issue. The question then becomes what are "legitimate issue?" No rule of construction can determine this question.

A good example of the kind of question that can come up is provided by *Re MacDonald*.[13] A testator left property to the issue of a grandson, and the grandson, who had died, left a daughter, Maria. The grandson had lived in Mexico, (the courts held that the grandson had acquired a domicile there) and under Mexican law Maria, though admittedly illegitimate, was entitled to succeed to the grandson's estate as if she were legitimate. The Supreme Court of Canada held that she could succeed as "issue". Ritchie J., delivering the judgment of the court said:[14]

"Maria . . . the sum total of whose capacities and obligations under the law of [Mexico] include all those of a child born in wedlock in Ontario, in my opinion has the status of a legitimate child in that Province for the purpose here in question and the fact that some social limitations may attach to her position in Mexico, and that her status in that country is therefore described as 'illegitimate', can, in my view have no effect on the standards required in order to qualify as a legitimate child for the purpose of benefiting as one of 'the issue' of the grandson of an Ontario testator".

The difficulty in analysing this case stems from the fact that it is very hard, in the light of the decision, to understand the purpose of the rule of construction that "issue" means "legitimate issue". If the rule expresses some valid concern of Ontario why should that concern be subordinated to the Mexican desire to treat all of a person's children equally? If Ontario testators are presumed to share the concerns of the barons at Merton in 1234,[15] are these concerns acknowledged by the decision of the Supreme Court of Canada? If we can assume that, since the testator had legal advice in setting up the scheme for disposing of his estate, he probably meant what the common law presumed that he meant, then what Mexican law might say to Mexican testators should be irrelevant in the case of a Canadian testator.

However, if we are realistic, it would seem to be unlikely that the testator ever addressed his mind to the situation that arose. If this is the case, have we done anything sensible in cutting Maria out? It would make sense in distributing an estate of this kind to consider all the persons in the class of beneficiaries as having equal shares to the testator's estate. Equal treatment can be regarded as being the fairest method of distribution. It is not then a big step to argue that to exclude a person who might be thought to be in the class requires that there be some good reason for doing so.[16]

The way in which the rule of construction and the alternative policy can be accommodated is to say that, if the testator has shown a clear intention to exclude someone who would otherwise be expected to be entitled to take as a member of a class of beneficiaries, then, subject to any statutory disability, he may do so. If he has no such intention, then, so far as possible, once we know who the members of the class are, all the members of the class of beneficiaries should be treated equally. When a court is free to consider the possible application of foreign law, then the scope of a court to be creative is far greater than under its own domestic law. The Supreme Court of Canada seized on the fact that, in Mexico, Maria enjoyed the incidents of any legitimate child even though she was regarded as illegitimate. The court was then able to reach a result that was consistent with the principle that I have suggested should govern.[17] As will be seen, the view of Mexican law as to Maria's rights to succeed indicated that there was no good reason to exclude her from the class of beneficiaries.

We now have to determine two questions in a case like *Re MacDonald:* is the claimant a member of the class of beneficiaries, and, if so, then, is there a good reason for excluding the claimant from taking? The second question cannot be answered by reference to the Ontario rule of construction, for we must have already determined that the testator had no intention of excluding the claimant from taking under his will before we can consider this question.

In any case where the gift is to "issue" or "children", we could answer the first question upon proof that the biological relationship of parent and child exists. While this may be a difficult enquiry in many cases, especially when there are no presumptions to help the court, it is not often going to be so and, in any case, mere difficulty is not a reason for not attempting the task (particularly when the task is done at the expense of the estate). The second question is much more difficult from the point of view of the law. The difficulty arises precisely because it is hard to know why we have such a rule in Ontario. The following justifications are offered in an attempt to show what might happen. (It should be clear that I offer these without any belief in their validity.) *One,* some taint attaches to bastardy, so that bastards should not take equally with legitimate children. *Two,* the sins of the parents should be visited on the heads of the children and the law should respect this moral position. *Three,* a parent may be expected to care more for his legitimate children than for his bastards. (If these reasons seem repulsive then it is only because our domestic law is so. If the purpose is grotesque, then so will be the law.)

If we consider the first reason for the rule excluding bastards from taking, then we may consider that, in the case of *Re MacDonald,* an Ontario court could exclude Maria from taking so that more of the testator's money would be available for legitimate children.[18] This might, then, be a good reason for denying her any right to succeed. If this be the reason for the rule, however, the decision of the Supreme Court of Canada frustrated it. The second and third reasons would appear to be solely the concern of Mexico, where Maria and her parents lived. If Mexico sees no reason to prevent her from succeeding to her father (or through her father) why should Ontario care?[19] There may be other and better reasons for excluding illegitimate children, but even if there are, I have indicated that one can consider each reason and then decide whether that reason justifies any particular result. We have a "fall-back" position in that we allow the child to share equally with others in the class, unless there is some good reason to deny her.

There are several important consequences of this method of analysis. First, there is no need to talk of status in the abstract. We are concerned with a simple question, "Can this child succeed?" To ask "Is this child the legitimate child of X?" is meaningless, for legitimacy is of no interest to us unless it helps to answer in a sensible way some question that bothers us. Secondly, we have posed and answered a choice of law question without having to consider some general statement, for example, that the question of legitimacy is to be decided by the law of some domicile at some point of time. It is true that in Ritchie J.'s judgment, and in most commentaries[20], the important question is not the status of the child but the incidents of that status. The step made here (that is missing there) is that here we have a starting point for our reasoning — the desire to treat all children equally — and a focus on reasons for not doing so in appropriate cases. As I have suggested, there may be a good reason why Ontario should be concerned about the distribution to illegitimate children of an estate governed by Ontario law. Thirdly, the problems we have with a conflict case stem directly from the unsatisfactory nature of the domestic Ontario rule. If the rule regarding illegitimate children made as much sense as most rules, say, of contract and tort, then we would not have most of the problems that we do in trying to apply it. As a result of the unsatisfactory nature of the common law rule one would expect that the courts (when given the chance) would frequently find a way around it. That is what has happened. In effect the child has the benefit of both rules. A child who can take under Ontario law, either because the testator intended that she should, or because under Ontario law[21] she is not excluded from a class intended to benefit, will then take. A child who cannot take under Ontario law, but who can take under some applicable foreign law will be allowed to take.[22] The courts are following sound instincts in doing this, but there are better reasons than their instincts to justify the sensible result.

The problems of the legitimacy of children are not confined to problems of testate succession. There are three other areas where the issue can be relevant. The first is intestate succession. The issue here is the same as with testate succession. The Devolution of Estates Act[23] at present (i.e. 1977) excludes illegitimate children from succeeding. This is regarded as a matter of the interpretation of the Act. The legal question of who are illegitimate children must still be answered. However, in the distribution of a deceased's estate one could adopt the same position as was suggested should govern testate succession: a presumption of equal treatment, rebutted in appropriate circumstances. There could then be a choice of law analysis in any conflict case to determine what an "appropriate circumstance" might be.

The second is support or maintenance *inter vivos*. The distinctions between illegitimate and legitimate children are of much less importance in this case. I do not propose to discuss this topic here since the operation of the legislation is very specialized and a discussion of the choice of law issues would require an explanation of the scheme of the Reciprocal Enforcement of Maintenance Orders Act,[24] and there is no scope for that here.

The third area is the Dependants' Relief Act.[25] Unlike the Devolution of Estates Act, the purpose of this Act is fairly clear. It exists to protect dependants whom it is felt have a claim to be supported by the deceased rather than by the state. If we suppose the typical case that a testator has died leaving his estate away from his immediate family, the justification for applying the Dependants' Relief Act will be the likelihood of the protected dependants being supported by the state in Ontario rather than by the person who should have done so.[26] The purpose of the Act will determine any choice of law issue, *i.e.,* any issue of the territorial scope of the Act. The traditional analysis has usually said that the application of the Act depends on the law governing the succession, *viz.,* the *lex situs* in the case of immovables, and the *lex domicilii* in the case of movables. Given the purpose of the Act, these rules are absurd.[27] If a jurisdiction where the dependants are living sees no reason to protect them then there is no reason for Ontario to do so, no matter whether the property is movable or immovable and in Ontario or not. The Ontario limitation that the testator must be domiciled in Ontario may cut down the possibility that, say, a New York wife or child could claim in Ontario the dependant's share out of Ontario land owned by a New York domiciliary. But even with this restriction, the purpose of the legislation must be the determining factor in any issue of its scope.

This analysis can provide the answer to the narrow problem we are considering. If Ontario excludes illegitimate children from the protection of the Act, one can simply say that that is Ontario's business. Since only those dependants who may rely on Ontario for support (if the testator is not compelled to support them) are affected, there can be no choice of law issue. If the application of the Act were not limited to those cases where the testator was domiciled in Ontario, one could have a case where a foreign testator dies leaving immovable property in Ontario and a dependant child in the Province. That child may or may not be the legitimate child of the testator, but, unless Ontario were to treat the illegitimate children of foreign testators more generously than the illegitimate children of Ontario testators, there would again be no reason to raise any issue of foreign capacity as opposed to status, and allow the child of the foreigner to take.[28]

The interesting feature of this analysis is that the purpose of the legislation has provided a very clear answer to the actual cases. The conflict cases are solved, not by any true choice of law analysis, but simply because the local legislation (as it has been interpreted by the courts) excludes any question of foreign capacity and always answers by a process of construction which limits the protection of the Act to those children who are legitimate by Ontario law. The remedy here is to broaden the range of the Act's protection to include all those who need it whether they are lawfully married, legitimate or not.

The issue of legitimation raises issues that are very similar to those of legitimacy. The Ontario Legitimacy Act provided[29] for legitimation by subsequent marriage. The Act, like most statutes did not indicate its own scope, but presumably it applied when the issue of legitimacy was raised in Ontario proceedings and where the case was governed by Ontario law. The effect of the Act was to narrow the situations where children were regarded as illegitimate, and it was, therefore, applicable in any case where, under the preceding analysis, the illegitimacy of a child by Ontario law would have excluded his or her right to succeed to an estate. The effect of legitimation by recognition, which must still come under the common law, will be similar. The common law rule requiring that the father be domiciled in a jurisdiction permitting such legitimation both at the date of the child's birth and subsequent recognition has little to recommend it.[30] If, for example, the child is domiciled in the appropriate foreign jurisdiction at the time when his legitimacy is challenged, for example, in an issue of succession, the argument which suggested that there would then be no good reason not to allow the child to succeed as a member of a class of beneficiaries, would obviously be applicable.[31] The case where a child moves from a jurisdiction where legitimation by recognition is possible to one where it is not, can only be dealt with under the general law governing legitimacy.[32] So long as legitimation by any method cuts down the chance of a child being held to be illegitimate, all issues of legitimation can be handled by the general approach that has been offered.

The third of the original three questions, "Is this child the adopted child of that person?", raises issues that are different from those of the other two. The reason is that the problems of adoption have a similarity with those of divorce. The crucial questions in all cases will be whether the Ontario court has jurisdiction to make the order that is requested, or whether the foreign court had jurisdiction to make the order that it made. The Child Welfare Act provides that both child and applicant must be resident in Ontario[33] and it also states that any foreign adoption "has the same effect in Ontario as an adoption" under the Ontario statute.[34]

From the point of view of the Ontario court, if it has jurisdiction, then the provisions of the Ontario Act will apply even though, for example, the consents required by the child's domicile or even by the applicant's domicile are not obtained. It is not true that there is, therefore, no choice of law issue. Rather the choice of law question is subsumed by the jurisdictional one: the answer to the latter disposes of the former. The same applies in the case of a foreign order.

The Ontario Act does not dispose of the issue of recognition of a foreign order, for, consistently with the courts' view of all foreign judgments, the Ontario court can test the jurisdiction of the foreign court to make the order. The rule applied in the English and Canadian cases is that the order of a foreign court will be recognized if it is at least the court of the domicile of the applicants.[35] It might also be thought that, since Ontario courts take jurisdiction on the basis of the parties' residence, residence of the parties might be sufficient.[36] Obviously a great number of variations are possible, but it will be more useful to analyze a few of the cases and issues that can come up to see if any general approach can be developed.

Since the issues of divorce are better known, it will be convenient to illustrate an approach that offers a fruitful method of analyzing most cases where a court is called upon to recognize a foreign divorce decree. The starting point must be to ask what is the purpose of our rules regarding the recognition of foreign divorces. I suggest that the principal purpose is to preserve Ontario from being forced to recognize foreign divorces which undermine the sanctity of an Ontario marriage. I shall not define an "Ontario marriage" except to suggest that the paradigm case is the marriage of two people domiciled and resident in Ontario.[37] This reason for the rule is not the same as that usually put forward. Judges have, for example, said that there are two concerns represented by the Common Law recogniton rules: *one*, to prevent limping marriages, and *two*, to require that the divorce be genuine.[38] It is easy to show that the actual rules applied by the courts frustrate the achievement of these concerns and that they are contradictory.[39] The adoption of the principle of *Armitage v. A.G.*,[40] for example, must sacrifice the concern for the genuineness of the divorce. The adoption of this latter concern in a case like *Mountbatten v. Mountbatten*[41] allows a marriage to limp. But where there is no reason to believe that the couple have sought to evade the rules that might normally be thought to govern (for example) an Ontario marriage, then there is no good reason to refuse to recognize any foreign divorce (perhaps so long as the parties have relied on it). The basic position could then be that we recognize all foreign divorces unless there is some good reason to the contrary.

Exactly the same analysis can deal with the issue of adoption. Divorces are too important in the lives of the parties to be refused recognition unless there is some very good reason to do so. Adoption orders are too important to be refused recognition unless there is a good reason. A case like *Re Valentine*[42] is therefore indefensible unless it could be shown that there was something objectionable in the "parents" having gone to another jurisdiction to evade some provision of the law of their domicile.

This analysis of divorce and adoption shows that the problem of recognition is really a choice of law problem. The real reason why a Nevada divorce of an Ontario couple is refused recognition in an Ontario court is that the Nevada court applied Nevada law. If it applied Ontario law, why should we care? The application of Nevada law is a choice of law issue. The kinds of objection that might properly be made against a foreign adoption are similar. Suppose that a child is kidnapped from its parents in Ontario, and taken to a jurisdiction where it is made the subject of an adoption order. If that child subsequently came to Ontario and its parents challenged the foreign order, an Ontario court is very likely to seek a reason for refusing recognition. This is basically a choice of law issue: the foreign court did not require the consents it should have, (or was prevented from doing so by fraud), and Ontario law will determine the nature of these consents. Between this extreme case, and the equally clear one of the foreign domiciliaries adopting a child domiciled and resident in the foreign jurisdiction, there are a multitude of cases that may force the court to face the issue of recognition. When that happens, the results will only be sensible if the courts have some clear guidelines to follow. I have suggested a starting point for their reasoning.

I have considered in this paper only a few fairly simple cases involving children and the conflict of laws. I think that most of the problems were the result of (then) unsatisfactory rules in Ontario. With changed rules, we may expect that the conflict cases will be easier to solve. I think, however, that it is unlikely that all conflict problems will disappear overnight and so the need remains to provide better methods of dealing with these problems. What I am suggesting is simply the application in the area of the conflict of laws of exactly the same method of analysis that any court must use in every case that comes before it.

1   This proposition is supported by Dicey and Morris, *The Conflict of Laws* (9th ed.) 765 (Rule 149) and by Cheshire, *Private International Law* (9th Ed.) 228. The Canadian cases cited in support are *Bondholders Securities Corpn. v. Manville* [1933] 3 W.W.R. 1, [1933] 4 D.L.R. 699 (Sask. C.A.) and *Charron v. Montreal Trust* [1958] O.R. 597, 15 D.L.R. (2d) 240 (C.A.). See Castel, Canadian Conflict of Laws, (1977), Vol.2, 515-544 (proper law), 547 (capacity and the *Bondholders* case).

2   Currie, "Married Women's Contracts: A Study in Conflict of Laws Method" (1958) 25 U. Chi. L. Rev. 227. Reprinted in B. Currie, *Selected Essays on the Conflict of Laws* (1963) 77.

3   *Bondholders Securities Corpn. v. Manville* (see note 1) is one of the classically absurd cases. It is a commentary on English and Canadian conflicts that it is even considered as authority for anything. *Charron v. Montreal Trust* (see note 1) is also wrong, but for different reasons. That case involved a separation agreement, but the case has always been regarded as an authority in commercial contract cases. The result of the case was to uphold a separation agreement made between a Quebec couple with the result that incompatible matrimonial regimes were mixed and the wife got more from her husband's estate than she would have under either Ontario or Quebec law had they been operating separately.

4   The term "true conflict" is discussed by Cavers, "The Choice of Law Process", *passim.*

5   This is the result suggested by Cavers, note 4, 181 and other writers, *e.g.* Weintraub, *Commentary on the Conflict of Laws* 292.

6   I have discussed the significance of the shift from choice of law rules of the traditional Anglo-Canadian type to choice of law principles developed to choose between competing individual rules. The importance of the suggested change in approach is that the law is now provided with a generally sound basis for decision. This is not the place to enter into a full-scale discussion of choice of law methodology. See Swan, "Annual Survey of Canadian Law, Conflict of Laws" (1976) 8 Ottawa Law Rev. 182.

7   Dicey and Morris, (see note 1) 592 (Rule 101).

8   Many rules present a strongly asymmetrical appearance so far as their effects are concerned. It is a far more serious thing to hold a contract, will or marriage to be *invalid,* than it is to hold one valid. Invalidity may defeat reliance and disappoint reasonable expectations. Such things should not be lightly done. The formal statement of most traditional conflicts rules does not acknowledge this asymmetry. See Swan, "A New Approach to Marriage and Divorce in the Conflict of Laws" (1974) 24 U.T.L.J. 17.

9   The cases are discussed in Swan, "Annual Survey of Canadian Law, Conflict of Laws" (1973) 6 Ottawa Law Rev. 128.

10 There is a problem here with the purpose of the rule of invalidity. The purpose of contractual incapacity in a minor can be seen as being for his protection: he has the option of affirming or avoiding the contract. The purpose of testamentary capacity is presumably some concern that the minor may be irresponsible: he or she may not have power to dispose of any property. I have, therefore, assumed, perhaps without adequate investigation, that if the law of the minor's settled residence holds that testamentary capacity is lacking, that law has some concern for the risks of irresponsibility. It may be that if there is, for example, no property of the minor in that jurisdiction that result cannot be justified.

11 The law of the situs of immovables may be justified in invalidating a will on the ground of incapacity. It should be noted that in such a strong case this result could be justified even though the minor had testamentary capacity when he made the will.

12 This paper will not touch on the issue of legitimacy as it arises when there may be a marriage valid in one jurisdiction but invalid in another. The assumption made in this paper is that there has been no marriage of any kind.

13 [1964] S.C.R. 317, 44 D.L.R. (2d) 208, affirming [1962] O.R. 762, 34 D.L.R. (2d) 14.

14 *Ibid.* at 215 (D.L.R.).

15 It was apparently at the Parliament of Merton in 1234 that the barons of England rejected the argument of the bishops that some relaxation should be made in the common law rules of bastardy. As to removal of bastardy in Ontario, see The Children's Law Reform Act which came into effect in 1978.

16   The basic policy, if it be accepted, can, of course, apply to all cases where there is a dispute over who can take under a will. However, so far as the Ontario courts are concerned, when there is no doubt about the application of Ontario law, they are bound by the consequences of the Ontario rule of construction and by the fact that a child whose parents are not married is illegitimate. (It is not necessary to consider here the extension of legitimacy under the Ontario Legitimacy Act, R.S.O. 1976, c.242.)

17   In a comment on the judgment of the Ontario Court of Appeal, Coutts (1963) 41 Can. Bar Rev. 265 supports the result though he finds the reasons surprising.

18   One might have to assume that the children lived in Ontario and that, under the will, this would be the effect of denying the right of Maria to take.

19   I have assumed that because Mexico grants Maria all the incidents of a legitimate child, Mexico does not accept any of the reasons that I have suggested to justify the common law rule.

20   *E.g.* see note 1, Dicey and Morris 441 and Cheshire 450. In both cases reference is made to *Re MacDonald* see note 13.

21   As would be the case if the Legitimacy Act, R.S.O. 1970, c. 242 had applied.

22   On the facts of *Re MacDonald,* see note 13, Mexican law was determined to be applicable because it was the domicile of Maria and her parents. Obviously, there are more difficult cases, and it is not possible to lay down any hard and fast rule that domicile is necessary. The determination of what foreign law is applicable will depend on the reasons for denying the child from taking. The fact that the child may take an interest in an immovable may be sufficient reason to make the *lex situs* applicable. This aspect of the rule may have to be worked out as the cases come up.

23   R.S.O. 1970, c. 129.

24   R.S.O. 1970, c. 403.

25   R.S.O. 1970, c. 126.

26   Under the Dependants' Relief Act (as at present, *i.e.* 1977) the judge must find that the testator has not made "adequate provision" for the future maintenance of his dependants (R.S.O. 1970, c. 126, s.2(1)). The phrase "adequate provision" and the way the courts have treated this section make my suggestion that only the Act stands between the dependants and welfare unrealistic. It is easiest for my purposes (and it does not weaken the general argument) to assume that the purpose of the Act is to keep the dependants from starving or going on welfare. The Act does not go so far as to force any testator to leave any dependant the share he or she would have got under the Devolution of Estates Act.

27   Such cases have occurred; *Williams v. Moody Bible Institute* [1937] 1 W.W.R. 688, reversed [1937] 2 W.W.R. 316, [1937] 4 D.L.R. 465 (Sask. C.A.). This case involved immovable property in the province and out-of-province dependants. Falconbridge, *Conflict of Laws* (2d ed., 1954) 656 appears to approve of these cases. The cases are absurd because the general freedom of testation is cut down for no good reason.

28   It makes no more sense to exclude illegitimate children from the protection of the Act, than it does to exclude them from taking under an Ontario will or intestacy. In fact, since the basis for relief under the Act is that the testator has provided inadequate support, the claim for relief by all actual dependants is stronger than in the other cases.

29   R.S.O. 1970, c. 242, s. 1(1).

30   *Re Luck* [1940] Ch. 864, [1940] 3 All E.R. 307 (C.A.). The requirement that the father be domiciled in an appropriate jurisdiction at the date of the child's birth has been criticized by Cheshire, see note 1, 457-458.

31   It should be noted that domicile is not necessarily the only basis for dealing with this issue. As I have suggested in regard to testamentary capacity, settled residence may be a preferable test to domicile if we are seeking some functional connection between a person and a system of law. A jurisdiction at the situs of immovable property may also choose to consider that there is not (or is) a good reason for excluding the child from the class of beneficiaries.

32   It is not yet possible to remove completely the category of illegitimate child and, so long as it remains in some jurisdictions, there are going to be cases where it will be applied to cut out a child from succeeding. If this is only done when the purpose of the rule would be

forwarded (whatever that purpose might be) then the chances of a child being affected by the rules governing illegitimate children will be reduced to a minimum.

33 R.S.O. 1970, c. 64 (as amended) s. 70(1).

34 *Ibid.* s. 85.

35 *Re Jensen* (1963) 42 W.W.R. 513, 40 D.L.R. (2d) 469 (B.C.). See also, Cheshire see note 1, 470-1.

36 The obvious analogy is to cases like *Indyka v. Indyka* [1969] 1 A.C. 33, [1967] 2 All E.R. 689 (H.L.)

37 An Ontario court might also refuse to recognize a divorce which could be regarded as undermining the sanctity of a B.C. or English marriage. It is simpler to consider the position from only one point of view. The problems are more extensively discussed in Swan, "Marriage and Divorce in the Conflict of Laws" (1974) 24 U.T.L.J. 17.

38 *Indyka v. Indyka* [1969] 1 A.C. 33, [1967] 2 All E.R. 689, especially Lord Pearce, at 88-89 and *Messina v. Smith* [1971] 2 All E.R. 1046, [1971] P. 322.

39 Swan, "Marriage and Divorce in the Conflict of Laws" (1974) 24 U.T.L.J. 17, 46. So long as there are different rules for divorce in the world and different rules for taking jurisdiction, there are going to be problems of "limping marriages". Any rule put forward to solve the problem of recognition must admit that it is inevitable that some marriages will limp and that some concerns for genuineness will have to be ignored.

40 [1906] P. 135.

41 [1959] P. 43, [1959] 1 All E.R. 99.

42 [1965] Ch. 831, [1965] 2 All E.R. 226 (C.A.). The facts were that a couple domiciled in S. Rhodesia adopted two children in South Africa. The court held that the adoptions could not be recognized because they were not made in the couple's domicile.